MICROCOMPUTERS AND MICROPROCESSORS

The 8080, 8085, and Z-80 Programming, Interfacing, and Troubleshooting

Second Edition

John Uffenbeck

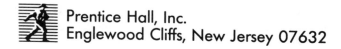
Prentice Hall, Inc.
Englewood Cliffs, New Jersey 07632

Library of Congress Cataloging in Publication Data

Uffenbeck, John E.
    Microcomputers and microprocessors : the 8080, 8085, and Z-80 :
programming, interfacing, and troubleshooting / John Uffenbeck. —
2nd ed.
        p. cm.
    Includes index.
    ISBN 0-13-584061-9
        1. Microcomputers.   2. Intel 8080 (Microprocessor)   3. Intel 8085
(Microprocessor)   4. Zilog Z-80 (Microprocessor)   I. Title.
QA76.5.U35   1991
004. 16—dc20   90-36041
                                                                      CIP

Editorial/production supervision: Tally Morgan, Wordcrafters Editorial
    Services, Inc.
Cover design: Butler/Udell Design
Manufacturing buyer: Ed O'Dougherty

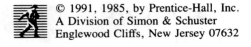 © 1991, 1985, by Prentice-Hall, Inc.
A Division of Simon & Schuster
Englewood Cliffs, New Jersey 07632

Printed in the United States of America

10   9   8   7   6   5   4

ISBN 0-13-584061-9

Prentice-Hall International (UK) Limited, *London*
Prentice-Hall of Australia Pty. Limited, *Sydney*
Prentice-Hall Canada Inc., *Toronto*
Prentice-Hall Hispanoamericana, S.A., *Mexico*
Prentice-Hall of India Private Limited, *New Delhi*
Prentice-Hall of Japan, Inc., *Tokyo*
Simon & Schuster Asia Pte. Ltd., *Singapore*
Editora Prentice-Hall do Brasil, Ltda., *Rio de Janeiro*

Contents

PREFACE   xii

1   INTRODUCTION TO THE MICROPROCESSOR   1

   1.1   Digital Computers: Some Basics   2
      The stored program computer   2
      Fetch and execute   4
      The three-bus architecture   4
      Computer programming   5

   1.2   Computer Codes   5
      Bits and bytes   6
      Binary, decimal, and hexadecimal numbers   7
      Codes   10

   1.3   Computer Languages   12
      Machine and assembly language programming   12
      High-level languages   14

   1.4   Implementing the Three-Bus Architecture in Hardware   16
      Digital signals   16
      Defining the three buses   19

   1.5   The CPU as a Complex Timer   21
      Machine cycle timing diagrams   21
      Instruction timing   23
      Processor timing   23

Chapter Summary   26
Lab Projects   27
Questions and Problems   28
Key Concept Answers   31

2   INTRODUCING THE 8080, 8085, AND Z-80
     MICROPROCESSORS   32

     2.1   Constructing the CPU Module   32
            The CPU module   33
     2.2   CPU Modules for the 8080, 8085, and Z-80
            Microprocessors   36
            The 8080 CPU module   36
            The 8085 CPU module   42
            The Z-80 CPU module   46
     2.3   Programming Models for the 8080, 8085, and Z-80
            Microprocessors   51
            A programming model for the 8080   51
            The 8080 flag register   52
            A programming model for the 8085   55
            A programming model for the Z-80   55
            The Z-80 flag register   55
     2.4   Introducing the Instruction Sets   57
            Instruction types   57
     2.5   Addressing Modes   66
     2.6   Putting It All Together: A Programming Example   68
     Chapter Summary   70
     Lab Projects   71
     Questions and Problems   72
     Key Concept Answers   76

3   PROGRAMMING THE MICROPROCESSOR   78

     3.1   Microprocessor Programming Examples   79
            Program 1: 8080/85 8-bit addition   79
            Program 2: Z-80 8-bit addition   81
            Program 3: 32-bit binary addition   84
            Program 4: 32-bit decimal addition   86
            Program 5: 8-bit multiplication   89
            Program 6: BCD-to-binary conversion   93
            Program 7: filling a block of memory   98
            Program 8: square-wave generator   102
            Program 9: serial communications test program   103
            Program 10: hex dump   105
            Program 11: 1-bit I/O port   110
            Program 12: frequency counter   112

Program 13: the game of nim   *116*
Program 14: computer music   *117*

3.2   Operating Systems   127
Some common operating systems   *128*
Features of CP/M   *128*
A sample session with CP/M   *130*
Linking programs to CP/M   *135*

Chapter Summary   138
Lab Projects   139
Questions and Problems   141
Key Concept Answers   143

4   BUILDING THE MICROCOMPUTER, PART 1:
THE BUSES   145

4.1   Generating the System Clock   146
The 8080 clock   *148*
The 8085 clock   *148*
The Z-80 clock   *150*

4.2   Resetting the Microprocessor   152
Starting up a "new" computer   *152*
Reset circuits for the 8080, 8085, and Z-80   *153*

4.3   Electrical Characteristics of a Bus   154
Noise immunity   *154*
Bus loading   *156*
Reflections   *157*

4.4   Bus Buffering Techniques   160
Type 1 bus   *160*
Tri-state buffers with hysteresis   *164*
Type 2 bus   *164*
Type 3 bus   *167*

4.5   CPU Modules for the 8080, 8085, and Z-80   172
The 8080 CPU module   *172*
The 8085 CPU module   *174*
The Z-80 CPU module   *174*
Summary   *177*

4.6   Single-Stepping the Microprocessor   177
Single-stepping the 8080   *179*
Single-stepping the 8085   *181*
Single-stepping the Z-80   *182*

4.7   A Power-On-Jump Circuit for the Z-80   183
Chapter Summary   185
Lab Projects   185
Questions and Problems   187
Key Concept Answers   191

Contents

5 BUILDING THE MICROCOMPUTER, PART 2: ADDING MEMORY   192

5.1   Memory Hierarchies   193

5.2   The Microprocessor Defines the Memory Timing   195
Memory-read-cycle timing   196
Memory-write-cycle timing   197
Memory interfacing requirements   199
Interfacing slow memory   199

5.3   Choosing Memory   201
ROM applications   202
RAM applications   202
The memory map   202

5.4   RAM and ROM Technologies   204
Mask-programmable ROMs   204
Field-programmable ROMs   204
Static and dynamic RAMs   214
RAM organization   216
The universal site   217

5.5   Interfacing Static RAM and ROM to the Microprocessor   219
Interfacing the 2764 8K-byte EPROM   220
Interfacing the 2167 16K static RAM   226
Interfacing a RAM/ROM module   229

5.6   Interfacing Dynamic RAM to the Microprocessor   236
Timing diagrams for dynamic RAM   236
Refresh   238
The 8203 DRAM controller   240
The Z-80 as a refresh controller   244

5.7   Conclusion   244
Chapter Summary   245
Lab Projects   246
Questions and Problems   248
Key Concept Answers   254

6 BUILDING THE MICROCOMPUTER, PART 3: INPUT/OUTPUT   256

6.1   Parallel I/O: Interfacing to a Type 3 Bus   257
I/O machine cycles and timing   257
Designing an 8-bit input port   260
Designing an 8-bit output port   262
Applications for the device select pulse   265

6.2   Memory-Mapped I/O   265
Designing an 8-bit memory-mapped input port   268
Designing a digital lock   268

6.3   Handshaking Logic   274
Busy, ready, and acknowledge flags   274

6.4   Programmed I/O   275
Polling   276

   Data transfer rate 279
   Priorities 279
 6.5 Interrupt-Driven I/O 281
   Generating an interrupt 283
   Maskable and nonmaskable interrupts 285
   Branching to the interrupt service routine 286
   Response time and transfer rate 290
   Multiple interrupts: the priority problem 293
   Summary points for the 8080, 8085, and Z-80 297
 6.6 Direct Memory Access 299
 Chapter Summary 302
 Lab Projects 303
 Questions and Problems 304
 Key Concept Answers 312

7 SPECIAL-PURPOSE SUPPORT DEVICES:
THE 8080/85 FAMILY   313

 7.1 The 8755A 16K EPROM with I/O 314
   Interfacing the 8755A ROM 315
   Interfacing the 8755A I/O ports 317
   Three-chip 8085 microcomputer system 319
 7.2 The 8255A Programmable Peripheral Interface 321
   Interfacing the 8255A 322
   Mode O: basic I/O 324
   The bit set/reset mode 328
   Electrical characteristics of the ports 329
   Mode 1: strobed I/O 330
   Mode 2: strobed bidirectional I/O 336
 7.3 The 8254 Programmable Interval Timer 341
   Interfacing the 8254 342
   Programming the 8254 343
   Mode definitions 347
   A design example 348
   8254 electrical characteristics 350
 7.4 The 8259A Programmable Interrupt Controller 351
   Interfacing the 8259A 352
   Arbitration modes 353
   Programming the 8259A 356
   Operation control words 359
 7.5 The 8237 Programmable DMA Controller 362
   Interfacing the 8237A 363
   Response time and transfer rate 368
   Programming the 8237 370
   *A design example: interfacing a floppy
   disk drive 378*
 7.6 Peripheral Controller Bus Buffering Techniques 382
 Chapter Summary 384
 Lab Projects 384

Contents

Questions and Problems   386
Key Concept Answers   392

8   SPECIAL SUPPORT DEVICES: THE Z-80 FAMILY   393

8.1   The Z8420 Parallel Input/Output Controller   394
Interfacing the Z-80 PIO   395
Programming the Z-80 PIO   397
Mode 0: output port with handshake   400
Mode 1: input port with handshake   401
Using the Z-80 PIO to interface a parallel printer   403
Mode 2: bidirectional I/O with handshake   404
Mode 3: bit-defined I/O   406
A design example: mode 3 control of a multiplexed LED display   408
Electrical characteristics of the ports   413

8.2   The Z8430 Counter/Timer Circuit   413
Interfacing the Z-80 CTC   414
Programming the Z-80 CTC: counter mode   416
Programming the Z-80 CTC: timer mode   420
Electrical characteristics   424

8.3   The Z8410 Direct Memory Access Controller   424
Interfacing the Z-80 DMA   425
Typical DMA transfer   426
Response time and transfer rate   429
Read/write registers   431
Programming the Z-80 DMA   435

8.4   Peripheral Controller Bus Buffering Techniques   437
Chapter Summary   437
Lab Projects   438
Questions and Problems   439
Key Concept Answers   444

9   SERIAL I/O TECHNIQUES   445

9.1   Asynchronous Serial Communications   446
Start bits, stop bits, and the baud rate   447
Generating and recovering asynchronous serial data   448
Standard asynchronous serial communications protocols   450
The UART   450

9.2   Synchronous Serial Communications   455
Bisync protocol   455
Serial data link control   456

9.3   Error Detection and Correction   457
Parity   458
Checksums   458
Cyclic redundancy checks   460
The Hamming code   461

9.4 The Intel 8251A USART 465
  Interfacing the 8251A 467
  Programming the 8251A: asynchronous mode 470
  Programming the 8251A: synchronous mode 472
9.5 The Zilog Z-80 SIO and Z-80 DART 474
  Comparing the SIO and the DART 475
  Interfacing the Z-80 SIO 477
  Programming the Z-80 SIO: asynchronous mode 479
  Controlling the Z-80 SIO in the asynchronous mode 483
  Using the Z-80 SIO in the synchronous mode 488
9.6 Remote Control Applications for Asynchronous Serial Data 490
9.7 Serial Data Interface Standards 492
  The EIA RS-232D standard 492
  The RS-422A and RS-423A standards 500
9.8 Telecommunications 503
  The basics 504
  Interfacing a 300-bps modem 506
  High-speed modems 510
Chapter Summary 512
Lab Projects 513
Questions and Problems 515
Key Concept Answers 521

10 FLOPPY AND HARD DISK DRIVES 522

10.1 Storing Data on a Magnetic Disk 523
  Flux transitions 523
  The media 523
10.2 The Components of a Disk Drive 525
  Floppy-disk drives 525
  Hard drives 526
10.3 Common Disk Drive Specifications 528
  Sectors 528
  Cylinders 530
  Clusters 530
  High and low level formatting 531
10.4 Data Encoding Techniques 533
  Single-density 534
  Double-density 535
  RLL (run length limited) 535
  Disk drive data rates 537
10.5 The Disk Drive Interface 540
  Floppy drives 540
  Hard drives 541
Chapter Summary 542
Questions and Problems 543
Key Concept Answers 544

11 MICROCOMPUTER CONTROL APPLICATIONS AND TROUBLESHOOTING TECHNIQUES 546

11.1 Detecting the Presence of an Analog Signal: The Comparator 547

11.2 ON/OFF Control of Analog Peripherals 550
DC control 552
AC control 555

11.3 Interfacing a Digital-to-Analog Converter 559
The digital-to-analog conversion process 560
Interfacing the MC1408 DAC 563
Interfacing the DAC1200 566

11.4 Interfacing an Analog-to-Digital Converter 569
The analog-to-digital conversion process 570
Interfacing the ADC0809 eight-channel ADC 579

11.5 Troubleshooting Techniques 582
Hardware troubleshooting tools 585
Summary 592

Chapter Summary 592
Lab Projects 593
Questions and Problems 595
Key Concept Answers 599

12 INTRODUCTION TO THE 8086 16-BIT MICROPROCESSOR 601

12.1 8086 Hardware Details and Basic System Timing 602
The queue 602
The min and max mode 604
Memory organization 605
Basic system timing 608
Special support chips 610

12.2 Min and Max Mode CPU Modules for the 8086 611
The min mode 612
The max mode 615

12.3 A Programming Model for the 8086 615
Internal register array 615
Segment registers 618
Addressing modes 621

12.4 Programming the 8086 622
Data transfer group 623
Arithmetic group 625
Bit manipulation group 626
Transfer group 626
Interrupts 629
String group 631
Processor control group 631
An example: two 8086 block fill programs 632

12.5   8086 Memory and I/O Interfacing   634
Interfacing a 16K-word memory   *634*
Interfacing the 8255A PPI   *636*

12.6   The 8086 Family of Microprocessors   639
The 8088   *639*
The 80286   *640*
The 80386   *641*
The 80486   *642*

Chapter Summary   642
Lab Projects   643
Questions and Problems   645
Key Concept Answers   648

ANSWERS TO SELECTED PROBLEMS   649

APPENDIX

Appendix A.1   655
Appendix A.2   656
Appendix B.1   657
Appendix C.1   664
Appendix C.2   667
Appendix C.3   670
Appendix D.1   675
Appendix D.2   677

Glossary   678

INDEX   685

Preface

This is a book about *microcomputer technology*. It is appropriate for use in an introductory microprocessor and microcomputer course. Its primary emphasis is an understanding of the hardware components of a microcomputer system and the role of software to control that hardware.

In order to make these topics "real," three compatible 8-bit microprocessor chips are studied. These are the Intel 8080, the Intel 8085, and the Zilog Z-80. Although none of these chips can be considered state-of-the-art, they do provide a very solid platform upon which subsequent courses may be built. They also provide a very "real" hardware setting for the study of microcomputer technology.

You will get maximum benefit from this book if you have a good understanding of dc and ac circuits. In addition, you should be familiar with digital logic circuits such as gates, flip-flops, decoders, and counters. The hexadecimal number system is used throughout the book and this topic is reviewed in Chap. 1.

FEATURES

Among the important features of this book are:

1. A "learn-by-doing" approach to software. After surveying the instruction sets, 14 detailed program examples help illustrate common programming techniques.
2. New components are learned by studying the actual manufacturer's data sheets which are included throughout the text.

3. Thorough coverage of the Intel and Zilog programmable peripheral controller chips is provided. These include the 8255 PPI, 8254 PIT, 8259 PIC, 8237 DMAC, 8251 USART, Z-80 PIO, Z-80 CTC, Z-80 DMA, and the Z-80 SIO and DART.

4. An introduction to the 16-bit 8086 microprocessor is provided in Chap. 12. This will allow you to compare 16-bit and 8-bit technologies side by side. Included in this chapter are specific examples of 8086 memory and I/O interfacing as well as several programming examples.

5. More than 70 laboratory projects are described. These should give you ideas on how to test and demonstrate the ideas presented in the chapters.

CHANGES

Many changes have been incorporated in this new addition. Most of these have been included to improve the "teachability" of the book.

1. Each section now includes a set of *Key Concept Questions*. Answers to these questions appear at the end of the chapter.

2. The Appendix has been expanded to include a *Glossary* of appropriate terms.

3. The end-of-chapter problems have been extensively rewritten and reorganized. They are now grouped by section and have been carefully worded to make it clear which processor they refer to. This should make it easier for Z-80-only or 8085-only users to select appropriate problems. Questions marked with an asterisk (*) refer to *troubleshooting* problems.

4. Laboratory projects are included at the end of each chapter. They are written in such a way that you should be able to adapt them to your particular hardware.

5. Chapter 10 on disk drives has been completely rewritten and updated. It now focuses on 5¼" and 3½" floppy disk drives as well as *double-density* and *RLL*-encoded hard drives.

THE THREE MICROPROCESSOR APPROACH

The surveys we received about this book indicated that some users liked everything but the Z-80 coverage. Others said the 8085 sections should be deleted. Still others felt that the 8080 was out of date and should not be covered. If we took all of this advice to heart, this would be a very short book indeed!

I believe that a first course in microprocessors should provide a solid foundation in the *technology* of microcomputers. This means learning the difference between RAM and ROM and how these two types of memory are interfaced to the microprocessor. It also means learning how an input or output port works, and how to construct a serial interface. None of these concepts depends on a particular microprocessor chip. We pick a particular chip because we need something real to work with. In that respect, an 8080 works as well as an 80386 (maybe even better—the 8080 is probably easier to understand).

Because the 8080, 8085, and Z-80 are all software compatible, it seems logical to cover all three of these at once. Even the hardware differences are minimal. Once the *CPU modules* have been designed (in Chap. 4), nearly all of the hardware interfaces presented in this book will work with any of the three processors (indeed, most of the interfaces will require only minor changes to work with *any* microprocessor).

Nevertheless, each section is clearly marked, and if you are an "8085-only person" or a "Z-80-only person," you should have no trouble spotting and skipping over the "offending" sections!

ACKNOWLEDGMENTS

I would like to thank all of the reviewers who took the time to respond to our survey. Each response was carefully studied and many of the suggestions are incorporated in this new edition (I particularly liked one of the reviewer's comments who said, "Great text! Don't screw it up!"). I also appreciate the assistance I have received from both Intel and Zilog for permission to reproduce the large number of data sheets that appear throughout this book.

John Uffenbeck
Wisconsin Indianhead Technical College

1

Introduction to the Microprocessor

What is a *microprocessor*? Some people might answer "a very small computer," others a "desktop or personal computer," still others might reply "a computer on a chip." The word "microprocessor" was coined in the semiconductor industry by Intel Corporation. They used the term to describe a newly designed 4-bit calculator-like integrated circuit.

Today we think of the microprocessor as the silicon chip around which a *microcomputer* is built. Thus we have the IBM Personal Computer, based on the Intel 8088 microprocessor; the Apple IIe, based on the Rockwell 6502; the Apple Macintosh, based on the Motorola 68000; and so on.

Some manufacturers have found it advantageous to use several microprocessors in one computer. One might be used to control the keyboard, a second to handle input/output operations, a third to control the mass storage devices (disk drives), and of course, a fourth as the main system processor. This technique is referred to as *distributed processing*.

Some microprocessor chips claim to be single-chip microcomputers. The Zilog Z-8* contains the central processing unit (CPU), a preprogrammed memory containing the operating system software, scratchpad memory for storing temporary results, logic for communicating with a computer terminal, and three parallel input/output ports for hardware control applications.

Despite the advances in semiconductor technology and microprocessors, the

---

* All figures and tables by Zilog were "Reproduced by permission © 1977, 1978, 1981 Zilog, Inc. This material shall not be reproduced without the written consent of Zilog, Inc." "Zilog Z-80® is a trademark of Zilog, Inc., with whom Prentice Hall is not associated."

1

basic architecture of the digital computer has remained unchanged for the last 35 years. This is the so-called *von Neumann* model of the stored program computer. In this chapter we will study the basic concepts of this model as it applies to the microprocessor.

We will also begin to take a look at the subject of microcomputer programming—perhaps from a point of view you have not taken before. This is to consider the effects each computer instruction has on the electrical lines or "buses" of the microprocessor chip itself.

The chapter concludes with an introduction to instruction timing diagrams. Armed with this information, we can predict exactly how long a given microcomputer program will take to execute (not too long!).

1.1 DIGITAL COMPUTERS: SOME BASICS

As you read this section, look for the answers to these Key Concept questions:

1.1.1. What are the three main parts of a stored program computer?

1.1.2. List the three buses used by the CPU to communicate with its memory and I/O devices.

1.1.3. The stored program computer can perform four different types of instruction cycles. What are they?

In the early 1960s the United States was caught up in a wave of new technology. The transistor, developed by a trio of scientists at Bell Laboratories shortly after the end of World War II, had finally begun to displace its rival, the vacuum tube. Suddenly everything from car radios to electric mixers carried the label *solid-state*.

New electronics companies seemed to spring up overnight, including a company based in Dallas, Texas, called Texas Instruments. TI (as it has become known) had just announced a new solid-state component called the *integrated circuit* (IC). Little did we know then that the electronics version of the industrial revolution was about to begin.

The Stored Program Computer. Figure 1.1 is a block diagram of a typical digital computer. The *central processing unit* or CPU, shown on the far left, is often likened to the human brain because it is here that all decisions are made and the system timing generated. The arithmetic logic unit or ALU is contained within the CPU and all the mathematical operations are performed there. The results of these calculations are left in a special register in the ALU called the *accumulator*.

The memory unit shown in Fig. 1.1 is used to store the specific sequence of commands that will be used to instruct the CPU to perform some task. These instructions are called the computer *program* (hence the name *stored program* computer).

Finally, no useful task can be performed by the computer without the input/output devices—the *I/O* in "computerese." It is with the keyboard that we input the instructions or commands about the task to be accomplished. The results are then viewed on the printer or CRT (cathode ray tube) screen.

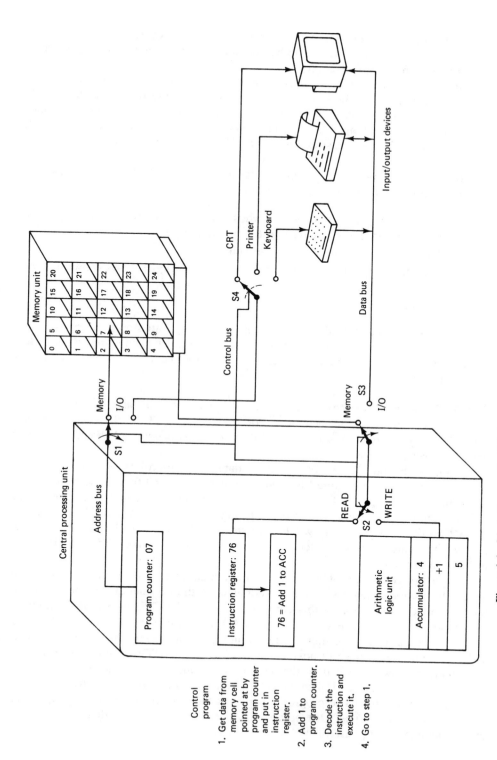

Figure 1.1 Block diagram of a digital computer. The three main blocks are the CPU (central processing unit), the memory unit, and the input/output (I/O) devices.

3

Studying the memory unit more closely, note that each cell in the memory has its own unique identifying number or *address* and that the total capacity of this particular memory unit is 25 cells.

If we were to examine the contents of these memory cells, we would see a strange collection of numbers having no particular meaning to us. Yet to the CPU these numbers would represent a concise set of commands instructing it to carry out some sequence of operations. These numbers represent the operation codes (*op-codes*) for the various instructions in the CPU's instruction set.

Fetch and Execute.   Continuing to refer to Fig. 1.1, note that the CPU has been designed to follow repeatedly four simple steps.

1. Fetch data from the memory cell whose address is currently in the program counter register. Put this data into the instruction register.
2. Add 1 to the address in the program counter.
3. Decode the command currently in the instruction register and do what it tells you.
4. Go to step 1.

These four steps constitute the principle of operation of all stored program digital computers. This includes the largest IBM mainframe to the tiniest microcomputer. The principle is called *fetch and execute* and is the key to understanding the activities of a microprocessor.

The Three-Bus Architecture.   The CPU, memory unit, and I/O devices must be able to communicate with each other. For example, the CPU must be able to specify which memory cell is to be selected, and if the contents of that cell should be read or new data written into the cell.

This is the purpose of the address, data, and control buses shown in Fig. 1.1. When the CPU is required to read the contents of a particular memory cell, it first outputs the proper address on its *address bus*. This is actually the contents of the program counter. Next, the *control bus* causes switches S1 and S3 to switch to the MEMORY position and switch 2 to the READ position. The *data bus* now carries the contents of the selected memory cell back to the CPU and into the instruction register.

As a further example of the three-bus architecture, let's assume that the command in the instruction register requires the contents of the accumulator to be output to the printer. The execution of this command requires the CPU to output the address of the printer on its address bus. Switch S4 will examine this address, and seeing that it is for the printer, switch to the printer position. Next, the control bus will switch S1 and S3 to the I/O position and S2 to the WRITE position. The data to be output can now be placed on the data bus and routed to the printer.

In summary, the CPU begins each command cycle with an instruction fetch from the memory unit. The program counter is then incremented in preparation for the next fetch cycle. Finally the op-code for the instruction is decoded and executed during the execution phase of the cycle.

TABLE 1.1 INSTRUCTION CYCLES OF A DIGITAL COMPUTER

Instruction type	Address bus	Control bus	Data bus
Memory read	Memory cell address	Select memory and read	Contents of selected memory cell
Memory write	Memory cell address	Select memory and write	Data to be written to memory
I/O read	I/O device address	Select I/O and read	Data from selected I/O device
I/O write	I/O device address	Select I/O and write	Data to be written to I/O device

From the standpoint of the three-bus architecture, there are only four unique instruction cycles possible. These are listed in Table 1.1 with the contents of the three buses specified for each case. When we study microprocessor programming in Chaps. 2 and 3 it will be interesting to note that all microprocessor instructions are made up of combinations of these four cycles (later in this chapter we will call them *machine cycles*).

Computer Programming. From the preceding discussion you can begin to see how the CPU controls the flow of data between itself, memory, and the I/O devices. The instruction set of a computer can be thought of as a list of commands that cause unique sequences to occur on the three buses.

As an example, the command LD A,(10)—load the accumulator with the contents of memory cell 10—would cause the address bus to output address 10, the control bus to establish a memory read cycle, and the data bus to input data from memory cell 10 and store it in the accumulator of the CPU.

Writing a computer program requires assembling the proper instructions and storing them sequentially in the memory unit of the computer. In Chaps. 2 and 3 we will study the instruction sets of the 8080, 8085, and Z-80 microprocessors and learn in detail how to program these processors.

1.2 COMPUTER CODES

As you read this section, look for the answers to these Key Concept questions:

1.2.1. How many different binary numbers can be written using 8 bits?

1.2.2. The hexadecimal number system is convenient because it "compresses" the size of a binary number. For example, 11010110 is equivalent to _____ hex and _____ decimal.

1.2.3. When encoded in ASCII, the letter "P" has the binary code _____.

One of the complications that we human beings have when working with a computer is that we cannot simply tell the computer what we want it to do. For example, suppose that I wish to add two numbers. As a human being I could ask you for the two numbers, add them in my head, and announce the result. Compare this to the steps required to make a computer do this.

1. Read the first number input from the keyboard.
2. Store this number in the memory unit.
3. Read the second number from the keyboard and store it in the accumulator.
4. Retrieve the first number from the memory unit and add it to the number in the accumulator, leaving the result in the accumulator.
5. Output the contents of the accumulator to the CRT screen.

There are so many operations required that it makes you wonder about the usefulness of the computer in the first place! Of course, the computer can do each operation rather quickly—usually in just a few microseconds. Once the program to add two numbers has been written, it will do so at lightning speed and never make a mistake. Of course, this is the advantage the computer has over us—once programmed to perform a task, it will flawlessly perform that task at rates approaching millions of operations per second!*

The problem becomes one of programming the computer, that is, telling it what we want it to do. Unfortunately, the computer does not speak our language and seems unwilling to learn (people are working on it, though). Therefore, the burden is on us to learn the instructions that will program the computer to perform a particular task.

Bits and Bytes. When typing at the keyboard of a microcomputer or time-shared terminal, it is easy to forget that computers are simply *ON* and *OFF* machines. The logic circuits controlling the computer's operations typically produce +5 V or 0 V. Because of this the binary number system is invoked to describe these digital signals. Assuming a positive logic convention, the +5-V level becomes a logic 1 and the 0-V level a logic 0.

A single digital line can therefore carry only two pieces of information—the line is a 1 or it is a 0. We solve this apparent lack of information-handling capability by combining many digital lines together. Such collections of lines are referred to as a *bus*.

Figure 1.2 shows eight such lines representing the data bus of a microprocessor. When written in binary the data on the bus is

$$11001011$$

---

*The CRAY X-MP supercomputer can perform 400 million operations per second. A 4-MHz Z-80 does 1 million operations per second.

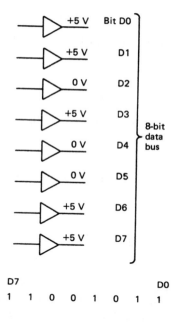

Figure 1.2 Eight digital lines make up the data bus of a microcomputer. The binary number system is used to describe the data on this bus. In this case the data word is 11001011.

where the D7 output is on the left and the D0 output on the right. Each digit in this binary number is referred to as a *bit* (*bi*nary digi*t*). It has become common practice to refer to 8 bits as a *byte*; 4 bits are often called a *nibble*.

The important result to note is that by combining eight lines, the information-handling capability of the bus has increased not by a factor of 8 but by a factor of 2^8. This is seen by writing down all possible combinations of the 8 bits: starting with 00000000, 00000001, 00000010, . . . , 11111110, and finally 11111111. In doing this exercise you will discover (or take my word for it) that there are 256 different combinations of 8 bits. The general result is that for n bits there are 2^n unique combinations.

This result is the key to the success of the modern digital computer. If enough bits are used in the data words, we can express even the largest of numbers. Furthermore, we can develop *codes* to represent the letters and punctuation marks of the alphabet. In this way the computer can process all types of written information.

Binary, Decimal, and Hexadecimal Numbers.

At first glance a binary number is imposing to most of us used to dealing with base 10 numbers. Is 11001011 a large number or a small one? How can we tell?

Any binary number can be converted to its decimal equivalent by adding the powers of 2 represented by its bit position. In binary this is particularly easy because each bit is either a 1 or 0. As with any number system, the weight of a digit is found as the base (2 in this case) raised to the power corresponding to the digit's position. Numbering the digit positions starting from the right and beginning with 0 results in

$$2^n \ldots 2^3 \, 2^2 \, 2^1 \, 2^0$$

The decimal value of the binary number in Fig. 1.2 is therefore found to be

$$
\begin{array}{cccccccc}
1 & 1 & 0 & 0 & 1 & 0 & 1 & 1 \\
1 \times 2^7 + & 1 \times 2^6 + & 0 \times 2^5 + & 0 \times 2^4 + & 1 \times 2^3 + & 0 \times 2^2 + & 1 \times 2^1 + & 1 \times 2^0 = \\
128 & + 64 & + 0 & + 0 & + 8 & + 0 & + 2 & + 1 \qquad = 203
\end{array}
$$

Experienced users of binary simply count 1, 2, 4, 8, 16, 32, and so on, adding up the appropriate powers of 2.

Example 1.1

Convert the following binary words to their decimal equivalents: (a) 101, (b) 11111111, (c) 1100001011.

Solution
(a) $101 = 4 + 1 = 5$
(b) $11111111 = 128 + 64 + 32 + 16 + 8 + 4 + 2 + 1 = 255$
(c) $1100001011 = 512 + 256 + 8 + 2 + 1 = 779$

Computers may like binary numbers but we human beings surely do not. It is very difficult to remember (or even recognize) that 11001011 is actually decimal 203. Because of this the *hexadecimal* number system is often used. Table 1.2 lists the binary and hexadecimal equivalents of the decimal numbers 0 through 15. The hexadecimal (or simply hex) number system defines a unique symbol for each of the 16 possible combinations of 4 bits. Note that this requires a little imagination after the symbol 9 has been used.

TABLE 1.2 BINARY
AND HEXADECIMAL
EQUIVALENTS OF THE DECIMAL
NUMBERS 0 THROUGH 15

Decimal	Binary	Hexadecimal
0	0000	0
1	0001	1
2	0010	2
3	0011	3
4	0100	4
5	0101	5
6	0110	6
7	0111	7
8	1000	8
9	1001	9
10	1010	A
11	1011	B
12	1100	C
13	1101	D
14	1110	E
15	1111	F

At first it might appear that we have only made matters worse. After all, what is the meaning of a number like E3D? The real utility of the hex number system is the ease with which binary numbers can be represented. Grouping the binary digits four at a time, we may convert a binary number to hex by inspection.

For example, our binary number 11001011 becomes CB in hex. Its decimal value is still unrecognizable perhaps, but it is a number that is more easily "carried around."

Example 1.2

Convert the binary numbers in Ex. 1.1 to hex.

Solution
(a) 101 = 5
(b) 11111111 = FF
(c) 1100001011 = 30B

When we begin programming the microprocessor in Chap. 2, the value of hex will become even more apparent. To be fully conversant in hex and binary you must be able to convert back and forth between the two and their decimal equivalents with ease. Several examples will review the techniques.

Example 1.3

Convert the following hex numbers to decimal and binary:
(a) 3C, (b) 2A92, (c) FFFF.

Solution. The conversion to binary can be made directly by writing the four binary digits representative of each hex digit.
(a) 3C = 0011 1100
(b) 2A92 = 0010 1010 1001 0010
(c) FFFF = 1111 1111 1111 1111
We could now count the binary weights to find the decimal equivalents, but there is a quicker way—convert the hex numbers directly to decimal.
(a) $3C = 3 \times 16^1 + 12 \times 16^0 = 60$
(b) $2A92 = 2 \times 16^3 + 10 \times 16^2 + 9 \times 16^1 + 2 \times 16^0 = 10,898$
(c) $FFFF = 15 \times 16^3 + 15 \times 16^2 + 15 \times 16^1 + 15 \times 16^0 = 65,535$

Example 1.4

Convert the following decimal numbers to binary: (a) 43, (b) 106, (c) 862.

Solution. This can be done by reversing the process used in Ex. 1.1.
(a) $43 = 32 + 8 + 2 + 1 = 2^5 + 2^3 + 2^1 + 2^0 = 101011$
(b) $106 = 64 + 32 + 8 + 2 = 2^6 + 2^5 + 2^3 + 2^1 = 1101010$
(c) $862 = 512 + 256 + 64 + 16 + 8 + 4 + 2 = 2^9 + 2^8 + 2^6 + 2^4 + 2^3 + 2^2 + 2^1 =$ 1101011110

Decimal numbers can also be converted to binary by using the repeated-division-by-2 technique. However, this is a rather laborious process. The next example will show a faster method.

Example 1.5

Convert the following decimal numbers to hexadecimal and then to binary: (a) 94, (b) 299, (c) 48,000.

Solution. These can be converted in a straightforward manner by accumulating the highest power of 16, similar to Ex. 1.4. The following technique makes use of a pocket calculator and is suitable for even the largest decimal numbers.

(a) $94/16 = 5.875$ Write down the 5.   5
    $.875 \times 16 = 14$ Write down the 14 (D).   D

The result is $94_{10} = 5D_{16} = 1011101_2$.

(b) $299/256 = 1.16796875$ Write down the 1.   1
    $.16796875 \times 256 = 43$
    $43/16 = 2.6875$ Write down the 2.   2
    $.6875 \times 16 = 11$ Write down the 11 (B).   B

The result is $299_{10} = 12B_{16} = 100101011_2$.

(c) $48,000/4096 = 11.71875$ Write down the 11 (B).   B
    $.71875 \times 4096 = 2944$
    $2944/256 = 11.5$ Write down the 11 (B).   B
    $.5 \times 256 = 128$
    $128/16 = 8.0$ Write down the 8.   8
    $0 \times 16 = 0$ Write down the 0.   0

The result is $48,000_{10} = BB80_{16} = 1011101110000000_2$.

Note: Once the conversion to hexadecimal has been made, the binary conversion is obtained almost for "free."

Codes. In Fig. 1.1 the program counter of our simple computer is "pointing at" memory cell 7. In that cell is the data word 76. Based on the preceding section, we now know that this data word would actually be stored in binary form as 01001100. But what does this number represent? Should we interpret it literally as decimal 76, or does it represent the *code* for some computer operation?

The answer to this question is that only the computer knows for sure. If the computer is looking for an operation code, it will interpret this byte as an operation code (even if we meant it to be a data byte). If the computer is looking for a data byte, it will be interpreted as data. It is up to the programmer to make sure that the proper codes are presented to the computer. This is what computer programming is all about.

The important point we need to make is that a byte may have many interpretations besides its decimal value. For example, the byte 01001100 is interpreted as decimal 76, hexadecimal 4C, by an 8080 microprocessor as the operation code MOV C,H (copy the contents of the H register into the C register), the operation code JMP by the 6502 microprocessor, and the operation code INCA (increment accumulator A) by the 6800 microprocessor.

There is still another interpretation for the byte. In 1968 the American National Standards Institute established a 7-bit code for all of the letters of the alphabet, the

TABLE 1.3 AMERICAN STANDARD CODE FOR INFORMATION INTERCHANGE (ASCII)[a]

Least significant bits	Most significant bits							
	0 0000	1 0001	2 0010	3 0011	4 0100	5 0101	6 0110	7 0111
0 0000	NUL	DLE	SP	0	@	P	`	p
1 0001	SOH	DC1	!	1	A	Q	a	q
2 0010	STX	DC2	"	2	B	R	b	r
3 0011	ETX	DC3	#	3	C	S	c	s
4 0100	EOT	DC4	$	4	D	T	d	t
5 0101	ENQ	NAK	%	5	E	U	e	u
6 0110	ACK	SYN	&	6	F	V	f	v
7 0111	BEL	ETB	'	7	G	W	g	w
8 1000	BS	CAN	(	8	H	X	h	x
9 1001	HT	EM	)	9	I	Y	i	y
A 1010	LF	SUB	*	:	J	Z	j	z
B 1011	VT	ESC	+	;	K	[	k	{
C 1100	FF	FS	,	<	L	\	l	|
D 1101	CR	GS	−	=	M	]	m	}
E 1110	SO	RS	.	>	N	^	n	~
F 1111	SI	US	/	?	O	—	o	DEL

[a] Bit 7 of the code is assumed to be 0.

numerals 0–9, the common punctuation symbols found on most typewriters, and several special-purpose control codes. They called their code the American Standard Code for Information Interchange or *ASCII* for short (pronounced ''ask-E''). A copy of this code is given in Table 1.3.

Although ASCII is a 7-bit code, it is often written in byte (8-bit) form with bit 8 ignored (assumed 0) or used for parity. Examining Table 1.3, we see that the byte 01001100 (4C hex) is the code for the capital letter L. Nearly all text information today is encoded in ASCII format, making it possible to transfer data between two different computer systems. Each time you type a key on a computer terminal the ASCII code for that key is generated and sent to the computer for processing.

Actually, there are many codes in addition to ASCII. There is the *BCD* code (binary-coded decimal), useful for decimal arithmetic; the *Gray* code, in which only one bit changes between successive entries in the code (useful for testing digital circuits); the *2's-complement* code shown in Table 1.4, in which the most significant bit of each word represents the sign (positive or negative) of the word; the *Baudot* or five-level code used on early teletype machines and now obsolete; the *Extended Binary-Coded Decimal Interchange Code* (EBCDIC) developed by IBM for its line of Selectric typewriters; and on and on.

So you can see that there is much more to a group of binary digits than their decimal value. It is up to the user to select and use the appropriate code for the application at hand.

TABLE 1.4 TWO'S-COMPLEMENT
SIGNED BINARY NUMBERS[a]

Decimal	Binary	Hexadecimal
−128	10000000	80
−127	10000001	81
−126	10000010	82
−125	10000011	83
−124	10000100	84
⋮	⋮	⋮
−3	11111101	FD
−2	11111110	FE
−1	11111111	FF
0	00000000	0
+1	00000001	1
+2	00000010	2
⋮	⋮	⋮
+125	01111101	7D
+126	01111110	7E
+127	01111111	7F

[a] Positive numbers are formed without change.
Negative numbers are formed by complementing all bits and adding 1. Thus −6 becomes
$00000110 \rightarrow 11111001 + 1 = 11111010$.

1.3 COMPUTER LANGUAGES

As you read this section, look for the answers to these Key Concept questions:

1.3.1. What is the name of a computer program that inputs instruction mnemonics and outputs binary object code?

1.3.2. A(n) _____ is a digital circuit that can be used to convert the closing of a switch into a binary number.

As mentioned previously, programming the computer requires learning a new language. But which one? There is machine language, assembly language, and a host of high-level languages. In this section we examine these different languages and discuss the merits of each.

Machine and Assembly Language Programming. Fundamentally, all computers must be programmed in binary. However, this can be very awkward for human beings. Consider an 8080 microprocessor program that adds two numbers input from a keyboard.

```
11011011
00000000
01000111
```

```
11011011
00000000
10000000
11010011
00000000
01110110
```

Not too clear, is it? Of course, it is crystal clear to an 8080 microprocessor. This type of program is referred to as *object code* and is the only code a computer can execute. However, it is nearly impossible for a human being to work with.

Consider the same program encoded in hexadecimal.

```
DB
00
47
DB
00
80
D3
00
76
```

Certainly this is more readable, but the function of the program is still not clear. Let's add the *mnemonics* (abbreviations for the instruction operation codes) corresponding to these hex codes.

Binary	Hex	Mnemonic	Comment
11011011	DB	IN	;INPUT THE FIRST NUMBER
00000000	00	0	;FROM PORT 0 AND SAVE IN REGISTER A.
01000111	47	MOV B,A	;PUT A COPY OF REGISTER A IN REGISTER B.
11011011	DB	IN	;INPUT THE SECOND NUMBER
00000000	00	0	;FROM PORT 0 AND SAVE IN REGISTER A.
10000000	80	ADD B	;ADD REGISTERS A AND B, LEAVE THE SUM ; IN REGISTER A.
11010011	D3	OUT	;OUTPUT REGISTER A
00000000	00	0	;TO PORT 0.
01110110	76	HLT	;HALT.

The function of the program now becomes clear. The two numbers to be added are first input from port 0 (where the keyboard is assumed connected). The first number is temporarily saved in register B so that the second input operation will not overwrite it. (*Note:* A register is a storage location within the CPU capable of storing data just as a memory cell can. The 8080 microprocessor has several such registers, labeled B, C, D, E, H, and L.) The ADD B instruction adds the contents of registers A and B, leaving the result in Register A (the accumulator). This value is then output to port 0 (where the CRT is assumed connected). Finally, the computer is instructed to halt.

Notice how the operation codes may be represented in binary, hex, or as a mnemonic. The comments on the far right help make the function of the program clear. Programming the computer by entering only the hexadecimal operation codes is referred to as *machine language* programming. Some computers allow the mnemonics to be entered directly. This is called *assembly language* programming.

Although it is obvious that assembly language is the easiest of the two forms to use, it is well to remember that the computer itself can accept only binary data (object code). What, then, is the usefulness of assembly language?

A special program called an *assembler* is required. When placed in the computer's memory, it will allow the operator to input the program in mnemonic form. The assembler program usually comes with some form of *editor* that allows for easy creation of the assembly language file (called the *source code*). When the source code version of the program is completed, the assembler is called on to "look up" the binary codes for the mnemonics and create a new file called the *object code*. This file contains the binary code, which can be loaded into memory and executed.

If you are using a microprocessor trainer to learn microcomputer programming, you will probably be writing your programs in mnemonic form. You will then be required to look up the hex codes for each mnemonic in an assembly language reference chart supplied with the documentation for your microprocessor. This process is called (strangely enough) *hand assembly*.

Now you might be wondering to yourself how your trainer can accept hex codes when the microprocessor can digest only binary codes. Figure 1.3 should help explain. This is the diagram for a 16 line-to-4 line encoder. This circuit accepts 16 different inputs (corresponding to the 16 keys 0 through F on your trainer's keyboard) and provides a 4-bit binary output 0000 through 1111. In this way you are allowed to input data in hex even though the computer itself will see this data as binary.

High-Level Languages.   The BASIC computer language has become very popular lately and is supplied with most personal computer systems. The program to add two numbers when written in BASIC becomes

```
10 INPUT N1,N2
20 PRINT "SUM = ";N1+N2
30 END
```

A comparison with the original binary program is striking. Of course, that is the intent of all high-level languages. Let the programmer communicate in a language as similar as possible to his or her own.

Programming in BASIC requires a BASIC *interpreter* or *compiler*. When using interpreted BASIC, the application program may be entered to memory without an editor. The command RUN is then given, causing the interpreter to examine each BASIC statement and then execute a sequence of machine code to perform the function.

The use of an interpreter may result in very slow program execution speed. If the computer is in a loop, the interpreter will continue to interpret the instructions

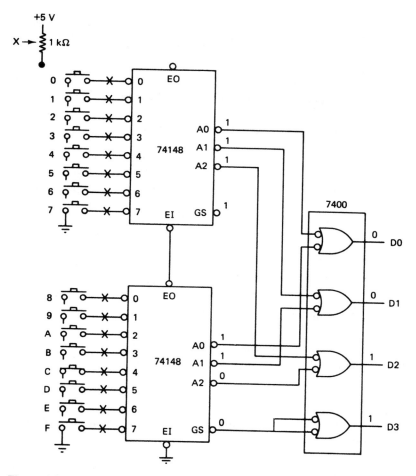

Figure 1.3 A 16 line-to-4 line encoder circuit allows hexadecimal input to a microprocessor trainer. In this example key C is closed and the binary output is 1100.

in that loop over and over. Of course, the computer is so fast that we often do not notice this delay.

For example, the BASIC program given previously to add two numbers might require 10 ms to calculate the sum and print the result. The machine language version could do it in 23 μs (8080 microprocessor with a 2-MHz clock). However, you would have to be pretty quick to notice the difference between 10 ms and 23 μs!

This time delay can become very noticeable when large amounts of computing must be done, however. For example, let's say that we had to perform the addition problem 1 million times. This would require 1,000,000 $\times$ 10 ms = 10,000 s or 2.8 hours with the BASIC program. The machine language version would require 1,000,000 $\times$ 23 μs = 23 s!

Sec. 1.3   Computer Languages

A *compiler* is used to convert a high-level language program to object code form. Using a compiler is similar to using an assembler because an editor must be used for creating the application program file.

When the compiler is called on, it compiles the high-level language program into a binary machine code file. This has several advantages over the interpreter. For one, the code does not have to be reinterpreted over and over when loops are encountered. In addition, the resulting object code file will run all by itself without the need for the compiler to be resident in memory. This saves memory space and allows for larger programs to be run.

The main disadvantage to using a compiler is that errors will require reinvoking the editor, correcting the errors, and recompiling the program. This can be frustrating when simple syntax errors—missing commas, for example—appear.

1.4 IMPLEMENTING THE THREE-BUS ARCHITECTURE IN HARDWARE

As you read this section, look for the answers to these Key Concept questions:

1.4.1. What are typical high- and low-level output voltages for a standard TTL gate?

1.4.2 Which microprocessor bus is used to indicate if the current instruction requires data to enter the CPU or leave the CPU?

In this section we introduce the typical 8-bit microprocessor. This chip has an 8-bit data bus, a 16-bit address bus, and a four-line control bus. A detailed understanding of these three buses is essential for anyone interested in microprocessor design and engineering.

Digital Signals. Figure 1.4 illustrates the *three-bus architecture* of a typical microprocessor. The 16 lines of the address bus are labeled A0 (least significant bit) through A15 (most significant bit). Similarly, the eight lines of the data bus are labeled D0 through D7. The four lines of the control bus are defined to be consistent with the four types of machine cycles introduced in Sec. 1.1 (I/O read and write and memory read and write).

Recall that a bus is defined as a collection of lines each carrying a discrete voltage level. When this voltage level is varying in time, we refer to the information on the line as a digital signal.

Nearly all microprocessors and digital circuits provide signals that are TTL (*transistor-transistor-logic*)-compatible. In this system any voltage level less than or equal to 0.4 V is considered a logic 0. A logic 1 is defined as a voltage level greater than or equal to 2.4 V. Typical values are 0.2 V and 3.4 V. Note that a TTL receiver is designed to accept voltages as high as 0.8 V for a logic 0 and as low as 2.0 V for a logic 1 (see Sec. 4.3 for a discussion of noise immunity).

Another popular logic family is CMOS (*complementary metal-oxide semiconductor*) and these devices produce typical logic levels of 0 V and 5 V. In most

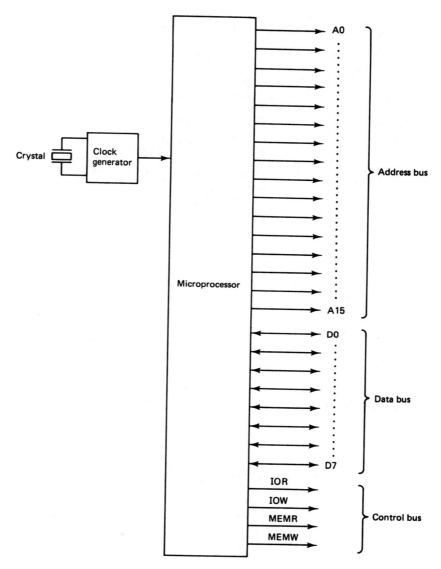

Figure 1.4 An 8-bit microprocessor showing the data, address, and control buses.

cases, TTL devices can drive a nearly unlimited number of CMOS devices (provided that pullup resistors are used to bring TTL's logic 1 level closer to 5.0 V), but CMOS is limited to one standard TTL load. More detail on TTL to CMOS and CMOS to TTL interfacing is provided in Chap. 4 and in most digital electronics textbooks.

It is important to remember that digital signals are nearly always switching in time. As an example, Fig. 1.5 shows an oscilloscope photograph of the two

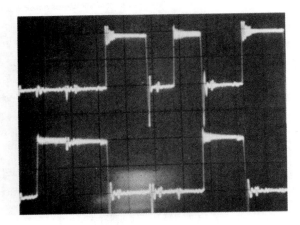

Figure 1.5 Oscilloscope photograph of address lines A0 and A1 on a Z-80 microprocessor. The vertical sensitivity is 2 V/div and the horizontal time base is 2 μs/div.

low-order (A0 and A1) address lines of a Z-80 microprocessor. We expect these lines to be switching quite frequently because they must change each time the microprocessor fetches a new instruction from memory. Also note that the idealized square waves usually drawn (with 0 ns rise and fall times and perfectly square edges) are not realized in practice.

With 16 address lines, eight data bus lines, and four control lines, the conventional dual-trace oscilloscope may not be the ideal tool for troubleshooting microcomputer systems. What is required is a multichannel instrument with memory that can store the contents of the buses over a period of time (several hundred cycles) and present the data in binary, hex, ASCII, or mnemonic form. Such an instrument

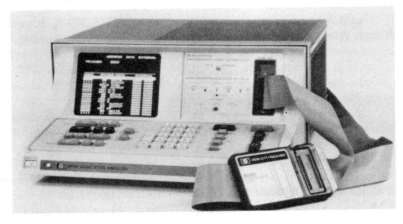

Figure 1.6 The Hewlett-Packard model 1611A logic-state analyzer. This device has 32 input channels and is ideal for monitoring the buses of a microprocessor system. When used with the optional personality module, the contents of the data bus can be disassembled and displayed in mnemonic form. (Courtesy of Hewlett-Packard.)

is called a logic or *data analyzer* and is an indispensable tool for locating hardware problems in microprocessors.

Figure 1.6 shows the Hewlett-Packard model 1611A logic-state analyzer. This instrument has 32 channels and will store 64 cycles of the input data. The screen display can be in binary, hex, ASCII, or with the appropriate personality module, the hex codes can be disassembled and the corresponding mnemonics displayed. Using the logic analyzer as a troubleshooting tool is discussed in detail in Chap. 11.

Defining the Three Buses.   The address bus in Fig. 1.4 carries the address of the memory cell the CPU wishes to read from or write to. With 16 address lines there are 2^{16} or 65,536 unique addresses that the CPU can output. These range from 0000 hex to FFFF hex. Strangely enough, this is referred to as *64K* of memory space. This apparent misnomer is due to the fact that there is no even power of 2 that comes out to 1000. The closest is 2^{10} or 1024. Therefore, 1K in binary is 1024 and a 1K-bit memory actually has 1024 memory cells. Similarly, a 2K-bit memory has 2048 memory cells, and so on.

Figure 1.7 shows two pictorial representations of the 16-bit address. In Fig. 1.7(a) the high-order 8 bits are shown defining 1 of 256 pages in a book (remember that there are 256 unique combinations of 8 bits). On each page there are 256 lines defined by the 8 low-order bits. The total capacity of the book is thus 256 pages with 256 lines per page or 65,536 total lines. Of course, each line of the memory actually stores one byte (8 bits), and a 64K memory system thus represents 64K × 8 or 512K total bits.

In Fig. 1.7(b) the memory space is shown as a *map* with 16 blocks. Each block corresponds to 4K of memory space. This division into 4K blocks is arbitrary but it is a convenient choice. This is because the most significant hex digit increments by 1 for each 4K block.

Memory maps are useful to show how much of the memory space of the microprocessor is actually implemented and if any I/O devices are mapped into this area (this is called *memory-mapped I/O* and is discussed in Chap. 6). We will return to the memory-map concept throughout this book.

Although the memory lines are all outputs from the microprocessor, the data bus lines must be capable of both inputting and outputting data. Such a bus is referred to as *bidirectional*. A microprocessor with an 8-bit data bus is referred to as an 8-bit machine. All of the microprocessors studied in this book are 8-bit machines, but of course there are 4-, 8-, 16-, and 32-bit microprocessors—how long will it be until the first 64-bit micro appears?

Last, we come to the control bus. This bus is necessary to control the direction of data flow on the bidirectional data bus and to differentiate between a memory address and an I/O address. For example, when the IOW (I/O write) line is active, the address on the address bus should be interpreted as an I/O address, and not that of a memory cell. Because it is a write cycle, the I/O device should be prepared to receive data from the microprocessor.

You should be able to see that the four lines of the control bus electrically define the type of instruction cycle the microprocessor is performing, as listed in Table 1.1.

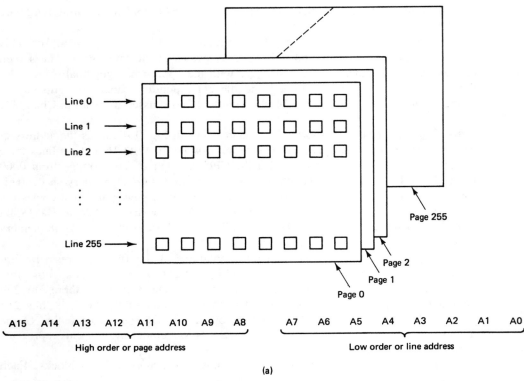

Line 0 →
Line 1 →
Line 2 →

Line 255 →

Page 255

Page 2

Page 1

Page 0

A15 A14 A13 A12 A11 A10 A9 A8

High order or page address

A7 A6 A5 A4 A3 A2 A1 A0

Low order or line address

(a)

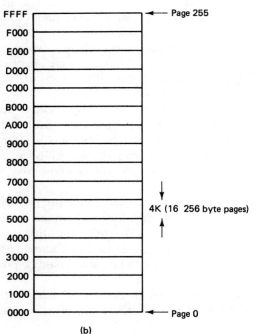

FFFF — Page 255
F000
E000
D000
C000
B000
A000
9000
8000
7000
6000
5000
4000
3000
2000
1000
0000 — Page 0

4K (16 256 byte pages)

(b)

Figure 1.7 Visualizing the memory space of a microprocessor: (a) the 16-bit address can be thought of as defining 256 pages in a book with 256 lines on each page; (b) the memory space is visualized as a two-dimensional map with memory cell 0 at the bottom and memory cell 65535 (FFFF) at the top.

1.5 THE CPU AS A COMPLEX TIMER

As you read this section, look for the answers to these Key Concept questions:

1.5.1 The CPU continually follows the sequence: _____ and _____.

1.5.2 Each computer instruction is made up of one or more _____ cycles, and each of these requires several clock cycles or _____ states.

One way of visualizing the microprocessor is as a complex timing unit. It outputs memory or I/O addresses on its address bus, reads and writes data on its data bus, and synchronizes these activities with its control bus.

The microprocessor controls the timing for the entire microcomputer system. Once set in motion, the CPU endlessly executes its sequence of fetch and execute. It will be up to the memory and I/O devices to be ready when their "turn" comes up. The microprocessor does not care, and it will not wait. It will just as soon read garbage as meaningful data.

We may think of the instructions stored in the memory unit as codes that will cause a particular sequence of events to occur on the CPU's three buses. Keeping this perspective in mind, let us sketch timing diagrams for a simple assembly language program.

Machine Cycle Timing Diagrams. Figure 1.8 is the listing of an assembly language routine that will input data from an I/O device at port 3, store this data at memory address 0700H (the capital H signifies that the address should be interpreted in hexadecimal), and halt. The hex instruction codes are shown in the middle of the listing on the same line as each mnemonic. The memory addresses correspond to the locations in memory where the instruction codes are stored.

Notice that the IN and STA instructions require two- and three-byte instruction codes, respectively. The first byte always represents the *op-code* for the instruction. Thus DB is the op-code for IN and 32 the op-code for STA.

We will see that the processors studied in this book use only 8-bits for the I/O address. For this reason the second byte of the IN instruction corresponds to the 8-bit I/O address—port 3 in this case.

The STA instruction requires a 16-bit address to identify the memory cell in which to store the data. Notice that the processor requires that these bytes be given

ADDRESS	OP-CODES	MNEMONICS	COMMENTS
0000	DB 03	IN 3	INPUT DATA FROM PORT 3 TO ACCUMULATOR
0002	32 00 07	STA 0700	STORE ACCUMULATOR AT PAGE 7 LINE 0
0005	76	HLT	HALT

Figure 1.8 Assembly language routine used for the machine cycle timing diagram in Fig. 1.9.

in reverse order, with the low-order address first (00) and the high-order address last (07).

Figure 1.9 is the machine-cycle timing diagram corresponding to this program. The presence of a control signal is shown by a pulse to the logic 1 level. The contents of the address and data buses are given in hex for better readability. The diagram is divided into three major time periods corresponding to the three separate instructions.

Each instruction begins with an op-code fetch (memory read machine cycle). This cycle is numbered *M1* in Fig. 1.9. Tracing the IN 3 instruction, the second machine cycle (M2) is also a memory read cycle. This is because during the M1 cycle only the op-code was read. This told the CPU it is to input data from a port. The M2 memory read cycle identifies the port address. Also notice that the address bus increments to 0001 for the M2 cycle.

Once the op-code and port address are known, the CPU can execute the instruction by inputting the data from port 3. The M3 cycle shows this execution phase. The IOR (I/O read) control line is pulsed, the address bus outputs 03 (the port

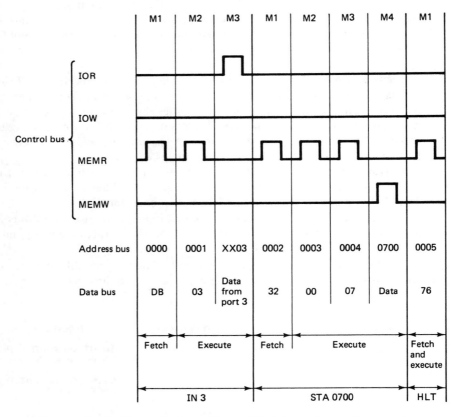

Figure 1.9 Machine cycle timing diagram. Each instruction produces a unique pattern on the three buses of the microprocessor. This diagram is for the program in Fig. 1.8.

address) on A0 through A7, and the bidirectional data bus is configured for data input. It is now up to the I/O device to place its data on the bus.

The M3 machine cycle ends the IN instruction and the next op-code is fetched from memory. We see 0002 on the address bus and the hex code 32 on the data bus. Two memory read cycles follow as first the low-order and then the high-order memory address for the STA instruction are read. Now that the CPU knows the proper memory address to store the data, it executes a memory write cycle during M4. This is observed by the memory write pulse on the control bus, address 0700H on the address bus, and the data byte appearing on the data bus.

Finally, the HLT instruction can be fetched. This instruction does not require further access to memory or I/O and thus it is just one machine cycle long. The CPU now halts in an idle loop, waiting for a reset to restart the fetch-and-execute sequence.

The main points to be learned from this diagram are:

1. Each instruction has an op-code fetch-and-execute phase.
2. The M1 machine cycle is always a memory read (op-code fetch).
3. The CPU can perform only one activity at a time and only one control line can thus be active at any given instant.
4. A single microprocessor instruction may require several bytes and several machine cycles; the Intel and Zilog processors studied in this book have a maximum of four bytes per instruction and six machine cycles per instruction.

Instruction Timing.   Figure 1.10 is an instruction set summary for the Intel 8080 microprocessor. The mnemonics are listed in alphabetical order followed by a brief description of the instruction. The binary equivalent of the op-code is also given. From this chart you can see that the IN instruction has the op-code 11011011 or DBH (again H indicates hex).

The chart also includes the number of clock cycles—sometimes called *T states*—required for each instruction. The IN instruction requires 10 clock cycles, the STA instruction requires 13, and the HLT instruction 7. From this information we can conclude that the program given in Fig. 1.8 will require 30 clock cycles. If the microcomputer system clock is 2.0 MHz, the time required to execute this program is

$$30 \text{ clock cycles} \times \frac{1}{2 \text{ MHz}} = 15 \text{ } \mu s$$

The chart in Fig. 1.10 does not indicate how these clock cycles are distributed over the various machine cycles involved. This information can be found (if you care) in the user's manual for the microprocessor. The important point to remember is that *not all machine cycles are of equal length* even though Fig. 1.9 gives that impression.

Processor Timing.   Figure 1.11 illustrates basic processor timing for memory read and write machine cycles. Each T state is identified as one pulse from the system

INSTRUCTION SET

Summary of Processor Instructions
By Alphabetical Order

Mnemonic	Description	Instruction Code [1]								Clock [2]
		D7	D6	D5	D4	D3	D2	D1	D0	Cycles
ACI	Add immediate to A with carry	1	1	0	0	1	1	1	0	7
ADC M	Add memory to A with carry	1	0	0	0	1	1	1	0	7
ADC r	Add register to A with carry	1	0	0	0	1	S	S	S	4
ADD M	Add memory to A	1	0	0	0	0	1	1	0	7
ADD r	Add register to A	1	0	0	0	0	S	S	S	4
ADI	Add immediate to A	1	1	0	0	0	1	1	0	7
ANA M	And memory with A	1	0	1	0	0	1	1	0	7
ANA r	And register with A	1	0	1	0	0	S	S	S	4
ANI	And immediate with A	1	1	1	0	0	1	1	0	7
CALL	Call unconditional	1	1	0	0	1	1	0	1	17
CC	Call on carry	1	1	0	1	1	1	0	0	11/17
CM	Call on minus	1	1	1	1	1	1	0	0	11/17
CMA	Compliment A	0	0	1	0	1	1	1	1	4
CMC	Compliment carry	0	0	1	1	1	1	1	1	4
CMP M	Compare memory with A	1	0	1	1	1	1	1	0	7
CMP r	Compare register with A	1	0	1	1	1	S	S	S	4
CNC	Call on no carry	1	1	0	1	0	1	0	0	11/17
CNZ	Call on no zero	1	1	0	0	0	1	0	0	11/17
CP	Call on positive	1	1	1	1	0	1	0	0	11/17
CPE	Call on parity even	1	1	1	0	1	1	0	0	11/17
CPI	Compare immediate with A	1	1	1	1	1	1	1	0	7
CPO	Call on parity odd	1	1	1	0	0	1	0	0	11/17
CZ	Call on zero	1	1	0	0	1	1	0	0	11/17
DAA	Decimal adjust A	0	0	1	0	0	1	1	1	4
DAD B	Add B & C to H & L	0	0	0	0	1	0	0	1	10
DAD D	Add D & E to H & L	0	0	0	1	1	0	0	1	10
DAD H	Add H & L to H & L	0	0	1	0	1	0	0	1	10
DAD SP	Add stack pointer to H & L	0	0	1	1	1	0	0	1	10
DCR M	Decrement memory	0	0	1	1	0	1	0	1	10
DCR r	Decrement register	0	0	D	D	D	1	0	1	5
DCX B	Decrement B & C	0	0	0	0	1	0	1	1	5
DCX D	Decrement D & E	0	0	0	1	1	0	1	1	5
DCX H	Decrement H & L	0	0	1	0	1	0	1	1	5
DCX SP	Decrement stack pointer	0	0	1	1	1	0	1	1	5
DI	Disable Interrupt	1	1	1	1	0	0	1	1	4
EI	Enable Interrupts	1	1	1	1	1	0	1	1	4
HLT	Halt	0	1	1	1	0	1	1	0	7
IN	Input	1	1	0	1	1	0	1	1	10
INR M	Increment memory	0	0	1	1	0	1	0	0	10
INR r	Increment register	0	0	D	D	D	1	0	0	5
INX B	Increment B & C registers	0	0	0	0	0	0	1	1	5
INX D	Increment D & E registers	0	0	0	1	0	0	1	1	5
INX H	Increment H & L registers	0	0	1	0	0	0	1	1	5
INX SP	Increment stack pointer	0	0	1	1	0	0	1	1	5
JC	Jump on carry	1	1	0	1	1	0	1	0	10
JM	Jump on minus	1	1	1	1	1	0	1	0	10
JMP	Jump unconditional	1	1	0	0	0	0	1	1	10
JNC	Jump on no carry	1	1	0	1	0	0	1	0	10
JNZ	Jump on no zero	1	1	0	0	0	0	1	0	10
JP	Jump on positive	1	1	1	1	0	0	1	0	10
JPE	Jump on parity even	1	1	1	0	1	0	1	0	10
JPO	Jump on parity odd	1	1	1	0	0	0	1	0	10
JZ	Jump on zero	1	1	0	0	1	0	1	0	10
LDA	Load A direct	0	0	1	1	1	0	1	0	13
LDAX B	Load A indirect	0	0	0	0	1	0	1	0	7
LDAX D	Load A indirect	0	0	0	1	1	0	1	0	7
LHLD	Load H & L direct	0	0	1	0	1	0	1	0	16
LXI B	Load immediate register Pair B & C	0	0	0	0	0	0	0	1	10
LXI D	Load immediate register Pair D & E	0	0	0	1	0	0	0	1	10
LXI H	Load immediate register Pair H & L	0	0	1	0	0	0	0	1	10
LXI SP	Load immediate stack pointer	0	0	1	1	0	0	0	1	10

Mnemonic	Description	Instruction Code [1]								Clock [2]
		D7	D6	D5	D4	D3	D2	D1	D0	Cycles
MVI M	Move immediate memory	0	0	1	1	0	1	1	0	10
MVI r	Move immediate register	0	0	D	D	D	1	1	0	7
MOV M, r	Move register to memory	0	1	1	1	0	S	S	S	7
MOV r, M	Move memory to register	0	1	D	D	D	1	1	0	7
MOV r1/r2	Move register to register	0	1	D	D	D	S	S	S	5
NOP	No-operation	0	0	0	0	0	0	0	0	4
ORA M	Or memory with A	1	0	1	1	0	1	1	0	7
ORA r	Or register with A	1	0	1	1	0	S	S	S	4
ORI	Or immediate with A	1	1	1	1	0	1	1	0	7
OUT	Output	1	1	0	1	0	0	1	1	10
PCHL	H & L to program counter	1	1	1	0	1	0	0	1	5
POP B	Pop register pair B & C off stack	1	1	0	0	0	0	0	1	10
POP D	Pop register pair D & E off stack	1	1	0	1	0	0	0	1	10
POP H	Pop register pair H & L off stack	1	1	1	0	0	0	0	1	10
POP PSW	Pop A and Flags off stack	1	1	1	1	0	0	0	1	10
PUSH B	Push register Pair B & C on stack	1	1	0	0	0	1	0	1	11
PUSH D	Push register Pair D & E on stack	1	1	0	1	0	1	0	1	11
PUSH H	Push register Pair H & L on stack	1	1	1	0	0	1	0	1	11
PUSH PSW	Push A and Flags on stack	1	1	1	1	0	1	0	1	11
RAL	Rotate A left through carry	0	0	0	1	0	1	1	1	4
RAR	Rotate A right through carry	0	0	0	1	1	1	1	1	4
RC	Return on carry	1	1	0	1	1	0	0	0	5/11
RET	Return	1	1	0	0	1	0	0	1	10
RLC	Rotate A left	0	0	0	0	0	1	1	1	4
RM	Return on minus	1	1	1	1	1	0	0	0	5/11
RNC	Return on no carry	1	1	0	1	0	0	0	0	5/11
RNZ	Return on no zero	1	1	0	0	0	0	0	0	5/11
RP	Return on positive	1	1	1	1	0	0	0	0	5/11
RPE	Return on parity even	1	1	1	0	1	0	0	0	5/11
RPO	Return on parity odd	1	1	1	0	0	0	0	0	5/11
RRC	Rotate A right	0	0	0	0	1	1	1	1	4
RST	Restart	1	1	A	A	A	1	1	1	11
RZ	Return on zero	1	1	0	0	1	0	0	0	5/11
SBB M	Subtract memory from A with borrow	1	0	0	1	1	1	1	0	7
SBB r	Subtract register from A with borrow	1	0	0	1	1	S	S	S	4
SBI	Subtract immediate from A with borrow	1	1	0	1	1	1	1	0	7
SHLD	Store H & L direct	0	0	1	0	0	0	1	0	16
SPHL	H & L to stack pointer	1	1	1	1	1	0	0	1	5
STA	Store A direct	0	0	1	1	0	0	1	0	13
STAX B	Store A indirect	0	0	0	0	0	0	1	0	7
STAX D	Store A indirect	0	0	0	1	0	0	1	0	7
STC	Set carry	0	0	1	1	0	1	1	1	4
SUB M	Subtract memory from A	1	0	0	1	0	1	1	0	7
SUB r	Subtract register from A	1	0	0	1	0	S	S	S	4
SUI	Subtract immediate from A	1	1	0	1	0	1	1	0	7
XCHG	Exchange D & E, H & L Registers	1	1	1	0	1	0	1	1	4
XRA M	Exclusive Or memory with A	1	0	1	0	1	1	1	0	7
XRA r	Exclusive Or register with A	1	0	1	0	1	S	S	S	4
XRI	Exclusive Or immediate with A	1	1	1	0	1	1	1	0	7
XTHL	Exchange top of stack, H & L	1	1	1	0	0	0	1	1	18

NOTES: 1. DDD or SSS — 000 B — 001 C — 010 D — 011 E — 100 H — 101 L — 110 Memory — 111 A.
2. Two possible cycle times, (5/11) indicate instruction cycles dependent on condition flags.

Figure 1.10 Instruction set of the 8080 microprocessor. (Courtesy of Intel Corporation.)

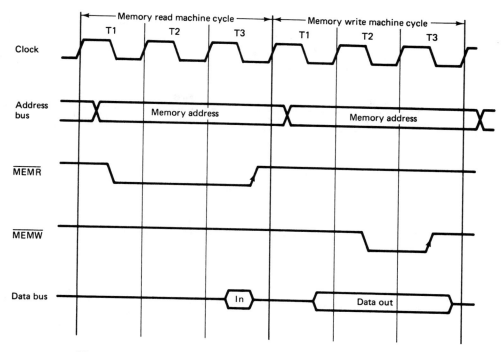

Figure 1.11 Processor timing for memory read and write machine cycles.

clock. In this instance both machine cycles are shown as three T states long, but this may not always be true.

Rather than try to show 16 separate lines for the address bus, it is shown as two parallel lines symbolizing that some of the lines are a logic 1 level and some a logic 0 level. When these lines cross, a new address is output by the CPU. Similarly, the eight lines of the data bus are defined only when valid data is present and left unknown elsewhere.

Examining the memory read machine cycle in Fig. 1.11, the contents of the address bus become valid during the T1 clock cycle. Near the end of this machine cycle the MEMR (memory read) line becomes active (the bar drawn above MEMR signifies that this line goes low when active). The memory unit now has the time until the falling edge of the clock during the T3 cycle to find the data requested by the CPU and place it on the data bus. This time is referred to as the *access time* of the memory.

Notice that the data bus is expected to receive valid data from the memory when the falling edge of T3 occurs, and at no other time during this machine cycle is data valid on the bus.

The memory write cycle is similar to the memory read cycle except that the processor now outputs the data instead of the memory unit. To give the memory plenty of time to latch the data, the data bus contains valid data early in the machine cycle. When the MEMW (memory write) line goes high, the memory unit will

Sec. 1.5   The CPU as a Complex Timer

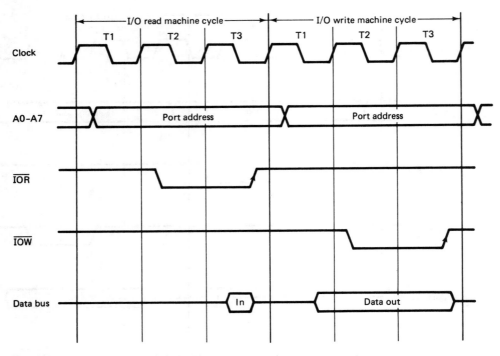

Figure 1.12   Processor timing for I/O read and write machine cycles.

store the byte on the data bus at the address specified by the A0 through A15 address lines.

Figure 1.12 illustrates processor timing for I/O read and write operations. You should be able to see that these are identical to memory read and write cycles except that the $\overline{\text{IOR}}$ and $\overline{\text{IOW}}$ lines will be active instead of $\overline{\text{MEMR}}$ and $\overline{\text{MEMW}}$.

CHAPTER SUMMARY

1. The three main units of a digital computer are the central processing unit (CPU), the memory unit, and the input/output devices.
2. The CPU is hard-wired to follow continually the sequence: fetch an operation code from memory, increment the program counter, execute the instruction.
3. The microprocessor communicates with the other components in the microcomputer system via the data, address, and control buses.
4. At any given instant in time the CPU is either performing a memory read or write operation, an I/O read or write operation, or an internal activity.
5. All digital computers are designed with binary circuits that switch between an ON and an OFF state. In binary an individual digit is called a bit and a group of 8 bits is referred to as a byte.

6. The hexadecimal number system provides a convenient means of expressing binary numbers.

7. The binary data in a microcomputer's memory may be coded and represent instruction operations, ASCII characters, BCD numbers, or other codes.

8. Programming the computer by supplying the instruction operations in hex or binary is called machine language programming.

9. A mnemonic is an abbreviation for a computer instruction that suggests the intent of that instruction. Supplying the microcomputer with mnemonics is called assembly language programming.

10. Digital signals switch between logic 1 and 0 levels. Most microcomputer systems use TTL logic circuits in which a logic 1 is a voltage greater than or equal to 2.4 V and a logic 0 a voltage less than or equal to 0.4 V.

11. The typical 8-bit microprocessor with 16-bit address bus can access 65,536 8-bit memory locations. This is referred to as 64K of memory space.

12. Each microprocessor instruction can be broken into several machine cycles, during which the CPU does one of four specific operations: memory read, memory write, I/O read, or I/O write.

13. The time to execute a microcomputer program can be found by adding up the total clock cycles or T states required for all instructions in the program.

LAB PROJECTS

1.1. BASIC has two functions—CHR$(n) and ASC(''X'')—which can be used to print the ASCII equivalent of the number n or the ASCII code of character ''X''. Use these functions to write the following BASIC programs.
  (a) Input a decimal number, output its ASCII character equivalent.
  (b) Input an ASCII character, output its ASCII numeric code.
  (c) Print the entire ASCII character set corresponding to all combinations of 8 binary bits.

1.2. The four-line BASIC program shown below can be used to convert a decimal number to its 8-bit binary equivalent [stored in the array B(J)]. Modify this program so that it will accept decimal numbers as large as 65,535, convert to a 16-bit binary number, and print the result.

```
10 INPUT N
20 FOR J = 7 to 0 STEP −1
30 IF N − 2^J < 0 THEN B(J) = 0 ELSE B(J) = 1: N = N − 2^J
40 NEXT J
```

1.3. The BASIC statement A$ = HEX$(n) stores the hexadecimal equivalent of n in string variable A$. Using this function, modify the program of Lab 1.2 to also print the hexadecimal equivalent of the input number.

1.4. Test the keyboard encoder circuit shown in Fig. 1.3. If a 16-key keypad is unavailable, two 8-switch DIP switches can be substituted.

(a) Test the output with 2 or more keys down.

(b) Test the output with no keys down.

(c) Modify the circuit to include a KEYDOWN signal that will be active only when one or more of the 16 keys are pressed.

(d) Add a seven-segment decoder and display to the output so that each key code can be viewed directly.

QUESTIONS AND PROBLEMS

Section 1.1

1.1. Explain the purpose of the address, data, and control buses. Which are bidirectional?

1.2. Indicate the source and destination of data for each of the following machine cycle types:

(a) memory read

(b) memory write

(c) I/O read

(d) I/O write

1.3. Referring to Fig. 1.1, describe the contents of the address, data, and control buses when the CPU is writing the data word 26 to memory cell 16.

1.4. One problem with all stored program computers is that when first turned on the memory unit contains random data (the flip-flops that make up the memory cells will power-on in a random fashion). Because this random data cannot be executed with predictable results, the computer is not usable. Can you suggest a different type of memory that could be used to ''boot up'' the computer when power is first applied solving this problem?

Section 1.2

1.5. How many different memory locations can a microprocessor with a 24-bit address bus access?

1.6. Most 8-bit microprocessors have 16 address lines and can therefore access 64K bytes of memory. What happens to this memory capacity when one additional memory line is added? State the general result for adding n additional memory lines.

1.7. Convert the following hex numbers to binary and to decimal.

(a) FE

(b) 13

(c) CC00

(d) FE027C

1.8. Convert the following decimal numbers to binary and to hex.

(a) 19

(b) 99

(c) 251

(d) 57,629

1.9. Perform the following hexadecimal arithmetic problems. Express your answer in hex and in decimal.

    (a) 2AH + 13H

    (b) BCH + 36H

    (c) 6BH − 3CH

    (d) E2 − D7

1.10. One way of expressing a negative number in binary is to use the 2's complement. This is found by complementing all bits and adding 1. Positive numbers are left unchanged. Express the following decimal numbers in 8-bit 2's complement form.

    (a) −23

    (b) −102

    (c) −128

    (d) +47

1.11. Using the 2's complement, a positive number is indicated when the most significant bit (MSB) of a signed number is a 0. If the MSB is a 1, a negative number is indicated (see Table 1.4) and its magnitude can be found by forming the 2's complement and converting to decimal. Following these rules, convert the following 8-bit signed numbers to decimal.

    (a) 11010110

    (b) 10001111

    (c) C3H

    (d) 66H

1.12. When the hexadecimal numbers 3C and 92 are added together the result is CE. Show that in *unsigned* binary this problem corresponds to the decimal addition of 60 + 146 = 206. Now show that using *signed* binary, the same problem corresponds to 60 − 110 = −50.

1.13. Determine the ASCII equivalent of the following hexadecimal numbers.

    (a) 26H

    (b) 64H

    (c) 07H

    (d) 1BH

Section 1.3

1.14. What does it mean to "hand assemble" a machine language computer program?

1.15. When you buy an expensive software program, the manufacturer will always supply the object code but seldom the source code. What is the reasoning behind this?

1.16. Consider a program written in assembly language, interpreted BASIC, and compiled BASIC. Which version will have the shortest execution time? Which one do you think is the easiest to write? Explain why.

1.17. Refer to the keyboard encoder circuit shown in Fig. 1.3. If keys 4 and 5 are both held down, what is the binary output code that will be produced?

*1.18. Refer to Fig. 1.3. Assume the connection between EO and EI of the two encoders breaks open. What would the *symptom* of this problem be? (Hint: TTL circuits interpret open pins as logic 1s.)

Section 1.4

1.19. How many decimal memory words are there in an 8K-byte memory unit? How many address lines would be required to access all locations in this memory?

1.20. Refer to Fig. 1.7(a). What is the hexadecimal address corresponding to decimal page 48 line 203?

1.21. A certain microcomputer has a 1K byte memory beginning at address 1000H. What is the hex address of the *last* byte in this memory?

1.22. Redraw the memory map shown in Fig. 1.7(b) using 8 8K-byte blocks. Indicate the starting address of each block.

Section 1.5

1.23. A single-step circuit will "freeze" all data on the buses of a microcomputer system. Assume that such a circuit is used to test a microprocessor and that the data bus lines are measured with a voltmeter. The results are as follows:

bit D0 = 3.8 V	bit D1 = 3.5 V
bit D2 = 0.1 V	bit D3 = 0.1 V
bit D4 = 3.5 V	bit D5 = 3.4 V
bit D6 = 0.2 V	bit D7 = 0.1 V

What is the data byte on the bus if it is interpreted in hexadecimal? What character does it represent as an ASCII code? What operation code does it represent as an 8080 microprocessor instruction?

1.24. The first machine cycle of every instruction is always:
   (a) memory read
   (b) memory write
   (c) I/O read
   (d) I/O write

1.25. The 8080/8085 instruction IN 3 requires three machine cycles. What are they?

1.26. True or false: One machine cycle requires one T state or clock cycle.

1.27. Refer to Fig. 1.13. How many total bytes does this program require?

1.28. In Fig. 1.13 memory location 0005 holds the data byte FF. How will the CPU interpret this byte when the program is run?

1.29. If it is desired to output 26H to I/O port 5, what change should be made to the program in Fig. 1.13?

1.30. Draw a machine cycle timing diagram for the program in Fig. 1.13. Follow the format shown in Fig. 1.9.

* Throughout the text, problems marked with a * indicate troubleshooting problems.

ADDRESS	OP-CODES	MNEMONICS	COMMENTS
0000	3E 32	MVI A,32H	LOAD ACCUMULATOR WITH 32H
0002	D3 05	OUT 5	OUTPUT THE CONTENTS OF THE ACCUMULATOR TO I/O PORT 5
0004	32 FF 06	STA 06FFH	STORE THE ACCUMULATOR AT MEMORY LOCATION 06FFH
0007	76	HLT	HALT

Figure 1.13 8080 microprocessor assembly language routine used for Probs. 1.27 through 1.31.

1.31. Calculate the total time required to execute the program in Fig. 1.13 if the system clock frequency is 2 MHz. Figure 1.10 provides T-state information for each 8080 microprocessor instruction.

1.32. The access time of a memory chip is defined as the time from receipt of the memory address until valid data is output by the chip. Referring to Fig. 1.11, estimate the access time required of the memory assuming a 4-MHz clock signal.

KEY CONCEPT ANSWERS

1.1.1. CPU, memory, I/O

1.1.2. address, data, control

1.1.3. memory read and write, I/O read and write

1.2.1. 256

1.2.2. D6, 214

1.2.3. 1010000

1.3.1. assembler

1.3.2. encoder

1.4.1. 3.4 V and 0.2 V

1.4.2. control bus

1.5.1. fetch, execute

1.5.2. machine, T

2

Introducing the 8080, 8085, and Z-80 Microprocessors

In Chap. 1 we studied the basic elements of the stored program computer. We now apply these concepts to some "real" hardware in the form of the Intel 8080 and 8085 and the Zilog Z-80 microprocessors.

We begin this task by forming the basic *CPU module* for each chip. This module will be consistent with the definition of the CPU presented in Chap. 1. Next we carefully "peel the covers off" each processor and develop *programming models* for each chip. Think of the CPU module as the hardware designer's view of the microprocessor, whereas the programming model presents the software designer's view.

The chapter concludes with an introduction to the instruction sets of the three processors, a discussion of addressing modes, and a sample program written in assembly language with hexadecimal instruction codes.

2.1 CONSTRUCTING THE CPU MODULE

As you read this section, look for the answer to this Key Concept question:

2.1.1. List two different design techniques commonly used to build a microcomputer system.

As discussed in Chap. 1, a typical computer consists of the CPU, the memory unit, and the I/O (input/output) devices. In a practical microcomputer system these functions are often constructed on separate plug-in cards that mate to parallel connectors on a *motherboard*. This technique is shown in Fig. 2.1.

This type of microcomputer design is referred to as *bus-oriented* because all of the parallel connectors form a common bus. But if this bus is to be truly useful, everyone must agree on the signal definitions for each pin of the bus. As an example, consider the *IEEE-696* (or S-100) bus, whose pin definitions are given in Fig. 2.2. All told, 100 pins are specified, including three power supply voltages, a system clock signal, numerous control signals, and the address and data bus lines.

Other buses exist, such as the *STD* bus (Pro-Log Corporation), the *Unibus* (Digital Equipment Corporation), the *Multibus* (Intel Corporation), and the IBM PC bus. The main advantage of a bus-oriented computer is flexibility. If you want to change the memory or I/O configuration, this can be done by simply plugging in a new memory or I/O board. Indeed, it is even possible to change the CPU board and operate with an entirely new microprocessor.

With the advances in integrated-circuit technology, it has become possible to construct the entire computer on a single board. An example of a *single-board computer* (SBC) is shown in Fig. 2.3. The CPU, I/O, and memory unit are all contained on this single card. The advantage to this technique is the compact design that results and low cost.

The CPU Module. In this chapter we are concerned primarily with the CPU portion of the microcomputer system. This module must generate a system clock signal and

Figure 2.1 A bus-oriented computer consists of several plug-in boards each mating to a connector on a motherboard. This photo illustrates an S-100 (standard 100-pin connector) computer. The disk drives and power supply are in the right-hand compartment. (Courtesy of North Star Computers.)

pin 1	+8 V (B)		pin 51	+8 V (B)	
pin 2	+16 V (B)		pin 52	−16 V (B)	
pin 3	XRDY (S)	H	pin 53	0 volts	
pin 4	VI0* (S)	L	pin 54	SLAVE CLR* (B)	L
pin 5	VI1* (S)	L	pin 55	TMA0* (M)	L
pin 6	VI2* (S)	L	pin 56	TMA1* (M)	L
pin 7	VI3* (S)	L	pin 57	TMA2* (M)	L
pin 8	VI4* (S)	L	pin 58	sXTRQ* (M)	L
pin 9	VI5* (S)	L	pin 59	A19	H
pin 10	VI6* (S)	L	pin 60	SIXTN* (S)	L
pin 11	VI7* (S)	L	pin 61	A20 (M)	H
pin 12	NMI* (S)	L	pin 62	A21 (M)	H
pin 13	PWRFAIL* (B)	L	pin 63	A22 (M)	H
pin 14	TMA3* (M)	L	pin 64	A23 (M)	H
pin 15	A18 (M)	H	pin 65	NDEF	
pin 16	A16 (M)	H	pin 66	NDEF	
pin 17	A17 (M)	H	pin 67	PHANTOM* (M/S)	L
pin 18	SDSB* (M)	L	pin 68	MWRT (B)	H
pin 19	CDSB* (M)	L	pin 69	RFU	
pin 20	0 V		pin 70	0 V	
pin 21	NDEF		pin 71	RFU	
pin 22	ADSB* (M)	L	pin 72	RDY (S)	H
pin 23	DODSB* (M)	L	pin 73	INT* (S)	L
pin 24	φ (B)	H	pin 74	HOLD* (M)	L
pin 25	pSTVAL* (M)	L	pin 75	RESET* (B)	L
pin 26	pHLDA (M)	H	pin 76	pSYNC (M)	H
pin 27	RFU		pin 77	pWR* (M)	L
pin 28	RFU		pin 78	pDBIN (M)	H
pin 29	A5 (M)	H	pin 79	A0 (M)	H
pin 30	A4 (M)	H	pin 80	A1 (M)	H
pin 31	A3 (M)	H	pin 81	A2 (M)	H
pin 32	A15 (M)	H	pin 82	A6 (M)	H
pin 33	A12 (M)	H	pin 83	A7 (M)	H
pin 34	A9 (M)	H	pin 84	A8 (M)	H
pin 35	DO1 (M)/ED1 (M/S)	H	pin 85	A13 (M)	H
pin 36	DO0 (M)/ED0 (M/S)	H	pin 86	A14 (M)	H
pin 37	A10 (M)	H	pin 87	A11 (M)	H
pin 38	DO4 (M)/ED4 (M/S)	H	pin 88	DO2 (M)/ED2 (M/S)	H
pin 39	DO5 (M)/ED5 (M/S)	H	pin 89	DO3 (M)/ED3 (M/S)	H
pin 40	DO6 (M)/ED6 (M/S)	H	pin 90	DO7 (M)/ED7 (M/S)	H
pin 41	DI2 (S)/OD2 (M/S)	H	pin 91	DI4 (S)/OD4 (M/S)	H
pin 42	DI3 (S)/OD3 (M/S)	H	pin 92	DI5 (S)/OD5 (M/S)	H
pin 43	DI7 (S)/OD7 (M/S)	H	pin 93	DI6 (S)/OD6 (M/S)	H
pin 44	sM1 (M)	H	pin 94	DI1 (S)/OD1 (M/S)	H
pin 45	sOUT (M)	H	pin 95	DI0 (S)/OD1 (M/S)	H
pin 46	sINP (M)	H	pin 96	sINTA (M)	H
pin 47	sMEMR (M)	H	pin 97	sWO* (M)	L
pin 48	sHLTA (M)	H	pin 98	ERROR* (S)	L
pin 49	CLOCK (B)		pin 99	POC* (B)	
pin 50	0 V		pin 100	0 V	

Figure 2.2 Signal definitions for the S-100 bus. (Courtesy of The Institute of Electrical and Electronic Engineers, Inc.)

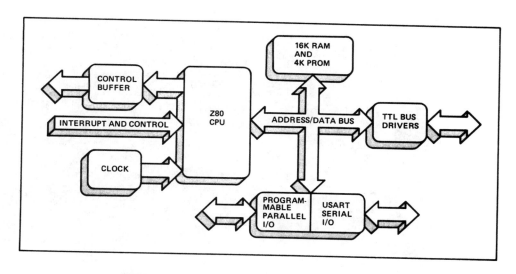

Figure 2.3 Single-board computer (SBC) based on the Zilog Z-80 microprocessor. (Courtesy of Zilog, Inc.)

provide access to the three-bus architecture discussed in Chap. 1. In most cases this means that several TTL packages will be required to support the microprocessor as the CPU module is assembled. As an example, consider the Z-80 CPU card shown in Fig. 2.4. As you can see, several ICs are required in addition to the microprocessor chip itself (the long 40-pin device in the figure).

In the next section we begin to detail the requirements for practical CPU modules for the 8080, 8085, and Z-80 microprocessors.

Figure 2.4 Z-80 CPU card for the S-100 bus. (Courtesy of North Star Computers.)

2.2 CPU MODULES FOR THE 8080, 8085, AND Z-80 MICROPROCESSORS

As you read this section, look for the answers to these Key Concept questions:

2.2.1. The 8080 CPU module requires two support chips—the _____ clock generator and the _____ system controller.

2.2.2. The 8085 CPU module requires an 8-bit latch to demultiplex the _____ and _____ lines.

2.2.3. The Z-80 CPU module requires only an external TTL-compatible _____ generator.

The 8080 CPU Module.   In its day, Intel's 8080 microprocessor was one of the most popular microprocessors in the industry. Indeed, this chip and Motorola's 6800 singlehandedly begat the microprocessor revolution still ongoing today.

The first samples of the 8080 became available in December 1971, so it is not a new device. However, it is a tribute to the original designers (and the circuit's popularity) that all of the processors studied in this book remain software-compatible.

Figure 2.5 provides a pinout for the 8080 and a word description for the function of each pin. The 8080 shows its age by requiring three power supplies (+5 V, −5 V, and +12 V) and a two-phase nonoverlapping, non-TTL-compatible clock signal shown in Fig. 2.6.

The 8080 does not directly provide the control bus signals we are familiar with from Chap. 1. Instead, it provides a *SYNC* signal that pulses high during the first T cycle of each M1 machine cycle (that is, the first clock pulse of each instruction

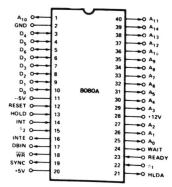

Symbol	Type	Name and Function
A_{15}-A_0	O	**Address Bus:** The address bus provides the address to memory (up to 64K 8-bit words) or denotes the I/O device number for up to 256 input and 256 output devices. A_0 is the least significant address bit.
D_7-D_0	I/O	**Data Bus:** The data bus provides bi-directional communication betweeen the CPU, memory, and I/O devices for instructions and data transfers. Also, during the first clock cycle of each machine cycle, the 8080A outputs a status word on the data bus that describes the current machine cycle. D_0 is the least significant bit.
SYNC	O	**Synchronizing Signal:** The SYNC pin provides a signal to indicate the beginning of each machine cycle.
DBIN	O	**Data Bus In:** The DBIN signal indicates to external circuits that the data bus is in the input mode. This signal should be used to enable the gating of data onto the 8080A data bus from memory or I/O.
READY	I	**Ready:** The READY signal indicates to the 8080A that valid memory or input data is available on the 8080A data bus. This signal is used to synchronize the CPU with slower memory or I/O devices. If after sending an address out the 8080A does not receive a READY input, the 8080A will enter a WAIT state for as long as the READY line is low. READY can also be used to single step the CPU.
WAIT	O	**Wait:** The WAIT signal acknowledges that the CPU is in a WAIT state.
$\overline{WR}$	O	**Write:** The $\overline{WR}$ signal is used for memory WRITE or I/O output control. The data on the data bus is stable while the $\overline{WR}$ signal is active low ($\overline{WR}$ = 0).
HOLD	I	**Hold:** The HOLD signal requests the CPU to enter the HOLD state. The HOLD state allows an external device to gain control of the 8080A address and data bus as soon as the 8080A has completed its use of these busses for the current machine cycle. It is recognized under the following conditions: • the CPU is in the HALT state. • the CPU is in the T2 or TW state and the READY signal is active. As a result of entering the HOLD state the CPU ADDRESS BUS (A_{15}-A_0) and DATA BUS (D_7-D_0) will be in their high impedance state. The CPU acknowledges its state with the HOLD ACKNOWLEDGE (HLDA) pin.
HLDA	O	**Hold Acknowledge:** The HLDA signal appears in response to the HOLD signal and indicates that the data and address bus will go to the high impedance state. The HLDA signal begins at: • T3 for READ memory or input. • The Clock Period following T3 for WRITE memory or OUTPUT operation. In either case, the HLDA signal appears after the rising edge of ϕ_2.
INTE	O	**Interrupt Enable:** Indicates the content of the internal interrupt enable flip/flop. This flip/flop may be set or reset by the Enable and Disable Interrupt instructions and inhibits interrupts from being accepted by the CPU when it is reset. It is automatically reset (disabling further interrupts) at time T1 of the instruction fetch cycle (M1) when an interrupt is accepted and is also reset by the RESET signal.
INT	I	**Interrupt Request:** The CPU recognizes an interrupt request on this line at the end of the current instruction or while halted. If the CPU is in the HOLD state or if the Interrupt Enable flip/flop is reset it will not honor the request.
RESET[1]	I	**Reset:** While the RESET signal is activated, the content of the program counter is cleared. After RESET, the program will start at location 0 in memory. The INTE and HLDA flip/flops are also reset. Note that the flags, accumulator, stack pointer, and registers are not cleared.
V_{SS}		**Ground:** Reference.
V_{DD}		**Power:** +12 ±5% Volts.
V_{CC}		**Power:** +5 ±5% Volts.
V_{BB}		**Power:** −5 ±5% Volts.
ϕ_1, ϕ_2		**Clock Phases:** 2 externally supplied clock phases. (non TTL compatible)

Figure 2.5 8080 microprocessor pinouts and word descriptions for each pin. (Courtesy of Intel Corporation.)

SILICON GATE MOS 8080A

A.C. CHARACTERISTICS

$T_A = 0°C$ to $70°C$, $V_{DD} = +12V \pm 5\%$, $V_{CC} = +5V \pm 5\%$, $V_{BB} = -5V \pm 5\%$, $V_{SS} = 0V$, Unless Otherwise Noted

Symbol	Parameter	Min.	Max.	Unit	Test Condition
t_{CY}[3]	Clock Period	0.48	2.0	μsec	
t_r, t_f	Clock Rise and Fall Time	0	50	nsec	
$t_{\phi1}$	ϕ_1 Pulse Width	60		nsec	
$t_{\phi2}$	ϕ_2 Pulse Width	220		nsec	
t_{D1}	Delay ϕ_1 to ϕ_2	0		nsec	
t_{D2}	Delay ϕ_2 to ϕ_1	70		nsec	
t_{D3}	Delay ϕ_1 to ϕ_2 Leading Edges	80		nsec	

TIMING WAVEFORMS [14]

(Note: Timing measurements are made at the following reference voltages: CLOCK "1" = 8.0V "0" = 1.0V; INPUTS "1" = 3.3V, "0" = 0.8V; OUTPUTS "1" = 2.0V, "0" = 0.8V.)

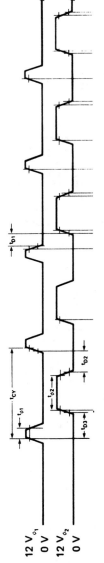

Figure 2.6 The 8080 requires a two-phase nonoverlapping clock signal. The clock levels are not TTL compatible. (Courtesy of Intel Corporation.)

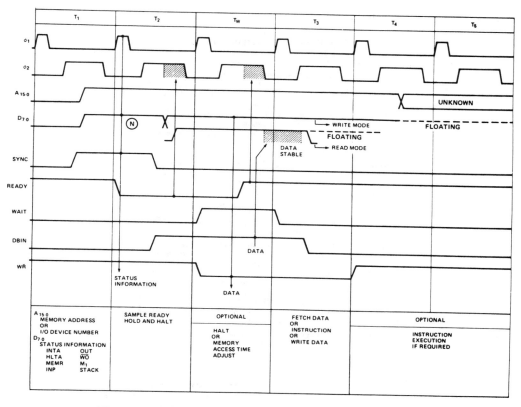

Figure 2.7 Basic 8080 instruction cycle timing. (Courtesy of Intel Corporation.)

fetch). When SYNC is high, the data bus carries *status* information that may be latched and decoded to provide a control bus.

Figure 2.7 illustrates basic 8080 instruction cycle timing. Note that when $\phi1$ is high and SYNC is high, the data bus carries a special *status word*. Table 2.1 is a chart listing the 10 unique status words that can be output by the 8080. Using this chart, a decoder can be designed to generate the four control bus signals necessary for I/O and memory read and write operations.

Example 2.1

Design a decoder circuit to generate the control bus signals $\overline{\text{MEMR}}$, $\overline{\text{MEMW}}$, $\overline{\text{IOR}}$, and $\overline{\text{IOW}}$ for an 8080 microprocessor.

Solution. Studying Fig. 2.7, note that the *DBIN* signal (data bus in) indicates a CPU read operation and the $\overline{\text{WR}}$ signal a CPU write operation. Referring to the status word chart in Table 2.1, only when data bus bit D6 is high is the current machine cycle an I/O read. Thus D6 can be latched and combined with DBIN to generate the $\overline{\text{IOR}}$ control bus signal. This is shown in Fig. 2.8. Only when DBIN is high and the latched data bus bit D6 is high will $\overline{\text{IOR}}$ be active (that is, low). The other three control signals are developed in a similar manner.

TABLE 2.1 8080 STATUS WORD CHART

STATUS INFORMATION DEFINITION

Symbols	Data Bus Bit	Definition
INTA*	D_0	Acknowledge signal for INTERRUPT request. Signal should be used to gate a restart instruction onto the data bus when DBIN is active.
$\overline{WO}$	D_1	Indicates that the operation in the current machine cycle will be a WRITE memory or OUTPUT function ($\overline{WO}$ = 0). Otherwise, a READ memory or INPUT operation will be executed.
STACK	D_2	Indicates that the address bus holds the pushdown stack address from the Stack Pointer.
HLTA	D_3	Acknowledge signal for HALT instruction.
OUT	D_4	Indicates that the address bus contains the address of an output device and the data bus will contain the output data when $\overline{WR}$ is active.
M_1	D_5	Provides a signal to indicate that the CPU is in the fetch cycle for the first byte of an instruction.
INP*	D_6	Indicates that the address bus contains the address of an input device and the input data should be placed on the data bus when DBIN is active.
MEMR*	D_7	Designates that the data bus will be used for memory read data.

*These three status bits can be used to control the flow of data onto the 8080 data bus.

STATUS WORD CHART

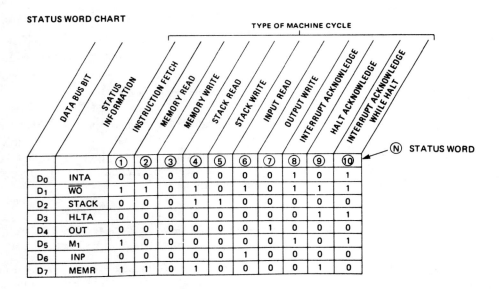

Data Bus Bit	Status Information	Instruction Fetch (1)	Memory Read (2)	Memory Write (3)	Stack Read (4)	Stack Write (5)	Input Read (6)	Output Write (7)	Interrupt Acknowledge (8)	Halt Acknowledge (9)	Interrupt Acknowledge While Halt (10)
D_0	INTA	0	0	0	0	0	0	0	1	0	1
D_1	$\overline{WO}$	1	1	0	1	0	1	0	1	1	1
D_2	STACK	0	0	0	1	1	0	0	0	0	0
D_3	HLTA	0	0	0	0	0	0	0	0	1	1
D_4	OUT	0	0	0	0	0	0	1	0	0	0
D_5	M_1	1	0	0	0	0	0	0	1	0	1
D_6	INP	0	0	0	0	0	1	0	0	0	0
D_7	MEMR	1	1	0	1	0	0	0	0	1	0

TYPE OF MACHINE CYCLE

(N) STATUS WORD

Source: Courtesy of Intel Corporation.

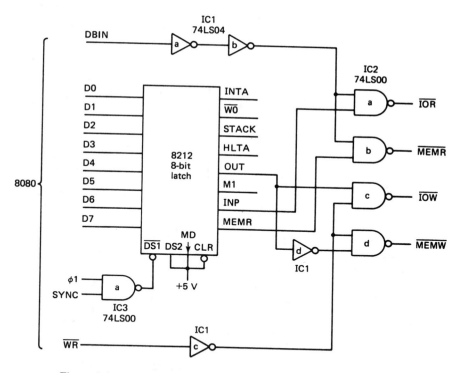

Figure 2.8 Decoding the 8080 status word to generate the control bus.

Note: Be sure that you understand the need to combine the status bit and DBIN or WR. The status word tells us what is about to happen (that is, the type of machine cycle), but DBIN and WR tell us that the microprocessor is now ready to make it happen. Because the status bits disappear after the T2 state, they must be latched until needed.

There is more information in the 8080 status word than is absolutely necessary for developing the control bus signals. For example, it is possible to distinguish between three types of memory reads—an _instruction fetch_, a _memory read_, and a _stack read_—by decoding status words 1, 2, and 4. Usually, this is not done and only the decoding shown in Fig. 2.8 is provided.

If you are beginning to picture the 8080 as a rather complex chip to interface, you are correct. To make this job simpler, Intel has provided two support devices for the 8080: the _8228 system controller_ and the _8224 system clock generator_. With these two chips we can finally draw the CPU module for an 8080-based microcomputer.

Figure 2.9 illustrates the circuit. The 8224 develops the two-phase clock signal from an external crystal. It divides the crystal frequency by 9, forms the two clock phases, and level-shifts the waveforms to the MOS levels required by the 8080. It also provides a TTL-level clock signal that may be used by other circuits in the

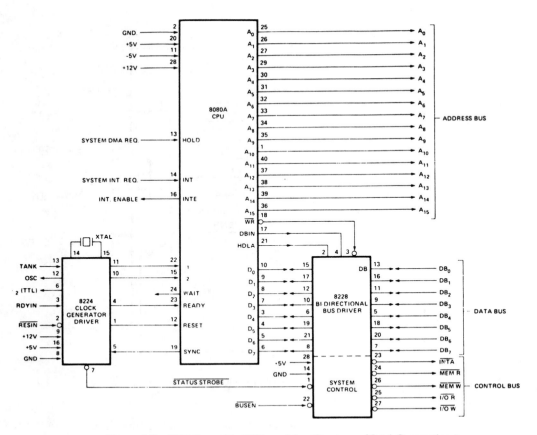

Figure 2.9 8080 three-chip CPU module. (Courtesy of Intel Corporation.)

system. Because of the divide-by-9 feature, a typical 8080A crystal is 18 MHz, resulting in a 2-MHz system clock.

The third chip in the CPU module is the 8228. This circuit takes the place of the 8212 latch and decoder circuitry shown in Fig. 2.8. In addition, it buffers (amplifies) the data bus lines so they will not be loaded down by the many chips connected to this bus.

In summary, the 8080 is actually a three-chip CPU module requiring the 8224 clock generator and the 8228 system controller. An external crystal determines the system clock frequency. A few lines remain to be explained in Fig. 2.9 and these are covered in Chaps. 4 and 6.

The 8085 CPU Module.   As the state of the art in semiconductor technology advanced, it became possible for Intel to redesign the 8080 and include the 8224 and 8228 in a single package. The result is the 8085 microprocessor. Although there are several differences when compared with the older 8080, the most important similarity is that the 8085 is *object code-compatible* with the 8080. This means that all software written for the 8080 will also run on the 8085 without any changes.

One of the problems that the 8085 designers (and indeed, all microprocessor designers) had to face was the limited number of pins available in the standard dual-in-line package (DIP). Most manufacturers have settled on the 40-pin package as a good compromise between a component that can be readily handled without breakage and still provide many lines of access to the chip itself.

Another solution to this problem is to share the package pins for several functions. This is what the designers of the 8085 chose to do. They maintained the standard 40-pin package but combined the low-order address lines (A0 through A7) with the data bus lines (D0 through D7). The resulting lines are labeled *AD0* through *AD7*.

For this scheme to work a new signal is required to identify when AD0–AD7 represent data and when they represent the low-order address. Intel calls this line *ALE* for *address latch enable*. When ALE is high, AD0–AD7 carry the low-order address; when ALE switches low, AD0–AD7 represent the bidirectional data bus.

Figure 2.10 provides a pinout and pin description for the 8085. The most significant differences when compared with the 8080 can be summarized as follows:

1. Only one power source is required, +5 V.
2. The clock signal is generated internally from an external crystal or *RC* network connected to X1 and X2. The internal clock runs at one-half the oscillation frequency of this circuit.
3. The low-order address lines (A0 through A7) and the data bus lines (D0 through D7) are *multiplexed* onto the same set of eight pins labeled AD0–AD7. The signal ALE is used to distinguish between the two.
4. The control bus is generated internally providing the three signals $\overline{RD}$, $\overline{WR}$, and IO/$\overline{M}$.

Figure 2.11 illustrates basic 8085 system timing. Notice that ALE pulses high during the T1 clock pulse of each machine cycle. This provides a means of *demultiplexing* the bus into separate A0 through A7 and D0 through D7 buses.

Figure 2.12 illustrates the technique in an 8085 CPU module for standard memory and I/O devices. The 8212 latch is used to demultiplex AD0–AD7. It is enabled by the ALE signal latching A0 through A7 on the falling edge of this signal. The gating array is used to form a control bus consistent with the 8080 CPU module.

Intel has developed special memory and I/O devices that support the multiplexed bus and control signals of the 8085 (see Chap. 7). When these devices are used, the 8085 becomes a single-chip CPU module. But if standard memory and I/O devices are selected, the CPU module in Fig. 2.12 must be used.

What has been gained by this multiplexing scheme? Several new *interrupt* inputs (special inputs to the microprocessor causing it to suspend its present task temporarily) have been provided giving the 8085 considerably more flexibility than the 8080 when servicing interrupts. In addition, two new I/O lines—*SID* and *SOD*—are provided and allow rudimentary serial input and output capabilities (serial I/O refers to transferring data bit by bit instead of byte by byte in parallel). Finally,

Symbol	Type	Name and Function
A_8–A_{15}	O	**Address Bus:** The most significant 8 bits of the memory address or the 8 bits of the I/O address, 3-stated during Hold and Halt modes and during RESET.
AD_0—$_7$	I/O	**Multiplexed Address/Data Bus:** Lower 8 bits of the memory address (or I/O address) appear on the bus during the first clock cycle (T state) of a machine cycle. It then becomes the data bus during the second and third clock cycles.
ALE	O	**Address Latch Enable:** It occurs during the first clock state of a machine cycle and enables the address to get latched into the on-chip latch of peripherals. The falling edge of ALE is set to guarantee setup and hold times for the address information. The falling edge of ALE can also be used to strobe the status information. ALE is never 3-stated.
S_0, S_1, and IO/$\overline{M}$	O	**Machine Cycle Status:**

S_0, S_1, and IO/$\overline{M}$ row continued:

IO/$\overline{M}$	S_1	S_0	Status
0	0	1	Memory write
0	1	0	Memory read
1	0	1	I/O write
1	1	0	I/O read
0	1	1	Opcode fetch
1	1	1	Opcode fetch
1	1	1	Interrupt Acknowledge
*	0	0	Halt
*	X	X	Hold
*	X	X	Reset

* = 3-state (high impedance)
X = unspecified

S_1 can be used as an advanced R/$\overline{W}$ status. IO/$\overline{M}$, S_0 and S_1 become valid at the beginning of a machine cycle and remain stable throughout the cycle. The falling edge of ALE may be used to latch the state of these lines.

Symbol	Type	Name and Function
$\overline{RD}$	O	**Read Control:** A low level on $\overline{RD}$ indicates the selected memory or I/O device is to be read and that the Data Bus is available for the data transfer, 3-stated during Hold and Halt modes and during RESET.
$\overline{WR}$	O	**Write Control:** A low level on $\overline{WR}$ indicates the data on the Data Bus is to be written into the selected memory or I/O location. Data is set up at the trailing edge of $\overline{WR}$. 3-stated during Hold and Halt modes and during RESET.

Figure 2.10 8085 microprocessor pin numbers and definitions. (Courtesy of Intel Corporation.)

Symbol	Type	Name and Function
READY	I	**Ready:** If READY is high during a read or write cycle, it indicates that the memory or peripheral is ready to send or receive data. If READY is low, the cpu will wait an integral number of clock cycles for READY to go high before completing the read or write cycle. READY must conform to specified setup and hold times.
HOLD	I	**Hold:** Indicates that another master is requesting the use of the address and data buses. The cpu, upon receiving the hold request, will relinquish the use of the bus as soon as the completion of the current bus transfer. Internal processing can continue. The processor can regain the bus only after the HOLD is removed. When the HOLD is acknowledged, the Address, Data $\overline{RD}$, $\overline{WR}$, and IO/$\overline{M}$ lines are 3-stated.
HLDA	O	**Hold Acknowledge:** Indicates that the cpu has received the HOLD request and that it will relinquish the bus in the next clock cycle. HLDA goes low after the Hold request is removed. The cpu takes the bus one half clock cycle after HLDA goes low.
INTR	I	**Interrupt Request:** Is used as a general purpose interrupt. It is sampled only during the next to the last clock cycle of an instruction and during Hold and Halt states. If it is active, the Program Counter (PC) will be inhibited from incrementing and an $\overline{INTA}$ will be issued. During this cycle a RESTART or CALL instruction can be inserted to jump to the interrupt service routine. The INTR is enabled and disabled by software. It is disabled by Reset and immediately after an interrupt is accepted.
$\overline{INTA}$	O	**Interrupt Acknowledge:** Is used instead of (and has the same timing as) $\overline{RD}$ during the Instruction cycle after an INTR is accepted. It can be used to activate an 8259A Interrupt chip or some other interrupt port.
RST 5.5 RST 6.5 RST 7.5	I	**Restart Interrupts:** These three inputs have the same timing as INTR except they cause an internal RESTART to be automatically inserted. The priority of these interrupts is ordered as shown in Table 2. These interrupts have a higher priority than INTR. In addition, they may be individually masked out using the SIM instruction.

Symbol	Type	Name and Function
RESET OUT	O	**Reset Out:** Reset Out indicates cpu is being reset. Can be used as a system reset. The signal is synchronized to the processor clock and lasts an integral number of clock periods.
X_1, X_2	I	**X_1 and X_2:** Are connected to a crystal, LC, or RC network to drive the internal clock generator. X_1 can also be an external clock input from a logic gate. The input frequency is divided by 2 to give the processor's internal operating frequency.
CLK	O	**Clock:** Clock output for use as a system clock. The period of CLK is twice the X_1, X_2 input period.
SID	I	**Serial Input Data Line:** The data on this line is loaded into accumulator bit 7 whenever a RIM instruction is executed.
SOD	O	**Serial Output Data Line:** The output SOD is set or reset as specified by the SIM instruction.
V_{CC}		**Power:** +5 volt supply.
V_{SS}		**Ground:** Reference.

Symbol	Type	Name and Function
TRAP	I	**Trap:** Trap interrupt is a nonmaskable RESTART interrupt. It is recognized at the same time as INTR or RST 5.5-7.5. It is unaffected by any mask or Interrupt Enable. It has the highest priority of any interrupt. (See Table 2.)
$\overline{RESET\ IN}$	I	**Reset In:** Sets the Program Counter to zero and resets the Interrupt Enable and HLDA flip-flops. The data and address buses and the control lines are 3-stated during RESET and because of the asynchronous nature of RESET, the processor's internal registers and flags may be altered by RESET with unpredictable results. $\overline{RESET\ IN}$ is a Schmitt-triggered input, allowing connection to an R-C network for power-on RESET delay (see Figure 3). Upon power-up, $\overline{RESET\ IN}$ must remain low for at least 10 ms after minimum V_{CC} has been reached. For proper reset operation after the power-up duration, $\overline{RESET\ IN}$ should be kept low a minimum of three clock periods. The CPU is held in the reset condition as long as $\overline{RESET\ IN}$ is applied.

Figure 2.10 (*Continued*)

Sec. 2.2   CPU Modules for the 8080, 8085, and Z-80 Microprocessors

45

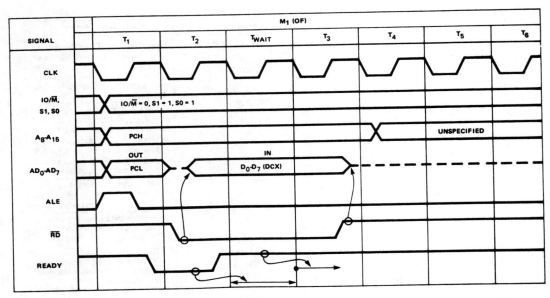

Figure 2.11 Basic 8085 instruction cycle timing. (Courtesy of Intel Corporation.)

status information is provided via the two pins *S0* and *S1*. They encode the bus activities as follows:

S1	S0	
0	0	Halt
0	1	Write
1	0	Read
1	1	Fetch

By combining these signals with IO/$\overline{\text{M}}$ it is possible to identify the type of machine cycle in progress (see Prob. 2.9). Because S0 and S1 are output *early* in the machine cycle, they can be used to generate early read and write control signals. This technique is useful for increasing memory access times allowed by the processor (and allowing slower memory parts to be interfaced).

In summary, the 8085 is software-compatible with the 8080, includes an on-chip clock oscillator, requires an external latch for interfacing standard memories, and will require some simple gating to generate 8080-compatible control bus signals.

The Z-80 CPU Module. The people responsible for the design of the 8080 micropro-cessor at Intel also designed the Z-80 for Zilog. In fact, Zilog is fond of calling the 8080 a *subset* of the Z-80. Of course, Intel considers the 8085 to be its version of an enhanced 8080.

Although neither the 8085 nor the Z-80 are pin-compatible with the 8080, the Z-80 more closely resembles the 8080 CPU module than does the 8085. The

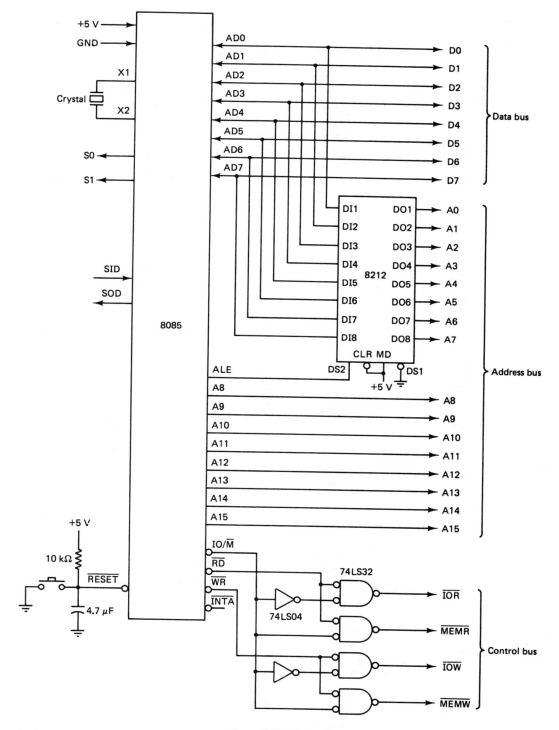

Figure 2.12 8085 CPU module.

Z80, Z80A-CPU Pin Description

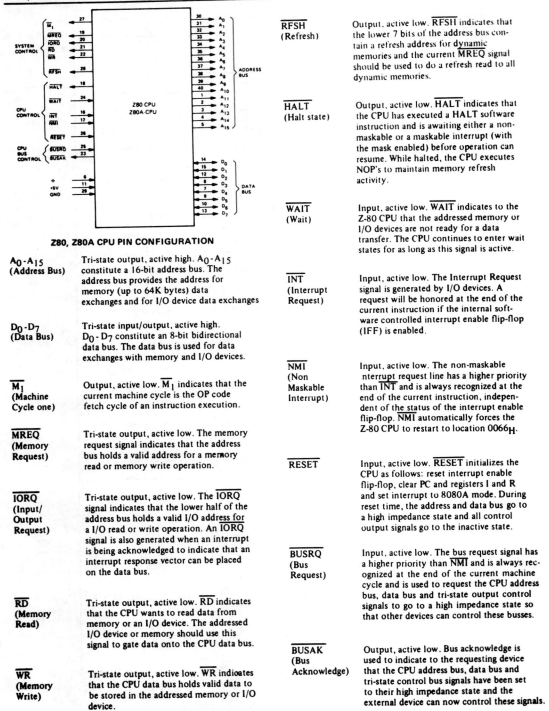

Z80, Z80A CPU PIN CONFIGURATION

A$_0$-A$_{15}$
(Address Bus) — Tri-state output, active high. A$_0$-A$_{15}$ constitute a 16-bit address bus. The address bus provides the address for memory (up to 64K bytes) data exchanges and for I/O device data exchanges

D$_0$-D$_7$
(Data Bus) — Tri-state input/output, active high. D$_0$-D$_7$ constitute an 8-bit bidirectional data bus. The data bus is used for data exchanges with memory and I/O devices.

$\overline{M_1}$
(Machine Cycle one) — Output, active low. $\overline{M_1}$ indicates that the current machine cycle is the OP code fetch cycle of an instruction execution.

$\overline{MREQ}$
(Memory Request) — Tri-state output, active low. The memory request signal indicates that the address bus holds a valid address for a memory read or memory write operation.

$\overline{IORQ}$
(Input/ Output Request) — Tri-state output, active low. The $\overline{IORQ}$ signal indicates that the lower half of the address bus holds a valid I/O address for a I/O read or write operation. An $\overline{IORQ}$ signal is also generated when an interrupt is being acknowledged to indicate that an interrupt response vector can be placed on the data bus.

$\overline{RD}$
(Memory Read) — Tri-state output, active low. $\overline{RD}$ indicates that the CPU wants to read data from memory or an I/O device. The addressed I/O device or memory should use this signal to gate data onto the CPU data bus.

$\overline{WR}$
(Memory Write) — Tri-state output, active low. $\overline{WR}$ indicates that the CPU data bus holds valid data to be stored in the addressed memory or I/O device.

$\overline{RFSH}$
(Refresh) — Output, active low. $\overline{RFSH}$ indicates that the lower 7 bits of the address bus contain a refresh address for dynamic memories and the current $\overline{MREQ}$ signal should be used to do a refresh read to all dynamic memories.

$\overline{HALT}$
(Halt state) — Output, active low. $\overline{HALT}$ indicates that the CPU has executed a HALT software instruction and is awaiting either a non-maskable or a maskable interrupt (with the mask enabled) before operation can resume. While halted, the CPU executes NOP's to maintain memory refresh activity.

$\overline{WAIT}$
(Wait) — Input, active low. $\overline{WAIT}$ indicates to the Z-80 CPU that the addressed memory or I/O devices are not ready for a data transfer. The CPU continues to enter wait states for as long as this signal is active.

$\overline{INT}$
(Interrupt Request) — Input, active low. The Interrupt Request signal is generated by I/O devices. A request will be honored at the end of the current instruction if the internal software controlled interrupt enable flip-flop (IFF) is enabled.

$\overline{NMI}$
(Non Maskable Interrupt) — Input, active low. The non-maskable interrupt request line has a higher priority than $\overline{INT}$ and is always recognized at the end of the current instruction, independent of the status of the interrupt enable flip-flop. $\overline{NMI}$ automatically forces the Z-80 CPU to restart to location 0066$_H$.

$\overline{RESET}$ — Input, active low. $\overline{RESET}$ initializes the CPU as follows: reset interrupt enable flip-flop, clear PC and registers I and R and set interrupt to 8080A mode. During reset time, the address and data bus go to a high impedance state and all control output signals go to the inactive state.

$\overline{BUSRQ}$
(Bus Request) — Input, active low. The bus request signal has a higher priority than $\overline{NMI}$ and is always recognized at the end of the current machine cycle and is used to request the CPU address bus, data bus and tri-state output control signals to go to a high impedance state so that other devices can control these busses.

$\overline{BUSAK}$
(Bus Acknowledge) — Output, active low. Bus acknowledge is used to indicate to the requesting device that the CPU address bus, data bus and tri-state control bus signals have been set to their high impedance state and the external device can now control these signals.

Figure 2.13 Z-80 microprocessor pin numbers and definitions. (Courtesy of Zilog, Inc.)

Z-80 also goes a step beyond the 8085 in that it is not only object code-compatible but has a greatly expanded instruction set when compared with the 8080. Indeed, some people feel that the instruction set is too complicated. You can judge this for yourself later in the chapter when the instruction sets of the three processors are presented.

Figure 2.13 is a pinout diagram and word description for the Z-80. Unlike the 8085, the clock signal must be generated external to the chip, but unlike the 8080, it is a single-phase TTL-compatible signal. A typical clock frequency for the Z-80 is 4 MHz. A single +5-V power source is required.

Also unlike the 8085, but similar to the 8080, the address and data buses are not multiplexed. Thus the Z-80 can be interfaced to standard memory and I/O devices without the need for a low-order address latch.

Basic system timing for an op-code fetch machine cycle is shown in Fig. 2.14. One of the more notable features of the Z-80 is the *refresh address* output on A0 through A7 during T3 and T4 of each M1 machine cycle. This address will increment with each successive M1 cycle and can be used to refresh dynamic memories. This is discussed in more detail in Chap. 5.

Figure 2.15 illustrates a typical Z-80-based CPU module. The 74LS04 inverters function as a crystal oscillator supplying the TTL-level clock signal. Zilog recommends pulling the clock output to +5 V through a 330-Ω resistor as shown. Again a simple gating array is required to produce an 8080-like control bus. Depending on the interface, this combination of gates may not always be needed or may be combined with the address decoding logic. We study this in more detail in Chaps. 4 through 8.

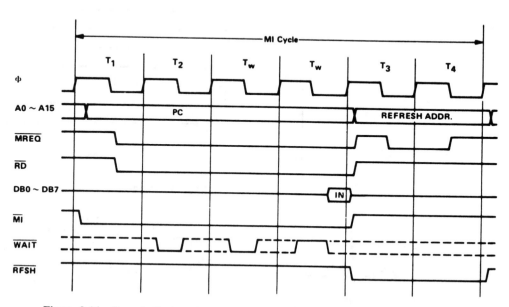

Figure 2.14 Op-code fetch cycle timing for the Z-80 microprocessor. (Courtesy of Zilog, Inc.)

Sec. 2.2   CPU Modules for the 8080, 8085, and Z-80 Microprocessors   **49**

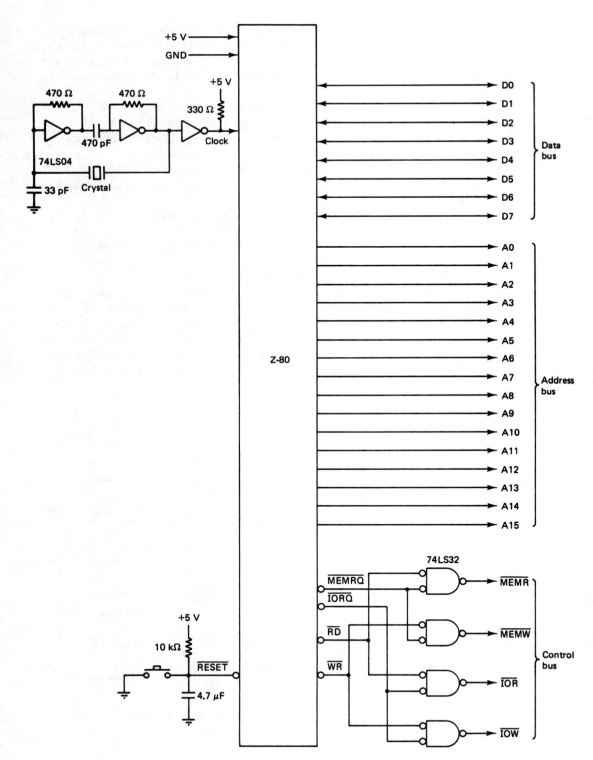

Figure 2.15 Z-80 CPU module.

Finally, there are several other control-oriented signals not shown in the CPU module. These are dealt with later when the subjects of *interrupts* and *DMA* (Chap. 6) and *WAIT* states (Chap. 5) are covered.

In summary, the Z-80 is an enhanced 8080 in a single IC package. Its bus structure is more straightforward than either the 8080 or the 8085. It does require an external clock generator, but this can be a simple 74LS04-based crystal oscillator. Its control bus is very similar to the 8080's and can be made to look exactly like the 8080 with a few simple gates.

2.3 PROGRAMMING MODELS FOR THE 8080, 8085, AND Z-80 MICROPROCESSORS

As you read this section, look for the answers to these Key Concept questions:

2.3.1. A diagram showing the internal CPU registers and flags of a computer is called the _____ _____.

2.3.2. Which CPU register stores the address of the next instruction to be fetched and executed?

2.3.3. After each instruction is executed, the _____ bits are updated to reflect the result of that instruction.

An understanding of the *CPU module* is essential when your goal is to design and construct a particular microcomputer system. However, when the goal is to develop *software* for a particular processor (that is, control and applications programs), a knowledge of the CPU module is less important.

For example, to write an 8080 assembly language program we do not need to know how the clock signal is generated or that status information is output at the beginning of each machine cycle. What we do need is a knowledge of the inner workings of the 8080 microprocessor itself. This information is usually presented in the form of a *programming model*.

The programming model is a diagram of the internal registers and flags within the CPU. Recall that we have already seen one special register in Chap. 1: the *accumulator*. In general, a register is a storage location in the CPU. The accumulator is special because data in this register can be manipulated mathematically or logically.

The nonaccumulator registers are called *general-purpose registers* and can be used to store temporary information (recall how the B register was used for temporary storage in the addition problem in Sec. 1.3).

Our goal in this section is to develop programming models for the three processors we are discussing. Once these models are understood, we will be able to make efficient use of the instruction sets of the processors and begin to write assembly language programs.

A Programming Model for the 8080. Figure 2.16 is a programming model for the 8080 microprocessor. The 8080 has six 8-bit general-purpose registers called

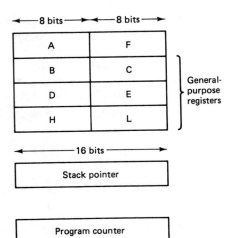

Figure 2.16 Programming model for the 8080 microprocessor.

the *B*, *C*, *D*, *E*, *H*, and *L* registers. The A register is the accumulator and register F is a special flag register.

There are also two 16-bit registers labeled register *SP* and register *PC*. Register PC is the *program counter* and its 16-bit length is consistent with the 16-bit address bus of the 8080. As mentioned in Chap. 1, the program counter holds the address of the next instruction the CPU will be fetching from memory.

Register SP is called the *stack pointer register*. It also holds a 16-bit address, but this address is interpreted as pointing to a special section of memory called the *stack*. The stack area of memory can be used to supply a nearly unlimited number of general-purpose registers *external* to the microprocessor. It is also used to save the return address when a subroutine call instruction is given. We will learn more about the stack later in this chapter.

Recall that all data for the 8080 is 8 bits in length. Therefore, when the CPU fetches an instruction from memory, it will issue a 16-bit address, but it will retrieve only 8 bits or one byte of data. The general-purpose registers are intended for storing data bytes, but the stack pointer and program counter registers are used to specify memory locations or addresses.

Some of the 8080 instructions allow the general-purpose registers to be grouped as *register pairs*. Thus we have the ''BC pair'' and the ''DE pair'' and the ''HL pair.'' Note that only these pairings are allowed. When used in this manner, the register pair can represent 16-bit numbers.

In some special cases the number in the register pair can be used as an address. For example, the 8080 instruction MOV M,B is interpreted to mean: ''Move the data in the B register to the contents of memory whose address is in the HL pair.'' This is referred to as *register-indirect* addressing. We will study the different addressing modes of the processors later in this chapter.

The 8080 Flag Register. Figure 2.17 illustrates the five condition flags of the 8080 and provides a definition for each. These flags are actually 1-bit flip-flops that

S	Z	0	AC	0	P	1	CY

Zero: If the result of an instruction has the value 0, this flag is set; otherwise it is reset.

Sign: If the most significant bit of the result of the operation has the value 1, this flag is set; otherwise it is reset.

Parity: If the modulo 2 sum of the bits of the result of the operation is 0, (i.e., if the result has even parity), this flag is set; otherwise it is reset (i.e., if the result has odd parity).

Carry: If the instruction resulted in a carry (from addition), or a borrow (from subtraction or a comparison) out of the high-order bit, this flag is set; otherwise it is reset.

Auxiliary carry: If the instruction caused a carry out of bit 3 and into bit 4 of the resulting value, the auxiliary carry is set; otherwise it is reset. This flag is affected by single precision additions, subtractions, increments, decrements, comparisons, and logical operations, but is principally used with additions and increments preceding a DAA (Decimal Adjust Accumulator) instruction.

Figure 2.17 8080 flag word and descriptions.

can be set to a logic 1 or reset to a logic 0. In general, each 8080 instruction will affect all, some, or none of these flags.

You can best understand the flags by studying several examples.

Example 2.2

If register B = 03H and register A = 03H, what is the state of the flags after the command SUB B is given?

Solution. The word description for SUB B is: "Subtract the contents of register B from register A, leaving the result in register A." It is obvious that for this example register A must contain 0. Because the result is 0, the Z flag will be set. The sign flag will be reset, the P flag will be set, and the AC and CY flags will both be reset.

Ignoring the last four flags for the moment, the point you should note is that the Z flag is set when the result of an arithmetic (or logical) operation is 0.

Example 2.3

If register B = 80H and register A = 03H, what is the state of the flags after the command ADD B is given?

Solution. The word description for ADD B is: "Add the contents of register B to register A, leaving the result in register A." Thus register A must contain 83H (10000011). In this case the Z flag will be reset because the result is not zero. Because there were no carries generated, the AC and CY flags will also be reset. The parity flag is reset because the number of 1's in 83H is three (odd parity). The sign flag will be set because the most significant bit of the result is a 1.

Note: Using 2's-complement arithmetic the number in the B register actually corresponds to −128 decimal. The 03H in register A represents +3 decimal. When the

ADD B instruction is given, a *subtraction* operation is actually indicated $(-128 + 3)$ and the result of 83H is equivalent to -125 decimal. The steps in realizing this are:

1. 80H = 10000000 and because bit 7 is a 1, a negative number is indicated.
2. To determine the decimal value of 80H find the 2's complement by inverting all bits and adding 1:

$$
\begin{array}{r}
01111111 \\
+ \qquad 1 \\
\hline
10000000 \qquad \text{or} \ -128_{10}
\end{array}
$$

3. Obviously, $-128 + 3 = -125$ and this can be verified by finding the 2's complement of the result 83H.

$$
\begin{array}{rl}
10000011 = & 83H \\
01111100 & \text{invert all bits} \\
+ \qquad 1 & \text{add 1 to form 2's complement} \\
\hline
01111101 = & 7DH \ \text{or} \ 125_{10} \qquad \text{as expected}
\end{array}
$$

Example 2.4

If register B = 01H and register A = FFH, what is the state of the flags after the command ADD B is given?

Solution. Register A will contain FF + 01 = 00. The S flag will be reset because bit 7 is 0; the Z flag will be set because the result is 0; the AC flag will be set because a carry occurred from bit 3 to bit 4; the P flag will be set because the parity is even and the CY flag will be set because of the carry out of bit 7.

The point to note here is that an *overflow* during an addition operation will set the CY flag. You will also find that the CY flag will act as a borrow flag for subtraction. For example, if A = 02H and B = 03H, the command SUB B will leave FF in the accumulator and set the CY flag.

The real utility of the flags is that they can be tested by various branch or jump instructions, allowing decision blocks in your program. For example, Fig. 2.18 is a brief 8080 machine language program that will loop through the last two instructions 255 decimal times. This can be useful for generating time delays.

ADDRESS	OP-CODES	MNEMONICS	COMMENTS
0000	06 FF	MVI B,FF	PUT FF INTO REGISTER B
0002	05	DCR B	SUBTRACT 1 FROM B
0003	C2 02 00	JNZ 0002	IF THE RESULT IS NOT ZERO JUMP TO LOCATION 0002

Figure 2.18 8080 machine language program demonstrating a technique for testing the Z flag.

The MVI B,FF instruction loads register B with 255 decimal. In the second line the contents of register B is decremented by 1. The JNZ 0002 instruction (jump if not zero to location 0002) tests the Z flag. If not set, that is, the result is not zero, the DCR B instruction is repeated. After 255 cycles the result will be zero and control will pass to the program segment following the JNZ instruction.

A Programming Model for the 8085. From a programmer's standpoint the 8085 is nearly identical to the 8080. The programming model shown in Fig. 2.16 still applies and the flag register shown in Fig. 2.17 is also the same. In fact, the only difference between the two is the inclusion of two new instructions with mnemonics *RIM* (read interrupt masks) and *SIM* (set interrupt masks). These commands allow the 8085 to service interrupting devices using its expanded interrupt capabilities. They also allow the input and output of serial data through register A and the SID and SOD pins. An example using these instructions and the SID and SOD pins is given in Chap. 3.

A Programming Model for the Z-80. The programming model for the Z-80 microprocessor is shown in Fig. 2.19. As can be seen, the Z-80 is almost like two 8080s in one package. All of the 8080 general-purpose registers, including the A and F registers, have been duplicated. These are called the *alternate register* set and are identified with the prime (') symbol.

In addition to the duplicate set of 8080 registers, the Z-80 contains two new 16-bit registers labeled *IX* and *IY*. These registers are referred to as the X and Y index registers and provide a new addressing mode called *indexed addressing*. For example, the Z-80 mnemonic LD A,(IX+5) is interpreted as "Load register A with the data in the memory location whose address is in index register X offset by 5." The offset is variable and is summed with the contents of register IX using 2's-complement arithmetic.

In addition to registers IX and IY there are two new 8-bit registers labeled *I* and *R*. The I register is used for mode 2 interrupts and is discussed in Chap. 6. The R register is used for refreshing dynamic memories. The low 7 bits of this register are placed on the low-order address lines (A0 through A6) during T3 and T4 of each M1 machine cycle. The R register is incremented automatically after each M1 machine cycle.

Although the Z-80's general-purpose register set is impressive, you should note that *only one set is accessible at a time*. The instruction *EXX* will exchange the contents of BC, DE, and HL with BC', DE', and HL'. The instruction EX AF,AF' performs a similar function with the accumulator and flag registers.

The Z-80 Flag Register. Figure 2.20 compares the 8080/85 flag register with the Z-80 flag register. The Z-80 has the same flags as the 8080 but includes two new flags labeled *P/V* and *N*. The P/V flag is set depending on the operation being performed. It represents an overflow condition for signed binary arithmetic and when set indicates an erroneous result due to data too large to fit into the data space allowed (greater than $+127$, less than -128).

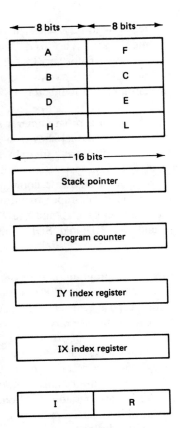

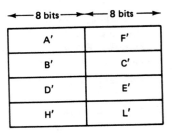

Figure 2.19   Programming model for the Z-80 microprocessor.

For input and logical operations the P/V flag is set according to the parity of the result—even parity sets the flag, odd parity resets it.

The N flag is used for internal operations and is not testable by the programmer. It is set to a 1 for all subtract operations and a 0 for all additions. Also note that in Zilog literature the AC flag is called the H flag (for half carry).

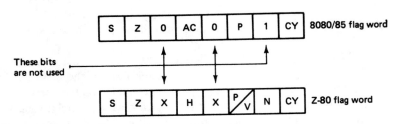

Figure 2.20   8080 and Z-80 flag words compared.

2.4 INTRODUCING THE INSTRUCTION SETS

As you read this section, look for the answers to these Key Concept questions:

2.4.1. Although the Z-80 uses different mnemonics than the 8080/85, the _____ codes for similar instructions are identical.

2.4.2. The data transfer group of instructions allow three different combinations for the source and destination of data. What are they?

2.4.3. Via this group of instructions, the sequential flow of a computer program can be altered. What is this group?

2.4.4. Which CPU register identifies the memory location corresponding to the current top-of-stack?

The instruction set of a microprocessor represents the unique codes that the CPU can interpret, decode, and execute. Recalling the CPU model from Chap. 1, these codes are fetched from the memory unit during the M1 machine cycle, stored in the instruction register, decoded by the CPU, and finally, executed.

The instruction codes cause data to be moved between the general-purpose registers, memory, and I/O devices. They also permit mathematical and logical operations to be performed. The complete set of all operation codes is referred to as the *instruction set*. For the 8080 microprocessor there are 244 unique operation codes that the processor can recognize.

When programming the microprocessor it is absolutely necessary that the programmer understand the programming model for that processor. In addition, he or she must be aware of all *types* of instructions in that processor's instruction set.

Take the time now to browse through the appendices. Included here are word descriptions of the 8080/85 and Z-80 instruction sets, hexadecimal operation codes, information on T states and machine cycles for each instruction, and details of how each instruction affects the condition flags.

The task before us is to become familiar with this information so that we can begin to write simple (and some not so simple) machine and assembly language programs. But how shall we do this? One approach would be to provide a *blow-by-blow* description of each instruction. But considering that the 8080 and 8085 have over 200 instructions and the Z-80 has over 600 instructions, this would be extremely tedious.

Instead, let us study the instructions in logical *groups*. In particular, we will choose seven types of instructions and study an example for each. This will be a "fast tour" designed to give you an overview of the types of instructions available.

In Chap. 3 you will find a number of programming examples that collectively illustrate the use of most of the processor's instructions in real-world applications. Studying these examples will allow you to compare and contrast the different processors.

Instruction Types. Consider the following seven groups of instructions for the 8080/85 and Z-80 microprocessors.

1. Data transfer group
2. Arithmetic group
3. Logical and rotate group
4. Branch group
5. Stack, I/O, and machine control group
6. Exchange, block transfer, and search group
7. Bit manipulation group

The data transfer group. Instructions in this group move data from register to register, memory to a register, or a register to memory. The data transferred can be 8 or 16 bits (one or two bytes) in length.

Figure 2.21 illustrates three examples. In the first, data is moved from register B to register A. There are many different versions of this register-to-register transfer corresponding to all of the 8-bit register combinations.

Although the 8080 (and 8085) have a different mnemonic for this instruction than that of the Z-80, the binary (and hex) op-code is the same for both. Of course, all of the 8080/85 codes have been duplicated by the Z-80, as mentioned previously.

The second example in Fig. 2.21 illustrates a 16-bit load operation. In this case the HL register pair is being loaded with the 16-bit word 0700H (the H indicates a hex number). Notice that this is a three-byte instruction and that when coded, the order of the data is *backward* (low-order byte first, high-order byte last).

The last example in Fig. 2.21 is unique to the Z-80. In this case the X index register is being loaded with the two data bytes at memory location 0700H and 0701H. Notice how the parentheses are used to indicate the *contents* of a memory location. The instruction LD IX,0700H (no parentheses) would load 16-bit register X with 0700H.

It is interesting to note that the LD IX,(nnnn) instruction has a two-byte op-code (DD 2A). This is the technique the designers of the Z-80 used to obtain more

Hex Op-code	Mnemonic		Symbolic Operation	Description
	8080/85	Z-80		
78	MOV A,B	LD A,B	A ← B	Place a copy of register B in register A.
21 00 07	LXI H,0700	LD HL,0700	HL ← 0700	Load the HL register pair with 0700
DD 2A 00 07	none	LD IX,(0700)	IX ← (0700)	Load the X index register with the contents of memory location 0700 (LSB)* and 0701 (MSB)*.

*Least Significant Byte.
*Most Significant Byte.

Figure 2.21 Examples of a register-to-register data transfer and two 16-bit load operations.

Hex Op-code	Mnemonic 8080/85	Mnemonic Z-80	Symbolic Operation	Description
80	ADD B	ADD A,B	A ← A+B	Register B is added to register A. The result is left in register A.
09	DAD B	ADD HL,BC	HL ← HL+BC	Register pair BC is added to register pair HL. The result is left in HL.

Figure 2.22 Examples from the arithmetic group of instructions.

than 600 instructions with an 8-bit word size. The DD op-code was not implemented in the 8080/85.

The arithmetic group. This group includes all of the mathematical commands, such as add, subtract, increment, and decrement. Again 8- and 16-bit operations are possible.

Figure 2.22 illustrates the basic add operation. The mathematical instructions always occur in the accumulator. Thus the command ADD B,C does not exist.

The second example in Fig. 2.22 shows a 16-bit addition with the BC and HL register pairs. Sixteen-bit additions are restricted to using the HL pair with one of the other register pairs.

The logical and rotate group. This group includes the logical operators AND, OR, and EXCLUSIVE-OR. The first example in Fig. 2.23 illustrates the AND operation. Note that each operation is performed *bit by bit*. For example, if register A = 7FH and register B = 9AH, the result of the 8080 instruction ANA B is:

$$A = 7F = 01111111$$
$$B = 9A = \underline{10011010}$$
$$A \cdot B = 1A = \overline{00011010}$$

Figure 2.23 also shows a compare instruction. In this case the accumulator is compared against a memory location whose address is held in the HL register pair— *register indirect* addressing. Note that the contents of the accumulator are unchanged

Hex Op-code	Mnemonic 8080/85	Mnemonic Z-80	Symbolic Operation	Description
A0	ANA B	AND B	A ← A·B	Register A is ANDed bit-by-bit with register B. The result is left in register A.
BE	CMP M	CP (HL)	A − (HL)	The contents of the memory location whose address is contained in HL is subtracted from the accumulator. The accumulator is unchanged but the condition flags are set.

Figure 2.23 Examples from the logical group of instructions.

Sec. 2.4   Introducing the Instruction Sets

by this operation. However, the Z flag is set if the two bytes compare; the CY flag is set if register A < (HL).

Table 2.2 illustrates all of the rotate and shift instructions. The 8080/85 supports only the first four. Notice how the carry flag is used to extend the accumulator to 9 bits for these operations. The 8080/85 restrict the rotates to register A. The Z-80 can rotate any of the general-purpose registers or memory locations.

The branch group. Branch instructions are also referred to as jump commands. These commands cause control of the program to be transferred to a new address breaking the normal sequential flow of a program. The jump instruction can be *conditional* or *unconditional*. In Fig. 2.18 we saw the 8080/85 mnemonic JNZ (jump if not zero). This is a conditional jump.

There are several conditional jump instructions allowing each of the processor condition flags to be tested for a true-or-false condition. For example, jump if the carry flag is set (JC), or jump if the carry flag is not set (JNC).

The first example in Fig. 2.24 is an *unconditional* jump. Note how this is implemented. The second and third bytes of the instruction are placed in the program counter so that the next instruction fetch cycle automatically occurs from the desired address. Again, the order of these two bytes is "backward."

The Z-80 supports a second type of branch command called the *relative jump*. This is the second example in Fig. 2.24. In this two-byte instruction the first byte specifies the op-code for the condition to be tested (JR C, JR NC, JR Z, etc.) The second byte specifies a 2's-complement offset to be added to the current value of the program counter to determine the new address. This type of relative branching allows a jump forward of 127 bytes or backward of 128 bytes.

The subroutine call is a third type of branch instruction. This is the third example in Fig. 2.24. The CALL instruction differs from the jump instruction in that control will be transferred back to the instruction following the CALL when a special RETurn instruction is encountered. This allows the subroutine to be used many times from different places in the same program.

The symbolic description of the CALL is rather complex. With reference to Fig. 2.24, the following sequence occurs:

1. The memory location pointed at by register SP-1 (the stack pointer less one) is loaded with the high-order byte of the program counter.
2. The memory location pointed at by register SP-2 is loaded with the low-order byte of the program counter. In other words, the program counter is saved on the stack.
3. The program counter is loaded with the address of the subroutine, in this case 0100H.
4. Register SP is decremented by 2. This protects the stack from being overwritten by another subroutine call and allows *nested* subroutines.

The program now resumes but at the new address (0100H in this example). When an RET instruction is encountered (see the last example in Fig. 2.24), register

TABLE 2.2 ROTATE AND SHIFT INSTRUCTIONS
FOR THE 8080/85 AND Z-80
MICROPROCESSORS

Mnemonic		Symbolic operation
8080/85	Z-80	
RLC	RLCA	
RAL	RLA	
RRC	RRCA	
RAR	RRA	
None	RLC r	
None	RLC (HL)	
None	RLC (IX+d)	
None	RLC (IY+d)	
None	RL m	
None	RRC m	
None	RR m	
None	SLA m	
None	SRA m	
None	SRL m	
None	RLD	
None	RRD	

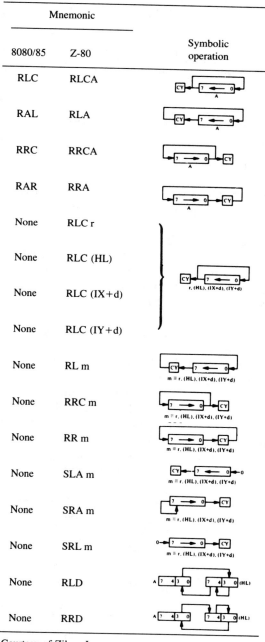

Courtesy of Zilog, Inc.

Sec. 2.4   Introducing the Instruction Sets

Hex	Mnemonic		Symbolic	Description
Op-code	8080/85	Z-80	Operation	
C3 00 01	JMP 0100	JP 0100H	PC ← 0100H	Control is transferred to the address given in bytes 2 and 3 of the instruction.
30 (offset)	none	JR NC, 0100H	PC ← PC+offset	Control is transferred to the address in the PC + offset.
CD 00 01	CALL 0100	CALL 0100H	(SP−1) ← PCH (SP−2) ← PCL PC ← 0100 SP ← SP−2	Control is transferred to the subroutine at 0100H. The return address is stored on the stack. The stack pointer is decremented by 2.
C9	RET	RET	PCL ← (SP) PCH ← (SP+1) SP ← SP+2	Control is transferred to the address on the stack top. The stack pointer is incremented by 2.

Figure 2.24 The branch group includes both conditional and unconditional jumps. Subroutine calls are also included in this group.

SP is incremented by 2 back to its ''old'' value and the data on the stack (the return address) is ''popped'' into the program counter.

Fortunately for the programmer, all of this is *transparent* and you need only remember to balance each subroutine call with a RET instruction. Subroutines are covered in more detail in Chap. 3.

The stack, I/O, and machine control group. We have already seen how the CALL and RET instructions affect the stack. There are two other instructions that utilize this area of memory. These are the *PUSH* and *POP* commands. Figure 2.25 illustrates the PUSH B and POP B instructions. The PUSH instructions are useful for saving any of the general-purpose registers, the flag register, or the accumulator. There are four versions: PUSH B, PUSH D, PUSH H, and PUSH PSW (using the 8080/85 mnemonics). PSW is the processor status word and is made up of register A and the flag register. The Z-80 mnemonic is PUSH AF.

Once pushed onto the stack, these registers are free to be used for some other purpose. The POP command reverses the process, popping the top of the

Hex	Mnemonic		Symbolic	Description
Op-code	8080/85	Z-80	Operation	
C5	PUSH B	PUSH BC	(SP−1) ← B (SP−2) ← C SP ← SP−2	The BC register pair is pushed onto the stack top. The stack pointer is decremented by 2.
C1	POP B	POP BC	C ← (SP) B ← (SP+1) SP ← SP+2	The top of the stack is popped into the BC pair. The stack pointer is incremented by 2.

Figure 2.25 The PUSH instruction can be used to store any of the register pairs in the stack area of memory. The POP command pops data off the stack and into the selected register pair.

stack into the selected register pair. This is shown as the second example in Fig. 2.25. Great care must be taken when using the stack, as it is a "last-in, first-out" type of memory. This means that registers should be popped off the stack in the reverse order in which they were pushed on.

Example 2.5

Explain the operation of the following 8080/85 program.

```
LXI SP,07FFH
PUSH B
PUSH H
POP B
POP H
HLT
```

Solution. The program begins by loading register SP with 07FFH. Now the BC and HL register pairs are pushed onto the stack. Figure 2.26 shows the stack at this point. Next, the top of the stack (containing the HL pair) is popped into the BC register pair, the stack pointer is incremented by 2, and the (new) stack top (containing the BC pair) popped into the HL register pair. The effect is to exchange the contents of register pairs BC and HL.

Note: This is the "wrong" way of using the stack when the intent is to save these registers temporarily. In this example it is an effective way of swapping two register pairs.

This group also includes the input/output instructions for the three processors and these are summarized in Table 2.3. The 8080 and 8085 have only two—IN n and OUT n—input the data from port n to the accumulator, or output the data in

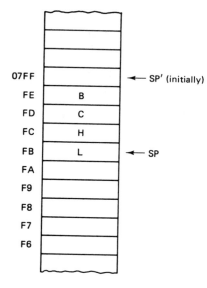

Figure 2.26 After pushing the BC and HL pairs onto the stack the stack pointer contains 07FBH. The contents of the HL pair now rest on the "top" of the stack.

TABLE 2.3 INPUT AND OUTPUT
INSTRUCTIONS FOR THE 8080/85 AND Z-80
MICROPROCESSORS

| Mnemonic | | Symbolic |
8080/85	Z-80	operation
In n	IN A, (n)	A ← (n)
None	IN r, (C)	r ← (C) If r = 110, only the flags will be affected
None	INI	(HL) ← (C) B ← B − 1 HL ← HL + 1
None	INIR	(HL) ← (C) B ← B − 1 HL ← HL + 1 Repeat until B = 0
None	IND	(HC) ← (C) B ← B − 1 HL ← HL − 1
None	INDR	(HL) ← (C) B ← B − 1 HL ← HL − 1 Repeat until B = 0
Out n	OUT (n), A	(n) ← A
None	OUT (C), r	(C) ← r
None	OUTI	(C) ← (HL) B ← B − 1 HL ← HL + 1
None	OTIR	(C) ← (HL) B ← B − 1 HL ← HL + 1 Repeat until B = 0
None	OUTD	(C) ← (HL) B ← B − 1 HL ← HL − 1
None	OTDR	(C) ← (HL) B ← B − 1 HL ← HL − 1 Repeat until B = 0

Source: Courtesy of Zilog, Inc.

the accumulator to port n. Note that for either instruction the data must pass through the accumulator.

This is not so for the Z-80. The Z-80 commands IN r,(C) and OUT (C),r allow I/O through any of the general-purpose registers except register C, which is used to identify the 8-bit port address.

In addition, data can be input or output from the memory location specified by the HL pair. In this case register B is used as a counter. It is decremented with each execution of the instruction. The INI and OUTI commands cause the address in HL to increment with each execution, while the IND and OUTD commands cause the HL address pointer to be decremented.

The INIR, INDR, OTIR, and OTDR instructions automatically repeat until the B register contains 0. All of these commands are useful for moving tables of data into or out of memory. One must be careful not to exceed the speed capabilities of the I/O device, however (see Chap. 6 for a discussion on synchronizing the microprocessor to the I/O device).

The exchange, block transfer, and search group. These instructions are unique to the Z-80 microprocessor. Figure 2.27 illustrates the EXX command, which swaps all of the Z-80 general-purpose registers with the alternate set of registers.

Another example is the LDDR command. This instruction moves data from the memory location pointed at by register pair HL to the memory location pointed at by register pair DE. It automatically decrements the HL and DE register pair pointers. It is assumed that register pair BC is loaded with the number of bytes to be transferred. After each transfer the BC byte counter is decremented, and if not zero, the instruction continues until all bytes in the block have been moved. Notice that this instruction has a two-byte op-code. There are four versions, labeled LDI (increment HL and DE), LDD (decrement HL and DE), LDIR (increment and repeat), and LDDR (decrement and repeat).

Hex Op-code	Mnemonic 8080/85	Mnemonic Z-80	Symbolic Operation	Description
D9	none	EXX	BC $\leftrightarrow$ B'C' DE $\leftrightarrow$ D'E' HL $\leftrightarrow$ H'L'	The primary and alternate register pairs are exchanged.
ED B8	none	LDDR	(DE) ← (HL) DE ← DE−1 HL ← HL−1 BC ← BC−1	Load location (DE) with location (HL), decrement DE, HL and BC; repeat until BC = 0.
ED A1	none	CPI	A − (HL) HL ← HL + 1 BC ← BC − 1	Compare location (HL) with the accumulator, increment HL and decrement BC. The accumulator is unchanged but the condition flags are set.

Figure 2.27 The Z-80 has several block-oriented commands. EXX allows switching between the primary and alternate set of registers. LDDR transfers a block of data from one location in memory to another. CPI is used to compare the accumulator with all data bytes in a block of memory.

Hex Op-code	Mnemonic		Symbolic Operation	Description
	8080/85	Z-80		
CB 61	none	BIT 4,C	$Z \leftarrow \bar{C}_4$	Test bit 4 of register C and set the Z flag accordingly.
CB 74	none	SET 6,H	$H_6 \leftarrow 1$	Set bit 6 of register H.
CB 97	none	RES 6,H	$H_6 \leftarrow 0$	Reset bit 6 of register H.

Figure 2.28 Bit setting, resetting, and testing is easily accomplished with the Z-80 bit-manipulation instructions.

Also shown in Fig. 2.27 is the CPI instruction. This is similar to the compare shown in Fig. 2.23 but uses the BC pair as a counter, automatically decrementing the pair with each execution. If the compare is true, the Z flag is set.

There are four versions of this instruction, labeled CPI, CPD, CPIR, and CPDR. The I represents increment HL and the D decrement HL. Instructions with the R suffix automatically repeat until BC = 0 or a true compare occurs.

The bit manipulation group. Included in this group are instructions that allow individual bits of a register or a memory location to be set, reset, or tested. The first example in Fig. 2.28 shows how bit 4 of register C can be tested. If zero, the Z flag will be set, reset if not.

In the second and third examples, bit 6 of register H is set to a 1 or reset to a 0. Although the 8080 and 8085 have no such instructions, the logical AND and OR instructions can be used to achieve the same result (see Probs. 2.29 and 2.30).

2.5 ADDRESSING MODES

As you read this section, look for the answers to these Key Concept questions:

2.5.1. Each computer instruction has a source and destination of data. The _____ _____ specify the way these data locations are accessed.

2.5.2. The _____ addressing mode uses a register pair to specify the address of a memory location.

A microprocessor has several ways of addressing data stored in memory or in its register array. For example, in the *direct* addressing mode the full 16-bit address is specified as part of the instruction. The 8080/85 mnemonic LDA 1000H has the word interpretation "Load register A with the contents of memory location 1000H." The hex op-code for this instruction is 3A 00 10.

The direct addressing mode is a straightforward way of accessing memory but has the drawback of requiring three memory fetches per instruction—one for the op-code and two for the 16-bit address. Programs requiring a large number of memory accesses will execute slowly with this addressing mode due to the relatively high number of T states required. To solve this problem microprocessor designers usually include a number of general-purpose registers that can be addressed with a single byte. For example, the 8080/85 instruction MOV A,B copies the data byte stored in register B to register A. This is called *register* addressing.

Of course, some means of loading the general-purpose registers must be provided. The *immediate* addressing mode is intended for this purpose. The 8080/85 instruction MVI A,00 has the hex op-code 3E 00 and the word interpretation "Load register A with the data byte immediately following this op-code." In this case the accumulator is loaded with the data byte 00. The Z-80 mnemonic is LD A,00. The immediate mode can also be used to load a register pair with 16 bits of data.

Even with the general-purpose registers, it is still necessary to use memory to store large tables of data or messages that are to be printed when a certain condition occurs. Indeed, *word processors* may need to store tens of thousands of data bytes. To access this large amount of data without having to specify the full 16-bit address for each access, the *register indirect* addressing mode has been developed.

In this mode the HL register pair is preloaded with a memory address. Now any of a number of special register indirect instructions may be given. For example, the 8080/85 mnemonic MOV A,M has the word interpretation "Move to register A the data stored in the memory location pointed at by the HL register pair." The Z-80 mnemonic is more concise: LD A,(HL), where the parentheses indicate the memory location addressed by HL. The hex op-code is the single byte 7E.

Table 2.4 summarizes the four addressing modes of the 8080/85 microprocessors. The mnemonics shown are for the 8080/85, but all four modes are also supported by the Z-80.

When the Z-80 was designed, two new addressing modes were included. The first is called *relative* addressing. It affects only the Z-80 branch instructions. Normally, the branch instruction requires three bytes, one for the op-code and two for the address. This is the *direct* addressing mode supported by the 8080/85. In addition to supporting this direct jump command, the Z-80 has a two-byte jump relative command (review the branch group in Sec. 2.4). For example, the instruction JR addr will unconditionally transfer control up to 127 locations forward or 128 locations backward relative to the present value of the program counter.

Besides saving one byte, the relative jump has the advantage that the resulting code is *position independent*. This means that programs written with relative jumps

TABLE 2.4 8080/85 ADDRESSING MODES[a]

Addressing mode	Sample mnemonic	Symbolic operation	Hex op-code
1. Direct	LDA 1000H	A ← (1000H)	3A 00 10
2. Register	MOV A,B	A ← B	78
3. Register indirect	MOV A,M	A ← (HL)	7E
4. Immediate	MVI A,00	A ← 00	3E 00

[a] All four are also supported by the Z-80.

TABLE 2.5 ADDRESSING MODES OF THE Z-80

Addressing mode[a]	Sample mnemonic	Symbolic operation	Hex op-code
1. Direct	LD A,(1000H)	A ← (1000H)	3A 00 10
2. Register	LD A,B	A ← B	78
3. Register indirect	LD A,(HL)	A ← (HL)	7E
4. Immediate	LD A,00	A ← 00	3E 00
5. Relative branching	JR PC + 20H	PC ← PC + 20H	18 20
6. Indexed	LD A,(IX+20H)	A ← (IX+20H)	DD 7E 20

[a] Modes 1 to 4 are also supported by the 8080/85.

can be loaded anywhere in memory and they will execute properly. We investigate the Z-80's relative addressing mode in more detail in the next chapter.

The sixth addressing mode for the Z-80 is called *indexed* addressing. This mode utilizes the two 16-bit index registers X and Y. These registers are used as pointers similar to the HL pair, but with one difference. The instruction specifies an *offset* to be added to the pointer value.

As an example, consider the Z-80 mnemonic LD A,(IX+20H), which has the word interpretation "Load register A with the contents of memory pointed at by index register X plus 20H." The hex op-code is DD 7E 20. The offset is added to register X or Y using *2's-complement* arithmetic. This means that the offset can range from +127 (7FH) to −128 (80H).

Table 2.5 summarizes the six addressing modes of the Z-80.

2.6 PUTTING IT ALL TOGETHER: A PROGRAMMING EXAMPLE

As you read this section, look for the answers to these Key Concept questions:

2.6.1. In general, the mnemonic for each microprocessor instruction will have two parts called the _____ and the _____.

2.6.2. There are two ways of generating the object code from the source code. What are they?

Let's use our newfound knowledge of the instruction sets to write a microcomputer program that adds two numbers; it is not exactly *Space Invaders* but it is a beginning! In Chap. 3 we will progress toward more elaborate and useful programs.

Example 2.6

Write a program to add the contents of memory locations 0700H and 0701H and leave the sum in memory location 0702H. Write the program beginning at location 0600H and show both the 8080/85 and Z-80 mnemonics.

Solution. Figure 2.29 is the 8080/85 solution. Note how this program has been laid out. A special form identifies the author, name, and data of the program and includes

Address	Object codes			Label	Op-code	Operand	Comments
0600	3A	00	07	SUM:	LDA	0700H	; GET FIRST BYTE
0603	47				MOV	B,A	; SAVE IN B
0604	3A	01	07		LDA	0701H	; GET SECOND BYTE
0607	80				ADD	B	; COMPUTE SUM
06C8	32	02	07		STA	0702H	; SAVE SUM
060B	76				HLT		; STOP

Program Name_____
Author_____   Date_____

Figure 2.29 8080/85 programming solution for Ex. 2.6.

six *fields* for the program itself. These are the *address field*, the *object code field*, the *label field*, the *op-code field*, the *operand field*, and the *comment field*. You are encouraged to follow this format as you develop your own programs.

For now we will only concern ourselves with the assembly language portion of the program and ignore the address and object code fields. The first instruction, LDA 0700H, is made up of the *op-code* LDA and the *operand* 0700H. As the comment field indicates, this instruction is used to fetch the first number to be added (the number stored in 0700H).

The label SUM: is optional and is used here simply to give the addition routine a name. In the next chapter we will see more useful applications for the label field.

Because additions must occur in the accumulator, the second instruction moves the data byte to register B for temporary storage. Now the LDA 0701H instruction brings in the second number and we are prepared for the addition: ADD B (add the contents of registers A and B). The sum, which is left in register A, is then stored in memory location 0702H with the direct addressing mode instruction: STA 0702H. HLT ends the program.

At this point the assembly language version of the program is complete. But of course the 8080/85 cannot execute mnemonics! What we have generated is called the *source code*, but what the microprocessor wants is called the *object code*. We now have two choices. If an 8080/85 assembler is available, the source code can be typed into the computer and the assembler told to assemble the program. If no assembler is available, you will have to "hand assemble" the program.

Hand assembly is a good way to learn machine language programming but is tedious for lengthy programs. To hand assemble this program, refer to the 8080/85 Instruction Set index (Appendix A.2) which provides a listing of all 8080 and 8085 instructions. Look up the LDA instruction. You will see: 3A LDA Adr. Recalling

Address	Object codes			Label	Op-code	Operand	Comments
0600	3A	00	07	SUM:	LD	A,(0700H)	; GET FIRST BYTE
0603	47				LD	B, A	; SAVE IN B
0604	3A	01	07		LD	A,(0701H)	; GET SECOND BYTE
0607	80				ADD	A, B	; COMPUTE SUM
0608	32	02	07		LD	(0702H), A	; SAVE SUM
060B	76				HALT		; STOP

Program Name_____

Author _____   Date _____

Figure 2.30 Z-80 programming solution for Ex. 2.6.

that 16-bit numbers are always entered "backward," we enter 3A 00 07 to the left of the LDA op-code under the field labeled "Object Code."

Continue in this manner, looking up the hex codes for each instruction. Finally, we can complete the address field, which must begin at address 0600H. Notice how the low-order address increases from instruction to instruction. Don't forget that you are counting in hex, so after address 0609 comes address 060A (not 0610!).

The program is now ready for testing. If you are using a microprocessor trainer, you may use your monitor program to enter the hex codes into memory starting at address 0600H. Before executing the program put two numbers in locations 0700H and 0701H. After running the program, the correct sum should be stored in location 0702H.

The Z-80 version of the program is shown in Fig. 2.30. This program is identical to the 8080/85 version except for the mnemonics. Note in particular that the object code is *exactly* the same. Appendix B.1 can be used to hand assemble the Z-80 version of this program.

CHAPTER SUMMARY

1. The CPU module of a microcomputer consists of the microprocessor, a clock signal generator, and logic circuitry to generate the control signals.

2. The 8080 requires a three-chip CPU module consisting of the 8080 microprocessor, the 8224 clock generator and the 8228 system controller.

3. The 8085 can be a single-chip CPU module, but when interfaced to standard

memory and I/O devices, it requires a low-order address latch and simple gating to generate an 8080-like control bus.

4. The Z-80 requires only a TTL-level clock oscillator circuit to construct its CPU module. Simple gating is required to generate an 8080-like control bus.

5. The programming model for a microprocessor shows the internal architecture of the processor. Typical elements are the accumulator, general-purpose registers, flag register, stack pointer register, program counter register, and index registers.

6. The condition flags in a microprocessor are flip-flops that are set or reset depending on the results of an instruction. Typical flags for the 8080/85 and Z-80 are the carry, zero, parity, half carry, sign, overflow, and subtract flags.

7. The condition flags are important because they can be tested and program flow altered based on their value.

8. The instruction set of a microprocessor is a list of all of the commands the CPU can decode and execute.

9. When learning a new microprocessor's instruction set it is convenient to group the instructions by type. For the 8080/85 and Z-80 we have the data transfer, arithmetic, logical and rotate, branch, stack, I/O and machine control, exchange, block transfer and search, and bit manipulation groups.

10. In general, each microprocessor instruction may have several different addressing modes. The 8080/85 has four addressing modes and the Z-80 has six.

11. When writing a microprocessor program it is important to be well organized. The following fields should always be included in the program: address, object code, label, op-code, operand, and comment fields.

12. When hand assembling a microprocessor program the hex code for each mnemonic must be looked up in an instruction set summary. Assemblers are programs that do this task for you.

LAB PROJECTS

2.1. Obtain a schematic diagram of the microcomputer you are using to support this text/course. Locate the following items on your schematic:
   (a) microprocessor chip
   (b) clock generator/crystal oscillator
   (c) 8 data bus lines
   (d) 16 address bus lines
   (e) I/O and memory control bus lines.

2.2. Sketch a *block diagram* of your computer showing all of the items from Lab 2.1. Save this diagram so that the memory and I/O can be added at a later time.

2.3. A good way to learn the instruction set of a microprocessor is to execute a single instruction and then return to the system monitor program to examine its effect on the CPU registers. For example, a typical sequence might be:

(a) Preload register A with 27H.

(b) Load the instruction ADI 3CH (8080/85) or ADD 3CH (Z-80). The hex codes are C6H 3CH.

(c) On paper predict the result:

$$\begin{array}{r} 27H \\ +3CH \\ \hline 63H \end{array}$$

(d) Run the "program."

(e) Examine A register to confirm your prediction.

Using this technique all of the instructions can be "tested." You should also be able to examine the flags to see how they are affected by each instruction.

2.4. Perform homework Question 2.42 or 2.44. Now take the hand-assembled listing and load this program into the memory of your computer. Run the program and verify the contents of register A and the flags.

2.5. Try the following changes to the program described in Lab 2.4 and predict the new results in register A and the flags:

(a) Change the data loaded into register B.

(b) Replace one of the rotates with a NOP.

(c) Change the rotates to RRC (8080/85) or RRCA (Z-80).

(d) Change the immediate data in the AND instruction.

(e) Change the AND instruction to an OR.

QUESTIONS AND PROBLEMS

Section 2.1

2.1. Compare and contrast single-board computers with bus-oriented designs. Which is best for economy, expandability, portability?

Section 2.2 (8080 microprocessor)

2.2. True or false: The M1 machine cycle is always an instruction fetch cycle.

2.3. What is the purpose of the 8080 SYNC signal? The 8085 and Z-80 do not need this signal. Why not?

2.4. While SYNC is high, the data bus of an 8080 microcomputer contains the data byte A2H. What type of machine cycle is indicated?

2.5. Refer to Table 2.1. Some 8080 machine cycle types can be identified by testing only a single bit. List all such machine cycle types.

2.6. Some 8080-based microcomputers include a front panel with LED indicators to display the different machine cycle types. Using an 8212 latch, several LEDs, and a few logic gates, design a circuit to display the following types of machine cycles: instruction fetch, memory read, stack read, stack write, memory write, input read, and output write.

2.7. In an 8080 system with 8228 controller, how many times will the $\overline{\text{MEMR}}$ control line pulse low during the following program?

```
MVI   A,10H
MVI   B,C9H
ADD   B
STA   0100H
HLT
```

Section 2.2 (8085 microprocessor)

2.8. True or false: ALE pulses high only during the T1 state of an op-code fetch (M1) machine cycle.

2.9. Complete the table below indicating the logic level on each control or status pin for the machine cycle types shown.

Machine cycle	$\overline{\text{RD}}$	$\overline{\text{WR}}$	$\text{IO}/\overline{\text{M}}$	S0	S1
memory read					
memory write					
I/O read					
I/O write					
op-code fetch					

2.10. Using the results of Prob. 2.9 design a logic circuit that will produce one active-high pulse for every 8085 M1 (op-code fetch) machine cycle.

2.11. Assume the program in Prob. 2.7 is run on an 8085. Give the name of each required machine cycle and the values of the S0 and S1 status signals for each cycle.

2.12. True or false: Any program written for the 8080 will run without changes on the 8085.

Section 2.2 (Z-80 microprocessor)

2.13. How does the Z-80 indicate that the current machine cycle is an op-code fetch (M1)?

2.14. Complete the table below indicating the logic level on each Z-80 control or status pin for the machine cycle types shown.

Machine cycle	$\overline{\text{RD}}$	$\overline{\text{WR}}$	$\overline{\text{MREQ}}$	$\overline{\text{IORQ}}$	$\overline{\text{M1}}$
memory read					
memory write					
I/O read					
I/O write					
op-code fetch					

2.15. True or false: Any program written for the 8080 will run without changes on the Z-80.

Chap. 2   Questions and Problems

2.16. True or false: Any program written for the Z-80 will run without changes on the 8085.

2.17. Design a logic circuit to detect and store the refresh address output on the Z-80 address bus. (*Hint*: Refer to Fig. 2.14 for refresh timing.)

Section 2.3 (8080/85 microprocessors)

2.18. If register B = C3H and register A = 3DH, determine the contents of register A and the value of the flags after the command ADD B is given.

2.19. Repeat Prob. 18 if the command is changed to SUB B.

2.20. Determine the value of the flags and register A after the program in Prob. 2.7 has been run.

2.21. If the addition in Prob. 2.7 is interpreted using 2's complement-signed binary numbers, the actual operation is a subtraction. Explain this by showing the decimal equivalent of the data in registers A and B and the result.

2.22. Assuming the program in Fig. 2.18 is run on an 8080 microprocessor with a 2-MHz system clock, how long will it take to execute? Use Fig. 1.10 to look up the number of T states required by each instruction. (*Hint*: The last two instructions are executed 255 times.)

Section 2.3 (Z-80 microprocessor)

2.23. In what ways is the Z-80 programming model the same as the 8080/85? In what ways is it different?

2.24. Repeat Prob. 2.18 assuming a Z-80 processor and the command ADD A,B is given.

2.25. Repeat Prob. 2.18 assuming a Z-80 processor and the command SUBB is given.

2.26. If register A = 60H and register B = 60H and the command ADD A,B is given, a 2's complement overflow results. Explain. How does the Z-80 indicate this condition?

Section 2.4 (8080/85 microprocessors)

2.27. Determine the contents of the accumulator after the following programs have run.

(a) MVI A,3CH	(b) MVI A,27H	(c) MVI C,7FH
ANI 07H	MOV B,A	MVI B,3EH
HLT	INR A	MOV A,B
	ANA B	RLC
	DCR A	RLC
	HLT	ANI 7FH
		HLT

2.28. Determine the value of the flags after each of the programs in Prob. 2.27 have run.

2.29. The instruction ANI 40H can be used to test bit 6 of register A. Explain.

2.30. An OR instruction can be used to force selected bits of a specified register high. What is the mnemonic of an instruction that will set bit 7 of register A without changing any of the other bits in this register?

2.31. What is the value of the stack pointer after the following program is run?

```
MOV    SP,07FFH
PUSH   B
CALL   Subroutine
POP    B
ADD    B
PUSH   B
HALT
```

Section 2.4 (Z-80 microprocessor)

2.32. Determine the contents of the accumulator after the following programs have run.

```
(a) LD    A,3CH      (b) LD    A,27H      (c) LD    C,7FH
    AND   07H            LD    B,A            LD    B,3EH
    HALT                 INC   A              LD    A,B
                         AND   B              RLCA
                         DEC   A              RLCA
                         HALT                 AND   7FH
                                              HALT
```

2.33. Refer to Appendix B.1 and determine the value of the flags after each of the programs in Prob. 2.32 have run.

2.34. The instruction AND 40H can be used to test bit 6 of register A. Explain.

2.35. An OR instruction can be used to force selected bits of a specified register high. What is the mnemonic of an instruction that will set bit 7 of register A without changing any of the other bits in this register?

2.36. Explain the difference between the instruction LD BC,(0600H) and the instruction LD BC,0600H.

2.37. What is the value of the stack pointer after the following program is run?

```
LD     SP,07FFH
PUSH   BC
CALL   Subroutine
POP    BC
ADD    A,B
PUSH   BC
HALT
```

Section 2.5 (8080/85 microprocessors)

2.38. Identify the addressing mode for each instruction in the program below.

```
MVI    H,07H
MVI    L,01H
MOV    C,B
INR    C
INR    M
LDA    0600H
```

2.39. In Prob. 2.38 the instruction INR M increments the contents of a memory location. What is the address of this memory location?

Section 2.5 (Z-80 microprocessor)

2.40. Identify the addressing mode for each instruction in the program below.

```
LD    IX,0701H
LD    B,(IX + 10H)
AND   B
INC   (HL)
LD    A,(0700H)
```

2.41. In Prob. 2.40 the instruction LD B,(IX + 10H) loads register A with the contents of a memory location. What is the address of this memory location?

Section 2.6 (8080/85 microprocessors)

2.42. Using a form similar to Fig. 2.29 hand assemble the program in Prob. 2.27(c) starting at address 0600H.

2.43. The codes listed below form an 8080/85 machine language program. Use Appendix A.2 to "decode" this program into the corresponding 8080/85 mnemonics. (*Caution:* Some of the codes represent data, not instructions, depending on the context of the instruction.)

Address	Code
0600	06
0601	3C
0602	DB
0603	03
0604	17
0605	D2
0606	02
0607	06
0608	A0
0609	D3
060A	05
060B	76

Section 2.6 (Z-80 microprocessor)

2.44. Using a form similar to Fig. 2.29, hand assemble the program in Prob. 2.32(c) starting at address 0600H.

KEY CONCEPT ANSWERS

2.1.1. bus and single-board

2.2.1. 8224, 8228

2.2.2. A0–A7 address, D0–D7 data

2.2.3. clock

2.3.1. programming model

2.3.2. program counter

2.3.3. flag

2.4.1. object

2.4.2. memory to register, register to memory, register to register

2.4.3. the conditional-jump or branch instructions

2.4.4. stack pointer (SP)

2.5.1. addressing modes

2.5.2. register indirect

2.6.1. op-code, operand

2.6.2. hand assembly, assembler program

3

Programming the Microprocessor

To be truly competent in the microcomputer field, you must be able not only to design microprocessor hardware, but also to program that hardware. If you have just designed and constructed an 8-bit *digital-to-analog converter* for a Z-80 microprocessor, how will you be able to tell if it works? A program is required that exercises that hardware and thoroughly tests its functions. Only then can you be sure that it has met all the design goals.

Like it or not, all of us hardware "types" are going to have to learn some software. We have already laid the groundwork for this task by covering programming models and instruction set groups in Chap. 2. In this chapter there are 14 programming examples for you to study. Each example identifies the processor the program is intended for, any special hardware requirements you will need, and provides a brief description of the new instructions introduced.

The first examples are easy, but they become more complex as you move further into the chapter. They are chosen to illustrate the instruction set groups, addressing modes, and programming techniques. Although you may only be interested in one of the processors studied in this book, you are encouraged to study the examples for the other processors as well. For example, in several cases the Z-80 and 8080 solutions to a problem are both provided. And in some of these cases the Z-80 cannot do the job any better than the older 8080. But in other cases the Z-80's greatly expanded instruction set can be taken advantage of to solve the problem more simply.

Finally, you will notice an introduction of *assembly directives* or *pseudo-ops*. These are not microprocessor instructions, but commands recognizable by an assembler program. Even if you do not have access to an assembler, you will find it convenient to use at least some of these directives in your machine language programs.

Unfortunately, you cannot become a computer programmer by reading a book. You cannot really remember that the low-order address must come first and then the high-order address until you have spent a half hour (or maybe an hour) tracking down this bug! So if you can, run some of these programs yourself. At the end of this chapter you will find several programming problems. Use these to test your knowledge.

Think of learning to program as learning a new language. You can look up the meaning of each new word (instruction) in a dictionary (instruction set) but you won't truly understand that word until you use it in context. The examples in this chapter will give you that "real-life" context.

In the last section of the chapter we discuss microcomputer *operating systems*. These are control programs that manage the overall operation of the computer. They can range from simple machine language monitors for microprocessor trainers to complex disk-based operating systems similar to those found on minicomputers. A sample session using CP/M (a popular control program for 8080/85 and Z-80 microcomputers) to develop an assembly language program will be given.

3.1 MICROPROCESSOR PROGRAMMING EXAMPLES

Each of the examples in this section is in the same format, with the following information given:

1. *Program name and number*.
2. *Processor*: the microprocessor for which the program is intended.
3. *Hardware*: the special (if any) hardware needed to test this program. This generally means a parallel output port or standard video terminal.
4. *Problem statement*: a word description of the problem to be solved.
5. *Sample output*: a sample of the output the program should produce.
6. *Discussion*: a brief explanation of the programming technique and flowcharting of the problem.
7. *New instructions*: a word description for each new instruction that the example introduces. Included are assembly directives.
8. *Problem solution*: a standard assembly language listing is provided, including the hexadecimal object code.
9. *Summary*: a summary of the key points to be learned.

PROGRAM 1: 8080/85 8-Bit Addition

As you read this section, look for the answer to this Key Concept question:

3.1.1. Rather than specify the address as part of each instruction, the register indirect addressing mode uses the _____ register pair to point to the memory location.

Hardware. Required is a machine language monitor capable of examining memory, depositing data to memory, and running a program.

Problem Statement. Add the contents of memory locations 0700H and 0701H. Place the sum in memory location 0702H.

Sample Output:

$$(0700) = 23H$$
$$(0701) = 6AH$$

Then

$$(0702) = 8DH$$

Discussion. This problem was first solved at the end of Chap. 2 using the *direct* addressing mode. In this example we will use *register indirect* addressing. This technique uses the HL register pair as a pointer to a memory location. The INR L command can be used to change the position of the pointer.

New Instructions:

ORG The ORG command is an assembly language *directive*. It instructs the assembler to begin assembly of the following mnemonics at the address specified in the operand field (in this program address 0600H). There can be any number of ORG commands within a particular program.

LXI H,Addr Byte 3 of the instruction is moved into register H. Byte 2 of the instruction is moved into register L. This is a 16-bit register pair load operation using the immediate addressing mode. Other forms are LXI B, LXI D, and LXI SP.

INR L The content of register L is incremented by 1. Any of the general-purpose registers may be specified. Similarly, **DCR r** decrements a register.

MOV A,M The content of the memory location, whose address is in registers H and L, is moved to register A. This is a one-byte instruction using the register indirect addressing mode. It saves two bytes and six clock cycles compared with the direct addressing mode technique (LDA Addr). It may be used with any of the general-purpose registers (MOV B,M, MOV C,M, etc.).

MOV M,A The content of register A is moved to the memory location whose address is in registers H and L. This instruction also uses the register indirect addressing mode. It can be used with any of the general-purpose registers (MOV M,B, MOV M,C, etc.).

ADD M The content of the memory location whose address is contained in the H and L registers is added to the content of the accumulator. The result is placed in the accumulator. This instruction uses register indirect addressing.

HLT The processor is stopped. The registers and flags are unaffected. You may want to replace this instruction with a RET or JMP back to your monitor. If not, only a reset will restart the computer.

```
                            ;8080/85 8-BIT ADDITION
                            ;
                            ;THIS PROGRAM WILL ADD THE CONTENTS
                            ;OF MEMORY LOCATIONS 0700H AND
                            ;0701H AND STORE THE SUM IN 0702H.
    0600                    ;
    0600  210007            ORG     0600H    ;START AT LOCATION 0600H
    0603  7E                LXI     H,0700H  ;HL POINTS AT FIRST BYTE
    0604  2C                MOV     A,M      ;SAVE FIRST BYTE IN A
    0605  86                INR     L        ;NOW POINT AT SECOND BYTE
    0606  2C                ADD     M        ;ADD IT TO A
    0607  77                INR     L        ;ADVANCE POINTER
    0608  76                MOV     M,A      ;SAVE SUM HERE
    0609                    HLT              ;STOP
                            END
```

Figure 3.1   Program 1 8080/85 8-bit addition.

END   END is another (optional) assembly directive and must be the last statement in an assembly language program. All statements following END will be ignored by the assembler.

Program Solution.   Figure 3.1 provides a solution to this problem. The program begins by loading the HL pair with the address of the first byte. Now the MOV A,M command brings this byte into the accumulator. Incrementing L results in HL pointing at the second byte. ADD M adds this to the accumulator. A second INR L causes HL to point at the location to store the sum and MOV M,A accomplishes this. Statements beginning with a semicolon are comments and are ignored by the assembler.

Summary.   This program solves the addition problem first presented in Chap. 2, with seven instructions versus six for that solution. However, the total number of bytes has been reduced from 12 to 9 due to use of the register indirect addressing mode.

PROGRAM 2: Z-80 8-Bit Addition

As you read this section, look for the answer to this Key Concept question:

3.1.2. Via a 2's complement offset, the _____ addressing mode allows access to 256 consecutive memory locations without the need to increment a memory pointer.

Processor—Z-80

Hardware.   Required is a machine language monitor capable of examining memory, depositing data to memory, and running a program.

Problem Statement.   Add the contents of memory locations 0700H and 0701H. Place the sum in memory location 0702H.

Sample Output:

$$(0700) = 23H$$
$$(0701) = 6AH$$

Then

$$(0702) = 8DH$$

Discussion.   This is another solution to the addition problem in Program 1. The Z-80 *indexed* addressing mode is used. This technique allows reference to a memory location pointed at by the X or Y index registers but with a 2's-complement offset. This is convenient when you need to pull values from a table or list with a known offset. Note, however, that the offset cannot be computed at run time.

New Instructions:

ORG   The ORG command is an assembly language directive. It instructs the assembler to begin assembly of the following mnemonics at the address specified in the operand field (in this program, address 0600H). There can be any number of ORG commands within a particular program.

LD IX,nnnn   This command is used to initialize the X index register with a 16-bit value. It uses the immediate addressing mode and requires four bytes. Any of the register pairs (IY, SP, BC, DE, HL) can be loaded in this manner (LD rp,nnnn).

LD A,(IX+0)   The accumulator is loaded with the contents of memory pointed at by the X index register offset by 0. Recall the Z-80 convention of using parentheses to indicate the contents of a memory location. Any of the general-purpose registers can be loaded in this manner. The offset can vary from -128_{10} to $+127_{10}$.

ADD A,(IX+1)   The indexed addressing mode is not restricted to the load instructions. This command adds the contents of memory pointed at by register IX+1 to the accumulator. This makes it unnecessary to use a general-purpose register for temporary storage. Only register A can be specified for this instruction.

HALT   The processor is stopped. The registers and flags are unaffected. You may want to replace this instruction with a RET or JMP back to your monitor. If not, only a reset will restart the computer.

END   END is another (optional) assembly directive and must be the last statement in an assembly language program. All statements following END will be ignored by the assembler.

Problem Solution.   Figure 3.2(a) is a listing of the solution to this problem. The program begins by loading the X index register with the address of the first byte. Now the LD A,(IX+0) command brings this byte into the accumulator. ADD A,(IX+1) adds the two numbers without the need of incrementing a pointer. Similarly, LD (IX+2),A stores the sum. Figure 3.2(b) shows how the X index register is used in this problem.

```
ADDR    CODE          STMT  SOURCE STATEMENT
                      0001        ;Z-80  8-BIT ADDITION
                      0002        ;
                      0003        ;THIS PROGRAM WILL ADD THE CONTENTS
                      0004        ;OF MEMORY LOCATIONS 0700H AND
                      0005        ;0701H AND STORE THE SUM IN 0702H.
  >0600               0006        ;
 '0600   DD210007     0007  ORG       0600H          ;START AT LOCATION 0600H
 '0604   DD7E00       0008  LD        IX,0700H       ;IX POINTS AT FIRST BYTE
 '0607   DD8601       0009  LD        A,(IX+0)       ;SAVE IT IN A
 '060A   DD7702       0010  ADD       A,(IX+1)       ;ADD THE SECOND BYTE
 '060D   76           0011  LD        (IX+2),A       ;SAVE THE SUM
                      0012  HALT                     ;STOP
                      0013  END

ERRORS=0000
```

(a)

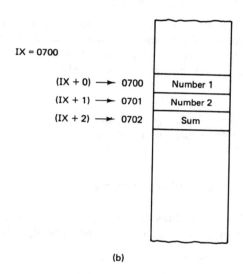

(b)

Figure 3.2 (a) Program 2 Z-80 8-bit addition; (b) the X index register is used to access all three memory locations.

Summary. The 8-bit addition problem has now been solved three ways. Of the three, the Z-80 solution requires the fewest number of instructions—just five. This is due to the *indexed* addressing mode. However, it requires just as many bytes as the 8080 *direct* addressing mode solution in Chap. 2 and three more bytes than the 8080 *register indirect* solution in Program 1. This is because the Z-80 indexed instructions all require two-byte op-codes plus an offset.

In general, the indexed addressing mode is most useful when the memory locations are not sequential. The register indirect mode is best for sequential data because the one-byte command INC HL can be used to advance the memory pointer through the table without the need to specify absolute addresses or an offset.

PROGRAM 3: 32-Bit Binary Addition

As you read this section, look for the answer to this Key Concept question:

3.1.3. When it is necessary to repeat a group of instructions several times, the _____ and _____ instructions can be used to decrement a loop counter and test for zero.

Processor—8080/85

Hardware. Required is a machine language monitor capable of examining memory, depositing data to memory, and running a program.

Problem Statement. Add the four-byte binary number in 0700H (LSD—least significant digit) through 0703H (MSD—most significant digit) to the four-byte binary number in 0704H (LSD) through 0707H (MSD). Store the sum as a four-byte binary number in 0708H (LSD) through 070BH (MSD).

Sample Output:

$$(0703–0700) = 05 \ 62 \ 21 \ 4F$$
$$(0707–0704) = 58 \ F3 \ CD \ 09$$

Then

$$(070B–0708) = 5E \ 55 \ EE \ 58$$

Discussion. Figure 3.3 shows how the 12 bytes of memory are used. In each case the least significant digit is stored first and the most significant digit last.

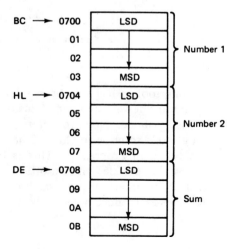

Figure 3.3 Memory organization for the 32-bit binary addition problem.

The program sets up four trials and proceeds to add the LSDs of the two numbers. The sum is placed in the LSD position of the sum. The process is repeated until all four bytes have been added.

New Instructions:

DS Define storage. This is an assembly directive and is used to tell the assembler to set aside a certain number of bytes at the current program position. For example,

TEMP   DS   1

reserves one byte of storage with the label (or name) TEMP.

ANA A The logical AND instructions perform a bit-by-bit AND operation with the accumulator. Any of the general-purpose registers may be specified or (HL). In this case A is being ANDed with itself. This seems illogical since A will not change. However, the carry flag will be reset. In effect, this is a *reset carry* instruction. Other forms of this instruction are ORA r (OR the accumulator with register r) and XRA r (exclusive-OR the accumulator with register r).

MVI A,nn All of the general-purpose registers can be loaded in the immediate mode. This two-byte instruction moves the second byte to the selected register.

STA addr Store the accumulator at the address in the second and third bytes of the instruction. This is the direct addressing mode and only the accumulator can be stored in this manner.

LDAX B This instruction is identical to MOV A,M except that register pair B is used as the memory pointer. The other form is LDAX D. Note that LDAX H is not a valid mnemonic—use MOV A,M.

ADC M Add the contents of memory pointed at by the HL pair, including the carry flag, to the accumulator. Any of the general-purpose registers may be specified (ADC B, ADC C, etc.). It is also possible to add without the carry. In this case the mnemonic is ADD M (also ADD B, ADD C, etc.).

INX B Increment register pair BC. Other forms are INX H, INX D, and INX SP. Note that no flags are affected (*very important!*).

JNZ addr Jump if not zero to addr. This instruction tests the zero flag allowing control to transfer to an instruction out of the sequential program path.

Program Solution. Figure 3.4 is the assembly language listing. All three register pairs are used as pointers, leaving the accumulator to hold the number of trials. However, the accumulator must also be used to accumulate the sums. For this reason a temporary storage location is created called TEMP. LDAX fetches the first number and ADC M adds the second to it. STAX D stores the sum. The process is repeated four times by decrementing TEMP and testing for 0 with JNZ NEXT. Note how the label NEXT is used to specify the location to jump to. The whole point of using labels is to avoid the use of specific addresses or variables in the program listing; let the assembler worry about this.

Summary. Multibyte addition is just an extension of 8-bit addition. One must take care to be sure that the carry propagates along with each addition (but is zero to start with).

Sec. 3.1   Microprocessor Programming Examples

```
                              ;32 BIT BINARY ADDITION
                              ;
                              ;THIS PROGRAM WILL ADD THE 32 BIT NUMBER
                              ;STORED AT 0700H THROUGH 0703H TO THE 32
                              ;BIT NUMBER STORED AT 0704H THROUGH 0707H.
                              ;THE 32 BIT SUM WILL BE STORED AT 0708H
                              ;THROUGH 070BH.
                              ;
     0600                     ORG    0600H        ;START AT LOCATION 0600H
     0600 010007             LXI    B,0700H       ;FIRST NUMBER LSD
     0603 210407             LXI    H,0704H       ;SECOND NUMBER LSD
     0606 110807             LXI    D,0708H       ;SUM LSD
     0609 A7                 ANA    A             ;CLEAR CARRY FLAG
     060A 3E04               MVI    A,4           ;FOUR TRIALS
     060C 321D06     NEXT    STA    TEMP          ;SAVE TRIALS HERE
     060F 0A                 LDAX   B             ;GET FIRST NUMBER
     0610 8E                 ADC    M             ;ADD WITH CARRY TO SECOND
     0611 12                 STAX   D             ;SAVE THE RESULT
     0612 03                 INX    B             ;ADVANCE POINTERS
     0613 23                 INX    H
     0614 13                 INX    D
     0615 3A1D06             LDA    TEMP          ;RECOVER TRIALS
     0618 3D                 DCR    A             ;ONE LESS
     0619 C20C06             JNZ    NEXT          ;CONTINUE TILL DONE
     061C 76                 HLT
     061D            TEMP    DS     1             ;ONE BYTE OF STORAGE
     061E                    END
```

Figure 3.4 Program 3 32-bit binary addition.

PROGRAM 4: 32-Bit Decimal Addition

As you read this section, look for the answers to these Key Concept questions:

3.1.4. When it is necessary to repeat a group of instructions several times, the _____ and _____ instructions can be used to decrement a loop counter and test for zero.

3.1.5. Following the addition of two BCD numbers, the _____ instruction should be used to ensure that the result is a valid BCD number.

Processor—Z-80

Hardware. Required is a machine language monitor capable of examining memory, depositing data to memory, and running a program.

Problem Statement. Add the four-byte BCD number stored in locations 0700H (LSD) through 0703H (MSD) to the four-byte BCD number in locations 0704H (LSD) through 0707H (MSD). Store the four-byte BCD sum in locations 0708H (LSD) through 070BH (MSD).

Sample Output:

$$(0703\text{--}0700) = 05\ 62\ 21\ 56$$
$$(0707\text{--}0704) = 58\ 53\ 38\ 09$$

Then

Discussion. Figure 3.3 shows how the 12 bytes of memory are used. In each case the least significant digit (LSD) is stored first and the most significant digit (MSD) last. The program sets up four trials and proceeds to add the LSDs of the two numbers. After each addition a *decimal adjust* must be made. This causes a half carry or full carry whenever the sum exceeds 9 (1001). The result is placed in the LSD position of the sum. The process is repeated until all four bytes have been added.

New Instructions:

EQU The EQU assembly directive allows an 8- or 16-bit value to be assigned to a label. This label can then be used throughout the program, making it more readable. In addition, if it is necessary to define a new value, only the EQU statement need be changed and the program reassembled. For example,

NUMB1   EQU   0700H

assigns the value 0700H to the name NUMB1.

AND A The logical AND instructions perform a bit-by-bit AND operation with the accumulator. Any of the general-purpose registers may be specified or (HL). In this case A is being ANDed with itself. This seems illogical at first because A will not change. However, the carry flag will always be reset. In effect, this is a *reset carry* instruction. Other forms of this instruction are OR r (OR the accumulator with register r) and XOR r (exclusive-OR the accumulator with register r).

EX AF,AF' The Z-80 has an alternate set of general-purpose registers, two accumulators, and two sets of flags. Only one set is active at a particular time and the exchange command flips back and forth between the two; it is up to you to know which set is active! EX AF,AF' exchanges the accumulator and flags. EXX exchanges the general-purpose registers (B, C, D, E, H, and L). You can also exchange the HL and DE registers within a particular set with the command EX HL,DE.

LD A,nn This is an 8-bit load operation using the immediate addressing mode. The second byte of the instruction is moved to register A. Any of the general-purpose registers or the accumulator may be specified.

LD A,(BC) This instruction uses register indirect addressing to load the accumulator with the contents of memory pointed at by register pair BC. Any of the register pairs may be used when A is the destination. If a general-purpose register is the destination, only the HL pair is allowed as the pointer.

ADC A,(HL) Add the contents of memory pointed at by the HL pair, including the carry flag, to the accumulator. Any of the general-purpose registers may be specified (ADC A,B, ADC A,C, etc.). It is also possible to add without the carry. In this case the mnemonic is ADD A,(HL) (also ADD A,B, ADD A,C, etc.).

DAA This instruction is used after an addition or subtraction operation to adjust the accumulator to a valid BCD number. This is necessary because of the six invalid BCD codes 1010 through 1111. For example, if the accumulator contains 59H and the command INC A is given, the result is 5AH. Now, if a DAA is executed, the result is 60H.

INC BC   Increment register pair BC. Other forms are INC HL, INC SP, INC IX, and INC IY. Note that no flags are affected (*very important!*). The DEC rp command similarly does not affect any of the flags.

DEC A   Decrement register A. Any of the general-purpose registers may be specified. Similarly, INC r increments a general-purpose register. All flags are affected by these instructions.

JR cc   Jump relative if the specified condition is true; otherwise, continue. This is a two-byte command with the second byte a 2's-complement offset, indicating a jump forward or backward. A significant advantage to using relative jumps in your programs is that *no absolute addresses need be specified*. This means that the resulting code is position independent.

   Program Solution.   Figure 3.5 is the assembly language listing. All three register pairs are used as pointers, leaving the accumulator to hold the number of trials. Because the accumulator must also be used to accumulate the sums, the EXX AF,AF' command is useful to swap accumulators (and carry flags) and provide

```
                                    Lifeboat Assoc. Z80 Assembler Page 0001
  ADDR   CODE        STMT SOURCE STATEMENT

                     0001          ;32-BIT DECIMAL ADDITION
                     0002          ;
                     0003          ;THIS PROGRAM WILL ADD THE 32 BIT BCD
                     0004          ;NUMBER STORED AT 0700H THROUGH 0703H TO
                     0005          ;THE 32 BIT BCD NUMBER STORED AT 0704H
                     0006          ;THROUGH 0707H.   THE 32 BIT BCD SUM WILL
                     0007          ;BE STORED AT 0708H THROUGH 070BH.
                     0008          ;
  >0700              0009 NUMB1    EQU     0700H
  >0704              0010 NUMB2    EQU     0704H
  >0708              0011 SUM      EQU     0708H
                     0012          ;
  >0600              0013          ORG     0600H             ;PROGRAM STARTS AT 0600H
  '0600  010007      0014          LD      BC,NUMB1          ;POINT AT NUMB1
  '0603  210407      0015          LD      HL,NUMB2          ;POINT AT NUMB2
  '0606  110807      0016          LD      DE,SUM            ;POINT AT SUM
  '0609  A7          0017          AND     A                 ;CLEAR CARRY
  '060A  08          0018          EX      AF,AF'            ;SAVE CARRY STATUS
  '060B  3E04        0019          LD      A,4               ;FOUR TRIALS
  '060D  08          0020 NEXT     EX      AF,AF'            ;RECOVER CARRY
  '060E  0A          0021          LD      A,(BC)            ;GET FIRST NUMBER
  '060F  8E          0022          ADC     A,(HL)            ;ADD TO SECOND WITH CARRY
  '0610  27          0023          DAA                       ;ADJUST FOR BCD
  '0611  12          0024          LD      (DE),A            ;SAVE SUM
  '0612  03          0025          INC     BC                ;ADVANCE POINTERS
  '0613  23          0026          INC     HL
  '0614  13          0027          INC     DE
  '0615  08          0028          EX      AF,AF'            ;RECOVER TRIALS
  '0616  3D          0029          DEC     A                 ;ONE LESS
  '0617  20F4        0030          JR      NZ,NEXT           ;CONTINUE FOR FOUR BYTES
  '0619  76          0031          HALT                      ;STOP
                     0032          END

ERRORS=0000
```

Figure 3.5   Program 4 32-bit decimal addition.

temporary storage for the trials counter. LD A,(BC) fetches the first number and ADC A,(HL) adds the second to it. After adjusting for decimal, LD (DE),A saves the sum in memory. The process is repeated four times by decrementing the trials counter in A. Notice how the label NEXT is used to specify the location to jump to. The whole point of using labels is to avoid the use of specific addresses in the program listing—let the assembler worry about this.

Note: If you do not have an assembler, you will have to figure out the argument for each relative jump yourself. There are two techniques. First you must realize that the program counter will be pointing at the instruction *following* the JR. In Fig. 3.5 this means that the PC = 0619. We want to branch back to location 060D. This is a total of 12 bytes (page 6 line 25 − page 6 line 13). Find the 2's complement of 12:

$$00001100 \rightarrow 11110011 + 1 = 11110100 = \text{F4}$$

Another technique is useful when the distance to branch is not too far. Starting at location 0618 (the last byte of the JR), count *backward* from FF until the desired location is reached. Try it. It really works!

Summary. Multibyte decimal addition is just an extension of 8-bit decimal addition. One must take care to be sure that the carry propagates along with each addition (but is zero to start with) and that the accumulator is properly adjusted for decimal.

PROGRAM 5: 8-Bit Multiplication

As you read this section, look for the answers to these Key Concept questions:

3.1.6. Two 8-bit numbers can be multiplied by repeatedly rotating the partial product left and adding the multiplicand for each 1 bit of the _____ .

3.1.7. To rotate the contents of the HL register pair left one bit, the instruction _____ should be given.

Processor—Z-80

Hardware. Required is a machine language monitor capable of examining memory, depositing data to memory, and running a program.

Problem Statement. Multiply the byte in 0700H (the multiplier) times the byte in 0701H (the multiplicand) and store the 16-bit product in 0702H (LSB) and 0703H (MSB).

Sample Output:

$$(0700) = \text{A3H} = 163_{10}$$
$$(0701) = \text{3AH} = 58_{10}$$

Sec. 3.1   Microprocessor Programming Examples

Then

$$(0702) = \text{EEH}$$
$$(0703) = \text{24H} \ (24\text{EEH} = 9454_{10})$$

Discussion. Figure 3.6(a) illustrates the conventional method for forming the product of two 8-bit numbers. Note the following points:

1. The partial product grows in size with each addition. It is 9 bits long after the second bit is considered and 10 bits long after the third bit is considered. Eventually, it becomes the product and can be 16 bits long.
2. Although it appears that we can simply rotate the multiplicand left with each addition for which the multiplier bit is a 1, this will require a 16-bit register for the multiplicand and another for the partial products.
3. There are no Z-80 instructions for rotating a 16-bit register. However, the command ADD HL,HL will double the contents of the HL pair (effectively, a shift left).
4. Consider the technique shown in Fig. 3.6(b). This multiplication is done by starting with the leftmost bit of the multiplier and shifting right. The result is the same, however.
5. Assume that the HL pair is used to hold the partial products and a general-purpose register is used to hold the multiplicand. Figure 3.7 shows the addition corresponding to line 3 of Fig. 3.6(b). IF the HL pair is rotated left one bit position, the addition will be correct.

The programming algorithm is now clear. We add HL to itself to perform a rotate left and then test the leftmost bit of the multiplier. If set, the multiplicand is added to the partial product. If this bit is reset, no action need be taken (there is no point in adding 0). When all 8 bits have been tested, HL contains the answer.

New Instructions:

ADD HL,HL This was discussed above. The Z-80 allows 16-bit addition, but the result must always be in the HL pair. Any of the register pairs may be added to HL (ADD HL,BC, ADD HL,DE, and ADD HL,SP). The zero flag is not affected, but the carry flag will be set if a carry out of bit 15 occurs.

RLCA Rotate the contents of the accumulator left circular. Bit 7 is rotated into the carry and into bit 0. The Z-80 features many different rotates and shift instructions (see Table 2.2) including the ability to rotate (HL).

DJNZ Decrement the B register and jump relative if not zero. This is a handy instruction that utilizes the B register as a counter. There are no other forms of this instruction.

LD (addr),HL Save the HL pair at address addr (L) and addr+1 (H). Any of the register pairs may be specified, including the X and Y index registers.

LD L,D Any general-purpose register may be copied into any other general-purpose register. In this case a copy of D is placed in L. D remains unchanged.

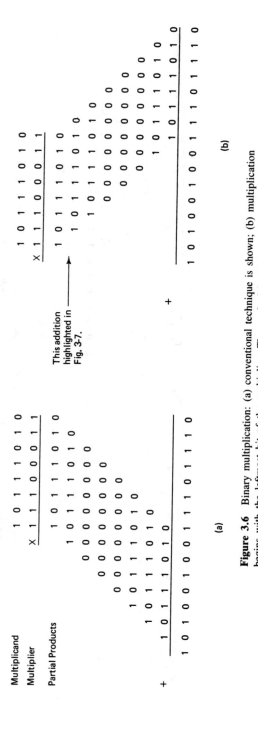

Figure 3.6 Binary multiplication: (a) conventional technique is shown; (b) multiplication begins with the leftmost bit of the multiplier. The method in (b) is easiest to implement with the Z-80.

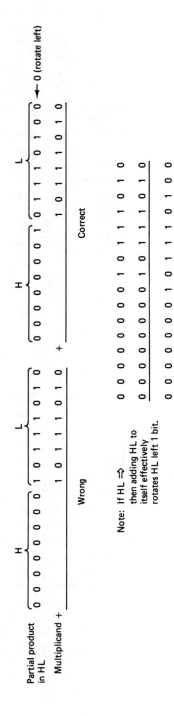

Figure 3.7 The partial product addition in line three of Fig. 3.6(b) is shown. If the partial product in the HL pair is first rotated left, the addition will be correct.

```
ADDR    CODE        STMT SOURCE STATEMENT

                    0001            ;Z-80  8-BIT MULTIPLICATION
                    0002            ;
                    0003            ;THIS PROGRAM WILL MULTIPLY THE 8-BIT
                    0004            ;NUMBER IN 0700H TIMES THE 8-BIT NUMBER
                    0005            ;IN 0701H.   THE 16-BIT PRODUCT WILL BE
                    0006            ;STORED IN 0702H (LSB) AND 0703H (MSB).
                    0007            ;
>0700               0008 DATA   EQU      0700H           ;ADDRESS OF FIRST BYTE
>0702               0009 PRDCT  EQU      0702H           ;ADDRESS OF PRODUCT
                    0010        ;
>0600               0011        ORG      0600H           ;PROGRAM STARTS AT 0600H
'0600   0608        0012        LD       B,8             ;BIT COUNTER
'0602   210007      0013        LD       HL,DATA         ;POINT AT MULTIPLIER
'0605   7E          0014        LD       A,(HL)          ;GET IT
'0606   23          0015        INC      HL              ;ADVANCE POINTER
'0607   5E          0016        LD       E,(HL)          ;E HOLDS MULTIPLICAND
'0608   1600        0017        LD       D,0             ;PREPARE FOR 16-BIT ADD
'060A   6A          0018        LD       L,D             ;HL MUST START WITH 0
'060B   62          0019        LD       H,D             ;
'060C   29          0020 MTPY   ADD      HL,HL           ;ROTATE PART PROD LEFT
'060D   07          0021        RLCA                     ;TEST MULTIPLIER
'060E   3001        0022        JR       NC,SKIP         ;NO ADD IF 0
'0610   19          0023        ADD      HL,DE           ;ADD MULTIPLICAND
'0611   10F9        0024 SKIP   DJNZ     MTPY            ;DO 8 TIMES
'0613   220207      0025        LD       (PRDCT),HL      ;SAVE THE PRODUCT
'0616   76          0026        HALT                     ;STOP
                    0027        END

ERRORS=0000
```

Figure 3.8 Program 5 Z-80 8-bit multiplication.

Program Solution.   Figure 3.8 is the assembly language listing of the program. The B register is used as the bit counter—thinking ahead to the DJNZ instruction. The multiplier is loaded into the accumulator and register E holds the multiplicand. Register D is zeroed in preparation for the ADD HL,DE which forms the partial product. The program now proceeds as described in the Discussion. RLCA is used to test the multiplier bit and the 16-bit sum is finally stored using the LD (PRDCT),HL command.

Summary.   Most 8-bit microprocessors do not have multiplication (or division) instructions and (rather complex) routines must be written to accomplish this function. The problem is further compounded by a lack of 16-bit rotate instructions. The ADD HL,HL instruction can be used to advantage in this instance.

PROGRAM 6: BCD-to-Binary Conversion

As you read this section, look for the answers to these Key Concept questions:

3.1.8. To divide a register by 2, rotate the contents of that register _____ one bit. The remainder if any will be stored in the _____ flag.

3.1.9. After the instruction BIT 7,A, the zero flag will be _____ if bit 7 of register A is a 1.

Sec. 3.1   Microprocessor Programming Examples   **93**

Processor—Z-80

Hardware.   Required is a machine language monitor capable of examining memory, depositing data to memory, and running a program.

Problem Statement.   Convert the eight-digit BCD number stored in 0700H through 0703H to a 24-bit binary number and store in 0704H through 0706H.

Sample Output.   Figure 3.9 illustrates the memory usage and shows the BCD number 13,964,829 stored in 0700H through 0703H. The 24-bit binary result is D5161DH and is stored in 0704H through 0706H.

Discussion.   This problem can be solved by using the *repeated-division-by-2* technique for converting decimal numbers to binary. In this method the decimal number is repeatedly divided by 2 and the remainder (which must be 0 or 1) recorded. The first remainder becomes the LSB (least significant bit) and the remainder from the last division is the MSB (most significant bit).

Figure 3.10(a) illustrates the method (for 8 bits) in decimal and Fig. 3.10(b) shows the same problem done in binary. Note that in binary, division by 2 is simply a rotate-right operation. We must be careful to be sure that the result is always a valid BCD number, however. Whenever a rotate operation results in bit 7 or 3 being set, 3 must be subtracted from the corresponding nibble to achieve the correct result.

The solution to this problem requires that we rotate the four-byte eight-digit BCD number right one bit; test bits 3 and 7 of each byte, and then use the carry flag to accumulate the binary result. A flowchart is presented in Fig. 3.11.

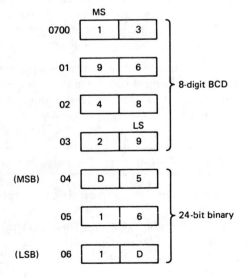

Figure 3.9 Memory usage for the BCD to binary conversion program. Four bytes are required for the eight-digit BCD number and the result is stored as a 24-bit binary number.

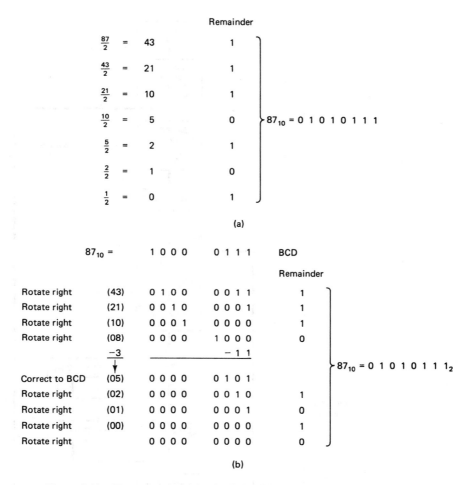

Figure 3.10 The repeated-division-by-2 algorithm applied to (a) a decimal number and (b) its BCD equivalent.

New Instructions:

PUSH AF and **POP AF** The accumulator and flag registers are pushed onto the top of the stack area of memory. The stack pointer register is decremented by 2. This is a convenient and quick way of saving a register pair when it must temporarily be used for something else. In this example the carry status needs to be saved, but the status of bits 3 and 7 of the accumulator must also be tested and corrected. PUSH AF is used to save the carry value and POP AF recovers it. In general, PUSH rp loads the top of the stack with a register pair, and POP rp pops the top of the stack into the selected register pair. Because PUSH and POP access only the top of the stack, great care must be taken to ensure that you know what is currently on the stack top. If not, erroneous data may be popped into your register pair.

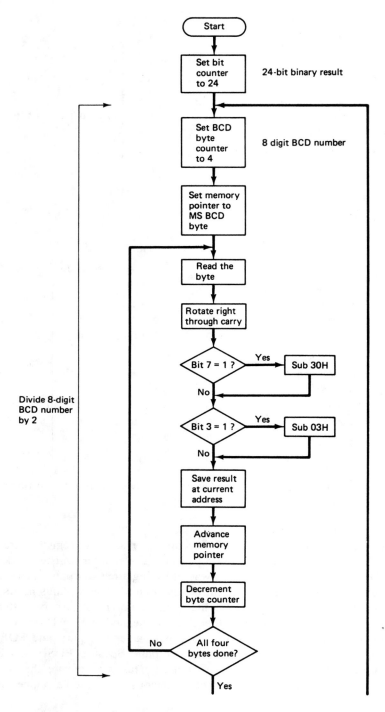

Figure 3.11   Flowchart for the BCD-to-binary conversion routine.

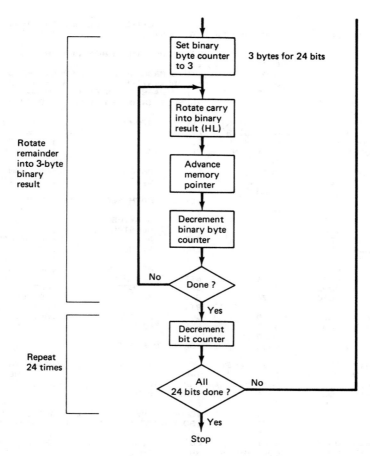

Figure 3.11 *(Continued)*

BIT 7,A   AND register A with 10000000 and set the zero flag accordingly. This instruction can be used to test any bit of any register, indexed memory location, or (HL). Similar instructions exist to set any bit (SET b,r) or reset any bit (RES b,r).

SUB nn   Subtract the immediate data byte nn from the accumulator. Other forms allow the contents of a general-purpose register or memory location to be subtracted from the accumulator [SUB r, SUB (HL), etc.]. Similar forms exist for the add instruction [ADD nn, ADD r, ADD (HL), etc.].

Program Solution.   Figure 3.12 is the assembly language listing for the program. It follows the flowchart very closely.

Summary.   Converting a BCD number to binary is a straightforward process once the repeated-division-by-2 algorithm is understood. In this process the rotate commands are useful for dividing or multiplying by 2 and extracting the remainder.

```
ADDR     CODE        STMT  SOURCE STATEMENT

                     0001        ;Z-80 BCD TO BINARY CONVERSION ROUTINE
                     0002        ;
                     0003        ;THIS PROGRAM WILL CONVERT THE 8 DIGIT BCD
                     0004        ;NUMBER STORED IN 0700H (MSB) THROUGH 0703H
                     0005        ;TO A 24-BIT BINARY NUMBER AND STORE THE
                     0006        ;RESULT IN 0704H (MSB) THROUGH 0706H.
                     0007        ;
>0700                0008  START  EQU   0700H          ;MSB OF BCD NUMBER
>0018                0009  BITS   EQU   24             ;BITS IN BINARY RESULT
>0004                0010  BYTES  EQU   4              ;BCD BYTES
>0003                0011  BIN    EQU   3              ;BINARY BYTES IN RESULT
                     0012        ;
>0600                0013        ORG   0600H           ;PROGRAM STARTS AT 0600H
'0600   0E18         0014        LD    C,BITS          ;LOAD BIT COUNTER
                     0015        ;
                     0016        ;DIVIDE EACH BCD DIGIT BY TWO
                     0017        ;
'0602   0604         0018  LOOP   LD    B,BYTES        ;LOAD BCD BYTE COUNTER
'0604   210007       0019        LD    HL,START        ;MEMORY POINTER
'0607   A7           0020        AND   A               ;CLEAR CARRY
'0608   7E           0021  DIV    LD    A,(HL)         ;FETCH BYTE
'0609   1F           0022        RRA                   ;DIVIDE BY 2
'060A   F5           0023        PUSH  AF              ;SAVE CARRY STATUS
'060B   CB7F         0024        BIT   7,A             ;ERROR IF SET
'060D   2802         0025        JR    Z,TEST3         ;CHECK BIT 3 IF NOT
'060F   D630         0026        SUB   30H             ;CORRECT HIGH ORDER NIBBLE
'0611   CB5F         0027  TEST3  BIT   3,A            ;ERROR IF SET
'0613   2802         0028        JR    Z,SAVE          ;SAVE IT IF NOT
'0615   D603         0029        SUB   03H             ;CORRECT LOW ORDER NIBBLE
                     0030        ;
                     0031        ;SAVE THIS RESULT
                     0032        ;
'0617   77           0033  SAVE   LD    (HL),A         ;SAVE THE CORRECTED RESULT
'0618   23           0034        INC   HL              ;PREPARE FOR NEXT BYTE
'0619   F1           0035        POP   AF              ;RECOVER CARRY
'061A   10EC         0036        DJNZ  DIV             ;TEST FOR LAST BYTE
                     0037        ;
                     0038        ;CARRY FLAG HOLDS THE REMAINDER OF THE DIVISION
                     0039        ;SO ROTATE THIS INTO THE BINARY RESULT.
                     0040        ;
'061C   0603         0041        LD    B,BIN           ;BYTE COUNTER
'061E   CB1E         0042  ANSWR  RR    (HL)           ;(HL) ACCUMULATES RESULT
'0620   23           0043        INC   HL              ;NEXT BYTE
'0621   10FB         0044        DJNZ  ANSWR           ;TEST FOR DONE
                     0045        ;
                     0046        ;THIS MUST BE DONE 24 TIMES FOR A 24-BIT RESULT
                     0047        ;
'0623   0D           0048        DEC   C               ;BUMP BIT COUNTER
'0624   20DC         0049        JR    NZ,LOOP         ;AND CONTINUE
'0626   76           0050        HALT                  ;UNTIL ALL BITS TESTED
                     0051        END
```

Figure 3.12 Program 6 Z-80 eight-digit BCD-to-24-bit binary conversion program.

PROGRAM 7: Filling a Block of Memory

As you read this section, look for the answers to these Key Concept questions:

3.1.10. When decrementing or incrementing one of the 16-bit register pairs, _____ of the flags are affected.

3.1.11. The instruction ORA E will set the zero flag only if registers A and E are _____ .

3.1.12. The Z-80 instruction LDI transfers the byte in memory pointed to by _____ to the location pointed to by _____ .

Processor—8080/85 (version 1) and Z-80 (version 2)

Hardware. Required is a machine language monitor capable of examining memory, depositing data to memory, and running a program.

Problem Statement. Fill the block of memory whose beginning address is stored at BEGIN and with total number of bytes stored at BYTES. Fill the block with the character FILL. Provide 8080/85 and Z-80 solutions.

Sample Output. If

```
BEGIN = 0700H
BYTES = 1000H
FILL  = 2BH
```

then all memory from 0700H through 16FFH will contain 2BH.

Discussion. The 8080/85 solution to the problem uses the HL pair as a memory pointer and the MOV M,A instruction to fill the memory location. A second register pair is used as a byte counter. Because the DCX rp instruction does not affect any flags, the low-order register of rp is first moved to the accumulator and then the high-order register of rp is ORed with the accumulator. A zero result means the register pair is zero.

The Z-80 does not have to go through these contortions. Its powerful LDI command decrements the byte counter and moves data pointed at by HL to the address pointed at by DE. By holding the HL address constant (at FILL), the block is filled automatically.

New Instructions:

DW or **DEFW**   Define word. This is an assembly directive that allows you to define the contents of two consecutive memory locations. Usually, it is used with a label as

```
START       DW       0700H
```

Start then becomes an address whose contents are 07H (START + 1) and 00 (START). Be sure that you see the difference between DW and EQU. The EQU directive assigns a value to a label. DW assigns an address (two consecutive bytes) to a label and allows you to specify the contents of that address.

DB or **DEFB**   Define byte. This is the same as DW except that only one byte is defined.

Note: The following are new 8080 instructions.

EQU   The EQU assembly directive allows an 8- or 16-bit value to be assigned to a label. This label can then be used throughout the program making it more readable.

In addition, if it is necessary to define a new value, only the EQU statement need be changed and the program reassembled. For example,

$$\text{NUMB1} \qquad \text{EQU} \qquad \text{0700H}$$

assigns the value 0700H to the name NUMB1.

LDA addr   Load the accumulator with the contents of memory specified in bytes two and three of the instruction. Only register A may be loaded in this manner.

LHLD   Load register L with the contents of memory whose address is specified in bytes two and three of the instruction. Load register H with the contents of the next memory location. Only the HL pair may be loaded in this manner. A similar instruction is SHLD, which stores the HL pair at the address specified in the instruction.

XCHG   Exchange the HL pair with the DE pair. LHLD followed by XCHG is a convenient way of loading the DE register pair from memory.

PUSH PSW and **POP PSW**   The accumulator and flag registers are pushed onto the top of the stack area of memory. The stack pointer register is decremented by 2. This is a convenient and quick way of saving a register pair or the flags when they must temporarily be used for something else. In general, PUSH rp loads the top of the stack with a register pair, and POP rp pops the top of the stack into the selected register pair. Because PUSH and POP access only the top of the stack, great care must be taken to ensure that you know what is currently on the stack top. If not, erroneous data may be popped into your register pair.

DCX rp   Decrement register pair. *No flags are affected*!

MOV r,r   Copy data from one register pair to another. The source register is not changed.

JZ addr   Jump if zero to addr. This instruction tests the ZERO flag, which has been set or reset in a previous instruction. All of the 8080/85 condition flags can be tested in this manner. The jump instructions are what allow the processor to break out of its normal sequential flow and provide decision points in the program.

Note: The following are the new Z-80 instructions.

LDI   Transfer the data byte pointed at by HL to the memory location pointed at by DE. Decrement the BC register pair (acting as a byte counter) and increment HL and DE. There are several forms of this instruction, including LDD, LDDR, and LDIR. The LDD versions decrement HL and DE, the LDI versions increment HL and DE. The two commands ending with R repeat until BC = 0.

JP PE,Loop   Jump if parity even to LOOP. The P/V flag is set if BC $\neq$ 0 after the LDI instruction. Thus JP PE,Loop causes the program to loop until BC = 0 (and the P/V flag is reset).

Program Solutions.   Figure 3.13 is the 8080/85 solution and Fig. 3.14 is the Z-80 solution.

Summary.   Filling a block of memory requires two register pairs, one to act as a memory pointer and a second as a byte counter. With the 8080/85, loading

```
                                        ;8080/85 BLOCK FILL PROGRAM
                                        ;
                                        ;BLOCK BEGINS AT ADDRESS (START)
                                        ;(BYTES) IS TOTAL BYTES IN THE BLOCK
                                        ;(FILL) IS THE CHARACTER TO WRITE TO THE BLOCK
                                        ;
        0600                    ORG     0600H       ;PROGRAM STARTS AT 0600H
        0600 3A1D06             LDA     FILL        ;GET FILL CHARACTER
        0603 2A1B06             LHLD    BYTES       ;GET NUMBER OF BYTES
        0606 EB                 XCHG                ;DE NOW BYTE COUNTER
        0607 2A1906             LHLD    START       ;HL HOLDS START ADDRESS
        060A 77         LOOP    MOV     M,A         ;WRITE A BYTE
        060B F5                 PUSH    PSW         ;SAVE A
        060C 23                 INX     H           ;ADVANCE MEMORY POINTER
        060D 1B                 DCX     D           ;BUMP BYTE COUNTER
        060E 7A                 MOV     A,D         ;PREPARE TO TEST IF
        060F B3                 ORA     E           ;D=E=0
        0610 CA1706             JZ      DONE        ;IF SO THEN DONE
        0613 F1                 POP     PSW         ;ELSE RECOVER A
        0614 C30A06             JMP     LOOP        ;AND WRITE ANOTHER BYTE
        0617 F1         DONE    POP     PSW         ;RESTORE STACK POINTER
        0618 76                 HLT                 ;STOP
                                        ;FILL THESE LOCATIONS WITH THE DESIRED
                                        ;BLOCK DATA
        0619 0007      START    DW      0700H       ;BLOCK STARTING ADDRESS
        061B 0010      BYTES    DW      1000H       ;NUMBER OF BYTES
        061D 2B        FILL     DB      2BH         ;FILL CHARACTER
```

Figure 3.13 Program 7 8080/85 version of the block fill program.

and testing these register pairs requires several instructions. With the Z-80, the LDI instruction makes the job much simpler. The final result is:

8080/85:   15 instructions and 25 bytes
Z-80:   7 instructions and 18 bytes

Lifeboat Assoc. Z80 Assembler Page 0001

```
ADDR    CODE        STMT  SOURCE STATEMENT

                    0001        ;Z-80  BLOCK FILL PROGRAM
                    0002        ;
                    0003        ;BLOCK BEGINS AT ADDRESS (START).
                    0004        ;(BYTES) IS TOTAL BYTES IN THE BLOCK.
                    0005        ;(FILL) IS THE CHARACTER TO WRITE TO THE BLOCK.
                    0006        ;
  >0600             0007        ORG     0600H           ;PROGRAM STARTS AT 0600H
'0600  ED5B1206'    0008        LD      DE,(START)      ;DE HOLDS FILL ADDRESS
'0604  ED4B1406'    0009        LD      BC,(BYTES)      ;BC IS BYTE COUNTER
'0608  211606'      0010        LD      HL,FILL         ;HL POINTS AT BYTE TO XFER
'060B  EDA0         0011  LOOP  LDI                     ;FILL THE LOCATION
'060D  2B           0012        DEC     HL              ;POINT AT SAME BYTE
'060E  EA0B06'      0013        JP      PE,LOOP         ;CONTINUE UNTIL BC=0
'0611  76           0014        HALT                    ;STOP
                    0015        ;
                    0016        ;FILL THESE LOCATIONS WITH THE
                    0017        ;DESIRED BLOCK DATA
'0612  0007         0018  START DEFW    0700H           ;BLOCK STARTING ADDRESS
'0614  0010         0019  BYTES DEFW    1000H           ;NUMBER OF BYTES
'0616  2B           0020  FILL  DEFB    2BH             ;FILL CHARACTER
                    0021        END

ERRORS=0000
```

Figure 3.14 Program 7 Z-80 version of the block fill program.

Sec. 3.1   Microprocessor Programming Examples

PROGRAM 8: Square-Wave Generator

As you read this section, look for the answer to this Key Concept question:

3.1.13. A _____ _____ can be achieved by preloading a register and then repeatedly decrementing that register to 0.

3.1.14. The _____ instruction allows control to transfer to a subroutine, which when complete, issues the _____ instruction to return control to the main program.

Processor—8080

Hardware. Required are a machine language monitor and a latched output port.

Problem Statement. Create a variable-rate square-wave generator using bit 0 of an available output port.

Sample Output. When the program is running and with a logic probe or oscilloscope connected to bit 0 of the chosen output port, a pulse condition should be observed.

Discussion. Generating a square wave with a microprocessor is much easier than it might at first seem. By simply incrementing the accumulator and giving the OUT command, bit 0 of the output port will toggle back and forth between a 1 and a 0—hence a square wave. Controlling the frequency of this oscillation is not so easy. In this example a subroutine will be called causing the microprocessor to count down to 0 from some large number. By calculating the number of clock cycles required and knowing the system clock frequency, the period for one-half cycle can be calculated.

New Instructions:

OUT nn The contents of the accumulator is output to the port whose address is specified in byte two of the instruction. The corresponding input instruction is IN nn. Note that for both instructions the data must go through the accumulator; no general-purpose registers may be specified.

CALL addr Jump to the subroutine at the address specified in bytes two and three of this instruction. Save the return address on the stack top. Subroutines are very useful because they represent sections of a program that can be shared by other parts of the program. This, in turn, saves memory space that would otherwise be filled duplicating the subroutine function. What makes the CALL different from a JMP is the RET instruction.

RET Return to the address stored on the stack top. Unlike the JMP, a subroutine can return to the main program when it is complete. It should be obvious that great care must be taken to balance each CALL with a RET. Similarly, PUSHes and POPs must be balanced or you may return from a subroutine using a PUSHed (but not POPed) register pair as the address!

```
                    ;8080 SQUARE WAVE GENERATOR
                    ;
                    ;CHANGE THE OPORT EQU TO MATCH YOUR HARDWARE
                    ;
                    ;TOTAL CLOCK CYCLES ARE:
                    ;(24 X DE) + 62(SUB) + 42(MAIN ROUTINE)
                    ;THE 24 CYCLES OF THE LOOP ARE HIGHLIGHTED.
                    ;IF DE = 20829 = 515DH THEN THE TOTAL CLOCK
                    ;CYCLES WILL BE 500,000.  FOR A 1MHZ COMPUTER
                    ;THIS RESULTS IN A 1HZ SQUARE WAVE AT BIT 0.
                    ;
0001 =        OPORT  EQU     1          ;OUTPUT PORT 1
515D =        DELAY  EQU     515DH      ;1HZ SQUARE WAVE
                    ;
0600                 ORG     0600H      ;START AT 0600H
0600 D301     AGAIN  OUT     OPORT      ;OUTPUT A LEVEL          (10)
0602 CD0906          CALL    WAIT       ;NOW WAIT                (17)
0605 3C              INR     A          ;TOGGLE THE OUTPUT BIT    (5)
0606 C30006          JMP     AGAIN      ;MAKE A SQUARE WAVE      (10)
                    ;
                    ;THIS IS THE WAIT SUBROUTINE
0609 D5       WAIT   PUSH    D          ;SAVE DE                 (11)
060A F5              PUSH    PSW        ;AND PSW                 (11)
060B 115D51          LXI     D,DELAY    ;16 BIT COUNT            (10)
060E 1B       LOOP   DCX     D          ;BUMP COUNTER           .(5)
060F 7A              MOV     A,D        ;PREPARE TO TEST        .(5)
0610 B3              ORA     E          ;FOR DE = 0             .(4)
0611 C20E06          JNZ     LOOP       ;IF NOT - CONTINUE      .(10)
0614 F1              POP     PSW        ;DONE SO RECOVER PSW     (10)
0615 D1              POP     D          ;AND DE - NOTE THE ORDER (10)
0616 C9              RET                ;TIMES UP                (10)
0617                 END
```

Figure 3.15 Program 8 8080 square-wave generator.

Program Solution.   Figure 3.15 provides a solution to this problem. The number of clock cycles for each instruction are indicated at the far right of the listing. This information can be obtained from the instruction set summary in Table A.1 of Appendix A. By changing the DELAY equate, the frequency of the square wave can be controlled. The PUSH D and PUSH PSW instructions make the subroutine "transparent"—the contents of the registers and flags are not changed. As discussed in Program 7, the DCX instruction does not affect the flags and therefore the MOV A,D and ORA E instructions are used to determine when DE has been counted down to zero.

Summary.   Time delay routines are good choices for subroutines. Using a 16-bit counter, a wide range of delay values can be achieved. However, care must be used when testing for 0 because the 16-bit decrement instructions do not affect any flags.

PROGRAM 9: Serial Communications Test Program

As you read this section, look for the answer to this Key Concept question:

3.1.15. A _____ is a binary pattern that allows specific bits to be tested via an AND instruction.

Processor—Z-80

Hardware.   Required are a machine language monitor and serial terminal with bit-testable receiver and transmitter ready flags. The terminal must be set to the *full-duplex* mode.

Problem Statement.   Monitoring the receiver and transmitter ready flags, "echo" each keystroke from the terminal's keyboard back to the terminal for display. This will verify the communications link between computer and terminal.

Sample Output.   With the test program running, the terminal will appear to be a typewriter displaying each character exactly as it is typed on the keyboard. Stopping the program will cease all output.

Discussion.   Computer terminals (or video terminals) are most often interfaced to a computer via a serial data link. Because the computer can input or output data to the terminal much faster than the terminal can accept it, *ready flags* are required. The receiver ready flag says "I am ready to give you a byte of data." Similarly, the transmitter ready flag says "I am ready to transmit another byte of data." Using these ready flags, the computer is *synchronized* to the slower data rate of the terminal. More detail on interfacing a terminal to a microcomputer is presented in Chap. 9.

New Instructions:

IN A,(nn) and **OUT (nn),A**   These are the basic input and output commands compatible with the 8080 and 8085. The port address is restricted to 8 bits and all data must flow through the accumulator.

IN r,(C) and **OUT (C),r**   The Z-80 can also input or output data with any of the general-purpose registers. In these instructions register C holds the port address. A third group of I/O instructions use (HL) as the source or destination of data. These are listed in Table 2.3.

Problem Solution.   Figure 3.16 is the assembly language listing of the program. If you wish to test this program, change the equates to match your hardware. RMSK and TMSK are logical *masks*. When ANDed with the accumulator the result is zero if the test bit is zero, and not zero if the test bit is set. The program begins by waiting for the receiver ready flag to be set, indicating that a character has been typed. The IN B,(C) command works nicely here, saving the character in B while the program continues by testing the transmitter ready flag. When set, the contents of register B—the received character—is echoed back to the terminal.

Summary.   An "echo back" program is an effective and simple way to test a serial communications line. Care must be taken to synchronize the computer to the data rate of the terminal. This can be accomplished by monitoring receiver and transmitter ready flags.

```
                      0001        ;SERIAL COMMUNICATIONS TEST PROGRAM
                      0002        ;
                      0003        ;THIS PROGRAM WILL ECHO EACH KEYSTROKE
                      0004        ;BACK TO THE TERMINAL FOR DISPLAY.
                      0005        ;
                      0006        ;CHANGE THE EQUATES BELOW TO MATCH YOUR
                      0007        ;SYSTEM HARDWARE.
                      0008        ;
                      0009        ;SPORT IS THE STATUS PORT AND DPORT IS
                      0010        ;THE DATA PORT.  TMSK AND RMSK ARE THE
                      0011        ;MASKS REQUIRED TO TEST THE TERMINAL
                      0012        ;READY FLAGS.
                      0013        ;
>0003                 0014 SPORT  EQU    3               ;STATUS PORT
>0002                 0015 DPORT  EQU    2               ;DATA PORT
>0001                 0016 TMSK   EQU    1               ;BIT 0 IS XMTR READY
>0002                 0017 RMSK   EQU    2               ;BIT 1 IS RECEIVER READY
                      0018        ;
>0600                 0019        ORG    0600H           ;PROGRAM BEGINS AT 0600H
                      0020        ;
'0600  0E02           0021        LD     C,DPORT         ;C IS THE DATA PORT ADDR
'0602  DB03           0022 CIN    IN     A,(SPORT)       ;GET READY STATUS
'0604  E602           0023        AND    RMSK            ;TEST RECEIVER
'0606  28FA           0024        JR     Z,CIN           ;WAIT FOR A KEYSTROKE
'0608  ED40           0025        IN     B,(C)           ;READ IT
                      0026        ;
                      0027        ;REGISTER B HOLDS THE CHARACTER.  NOW ECHO
                      0028        ;IT BACK TO TERMINAL.
                      0029        ;
'060A  DB03           0030 COUT   IN     A,(SPORT)       ;GET READY STATUS
'060C  E601           0031        AND    TMSK            ;TEST TRANSMITTER
'060E  28FA           0032        JR     Z,COUT          ;WAIT UNTIL READY
'0610  ED41           0033        OUT    (C),B           ;NOW TRANSMIT IT
'0612  18EE           0034        JR     CIN             ;LOOP FOREVER

ERRORS=0000
```

Figure 3.16   Program 9 serial communications test program.

PROGRAM 10: Hex Dump

As you read this section, look for the answers to these Key Concept questions:

3.1.16. By adding 30H (0–9) or 37H (A–F) a hexadecimal number is converted to its _____ equivalent.

Processor—8080/85

Hardware.   Required are a machine language monitor and serial terminal with bit-testable receiver and transmitter ready flags.

Problem Statement.   Using a standard 24-line by 80-character per line video terminal, output the contents of memory beginning with the address stored in (START). The contents of (BYTES) holds the total number of bytes to be dumped.

```
0700 A3 67 E6 2F 55 9F E6 22 21 5B C6 99 1C 9A AF 48

0710 4A 6B 7E 88 38 17 29 8C CE D4 B3 5A 22 71 2B 9E

0720 BC 4E 6A 73 88 19 26 37 3D EE 6A BE A5 62 77 21

0730 CC 42 75 49 A0 E2 8C 3B 11 AA 72 9B 1E 8A 90 EC
```

Figure 3.17 Sample output from the 8080/85 hex dump program.

Sample Output.   Figure 3.17 shows the output of the program with (START) = 0700H and (BYTES) = 0040H (the data shown represent random data at these locations in memory).

Discussion.   The main difficulty in solving this problem is converting the hexadecimal data stored in memory to ASCII format so that it will be readable on the terminal. The hex numbers 0 through 9 must be translated to 30H through 39H—simply add 30H. The hex letters A through F must be translated to 41H through 46H—add 37H (for example, 0AH + 37H = 41H = ASCII A).

Another feature of the program will require that the terminal's transmitter ready status be monitored before each character is output (refer to the Discussion in Program 9).

Finally, the output should be formatted on the screen with the address shown on the left, spaces between bytes of data, and line feeds between successive lines.

New Instructions:

CPI nn   Compare the contents of the accumulator with the immediate data byte that follows. The accumulator is not changed by this instruction but the condition flags are affected. The Z flag is set if the compare is true. If the accumulator is *less than* the data byte, the carry flag is set. The instruction CPI 0AH will set the carry flag if the accumulator is less than 0A (this can be used to identify the hex numbers 0 through 9). Other forms of the instruction are CMP r (compare the accumulator with a general-purpose register) and CMP M (compare the accumulator with the contents of memory pointed at by HL).

RZ   Return if the zero flag is set. Any of the condition flags can be tested in this manner. Be careful. If the condition never occurs, you will never return!

Problem Solution.   Figure 3.18 is a flowchart of the problem. Two subroutines have been incorporated into the program. COUT waits for the terminal to be ready and then outputs the character in the B register. HXAS converts the two-digit hex number in register A to two separate ASCII numbers and passes them on to COUT, where they are printed. The assembly language solution to the problem is presented in Fig. 3.19.

Note: Studying a program as complex as the one in Fig. 3.19 lets you appreciate the power of an assembler program. Much more than generating the machine codes,

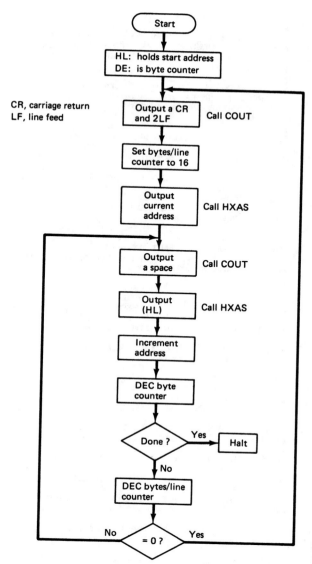

CR, carriage return
LF, line feed

Figure 3.18 Flowchart of the 8080/85 hex dump program.

the assembler lets you *document* your program so that it can be easily modified at a later date. Figure 3.20 is a copy of the hex dump program but without any of the comments. Try figuring out what it does!

Summary. A hex dump routine is a useful utility as part of a monitor program. The main problems to be overcome in its development are the conversion to ASCII of the hex data and the necessary screen formatting.

```
                         ;8080/85 HEX DUMP ROUTINE
                         ;
                         ;THIS PROGRAM WILL DUMP THE CONTENTS OF
                         ;MEMORY WITH BEGINNING ADDRESS STORED IN
                         ;(START) AND WITH TOTAL NUMBER OF BYTES
                         ;STORED IN (BYTES).
                         ;
                         ;THE FOLLOWING HARDWARE EQUATES CAN BE
                         ;CHANGED TO MATCH YOUR HARDWARE.  AN
                         ;80 CHARCATER BY 24 LINE CRT TERMINAL IS
                         ;ASSUMED.
0003 =          SPORT    EQU      3          ;TERMINAL STATUS PORT
0001 =          TMSK     EQU      1          ;TRANSMITTER READY FLAG MASK
0002 =          DPORT    EQU      2          ;TRANSMITTER DATA PORT
                         ;
                         ;THE FOLLOWING EQUATES WILL MAKE THE PROGRAM
                         ;MORE READABLE.
000D =          CR       EQU      0DH        ;CARRIAGE RETURN IN ASCII
000A =          LF       EQU      0AH        ;LINE FEED
0020 =          SPACE    EQU      20H        ;SPACE
0010 =          BLINE    EQU      16         ;BYTES/LINE IN THE DUMP
                         ;
0600                     ORG      600H       ;START AT 600H
                         ;BEGIN BY LOADING HL WITH START ADDRESS AND
                         ;DE WITH THE NUMBER OF BYTES TO OUTPUT
                         ;
0600 2A3B06             LHLD     BYTES      ;GET NUMBER OF BYTES
0603 EB                 XCHG                ;DE IS BYTE COUNTER
0604 2A3906             LHLD     START      ;HL IS MEMORY POINTER
                         ;
                NEWL     ;BEGIN EACH NEW LINE WITH A CR AND 2 LF
                         ;
0607 060D               MVI      B,CR       ;CARRIAGE RETURN
0609 CD5906             CALL     COUT       ;PRINT IT
060C 060A               MVI      B,LF       ;LINE FEED
060E CD5906             CALL     COUT       ;PRINT IT
0611 CD5906             CALL     COUT       ;ONE MORE
                         ;
                         ;LOAD THE BYTES/LINE COUNTER AND SAVE
                         ;
0614 0610               MVI      B,BLINE    ;BYTES/LINE
0616 C5                 PUSH     B          ;COUT ALSO USES B
                         ;
                         ;PRINT THE STARTING ADDRESS FOR THIS LINE
                         ;
0617 7C                 MOV      A,H        ;GET THE HIGH ORDER ADR
0618 CD3D06             CALL     HXAS       ;CONVERT TO ASCII AND PRINT
061B 7D                 MOV      A,L        ;GET THE LOW ORDER ADR
061C CD3D06             CALL     HXAS       ;CONVERT TO ASCII AND PRINT
                         ;
                NEWC     ;NOW PRINT THE HEX EQUIVALENT OF THE MEMORY
                         ;BYTE POINTED AT BY HL
                         ;
061F 0620               MVI      B,SPACE    ;FIRST A SPACE
0621 CD5906             CALL     COUT       ;PRINT IT
0624 7E                 MOV      A,M        ;GET THE BYTE
0625 CD3D06             CALL     HXAS       ;CONVERT TO ASCII AND PRINT
                         ;
                         ;ADVANCE THE MEMORY POINTER AND
                         ;TEST FOR DONE
                         ;
0628 23                 INX      H          ;ADVANCE POINTER
```

Figure 3.19 Program 10 8080/85 hex dump program.

```
0629 1B          DCX    D        ;BUMP BYTE COUNTER
062A 7A          MOV    A,D      ;PREPARE TO TEST
062B B3          ORA    E        ;IF DE=0
062C CA3806      JZ     DONE     ;IF SO WE'RE DONE
                 ;
                 ;IF NOT DONE THEN TEST FOR END OF LINE
                 ;
062F C1          POP    B        ;RECOVER BYTES/LINE
0630 05          DCR    B        ;END OF LINE?
0631 CA0706      JZ     NEWL     ;GO TO NEWLINE
0634 C5          PUSH   B        ;ELSE SAVE BYTES/LINE
0635 C31F06      JMP    NEWC     ;AND GO TO NEW CHARACTER
                 ;
         DONE    ;THIS IS PROGRAM END.  IF YOU ARE USING
                 ;THIS ROUTINE AS PART OF A MONITOR YOU
                 ;CAN MAKE THIS A RET.
0638 76          HLT             ;STOP
                 ;
                 ;DEFINE SOME SPACE FOR THE STARTING
                 ;ADDRESS AND BYTES TO DUMP
                 ;
0639 0007 START  DW     0700H    ;0700 IS AN EXAMPLE
063B 4000 BYTES  DW     0040H    ;4 LINES FOR EXAMPLE
                 ;
                 ;
         HXAS    ;**********************************
                 ;*          HXAS                 *
                 ;*   SUBROUTINE TO CONVERT THE HEX *
                 ;*   CHARACTER IN A TO ASCII AND CALL *
                 ;*   COUT.   REGISTERS A,B AND C ARE *
                 ;*   SCRAMBLED UPON RETURN        *
                 ;**********************************
                 ;
063D 0E02        MVI    C,2      ;2 ASCII DIGITS PER BYTE
063F F5          PUSH   PSW      ;SAVE THE CHARACTER
0640 0F          RRC
0641 0F          RRC             ;EXCHANGE MSD WITH LSD
0642 0F          RRC
0643 0F          RRC
0644 E60F CONV   ANI    0FH      ;MASK THE HIGH 4 BITS
0646 FE0A        CPI    0AH      ;CHECK FOR 0-9 HEX
0648 DA4D06      JC     NUMB     ;AND GO TO NUMB
064B C607        ADI    07H      ;LETTERS HAVE A 37H OFFSET
064D C630 NUMB   ADI    30H      ;NUMBERS HAVE A 30H OFFSET
                 ;
                 ;REGISTER A NOW HOLDS THE ASCII BYTE.
                 ;PRINT IT AND THEN CHECK IF BOTH DIGITS
                 ;HAVE BEEN CONVERTED
                 ;
064F 47          MOV    B,A      ;COUT WANTS CHARAC IN B
0650 CD5906      CALL   COUT     ;PRINT IT
0653 0D          DCR    C        ;TEST DIGIT COUNTER
0654 C8          RZ              ;IF ZERO WE'RE DONE
0655 F1          POP    PSW      ;RECOVER THE CHARACTER
0656 C34406      JMP    CONV     ;ELSE DO ONE MORE
                 ;
                 ;
         COUT    ;
                 ;**********************************
                 ;*          COUT                 *
                 ;*   THIS SUBROUTINE WILL WAIT FOR THE *
                 ;*   TRANSMITTER READY FLAG AND THEN *
                 ;*   OUTPUT THE CONTENTS OF THE B *
                 ;*   REGISTER TO THE SERIAL DATA PORT *
                 ;**********************************
                 ;
0659 DB03        IN     SPORT    ;GET TRANSMITTER STATUS
065B E601        ANI    TMSK     ;MASK READY FLAG
065D CA5906      JZ     COUT     ;WAIT UNTIL READY
0660 78          MOV    A,B      ;GET THE CHARACTER
0661 D302        OUT    DPORT    ;SHOW IT
0663 C9          RET             ;DONE
0664             END
```

Figure 3.19 (*Continued*)

```
0600    LHLD  063B
0603    XCHG
0604    LHLD  0639
0607    MVI   B,0D
0609    CALL  0659
060C    MVI   B,0A
060E    CALL  0659
0611    CALL  0659
0614    MVI   B,10
0616    PUSH  B
0617    MOV   A,H
0618    CALL  063D
061B    MOV   A,L
061C    CALL  063D
061F    MVI   B,20
0621    CALL  0659
0624    MOV   A,M
0625    CALL  063D
0628    INX   H
0629    DCX   D
062A    MOV   A,D
062B    ORA   E
062C    JZ    0638
062F    POP   B
0630    DCR   B
0631    JZ    0607
0634    PUSH  B
0635    JMP   061F
0638    HLT
0639    NOP
063A    NOP
063B    NOP
063C    NOP
063D    MVI   C,02
063F    PUSH  PSW
0640    RRC
0641    RRC
0642    RRC
0643    RRC
0644    ANI   0F
0646    CPI   0A
0648    JC    064D
064B    ADI   07
064D    ADI   30
064F    MOV   B,A
0650    CALL  0659
0653    DCR   C
0654    RZ
0655    POP   PSW
0656    JMP   0644
0659    IN    03
065B    ANI   01
065D    JZ    0659
0660    MOV   A,B
0661    OUT   02
0663    RET
0664
```

Figure 3.20 Program 10 without the comments or assembly directives.

PROGRAM 11: 1-BIT I/O PORT

As you read this section, look for the answer to this Key Concept question:

3.1.17. To read the status of the 8085 SID input use the _____ instruction. To control the status of the 8085 SOD line use the _____ instruction.

Hardware. Required are a machine language monitor, 7404 inverter, LED (light-emitting diode), two resistors, and one switch, as shown in Fig. 3.21.

Problem Statement. Use the SID and SOD lines of the 8085 microprocessor and construct a 1-bit I/O port.

Sample Output. With the program running, opening the switch should light the LED; closing the switch should turn off the LED.

Discussion. The *SID* (serial input data) line of the 8085 can be tested with the *RIM* instruction, which will set bit 7 of the accumulator according to the SID status. In a similar manner, the *SIM* instruction will cause bit 7 of the accumulator to be output to the *SOD* (serial output data) line of the 8085. This output will remain unchanged until another SIM is executed.

New Instructions:

SIM   Set interrupt masks. This instruction allows any of the 8085 RST 5.5, RST 6.5, or RST 7.5 interrupt inputs to be "masked." When masked, interrupts on that pin are ignored by the processor. In addition, the RST 7.5 interrupt flag can be reset with a SIM instruction. Interrupts are discussed in detail in Chap. 6. If bit 6 of the accumulator is set when the SIM instruction is executed, bit 7 of the accumulator is output to the SOD line as discussed above.

RIM   Read interrupt masks. Executing this instruction causes the accumulator to be loaded with the current interrupt mask status (as set by the SIM instruction), the interrupt enable status, and the status of any hardware interrupts that are pending. It also reads the value of the SID input line and stores this value in accumulator bit 7.

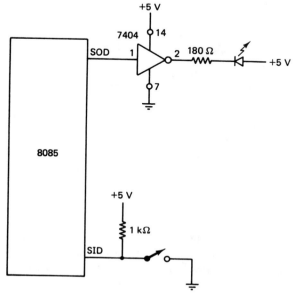

Figure 3.21   One-bit input and output port for the 8085.

```
                              ;8085 1-BIT I/O PORT
                              ;
                              ;THIS PROGRAM MONITORS A SWITCH CONNECTED
                              ;TO SID AND CONTROLS AN LED CONNECTED TO SOD.
                              ;WHEN THE SWITCH IS CLOSED THE LED IS OFF.
                              ;WHEN THE SWITCH IS OPENED THE LED LIGHTS.
                              ;
    0600                      ORG      0600H              ;PROGRAM STARTS AT 0600H
                              ;
                              ;TEST THE SID LINE AND BRANCH ACCORDINGLY
                              ;
    0600 20      CHECK        RIM                         ;GET SID STATUS
    0601 17                   RAL                         ;TO CARRY
    0602 D20B06               JNC      OFF                ;IF 0 TURN OFF LED
                              ;
                              ;ITS HIGH SO TURN ON LED
                              ;
    0605 3EC0                 MVI      A,0C0H             ;PROGRAM SOD HIGH
    0607 30                   SIM                         ;TURN ON LED
    0608 C30006               JMP      CHECK              ;CONTINUE MONITORING
                              ;
    060B 3E40   OFF           MVI      A,40H              ;PROGRAM SOD TO A 0
    060D 30                   SIM                         ;TURN OFF LED
    060E C30006               JMP      CHECK              ;CONTINUE MONITORING
```

Figure 3.22   Program 11 8085 1-bit I/O port.

Problem Solution.   Figure 3.22 is the assembly language listing of the program. The RIM instruction is used to test the status of the SID line. The SIM instruction is then used to turn the LED ON or OFF, depending on the switch position.

Summary.   The 8085 SID and SOD lines can be used to pass status information about an I/O device, to turn on valves, relays, LEDs, to detect switch closings, or to read and write serial data. The RIM instruction is used to test the SID input and the SIM instruction is used to control the SOD output.

PROGRAM 12: Frequency Counter

As you read this section, look for the answers to these Key Concept questions:

3.1.18. Falling edges of an input pulse can be counted in software by waiting for the input bit to be _____, and then to be _____.

3.1.19. One way of testing a bit is to give an AND instruction and then test the zero flag. Another way is to use a rotate instruction and test the _____ flag.

Processor—Z-80

Hardware.   Required are a machine language monitor, 5-Hz 50% duty cycle square wave, two decoded seven-segment displays, one 8-bit output port, and one square-wave generator to supply the unknown frequency to be measured. Refer to Fig. 3.23 for details.

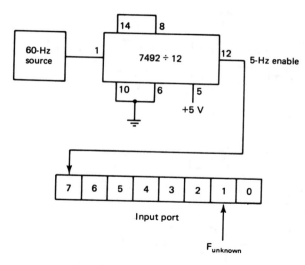

Figure 3.23 Hardware for the frequency counter program. The 7492 is connected as a divide-by-12 counter. It produces a 5-Hz 50% duty cycle enable signal from a TTL-compatible 60-Hz square-wave input.

Problem Statement. Measure the frequency of the input square wave by counting pulses during one-half period of the 5-Hz square wave. Display the frequency with a resolution of 10 Hz on the two seven-segment displays.

Sample Output. If the input square wave has a frequency of 654 Hz, the seven-segment displays should show 65. If the input frequency is 60 Hz, the displays should show 06.

Discussion. Figure 3.23 shows the hardware required for this problem. When using a microprocessor trainer, the two seven-segment displays could be replaced by the displays on the trainer. A video terminal can also be used with a hex-to-ASCII conversion routine.

The 5-Hz 50% duty cycle enable signal can easily be generated from a 60-Hz source (based on the line frequency) and divide-by-12 counter as shown.

Figure 3.24 illustrates the waveforms for the counter. In this figure the low period of the enable signal has arbitrarily been selected as the *count time*. If three pulses are counted during this 0.1-s interval, the frequency is 30 pulses per second or 30 Hz. Figure 3.25 is a detailed flowchart of the program.

New Instructions. There are none.

Problem Solution. Figure 3.26 is the assembly language listing of the program. Two methods of bit testing are used in this program. When the status bit to

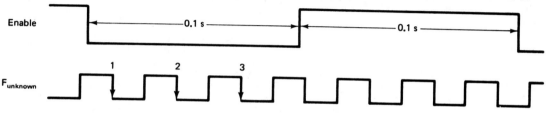

Figure 3.24 Typical waveforms for the frequency counter circuit. The computer will count three falling edges during the 0.1-s enable period and display 03 or 30 Hz.

Sec. 3.1   Microprocessor Programming Examples

113

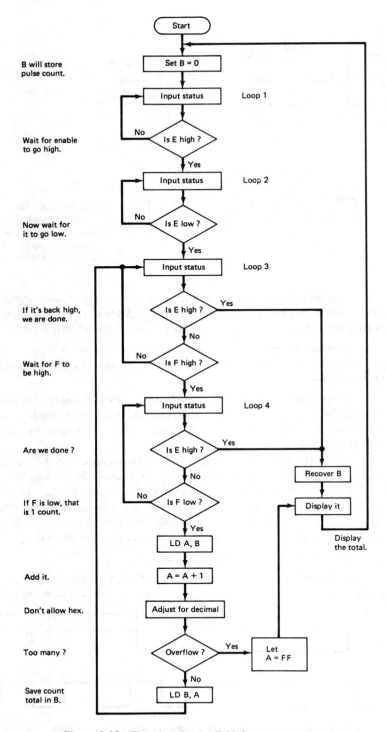

Figure 3.25 Flowchart for the Z-80 frequency counter.

```
ADDR    CODE      STMT SOURCE STATEMENT
                  0001          ;Z-80 FREQUENCY COUNTER
                  0002          ;
                  0003          ;5 HZ ENABLE SIGNAL (E) ON BIT 7 OF AN INPUT PORT.
                  0004          ;UNKNOWN FREQUENCY SQUARE WAVE (F)
                  0005          ;ON BIT 1 OF THE SAME INPUT PORT.
                  0006          ;
                  0007          ;TWO DECODED SEVEN SEGMENT DISPLAYS ARE
                  0008          ;ASSUMED CONNECTED TO AN OUTPUT PORT.
                  0009          ;
                  0010          ;RANGE IS 10 HZ TO 990 HZ DISPLAYED AS 01-99.
                  0011          ;OVERRANGE CAUSES THE DISPLAY TO GO DARK.
                  0012          ;
>00FF             0013 DARK     EQU    0FFH          ;CODE FOR DARK DISPLAY
>0001             0014 SPORT    EQU    1             ;THIS IS THE INPUT PORT
>0001             0015 DPORT    EQU    1             ;THIS IS THE OUTPUT PORT
                  0016          ;
>0600             0017          ORG    0600H         ;PROGRAM STARTS AT 0600H
                  0018          ;
'0600 0600        0019 START    LD     B,0           ;B COUNTS FALLING EDGES
                  0020          ;
'0602 DB01        0021 LOOP1    IN     A,(SPORT)     ;TEST E
'0604 17          0022          RLA                  ;BY ROTATING INTO CARRY
'0605 30FB        0023          JR     NC,LOOP1      ;WAIT FOR E TO BE HIGH
                  0024          ;
                  0025          ;E IS HIGH
                  0026          ;
'0607 DB01        0027 LOOP2    IN     A,(SPORT)     ;NOW WAIT
'0609 17          0028          RLA                  ;FOR E TO
'060A 38FB        0029          JR     C,LOOP2       ;GO LOW
                  0030          ;
                  0031          ;E IS LOW SO BEGIN COUNTING
                  0032          ;
'060C DB01        0033 LOOP3    IN     A,(SPORT)     ;CHECK E AGAIN
'060E 17          0034          RLA                  ;IF IT IS HIGH
'060F 3817        0035          JR     C,DONE        ;STOP COUNTING
'0611 CB4F        0036          BIT    1,A           ;CHECK F
'0613 28F7        0037          JR     Z,LOOP3       ;WAIT FOR F HIGH
                  0038          ;
                  0039          ;F IS HIGH
                  0040          ;
'0615 DB01        0041 LOOP4    IN     A,(SPORT)     ;CHECK E AGAIN
'0617 17          0042          RLA                  ;IF IT IS HIGH
'0618 380E        0043          JR     C,DONE        ;STOP COUNTING
'061A CB4F        0044          BIT    1,A           ;CHECK F
'061C 20F7        0045          JR     NZ,LOOP4      ;WAIT FOR F LOW
                  0046          ;
                  0047          ;FOUND 1 FALLING EDGE
                  0048          ;
'061E 78          0049          LD     A,B           ;RECOVER THE COUNT
'061F 3C          0050          INC    A             ;ADD 1
'0620 27          0051          DAA                  ;KEEP IT DECIMAL
'0621 3803        0052          JR     C,OVFL        ;TOO MANY?
'0623 47          0053          LD     B,A           ;SAVE THE COUNT
'0624 18E6        0054          JR     LOOP3         ;CONTINUE
                  0055          ;
'0626 06FF        0056 OVFL     LD     B,DARK        ;DARK DISPLAY
'0628 78          0057 DONE     LD     A,B           ;GET THE COUNT
'0629 D301        0058          OUT    (DPORT),A     ;SHOW IT
'062B 18D3        0059          JR     START         ;NEXT CYCLE
                  0060          END
ERRORS=0000
```

Figure 3.26 Program 12: Z-80 frequency counter.

Sec. 3.1   Microprocessor Programming Examples

be tested is bit 0 or 7, a rotate instruction followed by a test of the carry flag requires the fewest bytes. The Z-80 BIT n,r command can also be used but requires two bytes. The DAA instruction is used to prevent frequencies like 6A from being displayed (instead, 70 is shown).

Summary. This program presented an effective way to detect rising or falling edges of a pulse. Using this technique, a frequency counter is easily implemented. Other applications include detecting patterns on a serial pulse train, software UARTs (parallel-to-serial and serial-to-parallel converters), and real-time motor speed control.

PROGRAM 13: The Game of Nim

As you read this section, look for the answers to these Key Concept questions:

3.1.20. To set up a data table, point the _____ pair at the base of the table, then add the offset of the desired byte.

3.1.21. To store an ASCII message in memory, enclose the message between _____ and use the _____ operator to name that message.

Processor—8080/85

Hardware. Required are a machine language monitor and serial terminal.

Problem Statement. The game of Nim is played with 15 sticks. When it is your turn, you may pick 1, 2, or 3 sticks. The player to pick up the last stick wins. In this case the 8080/85 is to be programmed as the opponent.

Sample Output:

First move:	You pick 1—14 sticks remain.
	Computer picks 2—12 sticks remain.
Second move:	You pick 2—10 sticks remain.
	Computer picks 2—8 sticks remain.
Third move:	You pick 3—5 sticks remain.
	Computer picks 1—4 sticks remain.
Fourth move:	You pick 1 (sadly!)—3 sticks remain.
	Computer picks 3—It wins!

Discussion. The strategy behind this game is to have a table of choices for the computer to pick from depending on the number of sticks remaining. If each possible move is studied carefully, the computer can (almost always) be assured of winning.

The remainder of the problem is mainly one of formatting messages on the terminal's screen so that the user knows what the current state of the game is.

New Instructions:

LXI SP, addr   Load the stack pointer register with the 16-bit address that follows. This is an important instruction which is easily forgotten. When using a development system or microprocessor trainer, the stack is defined by the operating system as soon as power is applied. But if you are writing the operating system or developing a piece of stand-alone software, the stack pointer must be initialized.

XTHL   Exchange the top of the stack with the HL pair. This can be useful when it is desired to examine the top of the stack. It can also be used to cause a jump to the address stored on the stack. In this case the instruction PCHL—load the program counter with the address in HL—should be used. In this program XTHL is used because it takes a very large number of clock cycles—18 for the 8080 and 16 for the 8085. Putting a pair of these commands in a program loop does not change any CPU registers, but can generate a long time delay when this is desired.

Problem Solution.   Figure 3.27 is a flowchart for Nim and the assembly language listing of the program is presented in Fig. 3.28. Nim uses five subroutines and their functions are summarized in Fig. 3.29. Pay particular attention to the PRMSG—print message—subroutine. This routine greatly simplifies the task of outputting messages to the terminal. The HL pair is simply pointed at one of the eight messages (located at the end of the assembly listing) and PRMSG is called. Also note how the assembler allows the input of ASCII data between apostrophes (') but converts it to hex in the object code column.

Summary.   Game programs can be fun to develop and provide an interesting way of improving your assembly language skills. In such programs an extensive use of subroutines simplifies program development.

PROGRAM 14: Computer Music

As you read this section, look for the answer to this Key Concept question:

3.1.22.   To generate an audio tone, use the _____ instruction in a loop to complement one bit of an output port at an audio rate.

Processor—Z-80

Hardware.   Required are a machine language monitor, latched output port, loudspeaker, and transistor driver (see Fig. 3.30).

Problem Statement.   When the transistor in Fig. 3.30 is switched between *saturation* and *cutoff* at an audio-frequency rate, a tone will be heard from the speaker. Set up a song table in memory such that when the notes are pulled from the table, a simple song is played in the speaker.

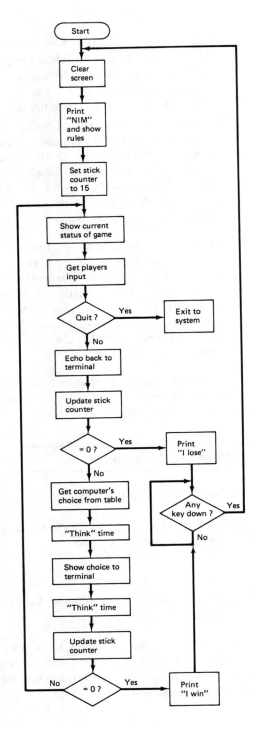

Figure 3.27 Flowchart for the game of NIM.

```
                    ;THE GAME OF NIM
                    ;
                    ;AN ASCII TERMINAL IS REQUIRED - CHANGE THE
                    ;FOLLOWING EQUATES TO MATCH YOUR HARDWARE
                    ;
                    ;ESCAPE THE GAME BY TYPING THE QUIT CHARACTER
                    ;YOU WILL RETURN TO SYSTEM (SEE EQUATES)
                    ;
                    ;
0000 =              SYSTEM    EQU  0     ;SYSTEM REBOOTS AT 0
0051 =              QUIT      EQU  'Q'   ;EXIT BY TYPING Q
001B =              ESC       EQU  1BH   ;ESCAPE SEQUENCE
000D =              CR        EQU  0DH   ;CARRIAGE RETURN
000A =              LF        EQU  0AH   ;LINE FEED
007A =              CSCREEN   EQU  7AH   ;ESC Z CLEARS SCREEN
0000 =              DELAY     EQU  0     ;ADJUST FOR 3-5S THINK TIME
0002 =              DPORT     EQU  2     ;TERMINAL DATA PORT
0003 =              SPORT     EQU  3     ;TERMINAL STATUS PORT
0002 =              RMSK      EQU  2     ;BIT 2 IS DATA READY
0001 =              TMSK      EQU  1     ;BIT 1 IS TRANSMITTER READY
                    ;
                    ;SET UP A STACK AND BEGIN PROGRAM AT 0100H
0100                          ORG  100H
0100 312E03                   LXI  SP,STKTOP
                    ;
                    ;AN IN DPORT WILL RESET DATA READY FLAG
0103 DB02           START     IN   DPORT    ;MAKE SURE FLAG RESET
                    ;
                    ;CLEAR THE SCREEN
0105 061B                     MVI  B,ESC     ;ESCAPE SEQUENCE
0107 CD8201                   CALL COUT
010A 067A                     MVI  B,CSCREEN ;CLEAR SCREEN
010C CD8201                   CALL COUT
010F CDA101                   CALL WAIT      ;TIME TO CLEAR SCREEN
                    ;
                    ;SHOW NIM
0112 21D701                   LXI  H,NIM     ;POINT AT NIM MESSAGE
0115 CD8F01                   CALL PRMSG     ;PRINT MESSAGE
                    ;
                    ;PRINT THE INSTR AND SET STICK COUNTER TO 15
0118 210E02                   LXI  H,INSTR   ;POINT AT INSTR
011B CD8F01                   CALL PRMSG
011E 160F                     MVI  D,0FH     ;D IS THE STICK COUNTER
                    ;
0120 CDB301         TURN      CALL UPDATE    ;SHOW STICKS REMAINING
                    ;
                    ;GET USERS CHOICE
0123 218802                   LXI  H,UCHCE   ;DISPLAY USERS CHOICE
0126 CD8F01                   CALL PRMSG     ;MESSAGE
0129 CD7B01                   CALL CRDY      ;WAIT FOR KEY DOWN
012C DB02                     IN   DPORT     ;AND READ THE KEY
012E FE51                     CPI  QUIT      ;TEST FOR QUIT
0130 CA0000                   JZ   SYSTEM    ;AND EXIT TO SYSTEM
0133 F5                       PUSH PSW       ;ELSE SAVE IT ON STACK
0134 47                       MOV  B,A       ;COUT WANTS IT IN B
0135 CD8201                   CALL COUT      ;ECHO TO TERMINAL
                    ;
                    ;UPDATE THE STICK COUNTER
0138 F1                       POP  PSW       ;RECOVER THE NUMBER
0139 E603                     ANI  3         ;STRIP OFF ASCII
013B 47                       MOV  B,A       ;SAVE IT
013C 7A                       MOV  A,D       ;GET STICK COUNTER
013D 90                       SUB  B         ;UPDATE IT
```

Figure 3.28 Program 13: The game of NIM.

```
019E  C1                        MOVR    POP   B
019F  F1                                POP   PSW
01A0  C9                                RET
                              ;
                              ;WAIT: WAIT A FEW SECONDS
01A1  F5                        WAIT    PUSH  PSW         ;MAKE TRANSPARENT
01A2  C5                                PUSH  B
01A3  010000                            LXI   B,DELAY     ;16 BIT COUNTER
01A6  E3                        LOOP    XTHL              ;18 CLOCK CYCLES
01A7  E3                                XTHL              ;MUST USE IN PAIRS
01A8  E3                                XTHL
01A9  E3                                XTHL
01AA  0B                                DCX   B           ;BUMP COUNTER
01AB  78                                MOV   A,B         ;TEST BC FOR 0
01AC  B1                                ORA   C           ;BY ORING THEM
01AD  C2A601                            JNZ   LOOP        ;LOOP UNTIL DONE
01B0  C1                                POP   B
01B1  F1                                POP   PSW
01B2  C9                                RET
                              ;
                              ;UPDATE: PRINT THE UPDATE MESSAGE
01B3  F5                        UPDATE  PUSH  PSW         ;MAKE TRANSPARENT
01B4  C5                                PUSH  B
01B5  21AA02                            LXI   H,UP1       ;POINT AT THERE ARE NOW
01B8  CD8F01                            CALL  PRMSG       ;AND PRINT IT
01BB  7A                                MOV   A,D         ;GET STICK COUNTER
01BC  FE0A                              CPI   0AH         ;IS IT LESS THAN 10?
01BE  DAC801                            JC    UNITS       ;YES
01C1  0631                              MVI   B,31H       ;FIRST DIGIT IS ASCII 1
01C3  CD8201                            CALL  COUT        ;PRINT IT
01C6  D60A                              SUI   0AH         ;OFFSET FOR SECOND DIGIT
01C8  C630                      UNITS   ADI   30H         ;FORM ASCII OFFSET
01CA  47                                MOV   B,A         ;COUT WANTS IT IN B
01CB  CD8201                            CALL  COUT        ;PRINT IT
01CE  21BC02                            LXI   H,MEND      ;POINT TO MESSAGE END
01D1  CD8F01                            CALL  PRMSG       ;PRINT IT
01D4  C1                                POP   B
01D5  F1                                POP   PSW
01D6  C9                                RET
                              ;
                              ;THESE ARE THE MESSAGES CALLED BY PRMSG
                              ;
01D7  2020202020                NIM     DB    '                       '
01F5  4E494D202D                        DB    'NIM - A GAME OF SKILL'
020A  0D0A0A00                          DB    CR,LF,LF,0
                              ;
020E  4920484156                INSTR   DB    'I HAVE 15 STICKS.   YOU MAY PICK '
022E  312C32204F                        DB    '1,2 OR 3 STICKS.   THEN I WILL '
024C  5049434B2E                        DB    'PICK.'
0251  0D0A                              DB    CR,LF
0253  594F552057                        DB    'YOU WIN IF YOU PICK UP THE LAST '
0273  312C203220                        DB    '1, 2 OR 3 STICKS.'
0284  0D0A0A00                          DB    CR,LF,LF,0
0288  594F555245                UCHCE   DB    'YOURE CHOICE:'
0295  00                                DB    0
                              ;
0296  0D0A                      LOST    DB    CR,LF
0298  594F552057                        DB    'YOU WIN!'
02A0  00                                DB    0
                              ;
02A1  0D0A                      WON     DB    CR,LF
02A3  492057494E                        DB    'I WIN!'
02A9  00                                DB    0
```

Figure 3.28 *(Continued)*

```
02AA 0D0A0A          ;
02AD 5448455245      UP1       DB    CR,LF,LF
02BB 00                        DB    'THERE ARE NOW '
                               DB    0
02BC 2053544943      ;
02CD 0D0A00          MEND      DB    ' STICKS REMAINING'
                               DB    CR,LF,0
02D0 4D59204348      ;
02DE 00              MCHCE     DB    'MY CHOICE IS: '
                               DB    0
02DF 0001020301      ;THIS IS THE TABLE OF SELECTIONS FOR THE COMPUTER
02E4 0102030101      TBL       DB    0,1,2,3,1
02E9 0101010102                DB    1,2,3,1,1
                               DB    1,1,1,1,2
                     ;SET UP THE STACK AREA HERE
02EE                 STACK     DS    64              ;STORAGE FOR STACK
032E =               STKTOP    EQU   $               ;TOP OF STACK
032E                 END
```

Figure 3.28   (*Continued*)

Subroutine Name	Function	Registers Changed
CRDY	Return when any key is pressed.	none
COUT	Print the character in register B.	none
PRMSG	Print the ASCII string pointed at by HL and terminated by 0.	HL is incremented to end of string.
WAIT	3–6 second time delay set by DELAY equate.	none
UPDATE	Print the message: "There are now xx sticks remaining."	HL is incremented to end of message.

Figure 3.29   Five subroutines used in the 8080/85 version of NIM.

Sample Output.   When the program is running, the song stored in memory is heard from the speaker. The note codes supplied with this program will play "Daisy."

Discussion.   The theory behind single-note computer music is quite simple. Substituting square waves for sine waves, time delays can be generated corresponding

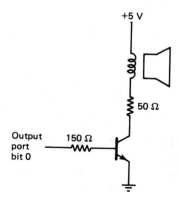

Figure 3.30   Driving a loudspeaker with 1 bit of an output port.

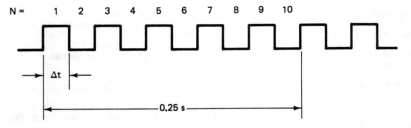

1. All notes will play for 0.25 s minimum.

2. Δt is determined by delay parameter in the E register.

3. N is found as 0.25 s/Δt.

4. Example: For middle C, f = 256 Hz

$$\Delta t = \frac{1}{2} \times \frac{1}{f} = 32 \times E \times \frac{1}{4\ MHz}$$

$$E = \frac{4\ MHz}{64f} = 244 = F4H$$

and N = 0.25s × 2 × f = 128 = 80H

Figure 3.31 Calculating E and N for the computer music program. The Δt time-delay loop has 32 × E clock cycles, where E is the contents of the E register.

to the periods of the various musical notes. Figure 3.31 illustrates the general case. The square wave shown has a one-half period of Δt. Consider the following time-delay routine (T states shown in brackets).

```
        CYCLE   LD    E,N         ;N is a number
[4]     LOOP    DEC   E
[4]             NOP
[4]             NOP
[4]             NOP
[4]             NOP
[12]            JR    NZ,LOOP
                CPL               ;COMPLEMENT ACCUMULATOR
                OUT   (nn),A
                JR    CYCLE
```

This routine has a loop with 32 × E clock cycles. As explained in Fig. 3.31, a 4-MHz Z-80 would require E = 244 to generate the proper period for middle C.

A not-so-obvious point is that higher-frequency notes will require less total time for the same number of cycles than is required by lower-frequency notes. If a fixed time period (say 0.25 s) is chosen for each note's duration, a second parameter can be calculated. Call this the number of cycles (N). Figure 3.31 also shows how to make this calculation. N is 128 for middle C. This means that 128 "half periods" of middle C will last for 0.25 s.

Now a two-byte-per-entry table can be created, holding the values of E (the time delay for the frequency generator) and N (the number of cycles) for each note it is desired to be able to play. This is shown in Fig. 3.32. This data table becomes a permanent part of the music program. A second table called the *note table* is also required. This table holds the note codes for the song to be played. A new song is created by changing the codes in this table.

A final problem remains to be solved. In music there are eighth notes, quarter notes, half notes, and full notes. Thus each note to be played should have two attributes: a note code and a duration code. With some sacrifice in the total number of notes possible, this information can be encoded into one byte. Figure 3.33 illustrates one technique.

***New Instructions*:**

RET NZ Return if the zero flag is not set. Any of the condition flags can be tested in this manner. Be careful. If the condition never occurs, you will never return!

CPL Complement accumulator. This instruction is useful to produce the toggling effect required in this program.

Address	Data	Note	Note code
0	80	Middle C	0
1	F4		
2	88	C#	1
3	E6		
4	90	D	2
5	DA		
6	98	D#	3
7	CD		
8	A2	E	4
9	C2		
A	AB	F	5
B	B7		
C	B5	F#	6
D	AD		
E	C0	G	7
F	A3		
10	CC	G#	8
11	99		
12	DB	A	9
13	91		
14	E4	A#	A
15	89		
16	F2	B	B
17	81		
18	00	High C	C
19	7A		

N
Δt

Figure 3.32 Data table for Program 14. Each note has two entries. The first number is N, the number of cycles required for a duration of 0.25 s. The second number is E, the value required in the time-delay loop for that note's frequency.

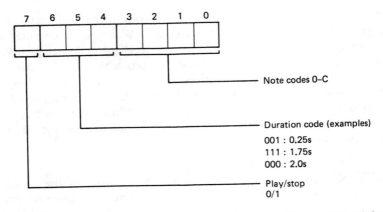

Figure 3.33 Each note in the song table is one byte long. The low 4 bits define 1 of 13 notes according to the code in Fig. 3.32. Bits 4 through 6 select one of eight note lengths from 0.25 s to 2.0 s. Bit 7 is used to detect the last note in the song table. If this bit is a 1, the program will quit.

RLD This instruction is difficult to explain in words but is clear when diagrammed as in Fig. 3.34. It amounts to a 12-bit rotate with the accumulator making up the top 4 bits and (HL) the bottom byte. The RRD instruction is similar but rotates the (HL) right. In this program RLD is useful for examining the two separate nibbles of the note code.

Program Solution. Figure 3.35 is a flowchart of the program. The tables are those mentioned previously. Each note is assigned a code between 0 and 12. Middle C is note 0 and high C is note 12 (0CH). If it is desired to play high C for 0.5 s, the hex code is 2C (2 × 0.25 s and note 12 or 0CH). If bit 7 is set in the note code, the program terminates.

The values for N and E are stored in the data table and selected by doubling the note code and adding to a pointer set at the top of the table. High C is found as the 25th and 26th entries in the table. Middle C corresponds to the first and second entries.

Figure 3.36 is the assembly language listing for the program.

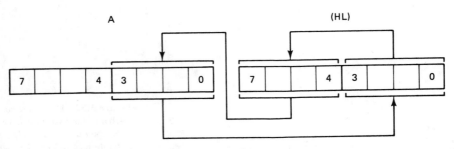

Figure 3.34 The Z-80 RLD instruction is actually a 12-bit rotate command in which bits 4 through 7 of the accumulator are unchanged.

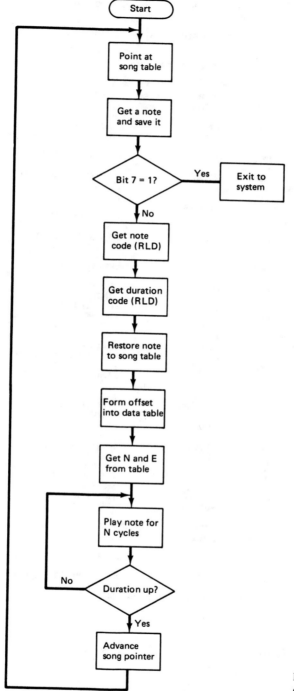

Figure 3.35 Flowchart for the Z-80 computer music program.

```
ADDR    CODE        STMT  SOURCE STATEMENT

                    0001  ;COMPUTER MUSIC WITH THE Z-80
                    0002  ;
                    0003  ;THIS PROGRAM WILL "PLAY" THE SONG STORED
                    0004  ;UNDER STBLE AT THE END OF THIS PROGRAM.
                    0005  ;
                    0006  ;CONNECT A LOUDSPEAKER AND TRANSISTOR
                    0007  ;DRIVER TO BIT 0 OF AN AVAILABEL OUTPUT PORT.
                    0008  ;REFER TO THE TEXT FOR THIS CIRCUIT.
                    0009  ;
 >0000             0010  PORT    EQU   0            ;THIS IS THE OUTPUT PORT
 >0000             0011  SYSTEM  EQU   0000         ;THIS IS RESTART ADDRESS
                    0012  ;
 >0600             0013          ORG   0600H        ;PROGRAM BEGINS AT 0600H
                    0014  ;
'0600   214A06'    0015          LD    HL,STBLE     ;POINT AT SONG TABLE
'0603   97         0016  NUNOTE  SUB   A            ;CLEAR ACCUMULATOR
'0604   CB7E       0017          BIT   7,(HL)       ;IF BIT 7 IS HIGH
'0606   C20000     0018          JP    NZ,SYSTEM    ;GO TO SYSTEM
'0609   4E         0019          LD    C,(HL)       ;SAVE THE NOTE
'060A   ED6F       0020          RLD                ;GET DURATION CODE
'060C   47         0021          LD    B,A          ;B HOLDS DURATION
'060D   ED6F       0022          RLD                ;A HOLDS NOTE CODE
'060F   71         0023          LD    (HL),C       ;RESTORE THE NOTE
'0610   87         0024          ADD   A,A          ;DOUBLE IT
'0611   113006'    0025          LD    DE,DTBLE     ;POINT AT DATA TABLE
'0614   83         0026          ADD   A,E          ;FORM AN OFFSET
'0615   5F         0027          LD    E,A          ;INTO THE DATA TABLE
'0616   EB         0028          EX    DE,HL        ;HL POINTS AT THE NOTE
'0617   D5         0029          PUSH  DE           ;DE HOLDS ADDR IN STBLE
'0618   56         0030  NOTE    LD    D,(HL)       ;GET NUMBER OF CYCLES
'0619   23         0031          INC   HL           ;AND
'061A   5E         0032  CYCLES  LD    E,(HL)       ;DELTA T
'061B   1D         0033  LOOP    DEC   E            ;THIS IS THE LOOP
'061C   00         0034          NOP                ;THAT DETERMINES
'061D   00         0035          NOP                ;THE NOTE FREQUENCY
'061E   00         0036          NOP                ;
'061F   00         0037          NOP                ;
'0620   20F9       0038          JR    NZ,LOOP      ;COUNT E DOWN
'0622   2F         0039          CPL                ;TOGGLE THE
'0623   D300       0040          OUT   (PORT),A     ;OUTPUT PORT
'0625   15         0041          DEC   D            ;BUMP CYCLE COUNTER
'0626   20F2       0042          JR    NZ,CYCLES    ;AND CONTINUE
'0628   2B         0043          DEC   HL           ;CORRECT POINTER
'0629   10ED       0044          DJNZ  NOTE         ;UNTIL DURATION IS UP
'062B   D1         0045          POP   DE           ;RECOVER ADDR IN STBLE
'062C   EB         0046          EX    DE,HL        ;NOW IN HL
'062D   23         0047          INC   HL           ;NEXT NOTE
'062E   18D3       0048          JR    NUNOTE       ;PLAY SOME MORE
                    0049  ;
                    0050  ;THIS IS THE DATA TABLE FOR THE 13 NOTES
                    0051  ;FROM MIDDLE C TO HIGH C.
                    0052  ;
'0630   80F488E6   0053  DTBLE   DEFB  80H,0F4H,88H,0E6H,90H,0DAH,98H,0CDH
        90DA98CD
'0638   A2C2ABB7   0054          DEFB  0A2H,0C2H,0ABH,0B7H,0B5H,0ADH,0C0H
        B5ADC0
'063F   A3CC99D8   0055          DEFB  0A3H,0CCH,99H,0D8H,91H,0E4H,89H
        91E489
'0646   F281007A   0056          DEFB  0F2H,81H,0,7AH
                    0057  ;
```

Figure 3.36   Program 14 computer music with the Z-80.

```
                         0058              ;THESE NOTES CORRESPOND TO "DAISY"
                         0059              ;
'064A   3C393530         0060 STBLE  DEFB  3CH,39H,35H,30H,12H,14H,15H,22H,15H,40H
        12141522
        1540
'0654   373C3935         0061        DEFB  37H,3CH,39H,35H,12H,14H,15H,27H,19H,47H
        12141527
        1947
'065E   191A1917         0062        DEFB  19H,1AH,19H,17H,3CH,19H,17H,45H,17H,29H
        3C191745
        1729
'0668   15221512         0063        DEFB  15H,22H,15H,12H,60H,10H,25H,19H,27H,10H
        60102519
        2710
'0672   25192719         0064        DEFB  25H,19H,27H,19H,1AH,1CH,19H,15H,27H,10H
        1A1C1915
        2710
'067C   7580             0065        DEFB  75H,80H

ERRORS=0000
```

Figure 3.36 (*Continued*)

Summary. The principle behind single-note computer music is simple, but implementing a useful program can be complex. To minimize the amount of memory required for each note, the note code and duration can be encoded into a single byte. The Z-80 RLD instruction is useful for such nibble-organized data.

3.2 OPERATING SYSTEMS

As you read this section, look for the answers to these Key Concept questions:

3.2.1. When using an editor to create the source code for a program named ZIP, CP/M expects this file to be named _____ .

3.2.2. Under CP/M, the executable (command) version of the program ZIP is called _____ .

3.2.3. CP/M function number _____ will read the input console and return with the ASCII value of the input in register _____ .

Before the advent of the floppy disk drive in the early 1970s, minicomputers (and microcomputers) used *paper tape* as a storage medium for important programs and data. The management of these programs was done by hand—you selected the program desired and loaded it into the paper tape reader. A directory of all your programs could be had by laying all the paper tapes in front of you.

The floppy disk changed all of this. One minifloppy disk drive can hold the data of more than 200 feet of paper tape. This means that many programs and data files can all be saved on one disk.

But the floppy disk also created some problems. A special program is needed to read the disk and convert the magnetic impulses stored there to logic ones and zeros. Another program is required to write data to the disk. Still another program is needed to list the contents of the disk: that is, print the directory. And what if I want to make a copy of one program and save it on another disk? Or perhaps I want to execute one of the programs stored on the disk? How do I do it?

Along with the hardware supporting the floppy disk, a new program is required. It must manage the storage and retrieval of data to and from the disk, and provide all of the functions (and more) listed in the preceding paragraph. This program is called the *disk operating system* or DOS.

In this section we study the general characteristics of operating systems and the *CP/M* (control program for microcomputers) operating system in particular.

Some Common Operating Systems.

Inserting a disk into the disk drive opening, closing the door, and turning on (or resetting) the computer has become known as *booting up* the computer. Once the computer has ''booted,'' the operating system takes hold. But now to communicate with the DOS, you must learn its language. For this purpose, entire books and user's manuals have been written helping you to learn how to use a particular operating system.

If you were talking to a Digital Equipment Corporation (DEC) VAX computer, you would use the *Digital Command Language* (DCL) to access the VAX/VMS operating system. Another popular minicomputer operating system (and becoming popular on 16-bit microcomputers) is *UNIX*. This DOS was developed by Bell Laboratories and is licensed by Western Electric.

Another 16-bit operating system popular on microcomputers is MS-DOS for *Microsoft Disk Operating System*. It has been made popular by the IBM Personal Computer and other IBM look-alikes.

The most popular operating system for the 8080/85 and Z-80 8-bit microcomputers is CP/M 80. This program was first written in the early 1970s by Gary Kildall of Microcomputer Applications Associates (later to be called Digital Research). MAA had just finished developing a new programming language called *PL/M* to replace assembly language programming for Intel's new 8080 microprocessor. CP/M was intended as a companion operating system for PL/M.

Over the years CP/M has undergone many changes, but its central theme remains—keeping applications software independent of the hardware it runs on. This is particularly important in the microcomputer world, where two computers may both use the 8080 microprocessor, but have totally different I/O configurations. Once CP/M has been installed—that is, configured to the particular hardware of the host computer—any program written under CP/M will run on this computer.

Features of CP/M.

When a CP/M computer is booted up, its memory is organized as shown in the memory map in Fig. 3.37. The bottom page of memory is used for storing system variables and holds the *warm start* boot address—this is a restart address after the system has been booted up for the first time.

The full DOS or *FDOS* is loaded into high memory and consists of the invariant *BDOS* (basic disk operating system) and the hardware-dependent *BIOS* (basic I/O system). It is the BIOS that must be customized for each computer.

The *CCP* is the console command processor and it accepts all input from the keyboard, decodes the commands, and loads the appropriate programs into the *TPA*

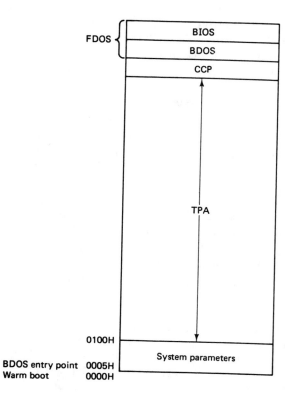

	BIOS
FDOS	BDOS
	CCP
	↑
	TPA
	↓
0100H	
	System parameters
BDOS entry point 0005H	
Warm boot 0000H	

Figure 3.37 Memory map for the CP/M operating system. The size of the TPA depends on the amount of available system memory.

(transient program area). The size of the TPA varies with the size of the CP/M system created when first installed.

Table 3.1 lists valid commands processed by the CCP. The built-in commands reside in the CCP and are executed immediately. The transient commands must be loaded off the disk into the TPA and then executed. These transient commands are actually complex programs of their own with several possible arguments. For example, the transient command

PIP LST:=B:TEST.ASM[t8]

TABLE 3.1 COMMON TRANSIENT AND BUILT-IN COMMANDS OF CP/M

	Transient command	Built-in command	
ASM	8080 assembler	ERA	Erase the file or files
ED	Text editor	DIR	Print disk directory
DDT	Dynamic debugging tool—monitor	REN	Rename a file
STAT	Print disk capacity remaining	TYPE	Print a copy of the file
PIP	Peripheral interchange program		
LOAD	Create a command file (.COM)		

will cause the peripheral interchange program (*PIP*) to load. PIP will, in turn, fetch a copy of the file TEST.ASM from drive B, expand the tabs to every eight columns, and send this file to the list device (usually a printer).

File names under CP/M are of the form

filename.type

The filename can be any combination of characters of maximum length eight. The file type is optional and can be no more than three characters long. When developing a program, CP/M will often append the file type to the primary file name. For example, let us consider the steps in creating an 8080 machine language program—TEST.

1. Using an editor, write the source code for the program. Call this TEST.ASM. The editor automatically creates a backup file, TEST.BAK.
2. Assemble the program by invoking the CP/M assembler. The result is TEST.HEX and TEST.PRN (explained below).
3. After debugging the program, create a command file with the command LOAD TEST. The result is the file TEST.COM.

In developing the program TEST, five files were created. The *.ASM* and *.BAK* files contain the ASCII source code of the program. The .ASM file is processed by the assembler and two new files are created. The first is the *.HEX* file, which contains the hex codes for the program in what has become known as Intel format. The second file is the *.PRN* file or print file. It contains the source code from the .ASM file and the object code created by the assembler. Any assembly errors detected by the assembler are also noted.

Finally, an exact memory image of the program is created by the LOAD command. This is the *.COM* file. All .COM files are directly executable by typing the primary file name—in this case, the single word TEST.

A Sample Session with CP/M.   CP/M is a very complex operating system and full details of its operation are beyond the scope of this book. However, it is possible to appreciate some of its capabilities by following through a sample program development session.

Figures 3.38 through 3.44 present examples of the stages in the development of the 8080 block fill program (call it PROG7) from Sec. 3.1. Let's look at each of these figures in detail.

1. *Figure 3.38*: Beginning at the top, CP/M has signed on to drive A—note the A> prompt—and the text editor ED has been invoked to create the new file PROG7.ASM (note ED's * prompt). The V command instructs ED to list line numbers and the I command indicates the insert mode. The source code is now entered with comments preceded by a semicolon.

After line 28 control Z (which is not printed) ends the insert mode and E indicates end the edit. The CCP is back in control—note the A> prompt—and the command STAT PROG7.* is entered. STAT is a transient command and in this

```
A>ED PROG7.ASM

NEW FILE
*V
    : *I
   1:             ;8080/85 BLOCK FILL PROGRAM
   2:             ;
   3:             ;BLOCK BEGINS AT ADDRESS (START)
   4:             ; (BYTES) IS TOTAL BYTES IN THE BLOCK
   5:             ; (FILL) IS THE CHARACTER TO WRITE TO THE BLOCK
   6:             ;
   7:             ORG     0600H     ;PROGRAM BEGINS AT 0600H
   8:             LDA     FILL      ;GET FILL CHARACTER
   9:             LHLD    BYTES     ;GET NUMBER OF BYTES
  10:             XCHG              ;DE NOW BYTE COUNTER
  11:             LHLD    START     ;HL HOLDS START ADDRESS
  12:     LOOP    MOV     M,A       ;WRITE A BYTE
  13:             PUSH    PSW       ;SAVE A
  14:             INX     H         ;ADVANCE MEMORY POINTER
  15:             DCX     D         ;BUMP BYTE COUNTER
  16:             MOV     A,D       ;PREPARE TO TEST IF
  17:             ORA     E         ;D=E=0
  18:             JZ      DONE      ;IF SO THEN DONE
  19:             POP     PSW       ;ELSE RECOVER A
  20:             JMP     LOOP      ;AND WRITE ANOTHER
  21:     DONE    HLT               ;STOP
  22:             ;FILL THESE LOCATIONS WITH THE DESIRED
  23:             ;BLOCK DATA
  24:     START   DW      0700H     ;BLOCK STARTING ADDRESS
  25:     BYTES   DW      1000H     ;NUMBER OF BYTES
  26:     FILL    DB      2BH       ;FILL CHARACTER
  27:             END
  28:
    : *E

A>STAT PROG7.*

RECS BYTS EX D:FILENAME.TYP
   6    1K  1 A:PROG7.ASM
   0    OK  1 A:PROG7.BAK
BYTES REMAINING ON A: 22K

A>ASM PROG7
CP/M ASSEMBLER - VER 1.4
061D
000H USE FACTOR
END OF ASSEMBLY

A>STAT PROG7.*

RECS BYTS EX D:FILENAME.TYP
   6    1K  1 A:PROG7.ASM
   0    OK  1 A:PROG7.BAK
   1    1K  1 A:PROG7.HEX
  10    2K  1 A:PROG7.PRN
BYTES REMAINING ON A: 19K

A>
```

Figure 3.38 Using the CP/M text editor (ED) and assembler (ASM) to write the 8080/85 block fill program. The stat command is used to observe the files created.

```
A>TYPE PROG7.PRN

                              ;8080/85 BLOCK FILL PROGRAM
                              ;
                              ;BLOCK BEGINS AT ADDRESS (START)
                              ;(BYTES) IS TOTAL BYTES IN THE BLOCK
                              ;(FILL) IS THE CHARACTER TO WRITE TO THE BLOCK
                              ;
          0600                ORG     0600H   ;PROGRAM BEGINS AT 0600H
          0600 3A1C06         LDA     FILL    ;GET FILL CHARACTER
          0603 2A1A06         LHLD    BYTES   ;GET NUMBER OF BYTES
          0606 EB             XCHG            ;DE NOW BYTE COUNTER
          0607 2A1806         LHLD    START   ;HL HOLDS START ADDRESS
          060A 77      LOOP   MOV     M,A     ;WRITE A BYTE
          060B F5             PUSH    PSW     ;SAVE A
          060C 23             INX     H       ;ADVANCE MEMORY POINTER
          060D 1B             DCX     D       ;BUMP BYTE COUNTER
          060E 7A             MOV     A,D     ;PREPARE TO TEST IF
          060F B3             ORA     E       ;D=E=0
          0610 CA1706         JZ      DONE    ;IF SO THEN DONE
          0613 F1             POP     PSW     ;ELSE RECOVER A
          0614 C30A06         JMP     LOOP    ;AND WRITE ANOTHER
          0617 76      DONE   HLT             ;STOP
                              ;FILL THESE LOCATIONS WITH THE DESIRED
                              ;BLOCK DATA
          0618 0007    START  DW      0700H   ;BLOCK STARTING ADDRESS
          061A 0010    BYTES  DW      1000H   ;NUMBER OF BYTES
          061C 2B      FILL   DB      2BH     ;FILL CHARACTER
          061D                END

A>
```

Figure 3.39   The print (.PRN) file created by the assembler.

case is used to find the status of all files with primary name PROG7. The .* is a *wild card*, which means that any file type with primary name PROG7 will match. In this case we see that two files have been created by ED: PROG7.ASM and PROG7.BAK (PROG7.BAK will be ''empty'' until PROG7.ASM is edited a second time).

Next the CP/M assembler is called on to assemble the source code. STAT is again used to see the new files created by the assembler. These are PROG7.HEX and PROG7.PRN.

2. *Figure 3.39*: The built-in command TYPE is used to examine the contents of the .PRN file. You can see the object code created by the assembler along the left side of the listing.

3. *Figure 3.40*: TYPE is used to examine the .HEX file. The hex codes are listed in Intel hex format as required by the load command.

4. *Figure 3.41*: The dynamic debugging tool (DDT) program has been loaded— note the (−) prompt. DDT is basically a monitor program designed for use with a serial terminal. In this case PROG7.HEX was also loaded with DDT.

```
A>TYPE PROG7.HEX
:100600003A1C062A1A06EB2A180677F5231B7AB33A
:0D061000CA1706F1C30A0676000700102B7A
:0000000000

A>
```

Figure 3.40   The hex (.HEX) file created by the assembler.

```
A>DDT PROG7.HEX
DDT VERS 1.4
NEXT  PC
061D 0000
-L600,617
    0600  LDA   061C
    0603  LHLD  061A
    0606  XCHG
    0607  LHLD  0618
    060A  MOV   M,A
    060B  PUSH  PSW
    060C  INX   H
    060D  DCX   D
    060E  MOV   A,D
    060F  ORA   E
    0610  JZ    0617
    0613  POP   PSW
    0614  JMP   060A
    0617  HLT
    0618
-A617
0617   RST 7
0618
-
```

Figure 3.41 DDT (dynamic debugging tool) has been used to load the hex version of the program. The L command is used to list the mnemonics. The in-line assembly command A is used to change the HLT to RST 7.

The command L600,617 lists the mnemonics for the codes stored between 600H to 617H. The in-line assembly command A (A617) is used to change the HLT in location 0617 to RST 7. RST 7 is a call to location 0038 and is used here to allow DDT to remain in control once the program is done executing. If not used, the HLT instruction would kill the system, requiring a reset.

5. *Figure 3.42*: XP requests DDT to supply the present value of the program counter used for the trace mode. It is changed to 0600 (the start of the program). Now the program is traced one instruction at a time. Note how the contents of all registers and flags are displayed after each trace. For example, after the first trace:

```
carry (C) = 0
zero (z) = 0
minus (M) = 0
parity (E) = 0
auxiliary carry = 0
register A = 00
registers BC = 0000
registers DE = 0000
registers HL = 0000
register SP = 0100
register PC = 0600
current instruction = LDA 061C
```

Tracing the first loop through the program all seems well. The command XD is used to examine and change the DE pair to 0001 (that is, one more loop remains). Now the end of the loop can be tested and is also observed to work properly.

6. *Figure 3.43*: Another feature of DDT is the dump memory command. Typing D0700,070F displays memory from 0700 to 070F in hex and ASCII (on the far right). In this example the beginning and end of the block to be written are dumped to show that they contain random data.

The G600 command (go to location 600H) executes the program and control

Sec. 3.2   Operating Systems

```
-XP
P=0000 0600
-T
COZOMOEOIO A=00 B=0000 D=0000 H=0000 S=0100 P=0600 LDA   061C*0603
-T
COZOMOEOIO A=2B B=0000 D=0000 H=0000 S=0100 P=0603 LHLD  061A*0606
-T
COZOMOEOIO A=2B B=0000 D=0000 H=1000 S=0100 P=0606 XCHG  *0607
-T
COZOMOEOIO A=2B B=0000 D=1000 H=0000 S=0100 P=0607 LHLD  0618*060A
-T
COZOMOEOIO A=2B B=0000 D=1000 H=0700 S=0100 P=060A MOV   M,A*060B
-T
COZOMOEOIO A=2B B=0000 D=1000 H=0700 S=0100 P=060B PUSH  PSW  *060C
-T
COZOMOEOIO A=2B B=0000 D=1000 H=0700 S=00FE P=060C INX   H*060D
-T
COZOMOEOIO A=2B B=0000 D=1000 H=0701 S=00FE P=060D DCX   D*060E
-T
COZOMOEOIO A=2B B=0000 D=0FFF H=0701 S=00FE P=060E MOV   A,D*060F
-T
COZOMOEOIO A=0F B=0000 D=0FFF H=0701 S=00FE P=060F ORA   E*0610
-T
COZOM1E1IO A=FF B=0000 D=0FFF H=0701 S=00FE P=0610 JZ    0617*0613
-T
COZOM1E1IO A=FF B=0000 D=0FFF H=0701 S=00FE P=0613 POP   PSW  *0614
-T
COZOMOEOIO A=2B B=0000 D=0FFF H=0701 S=0100 P=0614 JMP   060A*060A
-T
COZOMOEOIO A=2B B=0000 D=0FFF H=0701 S=0100 P=060A MOV   M,A*060B
-XD
D=0FFF 0001
-T
COZOMOEOIO A=2B B=0000 D=0001 H=0701 S=0100 P=060B PUSH  PSW  *060C
-T
COZOMOEOIO A=2B B=0000 D=0001 H=0701 S=00FE P=060C INX   H*060D
-T
COZOMOEOIO A=2B B=0000 D=0001 H=0702 S=00FE P=060D DCX   D*060E
-T
COZOMOEOIO A=2B B=0000 D=0000 H=0702 S=00FE P=060E MOV   A,D*060F
-T
COZOMOEOIO A=00 B=0000 D=0000 H=0702 S=00FE P=060F ORA   E*0610
-T
COZ1MOE1IO A=00 B=0000 D=0000 H=0702 S=00FE P=0610 JZ    0617*0617
-T
COZ1MOE1IO A=00 B=0000 D=0000 H=0702 S=00FE P=0617 RST   07*0617
-
```

Figure 3.42   The trace mode of DDT is used to single-step through the program.
Note how the contents of the DE pair is set to 0001 to test the exit from the
loop.

is regained by DDT on program completion (line 0617). Again the dump command
is used to observe that the block did indeed get written (in this case with the data
byte 2B or ASCII +).

   7. *Figure 3.44*: After returning to CP/M with the command G0 (G zero), the
LOAD command is issued. This transient reads the .HEX file and creates a memory
image of the program that is directly executable. The new file is called PROG7.COM.

   In summary, CP/M has the ability to create a file using ED, assemble it, test
and debug it using DDT, and finally install it as a new transient command on the
disk.

```
-D700,070F
0700 2B 2B 62 05 09 CD F3 02 C3 71 03 21 76 06 CD F3   ++b......q.!v...
-D16F0,170F
16F0 FD FD FD FD FD FD FD FD FD FD FD FD FD FD FD FD   ................
1700 FD FD FD FD FD FD FD FD FD FD FD FD FD FD FD FD   ................
-G600
*0617
-D700,70F
0700 2B 2B 2B 2B 2B 2B 2B 2B 2B 2B 2B 2B 2B 2B 2B 2B   ++++++++++++++++
-D16F0,170F
16F0 2B 2B 2B 2B 2B 2B 2B 2B 2B 2B 2B 2B 2B 2B 2B 2B   ++++++++++++++++
1700 FD FD FD FD FD FD FD FD FD FD FD FD FD FD FD FD   ................
-G0

A>
```

Figure 3.43 The DDT display command is used to examine memory before and after the block fill program is run.

Linking Programs to CP/M.

If the application program does not overlay the BIOS and BDOS, it is possible and even desirable to use the routines in these areas as part of your program. In fact, CP/M has a feature built in to support this concept. It is called the *function number*.

In all, there are 27 different function numbers. Functions 1 through 11 are listed in Table 3.2 and are concerned with basic I/O operations with the various peripherals. Functions 12 through 27 are called *disk access primitives* and allow for disk operations such as reading, writing, and disk head positioning.

When it is desired to use one of these functions, the C register is loaded with the desired function number and a call to location 0005 is executed. Data to be written is transferred in register E; data to be read is transferred in register A. When several characters are transferred—called a buffer—the DE pair is used as a pointer to the location of the buffer.

An example of a program that uses this function number concept is the MX-80 initialization routine shown in Fig. 3.45. This program is intended to program the Epson MX-80 printer to one of three print styles. These are 10 CPI (characters per inch) standard, 10 CPI emphasized, and 16.5 CPI standard.

```
A>LOAD PROG7

FIRST ADDRESS 0600
LAST  ADDRESS 061C
BYTES READ    001D
RECORDS WRITTEN 0B


A>STAT PROG7.*

RECS BYTS EX D:FILENAME.TYP
   6   1K  1 A:PROG7.ASM
   0   0K  1 A:PROG7.BAK
  11   2K  1 A:PROG7.COM
   1   1K  1 A:PROG7.HEX
  10   2K  1 A:PROG7.PRN
BYTES REMAINING ON A: 17K

A>
```

Figure 3.44 The CP/M LOAD command creates a new system command: PROG7. STAT shows the five files created.

TABLE 3.2 BASIC I/O FUNCTION CALLS IN CP/M

Function number (in register C)	Action	Parameters	
		On entry	On exit
1	Read console		ASCII char in A
2	Write console	Char in E	—
3	Read reader	—	ASCII char in A
4	Write punch	Char in E	—
5	Write list	Char in E	—
6	Direct console I/O	FFH in E	A = 00 if no char ready, else char in A
7	Get I/O byte	—	I/O byte in A
8	Set I/O byte	I/O byte in E	—
9	Print buffer	Buffer addr in DE terminated by $	—
10	Read buffer	Buffer addr in DE[a]	Buffer is filled with char until full or ⟨cr⟩
11	Console status	—	A = 0 if not ready A = FF if ready

[a] The read buffer is of the form

$$B1\ B2\ B3\ B4\ .\ .\ .\ Bn$$

where B1 is byte number 1 and represents the maximum length of the buffer (you must supply this byte). B2 represents the second byte and is the current length of the buffer. B3 through Bn are the input characters.

The program begins by calling the print message routine (PMSG) with DE pointing at the clear screen codes and then a sign-on message. PMSG in turn loads register C with function number 9 and calls location 0005 (BDOS). You can see this message stored at the end of the program. The end of the message is marked by a $.

Next, the program cancels all existing codes the printer may have received by outputting a series of cancel codes, this time using function number 5 (write list—write to the printer).

Function number 1—read console—is next loaded into register C to obtain the user's input in register A. This should be an ASCII number between 31H and 33H. If it is 31, the program terminates because the printer defaults to 10 CPI standard when all codes are canceled.

If the input is 32 or 33, the ASCII bias is stripped off and the code is doubled and added to register L to form a pointer into a two-byte-per-entry table. The E register is loaded with the first byte of the code to be transmitted, register C is loaded with function number five (write to the list device) and a call to BDOS (location 0005) is performed. This is done once more with the table pointer incremented by 1 for the second byte of the code.

```
                              ;MX-80 INITIALIZATION ROUTINE
                              ;USING THE CP/M FUNCTION CALLS
                              ;
     0100                     ORG      100H                ;START AT 100H
                              ;
     0000 =        CPM        EQU      0000                ;WARM BOOT ENTRY POINT
     0005 =        BDOS       EQU      5                   ;BDOS ENTRY POINT
     0009 =        PBUF       EQU      9                   ;PRINT BUFFER FUNCTION #
     0001 =        RDCON      EQU      1                   ;READ CONSOLE FUNCTION #
     0005 =        WRLIST     EQU      5                   ;WRITE LIST FUNCTION #
     000D =        CR         EQU      0DH                 ;CARRIAGE RETURN
     000A =        LF         EQU      0AH                 ;LINE FEED
     001B =        ESC        EQU      1BH                 ;ESCAPE
     0024 =        DONE       EQU      24H                 ;END OF STRING
                              ;
                              ;PRINT THE SIGN-ON MESSAGE
                              ;
     0100 115101              LXI      D,CSCREEN           ;POINT AT CLEAR SCREEN
     0103 CD4B01              CALL     PMSG                ;DO IT
     0106 115401              LXI      D,SIGNON            ;POINT AT SIGNON MESG
     0109 CD4B01              CALL     PMSG                ;PRINT MESG
                              ;
                              ;CANCEL ALL EXISTING CODES
                              ;
     010C 212E02              LXI      H,CANCEL            ;POINT AT CANCEL CODES
     010F 0E05      NEXT      MVI      C,WRLIST            ;WRLIST FUNCTION
     0111 7E                  MOV      A,M                 ;GET A CODE
     0112 FE24                CPI      DONE                ;DONE?
     0114 CA2101              JZ       GETCHR              ;YES SO GET INPUT CHAR
     0117 5F                  MOV      E,A                 ;NO SO PREPARE TO WRLIST
     0118 E5                  PUSH     H                   ;SAVE POINTER
     0119 CD0500              CALL     BDOS                ;WRITE IT TO PRINTER
     011C E1                  POP      H                   ;RECOVER POINTER
     011D 23                  INX      H                   ;BUMP POINTER
     011E C30F01              JMP      NEXT                ;NEXT CODE
                              ;
                              ;GET THE USERS RESPONSE
                              ;
     0121 0E01      GETCHR    MVI      C,RDCON             ;RDCON FUNCTION
     0123 CD0500              CALL     BDOS                ;GET 1 CHAR TO A
     0126 FE31                CPI      31H                 ;IS IT 10CPI STD?
     0128 CA4201              JZ       QUIT                ;YES SO DONE
     012B 213502              LXI      H,CODES             ;NO SO POINT AT CODE TABLE
     012E D632                SUI      32H                 ;STRIP OFF ASCII OFFSET + 2
     0130 87                  ADD      A                   ;DOUBLE IT FOR 2 BYTE TABLE
     0131 85                  ADD      L                   ;CALCULATE OFFSET
     0132 6F                  MOV      L,A                 ;ADD OFFSET TO POINTER
     0133 0E05                MVI      C,WRLIST            ;WRLIST FUNCTION
     0135 5E                  MOV      E,M                 ;GET THE CODE
     0136 E5                  PUSH     H                   ;SAVE POINTER
     0137 C5                  PUSH     B                   ;SAVE FUNCTION #
     0138 CD0500              CALL     BDOS                ;SEND TO PRINTER
     013B C1                  POP      B                   ;RECOVER FUNCTION #
     013C E1                  POP      H                   ;RECOVER POINTER
     013D 23                  INX      H                   ;ADVANCE POINTER
     013E 5E                  MOV      E,M                 ;GET SECOND CODE
     013F CD0500              CALL     BDOS                ;SEND TO PRINTER
                              ;
                              ;CLEAR THE SCREEN AND RETURN
     0142 115101    QUIT      LXI      D,CSCREEN           ;POINT AT CLEAR SCREEN
     0145 CD4B01              CALL     PMSG                ;DO IT
     0148 C30000              JMP      CPM                 ;DONE BACK TO CP/M
                              ;
```

Figure 3.45 CP/M-compatible MX-80 printer control program. This routine programs the printer for one of three print styles.

```
                                  ;SUBROUTINE TO CLEAR SCREEN
                                  ;
     014B 0E09        PMSG    MVI     C,PBUF          ;PRINT BUFFER FUNCTION #
     014D CD0500              CALL    BDOS            ;PRINT BUFFER
     0150 C9                  RET
                                  ;
                                  ;CLEAR SCREEN CODES
     0151 1B          CSCREEN DB      ESC
     0152 4524                DB      'E$'
                                  ;
                                  ;THIS IS THE SIGN-ON MESSAGE
                                  ;
     0154 0A0A0A      SIGNON  DB      LF,LF,LF
     0157 2020202020          DB      '                        '
     016E 4D582D3830          DB      'MX-80 INITIALIZATION ROUTINE'
     018A 0D0A0A              DB      CR,LF,LF
     018D 2020202020          DB      '                        '
     01A6 1B70                DB      ESC,70H         ;REVERSE VIDEO
     01A8 4245205355          DB      'BE SURE PRINTER IS ON LINE'
     01C2 1B71                DB      ESC,71H         ;NORMAL VIDEO
     01C4 0D0A0A0A0A          DB      CR,LF,LF,LF,LF
     01C9 454E544552          DB      'ENTER THE NUMBER OF YOUR CHOICE:'
     01E9 0D0A0A              DB      CR,LF,LF
     01EC 312E202031          DB      '1.  10 CPI (STANDARD)'
     0201 0D0A0A              DB      CR,LF,LF
     0204 322E202031          DB      '2.  16.5 CPI'
     0210 0D0A0A              DB      CR,LF,LF
     0213 332E202031          DB      '3.  10 CPI EMPHASIZED'
     0228 0D0A0A0A            DB      CR,LF,LF,LF
     022C 3F24                DB      '?$'
                                  ;
                                  ;THESE ARE THE CANCEL CODES
                                  ;
     022E 14121B461B  CANCEL  DB      14H,12H,1BH,46H,1BH,48H,24H
                                  ;
                                  ;THESE ARE THE PROGRAMMING CODES
                                  ;
     0235 0F0F        CODES   DB      0FH,0FH         ;16.5 CPI
     0237 1B45                DB      1BH,45H         ;10 CPI EMPHASIZED
```

Figure 3.45 *(Continued)*

The program terminates with a jump to the warm boot location on page 0. The obvious advantage of the function number concept is to transfer all I/O operations to CP/M. You needn't care how CP/M reads the console or outputs a character to the list device; just pass the proper function number in register C and the data in register A. Be sure to save any registers whose values are important; usually, CP/M will scramble their contents in processing the function.

CHAPTER SUMMARY

1. The register indirect and indexed addressing modes reduce the number of instructions and bytes required to access memory compared with the direct addressing mode.

2. The register indirect addressing mode is best suited for accessing sequential data and the indexed addressing mode is best for nonsequential data.

3. When doing multibyte addition, the add with carry instructions should be used to ensure proper results.

4. The DAA instruction should be used for all decimal arithmetic operations.

5. The rotate-right and rotate-left instructions can be used to achieve division and multiplication by 2.

6. Time delays are created by putting the processor in a counting loop for a specific number of clock cycles.

7. Slow peripherals are synchronized to a microprocessor by the use of ready flags. A masking technique can be used to monitor these flags.

8. The SID and SOD lines of the 8085 microprocessor are conveniently used as 1-bit input and output ports. The SIM and RIM instructions allow reading and writing to these lines.

9. Single-note computer music can be generated by toggling an output bit at an audio rate. The frequency of the note is controlled by the delay value in a loop.

10. Operating systems are file manager programs that allow reading and writing to a magnetic disk, copying of files, renaming of files, running programs, and other file management activities.

11. The CP/M operating system has facilities for writing, assembling, debugging, single-stepping, and installing assembly language programs.

LAB PROJECTS

3.1. Modify the 8-bit addition in Program 1 (8080/85 or) Program 2 (Z-80) so that the result of (0700)–(0701) is stored in 0702.

3.2. Write a Z-80 or 8080/85 program to move a block of data in memory beginning at address SOURCE to address DEST. Assume that the number of bytes in the block is stored in two sequential memory locations named NUMB. SOURCE and DEST are defined with EQU statements.

3.3. Write a Z-80 or 8080/85 program to search the source block of memory identified in Lab 3.2 for the smallest element. Store the result in memory location SMALL.

3.4. Write a Z-80 or 8080/85 program to search the source block of memory identified in Lab 3.2 for the byte stored in memory location OLD. Replace all occurrences with the byte stored in memory location NEW.

3.5. Write a Z-80 or 8080/85 program to convert the two hex digits stored in location 0700H to two ASCII digits and store in locations 0701H (LSD) and 0702H (MSD). For example, if (0700H) = A4H, then (0701H) = 34H and (0702H) = 41H.

3.6. Modify the communications test routine in Program 9 to send to the terminal an ASCII message stored in memory beginning at location MSG and terminated with the "$" symbol.

3.7. Rewrite the communications test routine in Program 9 using the read console and write console functions of CP/M. (*Note*: This can be tested only if you have the CP/M operating system).

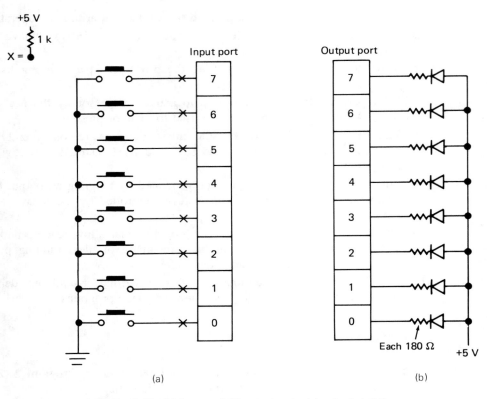

Figure 3.46 (a) Input and (b) output port wiring for Lab 3.8.

3.8. Connect a DIP switch and LEDs to an available input and output port as shown in Fig. 3.46. Write a Z-80 or 8080/85 program to "read" the value of the switches and turn on the corresponding LEDs (i.e., when switch 0 is closed, LED 0 should come on, etc.). Several other programs are possible. (*Example*: Turn all LEDs on only when switches 0 *and* 1 are closed *and* switches 3 *or* 4 are open, etc.)

3.9. Wire the 8085 circuit shown in Fig. 3.21. Now write a program that monitors the SID input line. When this line switches from high to low, turn on the LED connected to SOD. Turn off the LED on the next high-to-low transition of SID. Continue in this manner toggling the LED with each high-to-low SID transition.

3.10. Connect the seven segments of a common anode LED display to the output port of your computer as shown in Fig. 3.47. Connect an 8-switch DIP switch to an input port as shown in Fig. 3.46(a). Now write a Z-80 or 8080/85 program that reads switches 0–3 and displays the corresponding hex number on the display. (*Hint*: Use a data table for the seven-segment codes.)

3.11. With a seven-segment display connected as described in Lab 3.10, write a

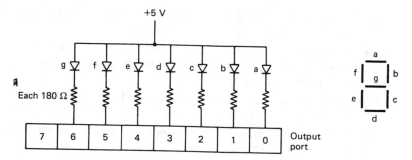

Figure 3.47 Seven bits of a computer output port can be used to drive a seven-segment display. There is no need for a conventional seven-segment decoder.

Z-80 or 8080/85 program that causes a slow count from 0 through F to appear in the display.

QUESTIONS AND PROBLEMS

8080/85 Specific Questions

3.1. List the changes required in Program 1 if the two numbers to be added are stored in locations C000H and C001H.

3.2. Compare the times required for the 8-bit addition in Program 1 using a 2-MHz 8080 and a 2-MHz 8085.

3.3. Why is it necessary to clear the carry flag at the beginning of Program 3?

3.4. Assume Program 3 is run with memory preloaded as follows:

0700	3C
0701	27
0702	FF
0703	80
0704	DE
0705	F9
0706	1A
0707	69

Determine the contents of memory locations 0708–070B after the program has run.

3.5. What is the address of the last byte in the memory block filled by the program in Fig. 3.13 (Program 7)? What character is written to the block?

*3.6. The instructions below are intended to form a time delay loop. However, debugging reveals that the loop is executed only once. What is wrong?

```
          LHLD    FFFFH
AGAIN     DCX     H
          JNZ     AGAIN
```

3.7. Assuming a 2-MHz 8080, what are the maximum and minimum square-wave frequencies produced by Program 8?

3.8. What is the frequency of the square wave at bit D7 of the output port in Program 8? What change is required to make all 8 bits of the output port operate at the same frequency?

3.9. Calculate the value of DELAY required for the WAIT subroutine in Program 8 to produce a 1-Hz square wave using a 3-MHz 8085AH.

3.10. In Program 10 the HXAS subroutine begins by exchanging the MSD and LSD. Explain why.

3.11. What change is necessary in Program 10 to cause the output to appear as follows?

```
0700   A3
0701   67
0702   E6
etc.
```

3.12. In Program 11 what change is required to make the LED light when the switch *closes*?

3.13. Analyze Program 13 and determine the number of sticks the computer will pick if 11 sticks remain and you pick 2.

3.14. Explain how the PRMSG subroutine in Program 13 detects the end of the string to be printed.

Z-80 Specific Questions

3.15. Describe the changes required in Program 2 if the two numbers to be added are stored in locations D780H and D781H. Assume the sum is to be stored in location D782H.

3.16. Calculate the time required to execute the 8-bit addition of Program 2 using a 4-MHz Z-80 processor.

3.17. In Program 4 the instruction JR NZ,NEXT has the op-code 20 F4. Show that F4 is actually the 2's complement of the displacement to memory location NEXT.

3.18. Refer to the sample output for Program 4. Determine the output produced by this program if the DAA instruction is omitted.

3.19. Determine the contents of the HL pair after the following instructions have been executed:

```
LD     HL,679A
ADD    HL,HL
```

Verify that the result is the same as rotating the HL pair left one bit.

3.20. Calculate the execution time for the 8-bit multiplication routine in Program 5 assuming a 4-MHz Z-80 processor.

3.21. What is the largest BCD number that Program 6 will convert correctly?

3.22. In Program 6, if the BCD number to be converted is 8,693,721 determine the contents of memory locations 0700–0706 after the first pass of the program (i.e., the first time the JR NZ,LOOP instruction in location 0624 is run). Assume locations 0704–0706 all initially store zeros.

3.23. What does the following program accomplish?

```
LD      DE,0100H
LD      BC,0100H
LD      HL,A000H
LDIR
HALT
```

3.24. How would the operation of Program 7 in Fig. 3.14 be changed if the DEC HL instruction in location 060D was deleted?

3.25. If the receiver ready flag in Program 9 was active in the low state instead of the high state, what changes would be required to make this program run correctly?

3.26. The terminal test routine in Program 9 can be stopped only with a processor reset. Modify the program so that typing control-R exits back to memory location MONITOR.

*3.27. Find all errors in the routine below, written to count rising edges of the signal applied to bit 0 of input port C3H.

```
TEST1   IN      A,C3H
        RLA
        JR      C,TEST1
TEST2   IN      A,C3H
        RRA
        JR      Z,TEST2
        INC     B           ;B is the edge counter
```

3.28. How could the frequency-divider hardware of Program 9 be modified to allow 1-Hz resolution without changing the program? What would the maximum count frequency be with this modification?

3.29. Refer to Program 14 and Fig. 3.32 and verify the calculations for E and N for note F (342 Hz).

3.30. Refer to Program 14 in Fig. 3.36. What is the first note of the song "Daisy"? How long is it played?

3.31. Determine the contents of register A and (HL) after the following instructions.

```
LD      A,D7H
LD      (HL),A
RLD
```

KEY CONCEPT ANSWERS

3.1.1. HL

3.1.2. indexed

3.1.3. DCR, JNZ or JZ

3.1.4. DEC, JR NZ

3.1.5. DAA

3.1.6. multiplier

3.1.7. ADD HL,HL

3.1.8. right, carry

3.1.9. reset

3.1.10. none

3.1.11. 0000 0000

3.1.12. HL, DE

3.1.13. time delay

3.1.14. CALL, RET

3.1.15. mask

3.1.16. ASCII

3.1.17. RIM, SIM

3.1.18. high, low

3.1.19. carry

3.1.20. HL

3.1.21 apostrophes, DB

3.1.22. CPL

3.2.1. ZIP.ASM

3.2.2. ZIP.COM

3.2.3. 1, A

4

Building the Microcomputer, Part 1: The Buses

The design of a microcomputer system must begin with the *CPU module*. This module will establish the basic system timing, provide an orderly means of starting up the processor, and provide access to the system buses. If the microcomputer is to be expandable, buffering and loading considerations must be taken into account when designing these buses.

It is also wise to think ahead to the testing phase of the design. Perhaps a *single-stepping* circuit should be designed into the module. This should allow the microprocessor to be stepped one machine cycle at a time—freezing all data, addresses, and control signals on the buses.

When reset, the 8080, 8085, and Z-80 all force their program counters to location 0000. This requires a startup program (usually in a read-only memory chip) permanently mapped to page 0 of the processor's memory space. However, low memory is often used by application programs; therefore, another useful addition to the CPU module is a *jump-on-reset circuit*. This circuit intercepts the reset signal and vectors the processor to a new location in memory.

Basic CPU modules for the 8080, 8085, and Z-80 microprocessors were presented in Chap. 2. In this chapter we expand on those designs and pay particular attention to the electrical characteristics of digital signals on a bus.

4.1 GENERATING THE SYSTEM CLOCK

As you read this section, look for the answers to these Key Concept questions:

4.1.1. Each computer instruction requires a specific number of clock cycles. Therefore, the higher the clock frequency, the _____ the computer will operate.

4.1.2. Comparing the 8080, 8085, and Z-80, only the _____ microprocessor has a "built-in" clock generator.

The design of a digital system may be *synchronous* or *asynchronous*. In an asynchronous digital network the outputs of the circuit change whenever the inputs change. That is, the outputs are not synchronized to any timing signal. Most combinational logic networks are examples of asynchronous logic.

Figure 4.1 illustrates a simple combinational logic circuit in which the inverter is assumed to have a propagation delay time twice that of the AND gate. As designed, the circuit is "looking for" the condition SELECT1 = 1 AND $\overline{\text{SELECT2}}$ = 0. Although this condition never occurs, a false output is produced due to the propagation delay time of the inverter.

Figure 4.2 shows how the same circuit is modified to become a synchronous logic circuit. The SENABLE (synchronized ENABLE) output is synchronized to the clock signal and can change only on the rising edge of the clock. By choosing

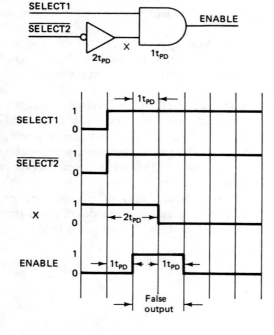

Figure 4.1 In an asynchronous logic network the outputs change when the inputs change. This may lead to temporary false outputs, due to the unequal propagation delay paths from input to output.

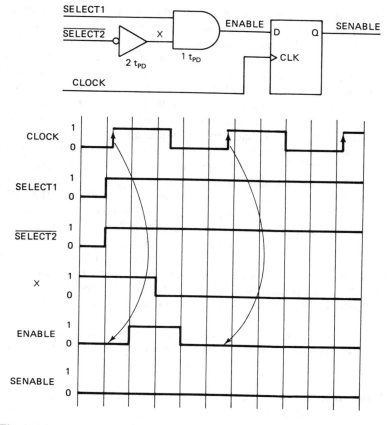

Figure 4.2 In a synchronous logic network the output can change only in synchronism with a clock signal. By choosing the clock period to exceed the worst-case propagation delay path, no false outputs occur.

the clock period long enough for all propagation delays to expire, false outputs are prevented.*

The maximum clock frequency of a microprocessor is determined by the propagation delays of its internal gates. These, in turn, are set by the type of technology used to manufacture the chip. For example, bipolar processors (using npn transistors) are faster than NMOS processors (using n-channel metal-oxide semiconductor transistors).

When choosing the clock frequency of a microcomputer, consideration must be given to the overall effect on the system. A 6-MHz 8085 processor may be desirable to minimize instruction execution times, but it will also require memory devices that can operate at this higher speed.

---

* The sum of the flip-flop set-up and hold times should exceed the pulse width of the false output.

The 8080 Clock.   The 8080 and 8085 microprocessors both use *two-phase non-overlapping* clock signals. This was shown in Fig. 2.6 for the 8080. The advantage of this type of clock signal is that two different timing periods and four clock edges are available. These can be used to synchronize different activities of the processor. For example, the 8080 and 8085 break each instruction into several machine cycles. Each machine cycle is further divided into several clock periods or T states.

Figure 4.3 shows the activities that take place during the four (or five) T states of an 8080 instruction fetch machine cycle. Note how the different timing intervals of the nonoverlapping clocks are used.

Generating the 8080 clock signal with discrete components is difficult because of the non-TTL levels and asymmetry of the two clock phases. As discussed in Chap. 2, Intel produces an integrated clock generator circuit for the 8080 called the 8224. This circuit is shown in Fig. 4.4. Interfacing the 8224 to the 8080 is extremely simple, as shown in Fig. 4.5. The clock frequency is determined by a crystal connected between pins 14 and 15. The crystal frequency should be nine times greater than the desired system frequency.

There are actually three different versions of the 8080 microprocessor and these are listed in Table 4.1. The maximum operating frequency is 3 MHz for the 8080A-1. The power dissipation is obtained from the dc characteristics data sheets in Table C.1 of Appendix C. Remember that the 8080 requires +5-V, +12-V, and −5-V power sources.

In summary, the 8224 clock generator is the logical choice for developing clock signals in 8080-based microprocessor systems. This chip is specifically designed to interface with the 8080 CPU and 8228 system controller.

The 8085 Clock.   Internally, the 8085 requires the same nonoverlapping clock signal as the 8080. However, in redesigning the 8080, the 8085 designers incorporated the 8224 clock generator (or its equivalent) on-board. As a result, generating the 8085

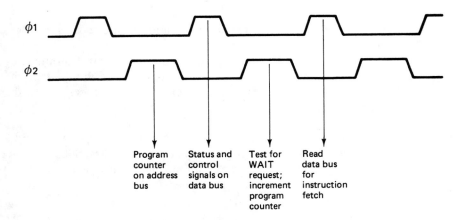

Figure 4.3   The 8080 and 8085 microprocessors use a two-phase nonoverlapping clock signal. The processor activities shown are for an 8080.

Schottky Bipolar **8224**

CLOCK GENERATOR AND DRIVER
FOR 8080A CPU

- **Single Chip Clock Generator/Driver for 8080A CPU**
- **Power-Up Reset for CPU**
- **Ready Synchronizing Flip-Flop**
- **Advanced Status Strobe**
- **Oscillator Output for External System Timing**
- **Crystal Controlled for Stable System Operation**
- **Reduces System Package Count**

The 8224 is a single chip clock generator/driver for the 8080A CPU. It is controlled by a crystal, selected by the designer, to meet a variety of system speed requirements.

Also included are circuits to provide power-up reset, advance status strobe and synchronization of ready.

The 8224 provides the designer with a significant reduction of packages used to generate clocks and timing for 8080A.

PIN CONFIGURATION

RESET	1		16	V_{CC}
$\overline{RESIN}$	2		15	XTAL 1
RDYIN	3		14	XTAL 2
READY	4	8224	13	TANK
SYNC	5		12	OSC
ϕ_2 (TTL)	6		11	ϕ_1
$\overline{STSTB}$	7		10	ϕ_2
GND	8		9	V_{DD}

BLOCK DIAGRAM

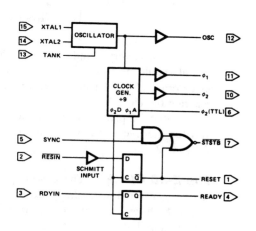

PIN NAMES

$\overline{RESIN}$	RESET INPUT		XTAL 1	CONNECTIONS
RESET	RESET OUTPUT		XTAL 2	FOR CRYSTAL
RDYIN	READY INPUT		TANK	USED WITH OVERTONE XTAL
READY	READY OUTPUT		OSC	OSCILLATOR OUTPUT
SYNC	SYNC INPUT		ϕ_2 (TTL)	ϕ_2 CLK (TTL LEVEL)
$\overline{STSTB}$	STATUS STB (ACTIVE LOW)		V_{CC}	+5V
ϕ_1	8080		V_{DD}	+12V
ϕ_2	CLOCKS		GND	0V

Figure 4.4 8224 clock generator. 8080 designers are strongly advised to use this circuit to generate the 8080 clock signals. (Courtesy of Intel Corporation.)

Sec. 4.1   Generating the System Clock

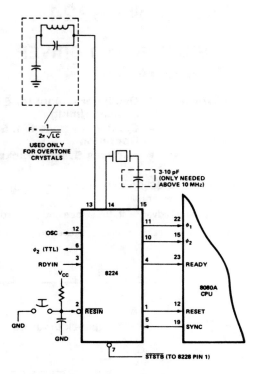

$$F = \frac{1}{2\pi\sqrt{LC}}$$

USED ONLY
FOR OVERTONE
CRYSTALS

3-10 pF
(ONLY NEEDED
ABOVE 10 MHz)

OSC

ϕ_2 (TTL)

RDYIN

V_{CC}

8224

RESIN

GND

GND

STSTB (TO 8228 PIN 1)

ϕ_1

ϕ_2

READY

8080A
CPU

RESET

SYNC

Figure 4.5 The 8224 connects directly to the 8080 requiring only an external crystal at nine times the system frequency. (Courtesy of Intel Corporation.)

clock signal is very simple. Figure 4.6(a) shows the connections. Unlike the 8080, the crystal should be twice the desired system operating frequency. You can also see that an external clock driver, an *LC* tuned circuit, or an *RC* circuit can all be used to generate the clock signal.

Table 4.2 provides data on the maximum operating frequency and power dissipation for the five versions of the 8085. This data is obtained from the data sheets in Table C.2.

The Z-80 Clock. The Z-80 requires a single phase 0 V to 5 V clock signal. This can be generated with the 74LS04 oscillator circuit shown in Fig. 4.7. Because the typical high-level output voltage of a TTL gate is only 3.3 V, and the minimum high level required at the Z-80 clock input is 4.4 V, a 330-Ω pullup resistor is required.

TABLE 4.1 SPEED AND POWER SPECIFICATIONS FOR THREE VERSIONS OF THE 8080 MICROPROCESSOR

	8080A	8080A-1	8080A-2
f_{max} (MHz)	2	3	2.5
P_D (mW)	1245	1245	1245

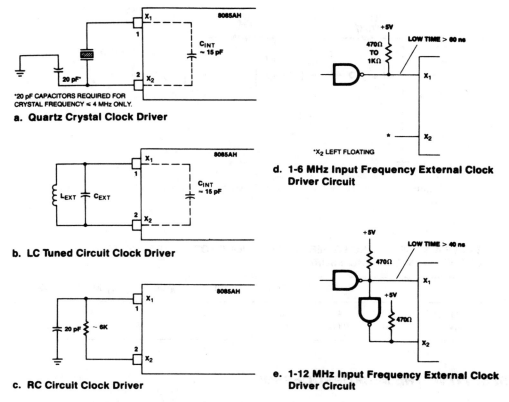

a. Quartz Crystal Clock Driver

*20 pF CAPACITORS REQUIRED FOR
CRYSTAL FREQUENCY ≤ 4 MHz ONLY.

b. LC Tuned Circuit Clock Driver

c. RC Circuit Clock Driver

d. 1-6 MHz Input Frequency External Clock Driver Circuit

*X₂ LEFT FLOATING

e. 1-12 MHz Input Frequency External Clock Driver Circuit

Figure 4.6 Different techniques for generating the 8085 clock signal: (a) quartz crystal clock driver; (b) *LC* tuned circuit clock driver; (c) *RC* circuit clock driver; (d) 1–6-MHz input frequency external clock driver circuit; (e) 1–12-MHz input frequency external clock driver circuit. (Courtesy of Intel Corporation.)

It is unfortunate that the Z-80 designers did not incorporate this clock circuit on-board as in the 8085, but two package pins are saved with this technique (compared to the 8085).

There are seven versions of the Z-80 and these are listed in Table 4.3. The Z-80L versions are appropriate for portable operation, where the power source must be a battery. Appendix C.3 is the source of this information.

TABLE 4.2 SPEED AND POWER SPECIFICATIONS FOR SEVERAL VERSIONS OF THE 8085 MICROPROCESSOR

	8085A	8085A-2	8085AH	8085AH-1	8085AH-2
f_{max} (MHz)	3	5	3	6	5
P_D (mW)	850	850	675	1000	675

Sec. 4.1   Generating the System Clock

151

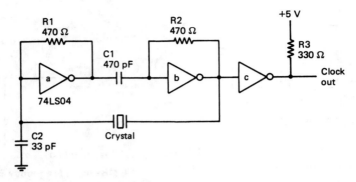

Figure 4.7 A TTL oscillator can be used to generate the Z-80 system clock signal.

TABLE 4.3 SPEED AND POWER SPECIFICATIONS FOR SEVERAL VERSIONS OF THE Z-80 MICROPROCESSOR

	Z-80	Z-80A	Z-80B	Z-80L	Z-80L-1	Z-80L-2	Z-80H
f_{max} (MHz)	2.5	4	6	1	1.5	2.5	8
P_D (mW)	750	1000	1000	150	175	225	1000

4.2 RESETTING THE MICROPROCESSOR

As you read this section, look for the answers to these Key Concept questions:

4.2.1. When reset, the 8080, 8085, and Z-80 all load their program counter with the address _____ .

4.2.2. Via a _____ - _____ - _____ circuit, the CPU's RESET input will be held low for several time constants, ensuring an orderly start-up of the computer.

Starting Up a "New" Computer. In Chap. 1 we conveniently sidestepped one significant problem of the stored program computer: How do we put the "very first" program in memory? Certainly, once it is there we can use the keyboard to enter new programs or give commands to load other programs from a magnetic tape or disk. But how did that first program get in?

What is needed is a permanent program stored in memory that can never be lost or written over, even when power is removed. I imagine that you are already ahead of me and realize that this is exactly the purpose of a read-only memory or *ROM*. A ROM chip is *nonvolatile*, which means that its contents are not lost when power is removed.

Usually, a ROM is used to hold a "bootstrap" loader. This is a special program that is called upon only once to "boot up" the operating system (usually stored on a magnetic disk). Once the operating system is loaded, the keyboard becomes active and new programs can be written or loaded from the disk.

But one problem still remains. When power is first applied to the microprocessor, all of its registers contain random data. This includes the program counter. Some means must be found to point the program counter at the bootstrap ROM. This is the purpose of the *reset* switch.

As mentioned earlier in this chapter, resetting the 8080, 8085, or Z-80 causes the program counter to be loaded with 0000. Therefore, this is the logical address for the bootstrap ROM chip (in Sec. 4.7 we show how to force a reset to any location in memory).

Reset Circuits for the 8080, 8085, and Z-80. Circuits for resetting the 8080, 8085, and Z-80 are shown in Fig. 4.8. The purpose of the switch should be clear, but the *RC* network requires some explanation.

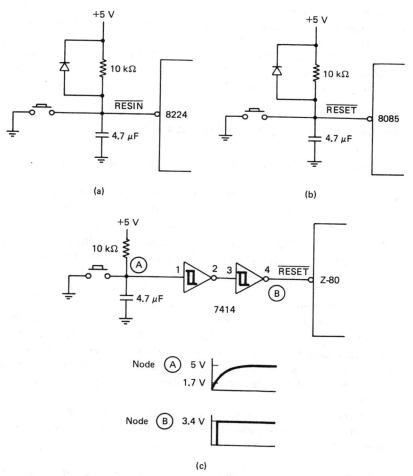

Figure 4.8 Reset circuits for the (a) 8080, (b) 8085, and (c) Z-80 microprocessors.

When power is first applied to the system it would be convenient to have the microprocessor reset itself without the need to push the reset button. In this way simply turning on the computer could cause the bootstrap program to load the operating system—this is sometimes called a *turnkey* system.

With the *RC* network connected to the reset input as shown in Fig. 4.8, the capacitor will hold the reset pin low for several time constants when power is first applied. The result is called a *power-on-reset* circuit.

Because the reset signal obtained across the capacitor is a rising exponential and not a sharp square wave, a Schmitt trigger is used to square up the wave shape. The 7414 shown in Fig. 4.8(c) will switch to a low-level output when its input exceeds 1.7 V. The input will now have to go below 0.9 V before the output will switch back high. That is, the logic 1 and logic 0 switching points are not the same.

A circuit with two different switching thresholds is said to have *hysteresis*. This property is characteristic of all *Schmitt* triggers and is useful for cleaning up wave shapes with excessive ringing or for signals that pass relatively slowly through the TTL switching threshold.

The 8224 and 8085 both incorporate Schmitt triggers at their reset inputs but the Z-80 does not. Note that this is another good reason for selecting the 8224 as a support component to the 8080.

4.3 ELECTRICAL CHARACTERISTICS OF A BUS

As you read this section, look for the answers to these Key Concept questions:

4.3.1. The difference between a transmitter's worst-case high- or low-level output voltage and a receiver's worst-case high- or low-level input threshold voltage is called _____ _____ .

4.3.2. As the number of receivers connected to a bus line increases, the transmitter's high-level output voltage will _____ and its low-level output voltage will _____ .

A bus can be defined as a set of lines used to transport data between a transmitter and a receiver. Usually, we lump together common signal lines and refer to them as a bus. Thus we have the *address bus*, the *data bus*, and the *control bus*. In many microcomputer systems these signals and others are all wired to a common *backplane* or *motherboard* and referred to as the system bus. Common system buses are the DEC UNIBUS, the Intel Multibus, the Zilog Z-bus, the Pro-Log STD bus, and the S-100 or IEEE-696 bus.

A properly designed system bus must consider such problems as noise immunity, ac and dc loading, reflection problems due to high-speed logic pulses, and crosstalk between parallel conductors.

Noise Immunity. In a microcomputer system there are typically three types of buses and these are described in Table 4.4. In all cases the transmitter places a logic 1

TABLE 4.4 MICROCOMPUTER BUSES

Type	Description	Example
1	One transmitter, many receivers	Address bus
2	One receiver, many transmitters	CPU control lines ($\overline{\text{WAIT}}$, $\overline{\text{INT}}$, etc.)
3	Many transmitters and receivers (bidirectional)	Data bus

(called V_{OH} for V_{out} high) or a logic 0 (called V_{OL} for V_{out} low) on the bus. This signal propagates down the bus line and is received as a V_{IL} (input voltage low) or V_{IH} (input voltage high).

The values for V_{OL}, V_{OH}, V_{IL}, and V_{IH} are dependent on the logic family used. Table 4.5 indicates values for TTL, CMOS, and LSTTL (low-power Schottky TTL). A minimum requirement for any bus system to work is

$$V_{OH} > V_{IH} \qquad \text{and} \qquad V_{OL} < V_{IL}$$

The amount by which these requirements are exceeded is called the *noise immunity*.

Example 4.1

Assume that a 7400 TTL gate is driving a bus line with a 74LS04 receiver. Calculate the worst-case noise immunity for the bus.

Solution. The minimum-output high level for the 7400 gate is 2.4 V. The 74LS00 will accept a logic 1 input as low as 2.0 V. Therefore, the logic 1 level noise immunity is 2.4 V − 2.0 V = 0.4 V.

TABLE 4.5 LOGIC-LEVEL SPECIFICATIONS FOR THE TTL, LSTTL, AND CMOS LOGIC FAMILIES

	Description	TTL	LSTTL	CMOS[a]
V_{OH}	Minimum logic 1 output voltage	2.4 V	2.7 V	4.6 V
V_{OL}	Maximum logic 0 output voltage	0.4 V	0.5 V	0.4 V
V_{IL}	Maximum acceptable logic 0 input voltage	0.8 V	0.8 V	1.5 V
V_{IH}	Minimum acceptable logic 1 input voltage	2.0 V	2.0 V	3.5 V
I_{IL}	Maximum logic 0 level input source current	−1.6 mA	−0.4 mA	−1 μA
I_{IH}	Maximum logic 1 level input sink current	40 μA	20 μA	1 μA
I_{OH}	Maximum logic 1 level output source current	−400 μA	−400 μA	−360 μA
I_{OL}	Maximum logic 0 level output sink current	16 mA	8 mA	0.36 mA

[a] Data given for the CD4001BC.

The maximum logic 0 level output voltage for the 7400 gate is 0.4 V. The 74LS00 will accept a logic 0 level input as high as 0.8 V, so the logic 0 level noise immunity is 0.8 V − 0.4 V = 0.4 V.

The 0.4 V of noise immunity calculated in this example means that the bus can tolerate a noise impulse that pulls the V_{OH} level down by 0.4 V or the V_{OL} level up by 0.4 V. Noise immunity levels for a CMOS transmitter driving a CMOS receiver are greater than 1 V.

Bus Loading.   Noise immunity is a characteristic of the logic family used and cannot be changed. However, a problem that can be designed out is the loading of the transmitter by the receiver or receivers on the bus. In general, each receiver added to the bus will require an additional amount of *source* current from the transmitter in the high state and an additional amount of *sink* current into the transmitter in the low state. This situation is diagrammed in Fig. 4.9.

All of the output voltage specifications in Table 4.5 are given for worst-case loading conditions, indicated as I_{OL} and I_{OH} in the bottom two lines of the table. Using this data we can expect a 7400 output to be no lower than 2.4 V when sourcing a 400-μA load and no greater than 0.4 V when sinking a 16-mA load. The amount of loading to be expected for a given logic family is given in Table 4.5 as I_{IL} and I_{IH}. Negative currents mean that the direction of the current is out of the device (that is, a source current).

Example 4.2

Calculate the number of 74LS04 receivers that a 7400 transmitter can safely drive without exceeding its drive capabilities.

Solution.   In the logic 1 state a 74LS04 presents one 20-μA load per input. The 7400 transmitter can supply 400 μA of drive current in the 1 state and thus the 7400 can safely drive 400 μA/20 μA = 20 74LS04 receivers.

In the logic 0 state the 74LS04 receiver presents a 0.4-mA load per input. The 7400 transmitter can supply 16 mA of drive current in the 0 state and thus can safely drive 16 mA/0.4 mA = 40 74LS04 receivers.

The logic 1 state is therefore the worst case and the bus should be limited to 20 74LS04 receivers.

Example 4.3

Calculate the number of CD4001 receivers that a 7400 transmitter can safely drive.

Solution.   The input loading factor for a CMOS gate is almost negligible (1 μA) and one would think that there would be no limit to the number of CMOS receivers a TTL transmitter could drive. However, there are two problems. The first is that the V_{OH} level for TTL does not meet the minimum V_{IH} requirement for CMOS. This means that the logic 1 output of a TTL gate may not be interpreted as a logic 1 input by the CMOS gate. This problem can be solved fairly simply by the use of a pullup resistor as shown in Fig. 4.10.

The second problem is caused by the capacitive nature of the CMOS input. A TTL gate typically has 1.5 pF of capacitance per input, but a CMOS gate can be as high as 7.5 pF per input.

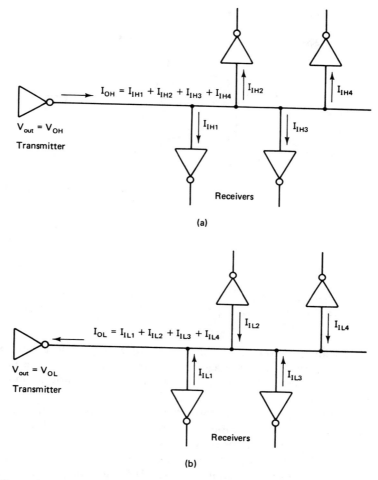

Figure 4.9 Transmitter sources current to the receiver when its output is high (a) and sinks current from the receiver when its output is low (b).

Consider a TTL transmitter driving 10 CMOS receivers. The total capacitive load (ignoring wiring capacitance) could be as high as 75 pF (compared to only 15 pF for 10 TTL loads). This large capacitive load will have the effect of distorting the output signal from the TTL gate as shown in Fig. 4.11. The effect will be to lower the bandwidth of the bus, that is, restrict the bus to low frequencies.

Reflections. The physical nature of a bus is usually a number of parallel traces on a printed circuit (PC) board or a bundle of wire-wrap wire. A pulse placed on this bus is affected in a similar manner to radio-frequency signals on a high-frequency transmission line.

Figure 4.12 illustrates the effect of placing a long and short pulse on an open-circuited bus line. This is a reasonable model for a microcomputer bus because of

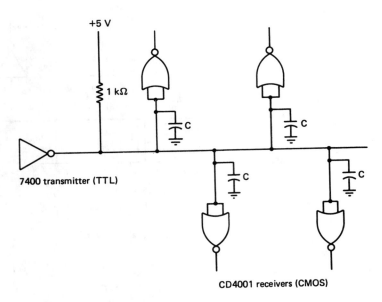

+5 V

1 kΩ

C

C

7400 transmitter (TTL)

C

C

CD4001 receivers (CMOS)

Figure 4.10 When a TTL transmitter is used to drive a bus line with CMOS receivers, a resistor is required to pull up the TTL V_{OH} level to near 5 V.

the high input resistance of a TTL or CMOS logic gate acting as a receiver. The pulse propagates down the line at approximately 2 ns/ft. Because of the open circuit, the current reaching the end of the line is forced to turn around and head back to the transmitter. This is called a *reflection*.

If the input pulse is very short, the effect is a series of reflected pulses. Depending on the amplitude and duration of these pulses, clocked devices such as flip-flops and latches may produce erroneous results.

The effect on longer input pulses is to produce a series of ripples (sometimes called *ringing*) in the transmitted pulse. The effect may be so severe as to produce momentary invalid logic levels.

Ideally, a receiver placed on the end of the transmission line would absorb all of the energy in the pulse and there would be no reflection. However, this occurs only if the input resistance of the receiver is *matched* to the resistance of

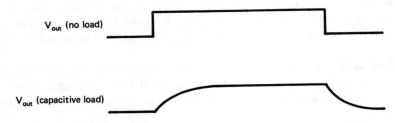

V_{out} (no load)

V_{out} (capacitive load)

Figure 4.11 When driving a capacitive load, the output of a logic gate will be delayed and become distorted as shown.

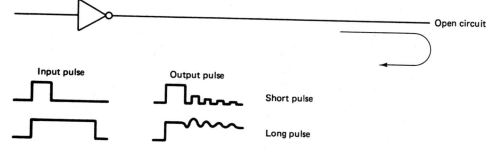

Figure 4.12 Effect of reflections on long and short pulses placed on an open-circuited bus line.

the transmission line. PC board traces and wire-wrap bundles exhibit a characteristic impedance (resistance plus reactance) of 100 to 200 Ω. Therefore, one means of minimizing reflections is to terminate each bus line with a 100- to 200-Ω resistor to ground. This is referred to as *passive termination*.

Unfortunately, this has the undesirable effect of producing a dc load on the transmitter. The V_{OH} level will be pulled down and the V_{OL} level pulled up. A better solution is to use a voltage-divider configuration that biases the bus line in the middle of the TTL-level threshold and simultaneously matches the characteristic impedance of the line. Such a circuit is called an *active terminator* and is shown in Fig. 4.13.

Because of the receiver input resistance and the resistance of the line, voltage division ensures that the amplitude of the reflected pulse will always be less than the amplitude of the incident pulse. Eventually, the reflections will die out. For this reason short bus lines (less than 3 ft) are not seriously affected by reflections. Of course, the closer the receiver is matched to the characteristic impedance of the bus line, the greater the attenuation factor for the reflected waves. There is no reflection with a matched load.

In some cases coaxial cable is used as a transmission line between receiver and transmitter. The center conductor in this cable is surrounded by a grounded

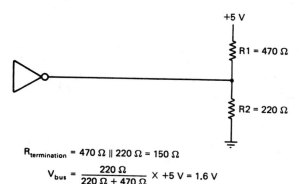

$R_{termination} = 470\ \Omega \parallel 220\ \Omega = 150\ \Omega$

$V_{bus} = \dfrac{220\ \Omega}{220\ \Omega + 470\ \Omega} \times +5\ V = 1.6\ V$

Figure 4.13 Active termination of a bus line minimizes reflections without producing a significant dc load on the transmitter.

Sec. 4.3   Electrical Characteristics of a Bus

"shield" or braid. This shielding prevents capacitive coupling between adjacent conductors called "crosstalk."

An alternative to coaxial cable is the "twisted pair." The signal wire and a ground conductor are twisted together to form an inexpensive transmission line. The ground wire again forms a protective shield.

With either type of transmission line the cable length should be restricted to 15 to 30 ft when driven by TTL. Greater cable lengths introduce unacceptably large capacitive loads. Special line drivers and receivers are available for these long lines.

4.4 BUS BUFFERING TECHNIQUES

As you read this section, look for the answers to these Key Concept questions:

4.4.1. Explain why it is advantageous to buffer receiver inputs as well as transmitter outputs.

4.4.2. An _____-_____ bus is useful when several transmitters share a common bus-request line.

4.4.3. The output of a tri-state bus buffer may be high, low, or an _____ _____ .

Bus buffering refers to the various methods required to ensure that valid logic levels are carried on the bus. In Sec. 4.3 we learned that a microprocessor has three types of buses (refer to Table 4.4). Each one of these requires a different buffering technique.

Type 1 Bus. The type 1 bus is characterized by a single transmitter and several receivers. The address bus is an example of a type 1 bus. The need for buffering can best be seen with an example.

Example 4.4

Assume that a Z-80 microprocessor is interfaced to a 32K-byte memory consisting of 16 HM6116 2K × 8 RAM chips. In addition to driving the RAM chips, assume that each address line must drive three TTL loads used for address decoding. Is a buffer required?

Solution. Figure 4.14 illustrates the interface for the A0 address line (in general, this is duplicated for all 16 address lines). Because the HM6116s are MOS devices, they require only a small drive current—10 μA in this case. The three TTL loads will require 1.6 mA each in the low state and 40 μA each in the high state. The total loading on the Z-80 A0 address line is thus

$$16 \times 10 \ \mu A = 160 \ \mu A$$
$$+ \ \ 3 \times 40 \ \mu A = 120 \ \mu A$$
$$\overline{280 \ \mu A \text{ in the logic 1 state}}$$

and

$$16 \times 10 \ \mu A = 160 \ \mu A$$
$$+ \ \underline{3 \times 1.6 \ mA = 4.8 \ mA}$$
$$4.96 \ mA \text{ in the logic 0 state}$$

The dc characteristics data sheet for the Z-80 in Appendix C.3 indicates an I_{OH} of 250 μA and an I_{OL} of 1.8 mA. The 32K memory interface will exceed both of these specifications and therefore a special buffer will be required.

The result of Ex. 4.4 should come as no surprise. Microprocessors are MOS devices and as such have very limited drive capabilities. As a general rule, a bus buffer should be used whenever the bus loading exceeds the drive capabilities of the microprocessor or when it is neccessary to drive receivers off the main CPU card. The latter requirement is due to the capacitive loading associated with the edge connectors and backplane wiring in a multicard system.

Special buffers are available for this application and Fig. 4.15 shows several common types. The 74LS241 and 74LS244 are particularly attractive because they contain eight buffers in one package. A data sheet for these devices is included as Fig. 4.16.

Example 4.5

Assume that a type 1 bus similar to Fig. 4.9 is to be buffered with a 74LS244 transmitter. Calculate the number of standard TTL loads that can be driven by this transmitter. How many loads can be driven if each input is also buffered by a 74LS244?

Solution. From the 74LS244 data sheet in Fig. 4.16, the high-level output drive capability is 3 mA at $V_{OH} = 2.4$ V. This means that 3 mA/40 $\mu A = 75$ standard TTL loads can be driven in the high state.

In the low state the 74LS244 can sink 12 mA and thus 12 mA/1.6 mA = 7.5 standard TTL loads can be driven.

When the loads are also buffered with 74LS244s, the high-level drive current required drops to 20 μA/input and 3 mA/20 $\mu A = 150$ loads can be driven.

In the low state the buffered load requires only 0.2 mA and the calculation is 12 mA/0.2 mA = 60 loads.

In summary, for a type 1 bus with 74LS244 transmitters, seven standard TTL loads can be driven or 60 74LS244 buffered loads.

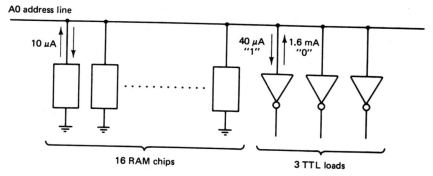

Figure 4.14 Loading considerations for the A0 address line in Ex. 4.4.

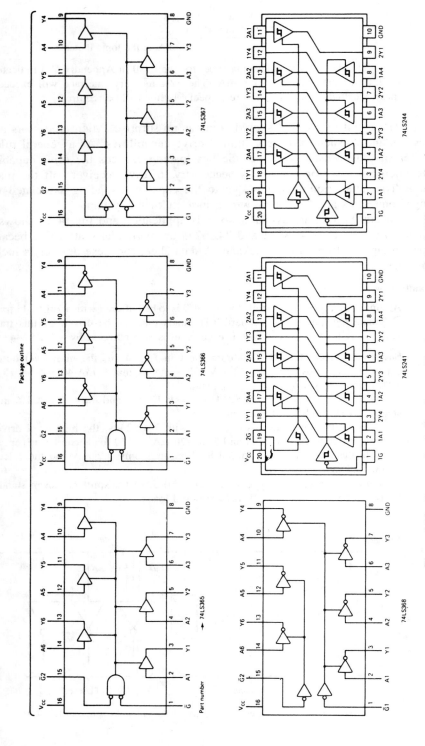

Figure 4.15 Common bus buffers for use with microprocessors. (From J. Uffenbeck, *Hardware Interfacing with the Apple II Plus*, Prentice-Hall, Inc., Englewood Cliffs, N.J., 1983 & Texas Instruments.)

recommended operating conditions

PARAMETER	SN54LS'			SN74LS'			UNIT
	MIN	NOM	MAX	MIN	NOM	MAX	
Supply voltage, V_{CC} (see Note 1)	4.5	5	5.5	4.75	5	5.25	V
High-level output current, I_{OH}			−12			−15	mA
Low-level output current, I_{OL}			12			24	mA
Operating free-air temperature, T_A	−55		125	0		70	°C

NOTE 1: Voltage values are with respect to network ground terminal.

electrical characteristics over recommended operating free-air temperature range (unless otherwise noted)

PARAMETER		TEST CONDITIONS†		SN54LS'			SN74LS'			UNIT
				MIN	TYP‡	MAX	MIN	TYP‡	MAX	
V_{IH}	High-level input voltage			2			2			V
V_{IL}	Low-level input voltage					0.7			0.8	V
V_{IK}	Input clamp voltage	V_{CC} = MIN,	I_I = −18 mA			−1.5			−1.5	V
	Hysteresis ($V_{T+} - V_{T-}$)	V_{CC} = MIN		0.2	0.4		0.2	0.4		V
V_{OH}	High-level output voltage	V_{CC} = MIN, V_{IH} = 2 V, V_{IL} = V_{IL} max, I_{OH} = −3 mA		2.4	3.4		2.4	3.4		V
		V_{CC} = MIN, V_{IH} = 2 V, V_{IL} = 0.5 V, I_{OH} = MAX		2			2			
V_{OL}	Low-level output voltage	V_{CC} = MIN, V_{IH} = 2 V, V_{IL} = V_{IL}max	I_{OL} = 12 mA			0.4			0.4	V
			I_{OL} = 24 mA						0.5	
I_{OZH}	Off-state output current, high-level voltage applied	V_{CC} = MAX, V_{IH} = 2 V, V_{IL} = V_{IL}max	V_O = 2.7 V			20			20	µA
I_{OZL}	Off-state output current, low-level voltage applied		V_O = 0.4 V			−20			−20	
I_I	Input current at maximum input voltage	V_{CC} = MAX,	V_I = 7 V			0.1			0.1	mA
I_{IH}	High-level input current, any input	V_{CC} = MAX,	V_I = 2.7 V			20			20	µA
I_{IL}	Low-level input current	V_{CC} = MAX,	V_{IL} = 0.4 V			−0.2			−0.2	mA
I_{OS}	Short-circuit output current♦	V_{CC} = MAX		−40		−225	−40		−225	mA
I_{CC}	Supply current	Outputs high	V_{CC} = MAX, Outputs open	All	17	27		17	27	mA
		Outputs low		'LS240	26	44		26	44	
				'LS241, 'LS244	27	46		27	46	
		All outputs disabled		'LS240	29	50		29	50	
				'LS241, 'LS244	32	54		32	54	

†For conditions shown as MIN or MAX, use the appropriate value specified under recommended operating conditions.
‡All typical values are at V_{CC} = 5 V, T_A = 25°C.
♦Not more than one output should be shorted at a time, and duration of the short-circuit should not exceed one second.

switching characteristics, V_{CC} = 5 V, T_A = 25°C

PARAMETER		TEST CONDITIONS		'LS240			'LS241, 'LS244			UNIT
				MIN	TYP	MAX	MIN	TYP	MAX	
t_{PLH}	Propagation delay time, low-to-high-level output	C_L = 45 pF, See Note 2	R_L = 667 Ω,		9	14		12	18	ns
t_{PHL}	Propagation delay time, high-to-low-level output				12	18		12	18	ns
t_{PZL}	Output enable time to low level				20	30		20	30	ns
t_{PZH}	Output enable time to high level				15	23		15	23	ns
t_{PLZ}	Output disable time from low level	C_L = 5 pF, See Note 2	R_L = 667 Ω,		15	25		15	25	ns
t_{PHZ}	Output disable time from high level				10	18		10	18	ns

NOTE 2: Load circuit and voltage waveforms are shown on page 3-11.

Figure 4.16 Electrical specifications for the 74LS240, 74LS241, and 74LS244. (Courtesy of Texas Instruments.)

Sec. 4.4   Bus Buffering Techniques

The lesson from this example should be clear. Not only is it advantageous to use a buffer for the transmitter, but also buffering each receiver input greatly increases the number of receivers that can be safely driven.

Tri-State Buffers with Hysteresis. Another advantage to the 74LS240 series of buffers is that each gate has a built-in *Schmitt* trigger. As mentioned previously, this is a circuit with a dual switching threshold—a property also called hysteresis. Figure 4.17 shows the effect that a Schmitt trigger can have on a waveform with excessive ringing due to reflections.

All of the buffers in Fig. 4.15 also have *tri-state* capability. This means that in addition to the two logic states, a third output state called the tri-state can be realized. This state is actually a high-impedance or open circuit. A model of a tri-state gate is shown in Fig. 4.18.

Tri-state buffers allow several transmitters to control the same bus line. By placing all but one transmitter in the tri-state mode (OFF), no interference occurs. This property will be taken advantage of in the type 3 bus.

Type 2 Bus. The type 2 bus has many transmitters but only one receiver. This type of bus cannot be realized with standard TTL gates. Figure 4.19 shows why. Everything is fine as long as both transmitters want the same level on the bus. But as shown in Fig. 4.19, when one output is high and the other is low, the bus line can become indeterminate. What is worse, an excessive current may flow from the logic 1 output to the logic 0 output, possibly damaging both devices. This is called *bus contention*.

One solution to this problem is to use tri-state gates for the transmitters. By enabling only one transmitter at a time, bus contention is eliminated. The problem with this technique is that extra logic will be required to ensure that only a single transmitter is enabled at a particular time.

Another solution is to use an *open collector* (or open drain) bus as shown in Fig. 4.20. In this scheme the transmitters have open-collector output stages. This means that they can pull the bus down to a logic 0—by saturating their output

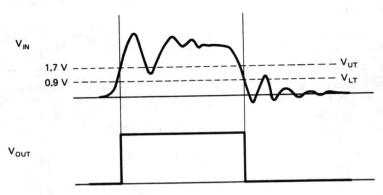

Figure 4.17 Effect of hysteresis on a waveform with excessive ringing. All 74LS240 series buffers have hysteresis.

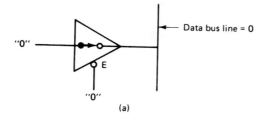

(a)

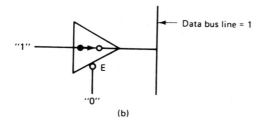

(b)

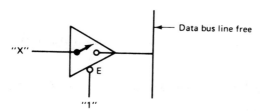

Figure 4.18 Tri-state gates are commonly used to gate data onto a data bus. In (a) and (b) the tri-state gate is enabled and the data bus line is connected to the input logic level. In (c) the tri-state gate is disabled and its output appears as an open circuit. The data bus line is now free to be controlled by another transmitter on the line. (From J. Uffenbeck, *Hardware Interfacing with the Apple II Plus,* Prentice-Hall, Inc., Englewood Cliffs, N.J., 1983.)

transistor—but they require an external pullup resistor to force a logic 1 onto the bus.

We can write the following logic equation for the WAIT signal in Fig. 4.20:

$$\overline{\text{WAIT}} = \overline{\text{TI}} + \overline{\text{T2}}$$

This connection is referred to as a "wired OR." An open-collector bus normally sits in the high state and is activated by any one transmitter pulling the bus line low. For this reason the receiver is normally a control function activated by a low

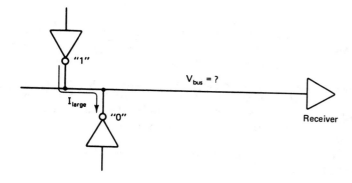

Figure 4.19 A type 2 bus has several transmitters and one receiver. If standard TTL gates are used, problems occur when one transmitter tries to drive the bus high and another tries to drive it low.

Sec. 4.4   Bus Buffering Techniques

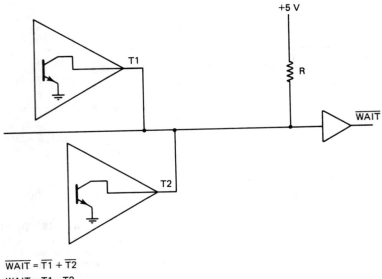

$$\overline{\text{WAIT}} = \overline{\text{T1}} + \overline{\text{T2}}$$
$$\text{WAIT} = \text{T1} \cdot \text{T2}$$

Figure 4.20 Type 2 bus realized with open-collector gates. This connection is called a "wired-OR."

logic level—that is, an active-low input. Examples are the Z-80 $\overline{\text{HALT}}$, $\overline{\text{WAIT}}$, $\overline{\text{INT}}$, $\overline{\text{NMI}}$, and $\overline{\text{BUSRQ}}$ inputs.

A disadvantage to this type of bus is that it is not possible to tell which transmitter pulled the bus line low. This may require the processor to read a status port—a technique called *polling*—to determine the activating device.

In many cases the CPU does not care what pulled the bus line low. For example, when the $\overline{\text{WAIT}}$ line is low, the microprocessor enters a wait or idling state. This is usually requested by a slow memory circuit that cannot respond quickly enough with data for the processor. In this case the processor waits until the memory is ready (when the $\overline{\text{WAIT}}$ line is released back high) and then continues. The specific memory device requesting the WAIT is unimportant.

The value of the pullup resistor used with an open-collector bus is not arbitrary. This is because loading of the transmitters must be considered.

Example 4.6

Assume that the open-collector bus in Fig. 4.20 has five transmitters each using a 7401 open-collector NAND gate. Assume that the receiver is the $\overline{\text{WAIT}}$ input of a Z-80 microprocessor. Calculate the value of the pullup resistor.

Solution. When all transmitters are OFF, the pullup resistor must supply a leakage current to each collector and the Z-80 input. According to the Z-80 dc characteristics data sheet in Appendix C.3, this is 10 μA for the $\overline{\text{WAIT}}$ input. The 7401 data sheet indicates 250 μA maximum leakage per collector. The total current is thus 5 × 250 μA + 10 μA = 1.26 mA.

The high level presented to the $\overline{\text{WAIT}}$ input must not be less than 2.4 V. Therefore, the pullup resistor must be less than

$$R \le \frac{2.6\ \text{V}}{1.26\ \text{mA}} = 2\ \text{k}\Omega$$

The general result is

$$R \le \frac{5\ \text{V} - 2.4\ \text{V}}{(n \times I_{\text{LKG}}) + I_{\text{IH}}}$$

The worst case for the bus line low occurs when only one output is low, as it must then sink all of the current from the pullup resistor. In this case the bus line must not exceed 0.4 V. The maximum sink current for the 7401 is 16 mA and I_{IL} for the Z-80 is 10 μA. The total sink current is thus 16.01 mA and the drop across R is 4.6 V. Thus the value of R must be greater than

$$R \ge \frac{4.6\ \text{V}}{16.01\ \text{mA}} = 287\ \Omega$$

The general result is

$$R \ge \frac{5\ \text{V} - 0.4\ \text{V}}{I_{\text{OL}} + I_{\text{IL}}}$$

For this particular bus, R must be greater than 287 Ω but less than 2 kΩ.

Type 3 Bus. The type 3 bus is a *bidirectional* bus in which there are many transmitters and many receivers. The most common example is the data bus of a microprocessor. Figure 4.21 illustrates data flow from an input device to the CPU. Note that all transmitters are shown as tri-state gates and all receivers are shown as latches (D-type flip-flops).

The neccessity for tri-state transmitters should be clear—only one transmitter can control the bus at a particular time. The need for receiver latches may not be

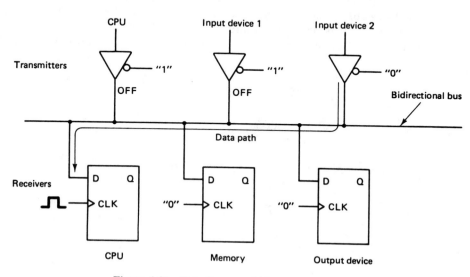

Figure 4.21 Data flow on a bidirectional bus line.

so clear. What we must remember is that data is placed on the bus for a very brief time. For example, when performing an input instruction the data bus holds the op-code for the IN instruction during the M1 machine cycle. During the next machine cycle it holds the port address. Finally, during the third machine cycle the input device is enabled and places the actual data onto the bus. Because each machine cycle is only four or five clock periods long, each receiver must quickly latch the data when its turn comes up.

And that is the main problem with the type 3 bus. How does a receiver (or transmitter) know when its turn is here? The answer to this question involves address bus and control bus *decoding* techniques, which are covered in detail in the next two chapters. But the concept is simple enough. If the control bus I/O read line is active, and if the address bus holds "our" port address, it is time to put the data on the bus (enable the tri-state transmitter).

On the other hand, if the I/O write line is active and the address bus holds "our" address, it is time to clock the flip-flop and store the present contents of the data bus. For this reason all three buses (control, address, and data) are involved in the transfer of data between a receiver and a transmitter on the data bus.

The CPU drive capabilities of its data bus lines are no better than the address lines. In addition, the routing of the data bus lines to other cards and peripherals will cause capacitive and reflective problems. Buffers will again be required.

The technique for buffering a data bus line is slightly more complex due to the bidirectional nature of the bus. Figure 4.22 shows the method. Two tri-state gates are required for each bus line with separate READ and WRITE enables. These enable signals must be derived from the control bus of the microprocessor.

Special bus transceivers are available for this application and Fig. 4.23 shows several common types. The 74LS245 is particularly well suited to this application. It contains eight tri-state pairs and has separate *enable* and *direction* controls.

A special circuit is available for the 8080 that combines the function of bidirectional bus buffer and status word decoder. This is the 8228 system controller shown in Fig. 4.24. It is designed to interface directly with the 8080 and uses the $\overline{\text{STSTB}}$ signal generated by the 8224 to latch the 8080 status word (see Sec. 2.2 for a

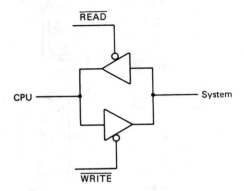

Figure 4.22 Bidirectional bus buffer. Only one gate is enabled at a particular time.

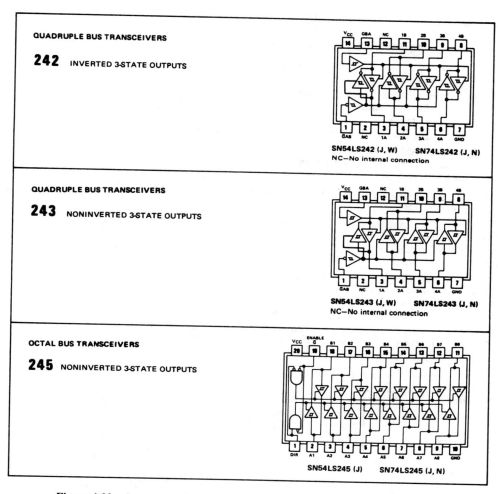

QUADRUPLE BUS TRANSCEIVERS

242 INVERTED 3-STATE OUTPUTS

SN54LS242 (J, W)   SN74LS242 (J, N)
NC—No internal connection

QUADRUPLE BUS TRANSCEIVERS

243 NONINVERTED 3-STATE OUTPUTS

SN54LS243 (J, W)   SN74LS243 (J, N)
NC—No internal connection

OCTAL BUS TRANSCEIVERS

245 NONINVERTED 3-STATE OUTPUTS

SN54LS245 (J)   SN74LS245 (J, N)

Figure 4.23 Common bus transceivers useful for buffering a microprocessor data bus. (Courtesy of Texas Instruments.)

discussion of the 8080 status word). Note that all of the common control bus signals are generated directly by the 8228.

The 8228 is an important support device for 8080-based microprocessor designs. It provides full data bus buffering, generates all control bus signals, and supports the 8080's vectored interrupt technique by allowing multiple-byte restart instructions or automatic insertion of an RST 7 instruction (details are provided in Chap. 6).

The 8228 has an I_{OH} of 1 mA and an I_{OL} of 10 mA compared to the 74LS245's 3 mA and 12 mA, respectively. Additional buffering of the 8228 data bus may therefore be required.

Schottky Bipolar **8228**

SYSTEM CONTROLLER AND BUS DRIVER
FOR 8080A CPU

- **Single Chip System Control for MCS-80 Systems**
- **Built-in Bi-Directional Bus Driver for Data Bus Isolation**
- **Allows the use of Multiple Byte Instructions (e.g. CALL) for Interrupt Acknowledge**
- **User Selected Single Level Interrupt Vector (RST 7)**
- **28 Pin Dual In-Line Package**
- **Reduces System Package Count**

The 8228 is a single chip system controller and bus driver for MCS-80. It generates all signals required to directly interface MCS-80 family RAM, ROM, and I/O components.

A bi-directional bus driver is included to provide high system TTL fan-out. It also provides isolation of the 8080 data bus from memory and I/O. This allows for the optimization of control signals, enabling the systems deisgner to use slower memory and I/O. The isolation of the bus driver also provides for enhanced system noise immunity.

A user selected single level interrupt vector (RST 7) is provided to simplify real time, interrupt driven, small system requirements. The 8228 also generates the correct control signals to allow the use of multiple byte instructions (e.g., CALL) in response to an INTERRUPT ACKNOWLEDGE by the 8080A. This feature permits large, interrupt driven systems to have an unlimited number of interrupt levels.

The 8228 is designed to support a wide variety of system bus structures and also reduce system package count for cost effective, reliable, design of the MCS-80 systems.

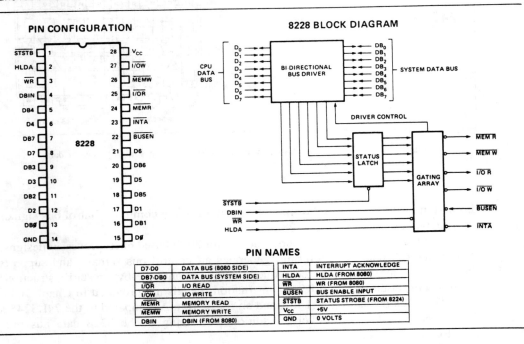

Figure 4.24 The 8228 system controller. This chip includes a bidirectional bus buffer and decoding logic to generate the 8080 control bus signals. (Courtesy of Intel Corporation.)

TOWARD MORE READABLE LOGIC DIAGRAMS

Have you ever noticed that most digital electronics textbooks seem to favor logic 1s over logic 0s? For example, a two-input AND gate is drawn as

and has the word interpretation: "*Output C will be high whenever inputs A AND B are high.*" But couldn't we also say: "*Output C will be low whenever inputs A OR B are low*"? This gate would have the symbol

In effect, this "new" gate is an OR gate that works on logic 0s instead of logic 1s. Sometimes this type of gate is called a *negative logic* OR gate. Unfortunately, the term "negative logic" scares a lot of folks. No one but the military would use negative logic!

But let's backtrack a moment. What's wrong with an OR gate that operates on 0s? I can think of many cases where the digital signal is asserted (applied or turned on) with a logic 0. The enable input on most buffers requires a 0. The asynchronous set and reset inputs of flip-flops are always active low (activated by a logic 0). Indeed, all of the control bus signals output by the microprocessor are active low.

So maybe there is some merit to this negative logic OR gate. Let's consider an example. As we have seen, the Z-80 control bus signals are similar but not identical to the 8080 control bus signals. If we wish to generate the 8080 $\overline{\text{IOR}}$ signal, we must note that the Z-80 indicates an I/O operation by asserting $\overline{\text{IORQ}}$. A read operation is indicated by $\overline{\text{RD}} = 0$.

Using conventional logic we would conclude that $\overline{\text{IOR}}$ can be generated by inverting $\overline{\text{IORQ}}$ and $\overline{\text{RD}}$, ANDing the two terms, and inverting the result.

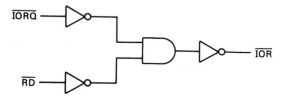

But why not let the word statement of the problem define the circuit? "*Whenever $\overline{\text{IORQ}}$ is low AND $\overline{\text{RD}}$ is low, generate a signal $\overline{\text{IOR}}$ that is low.*" The circuit is

You may not recognize this gate at first, but it is just an OR gate. Now we could have made up a truth table for this problem and recognized the OR function, but letting the problem speak for itself is much simpler.

In either case, recognizing the OR function, why not draw the OR symbol? This is an important point. If we were to use the OR gate symbol, the word interpretation would become: *"Whenever $\overline{IORQ}$ is high OR $\overline{RD}$ is high, output $\overline{IOR}$ should be high."* Although this is correct, it does not convey the designer's intent.

The key is to remember that there are really only two logic functions: AND and OR. If you need to AND two signals that are active low, draw the AND symbol with inversion circles on each input. If the output of this gate should also be active low, draw a circle on the output. If the output should be active high, omit the circle.

Forget about NAND and NOR gates. Let the problem define the logic symbol. Later you can go back and (using De Morgan's theorem if necessary) determine the part number of the symbol.

For example, the negative input positive output AND gate

is actually a NOR gate. This can be seen by applying De Morgan's theorem:

$$C = \overline{A} \cdot \overline{B} = \overline{A + B}$$

A convenient "trick" that makes this conversion easy to remember is to visualize the opposite gate type (ANDs become ORs and ORs become ANDs) with all inputs and outputs inverted.

Throughout this book you will find a "mixed logic" symbology. Positive and negative logic are intermixed—and not because I am trying to make the diagrams more confusing; just the opposite. Learn to "read" the word description of each logic function. Your logic diagrams will become clearer and fewer gates will be required.

4.5 CPU MODULES FOR THE 8080, 8085, AND Z-80

As you read this section, look for the answer to this Key Concept question:

4.5.1. Explain why the CPU module for the 8080, 8085, and Z-80 requires more than the CPU chip alone.

Basic CPU modules for the 8080, 8085, and Z-80 microprocessors were presented in Chap. 2. These were conceptual circuits that did not take into account real-world problems such as bus loading.

The 8080 CPU Module. As discussed in Chap. 2, the 8080 is really a three-chip microprocessor. This can be seen in Fig. 4.25. The 8224 clock generator is used to generate the two-phase clock signals and also to synchronize the WAIT and system reset requests. It also generates the status strobe signal required by the 8228.

The 8228 is used to buffer the system data bus and to generate the five control bus signals. A new control signal, $\overline{INTA}$—interrupt acknowledge—has been included

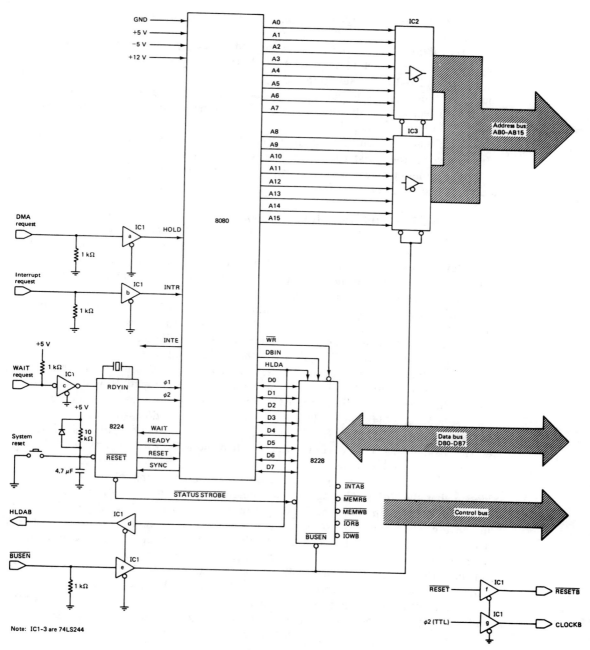

Figure 4.25 8080 CPU module.

in the control bus. This signal is important for interrupt-driven I/O and is discussed in Chap. 6.

The address bus is buffered by two 74LS244s. Note that the signal names have a "B" appended to indicate their buffered status. This is important. The signal A0 and AB0 are usually the same—but not always (for example, with direct memory access, A0 is tri-stated but AB0 is output by the direct memory access controller). Throughout this book, a signal name with the letter B appended represents a *buffered* version of that signal.

Note that all three buses can be tri-stated by driving the $\overline{\text{BUSEN}}$ input high. This allows another master to control the system buses.

The remaining signals—DMA request, interrupt request, INTE, and HLDAB—are explained in Chap. 6.

The 8085 CPU Module.   Unlike the 8080, no special support devices are required for the 8085. However, examining the CPU module diagram in Fig. 4.26 reveals a considerable number of TTL devices. There are two reasons for this. Because of the multiplexed address and data bus lines (AD0–AD7), a latch is required to separate the two buses. This is the function of IC6, a 74LS373 8-bit latch. It contains eight D flip-flops with a common active-high enable input (G).

AD0–AD7 carry the low-order address when the ALE (address latch enable) signal is high. When ALE switches low the 74LS373 stores this address.

The second reason for the complexity of the CPU module is the need to decode the control bus signals. This is done by IC8 and inverter IC5b. In Chap. 7 we will see that Intel supplies special memory and I/O devices that interface directly with the 8085's multiplexed address/data bus and are compatible with its control bus. If these devices are used, the CPU module can be simplified considerably.

Again 74LS244s are used to buffer the control and address buses. A 74LS245 is used to buffer the data bus. Note that the direction control of this device is derived from the $\overline{\text{RD}}$ control signal. Because IC8 and IC7 are 74LS parts, no buffering is required on the $\overline{\text{RD}}$ signal.

A $\overline{\text{BUSEN}}$ input is again provided to allow tri-stating of the three buses. Notice that the 74LS373 latch has the unique capability of tri-stating its outputs when $\overline{\text{OE}}$ is high. In addition, the output drive capability is identical to a 74LS244 in the low state and 2.6 mA (versus 3 mA for the 74LS244) in the high state. Thus the 74LS373 is ideally suited to this application. It latches the low-order address, allows its outputs to be tri-stated for direct memory access, and provides full buffering for AB0 through AB7. (*Note*:   The 8212 latch shown in Fig. 2.12 can also be used for this purpose but it has only 1 mA of high-level drive capability.)

Five active-high input interrupt requests are provided, labeled INTR, TRAP, and RST 5.5–7.5. The jumper connections allow these inputs to be grounded when not used. DMA request and HLDAB are discussed in Chap. 6.

The Z-80 CPU Module.   The Z-80 CPU module is presented in Fig. 4.27. Again no special support devices are required, although separate ICs are required to generate the clock signal and interface the system reset signal.

IC8 and 9 are used to generate an 8080-like control bus. If Zilog peripherals

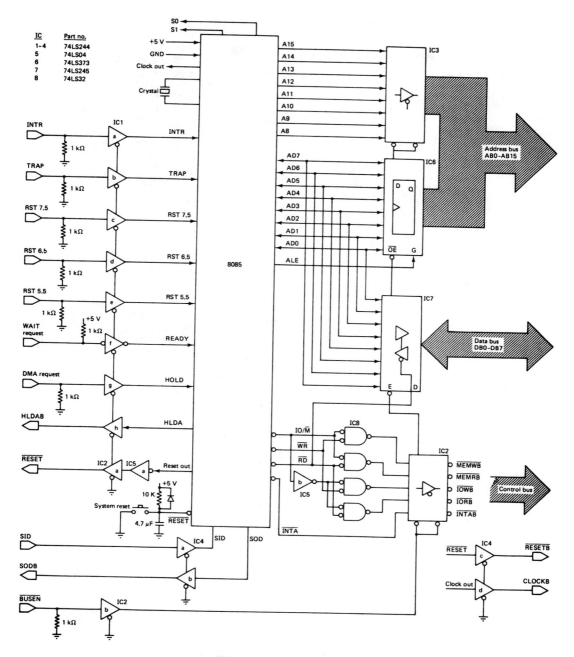

Figure 4.26 8085 CPU module.

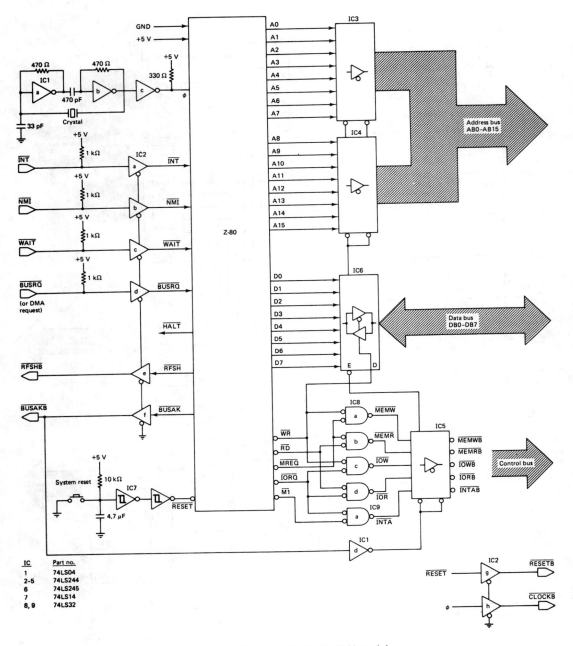

Figure 4.27 Z-80 CPU module.

are used, this will not be necessary. The $\overline{INTA}$ signal is not generated directly by the Z-80 but can be detected as a special M1 cycle during which $\overline{IORQ}$ is active. IC9a is used to decode this signal.

74LS244 and 74LS245 buffers are again used to buffer the address, control, and data buses. The $\overline{BUSEN}$ input can again be used to gain control of the system buses.

Two interrupt requests are provided, labeled $\overline{INT}$ and $\overline{NMI}$. These are active-low inputs and can be driven by open-collector gates. These signals and $\overline{BUSAKB}$ are discussed in Chap. 6.

Summary. The CPU module forms the "brain" of a microcomputer system. This module originates the system timing and controls all data transfers. When designing this module, expandability must be taken into account. Will the system be able to drive all of the RAM modules? Will it support direct memory access and interrupt-driven I/O?

Taking all of these factors into account, the CPU module becomes considerably more complex than first envisioned in Chap. 2. So, is the microprocessor a single-chip computer? Not really. At least not for the 8080, the 8085, or the Z-80 microprocessors.

4.6 SINGLE-STEPPING THE MICROPROCESSOR

As you read this section, look for the asnwers to these Key Concept questions:

4.6.1. When troubleshooting microprocessor hardware, which is more desirable, a circuit that single-steps instructions or machine cycles?

4.6.2. Machine cycle single-step circuits work by forcing the CPU into a _____ state in which valid data is held on all three buses.

The ability to *single-step* the microprocessor has several advantages. When developing an assembly language program a software single-step routine—like the TRACE command in the DDT utility of CP/M—can be invaluable. With it the contents of the various CPU registers and flags can be examined and changed at will. It becomes fairly simple to trace your program and find the spot where it goes astray.

A software single-stepper will not be of any use in debugging microcomputer hardware, however. Suppose that we have interfaced a digital-to-analog converter (DAC) to a Z-80 microcomputer but find that it does not work. The circuit might look something like Fig. 4.28.

Let's assume that a hardware single-stepper is available and attempt to debug this circuit. First we will need a simple test program (be sure to use a *simple* test program; we want to debug hardware, not software).

A suitable program might be

```
LOOP    LD      A,0      ;PUT A TEST PATTERN IN REGISTER A
        OUT     (3F),A   ;OUTPUT TO PORT 3F
        JP      LOOP     ;LOOP
```

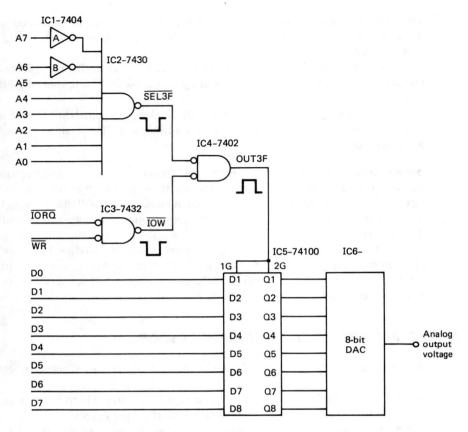

Figure 4.28 Digital-to-analog converter (DAC) interfaced to a Z-80 microprocessor.

Start the program running and then press the single-step switch. The program will stop in a *WAIT* state with all three buses holding valid data. Pushing the STEP key should cause the computer to execute one machine cycle. Now using a logic probe, we can examine each of the buses. What we are looking for is the M3 cycle of the OUT instruction. You can quickly find this cycle by monitoring the $\overline{\text{IORQ}}$ or $\overline{\text{WR}}$ control bus signals. When either of these lines goes low, you have found the M3 cycle. (Do you know why?).

Now checking the low-order address bus, the binary code 00111111 should be observed. This is the port address (3FH). All inputs to IC2 should be high and its output low. Because $\overline{\text{IORQ}}$ and $\overline{\text{WR}}$ are both low, the output of IC3 should also be low. Testing IC4 you should find both of its inputs low and its output high.

The IC4 output—labeled OUT3F—should pulse high once for each loop through the program. This pulse is used to clock the latch (IC5) which is used to store the data bus contents. Examining the data bus, you should see 00000000 and a similar result at the Q1 through Q8 outputs of the latch. This is the data output by the

OUT instruction. You can test the latch for different values of data by changing the test pattern in the LD instruction.

I think you can appreciate the power of the hardware single-stepper. By freezing the data on the microprocessor buses, it becomes a simple matter to test the hardware and locate any faults.

You might think that a good way to single-step a microprocessor would be to slow down the clock signal or manually pulse the clock input. In this way individual clock periods could be monitored. Unfortunately, this won't work. The reason is that internally the microprocessor uses *dynamic* logic. This is a circuit design technique that minimizes the number of circuit components by using the capacitive gate inputs of MOS transistors as storage elements. Because this charge will leak away in a few milliseconds, each gate must be repeatedly recharged. For this reason you will note that every microprocessor has a *minimum* clock frequency in addition to its maximum frequency specification.

Most single-step circuits utilize the built-in *WAIT* state capability of the micro-processor. In the WAIT state the microprocessor "idles," holding valid addresses, control signals, and data on its buses (this is true for most microprocessor chips but not all—to be sure, check the technical manuals for the chip that you are using).

Single-Stepping the 8080.   Figure 2.7 illustrates basic 8080 instruction-cycle timing. After the T1 state, in which the processor has output a valid memory or I/O address and setup its control signals, the READY input line is sampled. If this input is found low, a WAIT state is entered and identified by the WAIT output going high. The 8080 remains in this state sampling the READY input during each successive clock cycle. When READY is again found high, the instruction cycle continues with the T3 state.

The READY input is intended for interfacing slow memory devices to the 8080. Normally, the processor gives the memory three clock periods (until state T3) to place their data on the bus. This is shown in Fig. 2.7. If this is not enough time, a WAIT-state generator can be built to force a number of WAIT states to occur before state T3. It is important to note that the processor does not "automatically" insert these WAIT states—a circuit must be designed to request them.

An 8080 single-step circuit based on the WAIT state principle is shown in Fig. 4.29. The operation of this circuit is as follows.

1. With switch S1 in the RUN position, the output of IC1C will be high. As shown in Fig. 4.4, the RDYIN input of the 8224 is synchronized to the φ2 clock and applied to the 8080 READY input. Because RDYIN is high, the processor is in the RUN mode.

2. In the RUN mode the WAIT output is low and this asynchronously sets the D flip-flop IC2.

3. When S1 is switched to the single-step position, the output of IC1C goes low, forcing the READY input of the 8080 low on the next rising edge of the φ2 clock. The 8080 will enter the WAIT mode during the next T2 clock cycle and the three buses will become available for testing.

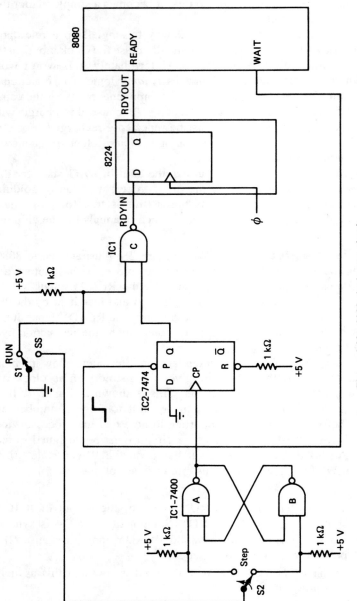

Figure 4.29 8080 single-step circuit.

4. To advance the program one machine cycle, the step switch can be pushed. This clocks IC2, forcing its Q output low, relinquishing the WAIT request. The processor again begins running—forcing WAIT low and setting IC2. Of course, this pulls the RDYIN line of the 8224 low and the 8080 will again enter the WAIT mode when the next T2 machine cycle occurs.

Single-Stepping the 8085.   WAIT-state timing for the 8085 is the same as for the 8080 and can be seen in Fig. 2.11. The main difference between the two processors is that no WAIT signal is available from the 8085. This turns out to not be a problem as the *ALE* signal (address latch enable) can be used in its place.

Figure 4.30 is the 8085 single-stepping circuit. Its operation is as follows.

1. With switch S1 in the run mode, the READY line of the 8085 is held high and the processor runs normally.
2. Because each machine cycle begins with an ALE pulse, the Q output of IC2 will be high.
3. Moving S1 to the single-step position causes the IC1C output to go low, and the 8085 will enter the WAIT mode after T2 of the next machine cycle.
4. Single-stepping by one machine cycle is accomplished by pushing S2. This clocks IC2 forcing its Q output low, relinquishing the WAIT request. The 8085 now runs until the next ALE pulse—one machine cycle later—and then reenters the WAIT mode.

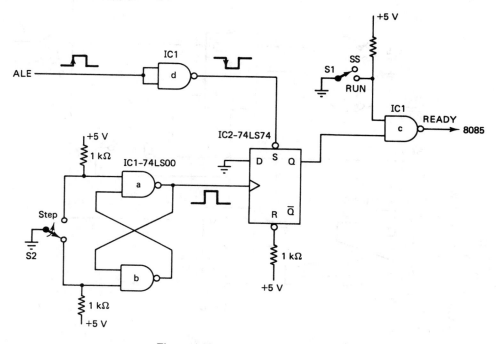

Figure 4.30   8085 single-step circuit.

Single-Stepping the Z-80. WAIT-state timing for the Z-80 is similar to the 8080 and 8085 and is shown in Fig. 2.14 for an op-code fetch machine cycle. Zilog prefers to call the READY input $\overline{\text{WAIT}}$, and this line is sampled with the falling edge of φ during the T2 clock period of each machine cycle. If $\overline{\text{WAIT}}$ is found low, the processor enters a WAIT state with valid addresses, control signals, and data on its buses. This WAIT state will persist indefinitely until the $\overline{\text{WAIT}}$ input is found high on the falling edge of φ. At this time program execution continues normally with the T3 state of the current machine cycle.

A single-step circuit for the Z-80 is shown in Fig. 4.31. The operation of this circuit is as follows.

1. When power is first applied, or when the reset switch (not shown) is pushed, IC2A is reset and IC2B is set.
2. With switch S1 in the RUN position, any I/O or memory request will set flip-flop IC2A and cause the $\overline{\text{WAIT}}$ line to go high. The processor will run normally.
3. When S1 is switched to the single-step position, any I/O or memory request will reset IC2A and cause $\overline{\text{WAIT}}$ to go low. This will cause the Z-80 to enter a WAIT state as soon as T2 of the next machine cycle occurs.
4. Pushing the STEP switch now resets IC2B, sets IC2A, and forces $\overline{\text{WAIT}}$ high. The $\overline{\text{Q}}$ output of IC2A also sets IC2B and this allows the next I/O or

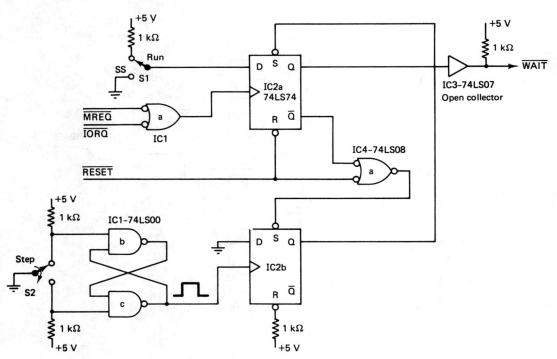

Figure 4.31 Z-80 single-step circuit.

memory request to again clock the $\overline{\text{WAIT}}$ line low. The effect is to execute one machine cycle each time the STEP switch is pushed.

4.7 A POWER-ON-JUMP CIRCUIT FOR THE Z-80

As you read this section, look for the answer to this Key Concept question:

4.7.1. What is the purpose of a jump-on-reset circuit?

As discussed in Sec. 4.2, resetting the 8080, 8085, or Z-80 microprocessors causes the program counter to be loaded with 0000. This generally means that a ROM chip must be mapped to page 0 in order to "boot up" the system. However, having a ROM in this location may be incompatible with some operating systems.

For example, *CP/M* uses page 0 for storing system variables. All three processors use locations on page 0 for storing *interrupt vectors* (see Chap. 6 for a discussion of interrupts). Commercial software is often written to begin in location 0.

What is needed is a *jump-on-reset* circuit that forces the processor to some location other than 0 when a reset occurs. Figure 4.32 is such a circuit for the Z-80. It basically "tricks" the microprocessor into reading the op-code for a jump instruction whenever the reset line is pulled low.

Because a jump instruction is three bytes long, three separate data bytes will have to be gated onto the Z-80 data bus. The circuit in Fig. 4.32 uses a three-stage shift register made up of three edge-triggered D-type flip-flops. The truth table in Fig. 4.32 indicates the action taken as the shift register sequences from 000 to 111.

The 74LS257 is a 4-bit word multiplexer routing word A or word B to its output dependent on the select (S) input. The outputs of the 74LS257 are tri-stated and active only when the enable ($\overline{\text{E}}$) input is low. This is necessary in order to drive the bus without conflicts.

The operation of the circuit is as follows.

1. When the $\overline{\text{RESET}}$ line is driven low, the shift register is reset to 000, causing the 74LS257 select input to be low (select word A).
2. When $\overline{\text{RESET}}$ returns high, the Z-80 begins an instruction fetch cycle and $\overline{\text{RD}}$ goes low. This enables the tri-state outputs of the 74LS257 through IC3C. The A inputs of the two multiplexers are hard-wired to 11000011 or C3H (the op-code for a JP instruction).
3. The multiplexer enable pulse also clocks the shift register to its next state, 100. This causes IC5 to select word B and the next memory read cycle causes the byte 00000000 to be gated onto the data bus. This will be interpreted as the low-order jump address.
4. Reading the low-order address also advances the shift register to the 110 state. Again word B is selected and the byte 11110000 (F0) is gated onto the data bus. This is the high-order jump address.

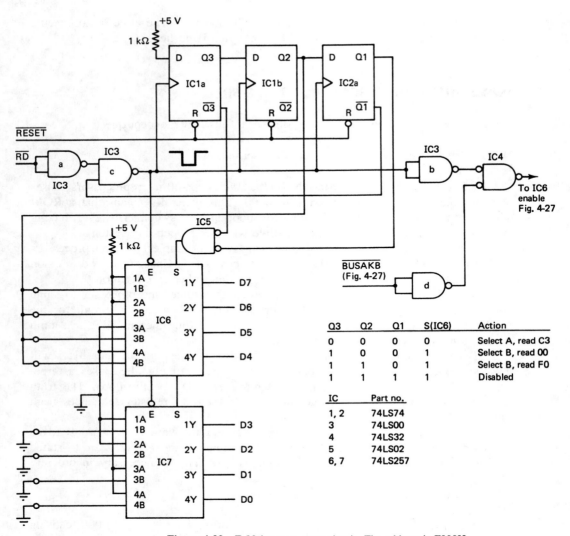

Figure 4.32 Z-80 jump-on-reset circuit. The address is F000H.

5. Reading the high-order address advances the shift register to the 111 state. The Q output of IC2A is now permanently high and the tri-state outputs of IC6 and 7 are permanently disabled. The circuit effectively "disappears." Program execution begins at F000H.

The circuit in Fig. 4.32 is designed to interface directly with the Z-80 data bus. Referring to Fig. 4.27, these are the lines labeled D0 through D7 (not DB0–DB7). The enable input (pin 19) of the 74LS245 transceivers must be disconnected from IC1D and connected to the output of IC4. This will turn off the external data bus when the jump-on-reset circuit is active.

CHAPTER SUMMARY

1. The 8080 requires a two-phase, nonoverlapping, non-TTL-compatible clock signal. It is best generated with the 8224 clock driver circuit and a crystal nine times the system operating frequency.

2. The 8085 incorporates an on-board clock oscillator circuit and to be operational requires only an external crystal at twice the system frequency.

3. The Z-80 requires an external 0 V to 5 V clock signal. It is easily built with three 74LS04 inverters, a crystal for the desired operating frequency, and a pullup resistor.

4. Because the microprocessor powers-on in a random state, a reset circuit is required to force the program counter to a known location (usually 0000).

5. There are three types of buses in a microprocessor system. These are buses with one transmitter and many receivers, one receiver and many transmitters, or a bidirectional bus with many transmitters and receivers.

6. Noise immunity is calculated as $V_{OH} - V_{IH}$ for the logic 1 level and as $V_{IL} - V_{OL}$ for the logic 0 level. Typical values are 0.4 V for TTL and 1.0 V for CMOS.

7. Bus buffers are required whenever the receiver loading exceeds the drive capability of the transmitters or when driving bus lines off card through connectors.

8. Open-collector gates are used for CPU control functions. In this application the bus line is normally held high with a pullup resistor and pulled low to activate the control function.

9. Tri-state buffers allow many transmitters to use the same bus. Special logic must be used to ensure that only one transmitter is driving the bus at a particular time.

10. Hardware single-step circuits are useful for debugging microprocessor hardware because they "freeze" the system buses and allow static testing of the logic signals.

11. A jump-on-reset circuit allows the microprocessor to jump to any location in memory upon reset. This allows read/write memory on page 0 for processors that normally reset to location 0.

LAB PROJECTS

4.1. Study the schematic diagram of the microcomputer you are using to support this text/course. Locate the following and redraw on a separate sheet of paper:
   (a) clock generator (note crystal frequency)
   (b) reset circuit (look for power-on-reset circuit)
   (c) address buffers (look for enable signal)
   (d) bidirectional data bus buffers (look for enable and direction control signals)

(e) control bus buffers (look for enable signal)

(f) single-step circuit

4.2. Use an oscilloscope to observe and measure the system clock signal. Compare with your predictions (Lab 4.1).

4.3. Set up an open-collector bus circuit like that shown in Fig. 4.33. Calculate a value for the pullup resistor.

(a) What is the normal (inactive) state of the bus?

(b) Make up a truth table in terms of SW1–SW3 and OUT.

(c) What equivalent logic function does the circuit perform?

4.4. Set up a bidirectional data bus circuit like that shown in Fig. 4.21. Use one 74LS244 for the transmitter and two 74LS74s for the receivers.

(a) With all transmitters disabled what is the logic level on the bus?

(b) Enable one of the transmitters. Note that its data input now controls the bus.

(b) Send data from one transmitter to one receiver (set the data, enable the transmitter, then clock the flip-flop of the receiver).

(d) Why don't the other receivers also store this data?

(e) What happens if two transmitters simultaneously try to control the bus (don't try it!)? What prevents this from happening in a practical computer system?

4.5. If your computer does not have a single-step circuit, try building and interfacing one of those presented in this chapter. You may want to make this a permanent addition to your computer.

4.6. Try running the single-step test program presented in Sec. 4.6. 8080/85 mnemonics are:

```
LOOP    MVI   A,0      ;test pattern
        OUT   3FH      ;any port will do
        JMP   LOOP     ;cycle forever
```

With the program running

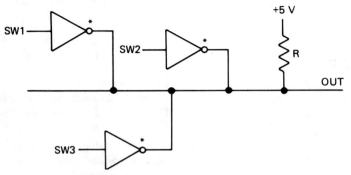

* Open collector outputs (7405, 7406, 7416, 7417, etc.)

Figure 4.33   Circuit for Lab 4.3.

(a) observe the $\overline{\text{IOW}}$, IO/$\overline{\text{M}}$, or $\overline{\text{IORQ}}$ line with a logic probe. It should be pulsing.

(b) switch to single-step mode. Repeatedly press the STEP switch until the I/O write machine cycle has been found.

(c) measure the contents of the data bus. You should see 00.

(d) measure the I/O address on address lines A7–A0. You should see 3FH.

(e) repeat (c) and (d) using a different test pattern and port address.

QUESTIONS AND PROBLEMS

Section 1.1

4.1. If the inverter and NAND gate in Fig. 4.1 have equal propagation delays, will the false output still occur?

4.2. If $t_{PD} = 0.5$ μs, what is the maximum clock frequency for the synchronous circuit in Fig. 4.2?

4.3. Refer to Appendix A and B and determine the minimum number of T states for any one 8080, 8085, or Z-80 instruction. Refer to Fig. 4.3 and describe the CPU activity for each state.

4.4. Assume you are designing CPU modules for the 8080, 8085, and Z-80. If the clock speed is to be 3 MHz, what crystal frequency should you select for each processor? Of the three CPU chips, which do you expect will require the most supply current?

Section 4.2

4.5. Why does a computer require a RESET input?

*4.6. Assume the capacitor in Fig. 4.8 becomes shorted. What would the *symptom* of this problem be?

4.7. What is the purpose of the Schmitt trigger buffers in the Z-80 reset circuit in Fig. 4.8?

Section 4.3

4.8. The 74LS00 can source 400 μA in the high state and sink 8 mA in the low state. Based on this information, how many standard TTL loads ($I_{IH} = 40$ μA and $I_{OL} = 1.6$ mA) can this chip drive?

4.9. Calculate the worst-case noise immunity for the interface described in Prob. 4.8.

4.10. What special considerations must be made when interfacing a TTL transmitter with several CMOS receivers?

4.11. What causes ''ringing'' on a bus line? How can its effect be minimized?

Section 4.4

4.12. If one unit load (1 UL) equals 40 μA of source current in the high state and 1.6 mA of sink current in the low state, what is the output drive capability

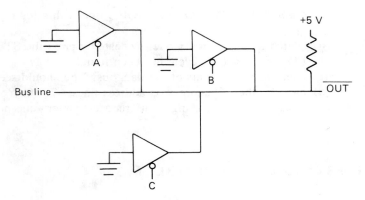

Figure 4.34 Circuit for Prob. 4.13.

of the 74LS244 expressed in unit loads (assume V_{OH} = 2.4 V and V_{OL} = 0.5 V)?

4.13. The circuit in Fig. 4.34 uses tri-state transmitters connected to a common bus line. Under what conditions will the bus line be low? Write the logic equation for $\overline{OUT}$ in terms of inputs A, B, and C.

4.14. Standard TTL provides 0.4 V of noise immunity in the high and low states. This can be improved by using a Schmitt trigger buffer with hysteresis such as the 74LS244. Assuming a high-level switching threshold of 1.7 V and a low-level threshold of 0.9 V, calculate the noise immunity for a TTL gate buffered with a 74LS244.

4.15. Assume the noisy ringing signal shown in Fig. 4.35 is applied to the 74LS244 buffer described in Prob. 4.14. Sketch the output waveform produced by this gate.

*4.16. What, if anything, is wrong with the microprocessor bus interface shown in Fig. 4.36?

4.17. Redesign the bus interface in Fig. 4.36 using 7405 open-collector gates. Calculate the value of the pullup resistor required.

4.18. Why do receivers on the data bus need to be *latches*, but not on the address bus?

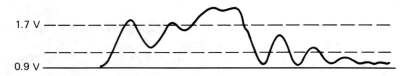

Figure 4.35 Waveform for Prob. 4.15.

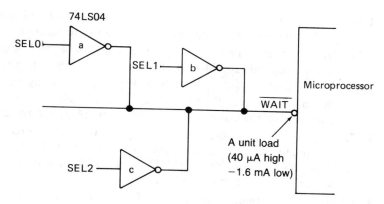

Figure 4.36 Circuit for Probs. 4.16–17.

4.19. Study the 74LS245 logic diagram in Fig. 4.23 and then complete the function table below.

DIR	ENABLE (G)	Description
0	0	B = input, A = output
0	1	
1	0	
1	1	

Section 4.5

4.20. Refer to the 8080 CPU module in Fig. 4.25. Which of the following is not a function of the 8228?
  (a) Bidirectional data bus buffer
  (b) Clock generator
  (c) Control bus decoder/buffer

4.21. Refer to the 8085 CPU module in Fig. 4.26. (a) Which chip decodes the multiplexed address/data bus? (b) What is the function of IC7? (c) Under what conditions will the $\overline{\text{MEMWB}}$ output be low?

4.22. Refer to the Z-80 CPU module in Fig. 4.27. (a) What is the purpose of IC1a–c? (b) What type of logic gate is IC8? (c) Under what conditions will output $\overline{\text{IORB}}$ be low?

Section 4.6

*4.23. If the output of IC2 in Fig. 4.28 is shorted to a logic 0, the circuit will still appear to work. What change to the test program will be required to detect this fault? How would you locate the bad IC?

*4.24. If $\overline{WR}$ is replaced by $\overline{RD}$ in Fig. 4.28, the circuit will not work. Describe the troubleshooting procedure you would use to locate this problem.

4.25. True or false: The single-step circuits in Figs. 4.29–31 cause the microprocessor to operate in "slow motion" one clock cycle at a time.

4.26. In the 8080 single-step circuit in Fig. 4.29, pushing the STEP switch in the SS mode forces RDYIN _____ causing the CPU to execute one machine cycle and the WAIT output to momentarily go _____ .

4.27. In the 8085 single-step circuit in Fig. 4.30, the Q output of the flip-flop is continually _____ by the rising edge of ALE. With the mode switch in the SS position, the READY input will be forced _____ at the beginning of each machine cycle.

4.28. In the Z-80 single-step circuit in Fig. 4.31 when S1 is in the SS position, the Q output of IC2a is continually _____ at the beginning of each memory or I/O machine cycle. Pushing the STEP switch momentarily _____ IC2a allowing the CPU to run one machine cycle.

4.29. Describe the function of the circuit in Fig. 4.37. (*Hint*: Consider the charging and discharging time constant paths.)

4.30. Modify the Z-80 single-step circuit so that it single-steps *instructions* instead of machine cycles.

*4.31. Assume the Q output of IC2 in the 8085 single-step circuit in Fig. 4.30 is stuck low. What would the symptom of this problem be? How would you troubleshoot this problem?

*4.32. Assume the Q output of IC2b in the Z-80 single-step circuit in Fig. 4.31 is stuck high. What would the symptom of this problem be? How would you troubleshoot this problem?

Section 4.7

4.33. In Fig. 4.32, what is the purpose of IC4?

4.34. Add a switch to the Z-80 jump-on-reset circuit in Fig. 4.32 so that in one position a normal reset to location 0000 occurs, and in the other, a jump to the hard-wired address occurs.

4.35. Modify the jump-on-reset circuit in Fig. 4.32 so that a jump to location D800H is performed upon reset.

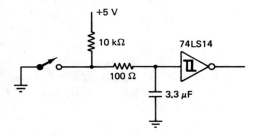

Figure 4.37 Circuit for Prob. 4.29.

KEY CONCEPT ANSWERS

4.1.1. faster

4.1.2. 8085

4.2.1. 0000

4.2.2. power-on-reset

4.3.1. noise immunity

4.3.2. decrease, increase

4.4.1. Buffered outputs have greater output current capabilities. Buffered inputs require minimal current from the driver.

4.4.2. open-collector

4.4.3. open circuit

4.5.1. A clock generator and reset circuit are required, as well as address, data, and control bus buffers.

4.6.1. A machine cycle single-stepper is most useful as it allows the data on the buses to be traced.

4.6.2. WAIT

4.7.1. Force the CPU to begin program execution at an address other than 0000 (perhaps because this address is used to store program data).

5

Building the Microcomputer, Part 2: Adding Memory

The concept of a memory unit is essential to the stored program computer. It is from this unit that the CPU fetches instructions directing it in some task. But within a particular computer system there may be several types of memories each with its own ranking or *hierarchy*.

Most important is the *main* or *prime* memory, which interfaces directly with the CPU over the system three-bus architecture. But there is also *secondary* memory for mass storage of application programs and data files. Still, a third type of memory, called *archival storage*, may be present in some systems for backup purposes.

The type and kind of memory used in a particular microcomputer system depends on the intended application for that system. Microcontrollers often store all of their program instructions in main memory and require no secondary storage. On the other hand, a microcomputer intended for business applications will require an extensive library of software stored on secondary storage devices such as floppy disks. In this chapter we are concerned only with main memory, leaving the topic of secondary storage to Chap. 10.

But even narrowing the discussion to main memory presents us with a myriad of memory technologies. There is, of course, *RAM* and *ROM*—random access and read-only memory—but there is also *PROM*, *EPROM*, E^2PROM, and *iRAM*—to name a few. And even RAM comes in two "flavors": *static* and *dynamic*. So nothing is simple anymore!

We will begin by letting the performance characteristics of memory define a hierarchy of memory systems. Next we will turn to the microprocessor to see that it defines the timing for all main memory. And we cannot change it. Our next task thus becomes one of choosing memory devices that will be compatible with the system needs and timing.

Our end goal is the design of a main memory module compatible with the CPU modules designed in Chap. 4. This is accomplished in Secs. 5.5 and 5.6.

5.1 MEMORY HIERARCHIES

As you read this section, look for the answers to these Key Concept questions:

5.1.1. Memory that interfaces directly to the address, control, and data bus of the microprocessor is called _____ memory.

5.1.2. List two examples of common secondary storage devices.

5.1.3. A tape drive is an example of an _____ storage device.

The fetch-and-execute principle mandates a main memory that interfaces with the microprocessor using the data, address, and control buses. The two qualifications for main memory are:

1. It must be able to communicate with the processor at the system frequency. This means that a 6-MHz processor will require faster memory devices than will a 1-MHz processor.

2. Each cell in the memory must be randomly accessible via its own unique address.

Main memory is *executable* memory. It must be capable of keeping up with the microprocessor. This means supplying data "instantly" when its address appears on the bus and allowing random storage of variables when needed.

Today main memory is built almost exclusively with semiconductor technology. In fact, one can measure the state of the art in semiconductor processing by observing the storage capacities of currently available memory parts. Table 5.1 highlights the developments to date.

But most computer systems will require more than main memory. Let's see why. A typical microcomputer used for data processing will require several high-level languages and application programs. Examples might include a 16K BASIC interpreter or compiler, a 35K word processor, a 24K data base management program, a 6K editor, and numerous application programs and data files from 1K to 40K bytes in length. It soon becomes apparent that all of these programs and languages cannot fit in main memory at once.

In fact, it is not uncommon for some large programs to exceed 64K bytes in length. These programs can be used only by loading smaller portions at a time into memory. For these reasons there is a need for a secondary storage medium with the following attributes:

TABLE 5.1 IMPORTANT DATES IN SEMICONDUCTOR MEMORY TECHNOLOGY

Date	Part no.	Organization	Description
1968	1101	256 × 1	Static RAM
1970	1103	1K × 1	Dynamic RAM
1972	2102	1K × 1	Static RAM
1973	4027	4K × 1	Dynamic RAM
1976	4116	16K × 1	Dynamic RAM
1977	2114	1K × 4	Static RAM
1981	4164	64K × 1	Dynamic RAM
1984	41256	256K × 1	Dynamic RAM
1987	511000	IM × 1	Dynamic RAM
1990	514000	4M × 1	Dynamic RAM

1. It must provide relatively fast access. An application program should load in 1 to 30 s.
2. Access can be random or sequential.
3. The storage medium must be portable so that programs and data files can be transported between machines or stored for safe keeping.
4. It must be nonvolatile.

A typical secondary storage device is the *floppy disk drive*. Data is transferred to main memory from a floppy disk at rates as high as 500,000 bits per second. This means that a 24K applications program could load in less than 1 s.

The data on a floppy disk is stored in sectors of 128 to 1024 bytes per sector. When reading data from a floppy disk, the data is read by locating the appropriate sectors. Data bytes within a given sector must be searched sequentially, meaning that the access is not truly random.

Floppy disks are made from a Mylar base and coated with a magnetic compound. Logic 1s and 0s are stored on the disk as flux transitions when current through the disk drive's read/write head is reversed. This makes them *nonvolatile* (the contents are not lost when removed from the disk drive) and easily transportable.

The main disadvantage to the floppy disk is the limited amount of storage available on one diskette. This can range from 100K bytes to over 1 MB (1 million bytes) in some double-sided drives. Although this sounds like a lot of storage capacity, computer programmers have been known to "eat" that much memory for breakfast!

For truly large amounts of storage a *rigid* or *hard disk* technology must be employed. This type of disk is available with capacities from 5 MB to over 300 MB. Once considered a luxury, nearly all microcomputers today came equipped with a hard drive.

Just like the floppy disk, hard disks are used for secondary storage, but they are less portable. This necessitates a third memory hierarchy called *archival storage*. The properties of this memory type are:

1. It must be nonvolatile.
2. It is accessed infrequently.

3. High speed and random access are not essential.
4. It must be portable.

Magnetic tape is commonly used for archival storage. It is relatively slow but can easily store 10 to 20 MB of data on one 2400-ft reel of $\frac{1}{2}$-inch tape. Some microcomputer systems use a magnetic tape cartridge similar to a cassette tape that can store up to 75 MB of data.

Archival storage is used for making backup copies of important data files that are infrequently used. It provides protection against loss of data due to operator error or system "crashes."

Table 5.2 summarizes the three major memory hierarchies. The remainder of this chapter will deal with main memory. Chapter 10 will consider secondary storage techniques in more detail.

TABLE 5.2 MICROCOMPUTER MEMORY HIERARCHIES

Memory type	Speed (access time/byte)	Capacity (bytes)	Example
Main	$<0.5\ \mu s$	1K to 4 M	Semiconductor RAM
Secondary	$<75\ \mu s$	100K to 300 M	Floppy disk
Archival	$<5000\ \mu s$	1 M to 100 M	Magnetic tape

5.2 THE MICROPROCESSOR DEFINES THE MEMORY TIMING

As you read this section, look for the answers to these Key Concept questions:

5.2.1. The length of time required by a memory chip to decode the memory address and output valid data is called the _____ _____ _____ .

5.2.2. To accommodate slow memory parts, a microprocessor can be slowed down by adding _____ states.

At first glance, interfacing main memory to a microprocessor can seem quite complex. There are read cycle times, chip-select access times, output enable access times, write cycle times, and numerous setup and hold times.

Naturally, these timing specifications should be carefully studied. However, if we view the microprocessor as the source of the timing signals, there is little we can do other than to verify that a certain memory chip will or will not meet the timing specifications for a particular processor.

Certainly, we cannot change the sequence of events that occur on the three buses during a memory read or write cycle. At best we can slow the processor down by adding wait states.

Memory-Read-Cycle Timing. Figure 5.1 is a sort of *generic* memory-read-cycle timing diagram. It shows the sequence of events on a microprocessor's address, data, and control buses when a memory read machine cycle is performed.

For clarity, the address bus is shown as two parallel lines. This should be interpreted as meaning that some of the address lines are high and others are low. When the lines cross, it indicates that a new address is output by the processor. The actual address is not important for this discussion.

A similar drafting convention is used for the data bus. Because the data on the bus may not always be valid, hash lines are used to indicate unknown or invalid data.

The memory cycle begins with the output of a memory address on A0 through A15. This is followed by the $\overline{\text{MEMR}}$ line going low, indicating that this is a memory read machine cycle. The microprocessor now turns its internal data bus around so that it is ready to receive data.

At this point it is up to the memory to place valid data on the data bus before the rising edge of $\overline{\text{MEMR}}$. When $\overline{\text{MEMR}}$ does go high, the contents of the data bus will be gated into the microprocessor and the memory read cycle will have ended.

There are three major time periods of importance in this read cycle.

t_{RD}: $\overline{\text{MEMR}}$ to valid data. This is the maximum amount of time after $\overline{\text{MEMR}}$ goes low that valid data can be placed on the bus by the memory. If this time is exceeded, the microprocessor may not be able to latch the data byte before $\overline{\text{MEMR}}$ goes high at the end of the cycle.

t_{ACC}: address access time. This is the maximum amount of time the memory has to decode the address and place the selected data byte on the data bus. If the memory requires more than this time, wait states will be required.

t_{CA}: $\overline{\text{MEMR}}$ to new address. This is the minimum amount of time after $\overline{\text{MEMR}}$ goes high before a new address will appear on the bus. This time does not have to be met by the memory but ensures that $\overline{\text{MEMR}}$ will be high when a

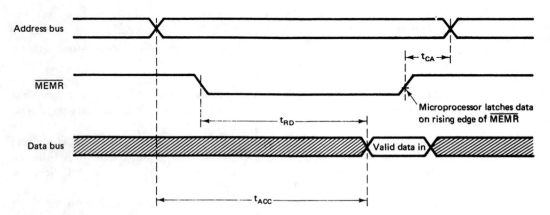

Figure 5.1 Typical memory read cycle for a microprocessor. The memory must respond with valid data t_{ACC} seconds after the memory address is placed on the bus by the processor.

new address is output by the processor. If this were not done, it would be possible for one memory device to be putting new data onto the bus while the previous memory device was still outputting its data. This could result in bus contention (two transmitters driving the same bus line).

Table 5.3 indicates values for these three times for the 8080A, the 8085AH, and the Z-80A microprocessors. This data is obtained from the ac characteristics data sheets in Appendix C. The terms in the equations refer to terminology used in these data sheets.

Note that the Z-80 timing specifications in Table 5.3 are for an op-code fetch machine cycle. When the Z-80 performs a general memory read (not an op-code fetch), an additional half clock period is allotted.

Memory-Write-Cycle Timing.

Figure 5.2 illustrates the sequence of events during a memory write cycle. The same drafting nomenclature is used as in the memory-read-cycle diagram.

The cycle begins with the output of an address on A0 through A15 by the microprocessor. In order to give the memory a *data write setup time*, valid data is output on D0 through D7 early in the machine cycle. The $\overline{\text{MEMW}}$ line then goes low, identifying the memory write cycle.

The memory now has until the rising edge of $\overline{\text{MEMW}}$ to latch the data. After this time the data bus contents will become undefined. There are two major time periods during this memory write cycle.

t_{DW}: data valid to end of write. This is the minimum amount of time that valid data will be held on the bus before $\overline{\text{MEMW}}$ goes high. This can be thought of as a *setup time* for the memory. If the memory requires more than this time, valid data may not be properly written.

t_{AW}: address valid to end of write. This is the minimum amount of time that a valid address will be held on the bus before $\overline{\text{MEMW}}$ goes high. This corresponds to the amount of time that the memory chip has to decode the address and write the data byte into the selected cell.

Table 5.4 lists times for these specifications for the 8080A, 8085AH, and the Z-80A microprocessors. This data is obtained from the ac characteristics data sheets in Appendix C. Again the terms used in the equations refer to specifications from the particular data sheet.

Note: The data in Tables 5.3 and 5.4 do not include time delays lost in buffers and decoders. This could easily account for another 100 to 150 ns and should be taken into account when comparing the specifications with a particular memory device (see Sec. 5.5).

Comparing t_{AW} in Table 5.4 with t_{ACC} in Table 5.3 reveals that the memory read timing is the most critical. For this reason, memory devices are usually characterized by their t_{ACC} specification—the address access time.

TABLE 5.3 MEMORY READ TIMING SPECIFICATIONS FOR THE 8080A, 8085AH, AND Z-80A MICROPROCESSORS

Microprocessor	t_{RD} (max)	Equation used	t_{ACC} (max)	Equation used	t_{CA} (min)	Equation used
8080A* (2 MHz)	464 ns	$2\,t_{CY} - t_{DSS} - t_{DC} - t_{DS2}$	650 ns	$2\,t_{CY} - t_{DA} - t_{DS2}$	330 ns	$t_{CY} - t_{DF} - t_{RR} + t_{DA}$
8085AH (3 MHz)	300 ns	t_{RD}	575 ns	t_{AD}	120 ns	t_{CA}
Z-80A (4 MHz)	195 ns	$t_3 + t_1 - t_{13} - t_{15}$	325 ns	$2\,t_{CY} - t_5 - t_{15} - t_6$	25 ns	$t_6 - t_{14}$

* Numbers obtained from the 8080A, 8224, and 8228 data sheets.

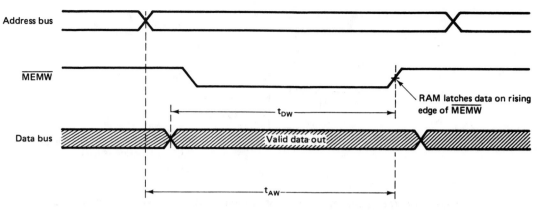

Figure 5.2 Typical memory write cycle for a microprocessor. The memory must latch the data word within t_{AW} seconds after its address is output by the microprocessor.

Memory Interfacing Requirements. The task of connecting a particular memory device to a microprocessor is called *memory interfacing*. From the timing diagrams presented in Figs. 5.1 and 5.2, we can define three general requirements.

1. Build a circuit that examines the address bus and outputs a pulse when the address is intended for the particular memory device. This circuit is called an *address decoder*.
2. Use the $\overline{\text{MEMW}}$ and $\overline{\text{MEMR}}$ control lines to control the direction of data flow to and from the memory.
3. Gate data onto or off the data bus but always in such a manner as to prevent bus contention.

In Sec. 5.4 we will study specific memory devices. In that section several examples are presented to illustrate how these three requirements are met.

Interfacing Slow Memory. What can be done about memory devices that do not meet the timing specifications listed in the preceding section? First, recognize that the memory cannot be "too fast" for the microprocessor—only too slow.

TABLE 5.4 MEMORY WRITE TIMING SPECIFICATIONS FOR THE 8080A, 8085AH, AND Z-80A MICROPROCESSORS

Microprocessor	t_{DW} (min)	Equation used	t_{AW} (min)	Equation used
8080A* (2 MHz)	656 ns	$2t_{CY} - t_{D3} - t_{DD} + t_{DC} + t_{WR}$	1176 ns	$3\,t_{CY} - t_{D3} - t_{DA} + t_{DC} + t_{WR}$
8085AH (3 MHz)	420 ns	t_{DW}	670 ns	$t_{AC} + t_{CC}$
Z-80A (4 MHz)	265 ns	$2\,t_{CY} - t_{53} - t_{12}$	500 ns	$t_2 + t_4 + 2\,t_{CY} + t_{32} - t_6$

* Numbers obtained from the 8080A, 8224 and 8228 data sheets.

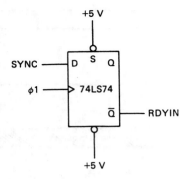

Figure 5.3 8080 WAIT-state generator. One clock period is added to all machine cycles.

Usually, the speed of a memory is measured by considering its address access time (or simply access time). Thus a Z-80A microprocessor will give a memory device 325 ns of access time (ignoring buffer propagation delays). A memory device with a 500-ns access time will be too slow. This means that it will not have enough time to decode the memory address and gate the proper data byte onto the data bus.

Nothing can be done to speed up the memory device—except to buy faster parts—but the microprocessor can be slowed down. Two methods are possible. In the first, the system clock can be set to a lower frequency. However, this penalizes the entire system because of one slow memory device.

A better solution is to have the slow memory device request a *WAIT* state (or states). This can be done by activating the processor's $\overline{\text{WAIT}}$ or READY input line. Recalling the single-step circuits in Chap. 4, the 8080, 8085, and Z-80 all

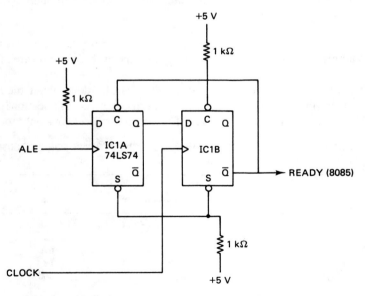

Figure 5.4 8085 WAIT-state generator. One clock period is added to all machine cycles.

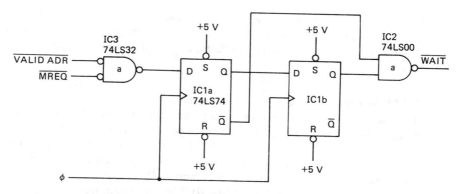

Figure 5.5 Z-80 WAIT-state generator. WAIT states will be generated only for the slow memory device.

examine this input during T2 of each machine cycle. If this input is found low, the processor enters an idle state but holds valid data on its address, data, and control buses.

This idle state will persist until the READY or $\overline{\text{WAIT}}$ input is found high one or more clock periods later. In this way an integral number of clock periods can be added to the access time provided the memory by the microprocessor.

Figure 5.3 is a simple *brute-force* WAIT-state generator for the 8080. It adds one WAIT state to all machine cycles (memory read or write and I/O read or write) regardless of the memory device selected. A similar circuit for the 8085 is shown in Fig. 5.4.

A WAIT-state generator for the Z-80 is shown in Fig. 5.5. The signal $\overline{\text{VALID ADR}}$ is presumed to go low whenever the slow memory device is accessed. As we will see, this can be derived from an address decoder. In this way WAIT states are requested only when the slow memory device is selected. See Prob. 5.11 for an analysis of the timing of this circuit.

5.3 CHOOSING MEMORY

As you read this section, look for the answers to these Key Concept questions:

5.3.1. List several applications of read–only memory.

5.3.2. Explain the terms volatile and nonvolatile.

5.3.3. A drawing showing the specific range of memory addresses associated with each of the memory devices in a computer is called a _____ _____ .

Choosing the memory components for a particular microcomputer system will depend on the intended application. A *controller* (such as used in a microwave oven) will require only a small prime memory configured almost entirely with read-only memory devices.

A word processor will require a large read/write prime memory for storing text and considerable secondary memory for storing data and program files. The amount of read-only memory in this type of system may be restricted to a bootstrap loader.

ROM Applications.   A read-only memory device or ROM has one main attribute that makes it very useful in a microcomputer system. It is *nonvolatile*. This means that its contents will not be lost when power is removed from the device.

ROMs are used in microcomputers to store bootstrap loader programs (see Sec. 4.2), software for dedicated controllers (the microwave oven example), and application programs in "turnkey" systems (a BASIC interpreter or a word processor program can be stored in one or two ROMs, for example).

The advantage of using ROM memory is that it is instantly available when power is applied. This allows the operator to simply *turn the key* and begin using the application program. In this respect ROM-based microcomputers can appear to be appliances rather than computers.

The disadvantage to a ROM is that it occupies memory space that cannot be written into. This may not be a problem in the dedicated controller, but can take away valuable prime memory from a word processor or other data processing system.

Another disadvantage is that ROMs are not easily programmed. Although custom devices can be programmed at the factory, this is practical only for large volumes (many thousands of units). Field-programmable devices must be programmed one at a time and must be individually removed from the circuit board—a slow and costly process.

RAM Applications.   Read/write memories are commonly referred to as RAMs or random-access memories. Of course, ROMs are also random-access memories, so the acronym is not really correct. Nevertheless, it has become common practice to refer to read/write memory as RAM memory—I suppose it would be difficult to pronounce RWM!

The most important property of a RAM is that it is *programmable*. Application programs can be quickly loaded into RAM from a disk or tape and then executed by the microprocessor. RAM is also used for storing temporary data such as BASIC program variables, the system "stack," and disk drive directories.

The amount of RAM a particular microcomputer system has available dictates the maximum size of an application program. Most microcomputer owners are familiar with the *OM* error—out of memory!

The single most important limitation to RAM memory is that it is *volatile*. Turn the power off and all information is lost. It is this property of the RAM that necessitates some form of secondary storage in most microcomputer systems.

The Memory Map.   Usually, a microcomputer system will have a mix of ROM and RAM memory. For example, there might be 16K of ROM, 12K of RAM, and the rest of the memory space may be left unimplemented or open. When developing software for such a system it is convenient (and perhaps mandatory) to know exactly where in the memory space of the processor this memory is located. This is the purpose of the *memory map*.

Example 5.1

A certain microcomputer has the following memory specifications:

1. 2716 2K ROM at address 0
2. 2732 4K ROM at address F000H
3. Eight HM6116 2K RAMs immediately following the 2716 in memory space

Draw the memory map for this computer.

Solution: In Chap. 1 we divided the 16-bit memory address into a *high-order* or page address and a *low-order* or line address (see Fig. 1.7). Keeping this analogy in mind, we can think of the high-order byte as a page counter. For a 2K memory there are eight 256-byte pages.

The 2716 ROM in this example will extend from location 0000 to location 07FFH. This is eight full pages with the ninth page beginning at address 0800H. In a similar manner the HM6116 RAM addresses can be found. This is shown in Fig. 5.6.

The 2732 is a 4K-byte ROM and thus occupies sixteen 256-byte pages. This corresponds to the range 0000 to 0FFFH (page 0 through page 15), with address 1000H marking the beginning of the second 4K block. Figure 1.7(b) shows a memory map marked in 4K-block segments. For this example the 2732 will occupy 16 pages of memory from F000H to FFFFH.

Note that most of the memory space is left open in this example.

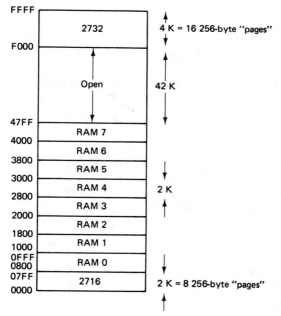

Figure 5.6 Memory map for Ex. 5.1.

5.4 RAM AND ROM TECHNOLOGIES

As you read this section, look for the answers to these Key Concept questions:

5.4.1. A _____-_____ ROM is selected when high volume production is required.

5.4.2. A PROM is a type of ROM that can be individually _____ by the user.

5.4.3. UV EPROMs can be erased by exposing the chip to _____ light.

5.4.4. _____ use an RS flip-flop as the basic storage cell, but _____ use a single MOS capacitor.

5.4.5. A memory chip organized as 64K × 8 has _____ storage locations, each _____ bits wide.

Although all RAM and ROM chips are semiconductor devices, several different types of semiconductor technologies are utilized. In this section we examine these technologies in detail.

Mask-Programmable ROMs. It is possible to view a ROM as a device with n inputs and m outputs. For each of the 2^n input combinations there is one output word of m bits. This is shown in Fig. 5.7.

A ROM is made up of an *address decoder*, a programmable *memory array*, and a set of output *buffers*. In Fig. 5.7 $n = 4$ and $m = 5$. When a 4-bit address is applied to the ROM, one of the 16 row lines will go low. A diode connected between a row line and a column line will program that output bit low. The absence of a diode will program a logic 1.

In essence, a ROM is nothing more than a truth table generator. It provides one m-bit output word for each possible input combination. Because of this, ROMs are often used to replace combinational logic networks (in Sec. 5.6 we will use a ROM as an address decoder).

A *mask-programmable* ROM is one in which the diode connections are programmed at the factory according to a truth table supplied by the user. In this way the manufacturer can sell the same ROM chip to many different customers, altering only the mask that defines the diode connections.

The economics of integrated-circuit manufacture are such that it would be impractical to make only one ROM chip. The integrated-circuit dies are grouped together on a wafer containing several hundred potential ROMs. Because there is no guarantee that a particular wafer will test as good, several wafers must be manufactured. For this reason, mask-programmable ROMs are limited to production runs of several thousand parts. Needless to say, it is imperative that the truth table supplied to the manufacturer be accurate!

Field-Programmable ROMs. There are several types of ROMs that can be programmed by the user in the field. These devices are referred to as *PROMs* or programmable read-only memories.

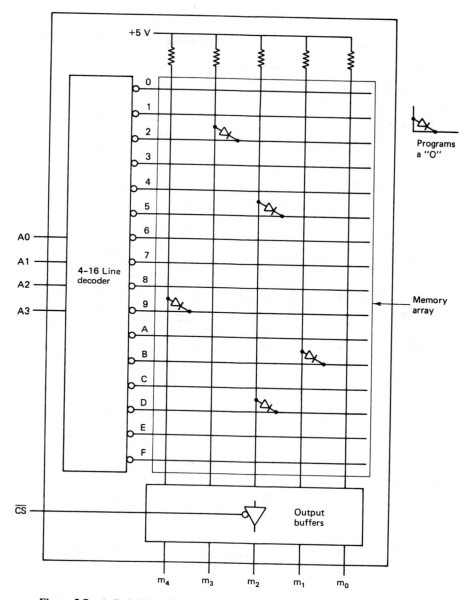

Figure 5.7 A diode ROM illustrating the n-input address decoder, $2^n \times m$ memory array and m output buffers.

Fusible-link PROMs. One type of PROM uses a low-current fusible link in series with the output. By applying a current pulse to the desired output, the fuse can be melted and a logic 1 or 0 permanently programmed. Figure 5.8 is a data sheet for a family of fusible-link PROMs manufactured by Texas Instruments.

- **Titanium-Tungsten (Ti-W) Fuse Links for Fast, Low-Voltage, Reliable Programming**
- **All Schottky-Clamped PROM's Offer:**
  **Fast Chip Select to Simplify System Decode
  Choice of Three-State or Open-Collector Outputs
  P-N-P Inputs for Reduced Loading on
  System Buffers/Drivers**

- **Full Decoding and Chip Select Simplify System Design**
- **Applications Include:**
  **Microprogramming/Firmware Loaders
  Code Converters/Character Generators
  Translators/Emulators
  Address Mapping/Look-Up Tables**

TYPE NUMBER (PACKAGES)		BIT SIZE	OUTPUT	TYPICAL ACCESS TIME (ns)	
−55°C to 125°C	0°C to 70°C	(ORGANIZATION)	CONFIGURATION	FROM ADDRESS	FROM CHIP SELECT
SN54186(J, W)	SN74186(J, N)	512 bits (64 W × 8 B)	open-collector	50	55
SN54188A(J, W)	SN74188A(J,N)	256 bits (32 W × 8 B)	open-collector	30	34
SN54S188(J, W)	SN74S188(J, N)		open-collector	25	12
SN54S288(J, W)	SN74S288(J, N)		three-state	25	12
SN54S287(J, W)	SN74S287(J, N)	1024 bits (256 W × 4 B)	three-state	42	15
SN54S387(J, W)	SN74S387(J, N)		open-collector	42	15
SN54S470(J)	SN74S470(J, N)	2048 bits (256 W × 8 B)	open-collector	50	20
SN54S471(J)	SN74S471(J, N)		three-state	50	20
SN54S472(J)	SN74S472(J, N)	4096 bits (512 W × 8 B)	three-state	55	20
SN54S473(J)	SN74S473(J, N)		open-collector	55	20

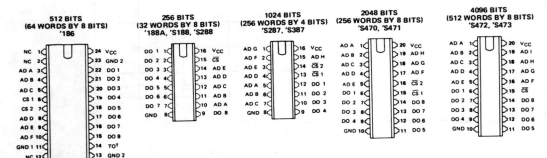

Pin assignments for all of these memories are the same for all packages.

NC–No internal connection
†TO is used for testing purposes.
The logic at TO is undefined.

description

These monolithic TTL programmable read-only memories (PROM's) feature titanium-tungsten (Ti-W) fuse links with each link designed to program in one millisecond or less. The Schottky-clamped versions of these PROM's offer considerable flexibility for upgrading existing designs or improving new designs as they feature full Schottky clamping for improved performance, low-current MOS-compatible p-n-p inputs, choice of bus-driving three-state or open-collector outputs, and improved chip-select access times.

The high-complexity 2048- and 4096-bit PROM's can be used to significantly improve system density for fixed memories as all are offered in the 20-pin dual-in-line package having pin-row spacings of 0.300 inch.

Figure 5.8 Specifications and package outlines for several common fusible-link PROMs. (Courtesy of Texas Instruments.)

UV-light-erasable PROMs (EPROM).

Probably the most popular type of PROM used in microcomputer systems is the erasable programmable read-only memory or *EPROM*. This device can be programmed, erased, and reprogrammed many times over by the user. A data sheet for the Intel 2764 8K-byte EPROM is given in Fig. 5.9.

EPROMs use a floating-gate avalanche-injection MOS (FAMOS) transistor cell to store charge. This is shown in Fig. 5.10(a). A special programming voltage (v_{PP}) causes a high electric field to be developed in the channel region of the transistor and causes electrons to jump the silicon dioxide barrier between the channel region and the floating gate.

During programming the select gate is given a positive bias which helps attract these electrons to the floating-gate electrode. Because the floating gate is surrounded by silicon dioxide (an excellent insulator), the injected charge is effectively trapped. The storage period is projected by Intel to exceed 20 years.

Cells with trapped charge cause the transistor to be biased ON, whereas those without charge are biased OFF. Virgin EPROMs have no trapped charge and each cell stores a logic 1. The EPROM can be erased by subjecting each gate to ultraviolet (UV) light which has a wavelength of 2537 angstroms. The electrons on the floating gate absorb photons from the UV-light source and acquire enough energy to reverse the programming process and return to the substrate.

EPROMs are packaged in special ceramic packages with quartz windows to allow erasure. Commercial erasers are available that will erase several EPROMs at once in 15 to 20 minutes.

In operation the EPROM window should be covered with an opaque label because normal room fluorescent lighting could erase the device (Intel reports that approximately three years of exposure to fluorescent lighting or one week of direct sunlight would be required).

As indicated in the mode selection chart in Fig. 5.9, the 2764 can be programmed in two ways. The first method is consistent with the programming technique used for the lower-density devices, such as the 2716 (2K byte) and 2732 (4K byte) EPROMs. In this technique pin 1, V_{PP}, is raised to 21 V, the chip is enabled, data applied to outputs 0 through 7, and the desired address applied to A0 through A12. Programming is accomplished by applying a 45 to 55-ms active-low TTL-level pulse to pin 27, the $\overline{PGM}$ pin.

Usually, the data written is then verified and the next address selected. The 2764 and 27128 (16K byte) EPROMs can also be programmed using what Intel refers to as an *intelligent programming algorithm*. A flowchart for this technique is given in Fig. 5.11. The advantage in using this algorithm is to reduce the programming time for a 2764 from nearly 7 minutes to less than 1½ minutes. V_{CC} equals 6.0 V for this mode.

PROM programmers are commercially available that allow programming of individual devices with a hex keypad, an external terminal, or an external computer. Universal "personality" modules allow most of the common EPROMs to be programmed with one machine. Figure 5.12 is a photo of the Pro-Log M980 PROM programmer.

The 2764 (and the 2732 and 27128) also support an *intelligent identifier* mode.

2764
64K (8K x 8) UV ERASABLE PROM

- **200 ns (2764-2) Maximum Access Time ... HMOS*-E Technology**
- **Compatible with High-Speed 8mHz iAPX 186...Zero WAIT State**
- **Two Line Control**
- **Pin Compatible to 27128 EPROM**

- **int_eligent Programming™ Algorithm**
- **Industry Standard Pinout ... JEDEC Approved**
- **Low Active Current...100mA Max.**
- **±10% V$_{CC}$ Tolerance Available**

The Intel 2764 is a 5V only, 65,536-bit ultraviolet erasable and electrically programmable read-only memory (EPROM). The standard 2764 access time is 250 ns with speed selection available at 200 ns. The access time is compatible with high-performance microprocessors such as Intel's 8 mHz iAPX 186. In these systems, the 2764 allows the microprocessor to operate without the addition of WAIT states. The 2764 is also compatible with the 12 MHz 8051 family.

An important 2764 feature is the separate output control, Output Enable ($\overline{OE}$) from the Chip Enable control ($\overline{CE}$). The $\overline{OE}$ control eliminates bus contention in microprocessor systems. Intel's Application Note AP-72 describes the microprocessor system implementation of the $\overline{OE}$ and $\overline{CE}$ controls on Intel's EPROMs. AP-72 is available from Intel's Literature Department.

The 2764 has a standby mode which reduces power consumption without increasing access time. The maximum active current is 100 mA, while the maximum standby current is only 40 mA. The standby mode is selected by applying a TTL-high signal to the $\overline{CE}$ input.

±10% V$_{CC}$ tolerance is available as an alternative to the standard ±5% V$_{CC}$ tolerance for the 2764. This can allow the system designer more leeway with regard to his power supply requirements and other system parameters.

The 2764 is fabricated with HMOS*-E technology, Intel's high-speed N-channel MOS Silicon Gate Technology.

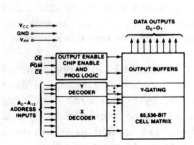

Figure 1. Block Diagram

Figure 2. Pin Configurations

MODE SELECTION

PINS \ MODE	CE (20)	OE (22)	PGM (27)	A$_9$ (24)	V$_{PP}$ (1)	V$_{CC}$ (28)	Outputs (11-13, 15-19)
Read	V$_{IL}$	V$_{IL}$	V$_{IH}$	X	V$_{CC}$	V$_{CC}$	D$_{OUT}$
Output Disable	V$_{IL}$	V$_{IH}$	V$_{IH}$	x	V$_{CC}$	V$_{CC}$	High Z
Standby	V$_{IH}$	X	X	X	V$_{CC}$	V$_{CC}$	High Z
Program	V$_{IL}$	V$_{IH}$	V$_{IL}$	X	V$_{PP}$	V$_{CC}$	D$_{IN}$
Verify	V$_{IL}$	V$_{IL}$	V$_{IH}$	X	V$_{PP}$	V$_{CC}$	D$_{OUT}$
Program Inhibit	V$_{IH}$	X	X	X	V$_{PP}$	V$_{CC}$	High Z
int_eligent Identifier	V$_{IL}$	V$_{IL}$	V$_{IH}$	V$_H$	V$_{CC}$	V$_{CC}$	Code
int_eligent Programming	V$_{IL}$	V$_{IH}$	V$_{IL}$	X	V$_{PP}$	V$_{CC}$	D$_{IN}$

1. X can be V$_{IH}$ or V$_{IL}$
2. V$_H$ = 12.0V ± 0.5V

PIN NAMES

A$_0$-A$_{12}$	ADDRESSES
$\overline{CE}$	CHIP ENABLE
$\overline{OE}$	OUTPUT ENABLE
O$_0$-O$_7$	OUTPUTS
PGM	PROGRAM
N.C.	NO CONNECT

*HMOS is a patented process of Intel Corporation

Figure 5.9 Specifications for the Intel 2764 8K-byte UV EPROM. (Courtesy of Intel Corporation.)

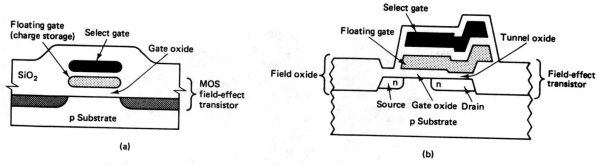

Figure 5.10 (a) Basic UV EPROM cell structure. A logic 0 is stored by trapping charge on the floating gate electrode. (b) The E²PROM has a thin tunnel oxide covering the drain diffusion of the MOS transistor. Electrons are able to "tunnel" through this thin oxide to or from the floating gate. In this way, programming and erasure are both done electrically. (Courtesy of Intel Corporation.)

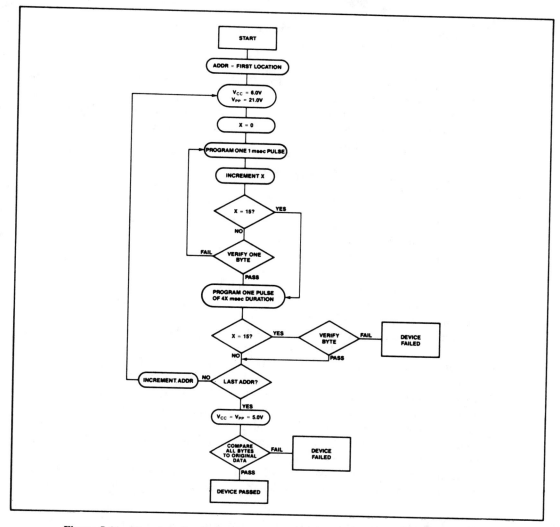

Figure 5.11 Flowchart for the Intel Intelligent Programming Algorithm. (Courtesy of Intel Corporation.)

Figure 5.12 The Pro-Log M980 PROM programmer. (Photo courtesy of Pro-Log Corporation, Monterey, Ca.)

In this mode address line A9 is raised to $+12$ V. Two identifier bytes may then be read from the PROM by forcing A0 to V_{IL} and then V_{IH}. The first byte represents a manufacturer code and the second byte a device code. This is intended to allow PROM programmers to "read" the device and automatically select the proper pinning and programming algorithm.

Electrically erasable PROMs (E²PROM). There are several disadvantages to the UV EPROM. These are:

1. The device must be removed from the circuit board to be erased.
2. Byte erasure is not possible—the entire contents of the chip must be erased.
3. The quartz window package is expensive.

Because of these problems much research has been devoted to developing an electrically erasable nonvolatile memory device. The result is the E²PROM. This device can be programmed and erased without removing the chip from its socket. In addition, both byte and bulk erasure modes are possible.

An example of an E²PROM is the Intel 2817, whose data sheet is given in Fig. 5.13. Figure 5.10(b) shows the difference between the FAMOS cell and the E²PROM cell. Like the FAMOS cell, a floating gate and select gate are used. However, a very thin tunnel oxide is provided over the drain diffusion of the MOS transistor in the E²PROM cell. With a positive voltage applied to the select gate, electrons are attracted to the floating gate and trapped as in the FAMOS cell. Reversing the process by grounding the select gate and applying a positive voltage to the drain terminal discharges the cell.

Because the gate oxide over the drain is so thin, the process is controlled by a *tunneling* phenomenon instead of avalanche injection. Tunneling has the advantage

intel®

2817   PRELIMINARY

16K (2K X 8) ELECTRICALLY ERASABLE PROM

- **Self Timed Byte Write with Automatic Erase**
- **Direct Microprocessor Interface Capability**
- **Static 21 Volt V_{PP}**
- **Reduces Support Component Requirement by 70% to 90% Over 2816 and 2815**

- **Fast Byte Write Time:**
  - **—Write Typical, 5 mS**
  - **—Cycle Typical, 10 mS**
- **Very Fast Read Access Time:**
  - **—2817, 250 nS**
  - **—2817-3, 350 nS**
  - **—2817-4, 450 nS**
- **Reliable Intel FLOTOX E^2PROM Technology**

The Intel 2817 is a 16,384 bit Electrically Erasable Programmable Read Only Memory. Like the Intel 2816 and 2815, it has completely Non-Volatile Data Storage. However, in addition, it offers a high degree of integrated functionality which enables in-circuit byte writes to be performed with minimal hardware and software overhead. The Intel 2817 is a product of Intel's advanced E^2PROM technology and uses the powerful HMOS*-E process for reliable, *non-volatile*, data storage.

The Intel 2817 eliminates all the interfacing hardware logic and firmware required to perform data writes. The device has complete self-timing which leaves the processor free to perform other tasks until the 2817 signals 'Ready.' With a transparent erase before write, the user benefits by saving an erase command contributing to efficient usage of system processing time. On chip latching further enhances system performance.

The Intel 2817's very fast read access time makes it compatible with high performance microprocessor applications. It uses Intel's proven 2-line control architecture which eliminates bus contention in a system environment. Combining these features with the 2817's 'Ready' signal makes the device an extremely powerful, yet simple to use, E^2 memory—available to the designer today.

The density, and level of integrated control, makes the Intel 2817 suitable for users requiring low hardware overhead, high system performance, minimal board space and design ease. Designing with, and using the 2817, is extremely cost effective as 70% of the required voltage and interfacing hardware required for other E^2PROM devices has been eliminated. See Figures 1, 2, and 3 for the Intel 2817's block diagram, pinout, and simple interface requirements.

*HMOS-E is a patented process of Intel Corporation.

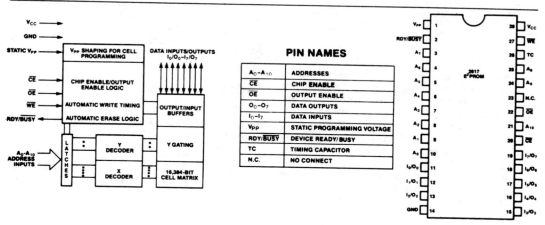

PIN NAMES

A_0–A_{10}	ADDRESSES
$\overline{CE}$	CHIP ENABLE
$\overline{OE}$	OUTPUT ENABLE
O_0–O_7	DATA OUTPUTS
I_0–I_7	DATA INPUTS
V_{PP}	STATIC PROGRAMMING VOLTAGE
RDY/$\overline{BUSY}$	DEVICE READY/BUSY
TC	TIMING CAPACITOR
N.C.	NO CONNECT

Figure 5.13   Specifications for the Intel 2817 E^2PROM. (Courtesy of Intel Corporation.)

Sec. 5.4   RAM and ROM Technologies

211

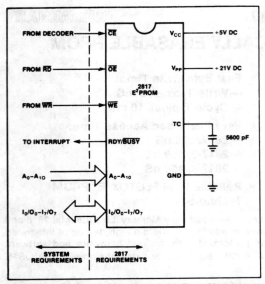

Figure 3. Simple 2817 Interface Requirements

DEVICE OPERATION

The Intel 2817 has 4 modes of user operation which are detailed in Table 1. All modes are designed to enhance the 2817's functionality to the user and provide total Intel E^2PROM microprocessor compatibility.

Table 1. $V_{CC} = +5V$, $V_{PP} = +21V$[1]

Mode \ Pin	$\overline{CE}$	$\overline{OE}$	$\overline{WE}$	I_0/O_0-I_7/O_7	RDY/$\overline{BUSY}$
Read	V_{IL}	V_{IL}	V_{IH}	D_{OUT}	V_{OH}
Standby	V_{IH}	X	X	High Z	V_{OH}
Write	V_{IL}	V_{IH}	⎍	D_{IN}	V_{OH}
Busy	X	X	X	High Z	V_{OL}

The Write Mode

The 2817 is programmed electrically in-circuit, yet it provides non-volatile storage without the constraint of ultraviolet erasure with EPROMs or of batteries with CMOS RAMs. Writing to non-volatile memory has never been easier as no external latching, erasing or timing is needed. When commanded to byte write, the 2817 automatically latches the address, data, and control signals, and starts the write. Concurrently, the 'Ready' line goes low indicating that the 2817 is Busy and that it can be deselected to allow the processor to perform other tasks. During the write, the static V_{PP} is used to perform an automatic byte erase, then write. The 2817 has on-chip verification to ensure successful byte programming. This is achieved by comparing the data written to the cell with the data latched on chip during the write request. The timing capacitor (TC) is used by the 2817 to generate the correct internal V_{PP} rise time constant for cell programming. Its value is 5600 pF ± 10%.

Should a regulated +24V DC be available in the system, the circuit shown in Figure 4 can be used to provide the required V_{PP} voltage. Should +24V not be available, the implementation in Figure 5 can be used to provide the static programming voltage. There are also many DC/DC converter modules available that convert +5V to +21V. See AP 148 (Using the Intelligent 2817 E^2PROM) for additional detail.

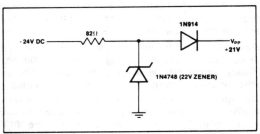

Figure 4. Voltage Stepdown from +24V DC to +21V DC

The Read Mode

One aspect of the 2817's high performance is its very fast read access time—typically less than 250 ns. It's read cycle is similar to that of EPROMS and static RAM's. It offers a 2 line control architecture to eliminate bus contention. The Intel 2817 can be selected using decoded system address lines to $\overline{CE}$ and then the device can be read, within the device selection time, using the processor's $\overline{RD}$ signal connected to $\overline{OE}$. As an option, the 2817 can be read with +5 volt on V_{PP}[2]

The Standby Mode

The 2817 has a standby mode in which power consumption is reduced by 50%. This offers the user power supply cost benefits when designing a system with Intel 2817's. This mode occurs when the device is deselected ($\overline{CE}$=1). The data pins are put into the high impedance state regardless of the signals applied to $\overline{OE}$ and $\overline{WE}$ concurrent with the reading and writing of other devices.

Figure 5.13 *(Continued)*

that a large amount of charge can be injected during the write cycle but only a small amount of charge is lost during a read cycle. Using the 21-V programming voltage, the ratio of charge current to leakage current is greater than 10^{11}. Data retention is projected to be greater than 10 years.

Because continuous read and write cycles cause a small amount of charge to be trapped in the gate oxide, E^2PROMs have a *lifetime* of 10^4 to 10^6 programming or erasing cycles.

Early E^2PROMs required extensive support circuitry. This included pulsing the V_{PP} line with a slow exponentially rising voltage waveform from 5 V to 21 V for all write cycles, a + 9- to 15-V V_{OH} level on the output enable pin for chip erasure, and the need to program all bits to a logic 1 before writing new data.

The 2817 requires no external support except for a static 21-V power source—the 2817A generates the 21-V source internally and is a 5-V-only part. An external 5600-pF capacitor should be connected to the TC pin and helps create the correct internal V_{PP} rise time for cell programming.

In some cases a write protection circuit will be required to prevent spurious writing of data when the system power is removed or applied. A recommended circuit is shown in Fig. 5.14. Read access times are comparable with present EPROM and RAM chips, but write times are slow (10 ms average) compared with conventional RAM devices. For this reason, WAIT states will be required when programming the device.

The 2817 provides a RDY/$\overline{\text{BUSY}}$ output that can be used to force the processor to enter a WAIT mode until the data has been safely written. In effect, a WAIT-state generator is incorporated on-chip.

What are some applications for the E^2PROM? Although it will not replace conventional RAM, it can be used to hold programs and data that are subject to frequent changes: for example, inventory price information (we all know which

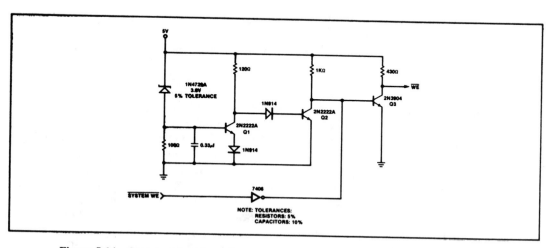

Figure 5.14 Care must be taken when power is applied to or removed from an E^2PROM. This circuit ensures that the $\overline{\text{WE}}$ input will be high during these power-on or power-off transitions. (Courtesy of Intel Corporation.)

Sec. 5.4   **RAM and ROM Technologies**

way that changes!), set points and end points in NC (numerically controlled) machine tools, and motion paths for industrial robots.

A particularly interesting application of the E²PROM is programming via a remote data link. Using a telephone interface called a modem, the central factory can "call up" the E²PROM field system and transfer new data or modify the system software. The cost savings can be substantial compared with conventional service calls and EPROM reprogramming techniques.

Static and Dynamic RAMs.   Two types of semiconductor RAM are popular. In the first, called *static RAM* (SRAM), four to six transistors are connected to form a simple RS flip-flop. The standard six-transistor static memory cell is shown in Fig. 5.15. Q1 and Q2 are the active devices, while Q3 and Q4 are biased as resistive loads. Transistors Q5 and Q6 are used to gate data onto the internal data bus.

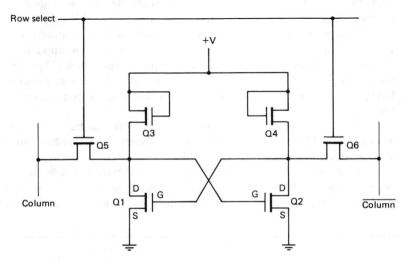

Figure 5.15   Basic six-transistor static memory cell.

As with all flip-flops, the latching mechanism is due to the *cross-coupling* of Q1 and Q2. If the Q1 drain is at 0 V, this level will hold Q2 OFF and its drain terminal will be high. This high level, in turn, holds Q1 ON and its drain low.

Data is written to the cell by applying the desired data (and its complement) to the column and $\overline{\text{column}}$ lines with Q5 and Q6 ON. Data is read out by enabling Q5 and Q6 and reading the column line. The static cell is volatile because it will lose its data if power is lost. Each cell will also power-on in an unknown state.

Static memories are best known for their ease of interfacing. No special timing circuits are required. We will see that the same is not true for the dynamic RAM. Table 5.5 lists several important specifications of popular static RAM chips.

If we assume that one of the goals of any memory technology is to produce a high-bit-density component, a part that requires six transistors per cell may not be the best choice. It is this basic flaw of the static RAM that has led designers to the *dynamic RAM* technology.

TABLE 5.5 COMMON STATIC RAM SPECIFICATIONS

Part no.	Total bits	Organization	Supplies	Access time (ns)	P_D(mW)	Pins
2114AL-1	4K	1K × 4	+5 V	100	200	18
2147H-1	4K	4K × 1	+5 V	35	900	18
2167	16K	16K × 1	+5 V	70	900	20
6116P-2	16K	2K × 8	+5 V	120	400	24
6264-1	64K	8K × 8	+5 V	100	30	28
62256-1	256K	32K × 8	+5 V	100	30	28

Dynamic RAMs or DRAMs are based on the well-known capacitive input nature of an MOS transistor. In this scheme the basic storage cell is shrunk to a single bit select transistor and storage capacitor. A portion of a dynamic RAM memory array is shown in Fig. 5.16.

The main advantage of the DRAM cell is its size. Compared with the SRAM we would expect a four- to six-fold density improvement. In practice the improvement may be even greater. In addition, because the dynamic cell draws no current unless it is being charged, power consumption is very low.

When compared with static RAM technology, the dynamic RAM shows some striking differences. The 2164 DRAM, for example, stores 65,536 total bits, consumes 275 mW of power, and is contained in a 16-pin package. Now consider that the HM6116 SRAM (introduced at about the same time as the 2164) stores 16,384 total bits, consumes 400 mW of power, and is contained in a 24-pin package. The static part stores fewer total bits, consumes more power, and requires a larger package.

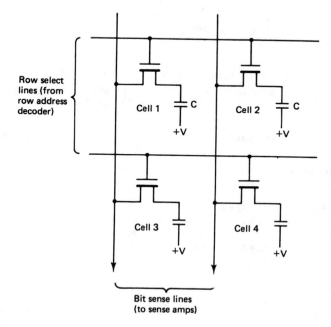

Row select lines (from row address decoder)

Cell 1 C +V

Cell 2 C +V

Cell 3 +V

Cell 4 +V

Bit sense lines (to sense amps)

Figure 5.16 Dynamic RAMs use an MOS capacitor as the basic storage cell.

Sec. 5.4   RAM and ROM Technologies

Table 5.6 provides information about other DRAMs and should be compared with Table 5.5 for the SRAMs.

Of course, you may already be familiar with the DRAM's greatest shortcoming— the storage node is not perfect; it *leaks*. This necessitates a *refresh* operation—that is, sense the charge, amplify it, and then rewrite it—on every cell in the memory at least once every 2 ms.

Refresh may not be as bad as it sounds. Referring to Fig. 5.16, each column in a DRAM has its own sense amplifier which can be used to recharge the bit cell in a given row. By sequencing through all *row* addresses the entire memory array can be refreshed. This means that a 64K DRAM will not require 64K refresh cycles.

DRAMs are purposely designed to facilitate the refresh process. For example, the 2164 is organized as four 128×128-bit cell quadrants. In this design the row address is common to all four quadrants and therefore a 7-bit refresh address is sufficient to access any row. This simplifies refreshing because only 128 rows need be sequenced each 2 ms. Some 64K DRAMs require sequencing through 256 rows every 4 ms.

To keep the packing density high, the industry has chosen to use the standard 300-mil-wide 16-pin DIP (dual-in-line package) for most DRAMs through the 21256 (256K bit). But because a 64K RAM will require 16 address lines, the address bus must be *multiplexed* and given to the chip as a row address followed by a column address. This has the negative effect of increasing the DRAM access time due to the setup times for the row and column addresses.

For these reasons the DRAM has become well known for its complex timing and interface circuitry. Later in this chapter a 2164-based 128K-byte DRAM interface will be presented and you will be able to judge for yourself.

In summary, static RAM is easier to interface and usually has a faster access time than dynamic RAM. However, dynamic RAMs consume less power and provide a four- to sixfold density improvement at any given time in the current state of the technology.

RAM Organization. From the manufacturer's standpoint (and for good marketing hype!), the most important number describing a memory component is the total bit capacity. But from a user's standpoint, it is just as important to know how this memory is *organized*.

The organization of a memory refers to the number of bits in the output

TABLE 5.6 COMMON DYNAMIC RAM SPECIFICATIONS

Part no.	Total bits	Organization	Supplies	Access time (ns)	P_D(mW)	Pins
2141-2	4K	$4K \times 1$	+5 V	120	350	18
PD4116-5	16K	$16K \times 1$	+12 V, −5 V, +5 V	120	460	16
2118-10	16K	$16K \times 1$	+5 V	100	135	16
2164A-15	64K	$64K \times 1$	+5 V	150	275	16
21256	256K	$256K \times 1$	+5 V	150	300	16
511000-10	1 M	$1 M \times 1$	+5 V	100	330	18

word. Referring to Tables 5.5 and 5.6, we see that this can range from *byte-wide* devices like the HM6116, to single-bit devices like the 2164 or 2147. DRAMs are all 1 bit wide because they are pin-limited in order to maintain the standard 16-pin DIP.

The advantage of the byte-wide devices is that a single chip can be used to provide a practical memory in a small memory system. This, in turn, helps keep the package count low and allows miniaturization of the overall hardware.

The single-bit chips will require eight devices to realize a useful memory but offer the advantage of higher board density in large memory systems. This is because there are only eight total data pins compared to eight data pins per chip with byte-wide devices.

Recently manufacturers have taken to mounting DRAM chips vertically on a small PC card. Called SIMMS, for *single in-line memory modules*, common configurations are 256K by 8 or 9 and 1 MB by 8 or 9. SIMMS plug into slot connectors on the computer's system board. Some computers can accommodate as many as 16 rows of SIMMS.

Example 5.2

It is desired to design a 32K-byte memory board. How many total RAM chips will be required if the board is built from 2114 RAMs? Repeat for 2147s, HM6116s, and 2167s.

Solution. The 2114s must be used in pairs to form the 8-bit word size and one pair will store a total of 1K bytes. Thus 64 2114s will be required for a 32K memory. Using 2147s the total is also 64. Using HM6116s or 2167s, 16 devices will be required.

Note: The best choice for this design (from a board-space standpoint) might be the 2167. This is because it comes in a 300-mil-wide 20-pin package compared to the 600-mil-wide 24-pin package of the HM6116.

The Universal Site. A number of semiconductor manufacturers have chosen to adopt a standard pinning configuration for byte-wide memories. This is called the *byte-wide universal memory site*. Figure 5.17 provides the details.

The universal memory site can accommodate EPROMs, E²PROMs, static

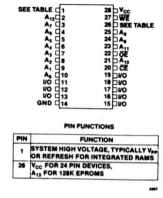

PIN	FUNCTION
1	SYSTEM HIGH VOLTAGE, TYPICALLY V$_{PP}$ OR REFRESH FOR INTEGRATED RAMS
26	V$_{CC}$ FOR 24 PIN DEVICES, A$_{13}$ FOR 128K EPROMS

Figure 5.17 Pin configuration for the byte-wide universal memory site. (Courtesy of Intel Corporation.)

RAMs, and quasi-static RAMs. Intel's line of universal products is shown in Fig. 5.18. Note that although the standard is based on a 28-pin package, 24-pin devices such as the 2716 EPROM can be used by plugging the device into the bottom 24 pins.

One of the advantages of this scheme is that developmental software can be debugged in static RAM, where changes are easily made. Once tested, an EPROM can be programmed and plugged into the same socket but with full confidence that the software has been debugged.

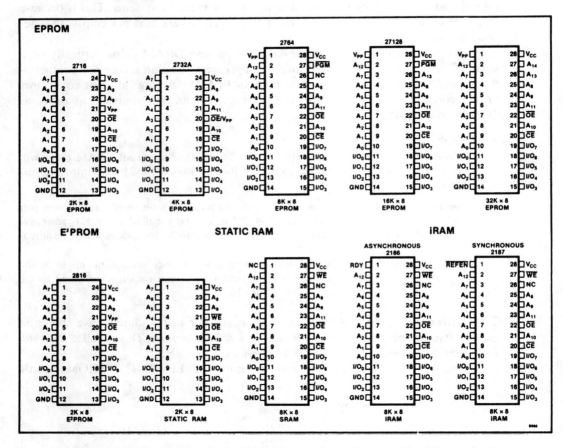

Figure 5.18   Intel family of universal memory products. (Courtesy of Intel Corporation.)

Example 5.3

Show how the universal memory site can be designed to accommodate the 2K 2716 EPROM or the 16K 27128 EPROM.

Solution.   Figure 5.19 is the circuit. The jumpers are shown in the 27128 position. The decoder is necessary to determine the value of the high-order address bits that will enable the EPROM. Notice that the 2716 plugs into the low 24 pins of the socket.

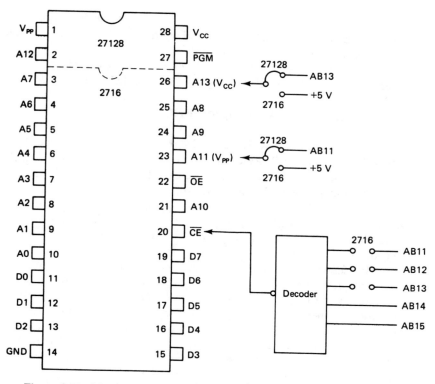

Figure 5.19 Memory design for a 2716/27128 EPROM interface. By using the universal memory site, 2716 designs can be upgraded to the larger 27128 without redesigning the circuit board.

5.5 INTERFACING STATIC RAM AND ROM TO THE MICROPROCESSOR

As you read this section, look for the answers to these Key Concept questions:

5.5.1. The _____ _____ determines the range of addresses occupied by a memory chip.

5.5.2. What is the effect of address and data bus buffers on memory timing?

5.5.3. When _____ decoding is used, the same memory block occupies more than one address.

5.5.4. All of the combinational logic of an address decoder can be replaced by a single _____ or _____ chip.

Connecting a memory device to the three-bus architecture of a microprocessor is called *memory interfacing*. This requires careful consideration of the control signals required by the memory component for compatibility with the host microprocessor. In addition, because the timing of the microprocessor cannot be changed (except to add wait states), the worst-case time delays of the interface circuitry and the memory device should be summed and verified to be within the specifications of the processor.

In this section we study examples of microprocessor memory interfacing. This includes a byte-wide 8K EPROM and a bit-wide 16K static RAM.

Interfacing the 2764 8K-Byte EPROM

Studying the EPROM data sheet. A data sheet for the 2764 8K EPROM is provided in Figure 5.9. Referring to the ac waveforms on this data sheet, note that two control lines are provided. These are called *chip enable* ($\overline{CE}$), an active-low input, and *output enable* ($\overline{OE}$), also an active-low input.

When the $\overline{CE}$ input is high, the 2764 operates in a *standby* mode and power consumption is reduced from 500 mW maximum to 200 mW maximum. The $\overline{CE}$ input should only be driven low when a valid address appears on the address bus from the microprocessor.

The second control input is $\overline{OE}$ and this line enables the internal tri-state buffers to place the data word on the output lines. Intel recommends that this line be driven by the processor $\overline{MEMR}$ control signal.

If you refer to the microprocessor memory read timing diagram in Fig. 5.1, you will notice that $\overline{MEMR}$ is always removed before the current address changes. Thus if $\overline{MEMR}$ is used to control $\overline{OE}$, the outputs of the memory will be in a high-impedance state (the tri-state) when the memory address changes. This is a safety precaution used to prevent bus contention.

The task of interfacing the 2764 to any of the three CPU modules presented in Chap. 4 should now be straightforward. Address lines AB0 through AB12 connect directly to the chip, as do data lines DB0 through DB7. The $\overline{MEMR}$ control signal can connect to the $\overline{OE}$ input. These connections are shown in Fig. 5.20(a).

Three address lines are unused in this scheme. These are AB13 through AB15. These lines should be *decoded* and used to control the $\overline{CE}$ input. For example, if the decoder requires that AB13 AND AB14 AND AB15 all be high to produce a low output, the EPROM will occupy the memory space from E000H through FFFFH, as shown in Fig. 5.20(b).

Because there are eight combinations of the three address lines AB13 through AB15, there are eight possible "slots" in the 64K memory space that this chip can occupy. These are listed in Fig. 5.20(b).

So what is in the box labeled *DECODER*? It must be a circuit that recognizes one of the eight patterns shown in Fig. 5.20(b) and causes a low-level output when that input appears. For the case AB13 = AB14 = AB15 = 1, the circuit is simply a three-input *NAND* gate. This is shown in Fig. 5.21(a). By adding inverters, any of the eight patterns can be decoded. Note that a three-input OR gate can also be used as a decoder, as shown in Fig. 5.21(c).

Verifying the timing. Now that we have determined the proper connections for the 2764 interface, we should verify that the timing specifications are compatible with the microprocessor.

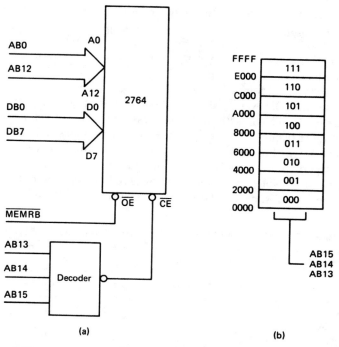

Figure 5.20 (a) 2764 EPROM interface to any of the CPU modules presented in Chap. 4; (b) address lines AB13 through AB15 are decoded to select one of eight possible 8K slots in the processor's memory space.

Consider first the *address access time* as defined in Fig. 5.1. This is the amount of time the processor will allow the memory to place valid data on the bus after it has output a memory address. For the 2764 this will require 250 ns maximum. Because we are deriving the $\overline{CE}$ signal from the address bus, the time t_{CE}

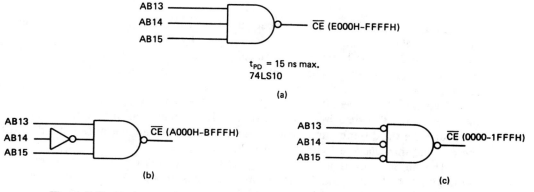

Figure 5.21 A three-input NAND (a) and (b) or a three-input OR gate (c) can be OR gate can be used to decode the three address lines in Fig. 5.20(a).

Sec. 5.5   Interfacing Static RAM and ROM to the Microprocessor   **221**

must also be considered. In reference to the data sheet in Appendix D, this is also 250 ns maximum.

Finally, the time t_{RD} in Fig. 5.1 (memory read to valid data) is considered. This corresponds to the time t_{OE} in the 2764 ac waveforms. It is specified as 100 ns maximum.

Table 5.7 compares these times with those calculated in Sec. 5.2 for the 8080A, the 8085AH, and the Z-80A. Be sure that you interpret these numbers correctly. In all cases the microprocessor provides a *timing window* in which the event must occur. For example, the 8080A provides a 590-ns access-time window during which the memory must decode the address and come up with valid data. In this particular case 250 ns is required by the memory, which is well within this specification. Notice, however, that the 2764 is too slow for the faster Z-80 processor and one WAIT state will be required (or select the 2764-2 part).

TABLE 5.7 TIMING PARAMETERS FOR THE 2764 EPROM INTERFACE IN FIG. 5.20

Processor	t_{ACC} (ns)[a]		t_{CE} (ns)[b]		t_{RD} (ns)[c]	
	μP	Memory	μP	Memory	μP	Memory
8080A (2 MHz)	590	250	555	250	404	100
8085AH (3 MHz)	515	250	480	250	218	100
Z-80A (4 MHz)	265	250	230	250	113	100

[a] Microprocessor times have been reduced by 60 ns from those given in Table 5.3. This accounts for the buffer delays as explained in Fig. 5.22.

[b] See note a. An additional 35 ns has been subtracted from the microprocessor times to account for the delay through the address decoder logic (see Fig. 5.22).

[c] See note a. An additional 22 ns has been subtracted from the 8085 and Z-80 times to account for the MEMR logic on the CPU module.

You will notice that the numbers used in Table 5.7 are shorter than those given in Table 5.3. Figure 5.22 helps explain why. When the microprocessor issues an address, it is buffered and placed on the system address bus. This introduces one time delay. Another buffer at the memory module site introduces a second delay.

The memory access time now occurs as the data byte is retrieved from the memory array. The data byte is then buffered and placed on the system data bus, introducing a third buffer time delay. Finally, the CPU module buffers the data off the bus and introduces a fourth buffer delay.

The propagation delay path for t_{CE} is further increased by the decoder logic (assume a NAND gate and inverter), and this adds another 35 ns of time delay to this parameter.

Finally, the memory read control bus logic (one 74LS32 OR gate) on the

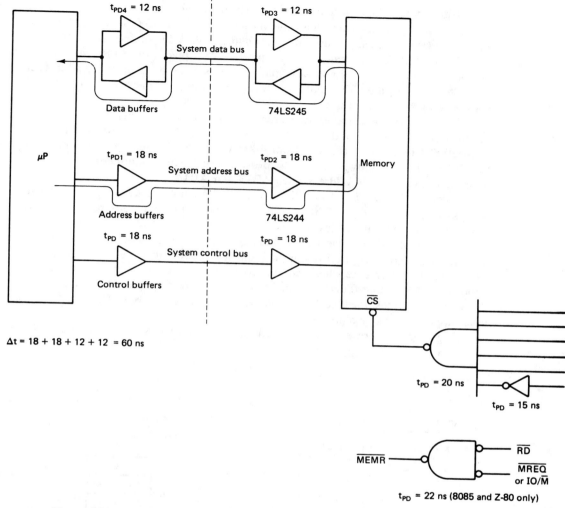

Figure 5.22 Buffers onto and off the system buses increase the total propagation delay times and have the effect of shortening the timing windows provided by the microprocessor.

Z-80 and 8085 CPU modules (see Figs. 4.26 and 4.27) contributes another 22 ns to their t_{RD} specifications.

The accumulation of all these buffer delays (each assumed worst case) deletes as much as 60 ns from the t_{AC} timing window, 95 ns from the t_{CE} timing window, and 82 ns from the t_{RD} timing window.

The timing considerations for the 8085 are more complex, still, due to the need for a low-order address latch. Assuming that a 74LS373 octal buffer/latch is used, as shown in Fig. 4.26, the worst-case time delays introduced by this buffer will be the same as if a standard buffer were used. Therefore, the same derating numbers can be applied to this processor.

Sec. 5.5   Interfacing Static RAM and ROM to the Microprocessor   **223**

Alternative decoding schemes. The decoding techniques shown in Fig. 5.21 all provide *full decoding*—all address lines are tested by the decoder. Sometimes, however, a *partial* decoding scheme is used in which some of the address lines are not tested.

Figure 5.23(a) illustrates a 2764 interface that places the EPROM in the first 8K slot of the processor's memory space. This is done by using only address line AB15 to generate the $\overline{CE}$ signal. When AB15 is low, the memory will be enabled and respond to addresses in the range 0000 to 1FFFH.

There is an undesirable side effect to this decoding scheme, however. The 8K memory "wraps around" or folds back on itself and also resides in the 8K slot from 2000H to 3FFFH, the slot from 4000H to 5FFFH, and the slot from 6000H to 7FFFH. This is shown in Fig. 5.23(b). These "extra" slots correspond to the unused combinations of address lines AB13 and AB14.

Because of the partial decoding, the 2764 cannot tell the difference between address 0000 and address 2000H. This is because the only difference is address line AB13, and this is not tested.

So why should we use partial decoding? In some microcomputer systems the amount of memory required is minimal and it is known that the system will not be expanded at a later date; these conditions might be met by a dedicated hardware controller such as that found in a microwave oven, for example. In this case, partial decoding simplifies the decoder logic by eliminating the NAND gate. This can save circuit-board space and help reduce costs.

Figure 5.24 shows another decoding scheme. In this circuit a 74LS138 3-8

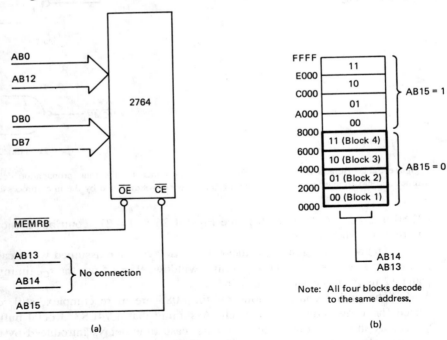

Figure 5.23 (a) The 2764 decoder is simplified by using only address line AB15 for the $\overline{CE}$ input; (b) the result is four 8K slots all decoding to the same chip.

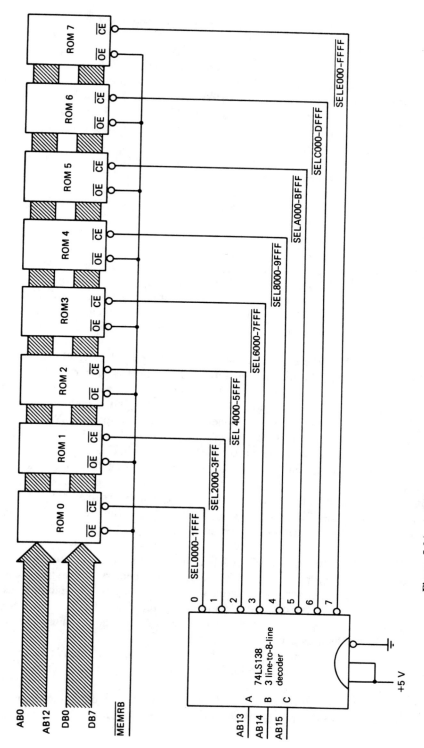

Figure 5.24 A 3 line-to-8 line decoder can be used to decode all eight 8K slots in the processor's memory space. In this case a 64K-byte EPROM interface is built.

225

line-to-line decoder (also made by Intel as the 8205) is used to generate eight separate EPROM select signals. These correspond to the eight memory slots shown in Figs. 5.20(b) and 5.23(b). By using these eight signals as $\overline{CE}$ inputs to eight separate EPROMS, a 64K-byte EPROM interface can be constructed.

Note that all address and data lines are connected in parallel in this interface. What allows this scheme to work is that only one EPROM can be enabled at a time, depending on the value of address lines AB13 through AB15. The output lines of the disabled devices will be in a high-impedance state and therefore not interfere with the selected EPROM.

The decoding technique shown in Fig. 5.24 is called *block decoding*, as it divides the memory space into eight separate memory blocks.

In summary, many different decoding schemes are possible, but the objective is always to prevent bus contention by enabling only one memory device at a time.

Interfacing the 2167 16K Static RAM

Chip architecture. Appendix D Table D.1 is a data sheet for the NEC µPD2167 16K $\times$ 1 static RAM. This is a very high-speed MOS RAM chip having a maximum access time of only 70 ns. It also has *separate* data-in and data-out lines. This means that data to be written should be applied to the data-in pin but read from the data-out pin. This feature will require special attention when interfacing to the system's bidirectional data bus.

Unlike the 2764, there is only one memory control line, called *chip select* ($\overline{CS}$). When $\overline{CS}$ is low, the memory is activated and data is placed on the data-out pin if the write enable ($\overline{WE}$) input is high. If $\overline{WE}$ is low, data placed on the data-in pin will be stored. $\overline{CS}$ should normally be kept high, as the data-out pin is then tri-stated and power consumption is reduced from 850 mW to 150 mW.

The 2167 competes with byte-wide devices like the HM6116 2K $\times$ 8 SRAM but offers the advantage of a narrow-profile package. This means that more DIPs can be accommodated on one circuit board, allowing large memory arrays to be constructed.

Its principal disadvantage is that it is not pin-compatible with any of the "universal memory components" discussed in Sec. 5.4. A board built with 2167s must be dedicated to an SRAM function of a particular size.

Verifying the timing. The 2167 is a very fast device, as is soon discovered when studying the timing parameters in Table 5.8. The memory access time is five to nine times faster than the window opening provided by any of the microprocessors. Note that the data sheet indicates two memory read cycles. Read cycle 1 occurs when the $\overline{CS}$ input is permanently enabled. Read cycle 2 is the more common case and occurs when the $\overline{CS}$ input is driven by an address decoder.

The microprocessor access times in Table 5.8 do not include time delays through the buffers and decoder logic, but it is clear that the 2167 is much faster than required.

A write cycle occurs when $\overline{CS}$ is brought low, output data is placed on the data-in pin, and the $\overline{WE}$ input is taken low. The $\overline{CS}$ input should be driven by an

Processor	t_{ACC} (ns)		t_{DW} (ns)		t_{AW} (ns)	
	μP	2167-2	μP	2167-2	μP	2167-2
8080A	650	70	656	30	1176	55
8085AH	575	70	420	30	670	55
Z-80A	325	70	265	30	500	55

address decoder and the $\overline{WE}$ input by the processor $\overline{MEMWB}$ control line. Using this convention, the write parameters agree exactly with the definitions in Fig. 5.2 for t_{DW} and t_{AW}. From Table 5.8 it is clear that the 2167 easily meets these requirements.

A 32K RAM module. Figure 5.25 is the diagram for a 32K RAM module based on the 2167 SRAM. Let's make several observations about this circuit.

1. Because the 2167 is 1 bit wide, eight chips are required to store a byte. For example, RAMs 0 and 8 store data bit 0, RAMs 1 and 9 store bit 1, and so on.
2. Two banks of 16K are required for the 32K module. BANK0 consists of RAMs 0 through 7; BANK1 consists of RAMs 8 through 15.
3. Address lines AB0 through AB13 are wired in parallel to each of the memory chips. However, only one bank of chips will be enabled at a particular time.
4. Address lines AB14 and AB15 are decoded to provide two bank select signals, $\overline{BANK0}$ and $\overline{BANK1}$. These signals are obtained from the wired-OR outputs of the open-collector *exclusive-OR* gates IC1a–d. For example, if switches S1 and S2 are open, then BANK0 will be selected only if AB14 AND AB15 are both low. If either of these address lines is high, $\overline{BANK0}$ will be held high and RAMs 0 through 7 disabled.
5. The purpose of switches S1 through S4 is to allow each 16K bank to be moved to one of four possible 16K slots in the memory space. In this way other memory modules can be accommodated that might otherwise conflict with a fixed address module. Figure 5.26 explains how the switches are to be set for a particular 16K slot.
6. The bidirectional data bus must be broken into separate data-in and data-out lines to accommodate the 2167. This is the purpose of tri-state buffers IC5 and 6.

During a memory read the processor outputs a 16-bit address on AB0 through AB15. The bank decoder examines AB14 and AB15 and depending on the settings of switches S1 through S4, causes one of the bank select lines to go low. This, in turn, chip-selects one row of RAM chips.

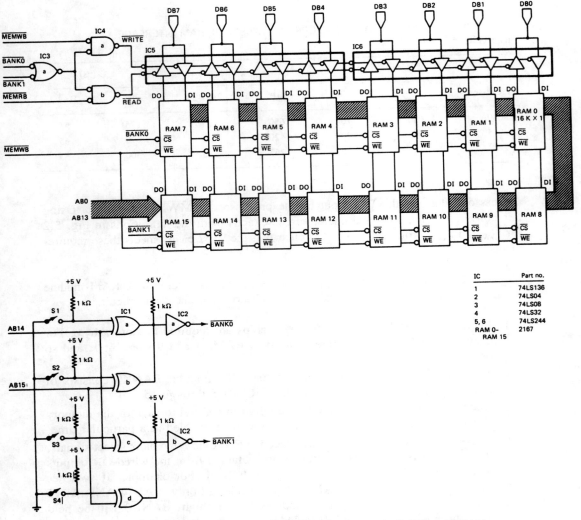

Figure 5.25 32K-byte RAM module based on the 2167 16K × 1 SRAM.

Each RAM chip in the selected row now decodes address lines AB0 through AB13 and places the selected bit on its data-out pin (DO).

The buffer control logic is enabled by either bank select signal, and because this is a memory read operation, the $\overline{\text{READ}}$ output goes low. This signal is used to enable the buffers connected to each data-out line and the data byte is thereby gated onto the microprocessor system data bus.

The sequence of events for a memory write is similar except that the $\overline{\text{MEMWB}}$ signal causes each RAM chip in the selected row to prepare to receive data on its data-in pin.

The buffer control logic causes $\overline{\text{WRITE}}$ to go low and enables the buffers connected to the data-in pin of each RAM. The microprocessor places the data

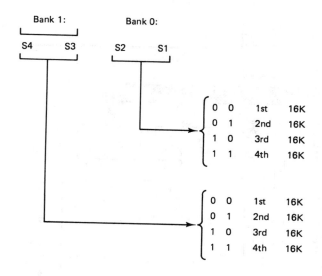

S4   S3   S2   S1

0	0	1st	16K
0	1	2nd	16K
1	0	3rd	16K
1	1	4th	16K

0	0	1st	16K
0	1	2nd	16K
1	0	3rd	16K
1	1	4th	16K

Example: S4 S3 S2 S1 = 1 1 0 1   (closed-closed-open-closed)
           Bank 0 = 4000–7FFF
           Bank 1 = C000–FFFF

Figure 5.26 Switches S1 through S4 select one of four 16K slots for each memory bank in Fig. 5.25.

byte to be written on the system data bus, allowing each RAM chip to latch its particular data bit. When $\overline{\text{MEMWB}}$ goes high, the cycle has ended.

Although not shown in Fig. 5.25, address lines AB0 through AB15 and the $\overline{\text{MEMRB}}$ and $\overline{\text{MEMWB}}$ control signals are all assumed to be buffered before connecting to the system address and control bus. The resulting RAM module can then be connected to any of the CPU modules designed in Chap. 4.

Interfacing a RAM/ROM Module.

A practical microcomputer system will require a certain amount of ROM memory for its operating system and a certain amount of RAM memory for read/write applications. In this section we study a RAM/ROM module that provides 12K of ROM and 16K of RAM.

Designing the hardware.

Combining ROM and RAM memory components in a single memory module is no more difficult than designing an all-ROM or all-RAM module. In this case we will use the 2167 16K-bit SRAM, the 2764 8K-byte EPROM, and the 2732 4K-byte EPROM. The main complication in this interface is the address decoding required for the three different block sizes.

Figure 5.27 is a schematic diagram of the module. The memory array consists of the eight 2167 SRAMs and the 2764 and 2732 EPROMs. The address bus is wired in parallel to each chip and the chip-select inputs driven with the signals $\overline{\text{RAM}}$, $\overline{\text{ROM1}}$, and $\overline{\text{ROM2}}$.

The system data bus must be broken into separate data-in and data-out lines to accommodate the 2167 SRAMs. Note that the EPROM data lines are wired in parallel with the data-out pins of the RAMs. This will not cause a conflict if the

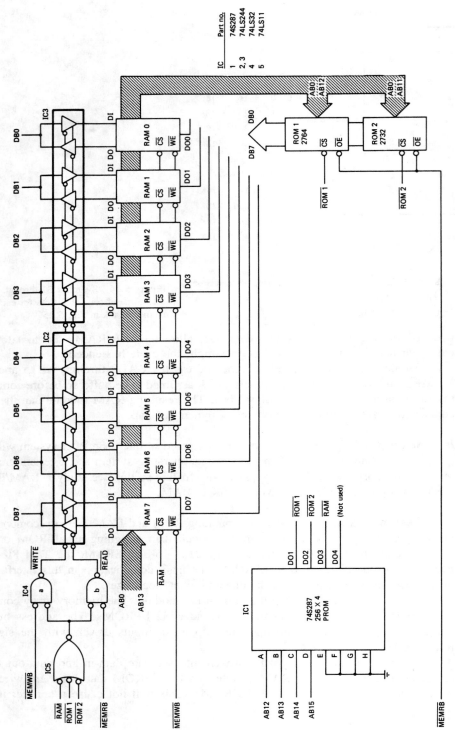

Figure 5.27 12 K-ROM 32K-RAM memory module using a fusible-link PROM decoder.

address decoding ensures that only one type of memory is enabled at a particular time (recall that the data lines of the memory devices go to a high-impedance state when their chip-select inputs are high).

Buffer control logic is again used to control the direction of data flow through the tri-state buffers IC2 and IC3. IC5 ensures that the buffers are disabled for addresses outside the range of this module.

ROM address decoder.   Perhaps the most interesting feature of the RAM/ROM module in Fig. 5.27 is the address decoder. Rather than use standard combinational logic, a 74S287 256 × 4 *fusible-link PROM* has been chosen. This has the advantage of allowing the memory map of the module to be *programmed* instead of hard-wired.

The desired memory map for the RAM/ROM module is given in Fig. 5.28. Because the smallest block size in the module is 4K, the PROM must have at least a 4K resolution. This means that address lines AB12 through AB15 must be examined by the PROM. The 16 combinations of AB12 through AB15 correspond to the 16 4K blocks of memory in the processor's 64K memory space. Similarly, address lines AB11 through AB15 would be required if a 2K resolution was desired.

The 74S287 has eight (address) inputs labeled A through H. We will require only lines A through D and connect these inputs to address lines AB12 through AB15. By grounding PROM inputs E through H, only the first 16 words in the 256-word PROM will be used.

What data should be stored in these 16 locations? To answer this question, we must develop a *truth table* and assign functions to each PROM output pin. This is done in Fig. 5.29.

Although there are four output pins (corresponding to the 4-bit word size),

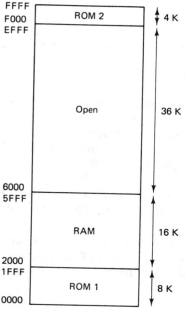

Figure 5.28   Memory map for the RAM/ROM module in Fig. 5.27.

H G F E	D C B A	DO4 (not used)	DO3 ($\overline{RAM}$)	DO2 ($\overline{ROM\ 2}$)	DO1 ($\overline{ROM\ 1}$)	
0 0 0 0	0 0 0 0	X	1	1	0	$\overline{ROM1}$
	0 0 0 1	X	1	1	0	
	0 0 1 0	X	0	1	1	
	0 0 1 1	X	0	1	1	$\overline{RAM}$
	0 1 0 0	X	0	1	1	
	0 1 0 1	X	0	1	1	
	0 1 1 0	X	1	1	1	
	0 1 1 1	X	1	1	1	
	1 0 0 0	X	1	1	1	
	1 0 0 1	X	1	1	1	
	1 0 1 0	X	1	1	1	Not used
	1 0 1 1	X	1	1	1	
	1 1 0 0	X	1	1	1	
	1 1 0 1	X	1	1	1	
	1 1 1 0	X	1	1	1	
0 0 0 0	1 1 1 1	X	1	0	1	$\overline{ROM2}$
0 0 0 1	0 0 0 0					
⋮			These addresses not programmed			
1 1 1 1	1 1 1 1					

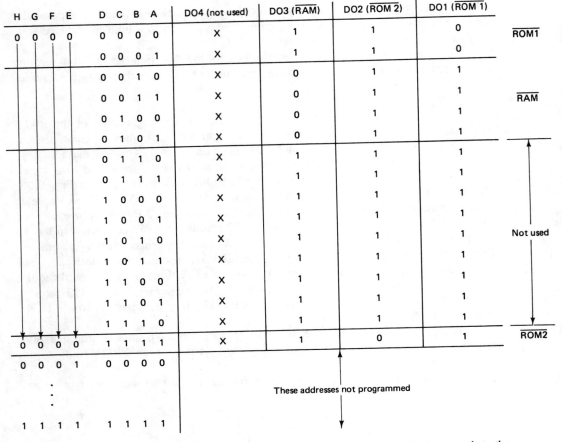

Figure 5.29 Truth table for the PROM decoder in Fig. 5.27. The table corresponds to the memory map in Fig. 5.28.

only three outputs are required. These are arbitrarily chosen as shown in Figs. 5.27 and 5.29.

Once the output definitions are determined, the truth table can be completed. Studying the addresses in the memory map in Fig. 5.28, the $\overline{ROM1}$ output should be low when AB15 through AB12 = 0000 or 0001. All other combinations should produce $\overline{ROM1}$ high.

Similarly, the RAM output should be low when AB15 through AB12 = 0010, 0011, 0100, or 0101. Finally, the 4K EPROM ($\overline{ROM2}$) is enabled when AB15 through AB12 = 1111.

Table 5.9 is a data table for the 74S287 PROM and lists in hex format the 4-bit data words to be stored in the PROM. Because an *unprogrammed* data bit stores a 1, the unused DO4 data bit is assumed 1 in this table.

TABLE 5.9 PROM DATA
TABLE

Address	Data
0	E
1	E
2	B
3	B
4	B
5	B
6	F
7	F
8	F
9	F
A	F
B	F
C	F
D	F
E	F
F	D
10	F
.	F
.	F
.	F
FF	F

The data in the truth table in Fig. 5.29 is converted to a PROM address and hex data word in preparation for programming.

Figure 5.30 lists the step-by-step programming procedure for the 74S287 as recommended by Texas Instruments.

PAL address decoder. Many designers today use *programmable arrary logic* devices or PALs instead of ROMs for replacing combinational logic. A PAL consists of a programmable array of AND and OR gates. Figure 5.31 shows an example of the PAL10L8. This chip has 10 input pins and 8 output pins. Note that each output is obtained from a two-input NOR gate, and each of these inputs are driven by AND gates. Inverters on each input pin allow the complement of each input to be easily obtained.

In Fig. 5.31 the intersection of a vertical and horizontal line represents a *possible* AND input. To program the chip you first place an "X" at each desired intersection to form a "map" of the intended circuit. For example, an X at row 0 column 5 and row 0 column 8 programs the product term:

$$\overline{\text{INPUT3}} \cdot \text{INPUT4}$$

step-by-step programming procedure

1. Apply steady-state supply voltage (V_{CC} = 5 V) and address the word to be programmed.

2. Verify that the bit location needs to be programmed. If not, proceed to the next bit.

3. If the bit requires programming, disable the outputs by applying a high-logic-level voltage to the chip-select input(s).

4. Only one bit location is programmed at a time. Connect each output not being programmed to 5 V through 3.9 kΩ and apply the voltage specified in the table to the output to be programmed. Maximum current out of the programming output supply during programming is 150 mA.

5. Step V_{CC} to 10.5 V nominal. Maximum supply current required during programming is 750 mA.

6. Apply a low-logic-level voltage to the chip-select input(s). This should occur between 10 μs and 1 ms after V_{CC} has reached its 10.5-V level. See programming sequence of Figure 3.

7. After the X pulse time (1 ms) is reached, a high logic level is applied to the chip-select inputs to disable the outputs.

8. Within 10 μs to 1 ms after the chip-select input(s) reach a high logic level, V_{CC} should be stepped down to 5 V at which level verification can be accomplished.

9. The chip-select input(s) may be taken to a low logic level (to permit program verification) 10 μs or more after V_{CC} reaches its steady-state value of 5 V.

10. At a Y pulse duty cycle of 35% or less, repeat steps 1 through 8 for each output where it is desired to program a bit.

NOTES: A) V_{CC} should be removed between program pulses to reduce dissipation and chip temperatures. See Figure 3.
B) When verification indicates that a bit did not program, repeat steps 3 through 9. If the bit did not program after the second application of a 1-ms X pulse, repeat steps 3 through 9 using an X pulse time of 10 to 20 ms. Regardless of the X duration, the total average pulse time of Y should be no more than 35% of the programming cycle.

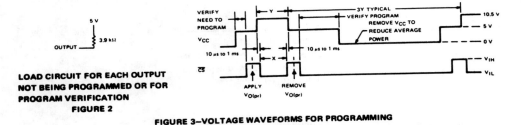

LOAD CIRCUIT FOR EACH OUTPUT
NOT BEING PROGRAMMED OR FOR
PROGRAM VERIFICATION
FIGURE 2

FIGURE 3–VOLTAGE WAVEFORMS FOR PROGRAMMING

Figure 5.30 Programming procedure for the 74S287 fusible-link PROM. (Courtesy of Texas Instruments.)

Two such product terms can be formed for each OR gate. In the preceding example we saw that the signal ROM1 should be active whenever AB15, AB14, and AB13 are low. This could be programmed via a PAL as:

$$O_{19} = \overline{INPUT1} \cdot \overline{INPUT2} \cdot \overline{INPUT3}$$

where pins 1, 2, and 3 are connected to AB13–15. Pin 19 then becomes the ROM1 output signal.

PALs are more easily programmed than ROMs because each output maps to a single programming combination. With a ROM, several hundred locations may have to be programmed for each output. PALs are programmed using a fusible-link technique similar to that of a bipolar PROM.

10L8

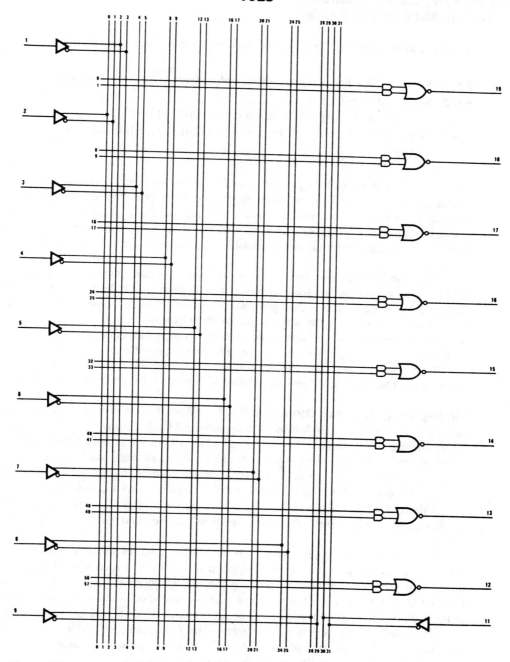

Figure 5.31 The PAL10L8 has 10 inputs and 8 outputs. (Courtesy of Monolithic Memories, Inc. PAL is a registered trademark of Monolithic Memories, Inc. PLF is a trademark of Monolithic Memories, Inc.)

Sec. 5.5   Interfacing Static RAM and ROM to the Microprocessor

235

5.6 INTERFACING DYNAMIC RAM TO THE MICROPROCESSOR

As you read this section, look for the answers to these Key Concept questions:

5.6.1. DRAM chips use a time multiplexed address bus. What does this mean?

5.6.2. Most DRAMs use a _____-_____ refresh in which each row address is output in sequence once every 2 ms.

5.6.3. Which refresh technique tries to "hide" the refresh cycles among inactive bus cycles?

One of the advantages of living in this era of "high technology" and microelectronics is that digital circuit design becomes simpler as time goes by. It was not so long ago that the design of a computer (any computer) required the skill of a computer scientist with many years of experience. Now a working microcomputer can be built by an ambitious junior high schooler with as few as three or four integrated circuits.

Fortunately, the same holds true for dynamic memory design. Early dynamic RAMs were notorious for their complex circuit designs. Indeed, some designers had little confidence in a memory technology that "forgets" and must be told to "remember." However, the advantages of the DRAM—high-bit density and low-power consumption—have caused the industry to increase its efforts to make this a useful technology. The result is the *dynamic RAM controller*.

In this section we examine the problems in designing a DRAM interface and see how the DRAM controller can be used to implement high-density RAM arrays.

Timing Diagrams for Dynamic RAM. Table D.2 in Appendix D contains a data sheet for the Intel 2164A 64K × 1 dynamic RAM. Referring to the logic symbol for this device, you will note that only eight address lines are provided. Normally, you would expect a 64K device to require 16 address lines. Because this many pins would require a large package, the designers have chosen to time-multiplex the address bus into a *row address* (A0 through A7) and a *column address* (A8 through A15).

Figure 5.32 illustrates basic timing for memory read and write cycles. Two clock signals are required: $\overline{RAS}$, row address strobe, and $\overline{CAS}$, column address strobe.

A read or write cycle begins with the falling edge of the $\overline{RAS}$ clock signal. This will latch the address currently applied to the chip, which should correspond to the low order or row address. During the timing window t_{RCD}, the row address must be held stable to meet the t_{RAH} row address hold specification and then changed to the high-order or column address. The falling edge of $\overline{CAS}$ will latch this address.

If a memory read cycle is in progress, the falling edge of $\overline{CAS}$ will also gate data onto the data-out pin of the RAM. The access time is measured from the falling edge of RAS to valid data at the data-out pin (t_{RAC}).

The memory read cycle must include the cycle *precharge* time t_{RP}. This is the time required to charge the bit sense line (see Fig. 5.16) in preparation for the

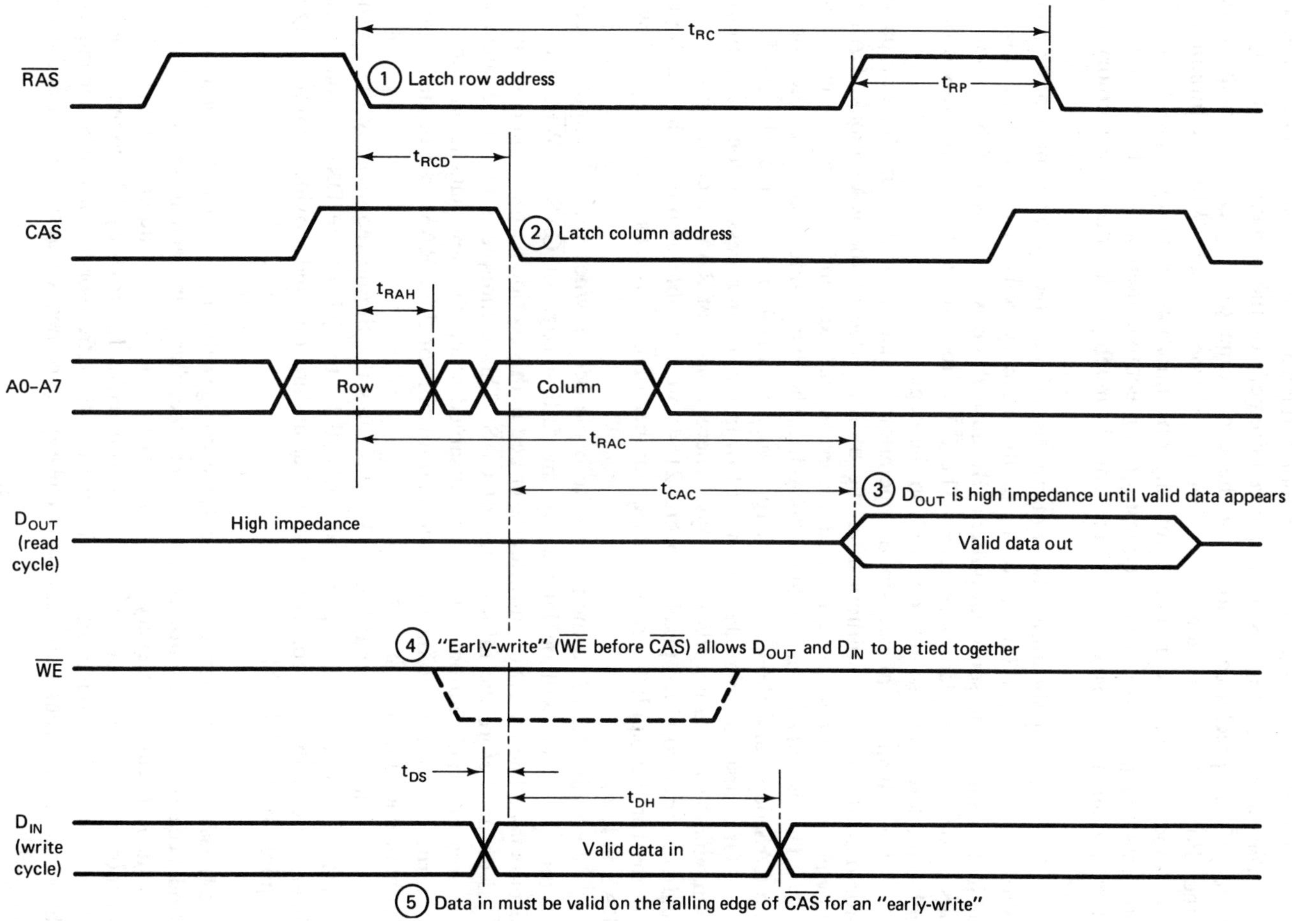

t_{RC}
$\overline{RAS}$
1 Latch row address
t_{RP}
t_{RCD}
$\overline{CAS}$
2 Latch column address
t_{RAH}
A0–A7
Row
Column
t_{RAC}
t_{CAC}
3 D_{OUT} is high impedance until valid data appears
D_{OUT} (read cycle)
High impedance
Valid data out
4 "Early-write" ($\overline{WE}$ before $\overline{CAS}$) allows D_{OUT} and D_{IN} to be tied together
$\overline{WE}$
t_{DS}
t_{DH}
D_{IN} (write cycle)
Valid data in
5 Data in must be valid on the falling edge of $\overline{CAS}$ for an "early-write"

Figure 5.32 Dynamic RAM timing diagrams. Two clock signals ($\overline{RAS}$ and $\overline{CAS}$) are required to latch the multiplexed row and column addresses.

next memory cycle. The memory read cycle time is the sum of t_{RAC} and t_{RP}. The 2164A-15 has a 150-ns access time (t_{RAC}) but a 260-ns cycle time.

From the microprocessor's standpoint, the access time is the important parameter. The precharge time is a unique requirement of the dynamic RAM only. The effect of the precharge is to cause the cycle time to be greater than the access time. Fortunately, this does not affect the microprocessor. Why? A minimum of four clock periods are required for any one microprocessor machine cycle. This prevents the processor from requesting consecutive memory cycles with periods shorter than 4T or 1μs at 4 MHz. This is much longer than the memory cycle time.

In certain applications the dynamic RAM can be operated in a *page mode*. When the $\overline{RAS}$ clock falls low, all of the memory cells in the selected row pass their data on to the sense amplifiers. Because the row address is 8 bits wide, 256 bits or one page of data is selected. The $\overline{CAS}$ clock now gates in the low-order or column address and selects one cell on the page.

The advantage of page-mode operation is that all of the data for one page is stored in the sense amplifiers after the trailing edge of the $\overline{RAS}$ clock. $\overline{CAS}$ can now be used to cycle through all addresses on that page and the access time becomes t_{CAC}. This is only 85 ns for the 2164A-15. The cycle time is equal to the width of the $\overline{CAS}$ pulse and the $\overline{CAS}$ precharge time. This is 125 ns for the 2164A-15.

Of course, page mode does not allow true random access. It does have applications in *bit-mapped graphics* displays, where a block of RAM is continually scanned and converted to video pixels. Special 2164s are available with extended $\overline{RAS}$ pulse widths for this application (so that a number of $\overline{CAS}$ pulses can be applied while $\overline{RAS}$ is low).

As with SRAM, a memory write cycle occurs when the $\overline{WE}$ input is active. In this case data will be latched by the falling edge of $\overline{CAS}$ or $\overline{WE}$, whichever occurs last. The DRAM controller described in this section performs an *early-write*—$\overline{WE}$ occurs before the falling edge of $\overline{CAS}$. This technique is preferred because it ensures that the data-out pin will be disabled when the new data is written. This, in turn, means that the data-out and data-in pins of the DRAM can be tied together without contention problems.

Be sure to note that Fig. 5.32 illustrates the timing required by the dynamic RAM chip, not the microprocessor. It will be the job of the DRAM controller to interface with the microprocessor three-bus architecture and provide the timing signals required by the DRAM.

Refresh.   As mentioned in Sec. 5.4, the storage cell for a dynamic RAM is a capacitor. And because this capacitor is not perfect, the charge in each memory cell must be rewritten at least once every 2 ms or data will be lost. In the case of the 2164, the memory array consists of four quadrants arranged as 128 rows by 128 columns. Because the row lines of all four quadrants are common, the refresh operation can be accomplished by sequencing through all 128 row addresses. This means that the refresh address is 7 bits wide.

Although a refresh operation will occur whenever a read or write cycle occurs, we cannot usually guarantee that every row of the DRAM will be accessed at least once every 2 ms (an exception to this might be "screen" memory used in a memory-mapped video display interface).

The technique most commonly used in DRAM controllers is called $\overline{RAS}$-only refresh and is illustrated in Fig. 5.33. In this scheme only a row address is output to the DRAM and no data is read or written during the cycle. Sequencing through all 128 row addresses will refresh the memory. Of course, during this time the processor will be unable to access the memory.

A third method of refreshing a DRAM is called *hidden refresh*. The timing is illustrated in Fig. 5.34. After completing a normal memory cycle, the $\overline{CAS}$ clock is left low. This will maintain data on the data-out pin. Now any number of $\overline{RAS}$ clocks can be applied as the row address is incremented. Hidden refresh is essentially a $\overline{RAS}$-only refresh but with the $\overline{CAS}$ clock held low. This technique can be used to "hide" refresh cycles among processor cycles which require that data be held on the bus but do not require a new memory or I/O access.

There are three methods of distributing the necessary refresh cycles over the 2-ms refresh period.

1. *Burst refresh*: In this technique the processor is forced into a WAIT state and all 128 rows are refreshed in one "burst." Normal processing is then resumed until the next refresh period is required. Because one refresh cycle can take 260 ns or longer, the time to refresh all 128 rows can exceed 30 μs. During this time the memory cannot be accessed.

2. *Distributed refresh*: Rather than refreshing the entire memory at once, the refresh cycles can be distributed over the entire 2-ms period. This will require

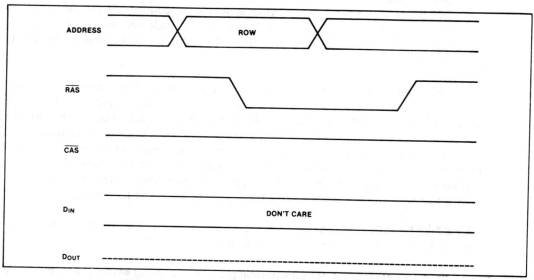

Figure 5.33 $\overline{RAS}$-only refresh cycle. The microprocessor cannot access the memory during this refresh time. (Courtesy of Intel Corporation.)

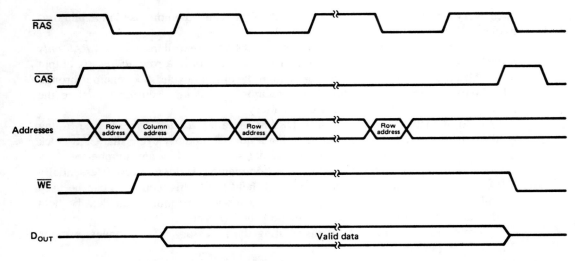

Figure 5.34 "Hidden refresh" cycle. Data-out is maintained valid throughout the cycle.

a refresh cycle every 2 ms/128 cycles = 15.6 μs. Most DRAM controllers use this technique.

3. *Transparent refresh*: Ideally, we would like to "sneak" the refresh cycles into the microprocessor timing at points when access to the memory is not required. In this way the refresh operations would be "transparent" and never slow the processor down. The usual technique is to identify the *M1* or opcode fetch machine cycle. After this fetch cycle several clock periods are often consumed for instruction execution. For example, the 8080 instruction INR r requires five T states. After state T3 the contents of the buses are no longer important. During states T4 and T5 the selected register is accessed and then incremented. One refresh cycle could easily be performed during this time.

Using transparent refresh the microprocessor must never cease fetching opcodes or data will be lost. This puts a restriction on certain types of processor activities, such as DMA transfers. Transparent refresh is also not suitable for the newer generation of high-speed microprocessors. This is because the execution phase of an instruction may not be sufficiently long at the faster clock speeds. Another problem occurs with processors such as the Intel 8086 16-bit microprocessor. This processor *prefetches* instructions while previous instructions are being executed. This effectively eliminates the "dead time" on the bus used for refresh.

The 8203 DRAM Controller.   There are several problems associated with interfacing a dynamic RAM memory. Among these are:

1. Address multiplexing. During normal processor read and write cycles the DRAM must receive a memory address from the processor, but during refresh operations it must receive a special "refresh address."

2. Each row in the DRAM memory must be refreshed at least once every 2 ms.
3. Timing signals must be generated to control $\overline{RAS}$, $\overline{CAS}$, and the address multiplexer.
4. Logic must be designed to decide if a refresh cycle or normal memory read or write cycle is to be performed. This is called *arbitration*.
5. When refresh interferes with normal processor activity, WAIT states must be requested.

This is a formidable list of problems to be solved (particularly with discrete logic gates). Fortunately, all of these problems have been solved in the form of the *dynamic RAM controller*.

Figure 5.35 presents a block diagram and pin configuration for the Intel 8203 dynamic RAM controller. It accepts a 16-bit address from the microprocessor at AH0–AH7 (the high-order or column address) and AL0–AL7 (the low-order or row address). These two bytes are then multiplexed with an 8-bit refresh counter and are available at outputs $\overline{OUT0}$ through $\overline{OUT7}$.

The refresh counter cycles through 256 states at least once every 4 ms. In this way the 8203 is compatible with 128-row or 256-row refresh RAMs. The refresh rate and all other system timing is controlled by a crystal connected to X0 and X1. Any frequency between 18.432 and 25 MHz can be used for this crystal.

Note that the 8203 directly generates the $\overline{CAS}$, $\overline{RAS}$, and $\overline{WE}$ signals required by the DRAM array. When used for controlling 16K devices, the $\overline{RAS0}$ through $\overline{RAS3}$ outputs allow four 16K banks. In this case the address is broken into two 7-bit groups: A0 through A6 and A7 through A13. A14 and A15 are then connected to B0 and B1 and determine which of the four banks is to be selected.

Figure 5.36 illustrates a 128K dynamic RAM interface using two banks of 2164 64K DRAMs. In this circuit the 8203 is used in the 64K mode by grounding pin 35 (16K/$\overline{64K}$). In this mode four of the pins change function. The number of banks is reduced to two, as the $\overline{RAS2}$ and $\overline{RAS3}$ outputs are now used for address output 7 and bank select input B0. The former bank select inputs, B0 and B1, are now used for the additional address inputs AL7 (A7) and AH7 (A15).

Refreshing of the two banks occurs automatically by the 8203 at least once every 2 ms. During the refresh time $\overline{RAS0}$ and $\overline{RAS1}$ are both enabled and therefore both 64K banks are refreshed simultaneously using the "RAS-only" technique.

Of course, the processors we have studied cannot directly access 128K of memory and do not have an address line AB16 (connected to B0 in Fig. 5.36). However, an output port (basically a flip-flop) could be used to control the 8203 B0 input. In this way an output instruction could be used to flip from one 64K bank to another.

The 8203 uses a *distributed refresh* technique and an internal refresh timer and arbitrator determines when to perform a refresh cycle so that RAM data is never lost. However, an external refresh can also be performed using the REFRQ input. This input would be used to implement "transparent refresh," for example.

Because the 8203 will perform a refresh cycle *asynchronously* with respect to the CPU, it is likely that the microprocessor will request a memory cycle during

8203
64K DYNAMIC RAM CONTROLLER

- Provides All Signals Necessary to Control 64K (2164) and 16K (2117, 2118) Dynamic Memories

- Directly Addresses and Drives Up to 64 Devices Without External Drivers

- Provides Address Multiplexing and Strobes

- Provides a Refresh Timer and a Refresh Counter

- Provides Refresh/Access Arbitration

- Internal Clock Capability with the 8203-1 and the 8203-3

- Fully Compatible with Intel® 8080A, 8085A, iAPX 88, and iAPX 86 Family Microprocessors

- Provides System Acknowledge and Transfer Acknowledge Signals

- Refresh Cycles May be Internally or Externally Requested (For Transparent Refresh)

- Internal Series Damping Resistors on RAS, CAS and WE Outputs

- Available in EXPRESS
  —Standard Temperature Range

The Intel® 8203 is a Dynamic Ram System Controller designed to provide all signals necessary to use 2164, 2118 or 2117 Dynamic RAMs in microcomputer systems. The 8203 provides multiplexed addresses and address strobes, refresh logic, refresh/access arbitration. Refresh cycles can be started internally or externally. The 8203-1 and the 8203-3 support Advanced-Read mode and an internal crystal oscillator. The 8203-3 is a ±5% Vcc part.

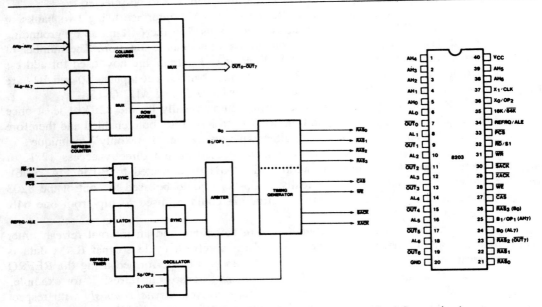

Figure 5.35   Intel 8203 dynamic RAM controller. (Courtesy of Intel Corporation.)

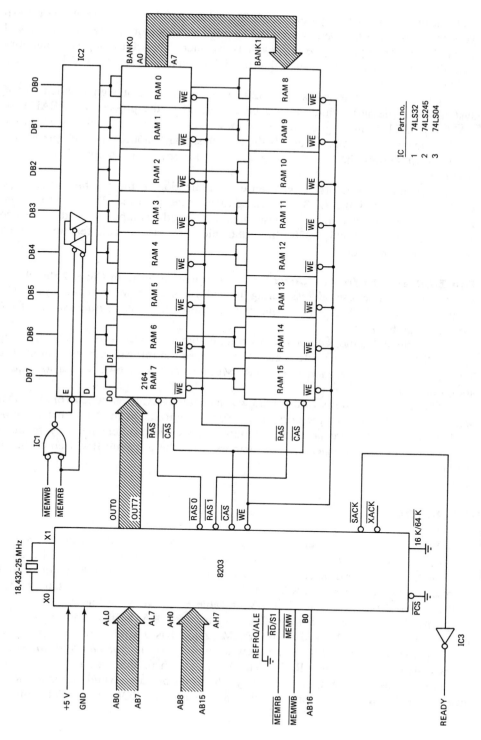

Figure 5.36 128K dynamic RAM module. For the 8080, 8085, or Z-80, A16 can be simulated with 1 bit of an output port.

a refresh operation. If this should occur, the arbitration logic will finish the refresh cycle and then honor the memory request. Similarly, a memory cycle will be allowed to complete before a pending refresh cycle is executed. The arbitrator gives a memory cycle the priority but also ensures that a refresh cycle will be delayed by at most one memory cycle.

For this scheme to work, the 8203 provides a control signal called $\overline{SACK}$ (system acknowledge), which should be connected to the processor's READY or $\overline{WAIT}$ input. This signal goes low early in a memory cycle and acknowledges the CPU's request for memory access. If the $\overline{SACK}$ signal is not received by the microprocessor, it knows that a refresh cycle is in progress and is forced to enter a WAIT state.

Some microprocessors provide an early indication of the machine cycle type which can be used by the 8203 to decrease memory access time. This is the purpose of the ALE and $\overline{RD}/S1$ inputs. These pins are directly compatible with the same signal names on the 8085, 8088, and 8086 microprocessors. This feature is called the *advanced read* mode.

The Z-80 as a Refresh Controller.   You may recall from Chap. 2 that the Z-80 outputs a 7-bit refresh address during T3 and T4 of every M1 machine cycle. The timing was shown in Fig. 2.14. Using this feature of the Z-80 a *transparent refresh controller* can be built.

Unfortunately, the $\overline{RAS}$ and $\overline{CAS}$ timing signals and the address multiplexing must still be built with discrete logic. And because the refresh address is limited to 7 bits, 256-row RAMs cannot be used. Multiple banks of 64K will also require additional bank select logic.

The refresh capability of the Z-80 was a decided advantage when 16K DRAMs were popular and 64K of memory space was thought adequate. Now that the 64K (and 256K) DRAMs are becoming popular, 128K (and larger) memory modules are not uncommon. For these larger memory sizes the dynamic RAM controller is the best choice.

5.7 CONCLUSION

This chapter has taken us on a (rather long) journey through the maze of memory technologies. Certainly, we have come to appreciate that the state of the art in semiconductor memories is continually changing. Reading through the industry trade journals we find that dynamic RAMs will soon be obsoleted by CMOS static RAMs, or that E²PROMs will obsolete the UV erasable EPROM. Who knows?

Intel has announced a new iRAM—integrated RAM—that appears static to the user but is internally a dynamic RAM. Zilog has a similar technology called the *pseudostatic* RAM. Still another new technology is the *nonvolatile RAM*, sometimes called the "shadow" RAM. The Intel version of this part is the 2004 and contains 512 bytes of storage. Internally, the 2004 has a conventional static RAM array but is backed up bit for bit with a nonvolatile E²PROM array. Performing a

STORE function transfers RAM data to the E²PROM and a *RESTORE* function is used to reload the RAM.

The shadow RAM and iRAM represent exciting new developments in memory technology. Perhaps one day we will be able to buy nonvolatile, easily interfaced, static memory parts that come in 1-megabyte plug-in modules (and sell for 25 cents each).

CHAPTER SUMMARY

1. Computer memories can be classified as main processor memory, secondary storage, and archival storage.

2. The microprocessor supplies timing windows in which the memory component must supply its data for a read operation or accept data for a write operation. Slow memory devices can be accommodated by adding *WAIT* states to the processor memory read and write cycles.

3. ROMs or read-only memories are characterized by their nonvolatility and find applications as bootstrap loaders and program storage in turnkey systems.

4. ROMs may be fusible-link programmable, mask programmable, UV-light erasable and electrically programmable (EPROM), or electrically erasable and programmable (E²PROM).

5. RAMs are used for temporary storage of application programs and data and for the stack area in ROM-based controllers.

6. Static RAMs (SRAMs) store data in a four- to six-transistor storage cell that requires no external refresh circuitry.

7. Dynamic RAMs use a single transistor and capacitor storage cell. This results in a very high bit density compared with SRAM technology but requires a special refresh controller.

8. When interfacing memory to a microprocessor, an address decoder is required to ensure that only one memory device drives the data bus at a particular time.

9. The simplest address decoder is a NAND gate but a PROM or PAL can also be used when the flexibility of a programmed decoder is desired.

10. Dynamic RAMs are refreshed by sequencing through all row addresses in a 2- or 4-ms period. This can be accomplished by normal memory read and write cycles, a $\overline{RAS}$-only cycle, or a hidden refresh cycle.

11. Refresh cycles can be performed in a burst mode, a transparent mode, or with a distributed refresh.

12. Dynamic RAM interfacing is greatly simplified with the aid of a DRAM controller. This circuit provides address multiplexing, generation of all timing, and arbitration logic to ensure that no memory accesses are lost while maintaining the required refresh intervals.

LAB PROJECTS

5.1. Study the schematic diagram of the microcomputer you are using to support this text/course. Now answer the following questions:
  (a) How much RAM does your system have?
  (b) How much ROM?
  (c) What types of memory chips are used? What is the organization of these chips (2K × 8, 16K × 1, etc.)?
  (d) Does your system buffer the address, data, and control buses?

5.2. On separate sheets of paper draw schematic diagrams of the RAM and ROM interfaces. Be sure to include the address decoding logic.

5.3. Sketch a *memory map* for your computer showing the address range occupied by each RAM and ROM chip. Can the memory of your computer be expanded? If so, include this information in your map.

5.4. Build a 16-word by 4-bit diode ROM similar to Fig. 5.7. On one side of a piece of perf board horizontally mount 16 bare copper wires—one for each byte. On the other side mount 8 vertical bit lines and 1K pullup resistors. Connect the word lines to the output of a 74LS154, connect the bit lines to the input of a 74LS244. For fun, program the ROM with the seven-segment codes for your name. Do this by soldering diodes between the appropriate row and column wires. Connect a binary counter to the address inputs and a seven-segment display to the data outputs.

5.5. The circuit in Fig. 5.37 can be used to test the operation of a 2K × 8 RAM. As shown, only 16 of the 2048 memory locations can be accessed because there are just 4 data switches. Write data to the RAM by selecting an address, hold the $\overline{WE}$ switch low, then set the data to be written on the DIP switch. When $\overline{WE}$ goes high, the data will be written. To read the data back, hold the $\overline{OE}$ switch low. (*Note:* Connect the memory data bus to an 8-bit input port of your computer. Now write a program to read the port and display its contents. This will make monitoring the memory's data bus very easy.)

5.6. If you have access to a PROM programmer and eraser, program a PROM to implement the following truth table.

I2	I1	I0	O0	O1	O2	O3
0	0	0	0	0	1	1
0	0	1	0	1	1	0
0	1	0	0	1	1	0
0	1	1	0	1	1	0
1	0	0	0	1	1	0
1	0	1	0	1	1	0
1	1	0	0	1	1	0
1	1	1	1	1	0	0

(*Note:* The four outputs correspond to the AND, OR, NAND, and NOR of the inputs I2, I1, and I0.)

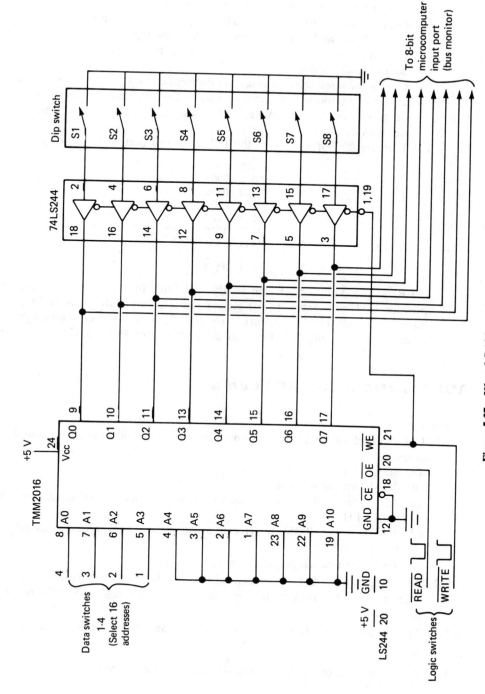

Figure 5.37 2K × 8 RAM test circuit for Lab 5.5.

5.7. Write a program to test the memory of your computer returning with the location of any error. Several different types of tests are possible.

   (a) *Checkerboard test*: Write AAH to the even bytes and 55H to the odd bytes. Read and verify all locations. Then repeat, reversing the even and odd bytes. (*Note*: This test is good for locating adjacent shorted data or address lines.)

   (b) *Complement test*: Read a byte, complement and save it, write it to memory. Compare memory with the saved byte. Complement memory and move on to the next byte. (*Note*: This test does not alter the contents of memory.)

   (c) *Walking-bit test*: (1) Write the following test pattern to memory.

$$
\begin{array}{cc}
0000 & 0000 \\
0000 & 0001 \\
0000 & 0010 \\
. & . \\
1000 & 0000 \\
1111 & 1110 \\
1111 & 1101 \\
. & . \\
0111 & 1111
\end{array}
$$

(2) Read the pattern back and verify. (3) Shift the test pattern by one bit position and go to step 1. (4) Repeat the test until all memory locations have stored all 17 data patterns. (*Note*: This test is very thorough and identifying the faulty RAM chip is quite easy—see Prob. 5.42.)

QUESTIONS AND PROBLEMS

Section 5.1

   5.1. Classify each of the following as main memory, secondary storage, or archival storage.
   (a) 360K-byte floppy disk drive
   (b) 20 M-byte hard drive
   (c) 32K bytes of RAM interfaced to a Z-80 microprocessor as address 0000 to 7FFFH
   (d) 32K bytes of ROM interfaced to an 8085 microprocessor as address 0000 to 7FFFH
   (e) 40 M-byte cartridge tape drive

   5.2. A certain floppy disk drive can store 1.44 MB of information. How can such a drive be used with a microcomputer that has only 64K bytes of memory space?

   5.3. True or false: Each byte of main memory has its own unique address.

Section 5.2

   5.4. A certain memory chip is advertised as having an *access time* of 100 ns. What does this mean?

5.5. Refer to Table 5.3. Which of the microprocessor chips listed will require the fastest memory parts? Why?

5.6. The 3-MHz 8085AH microprocessor expects to receive valid data from memory _____ ns after the $\overline{\text{MEMR}}$ signal becomes active.

5.7. A 4-MHz Z-80A microprocessor provides _____ ns of data-setup time before clocking the memory with the trailing edge of $\overline{\text{MEMW}}$.

5.8. Refer to Appendix C.2 and add an additional entry to Tables 5.3 and 5.4 for the 6-MHz 8085AH-1. *Hint*: Use the equations given in the tables.

5.9. Refer to Appendix C.3 and add an additional entry to Tables 5.3 and 5.4 for the 6-MHz Z-80B. *Hint*: Use the equations given in the tables.

5.10. Draw a timing diagram for the 8085 WAIT state generator in Fig. 5.4. Be sure to include the clock, ALE, Q1A, Q1B, and READY.

5.11. Draw a timing diagram for the Z-80 WAIT state generator in Fig. 5.5. Be sure to include the clock, $\overline{\text{MREQ}}$, Q1A, Q1B, and $\overline{\text{WAIT}}$.

5.12. Modify the 8085 WAIT state generator circuit in Fig. 5.4 so that it requests WAIT states only for memory read or write machine cycles—not I/O cycles.

*5.13. Assume a solder splash shorts to ground the SET inputs of IC1A and IC1B in the 8085 WAIT state generator circuit in Fig. 5.4. How would this fault affect the operation of this circuit?

Section 5.3

5.14. Can a practical microcomputer be built with ROM memory only (i.e., no RAM)? Explain.

5.15. True or false: In a typical microcomputer system ROM is used to store a bootstrap loader program, which in turn causes the applications software to be loaded into RAM.

5.16. An 8K-byte memeory is interfaced to a microcomputer system beginning at address A000H. What is the hex address of the *last* byte in this memory?

5.17. A microcomputer system has RAM from address 0000 to 5FFFH and ROM from C000H to FFFFH. How many total bytes of RAM does this system have? How many bytes of ROM? How much of the memory space is unused?

5.18. Draw a memory map showing the starting and ending address for each memory chip in the following system.
  (a) 2 8K-byte RAM chips beginning at address 0000.
  (b) 1 1K-byte RAM chip beginning at address B000H.
  (c) 4 2K-byte ROM chip beginning at address E000H

Section 5.4

5.19. What is the ''word'' stored at address 1101 in the diode ROM in Fig. 5.7?

5.20. Which of the following ROM types are user programmable?
  (a) fusible-link PROM
  (b) UV-EPROM
  (c) mask programmable ROM
  (d) E^2PROM

Chap. 5   Questions and Problems

5.21. Which of the ROM types listed in Prob. 5.20 are erasable?

5.22. Classify each of the following memory types as *volatile* or *nonvolatile*.
 (a) SRAM
 (b) UV-EPROM
 (c) floppy disk
 (d) DRAM

5.23. A 64K-byte memory is to be constructed using 64K × 1 DRAM chips or 8K × 8 SRAM chips. How many total chips are required for each design? What are the advantages and disadvantages of each choice?

5.24. True or false: To refresh a 64K-byte DRAM all 65,536 cell addresses must be accessed once every 2 ms.

5.25. Show how a 24-pin socket should be wired to accommodate a 2K × 8 2716 EPROM or a 2K × 8 6116 SRAM. Use jumper wires to select the ROM or RAM device.

Section 5.5

5.26. Refer to Fig. 5.38 for the following questions.
 (a) Is this a ROM or RAM memory interface?
 (b) What is the total memory capacity of the interface?
 (c) For what *range* of memory addresses is 2732B enabled?
 (d) How can the data buses of the two 2732s be wired in parallel without causing bus contention?

5.27. Redesign the memory interface in Fig. 5.38 to cover the address range 4000–5FFFH.

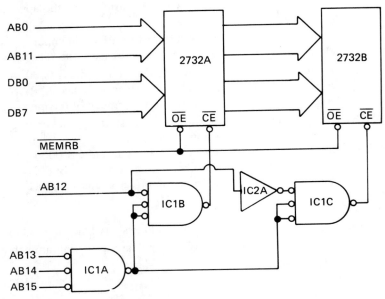

Figure 5.38 Memory interface for Probs. 5.26–29.

*5.28. Assume the output of ICIC in Fig. 5.38 fails in such a way that it is "stuck" high. How would this affect the operation of this circuit?

5.29. If address line AB15 is removed from IC1A in Fig. 5.38 and that input is grounded, the memory interface becomes *partially decoded*. To what range of addresses will each memory chip now respond?

5.30. The circuit in Fig. 5.39 is suitable as a ROM block decoder. For what *type* of bus cycles and *range* of memory addresses will output "C" be active? What size ROM chips should be used?

5.31. A certain memory interface uses buffers onto and off of the system address, data, and control buses. If the memory chips have a 150-ns access time, the address buffers a 25-ns propagation delay time, and the data bus buffers a 30-ns propagation delay time, calculate the minimum access time necessary to avoid WAIT states.

5.32. For each circuit in Fig. 5.40 determine the range of addresses for which the output is active, the active sense of the output (active-high or -low), and the total number of bytes in the address range.

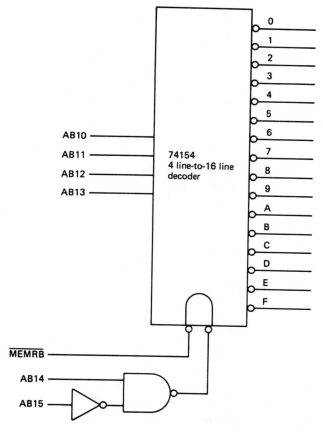

Figure 5.39 Circuit for Prob. 5.30.

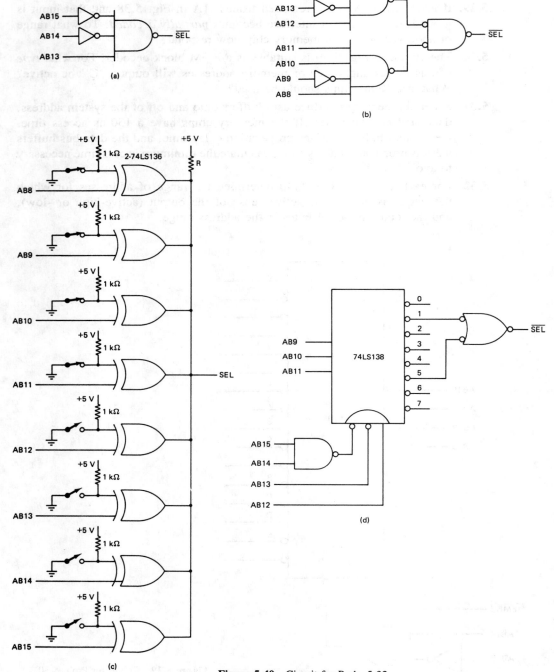

Figure 5.40 Circuit for Prob. 5.32.

5.33. Design a 2716 based 16-K-EPROM memory interface that begins at address 8000H. (*Hint*: Use a 74LS138 3–8 line-block decoder.)

5.34. Refer to the 32K-byte RAM module in Fig. 5.25. What switch settings are required to map BANK0 to the range 0000–3FFFH and BANK1 to the range 4000–7FFFH?

5.35. Design a 2167 based 16K-byte memory interface that begins at address C000H. Be sure to include bi-directional data bus buffers.

5.36. The 74S287 PROM address decoder in Fig. 5.27 could be replaced by a 74LS154 4 line-to-16 line decoder. Show the connections required for this change.

5.37. Determine the new truth table and PROM data table for the memory interface in Fig. 5.27 if the memory map is changed to agree with Fig. 5.41.

5.38. Replace all of the combinational logic (except the buffers) in the memory interface in Fig. 5.27 with a single fusible-link PROM. Specify the PROM required, input and output assignments, truth table, and data table required.

5.39. Assume a PAL10L8 is to be programmed to replace the 74S287 PROM address decoder in Fig. 5.27. Write the logic equations for $\overline{ROM1}$, $\overline{ROM2}$, and $\overline{RAM}$ in terms of A15–A12. (Hint: Refer to the truth table in Fig. 5.29.)

*5.40. A memory test is run on the 32K-byte memory shown in Fig. 5.25 with BANK0 mapped to cover addresses 0000–3FFFH and BANK1 mapped to

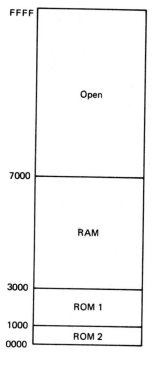

Figure 5.41 New memory map for the RAM/ROM module in Fig. 5.27.

cover addresses 4000–7FFFH. The test reports an error at address 57E3H bit 4. Which RAM chip is indicated?

*5.41. A memory test is run on the 32K-byte memory in Fig. 5.25 and reports errors at *all* memory locations. Further testing shows that each location appears to be storing random data despite attempts to write particular data patterns. What do you think is wrong with this interface? What would you check?

*5.42. The "walking 1's" memory test writes a 1 to each possible bit position. Which bit (0–7) do you think is in error in the walking 1's test report that follows?

Error at 2300H	wrote: 00000000	read: 00000001
Error at 2300H	wrote: 00000010	read: 00000011
Error at 2300H	wrote: 00000100	read: 00000101
Error at 2300H	wrote: 00001000	read: 00001001

Error at 2300H   wrote: 10000000   read: 10000001

Section 5.6

5.43. The *access time* of a DRAM chip is measured from the falling edge of _____ to _____ _____ .

5.44. If _____ occurs before _____ , the data-out and data-in pins of a DRAM can be shorted together. This is called an _____ write cycle.

5.45. How many address pins would you expect a 256K DRAM chip to have? Explain.

5.46. A certain DRAM requries a 7-bit refresh address and has a 300–ns cycle time. How long would a *burst refresh* cycle take for this memory chip? Express your answer as a percentage of the 2–ms refresh period.

5.47. In Fig. 5.36 which control signal selects the active 64K memory bank? Can both banks ever be active simultaneously?

5.48. Which of the following DRAM refresh controller components are "built-in" to the Z-80 microprocessor?
   (a) address multiplexer
   (b) RAS and CAS clock generator
   (c) refresh address generator

KEY CONCEPT ANSWERS

5.1.1. main
5.1.2. floppy and hard disk drives
5.1.3. archival
5.2.1. address access time

5.2.2. WAIT

5.3.1. Nonvolatile storage of a bootstrap loader, microcontroller software, applications software (BASIC in ROM)

5.3.2. Volatile: contents of memory lost when power is removed. Nonvolatile: contents of memory retained, even when power is removed.

5.3.3. memory map

5.4.1. mask-programmable

5.4.2. programmed

5.4.3. ultraviolet

5.4.4. SRAMs, DRAMs

5.4.5. 65536, 8

5.5.1. address decoder

5.5.2. They decrease the access time alloted the memory by the CPU.

5.5.3. partial

5.5.4. ROM, PAL

5.6.1. The address is split into a row and column address and clocked in separately on the same set of pins via the $\overline{\text{RAS}}$ and $\overline{\text{CAS}}$ clock signals.

5.6.2. $\overline{\text{RAS}}$-only

5.6.3. transparent

6

Building the Microcomputer, Part 3: Input/Output

The last block to be discussed in the building of our microcomputer is the input/output or I/O. We might call this the *user interface*. Try to imagine a microcomputer without any input or output devices. Internally, the CPU might be executing a "magnificent" program. But without a means to communicate with this program, the CPU might do as well executing NOPs.

There are basically two hardware techniques for getting data into and out of a computer. The first is the *parallel* interface and is the most natural for the microprocessor. Data is read and written from the I/O devices in 8-bit bytes much as from read/write memory. All data bits are transferred in parallel.

The second technique is the *serial* interface. This method does not come as naturally to the microprocessor, but it does have its advantages. A parallel-to-serial converter is used to transmit the 8 data bits serially—that is, one after the other in time. Similarly, a serial-to-parallel converter is used to reform the parallel data bytes. The advantage to this technique is that only three wires are required to implement the interface. These are serial data in, serial data out, and ground. The main disadvantage is a speed penalty. It will have to take at least eight times as long to transmit the byte one bit at a time as it will to transmit all 8 bits at once.

Nevertheless, serial data communications is quite popular today. Perhaps one reason is that many computer peripherals cannot handle data as fast as a parallel interface would like to output it anyway. Another reason is that three conductor cables are considerably cheaper than eight or nine conductor cables.

Finally, the 1s and 0s output by a serial computer interface can be converted into audio tones and transmitted over the telephone network by a *modem*. This allows communication over thousands of miles using the existing wiring of the various telephone companies.

Because serial communications is so popular, Chap. 9 is devoted entirely to this subject. In this chapter we concentrate on parallel I/O techniques. This would be a fairly simple topic if all computer peripherals were as fast as the microprocessor. But of course they are not. Data comes off a terminal as fast as the operator can type, and it can be output to a printer only as fast as the printer can type. Often, the microprocessor must sit and wait—sometimes for a relatively long time—until the peripheral is ready to receive or transmit more data.

A few peripherals are actually faster than the microprocessor. Magnetic disk interfaces, particulary rigid or "hard" disk drives, can transfer data at rates as high as 5 million bits per second. For these peripherals special data transfer processors (called *DMA controllers*) are required.

So once again we begin a chapter by saying: "Nothing is simple anymore!"

6.1 PARALLEL I/O: INTERFACING TO A TYPE 3 BUS

As you read this section, look for the answers to these Key Concept questions:

6.1.1. The 8080, 8085, and Z-80 output an _____-bit I/O address allowing access to _____ different I/O ports.

6.1.2. Which of the three processors—the 8080, 8085, or Z-80—adds a WAIT state to all I/O cycles?

6.1.3. The signal used to activate an I/O port is called the _____ _____ pulse.

The design of a microcomputer input or output port involves all three system buses. Figure 4.21 illustrated the data path from an input device to the microprocessor. Data is input to the CPU by tri-state transmitters and received by clocked latches. The bidirectional data bus is required for all data transfers. We defined this to be a *type 3* bus in Chap. 4.

Before we actually design an input or output port, let us review the timing for the two I/O operations, keeping in mind the type 3 bus model in Fig. 4.21.

I/O Machine Cycles and Timing.   Table 6.1 lists typical input and output instructions for the 8080, 8085, and Z-80 microprocessors. Notice that the 8080 and 8085 are restricted to using the accumulator for all I/O operations. The Z-80 can use register C to hold the port address and then input or output data with any of the other general-purpose registers. The Z-80 can also use (HL) as a source or destination of data.

Each I/O instruction leaves its own unique set of "footprints" on the three system buses. Understanding this information, microcomputer input and output ports can readily be designed.

Figure 6.1 summarizes the information in Table 6.1 in the form of a "generic"

TABLE 6.1 I/O INSTRUCTIONS FOR THE 8080, 8085, AND Z-80 MICROPROCESSORS

Microprocessor	Instruction	Data bus	Control bus	Address bus
8080	IN nn	Data	$\overline{IOR} = 0$	A0–A7 and A8–A15 = nn
	OUT nn	Accumulator	$\overline{IOW} = 0$	A0–A7 and A8–A15 = nn
8085	IN nn	Data	$IO/\overline{M} = 1$ $\overline{RD} = 0$	AD0–AD7 and A8–A15 = nn
	OUT nn	Accumulator	$IO/\overline{M} = 1$ $\overline{WR} = 0$	AD0–AD7 and A8–A15 = nn
Z-80	IN A,(nn)	Data	$\overline{IORQ} = 0$ $\overline{RD} = 0$	A0–A7 = nn A8–A15 = accumulator
	OUT (nn),A	Accumulator	$\overline{IORQ} = 0$ $\overline{WR} = 0$	A0–A7 = nn A8–A15 = accumulator
	IN r,(C)	Data	$\overline{IORQ} = 0$ $\overline{RD} = 0$	A0–A7 = C A8–A15 = accumulator
	OUT (C),r	r	$\overline{IORQ} = 0$ $\overline{WR} = 0$	A0–A7 = C A8–A15 = accumulator

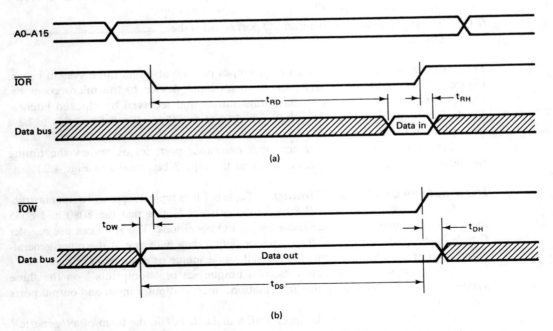

Figure 6.1 Timing relationships for (a) I/O read and (b) I/O write machine cycles.

timing diagram for an I/O read and I/O write machine cycle. The I/O read cycle [Figure 6.1(a)] is identical to a memory read cycle with the following changes:

1. The port address is 8 bits long instead of 16. The 8080 and 8085 duplicate this address on A0 through A7 and A8 through A15. The Z-80 outputs the port address on A0 through A7 only.
2. The $\overline{IOR}$ control signal is active instead of $\overline{MEMR}$. Remember that $\overline{IOR}$ is active when $IO/\overline{M} = 1$ and $\overline{RD} = 0$ for the 8085 and when $\overline{IORQ} = 0$ and $\overline{RD} = 0$ for the Z-80.
3. For the Z-80 only, one WAIT state is added.

The critical timing parameters for an I/O read cycle are t_{RD} and t_{RH}. t_{RD} is the time the microprocessor gives the input port select logic to gate its data onto the data bus. This amounts to the time required to enable the tri-state transmitter in Fig. 4.21.

t_{RH} is the amount of time the microprocessor requires that data be held stable after $\overline{IOR}$ returns high. This parameter is 0 ns for all three processors. This means that data can be removed as soon as $\overline{IOR}$ disappears. Specifications for t_{RD} and t_{RH} are given for the 8080A, 8085AH, and the Z-80A in Table 6.2.

Figure 6.1(b) illustrates an I/O write machine cycle. This cycle is identical to a memory write cycle with the following exceptions:

1. The port address is again 8 bits instead of 16.
2. $\overline{IOW}$ is active instead of $\overline{MEMW}$.
3. For the Z-80 only, one WAIT state is added.

The memory write cycle begins with the output of the port address on A0 through A15. Next the data to be written is placed on D0 through D7 and the $\overline{IOW}$ line is brought low. Table 6.2 provides specifications for the three timing parameters shown in Fig. 6.1(b).

The first is t_{DS}, the amount of time that data is on the bus before $\overline{IOW}$ is

TABLE 6.2 I/O TIMING SPECIFICATIONS FOR THE 8080, 8085, and Z-80 MICROPROCESSORS

Microprocessor	I/O read		I/O write		
	t_{RD} (max)	t_{RH} (min)	t_{DW} (min)	t_{DS} (min)	t_{DH} (min)
8080A (2 MHz)	464 ns	0	156 ns	656 ns	119 ns
8085AH (3 MHz)	300 ns	0	−40 ns	420 ns	100 ns
Z-80A (4 MHz)	475 ns	0	−10 ns	600 ns	60 ns

removed (goes high). Normally, data should be latched by the output port on the rising edge of $\overline{\text{IOW}}$ and thus t_{DS} corresponds to a setup time for the output port data latch.

The second important timing parameter is t_{DH}. This is the amount of time that data remains stable after $\overline{\text{IOW}}$ has gone high. This time is provided by the microprocessor to satisfy the hold-time requirements of many latches.

The last timing parameter is t_{DW} and is the amount of time that data is stable before the falling edge of $\overline{\text{IOW}}$. Referring to Table 6.2, you can see that t_{DW} is actually *negative* for the 8085 and Z-80 microprocessors. This means that $\overline{\text{IOW}}$ goes low *before* the data is stable. This is an important point. If the falling edge of $\overline{\text{IOW}}$ is used to clock the output port latch, erroneous information may be stored.

Designing an 8-Bit Input Port. Based on the preceding discussion, we can conclude that the hardware for a microcomputer input port must:

1. Examine the address bus for "its" port address.
2. When the port address is present AND $\overline{\text{IOR}} = 0$, generate a *device select pulse* (DSP).
3. Gate data onto the data bus through eight tri-state transmitters enabled by the DSP.

Example 6.1

Design a microcomputer interface to read the value set on an eight-position DIP switch. Use input port address 3FH. Calculate t_{RD} and verify that this specification is met for all processors listed in Table 6.2.

Solution. The circuit diagram is given in Fig. 6.2. Two inverters and an eight-input NAND gate are used to decode the port address output on address lines AB0 through AB7. The output of IC2 will go low each time the low-order address bus contains 3FH. Notice that this could occur many times in the execution of a typical program. This is because there are 256 separate pages that have a low-order address of 3FH.

When, and only when, the instruction IN 3FH [Z-80 mnemonic IN A,(3FH)] is executed, the low-order address will be 3FH AND the $\overline{\text{IOR}}$ line will be low. This will cause the output of IC3 to go low, generating a device select pulse (labeled $\overline{\text{IN3F}}$ in Fig. 6.2). The $\overline{\text{IN3F}}$ DSP is used to enable the 74LS244, causing the settings of the eight switches to be placed on the data bus. The microprocessor latches this data byte and stores it in the accumulator on the rising edge of $\overline{\text{IOR}}$.

The time delays associated with each component in this interface are shown as Δt in the figure. Also shown are the propagation delays associated with the address buffers, the 8085 and Z-80 $\overline{\text{IOR}}$ logic (actually on the CPU module), and the bidirectional bus buffers (also part of the CPU module).

First note that we do not need to consider the delays through the address decoder. This is because the port address is output well ahead of the $\overline{\text{IOR}}$ signal (180 ns for the Z-80A) and the $\overline{\text{SEL3F}}$ output thus arrives at IC3 well before $\overline{\text{IORB}}$. When $\overline{\text{IORB}}$ does arrive—delayed through buffers on the CPU module and I/O module—the $\overline{\text{IN3F}}$ DSP is generated. The total time delay to this point is

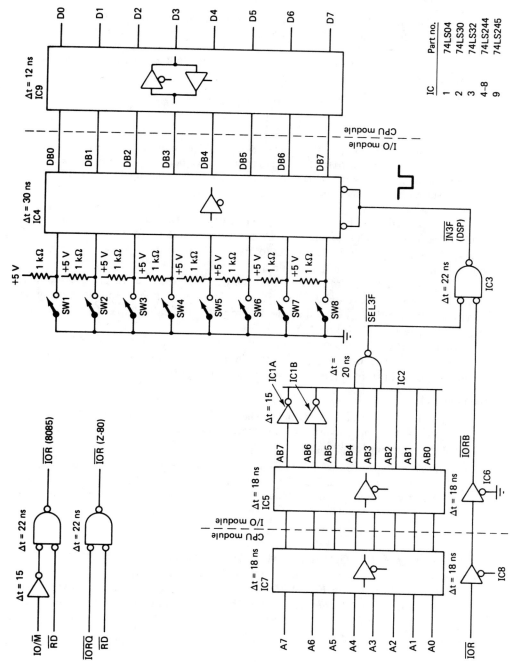

Figure 6.2 Hardware for the input port in Ex. 6.1.

IC	Part no.
1	74LS04
2	74LS30
3	74LS32
4-8	74LS244
9	74LS245

$$t_{DSP} = 2 \times t_{BUF} + t_{IC3}$$
$$= 36 \text{ ns} \quad + 22 \text{ ns}$$
$$= 58 \text{ ns}$$

This time should be increased by 37 ns for the 8085 and 22 ns for the Z-80 due to the $\overline{IOR}$ control logic shown in the upper left corner of Fig. 6.2.

Once the DSP is generated, the 74LS244 buffer responds (30 ns delay) and the data appears on the system data bus. The data bus buffers on the CPU module add an additional 12 ns of delay resulting in a total read time of

$$t_{RD} = t_{DSP} \quad + t_{BUF244} + t_{BUF245}$$
$$= 58 \text{ ns} \quad + 30 \text{ ns} \quad + 12 \text{ ns}$$
$$= 100 \text{ ns}$$

The results for the 8085 and Z-80 are 137 ns and 122 ns, respectively. This additional delay is due to the $\overline{IOR}$ logic, as mentioned before. Comparing these numbers to the specifications in Table 6.2, it is apparent that the input port in Fig. 6.2 is considerably faster than required.

It is interesting to note that the t_{RD} specification for the 6-MHz version of the 8085 drops from 300 ns to only 75 ns but is still 300 ns for the 6-MHz Z-80B. The Z-80 adds an extra WAIT state to its I/O instructions, purposely giving the select logic more time to output its data.

Also note that the time delays indicated in Fig. 6.2 are *worst-case* numbers. Typical devices will have delays only 50 to 60% of these times. However, designing to typical specifications means that the design will "typically" work! I would prefer to say that it will always work!

In summary, a microcomputer input port is built with tri-state buffers, an address decoder, and logic to generate the device select pulse. Figure 4.15 illustrates several types of buffers suitable for use in an input port.

Example 6.2

Write a Z-80 subroutine that detects when switches 1 and 4 or 2 and 7 are closed. If the condition is met, return with the accumulator cleared; if not met, return with the accumulator equal to FFH.

Solution. Figure 6.3 is the program listing. A *masking* technique is used to monitor bits 0 and 3 or bits 1 and 6. For example, if the accumulator is ANDed with 09H, the result will be 0 only if bits 0 and 3 are also 0. In this way any bit or combination of bits can be tested.

Designing an 8-Bit Output Port.

The design of a microcomputer output port requires the use of a latch to "catch" the data when it is output on the system data bus. This was illustrated in Fig. 4.21, where all receivers of data are shown as flip-flops. Again a *DSP* must be generated, this time by combining the address select signal and the $\overline{IOW}$ control signal. The DSP is then used to clock the latch connected to the system data bus.

```
EX6-2    IN     A, (3FH)     ;READ INPUT PORT
         LD     B,A          ;SAVE A COPY
         AND    09H          ;TEST BITS 0 AND 3
         JR     Z,DONE       ;IF ZERO RETURN
         LD     A,B          ;RETRIEVE COPY
         AND    42H          ;TEST BITS 6 AND 1
         JR     Z,DONE       ;IF ZERO RETURN
         LD     A,FFH        ;ELSE ACC = FF
DONE     RET
```

Figure 6.3 Program listing for Ex. 6.2.

Example 6.3

Design an 8-bit output port using partial decoding such that the port maps to any address between 80H and FFH. Calculate t_{DS} and t_{DH} for the circuit and verify that the specifications in Table 6.2 are met for all processors.

Solution. The circuit diagram is provided in Fig. 6.4. Because of the partial decoding requirement, there is no need for a separate address decoder circuit. This is because port addresses between 80H and FFH can easily be identified whenever address line A7 is high. The DSP signal used to clock the latch should combine A7 and $\overline{IOW}$. In this way, whenever the low-order address bus holds an address between 80H and FFH AND the $\overline{IOW}$ line is active, the data bus contents will be latched.

Notice that data is strobed into the latch on the rising edge of $\overline{IOW}$ when the data bus is guaranteed to hold valid data. Change IC2 to a NOR gate and problems could occur due to the t_{DW} specification.

This circuit will work correctly provided that the latch setup and hold-time specifications provided by the microprocessor are met. Let's consider t_{DS}, the *data setup time*, first. When data is output by the microprocessor, it must propagate through the CPU module buffers (40 ns delay) and then the I/O module buffers (18 ns delay). The 74LS374 latch requires that data be stable on its inputs for at least 20 ns prior to the strobe signal. Thus the setup time required by the output port interface in Fig. 6.4 is

$$t_{DS} = t_{BUFCPU} + t_{BUFI/O} + t_{SUlatch}$$
$$= 40 \text{ ns} \quad + 18 \text{ ns} \quad + 20 \text{ ns}$$
$$= 78 \text{ ns}$$

In reference to Table 6.2, 78 ns is well within the specifications for all of the processors.

Last we must consider the *hold-time* requirement. Some latches require that data be held for a brief period after the clock edge occurs. This ensures that data will be internally latched by the device. The 74LS374 latch used in Fig. 6.4 has a 0-ns hold-time requirement. This means that data need be held stable only until the clock edge occurs.

The 74LS374 clock signal (the $\overline{OUT80\text{-}FF}$ DSP) is derived from the address decoding logic and $\overline{IOW}$ signal. In this case, we are concerned with the trailing edge of $\overline{IOW}$, that is, the point in time when $\overline{IOW}$ returns high. To meet the hold-time specification of the 74LS374, data must be stable until the clock input goes high. Due to the CPU module and I/O module buffers and IC2, the rising edge of $\overline{IOW}$ will be delayed. During this time the data must be held stable. Thus the hold time for the circuit in Fig. 6.4 is

$$t_{DH} = t_{BUFCPU} + t_{BUFI/O} + t_{IC2}$$
$$= 18 \text{ ns} \quad + 18 \text{ ns} \quad + 22 \text{ ns}$$
$$= 58 \text{ ns}$$

Sec. 6.1   Parallel I/O: Interfacing to a Type 3 Bus

263

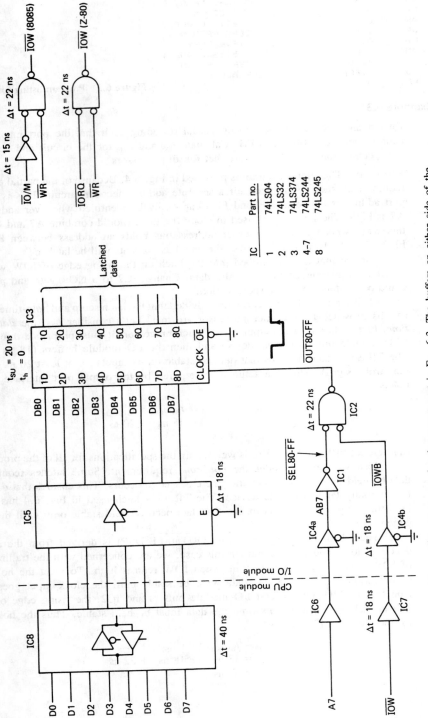

Figure 6.4 Hardware for the output port in Ex. 6.3. The buffers on either side of the dashed lines are part of the CPU module and I/O modules as recommended in Chap. 4.

This time must be increased to 95 ns for the 8085 and 80 ns for the Z-80 due to the extra $\overline{IOW}$ logic required for these processors. Checking with Table 6.2 we find that the 8080 and 8085 are within specifications (barely), but the Z-80 is 20 ns out of spec. One way of rationalizing this is to note that if the Z-80 does remove data 20 ns too soon, the 74LS374 will not realize this until after the propagation delays of the two data bus buffers. Assuming typical delays for these gates, 39 ns would be required and the hold time would be met with 19 ns to spare.

In summary, the design of a microcomputer output port requires decoding the port address, combining this signal with $\overline{IOW}$ to generate a DSP which is then used to clock a latch and store the data bus contents. Table 6.3 lists several commonly available latches suitable for microcomputer output ports.

Example 6.4

Write a Z-80 program that turns outputs 3 and 5 ON (high) in Fig. 6.4 if switches 1 and 4 or 2 and 7 of the input port in Fig. 6.2 are closed. If these switches are open, then turn on outputs 1 and 6.

Solution. The program listing is provided in Fig. 6.5. After turning all outputs off, the program checks the input port by calling the subroutine in Fig. 6.3. Depending on the status of the accumulator, the appropriate bit pattern is output to port 80H to turn on the proper output pins. The program loops continuously, responding immediately to a change at the input port.

Applications for the Device Select Pulse. For some control applications the device select pulse (DSP) alone is sufficient for the interface. An example of such a circuit is shown in Fig. 6.6. The $\overline{OUTFF}$ DSP is used to reset the flip-flop and the $\overline{INFF}$ DSP to set it. The Q output of the flip-flop is used to control a relay through the 74LS05 open collector buffer and transistor Q1.

The 8080/85 command OUT FF will reset the flip-flop and turn on the relay. The transistor is required because the relay coil requires 100 mA of current when energized—well beyond the sink capabilities of the flip-flop Q output. Chapter 11 provides more details on interfacing to non-TTL-compatible peripherals.

What data should be in the accumulator when the OUT FF command is given? Because no connection is made to the data bus, it does not matter. Only the DSP is used. Similarly, no data is input when the IN FF instruction is executed (due to the nature of a TTL gate—open inputs "look like" logic 1s—the accumulator will probably store FFH).

6.2 MEMORY-MAPPED I/O

As you read this section, look for the answers to these Key Concept questions:

6.2.1. When an I/O port is _____-_____, that port can be accessed using any of the processor's memory reference instructions.

6.2.2. List three problems that must be overcome to interface a keypad with a microprocessor.

TABLE 6.3 LATCHES SUITABLE FOR USE IN MICROCOMPUTER OUTPUT PORTS

MSI/LSI FUNCTIONS
FUNCTIONAL INDEX/SELECTION GUIDE

LATCHES

DESCRIPTION	NO. OF BITS	CLEAR	OUTPUTS	TYPICAL DELAY TIME	TYP TOTAL POWER DISSIPATION	DEVICE TYPE AND PACKAGE			
						−55°C to 125°C		0°C to 70°C	
MULTI-MODE BUFFERED	8	Low	Q	11 ns	410 mW	SN54S412	J	SN74S412	J, N
ADDRESSABLE	8	Low	Q	12 ns	300 mW	SN54259	J, W	SN74259	J, N
		Low	Q	17 ns	110 mW	SN54LS259	J, W	SN74LS259	J, N
TRANSPARENT	8	None	Q	19 ns	120 mW	SN54LS373	J	SN74LS373	J, N
		None	Q	7 ns	525 mW	SN54S373	J	SN74S373	J, N
DUAL 4-BIT WITH INDEPENDENT ENABLE	8	Low	Q	11 ns	250 mW	SN54116	J, W	SN74116	J, N
		None	Q	15 ns	320 mW	SN54100	J, W	SN74100	J, N
DUAL 2-BIT WITH INDEPENDENT ENABLE	4	None	Q, $\overline{Q}$	15 ns	160 mW	SN5475	J, W	SN7475	J, N
		None	Q, $\overline{Q}$	30 ns	80 mW	SN54L75	J	SN74L75	J, N
		None	Q, $\overline{Q}$	11 ns	32 mW	SN54LS75	J, W	SN74LS75	J, N
		None	Q	15 ns	160 mW	SN5477	W		
		None	Q	30 ns	80 mW	SN54L77	T		
		None	Q	10 ns	35 mW	SN54LS77	W		
		None	Q, $\overline{Q}$	12 ns	32 mW	SN54LS375	J, W	SN74LS375	J, N
QUAD $\overline{S}$-$\overline{R}$ (SSI)	4	None	Q	12 ns	90 mW	SN54279	J, W	SN74279	J, N
		None	Q	12 ns	19 mW	SN54LS279	J, W	SN74LS279	J, N

Source: Courtesy of Texas Instruments, Inc.

```
EX6-4     SUB    A          ;CLEAR ACCUMULATOR
          OUT    (80H),A    ;TURN ALL BITS OFF
LOOP      CALL   EX6-2      ;TEST BITS
          OR     A          ;SET FLAGS
          JR     NZ,NMET    ;CONDITION NOT MET
          LD     A,14H      ;BITS 2 AND 4 ON
          JR     CMET       ;CONDITION MET
NMET      LD     A,21H      ;BITS 0 AND 5 ON
CMET      OUT    (80H),A    ;PROGRAM THE PORT
          JR     LOOP       ;CYCLE AGAIN
```

Figure 6.5 Program listing for Ex. 6.4.

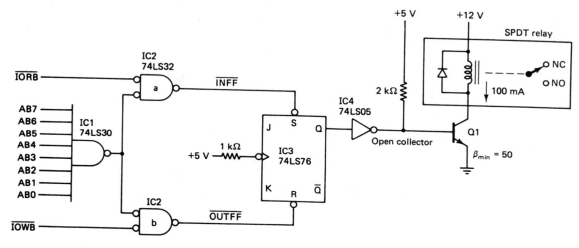

Figure 6.6 Using device select pulses (DSPs) to control a relay. An OUT FF instruction will turn on the relay and an IN FF instruction will turn it off.

We began Sec. 6.1 by noting the similarities between a memory read or write cycle and an I/O read or write cycle. Thinking about this similarity some more, we might note that a read/write memory is made up of (1-bit) latches for storing data and tri-state buffers for reading the data back out, the same hardware as that required for an I/O port. What if we designed a one-byte memory interface? For all intents and purposes this would, in fact, be an I/O port and not really a memory location.

This is the essence of *memory-mapped* I/O. All microprocessors are capable of memory-mapped I/O if they are capable of interfacing to memory. In fact, for many microprocessors, only memory-mapped I/O is possible. This is true for the 6800 and 6502 microprocessors, for example. These processors have no IN or OUT instructions; all I/O operations are performed using normal memory reference commands.

But this is precisely the advantage of memory-mapped I/O. The 8080 has only two I/O instructions, but it has numerous memory reference instructions. The instruction MOV M,B becomes an I/O instruction—copy the contents of register B into the output port whose address is stored in the HL pair.

In this section we will learn how to design a memory-mapped I/O port and use this technique to design a microcomputer controlled "digital lock."

Designing an 8-Bit Memory-Mapped Input Port.   Figure 6.7 is the schematic diagram of an 8-bit memory-mapped input port. This diagram should be compared with Fig. 6.2, which is the corresponding I/O mapped input port. (*Note*: *I/O mapped* is the term used for conventional I/O using the IN and OUT instructions.) The only difference between the two circuits is in the selection logic. Because a memory address is 16 bits long, the address decoder must decode more bits. In Fig. 6.7, two 74LS30s are required. In this case the port address is arbitrarily chosen to be FF3FH.

Any memory reference to address FF3FH will be decoded and cause $\overline{\text{SEL}}$ $\overline{\text{FF3F}}$ to go low. By combining this signal with $\overline{\text{MEMR}}$, any memory read from address FF3FH will cause the $\overline{\text{IN FF3F DSP}}$ signal to become active and enable the tri-state buffer.

Example 6.5

List several instructions that can be used to read the contents of the switch in the memory-mapped interface in Fig. 6.7.

Solution.   Many instructions can be used:

Mnemonic		
8080/85	Z-80	Comment
LDA FF3FH	LD A,FF3FH	;LOAD THE ACCUMULATOR DIRECT
LDAX B	LD A,(BC)	;BC = FF3FH
MOV C,M	LD C,(HL)	;HL = FF3FH
	LD D,(IX + d)	;IX = FF3FH AND d = 0

One of the disadvantages to memory-mapped I/O is the requirement to decode 16 bits versus 8 with the conventional I/O mapped interface. Because of this, *partial decoding* is often used. For example, if the portion of the decoder enclosed in dashed lines in Fig. 6.7 is removed—that is, A0 through A7 are no longer decoded—the resulting circuit is no more complex than Fig. 6.2. The price for this simplification is that the port now occupies memory from FF00H through FFFFH.

This points out the main drawback to memory-mapped I/O. It "steals" memory space away from the processor. Consider a memory implemented with 16K RAM chips and one memory-mapped input port at FFFFH. Because the memory and I/O cannot be allowed to have the same address, maximum memory capacity may be restricted to 48K. This problem can be overcome by detecting address FFFFH and disabling the RAM, but you can see the problem.

Memory mapping is a popular technique for interfacing a *video display generator*. Objects and characters on the screen can be manipulated at high speed using the processor's memory reference instructions. This technique also lends itself well to using dynamic RAMs. This is because the screen memory must be continually accessed (and therefore refreshed) in order to maintain the image on the CRT screen. In effect, refreshing is obtained for "free."

Designing a Digital Lock.   In this section we consider the use of the microprocessor as a controller. It will receive its input from a 10-digit memory-mapped keypad.

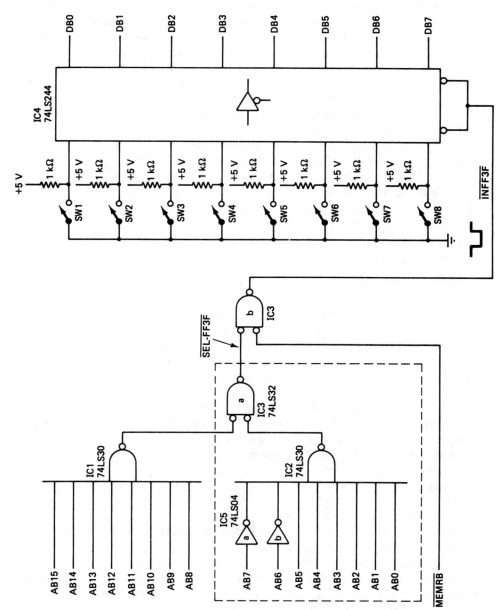

Figure 6.7 Memory-mapped input port at address FF3FH.

Its output will be a flip-flop controlled by two DSPs. The flip-flop will be used to activate a relay that controls an electronic door lock.

Problem statement.   Design the hardware and software for a microprocessor-controlled digital lock. The lock should be opened when the correct sequence of six digits is entered from a keypad. If an incorrect sequence is entered, the keypad should be disabled for at least 1 minute to discourage "trial and error."

Hardware.   The electronic lock will use the relay control circuit shown in Fig. 6.6. The relay contacts are assumed connected to the lock in such a way that an OUT FF command will turn ON the relay and open the lock. An IN FF command will turn OFF the relay and close the lock.

Figure 6.8 shows the memory-mapped keypad interface. The 10 keys are assumed to be normally open pushbutton switches arranged in two columns as shown.

Reading the keypad.   When interfacing any keyboard to a microcomputer three problems must be solved.

1. Detect that a key is down.
2. Debounce the key closure.
3. Encode the key.

In Fig. 6.8 a key closure is detected by doing a memory read from address FF03H. This will enable the tri-state buffers and cause the two column inverters, IC1A and IC1B, to put 0 V on the column lines. If no key is down, the row lines will be pulled high by the resistors and the data will be inverted and read as 00000000. However, if any key is down, the result will be nonzero—00010000 if key 4 is down, for example.

Whenever a mechanical switch is closed or opened, the contacts will "bounce" for several milliseconds. During this time the microprocessor will be lead into falsely interpreting these key bounces as legitimate key closures. The result will be a multiple input of the same key value. Switches can be *debounced* with hardware (using cross-coupled gates or see Prob. 4.29 for another technique) or with software.

Figure 6.9 is a flowchart illustrating how the keypad can be debounced in software. Because the microprocessor can execute the entire program before you can even take your finger off one key, the program begins by waiting until the keyboard is clear. Once this condition is detected, a 20-ms wait is inserted to allow the key to bounce upon being released.

Now the program waits for a key to be pressed. When this condition is detected, another 20-ms wait is inserted to allow the key to stop bouncing. Now the encoding process can begin. First, the column with the key closed must be determined. This is done by reading from address FF01 (column 1) and testing for a nonzero result. A zero result indicates that the key down must be in column 2 and address FF02 should be read.

Now that the proper column is known, a pointer into a data table is initialized.

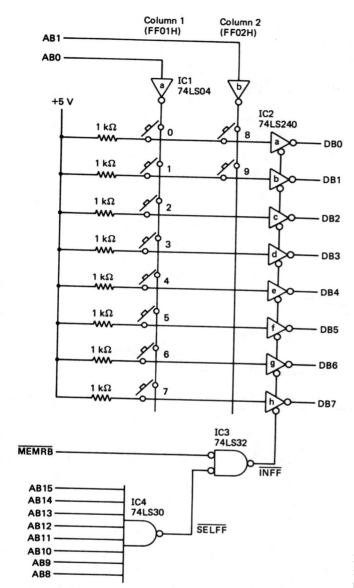

Figure 6.8 Memory-mapped keypad interface for the digital lock design problem.

In this table are stored the values we wish to assign each key: in this case, the numerals 0 through 9.

All that remains is to locate the actual key that is down. This is done by rotating the data word right and testing the carry flag. For example, after five rotate rights the carry flag will be set if key 4 was held down. By advancing the memory pointer with each rotate, it will end up pointing at 04. This character can be moved to a register and the routine ended.

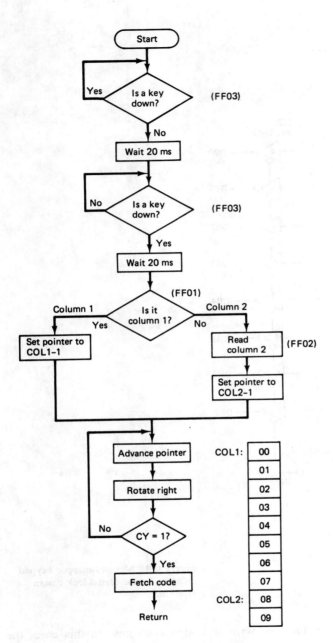

Figure 6.9 Flowchart to detect a key closure, debounce the key, and encode it using the hardware in Fig. 6.8.

Developing the control software. The keyboard encoding routine flowcharted in Fig. 6.9 is only part of the control program. The main program determines the number of digits in the sequence, checks each input as it is typed against the "secret code," and finally unlocks the door.

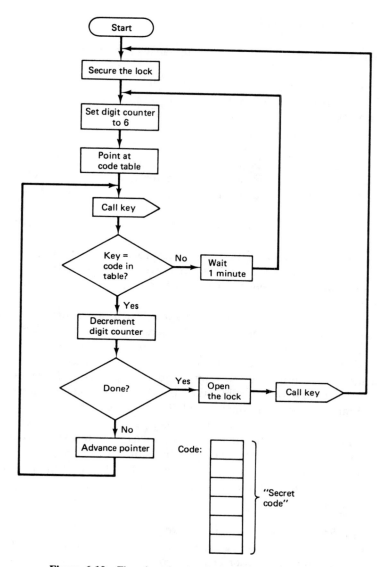

Figure 6.10 Flowchart for the digital lock control program.

A flowchart of this program is given in Fig. 6.10. The keyboard read routine is called as a subroutine returning with the key value. It is matched against a table (the "*secret code*") and if a match is found, the next digit is input. An incorrect digit causes a 1-minute time delay to be entered.

When all six digits match, the relay is turned on and the lock unlocked. Pushing any key will reactivate the lock and the program. The programs to go along with the flowcharts are not given but are included as Probs. 6.16 and 6.17.

6.3 HANDSHAKING LOGIC

As you read this section, look for the answers to these Key Concept questions:

6.3.1. "Handshaking" logic is required to _____ a fast microprocessor with a slow I/O device.

6.3.2. When a peripheral's BUSY/READY flag is _____, the I/O device is ready to receive new data.

Why was the block "Is a key down?" required in the digital lock problem? What would have happened if the microprocessor simply read the keyboard without waiting for this block? I think you know the answers to these questions. The data input from the keypad is *asynchronous* with respect to the microprocessor. Unless we wait for a key to be down, the program will try to process nonexistent data or it might read the same key many times over.

This is a critical point. The microprocessor must somehow *synchronize* itself with the peripheral. This means that the processor must be able to adjust to the data rate of the I/O device, whether the operator enters data at the rate of 5 characters per second or 1 character per hour.

In most cases the microprocessor is much faster than the peripheral. Consider a line printer capable of printing 100 characters per second (cps). This corresponds to one character every 10 ms. If the Z-80 instruction *OTIR* is used to output data to this printer, the Z-80A will output 190,476 characters per second! Unless some means of synchronizing the printer and microprocessor is found, data will be lost.

Most slow peripherals, such as printers and plotters are mechanical devices and limited in their maximum speed. To interface to these devices the microprocessor must be slowed down—certainly the peripheral cannot be speeded up.

For some peripherals, the microprocessor is too slow. A double-density 5¼-inch floppy disk transfers data at a rate of 250,000 bits per second. Rigid disks can transfer millions of data bits per second. Interfacing to these devices is particularly interesting because they cannot be slowed down and the microprocessor cannot be speeded up!

Busy, Ready, and Acknowledge Flags. It has become common practice, regardless of the interfacing technique used, to utilize a set of *handshaking* signals between the microprocessor and its peripherals. Figure 6.11 illustrates the technique. In addition to the data lines, the peripheral now supplies a *BUSY/READY* flag. When this line is high, the peripheral is busy and cannot accept new data. When low, the peripheral is ready for new data.

With reference to Fig. 6.11, the handshaking sequence begins with the processor checking the BUSY/READY flag of the peripheral. Finding it low (not busy), a strobe pulse (or DSP) is output by the processor. This tells the I/O device that data is on the bus and should be latched. The peripheral now sets its BUSY/READY flag while the character is being received and processed (printed in the case of a printer).

Eventually, an *acknowledge* signal is output by the peripheral. This signal

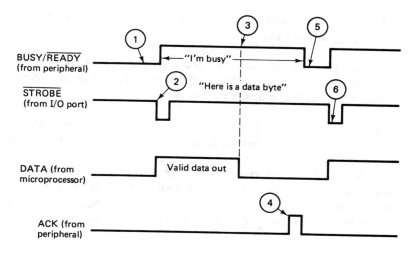

Microcomputer	Peripheral
1. Read BUSY/READY	BUSY/READY = 0
2. Strobe data to peripheral	BUSY/READY = 1
3. Read BUSY/READY	BUSY/READY = 1 (still busy)
4. —	ACK = 1 (data byte accepted)
5. Read BUSY/READY	BUSY/READY = 0
6. Strobe data to peripheral	BUSY/READY = 1

Figure 6.11 Handshaking signals allow the microprocessor and peripheral to be synchronized for data transfers.

acknowledges receipt of the data and indicates that new data can be placed on the bus. The term "handshake" comes from the CPU "extending its hand" with the strobe signal and the peripheral "extending its hand" back with the ACK signal.

Three techniques are commonly used to interface a peripheral using handshaking logic. These are listed below and are the subject of the remainder of this chapter.

1. Programmed I/O (Sec. 6.4)
2. Interrupt-driven I/O (Sec. 6.5)
3. Direct memory access (Sec. 6.6)

6.4 Programmed I/O

As you read this section, look for the answers to these Key Concept questions:

6.4.1. Programmed I/O requires that a software program _____ the I/O device to determine if it is ready to exchange data.

6.4.2. When is programmed I/O inefficient?

6.4.3. How are priorities determined when several peripherals are controlled via programmed I/O?

Programmed I/O is so called because a special I/O program is in full control of all data transfers. Using a software technique called *polling* the microprocessor is synchronized to the speed of the peripheral.

Polling. The classic example of programmed I/O is the parallel printer interface, sometimes called a "Centronics parallel printer interface" after the name of the printer manufacturer. Figure 6.12 illustrates the hardware.

A 74LS373 level-triggered latch (not edge triggered) is used to store the data byte. This latch is referred to as *transparent* because the data input is gated to the output pins whenever the latch's enable input is high. Data is latched when the enable input goes low. Be sure to notice that the requirement of latching the data with the rising edge of $\overline{\text{IOW}}$ is still met.

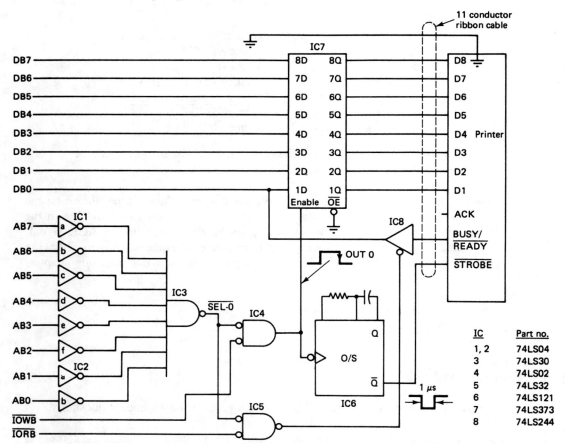

Figure 6.12 Parallel printer interface. Handshaking logic is used to synchronize the data flow from microprocessor to printer.

The address decoder is designed to decode port 0. Its output, $\overline{\text{SEL 0}}$, is shared with a 1-bit input port for the BUSY/$\overline{\text{READY}}$ flag and the output port latch.

The $\overline{\text{STROBE}}$ signal requires some explanation. $\overline{\text{STROBE}}$ is the signal generated by the I/O port that tells the printer that valid data is on the bus and should be latched and printed. At first glance it would appear that the $\overline{\text{OUT 0 DSP}}$ could be inverted and used for this purpose. However, most parallel printers have a *minimum* STROBE pulse width of 0.5 μs or longer. Assuming a 3-MHz 8085, the OUT 0 signal has only a 400-ns pulse width. Using a Z-80A, the pulse width is somewhat longer ($\sim$470 ns) due to the extra WAIT state inserted in Z-80 I/O cycles, but still a bit too fast for the printer. As a result, the $\overline{\text{OUT 0 DSP}}$ is used to trigger IC6, a 74LS121 one-shot. The pulse width is set for approximately 1 μs.

Finally, note that the interface will require an 11-conductor cable between the computer and printer. Because all signals are TTL levels, the cable length should be limited to 10 to 20 ft. This is one of the disadvantages of parallel I/O. An RS-232D serial port can do the same job, using only three wires, and drive a cable several thousand feet long. We discuss this in detail in Chap. 9.

Let's develop a program to control the flow of data from the output port to the printer in Fig. 6.12. We will write the program as a subroutine with the following assumptions:

1. The characters to be printed are stored in a table beginning at symbolic address DATA.

2. The number of bytes to be printed will be stored in a memory location called NUMB. (NUMB) must be a number less than 256.

An 8080/85 subroutine to accomplish the task is listed in Fig. 6.13. After pointing the HL pair at the head of the data table and loading register B with the number of bytes to be output, the program falls into a loop called POLL. In this loop the status of bit 0 of input port 0 is continually tested. In essence, the program is waiting for the printer to be READY.

When the BUSY/$\overline{\text{READY}}$ flag finally goes low, the character to be printed is output—generating the $\overline{\text{OUT 0 DSP}}$ and the 1 μs $\overline{\text{STROBE}}$ signal—the data pointer advanced, and the byte counter decremented. If more data remains to be output, control is transferred back to POLL; if not, the RET is executed.

The key point to note about this routine is the POLL loop. The technique of continually checking the peripheral's BUSY/$\overline{\text{READY}}$ flag is called "polling" and, in fact, programmed I/O is often referred to as polling. Polling has its advantages. The control program is always in control of the peripheral and the hardware required is not too complex.

Polling also has its disadvantages. The polling loop in Fig. 6.13 requires 24 T states using an 8080 or 12 μs with a 2-MHz clock. If the printer can accept characters at a 100-cps rate, 10 ms or 10,000 μs must elapse between each character. This means the subroutine in Fig. 6.13 will figuratively ask the question "*Are you ready?*" and receive the reply "*NO!*" 833 times before getting a "*YES!*" This is a rather *inefficient* use of the microprocessor.

What about this inefficiency? Does it really matter? Will the CPU wear itself

```
                    ;PARALLEL PRINTER CONTROL PROGRAM.
                    ;
                    ;THE CIRCUIT DIAGRAM IS SHOWN IN FIG. 6-12.
                    ;THE T STATES REQUIRED ARE SHOWN ALONG THE
                    ;RIGHT MARGIN.
                    ;
SPORT       EQU     0                       ;STATUS PORT
DPORT       EQU     0                       ;DATA OUTPUT PORT
                    ;
            ORG     0100H                   ;PROGRAM BEGINS AT 0100H
                    ;
                    ;BEGIN BY SETTING UP A POINTER AND BYTE COUNTER.
                    ;
            LXI     H,DATA                  ;POINT AT DATA TABLE
            LDA     NUMB                    ;FETCH BYTES TO OUTPUT
            MOV     B,A                     ;SAVE IN B
                    ;
                    ;NOW POLL THE STATUS PORT WAITING FOR READY.
                    ;NOTE THAT 24 T STATES ARE REQUIRED.
                    ;
POLL        IN      SPORT                   ;SAMPLE THE STATUS PORT  [10]
            RAR                             ;TEST BIT 0              [4]
            JC      POLL                    ;WAIT UNTIL LOW          [10]
                    ;
                    ;OUTPUT A BYTE FDOM THE TABLE TO THE PRINTER.
                    ;17 T STATES.
                    ;
            MOV     A,M                     ;FETCH DATA BYTE         [7]
            OUT     DPORT                   ;PRINT                   [10]
                    ;
                    ;ADJUST POINTER AND BYTE COUNTER
                    ;20 T STATES
                    ;
            INX     H                       ;ADVANCE DATA POINTER    [5]
            DCR     B                       ;DECREMENT BYTE COUNTER  [5]
            JNZ     POLL                    ;REPEAT                  [10]
                    ;
            RET                             ;RETURN WHEN DONE
                    ;
                    ;SET UP STORAGE LOCATION FOR NUMB AND A 256 BYTE AREA
                    ;FOR THE DATA TABLE.
                    ;
NUMB        DS      1                       ;1 BYTE FOR NUMB
DATA        DS      256                     ;256 BYTES FOR THE DATA TABLE
            END
```

Figure 6.13 Control program for the parallel printer interface in Fig. 6.12. A "polling" technique is used.

out continually testing the BUSY/READY flag? The answer is "not likely." The inefficiency is important only in a *multitasking* environment.

Multitasking means using the processor to do several tasks at once. This used to be a skill reserved for large mainframe computers and minicomputers, but no longer. It is becoming common practice to use a microcomputer to edit a file on a word processor while the same program is printing another file. And why not? Certainly, it is a better use of your time than waiting for the (perhaps lengthy) file to be printed.

However, to perform multitasking efficiently, special hardware is usually required (see Secs. 6.5 and 6.6). This can add additional cost and complexity to the microcomputer system.

Data Transfer Rate. An important characteristic of any I/O interface is the *maximum data transfer rate*. Let's calculate this number assuming an 8080 processor for the subroutine in Fig. 6.13. What we are interested in is the rate at which characters can be output by this program.

When run at its fastest rate, the polling routine will need to be executed only once for each output. This will require 24 T states, as mentioned previously. Once ready, data is fetched from the table, output, and the pointer and byte counter adjusted and tested. This requires an additional 37 T states. The total time for one cycle through the program is therefore 61 T states or 30.5 μs with a 2-MHz 8080 processor. This corresponds to 32,787 bytes per second.

Put this number into perspective by considering that a 5¼-inch double-density floppy disk transfers data at 31,250 bytes per second. Thus polling could be used to interface this peripheral. Note, however, that the transfer rate for a typical hard drive is greater than 500,000 bytes per second!

Example 6.6

Rewrite the polling routine in Fig. 6.13 assuming a Z-80 microprocessor. Calculate the maximum transfer rate with a 4-MHz clock.

Solution. The program is given in Fig. 6.14. The polling loop actually requires one additional T state when compared with the 8080 program, but the data output loop is reduced from 37 T states to 26 T states because of the special Z-80 output instruction *OUTI*. The cycle time of the program is 51×250 ns $= 12.75$ μs. The data transfer rate is 78,431 bytes per second.

Priorities. The polling concept can be extended to more than one peripheral. In this case a special status input port is dedicated to the BUSY/$\overline{\text{READY}}$ flags. This is shown in Fig. 6.15. One 8-bit input port can supply the status for eight peripherals.

A routine can now be written to poll each device (test bit 0, then bit 1, etc.) and branch to the appropriate peripheral service routine when ready. What happens if two devices are ready at the same time? Obviously, the first one to be polled will be serviced first. In fact, this suggests that the polling routine can be written in such a way that *priorities* are assigned to each peripheral.

For example, assume that we start polling with bit 0 and proceed to bit 7. Each time a flag is found ready, that peripheral is serviced and the polling restarts at bit 0. Using the device assignments shown in Fig. 6.15, this scheme assigns the highest priority to the floppy-disk drive and the lowest priority to the video terminal.

When several peripherals are controlled in a programmed I/O environment, the *response time* of the polling routine (in addition to the transfer rate) must be considered. For example, consider the polling program listed in Fig. 6.16. It inputs the status from port 0 and then proceeds to test each bit in order. Because so many devices have to be polled, the response time—the time from BUSY/$\overline{\text{READY}}$ = READY to the start of the service routine—can be quite long.

Example 6.7

Calculate the worst-case response time for the video terminal using the polling routine in Fig. 6.16. Assume that the service routine for each peripheral requires 50 T states and the system clock is 2 MHz.

```
;PARALLEL PRINTER CONTROL PROGRAM (Z-80 VERSION)
;
;THE CIRCUIT DIAGRAM IS SHOWN IN FIG. 6-12.
;THE T STATES REQUIRED ARE SHOWN ALONG THE
;RIGHT MARGIN.
;
SPORT   EQU     0                       ;STATUS PORT
DPORT   EQU     0                       ;DATA OUTPUT PORT
;
        ORG     0100H                   ;PROGRAM BEGINS AT 0100H
;
;BEGIN BY SETTING UP A POINTER AND BYTE COUNTER
;
        LD      HL,DATA                 ;POINT AT DATA TABLE
        LD      A,(NUMB)                ;FETCHES BYTES TO OUTPUT
        LD      B,A                     ;SAVE IN B
;
;WE WILL USE OUTI SO PUT DPORT IN C
;
        LD      C,DPORT                 ;C HOLDS DPORT ADDRESS
;
;NOW POLL THE STATUS PORT WAITING FOR READY.
;NOTE THAT 25 T STATES ARE REQUIRED.
;
POLL    IN      A,(SPORT)               ;SAMPLE THE STATUS PORT  [11]
        RRA                             ;TEST BIT 0              [4]
        JP      C,POLL                  ;WAIT UNTIL LOW          [10]
;
;OUTPUT A BYTE FROM THE TABLE TO THE PRINTER.
;NOTE THAT OUTI "AUTOMATICALLY" ADJUSTS HL AND B.
;26 T STATES
;
        OUTI                            ;OUTPUT BYTE             [16]
        JP      NZ,POLL                 ;REPEAT UNTIL 0          [10]
;
        RET                             ;RETURN WHEN DONE
;
;SET UP STORAGE LOCATION FOR NUMB AND A 256 BYTE AREA
;FOR THE DATA TABLE.
;
NUMB    DEFS    1                       ;1 BYTE FOR NUMB
DATA    DEFS    256                     ;256 BYTES FOR THE DATA TABLE
        END
```

Figure 6.14 Z-80 polling routine for the printer interface in Fig. 6.12.

Solution. In the worst case, the terminal's BUSY/READY flag will be ready just after servicing a previous character from the terminal. The terminal will have to wait for the JMP POLL instruction to execute, and then all of the other peripherals to be polled. In a "really bad" worst case, each of these devices will require service and the video terminal's service routine will not be entered until a total response time of

$$T = [10 + 11 + (14 + 50) \times 7] \times 500 \text{ ns} = 234.5 \text{ } \mu\text{s}$$

This example points out a major disadvantage to polling. Although the individual transfer rate can be quite high, the response time can be quite slow when many peripherals are involved. The scheme can become totally unacceptable when the response time is so long as to lose data.

In the case of the video terminal, it cannot accept data faster than one character every 469 μs (at 19,600 baud) and you certainly cannot type that fast. For this peripheral a 234.5-μs wait is no problem.

Video terminal	Modem	DAC	ADC	Plotter	Daisy-wheel printer	Line printer	Floppy disk
7	6	5	4	3	2	1	0

Figure 6.15 One 8-bit input port can be used to mointor the BUSY/READY status of eight separate peripherals.

```
POLL    IN      A,0                 ;READ STATUS PORT          [11]
        ;
        RAR                         ;TEST BIT 0                [4]
        JC      FD                  ;FLOPPY-DISK               [10]
        ;
        RAR                         ;TEST BIT 1                [4]
        JC      LP                  ;LINE PRINTER              [10]
        ;
        RAR                         ;TEST BIT 2                [4]
        JC      DW                  ;DAISY-WHEEL PRINTER       [10]
        ;
        RAR                         ;TEST BIT 3                [4]
        JC      PL                  ;PLOTTER                   [10]
        ;
        RAR                         ;TEST BIT 4                [4]
        JC      ADC                 ;ANALOG-DIGITAL CONV.      [10]
        ;
        RAR                         ;TEST BIT 5                [4]
        JC      DAC                 ;DIGITAL-ANALOG CONV.      [10]
        ;
        RAR                         ;TEST BIT 6                [4]
        JC      MOD                 ;MODEM                     [10]
        ;
        RAR                         ;TEST BIT 7                [4]
        JC      TERM                ;TERMINAL                  [10]
        ;
        JMP     POLL                ;REPEAT                    [10]
```

Figure 6.16 Polling can be extended to several peripherals. This routine tests the BUSY/READY status of all eight peripherals in Fig. 6.15. T states are listed along the right margin for an 8080.

Note: The "worst case" in Ex. 6.7 is not really the worst case. If we assume that each service routine branches back to address POLL in Fig. 6.16 (as it should), the floppy disk could require service continually and none of the other peripherals would ever be serviced. This is another disadvantage to polling; when several peripherals are involved, the highest-priority devices may cause the low-priority devices to become "starved" for service.

6.5 INTERRUPT-DRIVEN I/O

As you read this section, look for the answers to these Key Concept questions:

6.5.1. Why is interrupt driven I/O more efficient than programmed I/O?

6.5.2. What is an ISR?

6.5.3. What is a nonmaskable interrupt?

6.5.4. List three ways of transferring control to an ISR.

Sec. 6.5   Interrupt-Driven I/O

6.5.5. Why is it important for an ISR to save the CPU registers it is about to use?

6.5.6. List three methods suitable for prioritizing simultaneous interrupt requests.

One alternative to programmed I/O is to use the microprocessor's built-in interrupt capabilities. Most microprocessors have at least one interrupt input pin. This input is sampled by the processor during the last clock cycle of the last machine cycle of every instruction (the 8085 tests on the second last clock cycle). If the interrupt input is found active, control is transferred to a special *interrupt service routine* (ISR). This is illustrated in Fig. 6.17.

At time 1 normal processing is occurring—perhaps editing of a word processing file. At time 2 an interrupt occurs. The processor finishes its current instruction and then saves the program counter on the stack at time 3. Control is then transferred to the ISR at time 4 and this routine is executed during time 5. The ISR ends with a RET instruction at time 6, causing the program counter to be popped from the stack. Having recovered its "old address," normal processing continues at time 7.

Let's assume that the interrupt was generated by the BUSY/READY flag of a printer. In this case, the ISR would be a routine to "feed" the printer another character. This might require 20 to 100 μs of processing time. But remember, the printer requires 10,000 μs to print the character (at 100 cps). This leaves 9900 μs for the processor to continue its editing (or some other) task.

Interrupt-driven I/O has the advantage that the processor responds to the peripheral only when the peripheral is ready. And using the processor's special interrupt input, there is no need to poll for this condition. This allows more efficient use of the microprocessor.

In order to implement interrupt-driven I/O several problems must be solved. Among these are:

1. Hardware must be added to generate the interrupt.
2. The address of the ISR must be determined at interrupt time.
3. Some processor activities cannot be allowed to be interrupted or loss of data may result: disk operations, for example.

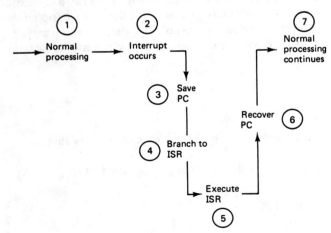

Figure 6.17 When an interrupt occurs, normal processing is suspended while a special interrupt service routine (ISR) is executed. Normal processing resumes when this routine is completed.

4. If several peripherals are to be interfaced, each must be recognized but have its own ISR.

5. What happens if two devices request interrupts simultaneously?

There is also a danger in using interrupts not present in programmed I/O. That is, hardware now controls the program flow instead of software. And because the source of the interrupt is *asynchronous* with respect to the processor, any program can be interrupted at any time. Too many interrupts can cause the microprocessor to become asynchronous—the programmer actually loses control of his or her own machine!

Generating an Interrupt. Throughout this book I have stressed the similarities between the various processors studied. Indeed, once the CPU modules have been designed, nearly all of the memory and I/O interfaces presented can be used with any 8-bit processor.

Not so with interrupts. Every processor seems to have its own unique way of handling interrupt requests. In this section we discuss interrupt-driven I/O in general and provide specific details for the 8080, 8085, and Z-80 microprocessors.

For most microprocessors (including the Z-80 but not the 8080 or 8085) the interrupt request input is interfaced using a type 2 bus. This is an open-collector bus line characterized by one receiver and many transmitters. In this way any number of interrupting devices may be interfaced (determining which device generated the interrupt is another matter, however). The type 2 interrupt bus is shown in Fig. 6.18(a).

Some processors, including the 8080 and 8085, require that the interrupt input be driven high. For these processors an OR gate must be used to provide the processor with a single interrupt request. This technique is shown in Fig. 6.18(b).

It is not uncommon for the microprocessor to have more than one interrupt input pin, and with these processors it may be possible for each peripheral to have its own dedicated interrupt input. Table 6.4 lists several important interrupt features of the 8080, 8085, and Z-80 microprocessors. In particular, note that the 8080 has

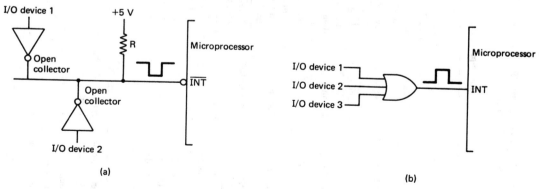

(a)

(b)

Figure 6.18 The interrupt request pin at the microprocessor may require (a) an active-low signal or (b) an active-high signal.

TABLE 6.4 IMPORTANT INTERRUPT FEATURES OF THE 8080, 8085, AND Z-80 MICROPROCESSORS

Micro-processor	Input	Interrupt request Type	Priority	Trigger	Interrupt response Type	Address	Acknowledge signal	PC saved?	Software maskable?	Type of return
8080	INTR	Maskable	—	High level until sampled	Vectored	RST pᵃ	$\overline{INTA}=0$	No[b]	No[c]	RET
8085	$\overline{TRAP}$	Nonmaskable	1	↑ Edge and level[d] / Latched	Direct	0024H	None	Yes	No	RET
	RST 7.5	Maskable	2	Latched	Direct	003CH	None	Yes	Yes	RET
	RST 6.5	Maskable	3	High level until sampled	Direct	0034H	None	Yes	Yes	RET
	RST 5.5	Maskable	4	High level until sampled	Direct	002CH	None	Yes	Yes	RET
	INTR	Maskable	5	High level until sampled	Vectored	RST pᵃ	$\overline{INTA}=0$	No[b]	No[c]	RET
Z-80	$\overline{NMI}$	Nonmaskable	1	High level until sampled	Direct	0066H	None	Yes	No	RETN[e]
	$\overline{INT}$ mode 0	Maskable	2	Low level until sampled / Latched	Vectored	RST pᵃ	$\overline{IORQ}=0$ M1 = 0	No[b]	No[c]	RET
	$\overline{INT}$ mode 1	Maskable	2	Low level until sampled	Direct	0038H	$\overline{IORQ}=0$ M1 = 0	Yes	No[c]	RET
	$\overline{INT}$ mode 2	Maskable	2	Low level until sampled	Indirect	I register + 7 bit vector points to vector table	$\overline{IORQ}=0$ M1 = 0	Yes	No[c]	RETI[f]

[a] A call instruction (or any other) may also be used.
[b] Using an RST instruction saves the PC.
[c] The DI instruction disables all maskable interrupts.
[d] Triggered on the rising edge but must be held high until internally sampled.
[e] Restores premaskable interrupt status.
[f] Used by Zilog peripherals to reset IEO flag.

only one interrupt input, the Z-80 has two, and the 8085 has five. The Z-80's $\overline{\text{INT}}$ input has three separate modes of operation controlled by software.

Remembering that the processor will not service an interrupt request until the end of the current instruction, care must be taken that the processor has indeed received the interrupt request. In most cases the processor will generate a special *interrupt acknowledge* signal called $\overline{\text{INTA}}$. This signal can be used to remove the interrupt request once it has been acknowledged as shown in Fig. 6.19.

The 8085 *RST 7.5* and Z-80 *NMI* inputs are edge triggered. An internal flip-flop will be set when the appropriate edge occurs, thus ensuring that the processor will "remember" that an interrupt is pending. The circuit in Fig. 6.19 is not required with these inputs.

The 8085's *RST 6.5* and *5.5* inputs are neither acknowledged nor edge triggered. When driving these input pins, care must be taken to ensure that the interrupt is long enough not to be missed by the processor, but not so long as to be counted twice.

The 8085 *TRAP* input is both level- and edge-triggered. On the rising edge of the TRAP signal, an internal latch is set, but the request will only be acknowledged provided that the TRAP input remains high. After the internal acknowledge has occurred, the interrupt request can be removed. The TRAP input will not be recognized again until it has returned low and then high. This feature prevents false triggering due to noise or logic glitches. For this reason, TRAP has a minimum pulse width but not a maximum.

Maskable and Nonmaskable Interrupts.

The interrupt inputs of a microprocessor can be classified as *maskable* or *nonmaskable*. A maskable interrupt is one that can be turned off or disabled by the CPU. For example, all three processors include the instruction *DI*—disable interrupts. When this command is given, maskable interrupts

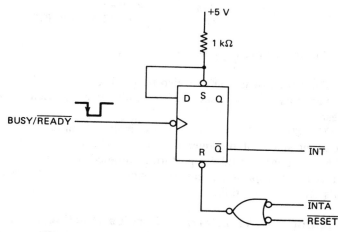

Figure 6.19 The microprocessor's interrupt acknowledge signal (INTA) can be used to remove the interrupt request after it has been received by the microprocessor.

Sec. 6.5   Interrupt-Driven I/O

cannot be serviced. Interrupts are automatically disabled whenever a $\overline{RESET}$ occurs or immediately after the receipt of an interrupt request.

The 8080 provides a special output signal called *INTE*—interrupts enabled. When high it indicates that interrupt requests will be honored by the processor. This signal turns out not to be too important, and neither the 8085 or Z-80 provides a similar output.

A nonmaskable interrupt cannot be ignored by the CPU. It must be serviced. Obviously, this type of interrupt should be used with great caution. Classically, it is reserved for a power-fail indication. If the computer system should lose power, the filter capacitors in the power supply will be able to hold up the supply voltages for several milliseconds. During this time important data in RAM can be quickly written to a disk or E^2PROM for safekeeping by the nonmaskable ISR.

The Z-80 $\overline{NMI}$ input and the 8085 TRAP input are both examples of nonmaskable interrupts. The 8080 does not have a nonmaskable interrupt.

When using the Z-80 NMI input, a special *RETN*—return from nonmaskable interrupt—should be used. This instruction restores the pre-$\overline{NMI}$ status of the internal interrupt enable flip-flop. This is necessary because an $\overline{NMI}$ request will reset this flip-flop, inhibiting further maskable interrupts.

In addition to the DI instruction, the 8085 has the command *SIM*—set interrupt mask. This instruction can be used to mask any combination of the RST 5.5 through 7.5 inputs. Figure 6.20(a) shows the bit assignments for the interrupt masks.

Example 6.8

Write an 8085 program that enables the RST 7.5 and RST 5.5 inputs.

Solution. The SIM instruction will copy the contents of the accumulator into the interrupt masks according to Fig. 6.20(a) if bit 3 is a 1. Thus the correct byte to load into the accumulator is X0X01010 (X implies a ''don't care'' condition). The program is

```
MVI A,0AH    ;MASK PATTERN
SIM          ;WRITE IT
EI           ;ENABLE INTERRUPTS
```

Note that DI overrides the SIM command.

The SIM instruction can also be used to reset the internal RST 7.5 flip-flop. However, this will be done automatically when servicing the RST 7.5 interrupt request.

The 8085 *RIM* command—read interrupt mask—can be used to determine the current status of the interrupt masks. The bit assignments are shown in Fig. 6.20(b). A RIM should be performed immediately after a TRAP occurs so that pre-TRAP interrupt status can be restored with a SIM. This is analogous to the Z-80's RETN instruction.

Branching to the Interrupt Service Routine. Once an interrupt occurs, control must be transferred to the address of the ISR. There are three techniques for doing this.

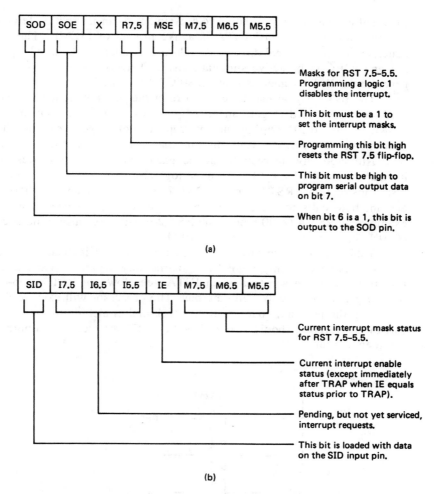

Figure 6.20 (a) The RST 5.5–7.5 inputs of the 8085 microprocessor can be masked using the SIM instruction; (b) the status of these interrupts can be read using the RIM instruction.

1. Vectored
2. Direct
3. Indirect

Vectored interrupts. When using *vectored* interrupts the interrupting device supplies a vector indicating the address of the ISR. All three processors support this type of interrupt, the 8080 and 8085 on the INTR pin, and the Z-80 on its $\overline{\text{INT}}$ pin. As indicated in Table 6.4, the Z-80 uses the $\overline{\text{INT}}$ pin for all three of its interrupt modes. The instructions IM 0, IM 1, and IM 2 are used to specify the desired technique: vectored, direct, or indirect.

During vectored interrupts a special interrupt acknowledge machine cycle is executed by the processor. This cycle is similar to an instruction fetch cycle except that the control bus signal $\overline{\text{INTA}}$ is active instead of $\overline{\text{MEMR}}$. The Z-80 does not generate the $\overline{\text{INTA}}$ signal directly, but during an interrupt acknowledge cycle causes $\overline{\text{M1}}$ and $\overline{\text{IORQ}}$ to be active simultaneously. These two signals can be combined to generate the $\overline{\text{INTA}}$ signal. See the Z-80 CPU module in Fig. 4.27.

The $\overline{\text{INTA}}$ signal can be used to reset the interrupt request as shown in Fig. 6.19. It is also used to gate an interrupt vector onto the system data bus. This is shown in Fig. 6.21. During the interrupt acknowledge cycle the CPU reads the data off the bus just as it would in a normal memory read cycle.

Although any instruction can be gated into the microprocessor during this interrupt acknowledge cycle, the most logical instruction to use is one of the eight restart instructions, RST 0 through RST 7 (8080/85 mnemonics). These instructions are one-byte calls to locations on page 0 of the processor's memory space. For example, an RST 4 (Z-80 mnemonic RST 20) will cause a subroutine call to address 0020H. Its op-code in binary is 11100111.

Table 6.5 lists the eight restart instructions and indicates the vector address for each. Note that only eight bytes of memory separate each address. Studying Fig. 6.21, you can see that when $\overline{\text{INTA}}$ goes low, an RST 4 (op-code = E7H) will be gated onto the system data bus. The processor will execute this instruction by saving the program counter on the stack and branching to location 0020H. The ISR in this location should terminate with a RET instruction and normal processing can then continue.

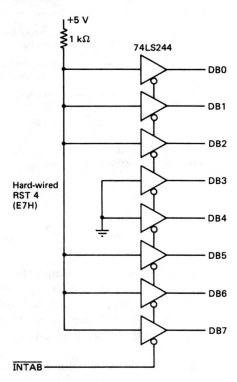

Figure 6.21 The $\overline{\text{INTA}}$ signal is used to gate a restart vector onto the microprocessor data bus.

TABLE 6.5 RESTART INSTRUCTIONS USED WITH
VECTORED INTERRUPTS

	Mnemonic		
Op-Code	8080/85	Z-80	Restart address
C7	RST 0	RST 0	0000H
CF	RST 1	RST 08	0008H
D7	RST 2	RST 10	0010H
DF	RST 3	RST 18	0018H
E7	RST 4	RST 20H	0020H
EF	RST 5	RST 28H	0028H
F7	RST 6	RST 30H	0030H
FF	RST 7	RST 38H	0038H

Direct interrupts. *Direct interrupts* are supported by the 8085 using the TRAP and RST 5.5 through 7.5 inputs. The Z-80 $\overline{\text{INT}}$ input is put in the direct interrupt mode by executing an IM 1 instruction. The Z-80 $\overline{\text{NMI}}$ input is also a direct interrupt.

Generating an interrupt on one of these pins causes a direct branch to a specific location in memory without the need for an interrupt vector. For example, activating the 8085's RST 5.5 input will cause a branch to location 002CH. In all cases, the program counter is automatically saved on the stack before the branch occurs.

Note that the 8085 TRAP input and the Z-80 $\overline{\text{NMI}}$ input are nonmaskable. All of the others are maskable.

Indirect interrupts. Only the Z-80 supports this mode. It is specified by executing an IM 2 instruction. This mode is similar to the vectored interrupt technique except that the vector gated onto the bus is combined with the Z-80's I register to form a 16-bit pointer into a vector table. The two consecutive bytes stored in this table are used as the address for the ISR.

Example 6.9

Using the interface shown in Fig. 6.21 determine the ISR address defined by the following Z-80 program.

```
IM 2        ;INTERRUPT MODE 2
LD A,0FFH   ;HIGH ORDER ADDRESS
LD I,A      ;IN REGISTER I
EI          ;ENABLE INTERRUPTS
```

Solution. The high-order address is specified by the contents of register I. In this case page FF is defined. When an interrupt occurs, the low-order address will be read from the interrupt acknowledge circuit but bit 0 will be ignored (the entries in the vector table must start at an even address). In this case the vector is 11100111, so the full address will be FFE6H. The processor will thus branch to the address stored in FFE6H (low-order address) and FFE7H (high-order address).

Indirect interrupts allow the ISR to be located anywhere in the processor's memory space. As such, they offer the maximum flexibility. Direct interrupts are the easiest to implement as no external hardware is required. Vectored interrupts offer the advantage that eight separate peripherals can share the same interrupt request line but each branch to a separate service routine. However, each routine is limited to eight bytes on page 0.

Response Time and Transfer Rate.   Interrupt-driven I/O is clearly a more efficient interfacing technique than programmed I/O. But how does it compare for *response time* and *transfer rate*?

Table 6.6 calculates the worst-case response time for each of the interrupt inputs on the 8080, 8085, and Z-80 microprocessors. This is the maximum time required from generation of the interrupt signal by the peripheral to execution of the first instruction in the ISR.

TABLE 6.6 INTERRUPT RESPONSE TIMES FOR THE 8080, 8085, AND Z-80 MICROPROCESSORS

Micro-processor	Interrupt input	Extra T state	One instruction: worst-case T states	WAIT states	RST T states	Total T states	Total time (μs)
8080A (2 MHz)	INTR	1	0–18	0	11	12–30	6–15
8085AH (3 MHz)	INTR TRAP RST 5.5–7.5	1	0–18	0	12	13–31	4.3–10.3
Z-80A (4 MHz)	NMI	1	0–23	0	10	11–34	2.8–8.5
	INT-Mode 0	1	0–23	2	11	14–37	3.5–9.3
	INT-Mode 1	1	0–23	2	10	13–36	3.25–9
	INT-Mode 2	1	0–23	2	17[a]	20–43	5–10.8

[a] 19 T states required to fetch low-order vector, save program counter, and branch to address in the vector table.

In the worst case, the interrupt request will occur just after the interrupt input is sampled in the last T state of an instruction. This means that the interrupt will not be serviced until the end of the following instruction. This could require as many as 18 T states for an 8080 or 8085 and 23 T states for a Z-80.

Unlike the 8080 or 8085, the Z-80 inserts two WAIT states in the interrupt acknowledge cycle for maskable interrupts. This is used to allow arbitration logic time to settle out and enable the highest-priority device. We will discuss this more in the next section.

After acknowledging the interrupt, a restart instruction is either fetched from the data bus (if the 8080/85 INTR or Z-80 $\overline{\text{INT}}$ mode 0 input is active) or automatically inserted by the processor (if the 8085 TRAP or RST 5.5–7.5 or Z-80 $\overline{\text{NMI}}$ or $\overline{\text{INT}}$ mode 1 input is active). In either case 10, 11, or 12 T states are required.

When using the Z-80 $\overline{\text{INT}}$ input in mode 2, 17 T states (plus 2 WAIT states) are required to fetch the low-order address vector, save the program counter on the stack, and get the jump address from the interrupt table in memory.

The total required T states shown in Table 6.6 can be compared with 24 or 25 T states for the response time for the polling routines in Figs. 6.13 and 6.14. Thus polling is slightly faster than interrupts when considering a worst case. In a best case, interrupts will be fastest.

But what happens as more peripherals are added? Considering the polling routine in Fig. 6.16, the daisy-wheel printer (DW) service routine will not be serviced until at least 53 T states have elapsed (11 + 14 + 14 + 14) and probably longer if one of the higher-priority devices is being serviced. If interrupts were used, as soon as the daisy-wheel printer requested service, the processor would respond. The total response time would still be found using the numbers in Table 6.6.

It should be clear that the response time for interrupt-driven I/O begins to excel programmed I/O as soon as a second peripheral is added to the polling routine.

Another advantage to interrupts is that one service routine can interrupt another. In fact, if the ISR is written so as to be *reentrant*, the interrupt can even interrupt itself. This prevents the response time from being degraded due to having to wait for a previous service routine to finish, as would occur with polling. Of course, the interrupted service routine will be suspended while the most recent interrupt is serviced. This will degrade the transfer rate of the first routine.

Let's consider the *transfer rate* of an ISR by developing a routine to service a printer each time its BUSY/$\overline{\text{READY}}$ flag indicates ready. We will assume the following:

1. A supervisor program is used to write into memory location DATA and DATA + 1 the address of a data table for the printer. This program also writes into memory location NUMB—the number of bytes that are to be printed.
2. When it is desired to print the data file, the supervisor enables interrupts, and then proceeds with some other activity.
3. When ready, the printer generates an interrupt and control is temporarily transferred to the printer ISR.
4. The printer ISR must fetch a data byte from the table, output it to the printer, test for the last byte, and reenable interrupts if more data is to be output.

Figure 6.22 is an 8080 listing for the printer ISR. Note that the routine is broken into six sections. In general, all ISRs must include these six activities.

1. Save the environment. If interrupts are to work at all, the ISR must not be allowed to change any CPU registers. If this is not done, the interrupted program may "crash" when the ISR returns control.

```
;SAMPLE INTERRUPT SERVICE ROUTINE FOR THE 8080.
;
;NOTE THE SIX ACTIVITIES PERFORMED BY THIS PROGRAM.
;T STATES ARE INDICATED IN THE RIGHT MARGIN.
;
;SUPERVISOR PROGRAM PRESUMED TO HAVE LOADED (DATA) AND (NUMB).
;
DPORT   EQU     1                       ;OUTPUT DATA PORT
        ;
        ORG     0100H                   ;PROGRAM BEGINS AT 0100H
        ;
        ;[1]    SAVE THE ENVIRONMENT
        ;
        PUSH    H                       ;                               [11]
        PUSH    PSW                     ;                               [11]
        PUSH    B                       ;                               [11]
        ;
        ;[2]    RESTORE PRINTING ENVIRONMENT
        ;
        LHLD    DATA                    ;(DATA) STORES ADDRESS OF       [16]
                                        ;CURRENT DATA BYTE TO BE OUTPUT
        LDA     NUMB                    ;(NUMB) STORES BYTES REMAINING  [13]
                                        ;TO BE OUTPUT
        MOV     B,A                     ;SAVE NUMB IN B                 [5]
        ;
        ;[3]    PRINT THE DATA BYTE - ADJUST POINTER AND COUNTER
        ;
        MOV     A,M                     ;FETCH THE BYTE                 [7]
        OUT     DPORT                   ;PRINT                          [10]
        INX     H                       ;ADVANCE POINTER                [5]
        DCR     B                       ;DECREMENT BYTE COUNTER         [5]
        JZ      DONE                    ;IF DONE SKIP EI                [10]
        ;
        ;[4]    SAVE PRINTING ENVIRONMENT
        ;
        SHLD    DATA                    ;SAVE POINTER                   [16]
        MOV     A,B                     ;FETCH BYTE COUNTER TO A        [5]
        STA     NUMB                    ;SAVE IT                        [13]
        EI                              ;REENABLE THE INTERRUPTS        [4]
        ;
        ;[5]    RESTORE CPU ENVIRONMENT
        ;
DONE    POP     B                       ;                               [10]
        POP     PSW                     ;                               [10]
        POP     H                       ;                               [10]
        ;
        ;[6]    RETURN
        ;
        RET                             ;                               [10]
                                                        TOTAL = [182]
        ;
        ;
        ;SET UP STORAGE LOCATION FOR DATA AND NUMB.
        ;
DATA    DS      2                       ;2 BYTES FOR DATA ADDRESS
NUMB    DS      1                       ;1 BYTE FOR THE BYTE COUNTER
        END
```

Figure 6.22 Typical ISR. This routine could be used to output data to a printer. Note that six specific activities are required of the program.

2. Variables used by the ISR must be recovered. Certainly, the CPU registers cannot be used to hold these values. It will be difficult to use the stack area because the top of the stack will contain a return address when the ISR is entered.

3. The peripheral can now be serviced. In this case data is output to the printer and a test is made for the last byte.

4. The variables used by the ISR must now be saved and interrupts reenabled. If EI is not given, the next interrupt (and all succeeding interrupts) will be missed.

5. Restore the environment. This restores any registers used by the ISR to their original values.

6. An RET instruction returns control to the interrupted program.

We can calculate the maximum transfer rate for this program by assuming that the next interrupt occurs just as the RET instruction is executed. In this case, control is immediately transferred back to the printer ISR and the next byte is output. The time required between bytes equals the response time in Table 6.5 (assuming no extra instruction) plus the time to execute the routine in Fig. 6.22— 182 T states for an 8080 processor. The total T states are thus 182 + 11 = 193 T states.

Assuming a 2-MHz 8080, 96.5 μs is required for each transfer. Of course, a 100-cps printer requires 10,000 μs per character, so the interrupt routine should work very nicely with this peripheral. But if the routine were used to read or write data from a floppy disk drive, it would be too slow—recall that a 5¼-inch double-density drive requires data every 32 μs.

It is interesting to note that the polling routine used to accomplish the same function (see Fig. 6.13) required only 61 T states and data could be transferred every 30.5 μs—fast enough to keep up with the floppy-disk drive. Why is the polling scheme faster than the interrupt-driven technique?

What we must remember is that although polling is inefficient, it is relatively fast when servicing a *single peripheral*. Interrupts, on the other hand, require a great deal of software overhead to save the program counter and any CPU registers used by the ISR. These instructions must be executed every time the ISR is executed. The polling routine may also have to save these registers, but it need only be done once when the polling routine is first entered.

In summary, we can say that when compared with interrupt-driven I/O, polling is an inefficient use of the resources of the microprocessor, but this matters only in a multitasking environment. When servicing a single peripheral, polling will usually result in the highest data transfer rate.

Multiple Interrupts: The Priority Problem. We have already mentioned that one ISR can interrupt another. This can only occur for either of two special cases:

1. The first ISR executes an EI instruction early in the routine.
2. The second interrupt is nonmaskable.

Remember that once an interrupt is acknowledged, maskable interrupts are automatically disabled. This is done to protect the ISR from being interrupted before it has had a chance to perform its task. A nonmaskable interrupt, however, can never be blocked even if the DI instruction is executed.

When *nested* interrupts are used—that is, interrupts within interrupts—care must be taken that the stack area does not grow so large as to overwrite the program or any of its data tables.

Example 6.10

Assume that an 8085 microprocessor received three interrupt requests in the following order: RST 7.5, RST 6.5, and RST 5.5. If these three interrupts are nested, to what depth does the stack penetrate if all registers within the CPU must be saved? Assume that the stack pointer initially points to location FFFFH.

Solution. Each ISR must begin with the sequence

```
PUSH PSW
PUSH B
PUSH D
PUSH H
EI
```

This means that the stack will "grow" by 10 bytes (do not forget the program counter) with each new interrupt request. Figure 6.23 illustrates that after the third interrupt the stack will have moved down 30 bytes to address FFE1.

This example again illustrates that caution must be used when using interrupts. When interrupts are enabled, the hardware is in control. If you forget this, one peripheral may cause hundreds of interrupts per second, quickly overwriting your program. The result is a "fatal" crash. This is especially hard to debug because there is no program left to examine!

It is also possible for the microcomputer to become *interrupt bound*. This occurs with long ISRs or multiple interrupt requests. The processor may never get back to its main task.

When this occurs, "software time" is no longer equal to "real time." A software timing loop that is repeatedly interrupted will become inaccurate. Monitoring edges of a pulse train is another example. If interrupted, the software may miss an edge. In both cases, the software is delayed by the ISR and no longer runs in real time.

Another problem to be considered with multiple interrupts is the possibility of two requests arriving simultaneously. Because the processor does not test for an interrupt request until the end of the current instruction, two interrupt requests do not actually have to arrive at the same instant to appear simultaneous to the microprocessor.

Interrupt no.		Stack address	
0		FFFFH	65,535
1	RST 7.5	FFF5H	65,525
2	RST 6.5	FFEBH	65,515
3	RST 5.5	FFE1H	65,505

Figure 6.23 Nested interrupts cause the stack to move downward in memory.

This problem has an easy solution and a hard one. The easy solution is provided by the microprocessor itself. The Z-80 and the 8085 both prioritize their interrupts. This is shown in Table 6.4. For the 8085, an RST 7.5 will be serviced before an RST 6.5 or RST 5.5.

Of course, a nonmaskable interrupt has the highest priority, but this priority extends only to *pending* interrupts, not working ISRs. For example, in Ex. 6.10, an RST 5.5 was used to interrupt an RST 6.5. When this is undesired, it is up to the programmer to be sure not to enable interrupts until the ISR has completed its task. In this way only a nonmaskable interrupt will be able to interrupt the executing ISR.

Prioritizing works well with direct interrupts, but another technique must be used when one interrupt line is shared by several peripherals. This is typically the case when the vectored interrupt line is used. In fact, it is the only technique available to the 8080.

As shown in Fig. 6.18, any number of peripheral devices can easily be connected to the interrupt request pin if an open-collector bus or an OR gate connection is used. The problem for the processor is determining who is requesting the interrupt and resolving any simultaneous requests by two or more devices. Three techniques are commonly used.

1. *Polling*: The interrupt request signal from each device can be used to set one bit of a register wired as an input port. When an interrupt occurs, the ISR polls this input port to "see" who requested service. A priority is automatically established by the order of the polling. This technique is very simple but has the negative effect of degrading response time.

2. *Priority interrupt controller* (PIC): Figure 6.24 illustrates a solution to the problem using hardware. The 8 line-to-3 line priority encoder (74148) generates a 3-bit binary code corresponding to the active input. If two or more inputs are present simultaneously, the highest numbered will be encoded. The 3 bits are inverted and combined to form a restart instruction that is enabled onto the data bus by $\overline{\text{INTA}}$. Note that the encoder $\overline{\text{GS}}$ output can be used to generate the interrupt request. The Intel 8259 PIC is covered in Chap. 7. This chip incorporates all of the features of the circuit in Fig. 6.24 but gates CALL instructions onto the data bus instead of restart instructions. The 8259 will accommodate 64 separate interrupts in a cascaded mode.

3. *Daisy chain*: This technique is illustrated in Fig. 6.25. Each peripheral has an interrupt enable input (IEI) and an interrupt enable output (IEO). An interrupt request can be made only if IEI is high. In Fig. 6.25 peripheral number 2 is requesting an interrupt causing its IEO to be low. This, in turn, disables devices 3 and 4. Note that device number 1 is still able to request an interrupt because it has a higher priority. The $\overline{\text{INTA}}$ signal can be used to reset IEO of the interrupting device.

Note: All Zilog peripheral interface chips support this daisy-chain technique, each having an IEI and IEO pin. Rather than use the $\overline{\text{INTA}}$ signal, a special return instruction can be output by the Z-80 called *return from interrupt—RETI*. The

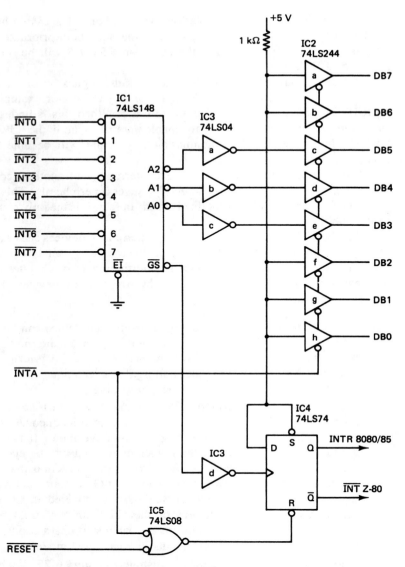

Figure 6.24 Hardware solution to the multiple-interrupts problem. This circuit will accept eight interrupt requests, prioritize them, and generate a separate restart instruction for each.

peripheral devices monitor the data bus for the unique RETI two-byte op-code ED 4D ($\overline{M1}$ is active for both bytes), and if IEI is high, reset IEO when this op-code is detected.

The daisy-chain technique is particularly versatile when the Z-80's mode 2 interrupts are selected. The peripheral devices can be programmed with the interrupt

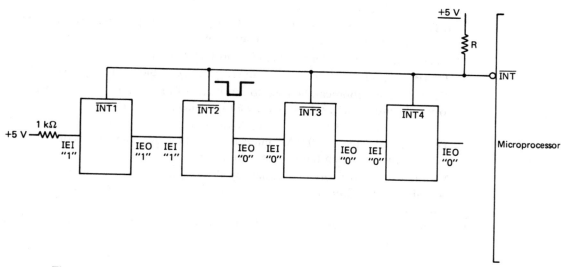

Figure 6.25 Daisy-chain approach to solving the multiple-interrupts problem. IEI is the interrupt enable input and IEO is the interrupt enable output. Only when IEI is high can the peripheral request an interrupt.

vector and this byte will automatically be gated onto the data bus during $\overline{\text{INTA}}$ ($\overline{\text{M1}}$ and $\overline{\text{IORQ}}$). Chapter 8 provides more detail on this topic.

Summary Points for the 8080, 8085, and Z-80.   As you have seen, each processor has its own unique methods of handling interrupt requests. The following is a summary of the important points for each processor.

The 8080:

1. There is one interrupt input, labeled INTR.
2. INTR can be masked with the DI instruction but is automatically disabled whenever an interrupt request is acknowledged.
3. INTR must be driven high to request an interrupt.
4. A vectored interrupt scheme is used. $\overline{\text{INTA}}$ is used to gate a restart instruction onto the data bus.
5. Eight different restart locations are possible.
6. Multiple interrupts are best handled using the 8259 programmable interrupt controller (PIC).
7. After a system reset INTR is disabled.

The 8085:

1. There are five interrupts, labeled TRAP, RST 7.5, RST 6.5, RST 5.5, and INTR.

2. Only TRAP is nonmaskable.

3. RST 7.5 is rising edge-triggered, TRAP is rising edge- and level-triggered. All of the others are active-high level-triggered.

4. INTR is a vectored interrupt identical to INTR on the 8080.

5. TRAP and RST 7.5–5.5 are direct interrupts. See Table 6.4 for the ISR address.

6. The SIM instruction can be used to mask any of the RST interrupts in addition to the DI instruction, which disables all maskable interrupts.

7. After a TRAP the RIM instruction should be the first instruction in the ISR. This will save the pre-TRAP interrupt status, which can be restored with a SIM instruction when the ISR is completed.

8. Multiple interrupts can be handled by dedicating a separate interrupt to each peripheral. The 8259 PIC can also be used when multiple interrupts are interfaced through INTR.

9. After a system reset all maskable interrupts are disabled and all three RST mask bits are set.

The Z-80:

1. The Z-80 has two interrupt pins, $\overline{\text{INT}}$ and $\overline{\text{NMI}}$.

2. $\overline{\text{NMI}}$ is a falling edge-triggered nonmaskable direct interrupt. Its restart address is 0066H.

3. The ISR for an $\overline{\text{NMI}}$ should end with RETN so that the pre-NMI maskable interrupt status will be retained.

4. $\overline{\text{INT}}$ is active-low level-triggered and can be used in three separate modes, labeled modes 0, 1, and 2.

5. When programmed for mode 0 (IM 0), $\overline{\text{INT}}$ behaves as a vectored interrupt identical to INTR on the 8080.

6. When programmed for mode 1 (IM 1), $\overline{\text{INT}}$ behaves as a direct interrupt with a restart address of 0038H.

7. When programmed for mode 2 (IM 2), $\overline{\text{INT}}$ behaves as an indirect interrupt using the address in memory pointed at by the contents of register I (high-order address) and the 7 most significant bits read from the data bus during interrupt acknowledge (low-order address).

8. After reset, the I register = 0, interrupt mode = 0, and maskable interrupts are disabled.

9. $\overline{\text{INTA}}$ must be derived from $\overline{\text{M1}} \cdot \overline{\text{IORQ}}$.

10. Multiple interrupts are best handled using Z-80 peripheral interface chips that support a daisy-chain priority technique. When this technique is used, all ISRs should terminate with the RETI instruction, as this is used by the support devices to reset the interrupt enable output status.

6.6 DIRECT MEMORY ACCESS

As you read this section, look for the answers to these Key Concept questions?

6.6.1. When DMA data transfers are used, the peripheral is synchronized to _____, not the microprocessor.

6.6.2. What is meant by simultaneous DMA?

6.6.3. List three DMA modes.

We have now seen two different methods of transferring data between a peripheral and a microcomputer. The polling technique synchronizes the microprocessor to the peripheral at the expense of processing efficiency. Interrupt-driven I/O is more natural—the processor responds only when called upon. This results in more efficient use of the microprocessor at the expense of greater software overhead. The result is a (usually) faster response time than with polling but a slower data transfer rate.

A third method of transferring data is called *direct memory access* or DMA. Using DMA, the peripheral is synchronized to main memory, not the microprocessor. Because memory access times are very short, the transfer rate can be very high.

To appreciate the DMA concept, you must understand that the real bottleneck in transferring data is the microprocessor itself. When a text file is output to a disk drive, we are concerned with transferring data from memory to that drive. The microprocessor acts as a "middleman" in this process, with the result that the data transfer rate is decreased.

The DMA approach is to "turn off" the processor and let the disk drive access the data file in memory itself: a sort of *direct memory access*. If the memory can supply a new byte of data every 200 ns, data can be transferred at a rate of 5 million bytes per second!

The challenge to DMA is building the controller that allows the peripheral to take over the job of the CPU temporarily while it directly accesses the system memory. Figure 6.26 illustrates one type of DMA controller (DMAC) similar to the Intel 8237. As you might imagine, all three system buses are involved in the interface.

A handshaking logic scheme is used between the DMAC and the microprocessor and between the peripheral and the DMAC. A DMA request is initiated by the peripheral by using its BUSY/$\overline{\text{READY}}$ flag to assert DMARQ. The DMAC responds by asserting $\overline{\text{BUSRQ}}$ (Z-80) or HOLD (8080/85). The microprocessor responds by finishing the current machine cycle and then asserting $\overline{\text{BUSAK}}$ (Z-80) or HOLDA (8080/85) and tri-stating its data, address, and control bus signals. The DMAC alerts the peripheral that it has been selected for DMA by applying DMACK.

The memory and I/O devices now find themselves directly interfaced to the DMAC, just as if it were the microprocessor. Two classes of DMA are now possible. In *sequential DMA* the DMAC performs a read operation fetching the data byte from the DMAC. Next a write operation is performed transferring the data byte to the I/O port. The opposite sequence is also possible—read a byte from the I/O

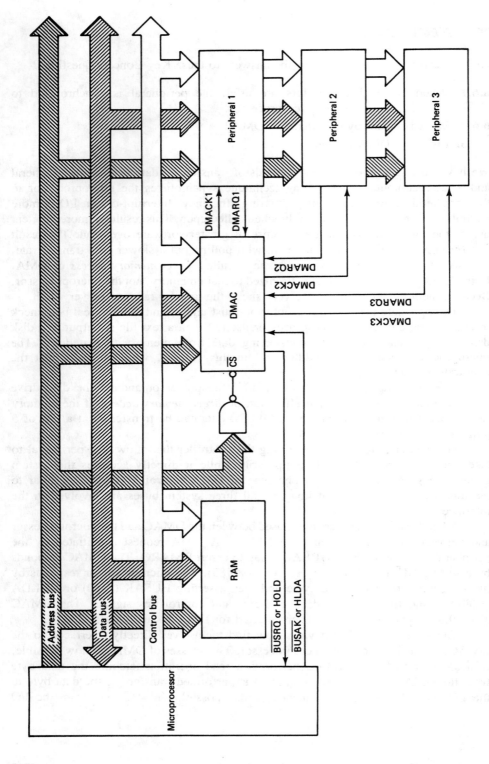

Figure 6.26 A DMA controller allows the peripheral to interface directly with memory without CPU intervention. This allows the data transfer rate to approach the access time of the memory.

port, write the byte to memory. Generally, two to four clock periods are required for each read or write operation (four to eight for the total transfer).

Simultaneous DMA provides the fastest transfers. With this technique the read and write operations are performed at the same time. This requires $\overline{MEMR}$ and $\overline{IOW}$ (or $\overline{IOR}$ and $\overline{MEMW}$) to both be active simultaneously. In this way data does not flow through the DMAC at all but directly from memory to the I/O port (or vice versa). The result is a twofold speed improvement compared to the sequential approach.

In either case the data transfer is done completely in hardware involving only the DMAC, the peripheral, and main memory. Because the CPU is not involved, there is no software overhead.

DMA requests take precedence over all other bus activities, including interrupts. In fact, no interrupts—maskable or nonmaskable—will be recognized during a DMA request.

Several types of DMA transfers are possible. These are:

1. Memory to peripheral
2. Peripheral to memory
3. Memory to memory
4. Peripheral to peripheral

The DMAC is usually interfaced to the microprocessor as an I/O port. Before any data transfers can occur, the CPU must program the DMAC for the type of transfer that is to take place, the destination and source addresses, and the number of bytes to be transferred.

If you consider sequential and simultaneous DMA to be separate "classes," then there are three modes of DMA within each class. These are shown in Fig. 6.27. In *byte* or single mode [Fig. 6.27(a)], the DMAC, after gaining control of the system buses, transfers a single data byte. Control of the buses is then relinquished until the peripherals's READY flag is again active.

The *burst* or demand mode, shown in Fig. 6.27(b), is intended for peripherals that have high-speed data buffers. After gaining control of the buses, data is transferred until the peripheral's READY flag is no longer active. Control of the buses is then relinquished to the CPU. When READY again becomes active, another burst of DMA occurs. The advantage of this technique is that the buffer can be filled very rapidly by the DMAC and then emptied at the peripheral's leisure.

A third type of DMA is called continuous or *block* mode DMA [Fig. 6.27(c)]. This is similar to burst mode except that control of the buses is not relinquished until the entire data block has been transferred. This technique is very effective with a high-speed peripheral that can keep up with the DMAC. Slow peripherals will cause long periods of inactivity on the buses as the DMAC waits for the READY flag.

Because the DMA request line is sampled at the end of each machine cycle (not instruction cycle), the response time for DMA will be no longer than one machine cycle plus one T state. This is a worst case of six T states for an 8080 or seven T states for an 8085 or Z-80.

Sec. 6.6   Direct Memory Access

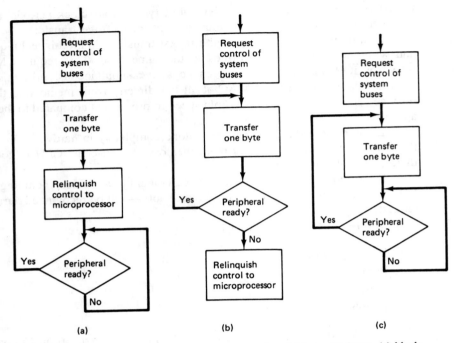

Figure 6.27 The three modes of DMA operation: (a) byte, (b) burst, (c) block.

The design of a DMA controller is not a simple task and this is probably the main disadvantage of the technique. The DMAC is actually a highly specialized *transfer processor* rivaling the microprocessor itself in complexity. Most microprocessors are now supported by special single-chip DMA controllers. Intel offers the 8237 Programmable DMA Controller to support the 8080 and 8085, and Zilog offers the Z-80 DMA to support the Z-80. These devices are discussed in detail in Chaps. 7 and 8.

CHAPTER SUMMARY

1. An 8-bit latch is required to store data output by the microprocessor during an I/O write operation.

2. Eight tri-state buffers are required to gate data onto the system data bus during an I/O read operation.

3. An input or output port has a specific address defined by its address decoder. The output of this circuit is combined with $\overline{IOR}$ or $\overline{IOW}$ to form a device select pulse. This signal is used to enable the latch of an output port or the buffers of an input port.

4. If $\overline{IOR}$ and $\overline{IOW}$ are replaced by $\overline{MEMR}$ and $\overline{MEMW}$ and the full 16-bit

address is decoded, a memory-mapped I/O port results. This port can be read from or written to just as if it were a memory location.

5. Most peripherals present data or accept data asynchronously with respect to the microprocessor. As a result, handshaking signals are interchanged between the microprocessor and peripheral to ensure a smooth transfer of data.

6. Programmed I/O or polling requires the microprocessor to monitor the BUSY/READY flag of the peripheral continually. This is an inefficient use of the microprocessor but provides a relatively fast response time and transfer rate if only one device is being monitored.

7. Interrupt-driven I/O provides an alternative to polling. The processor services the peripheral only when requested by the peripheral. This is a more efficient use of the resources of the microprocessor but requires software overhead to save the preinterrupt processing environment. The result is a slower data transfer rate.

8. Each microprocessor handles interrupts in a different way, but three techniques are common: vectored, direct, and indirect interrupts.

9. With interrupts or polling, a priority structure can be established that provides service to the most important (highest-priority) peripheral first.

10. Direct memory access (DMA) provides the fastest data transfer rate by synchronizing the peripheral to main memory. The software overhead is minimal, but a special DMA controller chip is required, complicating the hardware.

LAB PROJECTS

6.1. Study the schematic diagram of the microcomputer you are using to support this text/course. You should have a user-accessible 8-bit input and output port.[1]
 (a) What is the part number of the chip used as the output port latch?
 (b) What is the part number of the chip used as the input port buffer?
 (c) To what addresses (or range of addresses) are these ports mapped?

6.2. Sketch a schematic diagram of the input and output ports located in Lab. 6.1. Be sure to include the address decoding logic.

6.3. Sketch an I/O map for your computer showing the address ranges occupied by each input and output port. Identify the function of each port (e.g., keyboard, LED display, speaker, user, etc.).

6.4. Design an I/O port address decoder circuit that provides one input and one output device select pulse (DSP). Test your circuit by writing a program that causes each DSP to pulse at a 1-Hz rate. Use a logic probe to verify proper operation.

---

[1] Some systems use special parallel I/O chips like the 8255 PPI or Z-80 PIO. These are covered in detail in Chaps. 7 and 8.

6.5. Use the DSP signals from Lab. 6.4 to add an input and/or output port to your computer. Write a simple program to test your circuit.

6.6. Use the DSP signals from Lab. 6.4 to build a circuit similar to Fig. 6.6. Connect one bit of an input port to a switch and write a program to monitor the switch and turn a relay on and off. It can be fun to use a photocell in place of the switch.

6.7. Figure 6.28 is a 1-bit memory-mapped input port. Build this circuit and write a program to read the switch. (Note: You may have to adjust the address decoder to avoid conflicts with the memory of your computer. Refer to your system memory map.)

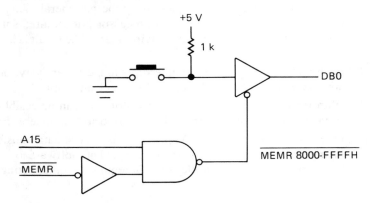

Figure 6.28   1-bit memory-mapped input port for Lab 6.7.

6.8. Using a technique similar to the one used in Chap. 3 Program 12 write a program to count and display the number of falling edges generated by the bouncing switch in Lab 6.7.

6.9. Design an interrupt interface such that pushing a switch will cause control to transfer to a vectored interrupt of your choice. Write a simple test program— jump to Monitor—to test your hardware.

6.10. Use the interrupt hardware from Lab 6.9 and write a "reaction timer" program. Have your program show 00 in its display and then begin a rapid count. When interrupted—by pushing the switch—the display should "freeze" showing the operator's reaction time.

QUESTIONS AND PROBLEMS

Section 6.1

6.1. Can an input port and an output port share the same address? Explain.

6.2. What data is output by the Z-80 program below? To which port(s) is the data output?

```
LD     C,27H
LD     B,3CH
OUT    (C),B
INC    C
OUT    (C),B
HALT
```

6.3. Write an 8080/85 program that is the equivalent of the Z-80 program in Prob. 6.2.

6.4. For all three processors valid data will be read by the CPU on the *falling/ rising* edge of the $\overline{\text{IOR}}$ control signal.

6.5. When designing an output port care must be taken *not* to latch the data bus on the falling edge of the $\overline{\text{IOW}}$ control signal. Explain.

6.6. Describe the changes required to the circuit in Fig. 6.2 if the port address is changed to 72H.

6.7. Redesign the address decoder in Fig. 6.2 so that the port address can be set to any one of 256 values via an 8-switch DIP switch. (Hint: Use two 74LS85 4-bit magnitude comparators.)

*6.8. A technician is troubleshooting the output port in Fig. 6.4. A logic probe connected to DB0–DB7 shows a pulsing condition on each line, but the 1Q–8Q latch outputs are steady. "There's the problem," he says. "The latch is bad." What is wrong with this logic?

*6.9. A technician testing the relay control circuit in Fig. 6.6 uses the following test program.

```
LOOP    IN     FFH
        CALL   DELAY      ;10 s delay
        OUT    FFH
        CALL   DELAY      ;10 s delay
        JMP    LOOP
```

Which of the following could be a cause for the relay to never come on?
(a) Register A must be loaded with 00 before the OUT instruction is given.
(b) The DELAY subroutine is changing the values of the CPU registers causing the program to fail.
(c) The 2k resistor is actually a 220k resistor.
(d) The flip-flop Q output is stuck low.

*6.10. How would you troubleshoot the hardware/software interface problem described in Prob. 6.9?

Section 6.2

6.11. Which of the following instructions could be used to output data to a memory-mapped output port?

8080/85 mnemonic		Z-80 mnemonic	
(a) MOV	A,B	LD	A,B
(b) STA	1000H	LD	(1000H),A
(c) STAX	D	LD	(DE),A
(d) PUSH	B	PUSH	BC
(e) MOV	M,C	LD	(HL),C

6.12. Study the circuit shown in Fig. 6.29. Is this an input or output port? Is it I/O-mapped or memory-mapped? To what address or *range* of addresses will this port respond?

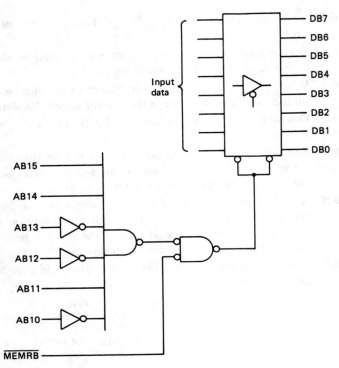

Figure 6.29 I/O port for Probs. 6.12 and 6.13.

6.13. Write a program to read the port in Fig. 6.29 and branch to location READY when bits 0 and 1 are both low.

6.14. Refer to the memory-mapped keypad interface in Fig. 6.8. Assume the instruction LDA FF03H (8080/85) or LD A, (FF03H) (Z-80) is given and the data byte 41H is read. Which key or keys are being held down?

6.15. If keys 3 and 7 are both held down, what key value will be encoded by the interface in Fig. 6.8 and software flowcharted in Fig. 6.9?

6.16. Write the program corresponding to the keyboard encoder flowcharted in Fig. 6.9.

6.17. Write the program corresponding to the digital lock flowcharted in Fig. 6.10.

6.18. Can the instruction SHLD 1000H (8080/85) or LD (1000H),HL (Z-80) be used as a 16-bit memory-mapped output instruction? Explain. What is the corresponding input instructon?

Section 6.3

6.19. Explain the handshaking signals exchanged between a computer and a peripheral by completing the table below.

Signal	Output by	Purpose
BUSY/READY		
STROBE		
ACK		

6.20. What is meant by *synchronizing* a microprocessor with a peripheral?

Section 6.4

6.21. Answer the following questions about the parallel printer interface in Fig. 6.12.
   (a) Is this interface-memory or I/O-mapped?
   (b) What is the data port address?
   (c) What is the size (bits) and purpose of the input port?
   (d) Sketch a timing diagram showing $\overline{IOW}$, the OUT0 DISP, and $\overline{STROBE}$.

6.22. Refer to the parallel printer control programs in Fig. 6.13 (8080/85) or Fig. 6.14 (Z-80).
   (a) What is the purpose of memory location NUMB?
   (b) Where is the data stored that is to be printed?
   (c) How does the program detect the end of data?

*6.23. A programmer plans to use the printer control programs in Figs. 6.13 and 6.14 to print a 700-byte document. His plan is to change the define storage operator to 1024 and then load NUMB with 700. Unfortunately, this will not work. Why not?

*6.24. Assume the printer cable in Fig. 6.12 is wired *incorrectly* such that the D2 and D1 printer data lines are exchanged. What would the symptom of this problem be?

6.25. Calculate the maximum transfer rate for the printer control program in Fig. 6.13 assuming a 6-MHz 8085AH-1. Remember to recalculate the T states for an 8085.

6.26. Calculate the maximum transfer rate for the printer control program in Fig. 6.14 assuming a 6-MHz Z-80B.

6.27. Assume a floppy disk drive and 100-cps printer are interfaced to a microcomputer. The BUSY/READY status bit assignments are shown in Fig. 6.30(a). Write a polling routine that monitors these flags and branches to the appropriate service routine as shown in Fig. 6.30(b). Write your program so that the disk drive has the highest priority.

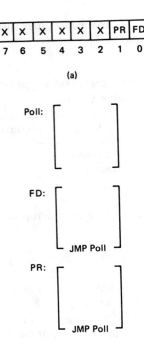

Figure 6.30 (a) Status bit assignments and (b) program organization for Prob. 6.27.

Section 6.5

6.28. List three situations that will cause maskable interrupts to be blocked by the 8080, 8085 or Z-80 microprocessors.

6.29. True or false: Nonmaskable interrupts have a higher priority than maskable interrupts.

6.30. True or false: When interrupts are enabled, a maskable interrupt can interrupt a nonmaskable interrupt service routine.

6.31. The 8085 SIM instruction returns the byte 34H. How is this byte interpreted?

6.32. Write an 8085 program to mask the RST 7.5 and RST 5.5 interrupt inputs. All others should be enabled.

6.33. Assume memory location 0030H stores a jump instruction to a printer interrupt service routine. Sketch a schematic diagram of the circuit required to *vector* to this interrupt.

6.34. The 8080/85 INTR and the Z-80 $\overline{\text{INT}}$ inputs are maskable and level-triggered. To guarantee acceptance by the CPU, how long must an interrupt request on one of these inputs be held active? Why is a circuit such as Fig. 6.19 useful with this type of interrupt?

6.35. Why do direct interrupts *not* require the interrupt acknowledge bus cycle?

6.36. A printer is to be interfaced to the Z-80 using mode 2 interrupts. The service routine begins at address 1000H and the interrupt vector is stored at address FE30H. Sketch a schematic diagram of the hardware required and write the instruction sequence needed to initialize the Z-80 for this interrupt.

*6.37. A technician is testing a Z-80 computer that uses interrupts. He finds that a mode 1 interrupt on $\overline{INT}$ is ignored if preceded by an interrupt on $\overline{NMI}$. However, if the machine is reset and the mode 1 interrupt occurs alone, the $\overline{INT}$ interrupt is serviced. The code for a system RESET, $\overline{INT}$ interrupt, and $\overline{NMI}$ interrupt is listed below. Studying this, the technician says, "Ah-ha, I see the problem." What has he found?

```
RESET       IM    1
            EI
            JP    MONITOR
INT_ISR     ......
            ......
            RET
NMI_ISR     ......
            ......
            RET
```

6.38. The circuit in Fig. 6.31 is intended as an 8085 program "break" key. Pushing the switch should force the CPU to run a *Monitor* program. Write the initialization sequence required to enable this circuit. At what address should the Monitor program (or a jump to the monitor program) be loaded?

6.39. Assume the ISR for the 8085 interrupt control circuit in Fig. 6.31 requires 30 μs to execute and then re-enables interrupts. Since it is not possible to hold the switch down for this short a time, it might appear that the CPU will run this interrupt several times. Why doesn't this happen? Is it really necessary to debounce the switch?

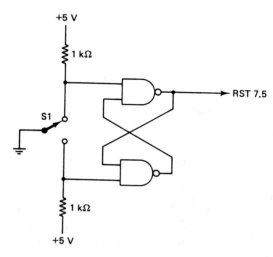

Figure 6.31 Circuit for Probs. 6.38 and 6.39.

```
ISR        PUSH    PSW              ;SAVE ENVIRONMENT
           PUSH    B
           ;
           POP     H                ;RECOVER OLD DATA POINTER
           POP     B
           ;
           MOV     A,M              ;PRINT THE CHARACTER
           OUT     1
           ;
           INX     H                ;ADJUST POINTER AND COUNTER
           DCR     B
           JZ      DONE
           ;
           PUSH    B                ;SAVE COUNTER AND POINTER
           PUSH    H
           EI                       ;REENABLE INTERRUPTS
           ;
DONE       POP     B                ;RESTORE CPU ENVIRONMENT
           POP     PSW
           RET
```

Figure 6.32   ISR for Prob. 6.41.

6.40. It is a common myth that a CPU's response time is much faster when using interrupts versus polling. Under what conditions is this true? When is it false?

*6.41. A programmer has written the ISR shown in Fig. 6.32 to control a printer connected to an 8080/85. What is wrong with his program?

6.42. Figure 6.33 is the schematic for a programmable interrupt controller (PIC) used to interface three peripherals: IREQ1, IREQ2, and IREQ3. Answer the following questions about this circuit.
   (a) What is the restart instruction associated with each interrupt?
   (b) What is the purpose of the 3-bit memory-mapped input port?
   (c) To what *range* of addresses will the memory-mapped port respond?
   (d) Write an ISR that will cause control to transfer to the addresses shown below when an interrupt occurs.

Input	Priority	Address
IREQ1	1	0100H
IREQ2	2	0200H
IREQ3	3	0300H

Section 6.6

6.43. Is the response time for DMA faster or slower than that for interrupts? Explain.

6.44. Some printers have buffers that allow them to accept several hundreds (or thousands) of characters before issuing the BUSY flag. The characters are then printed from this buffer at the speed of the printer. Which mode of DMA—byte, burst, or block—would be best suited for this type of peripheral?

Input	Priority	Address
IREQ1	1	0100H
IREQ2	2	0200H
IREQ3	3	0300H

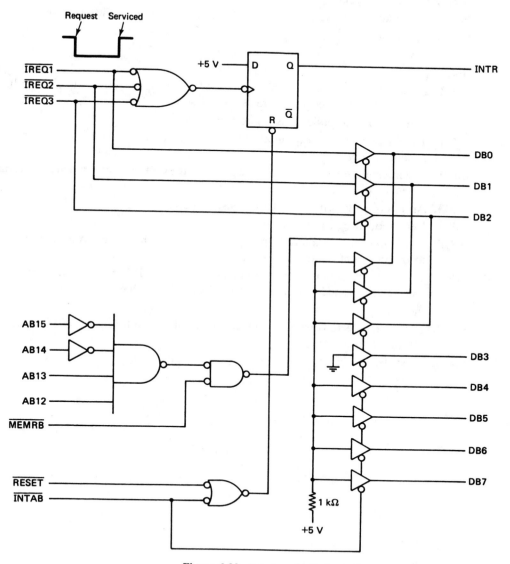

Figure 6.33 Interface for Prob. 6.42.

KEY CONCEPT ANSWERS

6.1.1. 8, 256

6.1.2. Z-80

6.1.3. device select

6.2.1. memory-mapped

6.2.2. detect key pressed, debounce the key, encode the key with a value

6.3.1. synchronize

6.3.2. low

6.4.1. poll

6.4.2. If the I/O device is very slow, the CPU will spend all of its time polling the peripheral to see if it is ready for new data.

6.4.3. The first device polled has highest priority.

6.5.1. The CPU is able to run another program while it waits for the peripheral to become ready.

6.5.2. The interrupt service routine—the program the CPU executes when an interrupt is received.

6.5.3. An interrupt to which the CPU must respond.

6.5.4. Vectored, direct, indirect

6.5.5. If the registers are altered, the system may "crash" when control is returned to the interrupted program.

6.5.6. Unless built into the microprocessor (8085 RST 7.5, 6.5, 5.5) priorities can be established via polling, a PIC, or a daisy-chain technique.

6.6.1. memory

6.6.2. Data is transferred directly between the peripheral and memory without passing through the DMAC.

6.6.3. burst, byte, block

7

Special-Purpose Support Devices: The 8080/85 Family

One of the unmistakable trends in microprocessor technology today is the integration of the special-purpose I/O interface circuitry into a single programmable device. These support devices interface to the microprocessor over the system data bus and are capable of receiving special initialization codes that program their function.

As an example, consider the Intel 8255 programmable peripheral interface (PPI). This 40-pin device has 24 separate I/O pins organized as three 8-bit ports. By giving the command

OUT (control port)

a control word can be written to the device. If, for example, the accumulator contains 90H, the PPI is programmed for 16 lines of output and eight lines of input.

In this chapter we examine several programmable I/O devices made by Intel Corp. to support the 8080 and 8085 microprocessors. Table 7.1 lists some of the devices available today. These range from the five chips designed especially for the multiplexed data and address bus of the 8085, to complex DMA processors, CRT controllers, floppy-disk controllers, and programmable keyboard/display interfaces.

Although these devices have been designed to interface with the 8080 or 8085, most can also be interfaced to the Z-80 (and most other 8-bit microprocessors). Of course, Zilog also supplies a family of support devices for the Z-80, and these are covered in detail in Chap. 8.

TABLE 7.1 I/O SUPPORT DEVICES FOR THE 8080
AND 8085 MICROPROCESSORS

Part number	Description
8155/56[a]	RAM with I/O and timer
8185[a]	1K × 8 RAM
8755/8355[a]	EPROM/ROM with I/O
8231	Arithmetic processing unit
8237	Programmable DMA controller
8251	Programmable communications interface
8254	Programmable interval timer
8255	Programmable peripheral interface
8256	Multifunction universal asynchronous receiver/transmitter
8259A	Programmable interrupt controller
8272	Single/double-density floppy-disk controller
8275	Programmable CRT controller
8279	Programmable keyboard display interface
8295	Dot matrix printer controller
82720	Graphics display controller

[a] Compatible with the 8085 multiplexed address and data bus.

7.1 THE 8755A 16K EPROM WITH I/O

As you read this section, look for the answers to these Key Concept questions:

7.1.1. The 8755 contains _____ bytes of ROM and _____ bit-programmable I/O ports.

7.1.2. To program port A of the 8755 so that pins PA0–PA3 are outputs and pins PA4–PA7 are inputs, output the byte _____ to DDRA.

Table 7.2 describes the memory and I/O capabilities of the five 8085 support devices available from Intel. The concept of combining memory and I/O functions on one chip was pioneered by Intel and allows a minimal 8085 microcomputer system to be built from three to five chips.

    All of the 8085 support devices interface directly to the processor's multiplexed address and data bus without the need for a low-order address latch. In this section we will cover the 8755A, which contains a 2K × 8 EPROM and two bit-programmable 8-bit I/O ports. Note that the 8355 is identical except that the ROM is mask programmable at the factory. All comments regarding the 8755A (except for EPROM programming instructions) apply equally to the 8355.

TABLE 7.2 SPECIAL SUPPORT DEVICES FOR THE 8085
MICROPROCESSOR

Device	Memory	I/O
8355	2K PROM	16-bit programmable I/O lines organized as two 8-bit I/O ports
8755	2K EPROM	Same as 8355
8185	1K × 8 RAM	None
8155[a]	256 × 8 RAM	Two 8-bit byte programmable I/O ports, one 6-bit control port for handshake, one 14-bit timer
8156[b]	256 × 8 RAM	Same as 8155

[a] Active-low CE input.

[b] Active-high CE input.

Interfacing the 8755A ROM.

Figure 7.1 is a block diagram and pinout of the 8755A. When interfacing to the ROM portion of this device, 11 address lines (A0–A10) are required to select one of the 2048 8-bit words in the memory array. The AD0 through AD7 bus lines from the 8085 connect directly to the 8755A, as does the multiplex control signal ALE.

Because the data on the bus can be directed to the I/O ports or the ROM, the 8085's $IO/\overline{M}$ output control signal is required to distinguish between an I/O address and a memory address. There are two chip-enable inputs, labeled $\overline{CE1}$ and CE2. Data from the ROM is placed onto the data bus by the 8755A when both chip select inputs are active, $IO/\overline{M} = 0$ and $\overline{RD} = 0$.

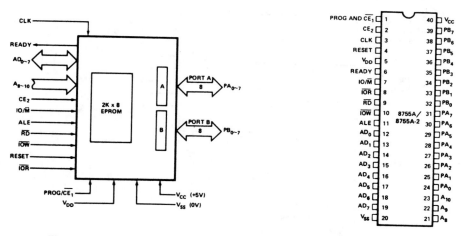

Figure 7.1 Block diagram and pinouts for the 8755A 2K × 8 EPROM with I/O. (Courtesy of Intel Corporation.)

Sec. 7.1   The 8755A 16K EPROM with I/O

Example 7.1

Design a fully decoded 8755A EPROM interface at address F800H through FFFFH.

Solution. The circuit diagram is shown in Fig. 7.2. The address/data bus connections and control bus connections are all straightforward ($\overline{IOR}$ and $\overline{IOW}$ will be explained in the next section), connecting to the same signal names on the 8085. The system clock signal is required to synchronize WAIT state requests (see below).

Address lines A11 through A15 define 32 different "slots" the 2K PROM can occupy in the 8085's 64K memory space. In this case the topmost slot is desired and the 74LS30 NAND gate functions as an address decoder for the range F800H through FFFFH. The CE2 input is not used and is therefore permanently enabled.

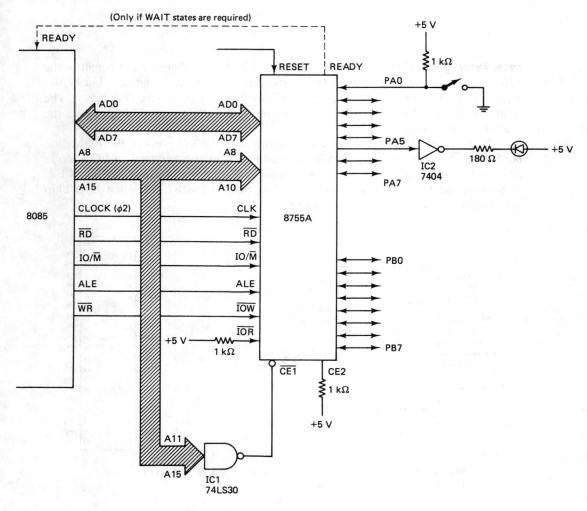

Figure 7.2 Interfacing the 8755A to the 8085 microprocessor.

The 8755A was intended to facilitate the design of minimum-package-count 8085 microcomputer systems. In such systems it is likely that the full memory space will not be implemented and partial decoding can be used. For example, in Fig. 7.2, connecting A15 to CE2 and grounding $\overline{CE1}$ would place the PROM in the top 32K of memory space from 8000H through FFFFH. No address decoder would be required. Up to five 8755As can be interfaced to the 8085 in this way without the need for an address decoder.

There are two speed versions of the 8755A. These are the 8755A with an access time of 450 ns and the 8755A-2 with a 300-ns access time. The first part is suitable in 8085 systems up to 3 MHz, while the 8755A-2 should be used in 5-MHz designs.

Automatic WAIT states are inserted by the 8755A if its READY output is connected to the 8085 READY input. Whenever the chip selects are active and ALE = 1, the READY output of the 8755A will go low for one clock period. If WAIT states are not desired, the READY output should be left open.

In larger 8085 systems, the buffer and address decoding logic may cause the chip-enable inputs to become valid after ALE has gone low. In this case the READY output will never go low and WAIT states cannot be requested. In this case the chip-enable logic will have to be redesigned to ensure a valid CE signal before ALE goes low.

The 8755A is programmed by raising the V_{DD} supply to 25 V and pulsing $\overline{CE1}$ to 5 V for 50 ms. Commercial programmers are available for this purpose. Erasure is accomplished by exposure to an ultraviolet-light source for 15 to 30 minutes.

Interfacing the 8755A I/O Ports.

The 8755A appears to the 8085 as four separate I/O ports defined by the four combinations of AD0 and AD1 (address lines A2 through A10 are not used when accessing the I/O ports). Table 7.3 lists the definitions of each of these ports. The data direction ports (DDRA and DDRB) control the direction of data at ports A and B. For example, writing F0H to DDRA will program PA0–PA3 as inputs and PA4–PA7 as outputs. Note that resetting the 8755A will clear both DDRs, configuring both ports as inputs.

It is also possible to read from a port defined as an output (read back the data written) or to write to a port defined as an input. In the latter case, the data

TABLE 7.3 I/O PORTS OF THE 8755A

AD1	AD0	Name	Function	Port address in Fig. 7.2
0	0	I/O port A	I/O on pins PA0–PA7	F8 or FC
0	1	I/O port B	I/O on pins PB0–PB7	F9 or FD
1	0	DDRA	Data direction for the 8 bits of port A*	FA or FE
1	1	DDRB	Data direction for the 8 bits of port B*	FB or FF

* A logic 1 programs an output bit, a logic 0 an input bit.

Sec. 7.1   The 8755A 16K EPROM with I/O

will be stored but not placed on the output pins until that pin is defined as an output.

When configured as an output port, each pin can supply 400 µA in the high state and sink 2 mA in the low state. This corresponds to one standard TTL load or five LSTTL loads. When configured as input ports, each pin presents a nearly insignificant 10 µA load.

When interfacing to the I/O ports of the 8755A, the 8085 $\overline{WR}$ output is normally connected to $\overline{IOW}$ as shown in Fig. 7.2. The $\overline{IOR}$ input should not be connected to $\overline{RD}$. This is because the $\overline{IOW}$ and $\overline{IOR}$ inputs override the IO/$\overline{M}$ and $\overline{RD}$ inputs. With $\overline{IOR}$ connected to $\overline{RD}$, a normal memory read cycle could access the PROM and one of the I/O ports simultaneously.

It is recommended that $\overline{IOR}$ be connected to +5 V and $\overline{IOW}$ connected to $\overline{WR}$. Table 7.4 describes the control bus combinations required to read the PROM or access the I/O ports.

Example 7.2

Determine the port addresses for the 8755A interface in Fig. 7.2.

Solution. Recall that the 8085 (and 8080) duplicate the I/O port address on A0–A7 and A8–A15 when performing an I/O operation. The port address can be broken into three parts:

1. A11–A15: These lines must be high to enable the 8755A via the $\overline{CE1}$ input.
2. AD0–AD1: These lines select one of four ports as shown in Table 7.3.
3. A8–A10: These lines are not used for the I/O portion of the interface in Fig. 7.2.

Because A10 is not decoded, two sets of ports are defined. These are F8H–FBH and FCH–FFH. Table 7.3 lists the two possible sets of port addresses. Address line A10 can be combined with the IO/$\overline{M}$ signal from the 8085 if partial decoding is not desired (see Prob. 7.2).

Figure 7.3 illustrates a decoding scheme that allows the ROM address and port address to be independent (at the expense of several more TTL gates).

TABLE 7.4 CONTROL BUS SIGNAL COMBINATION REQUIRED TO ACCESS THE PROM AND I/O PORTS OF THE 8755

$\overline{WR}$	$\overline{RD}$	IO/$\overline{M}$	Function	Active address lines
1	0	0	ROM read	AD0–AD10
0	1	0	Not allowed	—
1	0	1	I/O port read	AD0 and AD1[a]
0	1	1	I/O port write	AD0 and AD1[a]

[a] Table 7.3 defines the particular ports selected by the four combinations of the AD0 and AD1 address lines.

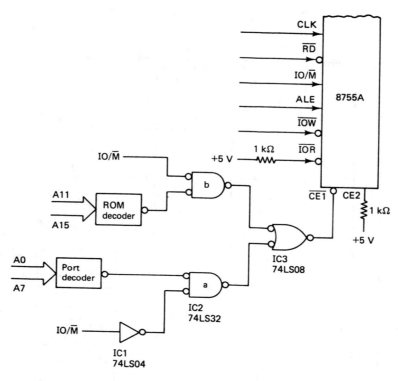

Figure 7.3 The ROM and I/O ports of the 8755 may have separate and independent addresses using this decoding scheme.

Example 7.3

Write a program to monitor the switch connected to PA0 in Fig. 7.2 and turn on the LED connected to PA5 when the switch is closed.

Solution. The program is given below. Because only PA0 and PA5 need to be defined, the DDRA control word is XX1XXXX0. Choosing the don't cares to be 0 results in the control word 20H.

```
        MVI   A,20H    ;DDRA CONTROL WORD
        OUT   FEH      ;DDRA ACCESS (COULD ALSO USE FAH)
LOOP    IN    FCH      ;SAMPLE PORT A (COULD ALSO USE F8H)
        RAR            ;TEST BIT 0
        JC    OFF      ;CY MEANS SWITCH IS OPEN
        MVI   A,20H    ;MAKE PA5 HIGH (LED ON)
        JMP   LED      ;
OFF     MVI   A,0      ;MAKE PA5 LOW (LED OFF)
LED     OUT   FCH      ;OUTPUT TO PA5
        JMP   LOOP
```

Three-Chip 8085 Microcomputer System. Figure 7.4 illustrates a complete 8085 microcomputer system requiring only three chips. It features 1K of RAM

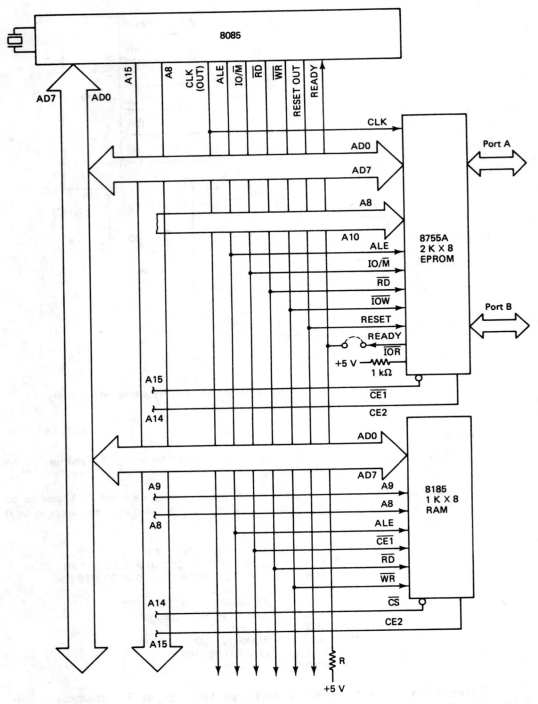

Figure 7.4 Three-chip 8085 microcomputer system with 1K of RAM, 2K of ROM, and 16 I/O pins.

using the 8185 1K × 8 static RAM, 2K of EPROM, and 16 I/O lines using the 8755A. Because the system is so small, no buffering is required and partial decoding can be used.

Is such a system practical? Absolutely. The 16 I/O lines could be used to monitor sensors and activate alarms in a home security system. In an automobile the I/O lines could be used to monitor engine operating conditions such as flow rates, temperatures, and pressures. A control program in the 8755A can supervise these activities using the 1K of RAM in the 8185 for a stack area and for storage of temporary variables.

The system could also be used as the basis for an 8085 microprocessor trainer. Using a memory-mapped keyboard similar to that developed in Chap. 6 and using port A or B of the 8755A to drive two seven-segment hex-decoded displays, one I/O port would remain for experimentation.

7.2 THE 8255A PROGRAMMABLE PERIPHERAL INTERFACE

As you read this section, look for the answers to these Key Concept questions:

7.2.1. When operated in mode 0, the 8255 contains _____ user I/O ports and _____ control port.

7.2.2. Which bit of the 8255 control port selects the mode-set or bit set/reset mode?

7.2.3. Which 8255 operating mode supplies two parallel I/O ports with handshaking signals?

7.2.4. What are the two main uses of the 8255 bit set/reset mode?

7.2.5. When operated in mode 2, the 8255 supplies one _____ I/O port and five handshaking signals.

The 8255A is a general-purpose I/O interfacing device. It provides 24 I/O lines organized as three 8-bit I/O ports labeled A, B, and C. Pin definitions and a block diagram are provided in Fig. 7.5. Unlike the 8755A, individual bits cannot be programmed as inputs or outputs. Instead, all of the bits in port A or B are programmed as one byte. The four high- and four low-order bits of port C can be programmed as two separate nibbles, however.

The 8255A is a very versatile device. It can be programmed to look like three simple I/O ports (mode 0), two handshaking I/O ports (mode 1), or a bidirectional I/O port with five handshaking signals (mode 2). The modes can also be intermixed. For example, port A can be programmed to operate in mode 2 while port B operates in mode 0. There is also a bit set/reset mode that allows individual bits of port C to be set or reset for control purposes.

Because the input/output block is a fundamental part of any microcomputer and because the 8255A is an excellent choice for a universal parallel I/O device, we cover this device in detail in this section. Several examples will be presented to help you appreciate its capabilities.

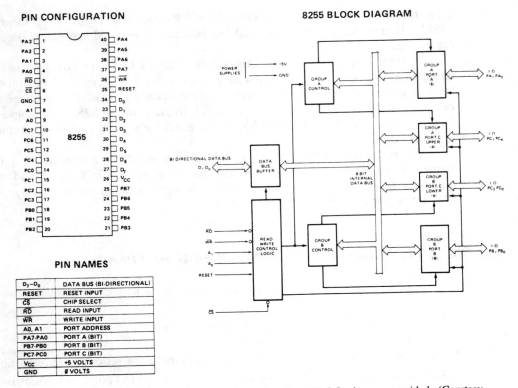

PIN CONFIGURATION

```
PA3  1        40  PA4
PA2  2        39  PA5
PA1  3        38  PA6
PA0  4        37  PA7
RD   5        36  WR
CS   6        35  RESET
GND  7        34  D0
A1   8        33  D1
A0   9        32  D2
PC7  10       31  D3
PC6  11  8255 30  D4
PC5  12       29  D5
PC4  13       28  D6
PC0  14       27  D7
PC1  15       26  Vcc
PC2  16       25  PB7
PC3  17       24  PB6
PB0  18       23  PB5
PB1  19       22  PB4
PB2  20       21  PB3
```

PIN NAMES

D_7–D_0	DATA BUS (BI-DIRECTIONAL)
RESET	RESET INPUT
CS	CHIP SELECT
RD	READ INPUT
WR	WRITE INPUT
A0, A1	PORT ADDRESS
PA7-PA0	PORT A (BIT)
PB7-PB0	PORT B (BIT)
PC7-PC0	PORT C (BIT)
Vcc	+5 VOLTS
GND	0 VOLTS

8255 BLOCK DIAGRAM

Figure 7.5 8255 programmable peripheral interface. 24 I/O pins are provided. (Courtesy of Intel Corporation.)

Interfacing the 8255A.

The 8255A is directly compatible with the three-bus architecture of the 8080 microprocessor. This is illustrated in Fig. 7.6. Because the CPU modules for the Z-80 and 8085 presented in Chap. 4 have been made to present 8080-like control buses, these processors will also interface directly.

Notice the bidirectional data bus connection. All communications with the programmable peripheral interface (PPI) occur over these eight lines. In fact, to the microprocessor, the 8255 appears to be four I/O locations corresponding to the four combinations of the A0 and A1 address line inputs. The specific port address is controlled by the chip-select ($\overline{CS}$) input. Only when this pin is low can the PPI be accessed.

Table 7.5 summarizes the possible read and write operations with the chip. When $\overline{RD}$ is low, any of the three data ports can be read by applying the appropriate combination to A0 and A1. When A0 and A1 are both high, the control port is accessed. This is a special register in the 8255A that controls the operating mode of the device. Note that this register can only be written to, not read from.

When the PPI is not accessed ($\overline{CS} = 1$ or $\overline{RD}$ AND $\overline{WR} = 1$), the data bus connections are in a high-impedance state and the processor is free to communicate with other devices in the microcomputer system.

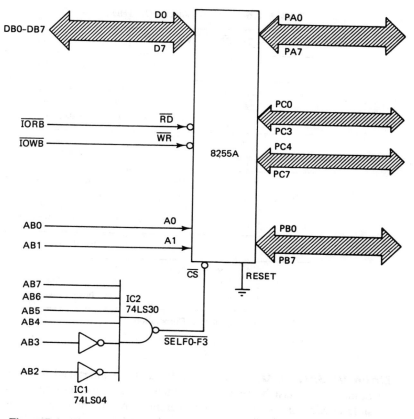

Figure 7.6 The 8255 interfaces directly to the three-bus architecture of the 8080 microprocessor.

Example 7.4

Determine the addresses of ports A, B, and C and the control port in the interface in Fig. 7.6.

Solution. The $\overline{CS}$ input will be driven low whenever the low-order address lines A2 through A7 = 111100. This can occur during memory or I/O machine cycles. However, the $\overline{RD}$ (connected to $\overline{IORB}$) and $\overline{WR}$ (connected to $\overline{IOWB}$) inputs are active only for I/O machine cycles. For example, port A is accessed as input or output port F0H (111100 00). For all four ports:

Port	I/O address
A	F0
B	F1
C	F2
Control	F3

TABLE 7.5 TRUTH TABLE FOR THE 8255A PPI

A_1	A_0	$\overline{RD}$	$\overline{WR}$	$\overline{CS}$	
					Input operation (READ)
0	0	0	1	0	Port A → data bus
0	1	0	1	0	Port B → data bus
1	0	0	1	0	Port C → data bus
					Output operation (WRITE)
0	0	1	0	0	Data bus → port A
0	1	1	0	0	Data bus → port B
1	0	1	0	0	Data bus → port C
1	1	1	0	0	Data bus → control
					Disable function
X	X	X	X	1	Data bus → 3-state
1	1	0	1	0	Illegal condition
X	X	1	1	0	Data bus → 3-state

Source: Courtesy of Intel Corporation.

Mode 0: Basic I/O. Once the PPI has been interfaced to the CPU module, the operating mode must be selected. As mentioned in the introduction, three modes are possible in addition to a bit set/reset operation. When unconditional or *nonhandshaking I/O* is required, mode 0 should be selected. But how is the mode determined?

A single control word written to the control port (port F3H in Fig. 7.6) determines the 8255A operating mode. Figure 7.7 shows the two types of control words possible. When bit 7 of the control word is a 0, the *bit set/reset* mode is selected. If bit 7 is a 1, any of the three port modes (0 through 2) can be selected. The bit set/reset mode is covered in the next section, so let's turn our attention to the mode set control word.

Studying Fig. 7.7, you can see that the three ports are broken into two groups for mode selection. Port A and the high-order bits of port C can be programmed for any of the modes 0 through 2. Port B and the low-order bits of port C can be programmed to operate in mode 0 or 1 only.

Example 7.5

The following mode 0 port configuration is desired:

Port A: input
Port B: output
Port C (*upper*): output
Port C (*lower*): input

Write the 8080/85 program required to initialize the 8255A assuming the interface circuit in Fig. 7.6.

Solution. Consulting Fig. 7.7, we can construct the control word. The result is: 1 00 1 0 0 0 1 or 91H. The 8080/85 initialization routine is very simple.

```
MVI   A,91H     ;CONTROL WORD
OUT   0F3H      ;CONTROL PORT
```

One of the most powerful features of the 8255A is that only one control word is required to program the mode selection—this is true no matter how complex the configuration may be.

Mode 0 is useful when the I/O device can always be assumed ready and no handshaking signals are required. Another example will illustrate the ease of programming and versatility of the 8255A.

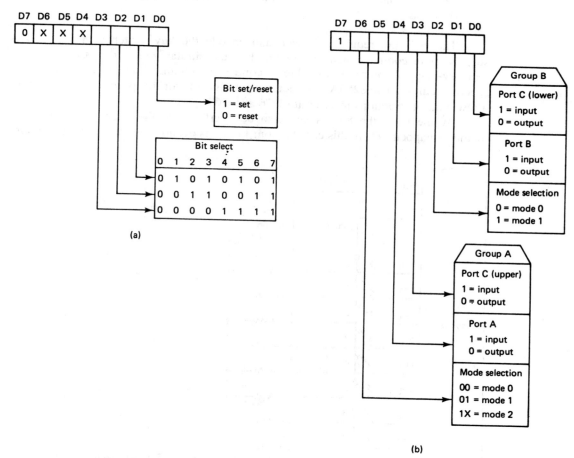

Figure 7.7 There are two types of 8255 control words. When bit 7 = 0, the bit set/reset mode is selected. When bit 7 = 1, any of modes 0–2 can be selected. (a) Bit set/reset format; (b) Mode definition format.

Sec. 7.2   The 8255A Programmable Peripheral Interface

325

Example 7.6

Use the 8255A and interface the 10-key matrix used in Chap. 6 for the digital lock design problem (see Fig. 6.8). Write the software to encode the 10-key switches using the flowchart in Fig. 6.9 as a guide.

Solution. The 8255A interface shown in Fig. 7.6 will be used with the key switches connected as shown in Fig. 7.8. Unlike the interface in Chap. 6, this circuit is *I/O mapped*. The column lines will be controlled by PC6 and PC7 programmed as outputs. The key matrix can be scanned by reading from port B.

In Chap. 6 the column lines were forced low by reading from the appropriate memory-mapped I/O address. In Fig. 7.8 the column lines are forced low by outputting 0s on PC6 and PC7. Although the row lines are not inverted, this is easily accomplished with the *CMA* instruction. The program solution is provided in Fig. 7.9. Notice that because port C (lower) and port B are not used, they can become "don't cares" when determining the 8255A control word. In this case their control bits were arbitrarily chosen as 0s.

The software required to scan and encode the key switches in Fig. 7.8 is slightly more complex than that required of the similar interface in Chap. 6. The memory-mapped interface was able to control the column lines by reading from a specific address. The 8255A interface must use port C for this purpose. This requires a few extra instructions to program PC6 and PC7.

By the way, the 8255A can also be interfaced to the microprocessor using memory-mapped I/O. In this case the four I/O ports occupy four consecutive memory

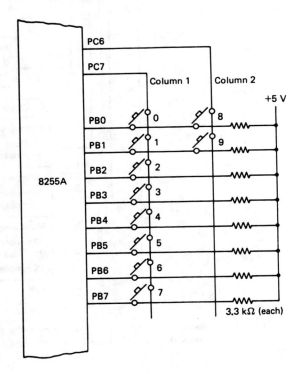

Figure 7.8 Interfacing a 10-key switch matrix to the 8255. Port B is programmed as an input port and port C (upper) as an output port.

```
                    ;PROGRAM TO READ THE MATRIX KEYBOARD IN FIG. 7-8
                    ;
                    ;BEGIN BY INITIALIZING THE 8255
                    ;
            MVI     A,82H                   ;8255 MODE 0 CONTROL WORD
            OUT     0F3                     ;CONTROL PORT
                    ;
                    ;PREPARE TO TEST BOTH COLUMNS BY MAKING PC6 AND PC7 LOW
                    ;
            SUB     A                       ;CLEAR ACCUMULATOR
            OUT     0F2                     ;PORT C
                    ;
                    ;LOOP UNTIL ALL KEYS ARE UP
                    ;
    KDWN    CALL    KREAD                   ;CHECK KEYBOARD
            JNZ     KDWN                    ;IF NOT ZERO A KEY IS DOWN
                    ;
                    ;WAIT FOR BOUNCE TIME AND THEN LOOP UNTIL A
                    ;KEY IS DOWN
                    ;
            CALL    DELAY                   ;10-20 MS DELAY
    KUP     CALL    KREAD                   ;CHECK KEYBOARD
            JZ      KUP                     ;IF ZERO NO KEYS ARE DOWN
                    ;
                    ;A KEY IS DOWN - BUT WHICH COLUMN?  TEST COLUMN 1
                    ;
            CALL    DELAY                   ;WAIT FOR IT TO STOP BOUNCING
            MVI     A,40H                   ;MAKE COLUMN 1 = 0
            OUT     0F2                     ;PORT C
            CALL    KREAD                   ;CHECK KEYBOARD
            JNZ     COL1                    ;IF NOT ZERO ITS COLUMN 1
                    ;
                    ;IT MUST BE COLUMN 2
                    ;
            MVI     A,80H                   ;MAKE COLUMN 2 = 0
            OUT     0F2                     ;PORT C
            CALL    KREAD                   ;CHECK KEYBOARD
                    ;
                    ;KEY VALUE IS IN ACCUMULATOR - SET COLUMN POINTER
                    ;
            LXI     H,COL2                  ;POINT AT COLUMN 2
            JMP     LKUP                    ;LOOK UP KEY VALUE
                    ;
    COL1    LXI     H,COL1                  ;POINT AT COL1
                    ;
                    ;LKUP NOW FINDS THE CORRECT KEY VALUE FROM A TABLE
                    ;
    LKUP    INX     H                       ;ADVANCE POINTER
            RAR                             ;TEST BIT
            JNC     LKUP                    ;CONTINUE UNTIL CARRY IS SET
            MOV     A,M                     ;FETCH THE CODE
            RET                             ;RETURN TO MAIN
                    ;
                    ;THIS IS THE KREAD SUBROUTINE
                    ;
    KREAD   IN      0F1                     ;READ PORT B
            CMA                             ;COMPLEMENT
            ORA     A                       ;SET FLAGS
            RET
                    ;
                    ;DEFINE BYTES FOR THE KEY VALUES
    COL1    DB      0,0,1,2,3,4,5,6 ;FIRST BYTE IS NEVER READ
    COL2    DB      7,8,9
```

Figure 7.9 This subroutine scans the key switch matrix in Fig. 7.8 and returns with the key value (0–9) in the accumulator.

Sec. 7.2   The 8255A Programmable Peripheral Interface

locations. This can have its advantages, especially with the Z-80. The IX or IY index register can be pointed at port A and then an offset used to access the other three ports without the need for specifying the full 16-bit address with each access.

The Bit Set/Reset Mode. When bit 7 of the 8255A control word is a 0, the bit set/reset mode is active. In this mode any one bit of port C can be set to a logic 1 or reset to a logic 0. Note that only one bit can be set or reset at a time. This feature can be taken advantage of to generate strobe signals.

Example 7.7

Use the 8255A and the bit set/reset feature of port C to interface a parallel printer. Write the control software assuming that a data table is stored at symbolic address DATA and a byte counter is stored at address NUMB.

Solution. The circuit diagram is shown in Fig. 7.10. Port A has been arbitrarily chosen as the data port and PC0 used to monitor the printer's BUSY/READY status. PC7 will be used to generate the strobe pulse. This interface can be compared to Fig. 6.12. Again an 11-conductor cable is required between computer and printer.

Of course, the software is what makes the circuit work. The control program for the printer is shown in Fig. 7.11. The 8255A is programmed for mode 0 with port A an output, port C (lower) an input, and port C (upper) an output. Port B is a "don't care" condition. After writing the control word to port F3 (the control port), the bit set control word 0XXX1111 is used to hold PC7—the printer STROBE input—high.

The program then drops into a polling routine testing PC0 for a 0. When ready, data is output to port A and the printer's STROBE input brought low (control word 0XXX1110). This begins the STROBE pulse. The INR A instruction and OUT F3 force the STROBE line back high. STROBE will be low during these two instructions—

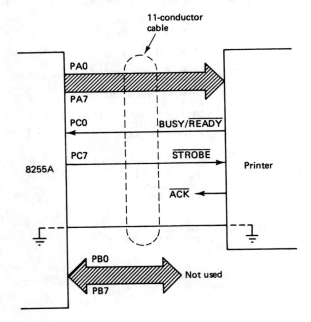

Figure 7.10 Parallel printer interface using the 8255 in a combined bit set/reset and mode 0 format.

```
;8255 PARALLEL PRINTER CONTROL PROGRAM
;
;THE HARDWARE INTERFACE IS IN FIG. 7-10.
;A COMBINED BIT SET/RESET AND MODE 0 ARE USED.
;
DATA    EQU     ADDR1           ;ADDR1 IS ADDRESS OF DATA TABLE
NUMB    EQU     ADDR2           ;ADDR2 IS ADDRESS OF BYTE COUNTER
;
;PROGRAM BEGINS BY INITIALIZING THE 8255 AND MAKES
;SURE THE PRINTER STROBE INPUT IS HIGH.
;
        MVI     A,81H           ;MODE 0 CONTROL WORD
        OUT     0F3H            ;CONTROL PORT
        MVI     A,0FH           ;BIT SET PC7 HIGH
        OUT     0F3H            ;CONTROL PORT
;
;POINT AT THE DATA TABLE AND RETRIEVE BYTE COUNTER
;
        LXI     H,DATA          ;TABLE BEGINS AT LOCATION DATA
        LDA     NUMB            ;GET NUMBER OF BYTES TO OUTPUT
        MOV     B,A             ;SAVE IN B
;
;POLL THE BUSY/READY FLAG
;
POLL    IN      0F2H            ;PORT C BUSY/READY STATUS
        RAR                     ;POLL PC0
        JC      POLL            ;LOOP UNTIL READY
;
;PRINTER IS READY - FETCH DATA BYTE AND OUTPUT IT
;
        MOV     A,M             ;RETRIEVE BYTE FROM TABLE
        OUT     0F0H            ;PORT A
;
;PULSE PC7 TO STROBE THE PRINTER
;
        MVI     A,0EH           ;BIT RESET PC7 LOW
        OUT     0F3H            ;CONTROL PORT
        INR     A               ;BIT SET PC7 HIGH
        OUT     0F3H            ;CONTROL PORT
;
;ADVANCE POINTER AND TEST BYTE COUNTER
;
        INX     H               ;POINT AT NEXT BYTE
        DCR     B               ;BUMP BYTE COUNTER
        JNZ     POLL            ;CONTINUE TILL EMPTY
        RET                     ;AND THEN RETURN
```

Figure 7.11   Control program for the 8255 interface in Fig. 7.10.

15 T states with an 8080 or 14 T states with an 8085. This will produce a STROBE pulse width of 7.5 μs on a 2-MHz 8080.

The data pointer is then incremented and the byte counter decremented. If more data remains to be printed, control is transferred back to the polling routine. If not, the program RETurns.

This example also illustrates that the bit set/reset feature does not override the mode selection but works in addition to the selected mode (0 through 2). However, as we shall see, the main purpose of the bit set/reset feature is for setting *interrupt masks* in mode 1 and mode 2.

Electrical Characteristics of the Ports.   All three 8255A ports have an I_{OL} specification of 1.7 mA and an I_{OH} specification of 200 μA. This means that they can drive one standard TTL load or four LSTTL loads. A special feature of ports B and C is that any set of eight lines can source 1 mA at 1.5 V. This is useful for driving solid-state relays and transistor drivers (more detail on these techniques is provided in Chap. 11). Note that the outputs *cannot* sink the typical 10- to 20-mA current required to light an LED and a TTL buffer should be used as shown in Fig. 7.2 for the 8755A.

There are two speed versions of the 8255A. These are the 8255A and the 8255A-5. The first part has a t_{RD} specification of 250 ns, making it compatible with all versions of the 8080 and the 3-MHz version of the 8085. The 8255A-5 has a 200-ns t_{RD} specification. This is not fast enough for the 5- and 6-MHz versions of the 8085 but interestingly enough is compatible with the Z-80A and Z-80B processors. This is because the Z-80 inserts one WAIT state in its I/O operations.

Mode 1: Strobed I/O.   Mode 1 is intended for handshaking and interrupt-driven I/O interfaces. In this mode ports A and B are programmed as data ports and port C is programmed to carry status signals. One of the unique features of this mode is that data transfers can take place without direct CPU intervention.

There are four possible configurations for the 8255A when operated in mode 1. These are shown in Fig. 7.12. These correspond to the four combinations of ports A and B as inputs and outputs. The two separate control words shown in Fig. 7.12(a) and (b) illustrate the fact that port A or port B or both ports can be programmed for mode 1 operation. This means it is possible to program port A for mode 1 while using port B in mode 0, for example.

Input port timing.   When port A or B is programmed as an input port, three control signals are dedicated to supporting data transfers on this port. These are IBF, $\overline{STB}$, and INTR. Table 7.6 gives a word explanation for each of these signals and Fig. 7.13 illustrates the timing.

When the peripheral device has data for the microprocessor, it places that data on the port A or B input lines and then pulses the 8255A $\overline{STB}$ input. The PPI replies by latching this data and raising its IBF (input buffer full) line. This is a signal to the peripheral that data has been latched but not yet read by the microprocessor.

If the INTE (interrupts enabled) bit of the input port has been set, IBF will also cause the INTR output of that port to go high. The processor now has the choice of polling the IBF line by reading the mode 1 status word (see Fig. 7.14) or letting INTR generate an interrupt, thereby alerting the processor that the input buffer is full.

In either case the processor should branch to a routine that reads the data port. The falling edge of $\overline{RD}$ causes the 8255A INTR output to be reset and the rising edge of $\overline{RD}$ resets IBF. The data transfer is now complete and the peripheral (monitoring IBF) can strobe in the next byte of data.

Output port timing.   When ports A or B are programmed as mode 1 output ports, three lines of port C are dedicated to supporting this function. These are $\overline{OBF}$, $\overline{ACK}$, and INTR and their word descriptions are provided in Table 7.6. Figure 7.15 illustrates output port timing.

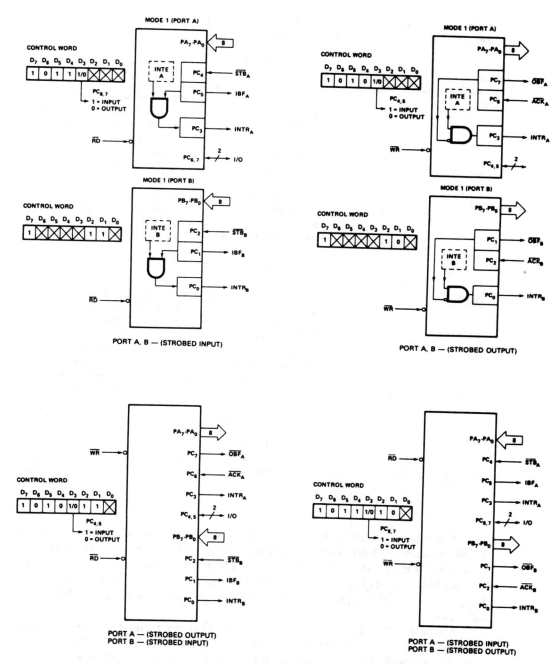

Figure 7.12 Four possible I/O configurations for ports A and B when the 8255 is programmed for mode 1 operation. Port C becomes a status port in this mode. (Courtesy of Intel Corporation and from J. Uffenbeck, *Hardware Interfacing with the Apple II Plus*, Prentice-Hall, Inc., Englewood Cliffs, N.J., 1983.)

TABLE 7.6 PORT C OF THE 8255A SUPPLIES SEVERAL HANDSHAKING SIGNALS WHEN PROGRAMMED FOR MODE 1 OPERATION

		Input Port
Signal	Direction	Description
IBF	OUT	A 1 on this output indicates that the data has been loaded into the input latch; in essence an acknowledgement. IBF is set by the falling edge of the $\overline{STB}$ input and is reset by the rising edge of the $\overline{RD}$ input.
$\overline{STB}$	IN	A 0 on this input loads data into the input latch.
INTR	OUT	A 1 on this output can be used to interrupt the CPU when an input device is requesting service. INTR is set by the rising edge of $\overline{STB}$ if IBF is a 1 and INTE is a 1. It is reset by the falling edge of $\overline{RD}$. This procedure allows an input device to request service from the CPU by simply strobing its data into the port. INTE A is controlled by bit set/reset of PC4 and INTE B by bit set/reset of PC2.

		Output Port
Signal	Direction	Description
$\overline{OBF}$	OUT	The $\overline{OBF}$ output will go low to indicate that the CPU has written data out to the specified port. The $\overline{OBF}$ flip-flop will be set by the rising edge of the $\overline{WR}$ input and reset by the falling edge of the $\overline{ACK}$ input signal.
$\overline{ACK}$	IN	A 0 on this input informs the 8255 that the data from port A or port B has been accepted. In essence, a response from the peripheral device indicating that it has received the data output by the CPU.
INTR	OUT	A 1 on this output can be used to interrupt the CPU when an output device has accepted data transmitted by the CPU. INTR is set by the rising edge of $\overline{ACK}$ if $\overline{OBF}$ is a 0 and INTE is a 1. It is reset by the falling edge of $\overline{WR}$. INTE A is controlled by bit set/reset of PC6 and INTE B by bit set/reset of PC2.

Source: J. Uffenbeck, *Hardware Interfacing with the Apple II Plus*, Prentice-Hall, Inc., Englewood Cliffs, N.J., 1983.

Assuming that data has been previously written to one of the data ports, the peripheral monitors $\overline{OBF}$ (output buffer full). When this line is low, data is available to be read by the peripheral. Using $\overline{OBF}$ as a $\overline{STROBE}$ input, the peripheral latches the data byte and responds with an $\overline{ACK}$ (acknowledge) pulse. The falling edge of this pulse resets $\overline{OBF}$ high and if INTE is high, the rising edge causes INTR to go high also.

Again the CPU has the choice of polling $\overline{OBF}$ by reading the mode 1 status word (see Fig. 7.14) or allowing INTR to alert it that $\overline{OBF}$ is high and the peripheral is ready for more data. In either case the processor should write a new byte of data to the output port. The falling edge of $\overline{WR}$ will reset INTR and the rising edge of $\overline{WR}$ will force $\overline{OBF}$ low. The peripheral, monitoring $\overline{OBF}$, can latch the new data byte and the cycle repeats.

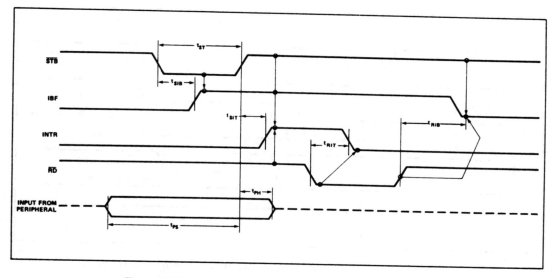

Figure 7.13 Mode 1 input port timing. (Courtesy of Intel Corporation.)

Polling versus interrupts. The advantages of polling and interrupts have been discussed previously. Let's make sure that we appreciate what is involved for each technique when using the 8255A in mode 1.

When polling is used, an input read from port C (an IN F2 instruction for the hardware shown in Fig. 7.6) will load the accumulator with the mode 1 status word shown in Fig. 7.14. Note that if port A is programmed as an input port and port B as an output, the status word will be made up of the GROUP A bits as an input and the GROUP B bits as an output. Standard bit-testing techniques can be used to monitor $\overline{OBF}$ or $\overline{IBF}$.

Note also that PC6 and 7 (port A = input) or PC4 and 5 (port A = output)

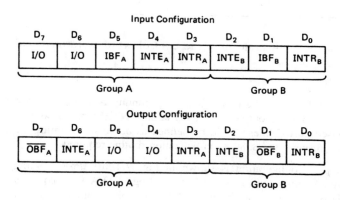

Figure 7.14 Mode 1 status word format.

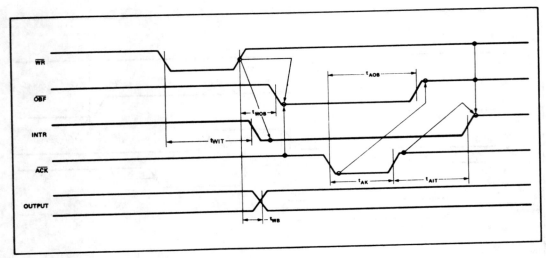

Figure 7.15 Mode 1 output port timing. (Courtesy of Intel Corporation.)

are not involved in the handshaking logic and can be programmed as general-purpose input and output lines. This is shown in Fig. 7.12. They can also be read as part of the mode 1 status word.

When interrupts are used, the INTR output will be set as $\overline{ACK}$ goes high (the buffer is available for more data) or as $\overline{STB}$ goes high (the input buffer contains data to be read). INTR can be set only if the corresponding INTE bit has been previously set by the processor. This is where the bit set/reset mode comes in.

Referring to Table 7.6, INTE is controlled as follows.

Port	Type	Name	Controlled by bit set/reset of:
A	Input	INTEA	PC4
A	Output	INTEA	PC6
B	Input	INTEB	PC2
B	Output	INTEB	PC2

A few examples should help illustrate how the control word is formed and interrupts enabled.

Example 7.8

Determine the 8255A control word to be used when programming port A as a mode 1 input port and port B as a mode 1 output port. INTEA and INTEB should both be enabled and the two unused port C lines should be defined as outputs. Assuming the hardware shown in Fig. 7.6, write the 8080/85 initialization routine required.

Solution. The desired port configuration is shown in Fig. 7.12(d). Programming PC6 and 7 as outputs, the control word is 1011010X. Setting INTEA will require a bit set for PC4 and INTEB will require a bit set for PC2. The initialization routine is

```
MVI   A,0B4H      ;CONTROL WORD
OUT   0F3H        ;CONTROL PORT
MVI   A,09H       ;BIT SET PC4
OUT   0F3H        ;CONTROL PORT
MVI   A,05H       ;BIT SET PC2
OUT   0F3H        ;CONTROL PORT
```

Example 7.9

Repeat Ex. 7.8 with port B programmed as a mode 0 output port. Program all free pins of port C as inputs.

Solution.   Refer to Fig. 7.12(a) to determine the port A portion of the control word. This is 10111XXX. Now refer to Fig. 7.7 for the GROUP B (or port B) portion of the control word. The last 3 bits should be 001. The resulting control word is 10111001. Only INTEA will need to be set, requiring a bit set operation on PC4. The program is given below. PC0 through PC2 and PC6 and PC7 are all available as general-purpose inputs.

```
MVI   A,0B9H      ;CONTROL WORD
OUT   0F3H        ;CONTROL PORT
MVI   A,09H       ;BIT SET PC4
OUT   0F3H        ;CONTROL PORT
```

As a final example, let's again use the 8255A to interface a parallel printer, but this time program the PPI for mode 1. To make the interface more interesting, we will use *interrupts* to control the flow of data. Refer to the timing diagram in Fig. 7.15 for the following discussion.

The circuit diagram is shown in Fig. 7.16. Port A has been chosen as the data output port requiring the $\overline{ACKA}$ signal from the printer to be connected to PC6. The $\overline{OBFA}$ output from the 8255 will serve as the $\overline{STROBE}$ input to the printer. Note that BUSY/$\overline{READY}$ is not used.

Assuming no data presently in the 8255A port A buffer, $\overline{OBFA}$ will be high, $\overline{ACKA}$ from the printer will be high, and if INTEA is set, INTRA will be high. Assuming that the processor has enabled its interrupt structure, the interrupt request will be honored. The interrupt service routine will respond to the interrupt request by fetching a data byte from a table and outputting it to port A. This will reset INTRA and force $\overline{OBFA}$ low, strobing the printer.

A period of time will now elapse as the character is printed. Eventually, $\overline{ACK}$ will go low as the printer acknowledges receipt and printing of the character. This will reset $\overline{OBFA}$ and force INTRA high, requesting another interrupt. The cycle then repeats until all of the data has been output.

It is interesting to note that INTRA is "automatically" removed by the 8255A when the processor does the I/O write to port A. Because of this, a synchronizing flip-flop is not required between INTRA and the processor.

Initializing the 8255A will require defining port A as a mode 1 output port and bit setting PC6 to enable INTEA. The 8080/85 code is

```
MVI   A,0A0H      ;CONTROL WORD = 1010XXXX
OUT   0F3H        ;CONTROL PORT
MVI   A,0DH       ;BIT SET PC6
OUT   0F3H        ;CONTROL PORT
```

Sec. 7.2   The 8255A Programmable Peripheral Interface

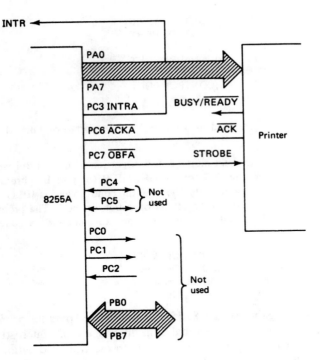

Figure 7.16 Interrupt-driven parallel printer interface using the 8255 in mode 1.

The interrupt service routine is identical to Fig. 6.22 with one change:

```
DPORT    EQU    0F0H    ;PORT A
```

Mode 2: Strobed Bidirectional I/O.

When operated in mode 2, port A of the 8255A becomes a *bidirectional* data port supported by five handshaking signals. This is shown in Fig. 7.17. The handshaking signals are identical to those provided in

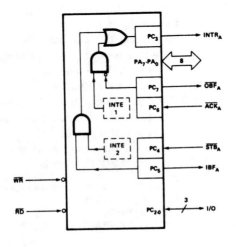

Figure 7.17 Mode 2 for the 8255. Port A is a bidirectional port in this mode, supported by five handshaking signals from port C. (Courtesy of Intel Corporation.)

mode 1 except that they now refer only to port A. This particular mode of operation is useful when transferring data between two computers (see the example later in this section).

When port A is programmed to operate in mode 2, port B can operate in mode 0 or mode 1. If programmed for mode 0, PC0–PC2 can be programmed as mode 0 inputs or outputs. If port B is programmed for mode 1, then PC0–PC2 become handshake signals for this port.

Considering all of the possible combinations, there are four configurations of the 8255A in mode 2. These are shown in Fig. 7.18. As an example, if we choose to program port A for mode 2, port B as a mode 0 input port, and PC0–PC2 as mode 0 output pins, the control word is 11XXX010.

Input port timing. Figure 7.19 is a timing diagram illustrating the sequence of events as a data byte is first transferred to the 8255 by the peripheral and then from the 8255A back to the peripheral. The numbers in the diagram are keyed to the explanation. We begin with the peripheral outputting a byte to the 8255A.

1. Data is output by the peripheral.
2. Peripheral applies a $\overline{STB}$ pulse to the 8255A.
3. When the data is latched, IBF goes high.
4. After $\overline{STB}$ returns high with IBF still set, INTR goes high, requesting an interrupt if this feature is used.
5. Polling or interrupts can now be used to service the peripheral. The 8255A buffer is read when $\overline{RD}$ goes low.
6. The falling edge of $\overline{RD}$ resets INTR.
7. The rising edge of $\overline{RD}$ resets IBF.

Output port timing. The following sequence occurs as the processor outputs a byte of data to the peripheral through the 8255A.

8. Data is output by the processor and latched by the 8255A (note that the peripheral bus is in a high-impedance state at this time).
9. The rising edge of $\overline{WR}$ causes $\overline{OBF}$ to switch low ("the output buffer is full").
10. The peripheral acknowledges $\overline{OBF}$ by causing $\overline{ACK}$ to go low.
11. On the falling edge of $\overline{ACK}$ the 8255A releases its data onto the bus.
12. $\overline{OBF}$ returns high ("the output buffer is empty").
13. The rising edge of $\overline{ACK}$ sets INTR, requesting an interrupt if this feature is used.
14. Polling or interrupts can now be used to write the next data byte to the 8255A.

A subtle point that we should not miss concerning mode 2 operation is that only a single INTR output is available. This raises the question of how the processor

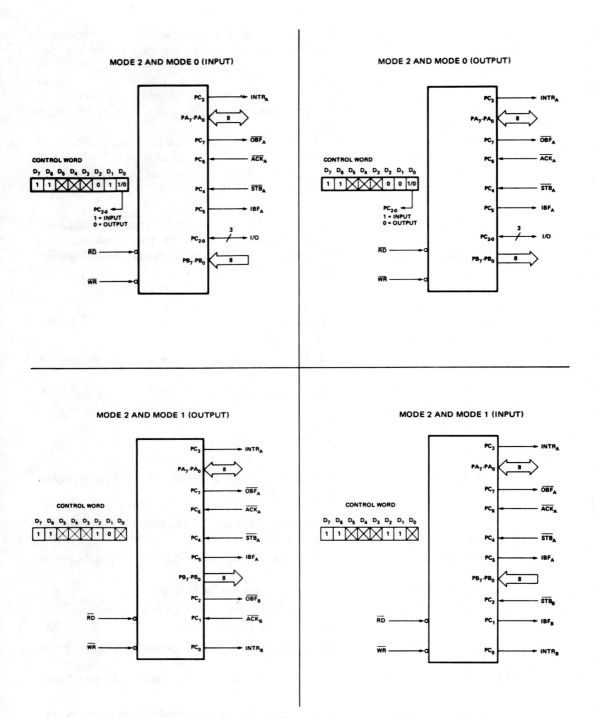

Figure 7.18 Four possible configurations of the 8255 when programmed for mode 2. (Courtesy of Intel Corporation.)

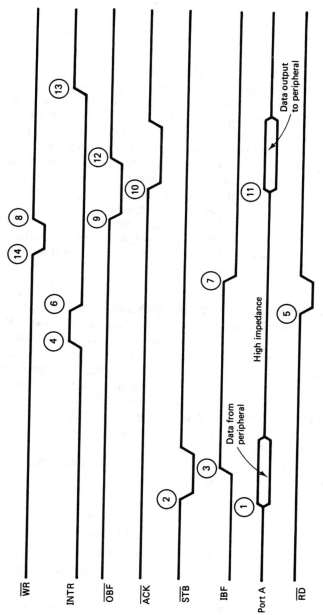

Figure 7.19 Input and output timing relationships for mode 2. The numbers are keyed to the text.

339

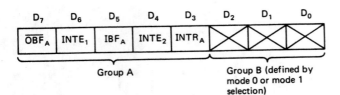

D₇	D₆	D₅	D₄	D₃	D₂	D₁	D₀

$\overline{OBF}_A$ | INTE₁ | IBF_A | INTE₂ | INTR_A | ✕✕✕✕✕✕

Group A

Group B (defined by mode 0 or mode 1 selection)

Figure 7.20 Mode 2 status word.

can determine if the interrupt requires data to be read or written—that is, who requested the interrupt? Two solutions are possible.

As discussed in Chap. 6, polling can be used when several interrupt requests must share the same input line. The mode 2 status word is shown in Fig. 7.20. With this technique the interrupt service routine (ISR) can poll port C testing IBFA and $\overline{OBFA}$. Control is then transferred to the appropriate routine.

A hardware solution is also possible. The interrupt request can be combined with $\overline{OBF}$ or IBF to generate two separate interrupts. These could be connected to the 8085's RST 5.5 and 6.5 inputs or a PIC (programmable interrupt controller) could be used to generate unique restart instructions.

Note that it is possible to mask interrupts generated by IBF or $\overline{OBF}$. This is done by resetting INTE1 or INTE2 with a *bit reset* operation. PC6 corresponds to INTE1 and PC4 to INTE2. The same bits must be set if interrupts are to be enabled. This can be seen by studying Fig. 7.17.

Exchanging data between two computers.   Figure 7.21 illustrates a technique for exchanging data between two computers using the 8255A in mode 2. Port A becomes a common data path between the two processors with the output port control signals of one connected to the input port control signals of the other.

When CPU-A outputs data to its 8255A, the $\overline{OBF}$ signal strobes 8255B, causing the IBF signal (inverted) to come back as an acknowledge pulse. This, in turn, gates data onto the bidirectional data bus. CPU-B reads the data, terminating the IBF pulse, and forcing $\overline{ACK}$ of 8255B high. This, in turn, releases $\overline{OBF}$ and the transfer is complete. The process works in reverse when CPU-B wishes to write a byte of data to CPU-A.

Each processor in Fig. 7.21 will require four separate routines for the data transfer to work. These are:

1. 8255A initialization routine
2. ISR or polling routine to monitor IBF and $\overline{OBF}$
3. A receiver program to read the data byte when IBF goes high
4. A transmitter program to output a data byte when $\overline{OBF}$ goes low

One of the interesting features about the interface in Fig. 7.21 is that it will allow the transfer of data files between two dissimilar computers. For example, one processor could be an 8085 and the other a 6800. Of course, 8085 binary object code files will not run on a 6800, but high-level language ASCII files could

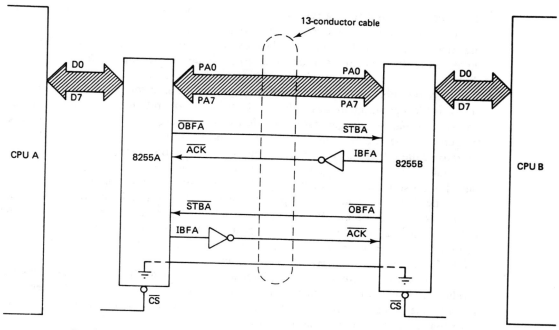

Figure 7.21 Two 8255s can be used to interface two dissimilar computers over a common data bus.

be transferred. Another application would be transferring data files between two computers with a similar processor but different floppy-disk formats.

7.3 THE 8254 PROGRAMMABLE INTERVAL TIMER

As you read this section, look for the answers to these Key Concept questions:

7.3.1. The 8254 contains _____ programmable counter/timers in one package.

7.3.2. What are the three types of control words that can be output to the 8254?

7.3.3. Which 8254 operating mode should be selected to produce a 50% duty cycle square wave?

7.3.4. When operated as a counter, the 8254 can be programmed to count in binary or _____.

Many microprocessor interfacing problems require accurate time delays for generating square-wave signals and strobe pulses. In some cases the microprocessor is called upon to count events and take some action after a prescribed number of pulses. In a real-time clock, for example, a 1-Hz interrupt signal is required to provide the "heart beat" for the clock.

It is for these kinds of applications that the 8254 has been designed. It provides three separate 16-bit timing registers, each of which can be programmed as a *timer* or an *event counter*. For example, by loading counter 0 with 868_{10} and specifying mode 3, a divide-by-868 50% duty cycle square wave is generated. The clock input can be the system clock or an external signal with an upper limit of 10 MHz (8254-2).

Programming consists of writing a byte to the control port selecting one of six possible operating modes. These modes allow operation as an event counter, one-shot, square-wave generator, divide-by-N counter, or hardware- or software-triggered strobe. Each counter can hold a 16-bit number, which is counted down to zero (called *terminal count*) at a rate set by that register's clock input. When terminal count occurs, an interrupt can be requested, a strobe pulse generated, a one-shot pulse terminated, or the logic level of a square wave toggled.

The 8254 is actually a "superset" of the 8253 timer. It has the exact same pinout as this device and is software-compatible. There are two differences. The 8253 has no read-back mode, which means that the status of a particular counter cannot be read back once it has been programmed. The second difference is that the 8253 is limited to 2 MHz for its maximum clock frequency.

In this section we see how to interface the 8254 to the microprocessor CPU module and how to program the device for each of its six modes of operation. Finally, the frequency counter program written in Chap. 3 (Program 12) will be rewritten using the 8254 as the interfacing element.

Interfacing the 8254. Figure 7.22 provides a block diagram and pinout for the 8254 programmable timer. To the microprocessor, it appears to be four separate I/O ports selected by the A0 and A1 input address lines. The $\overline{RD}$ and $\overline{WR}$ inputs determine if data is to be read or written using the eight lines of the bidirectional data bus. Table 7.7 lists the possible I/O operations. Like the 8255A, no operation is possible unless

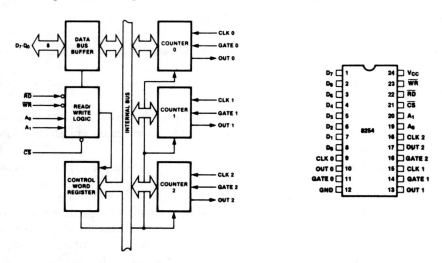

Figure 7.22 Block diagram and pin descriptions for the 8254 programmable interval timer. Three separate timer/counters are provided. (Courtesy of Intel Corporation.)

TABLE 7.7 READ/WRITE OPERATION
SUMMARY FOR THE 8254 PIT

$\overline{CS}$	$\overline{RD}$	$\overline{WR}$	A_1	A_0	
0	1	0	0	0	Write into Counter 0
0	1	0	0	1	Write into Counter 1
0	1	0	1	0	Write into Counter 2
0	1	0	1	1	Write Control Word
0	0	1	0	0	Read from Counter 0
0	0	1	0	1	Read from Counter 1
0	0	1	1	0	Read from Counter 2
0	0	1	1	1	No-Operation (3-State)
1	X	X	X	X	No-Operation (3-State)
0	1	1	X	X	No-Operation (3-State)

Source: Courtesy of Intel Corporation.

the $\overline{CS}$ (chip select) input is low. Also note that reading from the control register (A0 A1 = 11, $\overline{RD}$ = 0) is not possible; the read-back control word should be used.

Figure 7.23 illustrates a typical I/O-mapped interface to the three-bus system architecture.

Example 7.10

Determine the I/O port addresses for the three counters and control port in the 8254 interface in Fig. 7.23.

Solution. Only when the $\overline{CS}$ input is low is the device selected. This occurs when AB7–AB0 = 111100XX. In this case, the Xs are not really "don't cares" but specify the counter to be accessed. The four addresses are

Address F0: counter 0

Address F1: counter 1

Address F2: counter 2

Address F3: control register

Programming the 8254. The 8254 is programmed by writing a single byte (for each counter) to the control port followed by one or two bytes to specify the *initial count*. Three forms of the control word are possible, as shown in Fig. 7.24. The standard control word is used to specify the operating mode and the selected counter. Note that each counter can have a different operating mode and be programmed to operate as a *binary* or *BCD* counter.

Example 7.11

Write a program to specify counter 0 for mode 0 BCD operation with an initial count of 3648_{10}. Program counter 2 for mode 3 operation binary with an initial count of FFH.

Solution. The control words must first be determined. For counter 0 this is 00 11 000 1, which selects counter 0, two bytes for the initial count, mode 0, and BCD.

Sec. 7.3   The 8254 Programmable Interval Timer

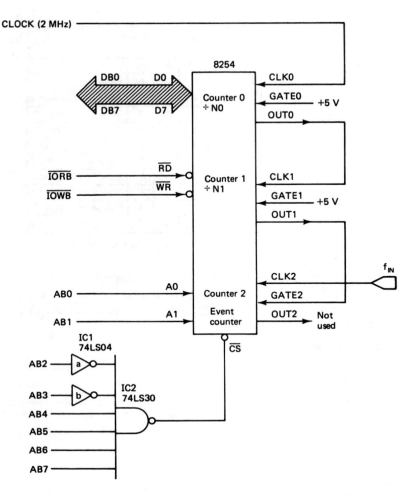

CLOCK (2 MHz)

8254

DB0   D0   CLK0

DB7   D7

Counter 0 ÷ N0   GATE0   +5 V

OUT0

$\overline{RD}$

$\overline{IORB}$ $\overline{WR}$ Counter 1 ÷ N1   CLK1

$\overline{IOWB}$

GATE1   +5 V

OUT1

CLK2 f_{IN}

AB0   A0   Counter 2   GATE2

AB1   A1   Event counter   OUT2   Not used

IC1 74LS04 $\overline{CS}$

AB2 — a

AB3 — b   IC2 74LS30

AB4

AB5

AB6

AB7

Figure 7.23 Interfacing the 8254 to the three-bus system architecture. Four I/O ports are required. The connections shown are for a frequency counter application.

For counter 2 the control word is 10 01 X11 0, which selects counter 2, one byte for the initial count, mode 3, and binary.

The program is shown in Fig. 7.25. First the control words are written followed by the two bytes for counter 0 and then the single byte to counter 2. Note that the order of programming does not matter except that the control word must be specified first. If two bytes are required for the initial count, both must be written.

When control bits D4 and D5 are 00, the *counter latch* command is specified. This mode latches the current value of the counter specified by bits D7 and D6. This is important because reading an unlatched counter may give erroneous results if the count is in the process of changing.

When the counter latch command is given, the count for that counter will be latched until read; the counter itself will continue to count. Also note that 16-bit

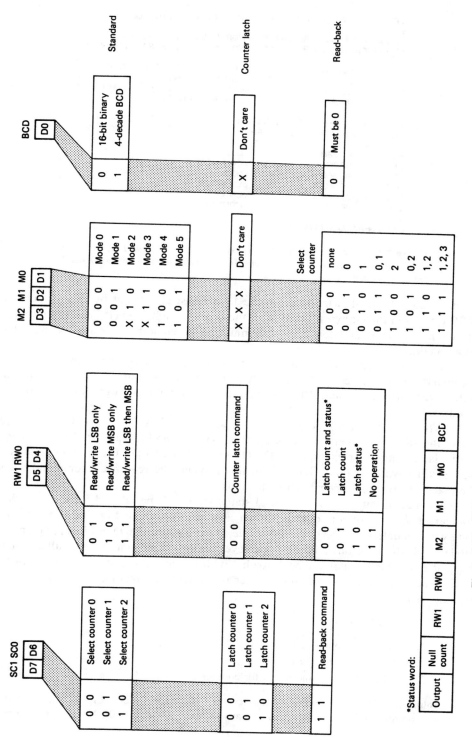

Figure 7.24 8254 control word. The standard form is used to specify the operating mode. The counter latch and read-back commands are used when the present count or status is to be read.

345

```
;PROGRAM TO DEMONSTRATE 8254 INITIALIZATION
;
;COUNTER 0 IS PROGRAMMED FOR MODE 0, BCD, 16-BITS
;COUNTER 2 IS PROGRAMMED FOR MODE 3, BINARY, 8-BITS
;
MVI     A,31H            ;COUNTER 0 CONTROL WORD
OUT     0F3H             ;CONTROL PORT
MVI     A,96H            ;COUNTER 2 CONTROL WORD
OUT     0F3H             ;CONTROL PORT
;
;LOAD COUNTER 0 WITH 3648H
;LOAD COUNTER 2 WITH FFH
;
MVI     A,48H            ;LSB
OUT     0F0H             ;COUNTER 0
MVI     A,36H            ;MSB
OUT     0F0H             ;COUNTER 0
MVI     A,0FFH           ;LSB
OUT     0F2H             ;COUNTER 2
;
;PROGRAM CONTINUES
```

Figure 7.25 Programming the 8254 consists of a control word followed by one or two bytes to specify the initial count. In this example only counters 0 and 2 are programmed.

counters must be read twice to fetch the LSB (least significant byte) and then the MSB (most significant byte). Once read, the counter latches revert back to following the count and another latch command must be given if it is desired to read the count again.

The third form of the control word facilitates the *read-back* command. This command allows the count to be latched at any or all counters and/or a special status word to be latched. Bits D6 and D7 must both be high for this control word.

When the read-back control word is specified, bits D4 and D5 are used to select the status or count latch modes. Bits D3, D2, and D1 are used to select the particular counter. For example, if D3 D2 D1 = 101 and D5 D4 = 01, counters 0 and 2 will have their count latched. In this respect, the read-back command takes the place of several counter latch commands.

By making bit D4 low, a special status word will be latched for the specified counter. The form of this byte is shown near the bottom of Fig. 7.24. From this byte you can determine the operating mode of the counter (BCD or binary, operating modes 0–5, 8- or 16-bit) and the logic level on the output pin. When null count is high, the counter has not yet been loaded with the initial count and should not be read. When null count is low, the counter is available for reading.

Example 7.12

Write a program that:

1. Latches the count for counter 0
2. Latches the status for counter 1
3. Latches the count and status for counter 2

Solution. The control word for counter 0 is 11 01 001 0 (refer to Fig. 7.24). Similarly, the control word for counters 1 and 2 are 11 10 010 0 and 11 00 100 0. The program is shown in Fig. 7.26. Note that it is possible to program all three counters at once if the same count/status is desired.

The only way that the current mode of a particular counter can be determined is by using the read-back command and specifying the status byte. Once this has been given, the selected counter can be read to obtain the status byte. If the status byte and count are both specified, the first read will return the status byte, the second byte (and the third if a 16-bit counter has been programmed) will return the latched count.

In all cases remember that the control word is written to the control port but all read operations must be from the selected counter, as specified with the A0 and A1 inputs.

Mode Definitions. As mentioned in the introduction, the 8254 can operate in one of six modes (selected by the standard form of the control word). The following is a brief description of each of these modes.

Mode 0: Event counter. If the GATE input is a 1, the counter will decrement from its initial count with the falling edge of the second pulse on the CLK input and each succeeding clock pulse thereafter. OUT will go high when the count reaches 0 (terminal count). OUT can be used as an interrupt input to the processor.

Mode 1: Hardware-triggered one-shot. On the rising edge of GATE, OUT will go low until the initial count has been decremented to 0. OUT will then return high. The active-low pulse width is equal to the initial count times the period of the CLK input.

Mode 2: Divide-by-N counter. If the GATE input is high, OUT will go low for one period of the signal at the CLK input after the initial count has been decremented to 1. The initial count will then automatically be reloaded and the cycle repeated. OUT is initially high.

Mode 3: Square-wave generator. This mode is identical to mode 2 except that the duty cycle of the output will be 50%. If the initial count is an odd number, OUT will be high for one more clock cycle than it is low.

```
;PROGRAM TO DEMONSTRATE THE 8254 READ-BACK COMMAND
;
MVI     A,0D2H          ;LATCH COUNT FOR COUNTER 0
OUT     0F3H            ;CONTROL PORT
;
MVI     A,0E4H          ;LATCH STATUS FOR COUNTER 1
OUT     0F3H            ;CONTROL PORT
;
MVI     A,0C8H          ;LATCH COUNT AND STATUS FOR
                        ;COUNTER 2
OUT     0F3H            ;CONTROL PORT
;
;INPUT INSTRUCTIONS CAN NOW BE USED TO READ THE STATUS
;AND COUNT OF A PARTICULAR COUNTER
```

Figure 7.26 Program for Ex. 7.12.

Mode 4: Software-triggered strobe. If the GATE input is high, OUT will go low for one period of the CLK input N clock cycles after writing the initial count (N). To produce the strobe a second time, the initial count must be rewritten.

Mode 5: Hardware-triggered strobe. The rising edge of the GATE input will cause the initial count to be decremented to 0. When terminal count occurs, OUT will go low for one period of the CLK input.

A Design Example. In Chap. 3, Program 12 presented the hardware and software to convert the Z-80 into a frequency counter. That circuit provided 10-Hz resolution and a maximum frequency of 990 Hz. In this example we will use the 8254 to provide a frequency counter with 1-Hz resolution and a maximum frequency of 9999 Hz. With a coarser resolution, frequencies approaching the 10-MHz limit of the (8254-2) clock input can be measured.

Hardware. Figure 7.23 shows the connections required. Counters 0 and 1 are programmed as divide-by-2000 square-wave counters. Assuming a 2-MHz system clock, this results in a frequency at OUT 1 of

$$\frac{2 \times 10^6}{2000 \times 2000} = 0.5 \text{ Hz}$$

A 0.5-Hz square wave has a 2-s period and by connecting this signal to GATE2, enables counter 2 (programmed as an event counter) for 1 s. During this counting interval, counter 2 will decrement from its initial count—9999—to some value dependent on the number of clock pulses received at its CLK2 input pin.

Software. The software must initialize the three counters and then monitor OUT1. When low, the counting period will have ended and the count can be recovered. By subtracting this number from 9999, the total number of clock pulses received during the 1-s counting interval (and thus the frequency) can be calculated.

Example 7.13

Assume that counter 2 contains 3275 just after OUT1 goes low. What is the frequency of the CLK2 input? Assume the hardware in Fig. 7.23.

Solution. The input frequency is found by subtracting 3275 from the initial count of 9999:

$$\begin{array}{r} 9999 \\ - \ 3275 \\ \hline 6724 \text{ Hz} \end{array}$$

It is interesting to notice that programming counter 2 for binary operation allows a maximum frequency of 65,535 Hz. However, a binary-to-decimal conversion routine will be required.

Figure 7.27 provides a solution to the 8254 frequency counter problem. You should note the following points:

1. Counters 0 and 1 are programmed to operate in mode 3 binary with an initial count of 2000.

```
;Program to use the 8254 as a frequency counter
;
;The hardware is shown in Fig. 7.23
;
;Program counters 0 and 1 for square wave mode
        MVI     A,36H           ;Counter 0, mode 3, binary
        OUT     OF3H            ;Control port
        MVI     A,76H           ;Counter 1, mode 3, binary
        OUT     OF3H            ;Control port
;
;Make each counter a divide-by 2000 (07D0H)
;
        MVI     A,0D0H          ;LSB
        OUT     OF0H            ;Counter 0
        OUT     OF1H            ;Counter 1
        MVI     A,07H           ;MSB
        OUT     OF0H            ;Counter 0
        OUT     OF1H            ;Counter 1
;
;Make counter 2 an event counter
;
CYCLE   MVI     A,0B1H          ;Counter 2, mode 0, BCD
        OUT     OF3H            ;Control port
        MVI     A,99H           ;Initial count is 9999
        OUT     OF2H            ;LSB
        OUT     OF2H            ;MSB
;
;Counter 2 is now counting pulses - done when
;OUT1 goes low
;
;Check to see if the counting period has ended
;
WAIT1   CALL    STAT            ;Counter 1 to carry
        JC      WAIT1           ;Wait until low
;
;Now latch count and status for counter 2 and test
;for overflow
;
        MVI     A,0C8H          ;Read-back counter 2
        OUT     OF3H            ;Control port
        IN      OF2H            ;First read is status
        RAL                     ;Test output
        JC      OVFLW           ;If set then overflow
;
;Read the count and adjust for display
;
        IN      OF2H            ;Get LSB
        CALL    ADJ             ;Subtract from 99
        INR     A               ;First clock pulse not counted
        OUT     0               ;LSB display assumed at port 0
        IN      OF2H            ;Get MSB
        CALL    ADJ             ;Subtract from 99
        OUT     1               ;MSB display assumed at port 1
;
;Check to see if the next counting period has begun
;
```

Figure 7.27 Frequency counter program for the 8254 interface in Fig. 7.23.

```
WAIT2   CALL    STAT            ;Counter 1 to carry
        JNC     WAIT2           ;Wait until high
        JMP     CYCLE           ;Start again
        ;
        ;If overflow then come here and show FF in displays
        ;
OVFLW   IN      0F2H            ;Finish the reads
        IN      0F2H            ;
        MVI     A,0FFH          ;Overflow display code
        OUT     0               ;LSB display
        OUT     1               ;MSB display
        JMP     WAIT2           ;Wait for next counting peri
        ;
        ;This routine subtracts the count from 99
ADJ     MOV     B,A             ;Move count to B
        MVI     A,99H           ;Initial count
        SUB     B               ;Adjust
        RET                     ;
        ;
        ;This routine reads the status of Counter 1
        ;and stores in the carry flag
STAT    MVI     A,0E4H          ;Read-back counter 1
        OUT     0F3H            ;Control port
        IN      0F1H            ;Counter 1 status
        RAL                     ;Move OUT1 to carry
        RET                     ;Done
        END
```

Figure 7.27   (*Continued*)

2. Counter 2 is programmed for mode 0 BCD. By letting this counter operate in BCD the (nontrivial) software required to convert from binary to decimal is avoided. However, the maximum frequency is limited to 9999 Hz.

3. Two decoded seven-segment displays are assumed wired to ports 0 and 1 to display the frequency. If an ASCII terminal is used, a BCD-to-ASCII conversion routine will be required.

4. The status of OUT1 is polled using the read-back command word for counter 1. When low, the event counter is disabled and the latched count (and status) read and subtracted from 9999.

5. If OUT2 is high, terminal count has been reached and an overflow condition is detected; FFFF is output to the displays.

6. The cycle repeats after rewriting 9999 to counter 2.

8254 Electrical Characteristics.   There are two speed versions of the 8254. The 8254 has a 220-ns access time and a maximum clock frequency of 8 MHz. The 8254-2 has a 185-ns access time and an upper frequency limit of 10 MHz.

The GATE and CLK inputs present 10 μA dc loads and the OUT output can source 400 μA in the high state and sink 2 mA in the low state. This means that one standard TTL load or five LSTTL loads can be driven.

7.4 THE 8259A PROGRAMMABLE INTERRUPT CONTROLLER

As you read this section, look for the answers to these Key Concept questions:

7.4.1. A single 8259A can accept as many as _____ different interrupt requests.

7.4.2. When an interrupt occurs, the 8259A automatically gates a three-byte _____ instruction onto the data bus of the microprocessor.

7.4.3. Which 8259A operating mode should be selected if all interrupting devices have equal priority?

7.4.4. What is the difference between an initialization control word (ICW) and an operation control word (OCW)?

Considering the 8080, 8085, and Z-80, the 8080 is the least capable when it comes to servicing interrupts. Only the single INTR line is provided compared to the 8085's five interrupt inputs and the two interrupt inputs of the Z-80. This is more an indication of the 8080's age than it is of a poor design. The solution to the problem is to expand the chip set required for an 8080 microcomputer system to include a *programmable interrupt controller* (PIC).

This is one of the rationales behind the 8259A PIC. It is designed to support any of the 8080, 8085, 8086, or 8088 series of microprocessors built by Intel. As such, it probably has more capabilities than are required by a 2-MHz 8080. And although it is compatible with the 8085's INTR input, it is difficult to imagine a situation where the 8085's present interrupt capabilities would be inadequate.

The 8259A PIC functions as an overall system interrupt manager designed to enhance the vectored interrupt capabilities of the 8080, 8085, 8086, and 8088 microprocessors. When operated in the 8080/85 mode it can:

1. Accept eight separate interrupt requests (cascadable to 64).
2. Gate the three bytes for a CALL instruction onto the system data bus in response to $\overline{\text{INTA}}$.
3. Assign priorities and arbitrate simultaneous interrupts.
4. Program the interrupt inputs for a level or edge trigger.
5. Program the vector address and a four- or eight-byte address interval.

The 8259A is a very powerful device and indeed has capabilities beyond the needs of most (relatively) low-speed 8080 or 8085 microcomputer systems. An 8-bit, 2-MHz 8080 microprocessor with more than a few interrupt inputs will quickly become overtaxed. In such systems, distributed processing techniques or higher-speed processors will usually provide better service.

On the other hand, a 16-bit, 10-MHz 8086 microprocessor might be used in a multiuser multitasking environment requiring several 8259As in cascade. Keep this perspective in mind. The 8259A is a very versatile but complex device, and many of its features are best taken advantage of with the 16-bit 8088 or 8086.

Interfacing the 8259A.   Figure 7.28 provides a block diagram of the PIC and gives the pin definitions. To the programmer the PIC appears to be two I/O ports (or memory locations) specified by the A0 address input. However, as we shall see later in this section, seven separate registers can be written to. The specific address of the PIC is controlled by an address decoder connected to the $\overline{CS}$ input.

Figure 7.29 illustrates a typical interface between the PIC and the three-bus system architecture. In this example ports F0H and F1H have been selected arbitrarily. The eight interrupt requests are received at IR0 through IR7 and can be programmed to be active-high, level-sensitive, or rising edge-triggered.

Assuming that the active interrupt is not masked, the 8259 requests an interrupt from the microprocessor by driving the $\overline{INTR}$ output high. The processor, upon completing its current instruction, issues $\overline{INTA}$, which is buffered and received by the 8259A as $\overline{INTAB}$. Three bytes are then gated onto the system data bus. The first is 11001101, the op-code for a CALL instruction. When this byte is received by the 8228 (in an 8080 system) or the 8085, two additional $\overline{INTA}$ pulses are output and used to gate in the 16-bit restart address corresponding to the active interrupt.

Note that the 8259A does not allow each interrupt input to have its own independent address. Instead, a base address can be programmed and a four- or eight-byte *interval* specified. For example, if the base address is 0100H and the

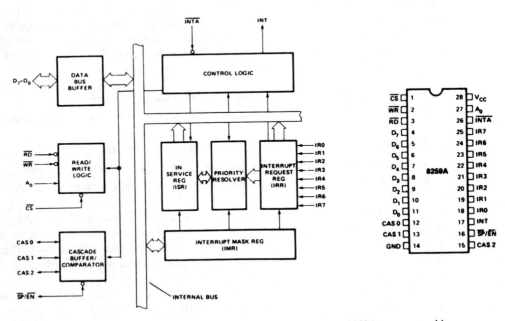

Figure 7.28   Block diagram and pin definitions for the 8259A programmable interrupt controller (PIC). (Courtesy of Intel Corporation.)

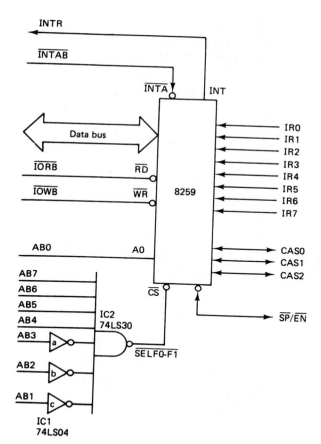

Figure 7.29 Interfacing the 8259A PIC to the three-bus system architecture. Two ports are required and in this case correspond to I/O port addresses F0H and F1H.

interval is four, eight restart locations will exist, as shown in Table 7.8. Normally, instructions to jump to the appropriate interrupt service routine would be stored in these locations and the 32 bytes of memory from 0100 to 011F referred to as a "jump table."

When cascading the 8259A the CAS0 through CAS2 input/output pins are used. This is illustrated in Fig. 7.30. One 8259A is defined to be the master ($\overline{SP/EN}$ = +5 V) and two other 8259As are defined as slaves ($\overline{SP/EN}$ = 0 V). CAS0 through CAS2 become outputs from the master and inputs to the slave. These lines are used by the master to identify the active slave device.

Notice that each 8259 in this design has its own I/O address (determined by the address decoder connected to the $\overline{CS}$ input) and communicates with the CPU over the bidirectional data bus. However, all interrupt requests to the processor must go through the master and no slave can respond to an $\overline{INTA}$ unless its CAS0 through CAS2 inputs are active.

Arbitration Modes. The 8259A has been designed to handle a large number of interrupt requests. Each of the eight interrupt inputs within one PIC can be assigned a

Interrupt request	Restart address
IR0	0100H
IR1	0104H
IR2	0108H
IR3	010CH
IR4	0110H
IR5	0114H
IR6	0118H
IR7	011CH

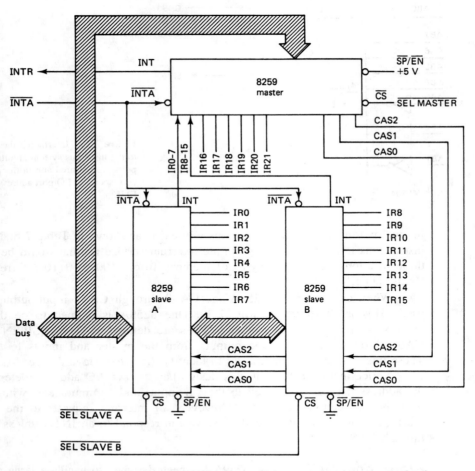

Figure 7.30 Cascading the 8259A. Up to 64 interrupts can be accommodated using one master and eight slaves.

priority for use in the event of a multiple interrupt request—that is, simultaneous interrupts. Six different operating modes can be programmed.

1. *Fully nested.* This is the default mode and assigns IR0 the highest priority and IR7 the lowest. In this mode, when one interrupt is being serviced, all others of equal or lower priority are remembered (in the interrupt request register—IRR) but not serviced. One bit of the in-service register (ISR) will be set corresponding to the active input.

When the interrupt service routine has finished, a special *nonspecific end-of-interrupt* (EOI) instruction must be given. This will reset the highest in-service bit (which in the fully nested mode will correspond to the active input). The EOI instruction is given by writing an *operation control word* (to be described shortly) to the command register. This instruction should be included as part of the interrupt service routine.

By writing a special *initialization control word*, it is also possible to program the 8259A to insert automatically the nonspecific end-of-interrupt command. In this case the in-service bit will be reset on the trailing edge of the last $\overline{\text{INTA}}$ pulse. Note that later in this section you will learn how to program the 8259A and write the initialization and operation control words.

2. *Rotating equal priority.* This mode is intended for applications where all devices have an equal priority. In this scheme, the currently executing interrupt is given the lowest priority after completing its service routine. The technique is shown in Fig. 7.31. Two interrupt requests are received, IR1 and IR6 in Fig. 7.31(a). IR1 has the highest priority and is therefore serviced first. After being serviced, IR1 is assigned the lowest priority. This is shown in Fig. 7.31(b).

IR6 is then serviced and assigned the lowest priority, as shown in Fig. 7.31(c). This technique prevents infrequent interrupt requests from being "starved" for service due to heavy traffic on other interrupt inputs.

The priority rotation can be accomplished automatically or with the special nonspecific EOI command (given at the end of the interrupt service routine).

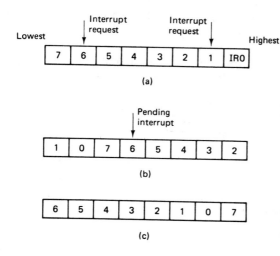

(a)

(b)

(c)

Figure 7.31 Rotating equal priority. In this technique the current interrupt is assigned lowest priority after being serviced. In (a) IR1 is serviced and then assigned lowest priority in (b). Next IR6 is serviced and then assigned lowest priority in (c).

3. *Rotating specific priority.* If a specific EOI control word is written to the 8259A, the priority structure after servicing the current interrupt can be fixed in the service routine. This is done by specifying the lowest-priority input as part of the EOI control word. Referring to Fig. 7.31(a), a specific EOI control word could assign IR7 the lowest priority with the result that the priority structure after servicing IR1 would look the same as Fig. 7.31(a), not like Fig. 7.31(b).

The advantage is that the service routine can set the priorities depending on program execution rather than a fixed rotation scheme. The result is greater flexibility for the programmer.

4. *Basic mask.* This mode allows any of the IR0 through IR7 inputs to be masked by writing a 1 to their corresponding bit position in the interrupt mask register (IMR). This interrupt will then be ignored in all other modes.

5. *Special mask.* Normally, a lower-priority interrupt cannot interrupt a higher priority. However, if the currently executing service routine writes a 1 to the interrupt mask register (IMR) ("masking itself") and the special mask mode is selected, interrupts of a lower (as well as higher)-priority level than the masked bit will be accepted.

6. *Polled.* In this mode the INT output is not used. Instead, the 8259A prioritizes the IR0 through IR7 inputs and provides a status port that can be polled. The status byte has the form shown in Fig. 7.32.

Programming the 8259A.   Programming the 8259A requires two to four *initialization control words* (ICWs). These bytes specify the vector address, select a four- or eight-byte interval between addresses, identify the single or cascaded mode, select the automatic or normal EOI mode, and program the type of trigger. Once these bytes have been written, the PIC is ready to receive interrupt requests.

The default arbitration scheme after initialization is the *fully nested* normal EOI mode in which only higher-level interrupt requests can interrupt an in–service request and an EOI command is required at the end of each interrupt service routine. In addition, the interrupt mask register (IMR) is cleared—that is, no masks are applied—IR7 is assigned lowest priority and the special mask mode is cleared. Changes to any of these operating modes will require writing one to three *operation control words* (OCWs).

Initialization control words.   Figure 7.33 describes the bit assignments for ICW1 through ICW4. In all cases, ICW1 and ICW2 must be written. These bytes

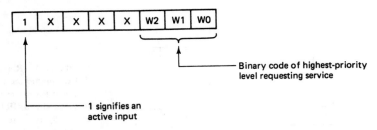

Figure 7.32   In the polled mode the 8259A acts as a prioritized status port.

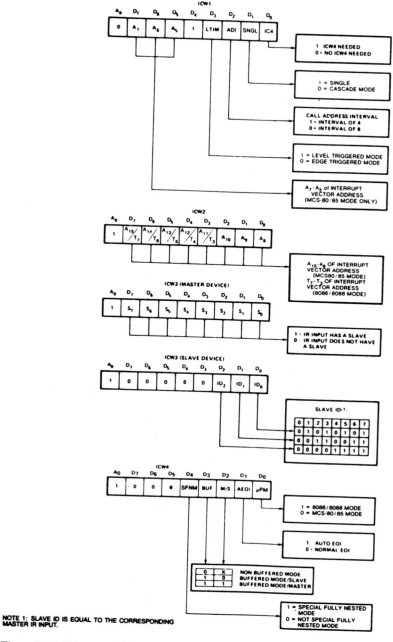

Figure 7.33 8259A initialization control word format. (Courtesy of Intel Corporation.)

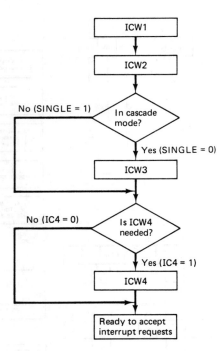

Figure 7.34 8259A initialization sequence. (Courtesy of Intel Corporation.)

program the base address that together with the interval will be gated onto the data bus during $\overline{\text{INTA}}$.

ICW3 should be written only when one or more slave PICs are to be used. ICW4 is required to specify an 8086 or 8088 processor, to enable the auto EOI mode and special fully nested mode (for cascaded PICs), and to select the buffered mode for slave and master. The latter selection is required when data bus buffers are used between the PIC and system data bus.

The steps required for 8259 initialization are shown in flowchart form in Fig. 7.34.

Example 7.14

The 8259A is to be used to interface eight level-triggered interrupt inputs. The following jump table will be used to service the interrupts.

Address	Op-code	Interrupt
E000	JMP ISR 0	IR0
E004	JMP ISR 1	IR1
E008	JMP ISR 2	IR2
E00C	JMP ISR 3	IR3
E010	JMP ISR 4	IR4
E014	JMP ISR 5	IR5
E018	JMP ISR 6	IR6
E01C	JMP ISR 7	IR7

Write the 8080/85 initialization routine assuming the hardware interface in Fig. 7.29.

Solution. Only ICW1 and ICW2 need be written. Note that ICW1 is accessed when A0 = 0 (thus port F0 in Fig. 7.29) and ICW1 is accessed when A0 = 1 (thus port F1 in Fig. 7.29).

```
MVI    A,1EH        ;000 1 1 1 0 (INIT. CODES)
OUT    0F0H         ;ICW1 PORT
MVI    A,0E0H       ;1110 0000 (BASE ADDRESS)
OUT    0F1H         ;ICW2 PORT
```

Note that if ICW3 and ICW4 are required, they are written to the same address as ICW2. The 8259A, by noting bits D0 and D1 of ICW1, will interpret the next two writes as ICW3 and ICW4.

Operation Control Words.

As explained previously, the operation control words (OCWs) are required only when the default conditions (obtained after initialization) must be changed and to give the nonautomatic EOI command at the end of each service routine.

Figure 7.35 details the bit definitions for the three operation control word registers. OCW1 controls the interrupt masks—logic 1s written to OCW1 will cause the selected interrupts to be masked and ignored by the 8259A.

The operating modes (see Arbitration Modes) are selected by writing to OCW2. Eight commands can be given—usually at the end of the interrupt service routine.

1. Nonspecific EOI—use this command at the end of each service routine when operating in the fully nested mode. It resets the highest in-service interrupt bit. While this bit is set, interrupts of equal or lower priority are inhibited. This command is automatically inserted by the 8259A if bit D1 of ICW4 is programmed high.

2. Specific EOI—use this command to force a specific in-service bit to be reset. This command should only be used when the fully nested structure is not implemented. Bits 0–2 select the in-service bit.

3. Rotate on nonspecific EOI—this command should be given when all peripherals have equal priority. It causes an automatic rotation of the priorities as illustrated in Figure 7.31.

4. Rotate in automatic EOI mode (Set)—this command activates the automatic rotate on nonspecific EOI mode (effectively the same as the mode 3 command above).

5. Rotate in automatic EOI mode (Clear)—this command deactivates the automatic rotate on nonspecific EOI mode.

6. Rotate on specific EOI—this command allows the programmer to specify the bottom priority in the rotate mode. For example, if IR4 is programmed as the lowest priority device, then IR5 will have the highest priority.

7. Set priority—this command alters the priority by specifying the lowest priority device. Note that this is not an EOI command however.

8. No operation.

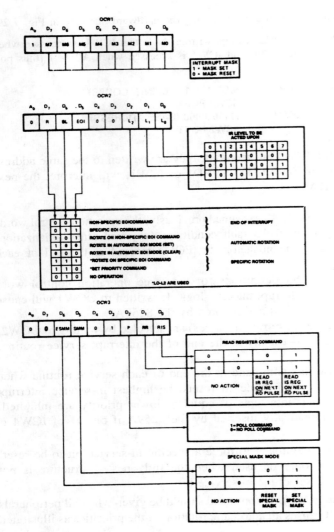

Figure 7.35 8259A operation control word (OCW) format. (Courtesy of Intel Corporation.)

OCW3 is used to enable the *interrupt request register*, IRR (that is, the status of pending interrupts), or the *in-service register*, ISR (that is, the interrupts currently being serviced), for a subsequent read operation. The polling mode is selected with bit D2. Bits D5 and D6 control the special mask mode.

The correct address to use when writing the ICWs and OCWs can be confusing and Table 7.9 should help explain. ICW1 is written with A0 = 0 and has bits 4,3 = 1X. The PIC recognizes this pattern as ICW1 and expects the initialization sequence, ICW2 through ICW4, to follow.

The OCWs are more complex. All write operations with A0 = 1 *after initialization is complete* will be directed to OCW1. If A0 = 0, bits 4 and 3 determine if the byte is to be interpreted as OCW2, OCW3, or ICW1 (begin a new initialization).

TABLE 7.9 8259A INITIALIZATION AND OPERATION CONTROL WORD SUMMARY

Name	RD	WR	A0	Special requirements	Comments
Initialization begins.					
ICW1	1	0	0	Bits 4,3 = 1X	This begins initialization sequence.
ICW2	1	0	1	None	First write with A0 = 1 after ICW1 must be ICW2.
ICW3	1	0	1	None	This write must follow ICW2 if specified in ICW1 (bit 1 = 0).
ICW4	1	0	1	None	This write must follow ICW3 if specified in ICW1 (bit 0 = 1).
Initialization is now complete.					
OCW1	1	0	1	None	This write sets the interrupt mask bits.
OCW2	1	0	0	Bits 4, 3 = 00	Bits 4, 3 identify as noninitialization command. Used to select mode.
OCW3	1	0	0	Bits 4, 3 = 01	Bits 4, 3 separate ICW1, OCW2, and OCW3. Bits 0, 1 determine input status registers to be read.
The following read operations may be specified.					
IRR	0	1	0	None	If OCW3 bits 1, 0 = 10, the pending interrupts will be read.
ISR	0	1	0	None	If OCW3 bits 1, 0 = 11, the current in-service interrupts will be read.
IMR	0	1	1	None	Read the interrupt mask bits. This is the read corresponding to OCW1.

Finally, note that three registers can be read. IRR and ISR are controlled by the data written to bits 0 and 1 of OCW3. The interrupt mask register, IMR, is read when A0 = 1 and a read cycle is performed.

Example 7.15

Assume that the initialization codes in Ex. 7.14 have been written to the 8259A in Fig. 7.29. Now write the proper operation control words for a fully nested priority structure. Mask IR1, IR3, and IR6 and enable the ISR for a read. What code should be used at the end of each interrupt service routine?

Solution. The fully nested structure defaults after initialization; thus only two control words are required. Refer to Fig. 7.35.

```
MVI    A,4AH      ;INTERRUPT MASK WORD – 01001010
OUT    0F1H       ;OCW1
MVI    A,0BH      ;READ ISR – 00001011
OUT    0F0H       ;BITS 4,3 = 01 => OCW3
```

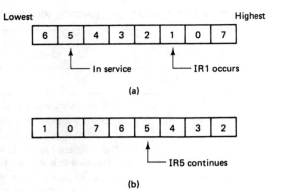

Lowest   Highest

| 6 | 5 | 4 | 3 | 2 | 1 | 0 | 7 |

— In service   — IR1 occurs

(a)

| 1 | 0 | 7 | 6 | 5 | 4 | 3 | 2 |

— IR5 continues

(b)

Figure 7.36 In-service register for Ex. 7.16.

Each interrupt service routine must end by giving the nonspecific EOI command (resetting the in-service bit). A typical routine would end with:

```
MVI   A,20H      ;NONSPECIFIC EOI - 00100XXX
OUT   0F0H       ;BITS 4,3 = 00 => OCW2
RET
```

Example 7.16

Assume that Fig. 7.36(a) shows the current interrupt priority and in-service status for the 8259A in Fig. 7.29. What changes are required to the OCWs given in Ex. 7.15 if the rotate in automatic EOI mode is desired? If IR1 occurs while IR5 is in service, will it be serviced? What will the new priority structure become?

Solution. The only change required to the OCWs in Ex. 7.15 is the inclusion of a rotate in automatic EOI mode command.

```
MVI   A,80H      ;ROTATE IN AUTOMATIC EOI - 10000XXX
OUT   0F0H       ;BITS 4,3 = 00 => OCW2
```

Because IR1 is of a higher priority than IR5, the IR5 service routine will be suspended and the IR1 routine executed. Figure 7.36(b) shows the priority structure after the IR1 routine has finished. IR1 has become the lowest priority and the IR5 service routine can now continue. When the IR5 routine finishes, it will become the lowest priority.

7.5 THE 8237 PROGRAMMABLE DMA CONTROLLER

As you read this section, look for the answers to these Key Concept questions:

7.5.1. What two signals are used by the 8080 and 8085 microprocessors to accept and acknowledge DMA cycles?

7.5.2. Why must the CPU tri-state its buses during DMA cycles?

7.5.3. When a peripheral is ready for a DMA transfer to begin, it activates one of the four _____ inputs of the 8237A.

7.5.4. How many different I/O ports does the 8237A occupy?

7.5.5. How does the 8237A know the source or destination memory address and the number of bytes involved in the DMA transfer?

DMA or *direct memory access* was introduced in Chap. 6. It is an alternative to programmed or interrupt-driven I/O. The main advantage is the high speed at which data transfers can take place. The 8237 DMA controller can transfer data between memory and an I/O port as fast as 1.6 MB/s (megabytes per second). This compares to less than 33,000 bytes per second using polling (with a 2-MHz 8080A).

Not all applications of DMA involve high-speed peripherals. Buffered printers can also be interfaced using DMA. Each time the printer's BUSY/READY flag indicates READY, the buffer of the printer can be filled using DMA at high speed, the DMA transfer is now complete, and the microprocessor resumes normal processing as the printer empties its buffer.

The advantage to using a DMA controller (DMAC) for this application is that the controller can be programmed to keep track of the source address and word count without CPU intervention. If interrupts were used, an interrupt service routine would be required and considerable processing time spent recovering and storing program variables.

The disadvantage to DMA is that the processor must idle while the DMA transfer takes place. This is not really a disadvantage when the transfer occurs in "bursts" as in the printer example. On the other hand, if the printer does not have a buffer and the DMAC must insert *WAIT* states to synchronize itself to the printer's data rate, interrupts would provide a better solution. This is because the processor would be allowed to perform some other task while waiting for the printer to be ready.

Another disadvantage to DMA is that no pre- or postprocessing can be done by the DMAC. If this is required, it will have to be done before or after the data has been transferred.

In the past the biggest limitation to using DMA has been the complexity of designing the DMA controller or DMAC. This is where the 8237A comes in. It provides all of the features required for DMA transfers in a single 40-pin chip and interfaces in a straightforward manner to the system three-bus architecture. Among the features of the 8237A DMAC are:

1. There are four DMA channels.
2. Each channel is capable of transferring up to 64K bytes.
3. Fixed or rotating priorities may be assigned.
4. Hardware or software may request the DMA transfer.
5. Block or single-byte transfers may be specified.
6. Data transfers between I/O and memory or from memory to memory are possible.

Interfacing the 8237A. Figure 7.37(a) is a block diagram and pinout definition for the 8237A programmable DMAC. Figure 7.37(b) provides a description of the pin

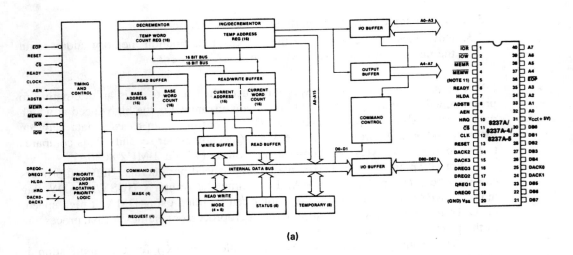

(a)

Symbol	Type	Name and Function
V_{CC}		**Power:** +5 volt supply.
V_{SS}		**Ground:** Ground.
CLK	I	**Clock Input:** Clock Input controls the internal operations of the 8237A and its rate of data transfers. The input may be driven at up to 3 MHz for the standard 8237A and up to 5 MHz for the 8237A-5.
CS	I	**Chip Select:** Chip Select is an active low input used to select the 8237A as an I/O device during the Idle cycle. This allows CPU communication on the data bus.
RESET	I	**Reset:** Reset is an active high input which clears the Command, Status, Request and Temporary registers. It also clears the first/last flip/flop and sets the Mask register. Following a Reset the device is in the Idle cycle.
READY	I	**Ready:** Ready is an input used to extend the memory read and write pulses from the 8237A to accommodate slow memories or I/O peripheral devices. Ready must not make transitions during its specified setup/hold time.
HLDA	I	**Hold Acknowledge:** The active high Hold Acknowledge from the CPU indicates that it has relinquished control of the system busses.
DREQ0–DREQ3	I	**DMA Request:** The DMA Request lines are individual asynchronous channel request inputs used by peripheral circuits to obtain DMA service. In fixed Priority, DREQ0 has the highest priority and DREQ3 has the lowest priority. A request is generated by activating the DREQ line of a channel. DACK will acknowledge the recognition of DREQ signal. Polarity of DREQ is programmable. Reset intializes these lines to active high. DREQ must be maintained until the corresponding DACK goes active

Symbol	Type	Name and Function
DB0–DB7	I/O	**Data Bus:** The Data Bus lines are bidirectional three-state signals connected to the system data bus. The outputs are enabled in the Program condition during the I/O Read to output the contents of an Address register, a Status register, the Temporary register or a Word Count register to the CPU. The outputs are disabled and the inputs are read during an I/O Write cycle when the CPU is programming the 8237A control registers. During DMA cycles the most significant 8 bits of the address are output onto the data bus to be strobed into an external latch by ADSTB. In memory-to-memory operations, data from the memory comes into the 8237A on the data bus during the read-from-memory transfer. In the write-to-memory transfer, the data bus outputs place the data into the new memory location.
IOR	I/O	**I/O Read:** I/O Read is a bidirectional active low three-state line. In the Idle cycle, it is an input control signal used by the CPU to read the control registers. In the Active cycle, it is an output control signal used by the 8237A to access data from a peripheral during a DMA Write transfer.
IOW	I/O	**I/O Write:** I/O Write is a bidirectional active low three-state line. In the Idle cycle, it is an input control signal used by the CPU to load information into the 8237A. In the Active cycle, it is an output control signal used by the 8237A to load data to the peripheral during a DMA Read transfer.
EOP	I/O	**End of Process:** End of Process is an active low bidirectional signal. Information concerning the completion of DMA services is available at the bidirectional EOP pin. The 8237A allows an external signal to terminate an active DMA

(b)

Figure 7.37 (a) Block diagram and pin definitions for the 8237A DMAC; (b) pin descriptions. (Courtesy of Intel Corporation.)

Symbol	Type	Name and Function
		service. This is accomplished by pulling the EOP input low with an external EOP signal. The 8237A also generates a pulse when the terminal count (TC) for any channel is reached. This generates an EOP signal which is output through the EOP Line. The reception of EOP, either internal or external, will cause the 8237A to terminate the service, reset the request, and, if Autoinitialize is enabled, to write the base registers to the current registers of that channel. The mask bit and TC bit in the status word will be set for the currently active channel by EOP unless the channel is programmed for Autoinitialize. In that case, the mask bit remains clear. During memory-to-memory transfers, EOP will be output when the TC for channel 1 occurs. EOP should be tied high with a pull-up resistor if it is not used to prevent erroneous end of process inputs.
A0–A3	I/O	Address: The four least significant address lines are bidirectional three-state signals. In the Idle cycle they are inputs and are used by the 8237A to address the control register to be loaded or read. In the Active cycle they are outputs and provide the lower 4 bits of the output address.
A4–A7	O	Address: The four most significant address lines are three-state outputs and provide 4 bits of address. These lines are enabled only during the DMA service.
HRQ	O	Hold Request: This is the Hold Request to the CPU and is used to request control of the system bus. If the corresponding mask bit is clear, the presence of any valid DREQ causes 8237A to issue the HRQ. After HRQ goes active at least one clock cycle (TCY) must occur before HLDA goes active.
DACK0–DACK3	O	DMA Acknowledge: DMA Acknowledge is used to notify the individual peripherals when one has been granted a DMA cycle. The sense of these lines is programmable. Reset initializes them to active low.
AEN	O	Address Enable: Address Enable enables the 8-bit latch containing the upper 8 address bits onto the system address bus. AEN can also be used to disable other system bus drivers during DMA transfers. AEN is active HIGH.
ADSTB	O	Address Strobe: The active high, Address Strobe is used to strobe the upper address byte into an external latch.
MEMR	O	Memory Read: The Memory Read signal is an active low three-state output used to access data from the selected memory location during a DMA Read or a memory-to-memory transfer.
MEMW	O	Memory Write: The Memory Write is an active low three-state output used to write data to the selected memory location during a DMA Write or a memory-to-memory transfer.

Figure 7.37 (b) (*Continued*)

functions. Before we begin a detailed study of this device, it would be wise to review the basic DMA concept.

DMA is an interfacing technique in which a special data transfer processor—the DMAC—takes over and controls the three buses of the microcomputer system. This is done by requesting a special *HOLD* state (called DMA REQUEST in Figs. 4.25 through 4.27) from the processor. The microprocessor acknowledges this request by asserting HLDA (hold acknowledge) and then tri-stating all of its system buses. These lines are then free to be controlled by the DMAC.

There is a problem in larger systems where all bus lines on the CPU module are buffered. Although the buffers "see" high impedances on their inputs (from the "tri-stated" microprocessor), they will (usually) convert this to logic 1 levels on their outputs, causing bus contention problems with the DMAC. For this reason, the CPU modules must include a signal (called $\overline{BUSEN}$ in Figs. 4.25 and 4.26) that will allow the bus buffers to be tri-stated. As shown in Figs. 4.25 and 4.26, driving $\overline{BUSEN}$ high disables all three system buses.

Figure 7.38 illustrates how the 8237A DMAC can be interfaced to any of the CPU modules presented in Chap. 4. Note that a high-order address latch is required. During the time when ADSTB is high and a DMA transfer is taking place, D0–D7 hold the high-order address bits. The falling edge of ADSTB latches this byte into the 74LS373 latch. For the remainder of the DMA transfer, D0–D7 function as a bidirectional data bus.

Sec. 7.5   The 8237 Programmable DMA Controller

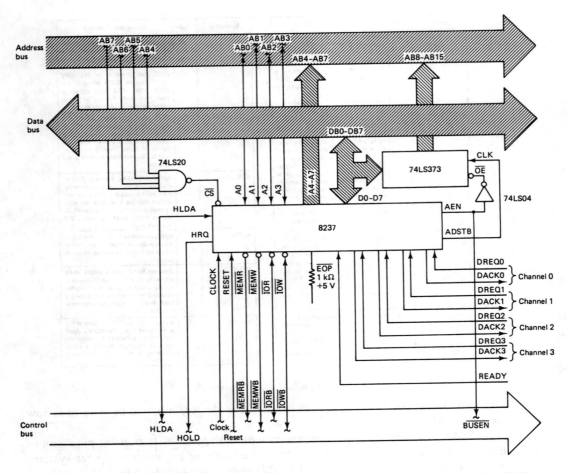

Figure 7.38 Interfacing the 8237A DMAC to the three-bus system architecture. Four DMA channels are provided.

Let's list the steps required for the 8237A in Fig. 7.38 to make a data transfer with a peripheral.

1. Before the transfer can take place, the DMAC must be programmed with the memory address, byte count, and type of transfer. In the case of the 8237A, the DMAC appears to be 16 consecutive I/O ports selected with A0–A3 and $\overline{\text{IOR}}$ and $\overline{\text{IOW}}$. Note that the device cannot be memory-mapped; $\overline{\text{MEMR}}$ and $\overline{\text{MEMW}}$ are output pins (for the DMAC) only.

2. A DMA transfer can now be requested on one of the four channels by a peripheral asserting DREQ.

3. If the 8237A is enabled and the active channel is not masked, the DMAC asserts HRQ, requesting a HOLD state from the CPU.

4. The CPU responds by completing the current machine cycle, tri-stating its buses, and then issuing HLDA.

5. The DMAC alerts the peripheral to this acknowledgment by outputting DACK to the peripheral. This signal is normally used to *chip select* the peripheral's data port.

6. The 8237A now outputs the high-order memory address on D0–D7 and raises AEN and ADSTB. This address represents the source or destination of the data transfer. AEN enables the tri-state outputs of the latch and is also used to disable the system buses via $\overline{\text{BUSEN}}$.

7. ADSTB then goes low, causing the high-order address to be latched. D0–D7 change to become the data bus and A0–A7 to the low-order address bus.

8. The DMAC is now in control of the buses and three types of data transfers are possible, as listed in Fig. 7.39. Highlighted in this figure is the transfer

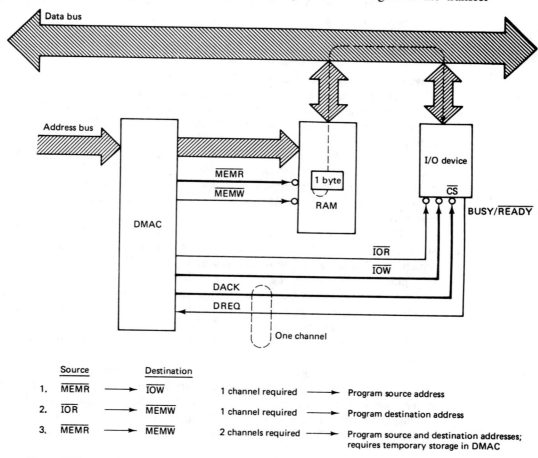

	Source	Destination		
1.	$\overline{\text{MEMR}}$	$\overline{\text{IOW}}$	1 channel required	Program source address
2.	$\overline{\text{IOR}}$	$\overline{\text{MEMW}}$	1 channel required	Program destination address
3.	$\overline{\text{MEMR}}$	$\overline{\text{MEMW}}$	2 channels required	Program source and destination addresses; requires temporary storage in DMAC

Figure 7.39 The 8237A can support three types of data transfers. The case highlighted is a transfer from memory to an I/O device. Note that $\overline{\text{MEMR}}$ and $\overline{\text{IOW}}$ are simultaneously low for this transfer.

of a data byte from memory to an I/O device. Note the unusual condition of the control bus—two signals are active simultaneously, $\overline{\text{MEMR}}$ and $\overline{\text{IOW}}$. Although this can never happen when the CPU is in control, it is the normal case when the DMAC is in control. Data read from the RAM is output directly to the I/O device; it does not go through the DMAC.

9. Only one channel of the 8237 is required for the transfer. In the special case of a memory-to-memory transfer, two channels are required; one is programmed with the source address (the 8237A requires channel 0) and the other with the destination address (channel 1 is required). In this case DREQ and DACK are not required.

10. Data is transferred between the RAM and I/O device (in Fig. 7.39) until the byte counter is zero (called *terminal count*). It is also possible to halt the transfer with an external EOP (end of process) input to the DMAC. In either case, HRQ and AEN are removed, relinquishing control of the system buses to the processor.

A timing diagram illustrating these same activities is presented in Fig. 7.40.

Response Time and Transfer Rate. As mentioned in Chap. 6, the CPU responds within one machine cycle of a HOLD request. This means that a maximum of six T states can elapse between the DMA request and the start of the DMA transfer. You might recall that using interrupts the 8080 and 8085 required 12–31 T states to respond to the request.

When a DMA transfer is to occur, the response time is usually not the main concern. This is because the DMA processor is dedicated to transferring large blocks of data—unlike interrupt-driven or polled I/O in which the processor must monitor a BUSY/$\overline{\text{READY}}$ flag and then quickly respond with a data byte before the next transaction is to occur.

The 8237A has two basic modes of operation, *idle* and *active*. In the idle state it can be programmed by the processor for an upcoming active state during which the DMA transfer will take place. Figure 7.41 illustrates the activities that take place during each of the six possible clock states.

After a DREQ occurs, the DMAC moves from state SI to S0 waiting for HLDA from the processor. In the S1 state the high-order address is output. Note that this address changes only once for every 256 data transfers. For this reason the 8237 automatically deletes state S1 except when the high-order address must change.

During S2 the low-order address is output and during S3 the control signals appear. The actual data transfer occurs during state S4. Assuming that the high-order address does not change, three clock states (S2, S3, and S4) will be required for one data transfer. The clock period ranges from 200 ns for the 8237A-5 to 320 ns for the 8237A. The transfer rate is thus found (for the 8237A-5) as

$$\frac{1}{3 \times 200 \text{ ns}} = \frac{1}{.6 \text{ } \mu\text{s}} = 1.6 \text{ MB/s}$$

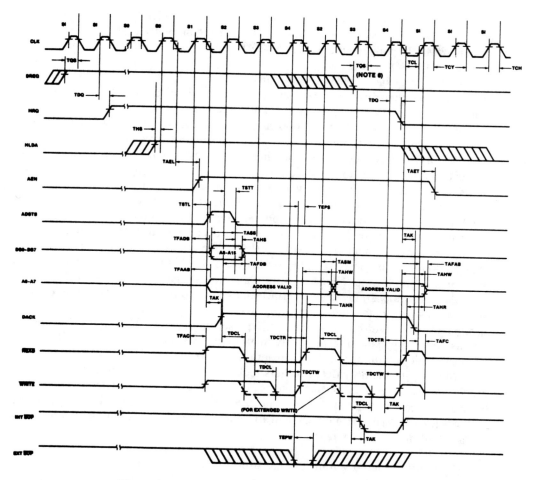

Figure 7.40 8237A DMA transfer timing. (Courtesy of Intel Corporation.)

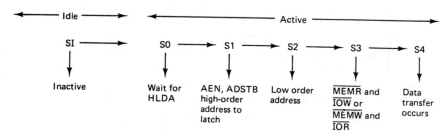

Figure 7.41 The 8237A has an idle and an active mode. When in the active mode, data transfers typically require only states S2, S3, and S4.

Sec. 7.5   The 8237 Programmable DMA Controller

369

In Chap. 6 we calculated the transfer rate for a 2-MHz 8080 using polling to be 32,787 bytes per second and 78,431 bytes per second with a 4-MHz Z-80. It's no wonder DMA is popular; the 8237A-5 has a transfer rate more than 20 times faster than the Z-80 polling rate!

Of course, the I/O device and memory must be able to keep up with the DMAC to achieve this high transfer rate. For semiconductor memory this is no problem. A memory read cycle (essentially the same as the address access time) consists of states S2–S4. This is 600 ns for the 8237A-5. But as we have seen in Chap. 5, memory access times of 600 ns are considered very slow.

The I/O device may be another matter, however. One of the most common applications of DMA is to interface a serial disk drive—a floppy disk or hard disk. A 5¼-inch double-density floppy disk will output (or require) a new data byte once every 32 μs—a very fast rate when polling is to be used, but very slow for a DMA transfer. To interface this peripheral, the READY input of the 8237A must be used. This line is pulled low by the floppy disk controller while it retrieves (or writes) a new byte of data. The DMAC's READY input is similar to the microprocessor's READY input and is sampled during state S3. If this input is found low, the three buses "mark time," holding valid data until READY again returns high.

Although the floppy disk interface does not require it, the 8237A is capable of an even faster data rate if *compressed timing* is used. In this mode state S3 is eliminated; it is used only to extend the pulse width of the $\overline{IOR}$ and $\overline{IOW}$ control signals, allowing data transfers only with states S2 and S4. This would require memory devices with access times of less than 400 ns for the 8237A-5.

Memory-to-memory data transfers require twice the time required for memory-to-I/O transfers. This is because one set of S states is required to read the data byte and another to write it; $\overline{MEMR}$ and $\overline{MEMW}$ cannot be allowed simultaneously low as they can with the memory and I/O control signals. In addition, a temporary register within the 8237A DMAC is required to save the data byte before the write cycle occurs.

Memory-to-memory transfers are useful when a large block of memory is to be transferred or when a block of memory is to be filled with a certain character.

Programming the 8237. Each channel of the 8237A has a 16-bit *current address register* and a 16-bit *current word register*. The current address register holds the memory address for the next DMA transfer. The current word register acts as a 16-bit down counter and is programmed with the total number of bytes to be transferred, less one. Terminal count occurs when this register rolls over from 0000 to FFFF.

Each of these registers is backed up by a *base address register* and *base word register* that contain the initial values when programmed. This allows an autoinitialize sequence to occur (if programmed) that rewrites the current address and current word registers when terminal count (or EOP) occurs.

Table 7.10 indicates the control signal codes required to access the registers for each channel. Note that the current address and word count registers can only be read, not written. Because the base address and word count are likely to require 16 bits, an internal flip-flop is used to gate these two bytes into the DMAC. In this way the first write to the base and current address register is interpreted as the

TABLE 7.10 ADDRESS REGISTER AND WORD COUNT REGISTER CONTROL CODES FOR THE 8237A DMAC

Channel	Register	Operation	$\overline{CS}$	$\overline{IOR}$	$\overline{IOW}$	A3	A2	A1	A0	Internal Flip-Flop	Data Bus DB0-DB7
0	Base and Current Address	Write	0	1	0	0	0	0	0	0	A0-A7
			0	1	0	0	0	0	0	1	A8-A15
	Current Address	Read	0	0	1	0	0	0	0	0	A0-A7
			0	0	1	0	0	0	0	1	A8-A15
	Base and Current Word Count	Write	0	1	0	0	0	0	1	0	W0-W7
			0	1	0	0	0	0	1	1	W8-W15
	Current Word Count	Read	0	0	1	0	0	0	1	0	W0-W7
			0	0	1	0	0	0	1	1	W8-W15
1	Base and Current Address	Write	0	1	0	0	0	1	0	0	A0-A7
			0	1	0	0	0	1	0	1	A8-A15
	Current Address	Read	0	0	1	0	0	1	0	0	A0-A7
			0	0	1	0	0	1	0	1	A8-A15
	Base and Current Word Count	Write	0	1	0	0	0	1	1	0	W0-W7
			0	1	0	0	0	1	1	1	W8-W15
	Current Word Count	Read	0	0	1	0	0	1	1	0	W0-W7
			0	0	1	0	0	1	1	1	W8-W15
2	Base and Current Address	Write	0	1	0	0	1	0	0	0	A0-A7
			0	1	0	0	1	0	0	1	A8-A15
	Current Address	Read	0	0	1	0	1	0	0	0	A0-A7
			0	0	1	0	1	0	0	1	A8-A15
	Base and Current Word Count	Write	0	1	0	0	1	0	1	0	W0-W7
			0	1	0	0	1	0	1	1	W8-W15
	Current Word Count	Read	0	0	1	0	1	0	1	0	W0-W7
			0	0	1	0	1	0	1	1	W8-W15
3	Base and Current Address	Write	0	1	0	0	1	1	0	0	A0-A7
			0	1	0	0	1	1	0	1	A8-A15
	Current Address	Read	0	0	1	0	1	1	0	0	A0-A7
			0	0	1	0	1	1	0	1	A8-A15
	Base and Current Word Count	Write	0	1	0	0	1	1	1	0	W0-W7
			0	1	0	0	1	1	1	1	W8-W15
	Current Word Count	Read	0	0	1	0	1	1	1	0	W0-W7
			0	0	1	0	1	1	1	1	W8-W15

Source: Courtesy of Intel Corporation.

low-order address and the second write as the high-order address. A similar arrangement is used with the word count register.

Example 7.17

Assume that channel 0 (the source) and channel 1 (the destination) of the DMAC interface in Fig. 7.38 are to be used for a memory-to-memory DMA transfer. Determine the port addresses for these two channels and write an 8080/85 initialization routine to load the address and word count registers if 100 bytes are to be transferred. Assume that the source address is 1000H and the destination address is F000H.

Solution. The 74LS20 connected to the $\overline{CS}$ input forces AB4–AB7 to be high to enable the 8237. Referring to Table 7.10 to select bits AB0–AB3, the following port addresses are found.

> *Port F0*: base and current address for channel 0
> *Port F1*: base and current word count for channel 0
> *Port F2*: base and current address for channel 1
> *Port F3*: base and current word count for channel 1

Sec. 7.5   The 8237 Programmable DMA Controller

The initialization program is as follows:

```
MVI   A,00      ;LSB SOURCE AND DESTINATION ADDRESS
OUT   0F0H      ;CHANNEL 0
OUT   0F2H      ;CHANNEL 1
MVI   A,10H     ;MSB SOURCE ADDRESS
OUT   0F0H      ;CHANNEL 0
MVI   A,0F0H    ;MSB DESTINATION ADDRESS
OUT   0F2H      ;CHANNEL 1
MVI   A,63H     ;LSB WORD COUNT LESS 1
OUT   0F3H      ;CHANNEL 1
MVI   A,00      ;MSB WORD COUNT
OUT   0F3H      ;CHANNEL 1
```

Note that you may intermix address and word count writes between the two channels. The first write will be interpreted as the LSB and the second write as the MSB. For memory-to-memory transfers it is necessary only to write the word count to channel 1.

The DMA *transfer mode* of the 8237 must also be programmed. There are four choices (modes 1 through 3 were flowcharted in Fig. 6.27):

1. *Single transfer*: A single byte is transferred, the word count is decremented, and the current address register incremented or decremented as programmed. DREQ must be held active until DACK is received. If DREQ is active throughout the transfer, control will be passed back to the microprocessor for one machine cycle before beginning the next transfer.

2. *Block transfer*: Data is transferred until TC (terminal count) or EOP occurs. DREQ must be held active until DACK occurs.

3. *Demand transfer*: Data is transferred as long as DREQ is active. When DREQ goes inactive, the current address and word count do not change, allowing the I/O device to resume the transfer where it left off. TC or EOP will terminate the transfer.

4. *Cascade mode*: In this mode one 8237A serves as a master and the other 8237As as slaves. This is shown in Fig. 7.42. Each of the slaves is programmed for one of the three transfer modes just listed. Each slave provides the memory address for the transfer, but the master prioritizes the HOLD requests from the slaves.

In addition to the four transfer modes listed, a *memory-to-memory* transfer mode can be specified, as illustrated in Ex. 7.17. This mode is limited to block transfers and channel 0 must be used for the source and channel 1 for the destination.

Four registers are used to program the transfer mode and select various operating features of the 8237A. Their bit descriptions are provided in Fig. 7.43. Each of these registers is *write-only*.

1. *Command register*: This register controls the operation of the 8237A. Note that the chip can be disabled by making bit D2 a 1. If rotating priority is selected, the last DREQ honored will be assigned the lowest priority.

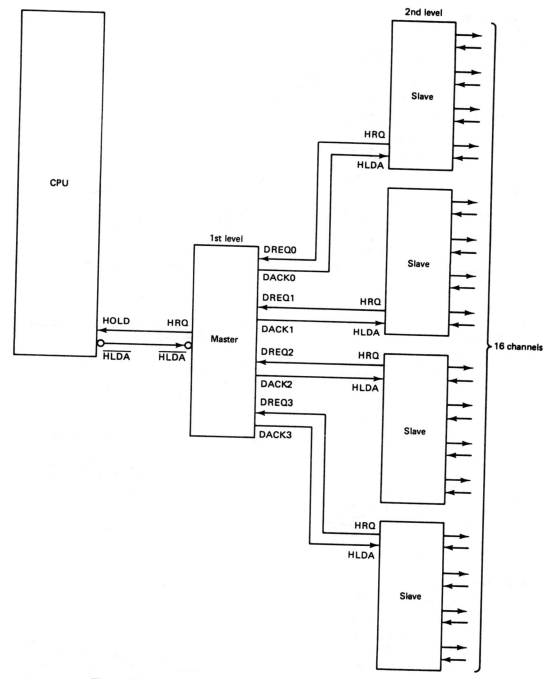

Figure 7.42 The cascade mode. All hold requests must be processed by the master.

Sec. 7.5   The 8237 Programmable DMA Controller

Command Register

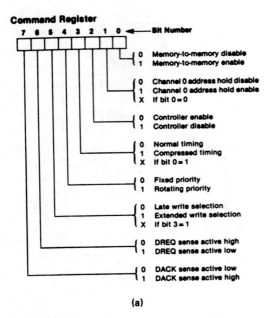

(a)

Mode Register

(b)

Request Register

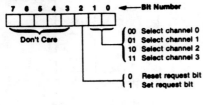

(c)

Mask Register

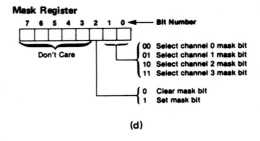

(d)

All four bits of the Mask register may also be written with a single command.

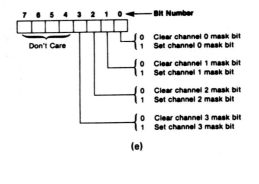

(e)

Figure 7.43 These four registers control the programming mode of the 8237A: (a) command register, (b) mode register, (c) request register, (d) and (e) mask register. (Courtesy of Intel Corporation.)

2. *Mode register*: The memory access portion of the DMA transfer may be programmed for a read, write, or verify operation. When programmed for verify transfers, the 8237 outputs addresses but not the control signals. The mode register is also used to program autoinitialization and address increment or decrement.

3. *Request register*: This register allows software to initiate the DMA transfer instead of DREQ. When programmed for memory-to-memory transfers, setting the request bit for channel 0 begins the transfer. Software requests are not maskable.

4. *Mask register*: This register is used to mask the DREQ for each channel. Clearing the mask bit enables that channel for DMA requests. Mask bits may be cleared individually or collectively as shown in Fig. 7.43(d).

Two registers are read-only. These are the status register shown in Fig. 7.44(a) and the temporary register shown in Fig. 7.44(b). The temporary register contains the last byte transferred during a memory-to-memory transfer.

Three ports of the 8237A are not really ports at all but use the *device select pulse* created by an OUT instruction.

1. *Clear first/last flip-flop*: This resets the internal flip-flop for ports 0–7 (see Table 7.10). The next memory access will therefore be the low-order byte for the memory address or word count.

2. *Master clear*: The 8237A enters the idle state with the command, status, request, and temporary registers and internal first/last flip-flop all reset and all mask register bits set.

3. *Clear mask register*: This command enables all four channels to accept DMA requests on their DREQ inputs by clearing all bits in the mask register.

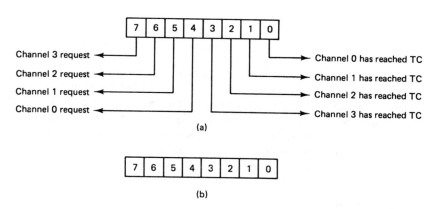

(a)

(b)

Figure 7.44 (a) The status register indicates (with a logic 1) which registers have reached TC and which channels have a pending DMA request. The bits are cleared upon reset and after a status read. (b) The temporary register holds data during a memory-to-memory DMA transfer. Reading this register reveals the last data byte transferred in the previous memory-to-memory transfer.

TABLE 7.11 PORT ADDRESSES OF THE 8237 DMAC

A3–A0	$\overline{\text{IOR}}$	$\overline{\text{IOW}}$	Function	
0	0	1	Read current address	
0	1	0	Write current address	Channel 0
1	0	1	Read current word count	
1	1	0	Write current word count	
2	0	1	Read current address	
2	1	0	Write current address	Channel 1
3	0	1	Read current word count	
3	1	0	Write current word count	
4	0	1	Read current address	
4	1	0	Write current address	Channel 2
5	0	1	Read current word count	
5	1	0	Write current word count	
6	0	1	Read current address	
6	1	0	Write current address	Channel 3
7	0	1	Read current word count	
7	1	0	Write current word count	
8	0	1	Read status register	
8	1	0	Write command register	
9	0	1	Illegal	
9	1	0	Write request register	
A	0	1	Illegal	
A	1	0	Write single mask register bit	
B	0	1	Illegal	
B	1	0	Write mode register	
C	0	1	Illegal	
C	1	0	Clear first/last flip-flop (DSP)	
D	0	1	Read temporary register	
D	1	0	Master clear (DSP)	
E	0	1	Illegal	
E	1	0	Clear mask register (DSP)	
F	0	1	Illegal	
F	1	0	Write all mask register bits	

Table 7.11 summarizes the possible read and write functions associated with each of the 16 (base) port addresses of the DMAC. Using the address decoder in Fig. 7.38, the 8237 requires I/O ports F0 through FF (ports FC, FD, and FE are controlled by device select pulses and do not actually transfer data).

Figure 7.45 flowcharts the steps required to initialize the 8237A and illustrates the action taken by the DMAC once programmed. Note that it might be wise to disable the DMAC until initialization is complete if a DREQ could be received during this time.

Example 7.18

In Ex. 7.17 the initialization program required to program the word count and address registers for a 100 byte memory-to-memory transfer was written. Using this as a base, write the complete initialization software required to fill 100 bytes of RAM beginning at address F000H with the data byte stored at 1000H.

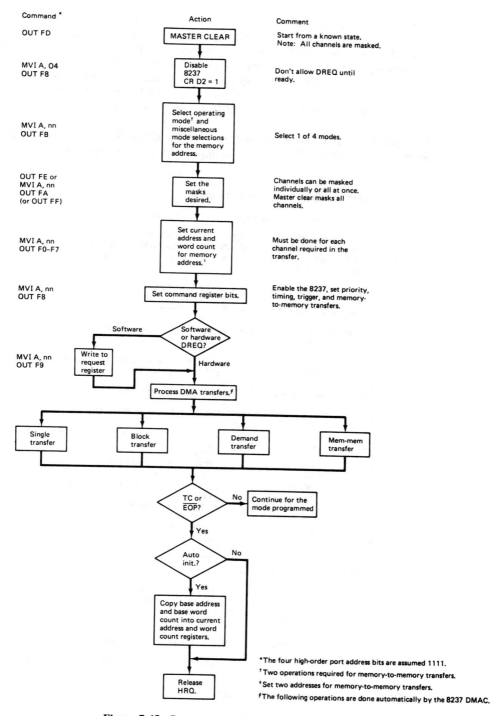

Command *	Action	Comment
OUT FD	MASTER CLEAR	Start from a known state. Note: All channels are masked.
MVI A, O4 OUT F8	Disable 8237 CR D2 = 1	Don't allow DREQ until ready.
MVI A, nn OUT FB	Select operating mode† and miscellaneous mode selections for the memory address.	Select 1 of 4 modes.
OUT FE or MVI A, nn OUT FA (or OUT FF)	Set the masks desired.	Channels can be masked individually or all at once. Master clear masks all channels.
MVI A, nn OUT F0–F7	Set current address and word count for memory address. ‡	Must be done for each channel required in the transfer.
MVI A, nn OUT F8	Set command register bits.	Enable the 8237, set priority, timing, trigger, and memory- to-memory transfers.
MVI A, nn OUT F9	Software or hardware DREQ?	

Software → Write to request register

Hardware → Process DMA transfers.ƒ

- Single transfer
- Block transfer
- Demand transfer
- Mem-mem transfer

TC or EOP? — No → Continue for the mode programmed

Yes ↓

Auto init.? — No →

Yes ↓

Copy base address and base word count into current address and word count registers.

Release HRQ.

*The four high-order port address bits are assumed 1111.

†Two operations required for memory-to-memory transfers.

‡Set two addresses for memory-to-memory transfers.

ƒThe following operations are done automatically by the 8237 DMAC.

Figure 7.45 Programmer's flowchart for the 8237A DMAC.

Sec. 7.5   The 8237 Programmable DMA Controller

Solution. The program is given in Fig. 7.46. Following a master clear, channel 1 is specified as the write mode register and programmed for autoinitialization and a block transfer with the address incrementing. Next the source, destination, and word count registers are written using the code from Ex. 7.17. The command register is then written specifying a memory-to-memory transfer but holding the source address constant (thus writing the same byte with each transfer). The transfer request is initiated by writing a 1 to bit 2 of the request register selecting channel 0.

A Design Example: Interfacing a Floppy Disk Drive.   Probably the most common application for DMA in a microcomputer system is a floppy disk drive interface.

```
;8237 MEMORY-TO-MEMORY TRANSFER ROUTINE
;
;THE HARDWARE IS SHOWN IN FIG. 7-38
;
;THIS PROGRAM WILL FILL THE 100 BYTES OF RAM
;BEGINING AT ADDRESS FOOOH WITH THE DATA BYTE
;STORED AT ADDRESS 1000H.  IT FOLLOWS THE FLOW
;CHART IN FIG. 7-45.
;
OUT        OFDH                 ;MASTER CLEAR
;
;SKIP THE DISABLE - NO OTHER DREQS ARE INVOLVED.
;
;PROGRAM CHANNEL 1 FOR WRITE MODE, AUTOINITIALIZATION,
;ADDRESS INCREMENT, BLOCK TRANSFER
;
MVI        A,95H                ;CHANNEL 1 OPERATING MODE
OUT        OFBH                 ;MODE REGISTER
;
;NO MASKS ARE REQUIRED (FOR SOFTWARE DMA REQUEST)
;
;PROGRAM THE SOURCE AND DESTINATION ADDRESSES
;
MVI        A,00                 ;LSB SOURCE AND DESTINATION ADD
OUT        OFOH                 ;CHANNEL O
OUT        OF2H                 ;CHANNEL 1
MVI        A,10H                ;MSB SOURCE ADDRESS
OUT        OFOH                 ;CHANNEL O
MVI        A,OFOH               ;MSB DESTINATION ADDRESS
OUT        OF2H                 ;CHANNEL 1
MVI        A,63H                ;LSB WORD COUNT LESS 1
OUT        OF3H                 ;CHANNEL 1
MVI        A,00                 ;MSB WORD COUNT
OUT        OF3H                 ;CHANNEL 1
;
;NOW PROGRAM COMMAND REGISTER FOR MEMORY-TO-MEMORY
;TRANSFER WITH ADDRESS HOLD FOR CHANNEL O
;
MVI        A,03                 ;CONTROL WORD
OUT        OF8H                 ;COMMAND REGISTER
;
;INITIALIZATION IS COMPLETE
;
;WRITE TO REQUEST REGISTER TO BEGIN TRANSFER
;
MVI        A,04                 ;SET REQUEST BIT FOR CHANNEL O
OUT        OF9H                 ;BEGIN THE TRANSFER
;
;DMA TRANSFER NOW OCCURS
```

Figure 7.46   DMA control program for the 8237A DMAC in Ex. 7.18.

This is because the floppy disk requires large blocks of data to be read or written at relatively high speed—a good match for the DMA controller.

Figure 7.47 is a diagram of an interface between the 8237A DMAC and the Western Digital WD2793 floppy disk controller (FDC).

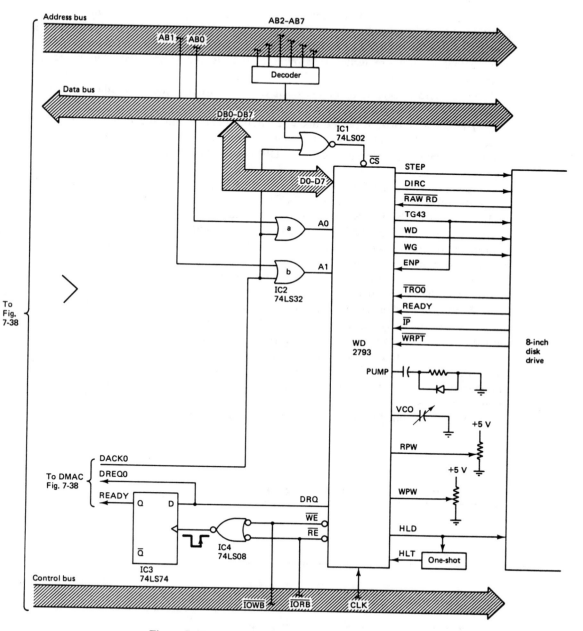

Figure 7.47 Interfacing a floppy disk controller (FDC) using DMA.

Similar to the other programmable controllers we have studied in this chapter, the WD2793 appears as four I/O or memory locations selected by A0 and A1 when its chip select input is low. Data is transferred to or from the FDC when A1 A0 = 11. The other three combinations of A0 and A1 select control functions and allow status to be read.

After programming is complete, the FDC is ready to transfer data with the 8237A DMAC. Typically, the control program will request a disk operation by writing to one of the three low port addresses of the FDC. As an example, let's assume that we wish to write 1024 bytes of data to the floppy disk. Upon receipt of the write sector command, the FDC loads the head (the head contacts the media), and the ID field is searched for the correct track number, sector number, and side number.

The correct position on the diskette having been found, the FDC asserts DRQ (data request). This signal indicates that the data register is empty and ready for one byte of data. Referring to Fig. 7.47, DRQ requests a DMA transfer from channel 0 of the 8237A.

Assuming that the DMAC has been properly programmed, DACK0 acknowledges the request, chip-selects the FDC, and accesses the data port of the WD2793 (A1 A0 = 11). The DMAC now fetches a data byte from its current address and transfers it directly to the FDC on D0–D7. The address is then incremented or decremented and the word counter decremented. If TC does not occur, the DMAC prepares to transfer another byte.

With four states per transfer and 200 ns per state, the entire operation requires 0.8 μs. But the floppy disk is not ready for the next byte for at least 32 μs (assuming a 5¼-inch double-density drive). For this reason the *READY* input of the DMAC must be controlled by the FDC to insert WAIT states until the next data byte can be read. This is the purpose of the D flip-flop in Fig. 7.47.

The timing diagram in Fig. 7.48 will help explain. When DRQ first goes high, the DMA request is passed on to the CPU. We will assume that the block transfer mode has been programmed and thus the full sector of data will have to be written before the microprocessor is again given control of its buses. The falling edge of $\overline{IOW}$ output by the DMAC resets DRQ and the disk drive writes the data

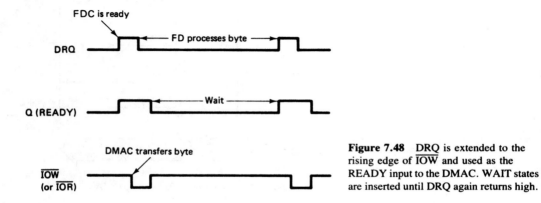

Figure 7.48 DRQ is extended to the rising edge of $\overline{IOW}$ and used as the READY input to the DMAC. WAIT states are inserted until DRQ again returns high.

byte (requiring 32 μs). The flip-flop is used to extend DRQ beyond the end of $\overline{\text{IOW}}$, preventing a WAIT-state request until the data byte has been transferred.

The rising edge of $\overline{\text{IOW}}$ (or $\overline{\text{IOR}}$ for a read operation) enables the flip-flop (which now follows DRQ) and a logic 0 is applied to the READY input of the DMAC. The DMAC samples this input during S3 and inserts WAIT states until READY again goes high. This occurs when the data byte has been written and the data register is again empty (DRQ = 1).

Although using the DMAC's READY input is an effective way of synchronizing the disk drive to the DMAC for block mode transfers, this technique may not always be the best choice. Assuming 0.8 μs for the data transfer and a worst-case response time to the DMA request of 3.5 μs (7 T states with a 2-MHz clock), 27.7 μs remains until the next DRQ pulse from the disk drive. If byte mode (instead of block mode) transfers are programmed, one or two CPU instructions can be

```
;INITIALIZATION ROUTINE FOR THE FDC IN FIG. 7-47
;
;THIS ROUTINE WILL WRITE 1K BYTES TO THE DISK WHEN
;THE FDC DRQ OUTPUT GOES HIGH.
;
;THE PROGRAM FOLLOWS THE FLOW CHART IN FIG. 7-45
;
OUT     OFDH             ;MASTER CLEAR
MVI     A,04             ;DISABLE DMAC UNTIL PROGRAMMED
OUT     OF8H             ;COMMAND REGISTER
;
;PROGRAM MODE REGISTER FOR CHANNEL 0, READ MODE,
;AUTOINITIALIZATION, ADDRESS INCREMENT, BLOCK MODE
;
MVI     A,98H            ;MODE WORD CHANNEL 0
OUT     OFBH             ;MODE REGISTER
;
;UNMASK CHANNEL 0 (AFTER MASTER CLEAR)
;
MVI     A,0              ;CLEAR CHANNEL 0 MASK
OUT     OFAH             ;MASK REGISTER
;
;PROGRAM CHANNEL 0 MEMORY ADDRESS AND WORD COUNT
;
MVI     A,0              ;LOW ORDER ADDRESS
OUT     OFOH             ;CHANNEL 0
MVI     A,80H            ;HIGH ORDER ADDRESS
OUT     OFOH             ;CHANNEL 0
MVI     A,OFFH           ;LOW ORDER WORD COUNT
OUT     OF1H             ;CHANNEL 0
MVI     A,3FH            ;HIGH ORDER WORD COUNT
OUT     OF1H             ;CHANNEL 0
;
;PROGRAM COMMAND REGISTER FOR DREQ AND DACK
;SENSE, LATE WRITE, FIXED PRIORITY, NORMAL TIMING,
;AND ENABLE CONTROLLER
;
MVI     A,80H            ;COMMAND WORD
OUT     OF8H             ;COMMAND REGISTER
;
;NORMALLY THE MICROPROCESSOR WOULD NOW SEND A "WRITE
;SECTOR" COMMAND TO THE FDC AND IT WOULD RESPOND BY
;RAISING DRQ INITIATIING THE 1K BYTE TRANSFER.
```

Figure 7.49   Initialization routine for Ex. 7.19.

performed during this "WAIT" time. This would be a more efficient use of the resources of the processor.

Example 7.19

Write the initialization routine required to transfer 1K of data from address 8000H to the disk drive interface in Fig. 7.47.

Solution. Following the steps outlined in the flowchart in Fig. 7.45, a master clear is given and then the mode register programmed for channel 0 select, autoinitialize, block mode, and write transfers. The address and word count registers are programmed next. After clearing the mask bit for channel 0, the command register programs the sense of DREQ and DACK to match the WD2793 and initialization is complete. The program is given in Fig. 7.49.

7.6 PERIPHERAL CONTROLLER BUS BUFFERING TECHNIQUES

As you read this section, look for the answer to this Key Concept question:

7.6.1. Why must the address and control bus buffers connected to a DMAC be bidirectional?

When interfacing any of the family support devices to the microprocessor, special buffering considerations must be taken. In Chap. 6, bus buffering for input and output ports was shown to be straightforward. See, for example, Fig. 6.2 for an input port. In this circuit the data bus buffer is the input port and is therefore obtained for "free."

In Fig. 6.4 an output port is illustrated. In this case the data bus is buffered into the latch. In both circuits the control and address bus buffers can be permanently enabled. Also note that the data bus buffers are unidirectional. Data either flows into or out of the port.

The family support devices we have discussed are all programmable and therefore by their very nature require a bidirectional data bus buffer. Although this is not hard to implement, we must consider one other problem. If a DMA controller is to be interfaced, the control and data bus lines must also be bidirectional. This is because during DMA the DMAC will be controlling all three system buses.

Figure 7.50 illustrates the bus buffering required to a general I/O module that includes a DMA controller. Bidirectional bus buffers are used on all three sets of bus lines. They are enabled by the signal $\overline{\text{MODULE SELECT} + \text{DMA}}$. This signal is obtained from an address decoder and the DMA acknowledge signal. It will go low when any support device in this module is selected or whenever a DMA operation is occurring.

The direction of the data bus buffer is controlled by $\overline{\text{DMA WRITE} + \text{CPU}}$ $\overline{\text{READ}}$. This signal is active whenever the CPU performs a read operation or when

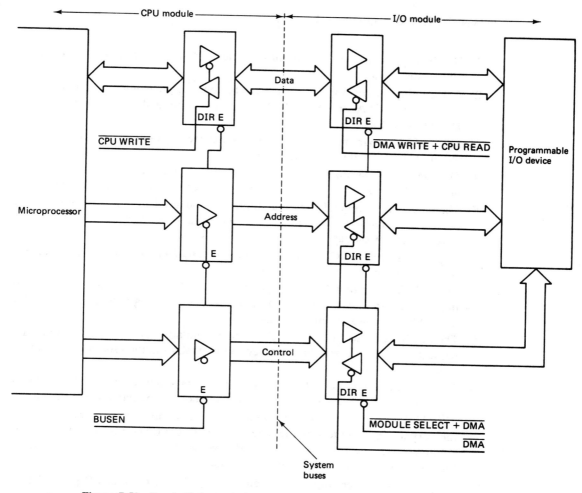

Figure 7.50 Bus buffering techniques for a general peripheral controller I/O module that includes a DMAC.

the DMAC is performing a write operation. If inactive, the buffers default to the write mode, presenting their inputs to the system data bus lines.

The last control signal is $\overline{\text{DMA}}$. This signal is active for DMA read or write cycles and is used to turn the control and address bus lines around (that is, make them outputs onto the bus) when DMA cycles are performed.

Of course, when DMA is not implemented, the control and address buffers can be unidirectional and left permanently enabled. In small systems, no buffering is required and the control, address, and data bus lines can be connected directly to the CPU. In this case, the CPU and DMAC will control the direction of the bus lines "automatically." Chapter 4 provides guidelines for determining what is considered a "small system."

CHAPTER SUMMARY

1. Nearly all microprocessor families are supported with special programmable interfacing devices.

2. A three-chip microcomputer system can be constructed using the 8085 microprocessor, the 8755A 2K-byte ROM with bit-programmable I/O, and the 8185 1K-byte RAM.

3. The 8255A programmable peripheral interface contains all of the circuitry required for three input or output ports.

4. The 8255A can be programmed for simple I/O, strobed I/O with full handshaking, or bidirectional I/O. Polled or interrupt driven techniques are both supported.

5. The 8254 programmable interval timer can be used as an event counter, a one shot, a divide-by-N counter, or a hardware- or software-initiated strobe pulse generator on each of three separate channels.

6. Applications for the 8254 include baud rate generator, real-time clock, square-wave generator, and frequency counter.

7. The 8259A programmable interrupt controller is designed to enhance the limited interrupt capabilities of the 8080 microprocessor and as a support device for the 8088 and 8086 16-bit microprocessors.

8. The 8259A uses the processor's INTR input and allows as many as 64 interrupt requests to be prioritized and vectored to jump tables in the processor's memory space.

9. The 8237A programmable DMA controller supports four separate DMA channels for memory-to-I/O, I/O-to-memory, and memory-to-memory DMA transfers.

10. The 8237A automatically takes care of incrementing (or decrementing) the memory address and testing the byte counter for the DMA transfer. This makes it attractive for interfacing high-speed peripherals such as floppy disk drives that are too fast for interrupt-driven techniques.

11. Peripheral controller chips require bus buffers similar to other I/O ports. However, when a DMA controller must be buffered all three buses require bidirectional buffers.

LAB PROJECTS

7.1. Study the schematic diagram of the microcomputer you are using to support this text/course and see if your computer uses an 8255 PPI. If so, answer the following questions about the interface.

(a) Is the PPI I/O- or memory-mapped?

(b) To what range of addresses is the chip mapped?

(c) List the I/O devices (if any) connected to ports A, B, and C.

7.2. Write a program to access your computer's 8255. For example, if a keypad and display are interfaced, write a program to read the keyboard and display the key's value. If a speaker is connected to one output bit, write a program to produce a tone (Program 14 in Chap. 3 provides an example of a computer music program).

7.3. Using Fig. 7.51 as a guide, build the memory-mapped 8255A interface shown. Probs. 7.12–15 suggest several control programs that can be written.

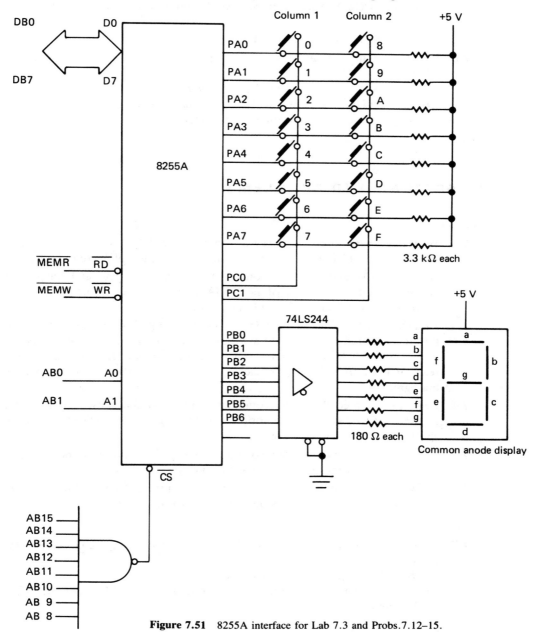

Figure 7.51 8255A interface for Lab 7.3 and Probs.7.12–15.

7.4. Construct the mode 0 8255A parallel-printer interface shown in Fig. 7.10. The program in Fig. 7.11 can be used to send (ASCII) data to the printer. By programming the 8255A for mode 1 and connecting INTRA to INTR of the CPU, the same interface can be used to control the printer in an interrupt-driven mode. This is shown in Fig. 7.16. A female DB-25 connector with long wires attached can be used to allow easy access to the printer signals.

7.5. Repeat Lab 7.1 for the 8254 PIT.

7.6. Using a circuit similar to Fig. 7.23, program one of the outputs of the 8254:

    (a) as a one-shot triggered by the gate input.

    (b) as a divide-by-N counter. Use a signal grenerator as the CLK input and observe the output on an oscilloscope.

QUESTIONS AND PROBLEMS

Section 7.1

    7.1. Write the instructions necessary to program the 8755A in Fig. 7.2 so that PA0–PA4 and PB0–PB6 are inputs and the remaining pins are outputs.

    7.2. Assume IO/$\overline{\text{M}}$ and A10 are combined via an AND gate and the output connected to the IO/$\overline{\text{M}}$ input of the 8755A in Fig. 7.2. Determine the resulting addresses of the four 8755A I/O ports.

    7.3. Assume that the three-chip 8085 computer in Fig. 7.4 has been built and that it is desired to test the two 8755A ports. Assuming the two ports are wired in parallel, devise a test program that outputs data to port A and reads it back from port B, branching to an error routine if the data does not agree.

    7.4. Refer to the three-chip 8085 computer in Fig. 7.4 and show how to add a matrix of 16 key switches memory mapped to page FF of the 8085's memory space. (*Hint*: Review Fig. 6.8.)

    7.5. Refer to the three-chip 8085 computer in Fig. 7.4 and show how to add two decoded seven-segment displays to port B.

    7.6. Draw a memory and I/O map for the 8085 computer in Fig. 7.4 including the keypad and LED displays described in Probs. 7.4 and 7.5.

Section 7.2

    7.7. Determine the control byte required for each of the following 8255A configurations.

    (a) Set PC5 using the bit set/reset mode.

    (b) Mode 0: port A = input, port B = output, PC7–PC4 = output, PC3–PC0 = input.

(c) Port A = mode 1 output, port B = mode 1 input, PC4 and PC5 = inputs.

(d) Port A is bidirectional, port B = mode 0 output, PC0–2 = inputs.

7.8. The following program is written to control the 8255A in Fig. 7.6. What does this program do?

```
SET    MVI    A,07H
       OUT    0F3H
       CALL   WAIT        ;0.5 ms time delay
       MVI    A,06H
       OUT    0F3H
       CALL   WAIT        ;0.5 ms delay
       JMP    SET
```

*7.9. A technician is testing the 8255A interface in Fig. 7.6 and has wired ports A and B in parallel. The test program in Fig. 7.52 is run but constantly jumps to the error routine. What do you think is wrong?

7.10. Answer the following questions about the 8255A keyboard interface and control program in Figs. 7.8 and 7.9.

(a) To read only column 1, PC6 must be _____ and PC7 must be _____ .

(b) If only key 6 is held down, what is the value of register A after the KREAD subroutine returns?

(c) If keys 4, 7, and 8 are all held down simultaneously, which key value will be encoded?

7.11. Explain how the parallel printer interface in Fig. 7.10 generates the printer STROBE pulse without using a one-shot.

7.12. Refer to the 8255A interface in Fig. 7.51 for the following questions.

(a) Specify the value of the required control byte.

```
       MVI    A,82H    ;A = output and B = input

       OUT    F2H      ;port C

       MVI    A,0      ;starting pattern

LOOP   MOV    B,A      ;save in B

       OUT    FOH      ;output to A

       IN     F1H      ;read back on B

       CMP    B        ;same ?

       JNZ    ERROR    ;if not then error

       INR    A        ;next pattern

       JNZ    LOOP     ;done?

       RET
```

Figure 7.52   8255A test program for Prob. 7.9.

(b) Is the PPI memory- or I/O-mapped?

(c) Specify the range of port addresses to which the PPI chip will respond.

(d) To read any of the keys 0–7, PC0 must be _____ and PC1 must be _____.

(e) What hex byte must be output to port B to cause the number 5 to appear in the seven-segment display?

7.13. Write a subroutine to read the key matrix in Fig. 7.51 and return with the key value (0–F) in register A bits 0–3.

7.14. Write a subroutine that reads the low four bits of the accumulator and displays the results as a hex number in the seven-segment display shown in Fig. 7.51. (*Hint*: Use A as the index into a 16-byte seven-segment code table.)

7.15. Combine the two subroutines from Probs. 7.13 and 7.14 to write a program that reads the key matrix and displays the last key pressed in the display.

7.16. Answer the following questions about the 8255A interrupt-driven printer interface in Fig. 7.16.

(a) How does the printer know when data is available to be read?

(b) What signal causes the $\overline{\text{STROBE}}$ pulse to terminate?

(c) How does the CPU know when to write another byte of data to the 8255A?

Section 7.3

7.17. Specify the 8254 control words required to:

(a) program counter 1 for mode 5, BCD, 16-bit count.

(b) latch the status of counter 0.

(c) latch the count of counters 0 and 1.

7.18. The following questions refer to the 8254 time-delay subroutine in Fig. 7.53. Assume the port addresses in Fig. 7.23.

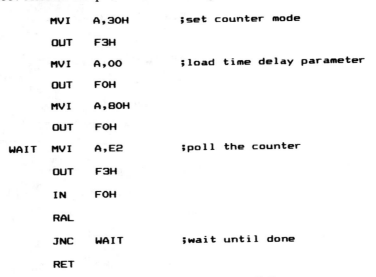

```
        MVI     A,30H       ;set counter mode

        OUT     F3H

        MVI     A,00        ;load time delay parameter

        OUT     F0H

        MVI     A,80H

        OUT     F0H

WAIT    MVI     A,E2        ;poll the counter

        OUT     F3H

        IN      F0H

        RAL

        JNC     WAIT        ;wait until done

        RET
```

Figure 7.53 Program for Prob. 7.18.

(a) Which of the 8254 counters is being used?

(b) What is the counter mode?

(c) Why is it necessary to *poll* the counter?

(d) If the clock input is 2 MHz, what is the time delay produced by this program?

7.19. What changes are needed in the frequency counter program in Fig. 7.27 to allow a maximum frequency of 99,990 Hz with 10-Hz resolution?

7.20. Assume the CLK2 input of the 8254 in Fig. 7.23 is connected to the 2-MHz system clock signal. Write the program required to produce a 1-KHz 50% duty-cycle square wave at OUT2. Assume GATE2 is wired high.

7.21. Study the 8254 interface in Fig. 7.54. Specify the port addresses of the three counters and control port.

7.22. Assume that counter 0 of the 8254 in Fig. 7.54 is to be used as a hardware triggered one-shot. Design the hardware and write the software to produce a 10-s pulse. Assume a 2-MHz system clock as the time base. (*Hint:* Use counter 1 to frequency divide the 2-MHz signal for counter 0.)

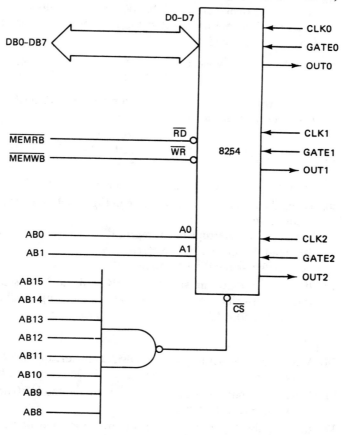

Figure 7.54 Circuit for Probs. 7.21 and 7.22.

7.23. Design the hardware and write the software to convert the 8254 into a digital stopwatch with .01-s resolution. Your design should provide a run/stop switch and accumulate times to 99.99 s.

Section 7.4

7.24. Assume a PIC is servicing an interrupt on IR5 while programmed for the *fully nested mode.* If an interrupt occurs on IR6, will the IR5 service routine be interrupted? Does the 8085 allow lower priority interrupts to interrupt higher priority service routines in progress?

7.25. Write the initialization routine to program the PIC in Fig. 7.29 for the following.
 (a) Jump table on page 8000H
 (b) Four-byte interval
 (c) Rising edge-trigger
 (d) Interrupts 0 and 1 masked
 (e) Rotating equal priority

7.26. Assume the PIC described in Prob. 7.25 currently has the interrupt priority structure shown below. If the IR3 service routine is in progress, can IR5 interrupt this routine? Sketch the new priority structure after IR3 and IR5 have been serviced.

lowest   highest

4   3   2   1   0   7   6   5   4

7.27. An interrupt service routine written for the PIC in Fig. 7.29 ends with the instruction sequence:

```
MVI   A,E2H
OUT   F0H
RET
```

How does the PIC interpret these instructions?

7.28. Using the port assignments shown in Fig. 7.29, write the instruction sequences required to:
 (a) read the interrupt mask register.
 (b) read the in-service register.
 (c) set the special mask mode.

7.29. If 8 interrupts occur simultaneously and the PIC is programmed for equal rotating priority, in the worst case, how long might one device have to wait for service?

Section 7.5

7.30. When doing a memory-to-I/O DMA transfer, the 8237A will simultaneously activate the _____ and _____ control bus signals.

7.31. What is the purpose of the $\overline{\text{BUSEN}}$ signal in the 8080 and 8085 CPU modules shown in Figs. 4.25 and 4.26?

7.32. Indicate the logic level (high or low) for each of the signals listed below for idle and active 8237A modes.

Signal	Idle mode	Active mode
HRQ		
HLDA		
AEN		
DREQn		
DACKn		
ADSTB		

7.33. One channel of the 8237 is required for I/O-to-memory and memory-to-I/O DMA transfers. However, memory-to-memory DMA transfers require two channels. Explain.

7.34. Calculate the time to fill 100 bytes of RAM using the DMA interface in Fig. 7.38 and the control program in Fig. 7.46. Assume noncompressed timing and a 200-ns 8237A clock period. Compare the time against the 8080/85 block-fill program—Fig. 3.13, Program 7. Assume a 2-MHz 8080 or 3-MHz 8085 CPU.

7.35. What byte should be written to the 8237A mode register if it is desired to transfer 16K bytes of data from memory to a disk drive using channel 2? Enable autoinitialization and select address increment.

Section 7.6

7.36. Figure 7.55 shows an 8255A interface with a bidirectional data bus buffer.

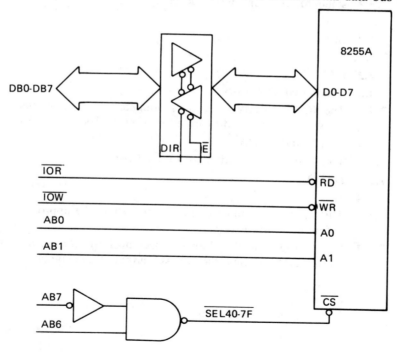

Figure 7.55 Circuit for Prob. 7.36.

What signals should be connected to DIR and $\overline{E}$ to properly control this buffer?

*7.37. A technician designing the 8255A interface in Fig. 7.55 connects $\overline{E}$ to ground and DIR to $\overline{IOR}$. He finds that the computer appears to power-on properly, but the keyboard now produces "odd" characters. What do you think is wrong?

KEY CONCEPT ANSWERS

7.1.1. 2K, 2

7.1.2. 0FH

7.2.1. 3, 1

7.2.2. bit 7 (1 → mode set, 0 → bit set/reset)

7.2.3. mode 1

7.2.4. Set or reset individual bits of port C, mask or enable interrupts on the mode 1 and 2 INTR outputs.

7.2.5. bidirectional

7.3.1. 3

7.3.2. standard, counter latch, read-back

7.3.3. mode 3

7.3.4. BCD

7.4.1. 8

7.4.2. CALL

7.4.3. rotating equal priority

7.4.4. The ICWs specify hardware parameters: vector address and trigger. The OCWs specify the software arbitration modes and masks.

7.5.1. HOLD and HLDA

7.5.2. To avoid bus contention with the DMAC.

7.5.3. DREQ

7.5.4. 16

7.5.5. This information must be programmed into the appropriate DMAC registers before the transfer begins.

7.6.1. When programmed, address and control signals are output to the DMAC. During DMA cycles, the DMAC outputs these signals.

8

Special-Purpose
Support Devices:
The Z-80 Family

The Z-80 microprocessor is supported by a number of special interfacing devices, as indicated in Table 8.1. These parts are designed to reduce the burden on the Z-80 in typical I/O interfaces. For example, the Z-80 PIO has two 8-bit I/O ports that can be programmed for any combination of input and output pins. Each port is also supported by two handshaking signals that simplify the task of synchronizing the microprocessor to the (usually) slower-speed peripheral.

The most powerful feature of the peripheral controllers is that they are *programmable* by the CPU. By writing to special control ports within the device, the "personality" of the part can be changed "on the fly." They also support the Z-80 "daisy-chain" priority structure and can be programmed to output any desired vector during $\overline{INTA}$.

Because the Z-80 CPU module can be made to look exactly like an 8080, all of the 8080 support devices covered in Chap. 7 can be interfaced to the Z-80. This includes the 8255A, 8254, 8259A, and 8237A. Of these, the 8255A programmable peripheral interface or PPI would be the most useful. It is similar to the Z-80 PIO but offers three I/O ports. The 8259A programmable interrupt controller can be interfaced to the Z-80, but it would not be logical. This is because the Z-80 processor already has similar interrupt capabilities.

The 8085 support devices covered in Chap. 7 cannot be interfaced to the Z-80 without considerable external logic. This is due to the multiplexed data bus of the 8085.

The Z-80 support devices to be discussed in this chapter include the Z-80 PIO, the Z-80 CTC, and the Z-80 DMA. These parts require decoding of $\overline{IORQ}$, $\overline{RD}$, and $\overline{M1}$ to generate $\overline{IOR}$, $\overline{IOW}$, $\overline{RESET}$, and $\overline{INTA}$. For this reason they are

TABLE 8.1 I/O SUPPORT DEVICES FOR THE Z-80
MICROPROCESSOR

Part number	Description
Z8410	DMA, direct memory access controller
Z8420	PIO, programmable input/output controller
Z8430	CTC, counter/timer circuit
Z8440	SIO, serial input/output controller
Z8470	DART, dual asynchronous receiver/transmitter
Z8530	SCC, serial communications controller
Z8531	ASCC, asynchronous serial communications controller
Z8536	CIO, counter/timer and parallel I/O unit

not compatible with the 8080 or 8085. In addition, they take advantage of the Z-80's mode 2 interrupts not supported by the 8080 or 8085.

8.1 THE Z8420 PARALLEL INPUT/OUTPUT CONTROLLER

As you read this section, look for the answers to these Key Concept questions:

8.1.1. The daisy-chain priority structure used by Z-80 peripherals requires that output IEO be connected to the IEI input of the next _____ priority peripheral.

8.1.2. The PIO can be programmed to generate an interrupt based on a logical _____ or _____ condition of the unmasked mode 3 input bits.

8.1.3. When the PIO is operated in mode 0 or mode 1, what signal is used by the peripheral to indicate that output data has been accepted or input data written?

8.1.4. What is the advantage of using a multiplexed LED display?

The Z8420 (usually called the Z-80 PIO) provides two 8-bit input/output ports each supported by two handshaking signals, labeled $\overline{\text{STB}}$ (strobe) and RDY (ready). The four operating modes of the PIO are defined and compared with the operating modes of the 8255A in Table 8.2. The two parts are comparable except for the

TABLE 8.2 OPERATING MODES OF THE Z-80 PIO

Mode	Function	8255A mode
0	8-bit output port with two handshaking signals	1
1	8-bit input port with two handshaking signals	1
2	Bidirectional data port with four handshaking signals[a]	2
3	Bit programmable input/output port	None[b]

[a] Port A is the bidirectional port; port B must be programmed for mode 3.
[b] Similar to 8255A mode 0, but each PIO pin can be individually programmed.

PIO having a bit-programmable mode not supported by the 8255A. The 8255A also has three I/O ports compared to the PIO's two.

Figure 8.1 provides a pinout diagram for the PIO. Note that three pins are devoted to interrupt control: $\overline{INT}$, interrupt enable in (IEI), and interrupt enable out (IEO). $\overline{INT}$ connects directly to the $\overline{INT}$ input of the Z-80 and IEI and IEO are used when several PIOs (or other support devices) are connected in a daisy-chain priority interrupt structure. When using this feature the PIO must be programmed for a (Z-80) mode 2 interrupt vector.

Interfacing the Z-80 PIO. Figure 8.2 illustrates an interface between the Z-80 microprocessor and the Z-80 PIO. You should note that the PIO is directly compatible with the Z-80 control signals (and therefore does not require the control bus decoding shown in the Z-80 CPU module in Fig. 4.27).

Another interesting feature is the omission of the $\overline{WR}$ control signal. Because of a limited number of package pins, Zilog has chosen to have the PIO internally decode $\overline{IORQ}$, $\overline{M1}$, and $\overline{RD}$. From these three signals five processor activities are decoded, as shown in Table 8.3. The $\overline{WR}$ signal is not required because $\overline{IOW}$ can be assumed when $\overline{IORQ}$ is active, $\overline{M1}$ inactive, and $\overline{RD}$ high.

The $\overline{INTA}$ decoding is standard, as the Z-80 does not output an $\overline{INTA}$ signal. The instruction fetch decoding is required so that the RETI op-code can be detected and the daisy-chain IEO output pin reset (refer to Chap. 6 for a detailed discussion of the Z-80's daisy-chain interrupt capabilities).

The designers ran out of pins when it came time to provide a reset. By holding

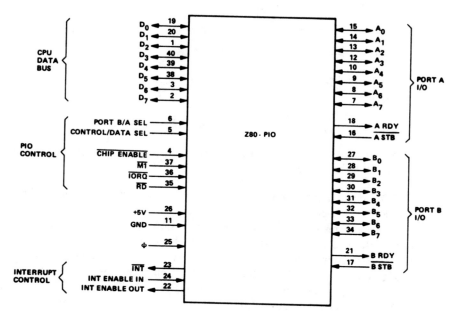

Figure 8.1 Pin definitions for the Z-80 PIO. (Courtesy of Zilog, Inc.)

Sec. 8.1   The Z8420 Parallel Input/Output Controller

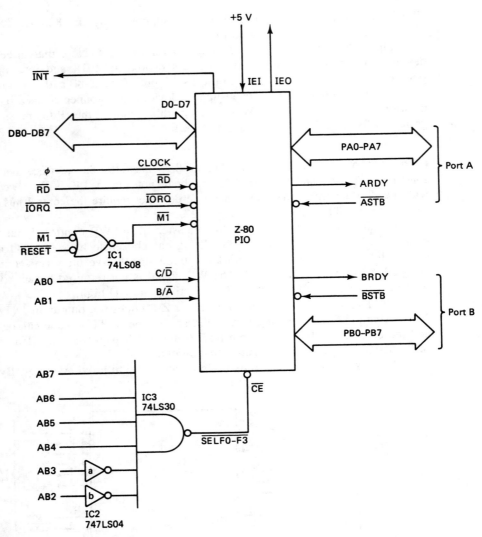

Figure 8.2 Interfacing the Z-80 PIO to the three-bus system architecture of the Z-80 microprocessor.

$\overline{\text{IORQ}}$ and $\overline{\text{RD}}$ inactive and applying 0 V to $\overline{\text{M1}}$, the reset function can be accomplished. The PIO also performs a power-on reset.

To the programmer the PIO appears to be four I/O ports (memory mapping is not allowed). Table 8.4 specifies the four port addresses for the circuit in Fig. 8.2. AB0, connected to $C/\overline{D}$, controls selection of the control port or data port. AB1, connected to $B/\overline{A}$, determines selection of the two ports, A or B.

IEI is shown connected to +5 V in Fig. 8.2. The daisy-chain priority structure allows an interrupt request only if IEI is a logic 1. When the request occurs, IEO

TABLE 8.3 INTERNAL PIO CONTROL BUS DECODING

$\overline{IORQ}$	$\overline{RD}$	$\overline{M1}$	Internally decoded to:
0	0	0	Inactive
0	0	1	$\overline{IOR}$
0	1	0	$\overline{INTA}$
0	1	1	$\overline{IOW}$
1	0	0	Instruction fetch
1	0	1	Inactive
1	1	0	Reset
1	1	1	Inactive

is forced low. By connecting IEO to the next-*lowest*-priority IEI input, lower-priority devices are prevented from interrupting higher-priority service routines. Figure 8.3 illustrates typical IEI and IEO connections when several PIO chips are involved.

The Z-80 acknowledges an interrupt request by outputting $\overline{IORQ}$ and $\overline{M1}$ low. The active PIO responds by placing its 7-bit interrupt vector onto the data bus at this time. Control is then transferred to the address stored in the memory location formed by register I (high-order address) and the 7-bit vector from the PIO.

The interrupt service routine is expected to terminate with an $\overline{RETI}$ instruction. The PIO detects the op-code for this instruction and resets its IEO output, allowing lower-priority devices access to the Z-80.

Programming the Z-80 PIO. Each PIO port is programmed by writing a control word (or words) to the corresponding control port. There are four basic control words:

1. Mode control word
2. Interrupt control word
3. Interrupt disable control word
4. Interrupt vector control word

TABLE 8.4 PORT DEFINITIONS AND ADDRESSES FOR THE Z-80 PIO INTERFACE IN FIG. 8.2

AB1 (B/$\overline{A}$)	AB0 (C/$\overline{D}$)	Figure 8.2 port address	Register selection
0	0	F0	Port A data
0	1	F1	Port A control
1	0	F2	Port B data
1	1	F3	Port B control

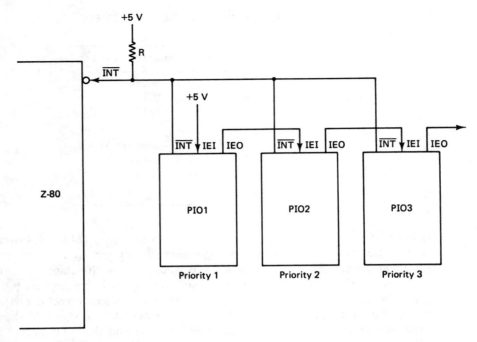

Figure 8.3 Several PIOs can be connected using a daisy-chain interrupt structure.

Table 8.5 illustrates the bit assignments for each of these control words. Although each word is written to the same address, the PIO examines bits 0–3 to determine which control word is being written. For example, if bits 0–3 are 1111, the mode control word is specified.

Note that in two cases—the mode control word and the interrupt control word—a two-byte sequence may be required. If the mode control word selects mode 3, a second write will be required to define each pin as an input or an output.

When the interrupt control word is selected, the PIO will generate an interrupt when a certain condition occurs on the port data pins (programmed as mode 3 inputs). In this case a mask word can be written, masking some of the input pins from consideration.

Example 8.1

Program port B of the PIO in Fig. 8.2 for mode 3 such that an interrupt will be generated if bit 0, 1, 4, *OR* 7 is high. Program bits 2, 3, and 6 as outputs and bits 0, 1, 4, 5, and 7 as inputs.

Solution. The program is given in Fig. 8.4. It begins by programming port B for mode 3 and then specifying the input/output pin combinations. Next, the interrupt control word is written, followed by a mask word for bits 0, 1, 4, and 7 (the only bits to be considered).

When interrupts are to be used, the (Z-80) mode 2 interrupt vector must be programmed into the PIO. This is the purpose of the interrupt vector control word.

TABLE 8.5 FOUR CONTROL WORDS ARE USED TO SPECIFY THE OPERATING CONDITIONS OF THE Z-80 PIO

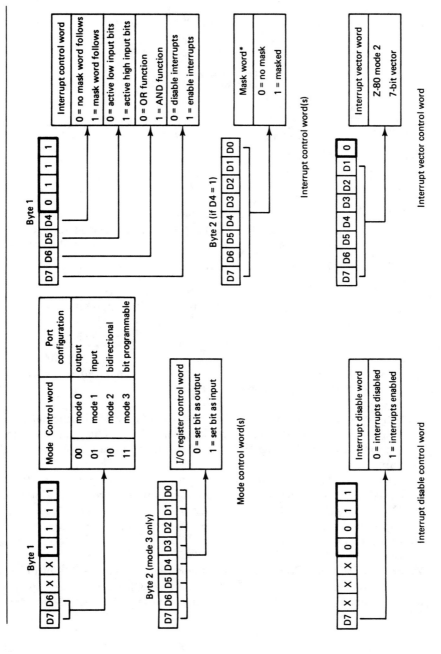

*The nonmasked pins must be defined as mode 3 inputs.

```
;PROGRAM TO DEMONSTRATE Z-80 PIO PROGRAMMING
;
;PORT 3 IS PROGRAMMED FOR MODE 3 SUCH THAT AN
;INTERRUPT IS REQUESTED IF BITS 0,1,4 OR 7 ARE HIGH.
;
LD      A,0CFH          ;MODE 3 CONTROL WORD
OUT     (0F3H),A        ;PORT B CONTROL
LD      A,0B3H          ;I/O BIT SELECTION
OUT     (0F3H),A        ;PORT B CONTROL
;
;PORT B IS NOW CONFIGURED
;NOW SPECIFY INTERRUPT CONDITIONS
;
LD      A,0B7           ;INTERRUPT CONTROL WORD
OUT     (0F3H),A        ;PORT B CONTROL
LD      A,6CH           ;MASK WORD FOR BITS 0,1,4 AND 7
OUT     (0F3H),A        ;PORT B CONTROL
;
;INITIALIZATION IS COMPLETE
```

Figure 8.4 Program for Ex. 8.1.

Example 8.2

Assume that the Z-80 maintains a jump table at memory address FC80H. Write the code required to enable an interrupt at PIO port B to vector to this address.

Solution. The program is as follows:

```
IM      2               ;MODE 2 INTERRUPTS
LD      A,0FCH          ;HIGH-ORDER ADDRESS
LD      I,A             ;COPY TO REGISTER I
LD      A,80H           ;LOW-ORDER ADDRESS
OUT     (0F3H),A        ;PORT B INTERRUPT VECTOR
```

The address of the ISR for port B should be stored in FC80 and FC81. Note that one page of RAM can accommodate 64 PIOs.

In some cases it might be desirable to be able to disable interrupts for the PIO without changing the interrupt control word. This is the purpose of the interrupt disable control word. Writing 03H to the desired port disables interrupts; 83H enables interrupts.

Finally, note that when reset both the port A and port B mask registers are set (masking all port data bits), the port data bus lines are set to a high impedance, ARDY and BRDY are low, and mode 1 is automatically selected. In addition, interrupts are disabled for both ports, but the vector address registers are not affected. Both port data registers are reset.

Mode 0: Output Port with Handshake. Figure 8.5 illustrates the timing

relationships among READY, $\overline{\text{STROBE}}$, and $\overline{\text{INT}}$ when a data port is programmed for mode 0 output. Because the PIO does not have a $\overline{\text{WR}}$ input, a pseudowrite signal ($\overline{\text{WR}}*$)
is derived from $\overline{\text{RD}}$ and $\overline{\text{IORQ}}$.

When data is written to the PIO in mode 0, the READY line is driven high on the first falling edge of the clock after the trailing edge of $\overline{\text{WR}}*$. This is an

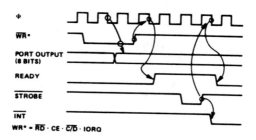

Figure 8.5 Mode 0 Z-80 PIO output timing. (Courtesy of Zilog, Inc.)

indication to the peripheral that data is available to be read. The PIO takes no further action.

The peripheral, upon "seeing" READY high, accepts the data and applies a STROBE pulse, indicating to the PIO that the data has been received. Following the trailing edge of STROBE, and assuming interrupts are enabled, the PIO will force INT low, requesting an interrupt from the Z-80. The READY line will also be reset on the first falling edge of φ after STROBE. In most cases the interrupt service routine will respond by writing a new data byte to the PIO.

Example 8.3

Explain the output obtained if the PIO's READY output is connected to the STROBE input as shown in Fig. 8.6(a).

Solution. The timing is shown in Fig. 8.6(b). Before the CPU initiates a write cycle, the READY output will hold the STROBE input low. READY will be forced high on the first falling edge of φ after WR∗. But because READY is reset by the rising edge of STROBE, it returns low on the falling edge of the next clock pulse. The result is an active-high pulse with a duration of one clock period.

Some peripherals require a STROBE pulse rather than a level-sensitive trigger achieved with the conventional PIO timing. In these cases the STROBE pulse is used by the peripheral to latch the data output by the PIO. However, the peripheral will usually require the PIO to monitor some form of BUSY/READY or ACK signal to synchronize the data transfers (and complete the "handshake"). This is where PIO mode 1 comes in.

Mode 1: Input Port with Handshake.

Figure 8.7 illustrates the timing relationships among STROBE, READY, and INT when a data port is programmed for mode 1 input. The transfer begins with the peripheral monitoring the READY output of the PIO. If high, the PIO is indicating that its input buffer is READY to receive a new data byte.

Detecting READY high, the peripheral strobes the PIO, causing the data byte to be latched and the READY line reset—this is done to prevent the peripheral from writing another data byte before the CPU has had a chance to read the last one. Assuming that the PIO interrupts are enabled, the STROBE signal also initiates INT, requesting an interrupt from the Z-80.

The interrupt service routine responds by reading the data byte from the PIO.

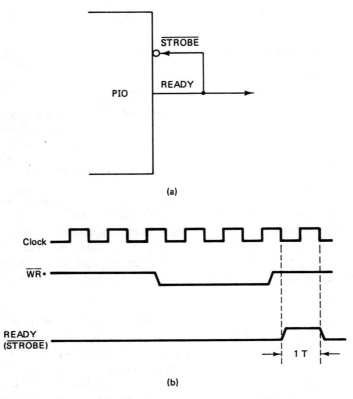

(a)

(b)

Figure 8.6 (a) Connecting the PIO's READY output to its $\overline{\text{STROBE}}$ input produces an active high pulse (b) for one clock period.

The rising edge of $\overline{\text{RD}}*$ causes READY to return high and a new data byte can be written to the PIO.

Note how the PIO mode 1 input port differs from a conventional input port discussed in Chap. 6. In the latter case data was presented to the CPU via eight tri-state buffers. That data had to be held stable until the CPU enabled the buffers and read the data. Using the PIO in mode 1, the peripheral can latch its data into the PIO even though the CPU has not yet read the data byte. Eventually, when READY

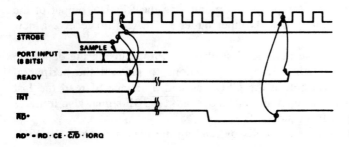

Figure 8.7 Mode 1 Z-80 PIO input timing. (Courtesy of Zilog, Inc.)

returns high, the peripheral "knows" that the data has been read and another data byte can be input.

It is possible to use the PIO in mode 0 or mode 1 for *unconditional* I/O transfers (comparable to the 8255A's mode 0). For mode 0 (outputs), data written by the CPU will always be latched by the PIO independent of $\overline{STROBE}$ and READY. Ignoring these two lines and disabling interrupts results in a simple 8-bit output port.

When programmed for mode 1 (inputs), input data can be permanently enabled into the PIO by holding the $\overline{STROBE}$ input low. The result is a simple 8-bit input port. As we will see, mode 3 can also be used for this purpose and offers the versatility of programmed input or output for each pin.

Using the Z-80 PIO to Interface a Parallel Printer.

Because of its built-in handshake logic and interrupt capabilities, the PIO is a natural choice for interfacing a parallel printer. Consider the circuit shown in Fig. 8.8. Port A of the PIO is programmed for mode 0 and used to output the data to the printer. READY and $\overline{ASTB}$ (port A $\overline{STROBE}$) are connected together so that the PIO "automatically" generates a one-clock-period $\overline{STROBE}$ signal. The inverter is required to change the sense to active low.

Two signals are available from the printer for handshake: the level-sensitive BUSY/$\overline{READY}$ and the strobe signal $\overline{ACK}$. If polling were to be used, BUSY/$\overline{READY}$ would be the logical choice. However, when interrupts are involved, $\overline{ACK}$ will work best. In this example an interrupt-driven scheme will be used.

When the data byte output by the PIO has been accepted and printed, the printer responds by pulsing $\overline{ACK}$. If port B is programmed for mode 1 input and $\overline{ACK}$ connected to $\overline{BSTB}$ through inverter IC1B, the falling edge of $\overline{ACK}$ (rising edge of $\overline{BSTB}$) will generate an interrupt request. The ISR can respond by fetching a new data byte and outputting it to port A. Note that interrupts for port A should be disabled.

PB0 (bit 0 of port B) is used to monitor the BUSY/$\overline{READY}$ flag of the printer. This is done to prevent the system from "hanging up" if the printer should be off line. Note that the printer $\overline{ACK}$ signal holds $\overline{BSTB}$ low allowing PB0 to monitor the BUSY/$\overline{READY}$ flag.

Example 8.4

Write the initialization routine required for the interrupt-driven parallel printer interface in Fig. 8.8. Assume that the ISR address is stored in memory locations E000H and E001H.

Solution. The program is shown in Fig. 8.9. Z-80 interrupt mode 2 is specified and then port A programmed for mode 0 and port B for mode 1. Register I is loaded with E0H, the high-order interrupt vector address, while the 7-bit interrupt vector for port B is programmed for 00. Interrupts are disabled for port A but enabled for port B. This will allow the printer's $\overline{ACK}$ signal to initiate the interrupt request.

Initialization of the PIO is now complete and need not be specified again unless a restart should occur. The system monitor can execute a CALL to address PRINT whenever data is to be output to the printer. Assuming that the B register holds the

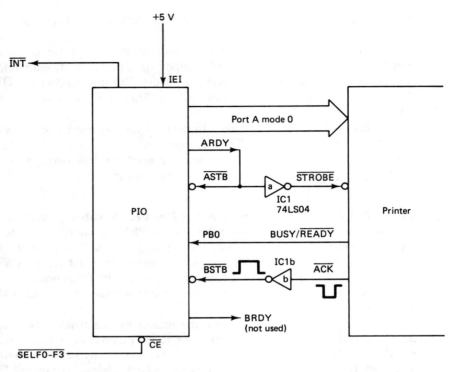

Figure 8.8 Using the Z-80 PIO to interface a parallel printer.

number of bytes to be printed, the PRINT routine writes this byte to address (NUMB). Next, the BUSY/READY status of the printer is polled to make sure that the printer is on line. If not, the message "Printer off line" is output. Interrupts can now be enabled and a CALL to the printer ISR executed to begin the sequence.

Note that after the initial CALL, data transfers will occur "automatically" under interrupt control and PRINT need not be called again. The printer ISR would look as shown in Fig. 6.22 with DPORT defined as port F0H. The RET instruction in this routine should be changed to RETI.

One word of caution about the printer interface in Fig. 8.8. The strobe signal generated by connecting ARDY and $\overline{\text{ASTB}}$ may be too short for some printers. For example, with a 4-MHz Z-80 processor, the pulse width will be 250 ns, yet a common printer specification is 0.5 μs minimum. The solution is a software strobe or an external one-shot triggered by ARDY.

Mode 2: Bidirectional I/O with Handshake. When mode 2 is selected, port A becomes a *bidirectional* data port supported by all four handshaking signals and port B must be programmed for mode 3. The timing relationships are shown in Fig. 8.10. As can be seen from studying this figure, mode 2 timing is a combination of mode 0 and mode 1 timing. The only difference is that data is not output onto the

```
            ;INITIALIZATION ROUTINE FOR THE INTERRUPT DRIVEN
            ;PARALLEL PRINTER INTERFACE IN FIG. 8-8.
            ;
            ;THE PRINTER ISR ADDRESS IS ASSUMED STORED IN
            ;E000H AND E001H.
            ;
            ;SPECIFY THE OPERATING MODES
            ;
   INIT     IM      2               ;Z-80 INTERRUPT MODE 2
            LD      A,OFH           ;MODE 0 - OUTPUT
            OUT     (OF1H),A        ;FOR PORT A
            LD      A,4FH           ;MODE 1 - INPUT
            OUT     (OF3H),A        ;FOR PORT B
            ;
            ;PROGRAM THE INTERRUPT VECTORS AND ENABLES
            ;
            LD      A,OEOH          ;HIGH ORDER JUMP TABLE ADDRESS
            LD      I,A             ;TO REGISTER I
            LD      A,OO            ;PORT B INTERRUPT VECTOR
            OUT     (OF3H),A        ;TO PORT B CONTROL
            LD      A,3             ;DISABLE INTERRUPTS
            OUT     (OF1H),A        ;FOR PORT A
            LD      A,83H           ;BUT ENABLE INTERRUPTS
            OUT     (OF3H),A        ;FOR PORT B
            ;
            ;INITIALIZATION IS NOW COMPLETE
            ;INIT IS NOT NEEDED AGAIN UNLESS A RESET OCCURS
            ;
            RET


            ;AFTER CALLING INIT A CALL TO PRINT WILL START THE
            ;PRINTING SEQUENCE BY LOADING (NUMB) WITH THE NUMBER
            ;OF BYTES TO BE OUTPUT, TESTING TO BE SURE THE PRINTER IS
            ;ON LINE, ENABLING INTERRUPTS AND BRANCHING TO THE PRINT
            ;ISR
            ;
   PRINT    LD      A,B             ;GET NUMBER OF BYTES
            LD      (NUMB),A        ;STORE IT IN (NUMB)
            ;
            ;NOW MAKE SURE PRINTER IS ON LINE
            ;
            IN      A,(OF2H)        ;READ PRINTER BUSY/READY
            RRA                     ;MOVE TO CARRY
            JP      C,MSG           ;PRINT "PRINTER OFF LINE"
            ;
            ;PRINTER IS READY
            ;
            EI                      ;ENABLE INTERRUPTS
            CALL    ISR             ;GO TO THE PRINT ROUTINE
            ;
            ;PRINT IS NOT NEEDED AGAIN UNTIL THE BUFFER IS EMPTY
            ;
            RET                     ;NORMAL PROCESSING RESUMES
```

Figure 8.9 Program for Ex. 8.4.

bidirectional bus until $\overline{ASTB}$ is brought low. The remainder of the time the bus is in a tri-state condition. This is done to prevent bus contention problems.

The general rule for mode 2 is strobe data off the bus only when ARDY is high and gate data onto the bus only when BRDY is high.

Figure 8.11 illustrates an application for this mode. PIO1 is assumed interfaced to one computer system and PIO2 to a second. By programming both PIOs for mode 2, data can be transferred between the two computers. One PIO will be pro-

Sec. 8.1   The Z8420 Parallel Input/Output Controller

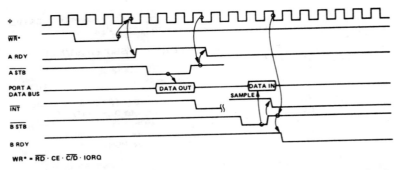

Figure 8.10 Mode 2 Z-80 PIO bidirectional timing. (Courtesy of Zilog, Inc.)

grammed as a transmitter and the other as a receiver. Note that the electrical connections are symmetric so that either PIO can function as a transmitter or a receiver, depending on which way data is to flow.

In Fig. 8.11, PIO1 is assumed the transmitter and PIO2 the receiver. The flowcharts describe the actions required of the PIOs under program control. The transmitter initiates the transfer. If BRDY2 is high, the input buffer of PIO2 is empty and ready to receive a data byte. Using PB7 to *poll* BRDY2, a data byte is written to PIO1, causing its ARDY1 output to go high.

No further action is taken by PIO1 until PIO2 generates a (software) $\overline{\text{STROBE}}$ signal on PB1. This $\overline{\text{STROBE}}$ gates data onto the bidirectional bus lines and the rising edge causes PIO2 to latch the data byte. BRDY2 now goes low, indicating that the data byte has been accepted by PIO2 but not yet read by CPU2. The PB1 strobe also resets ARDY1, indicating that the PIO1 transmitter buffer is empty.

When the data byte is read, BRDY2 returns high, indicating that PIO2 is again ready for data and the cycle repeats.

Mode 3: Bit-Defined I/O. When the PIO is programmed for mode 3, each of the eight pins of the data port can be individually assigned as an input or an output. The handshaking lines are not used in this mode. Turn back to the mode 3 control word in Table 8.5. Two bytes are required. The first is used to specify mode 3 and the second to indicate the input/output definitions.

This mode can be very useful when more control signals are required than are afforded by $\overline{\text{STROBE}}$ and READY. For example, PB0 and PB7 were programmed as polled inputs supporting the bidirectional data port in the preceding section. PB1 in that circuit was programmed as an output (used to generate the $\overline{\text{STROBE}}$ pulse).

Example 8.1 illustrated another feature of mode 3. An interrupt can be requested based on a logical OR or AND of the unmasked bits of this port. One application could be a control program required to poll bit 0 but generate an interrupt (alarm) if bits 0 AND 1 AND 4 should all be low (see Prob. 8.4).

Because no handshaking signals are involved, mode 3 is similar to the 8255A's mode 0. In fact, if all of the bits of one port are programmed the same, it is identical.

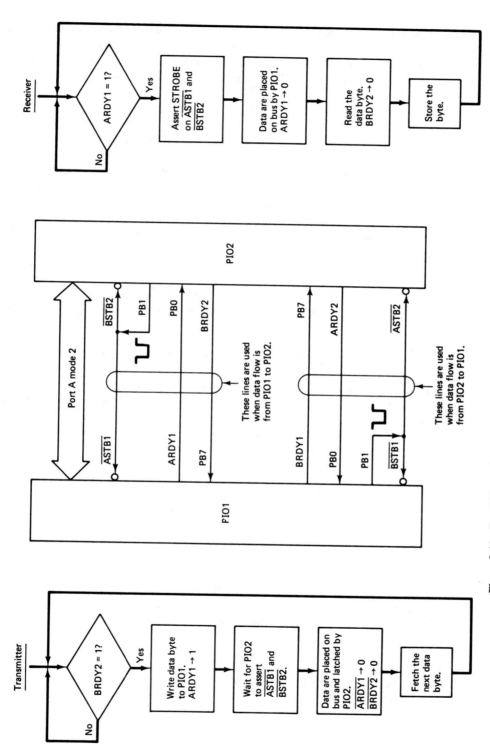

Figure 8.11 Two PIOs can be used to allow communications between two different computers.

A Design Example: Mode 3 Control of a Multiplexed LED Display.

We have seen in Chaps. 6 and 7 two methods for interfacing a matrix keyboard to a microcomputer system (see Secs. 6.2 and 7.2). In such systems a seven-segment display is often used as an output device. When interfacing this type of display, two problems must be solved.

1. Decode the BCD or hex encoded binary digits to seven-segment code.
2. Provide a driver circuit capable of handling the LED currents required.

Problem 1 can be solved by using a BCD-to-seven-segment or hex-to-seven-segment decoder. Problem 2 is solved by selecting a buffer or driver circuit capable of sinking or sourcing the LED currents.

Although this hardware approach works fine when only one or two displays are to be interfaced, it becomes very cumbersome when several digits of display are needed. For example, if a six-digit display is desired, you will require six displays, six decoders, and six drivers. Eighteen IC sockets and numerous connections will be required.

A better approach is to let the microprocessor do the decoding and *multiplex* the displays. Figure 8.12 illustrates this technique for a six-digit display controlled by a Z-80 PIO. Looking at the inset to the figure, note that each display has all of its cathodes connected together (called a "common-cathode display"). Grounding this common pin while applying $+1.5$ V to any of the pins a through g will light the appropriate segment.

The interface in Fig. 8.12 has the segment pins from each display connected in parallel and driven by IC1 and IC2, each a common-cathode *segment driver*. IC6, a common-cathode *digit driver*, is used to sink the segment currents. Figure 8.13 provides a description of these two devices.

The "trick" to making this circuit work is the software. Port A of the PIO is used to turn on one of the digits by forcing the selected digit line low. For example, if 04H is written to port F0 of the PIO (port A) and 6DH is written to port F2 (port B), digit 2 will light up and display a 5. If the software turns on each digit in sequence for a short time and can do this quickly enough, your eyes will be "fooled" into thinking that all six displays are on at once, even though only one digit is on at a time.

What have we gained by this multiplexing scheme? For one thing, only one set of drivers is required (instead of one set per display). Also, the decoder has been eliminated. And because this function is now accomplished with software, special characters (such as P, L, U, etc.) can be output in addition to the numerals 0–9 and letters A–F obtained with hardware decoders (this idea was presented in Lab. 3.10).

Example 8.5

Write a subroutine called *SCAN* that will scan and display the contents of a display buffer in memory called DSBF. Use the multiplexed display in Fig. 8.12.

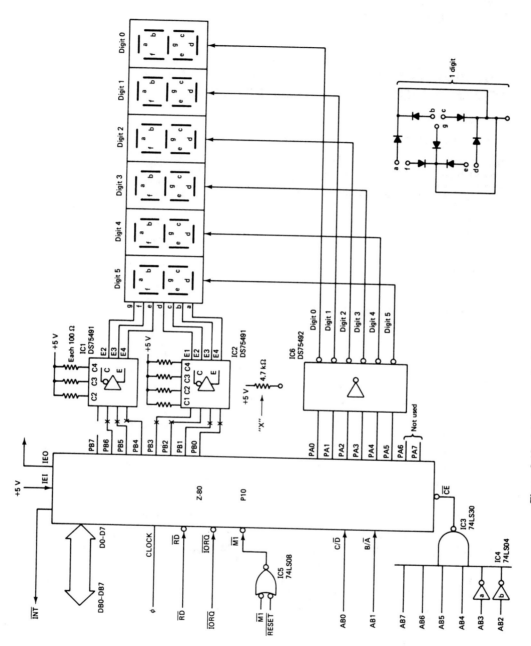

Figure 8.12 Interfacing a six-digit multiplexed display to the Z-80 PIO.

National Semiconductor

DS75491 MOS-to-LED Quad Segment Driver
DS75492 MOS-to-LED Hex Digit Driver

General Description

The DS75491 and DS75492 are interface circuits designed to be used in conjunction with MOS integrated circuits and common-cathode LED's in serially addressed multi-digit displays. The number of drivers required for this time-multiplexed system is minimized as a result of the segment-address-and-digit-scan method of LED drive.

Features

- 50 mA source or sink capability per driver (DS75491)
- 250 mA sink capability per driver (DS75492)
- MOS compatability (low input current)
- Low standby power
- High-gain Darlington circuits

Schematic and Connection Diagrams

DS75491 (each driver)

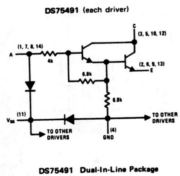

DS75492 (each driver)

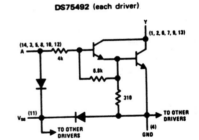

DS75491 Dual-In-Line Package

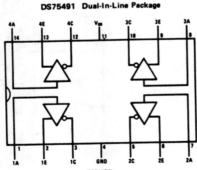

DS75492 Dual-In-Line Package

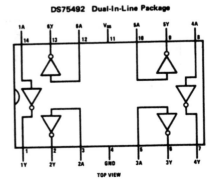

Figure 8.13 Segment and digit drivers for the six-digit display in Fig. 8.12. (Courtesy of National Semiconductor Corporation.)

Solution. The program will require two routines:

1. *HXSG*: Pass this subroutine the offset address (in register pair HL) of the hex digit to be converted to seven-segment code. It will return with the seven-segment encoded byte in register D.

2. *SCAN*: This subroutine will point HL at the display buffer and call HXSG. It will then output the contents of the D register to the segment driver (port B of the PIO) and turn on digit 0 for 1 ms. The process is repeated until all six digits have been converted and displayed.

The Z-80 program is shown in Fig. 8.14. In this program we assume that the PIO has been programmed with ports A and B specified as mode 3 output ports.

```
;                        SCAN

;A SOFTWARE DRIVER FOR THE MULTIPLEXED DISPLAY
;        PIO INTERFACE IN FIG. 8-12.
;
;SCAN IS A SUBROUTINE THAT DISPLAYS THE CONTENTS
;OF THE SIX BYTE DISPLAY BUFFER (DSBF).
;(DSBF) = RIGHTMOST DIGIT (#0).
;(DSBF+5) = LEFTMOST DIGIT (#5).
;
;NOTE: TO PREVENT THE DISPLAY FROM FLICKERING
;SCAN SHOULD BE CALLED AT LEAST ONCE EVERY 5-10 MS.
;
DIGT    EQU     OFOH        ;THIS IS THE DIGIT DRIVER PORT
SEGM    EQU     OF2H        ;THIS IS THE SEGMENT DRIVER PORT
DSBF    EQU     0000        ;CHOOSE A SUITABLE LOCATION
MS      EQU     0000        ;THIS SHOULD BE THE ADDRESS OF
                            ;A 1 MS SUBROUTINE
        ;
        ;BEGIN BY MAKING THE ROUTINE TRANSPARENT AND
        ;INITIALIZING SEVERAL REGISTERS.
        ;
SCAN    PUSH    AF          ;
        PUSH    HL          ;
        PUSH    BC          ;
        PUSH    DE          ;
        ;
        LD      HL,DSBF     ;THIS IS THE DISPLAY BUFFER
        LD      A,1         ;DIGIT CODE
        LD      B,6         ;DIGIT COUNTER
        LD      C,SEGM      ;SEGMENT PORT
        ;
        ;CALL HXSG TO CONVERT THE HEX DIGIT IN (HL) TO
        ;A SEVEN-SEGMENT CODE.  RETURN WITH THE CODE IN D.
        ;
NXD     CALL    HXSG        ;CONVERT TO SEVEN-SEGMENT
        OUT     (C),D       ;OUT TO SEGMENT PORT
        OUT     (DIGT),A    ;TURN ON ONE DISPLAY
        CALL    MS          ;1 MS DELAY SUBROUTINE
        RLA                 ;PREPARE FOR NEXT DIGIT
        INC     HL          ;ADVANCE POINTER
        DJNZ    NXD         ;DO FOR ALL 6 DIGITS
        ;
        ;TURN OFF ALL OF THE DISPLAYS AND RESTORE THE REGISTERS
        ;
        SUB     A           ;CLEAR ACCUMULATOR
        OUT     (DIGT),A    ;ALL DISPLAYS OFF
        OUT     (C),A       ;ALL SEGMENTS OFF
```

Figure 8.14 Z-80 control subroutine for the multiplexed display interface in Fig. 8.12.

```
                POP       DE              ;
                POP       BC              ;
                POP       HL              ;
                POP       AF              ;
                RET
                ;
                ;                         HXSG
                ;THIS SUBROUTINE LOOKS UP THE SEVEN-SEGMENT CODE FOR
                ;THE HEX DIGIT IN BITS 0-3 OF (HL).   THE RESULT IS
                ;RETURNED IN REGISTER D.
                ;
HXSG            PUSH      AF              ;DO NOT CHANGE SCAN REGISTERS
                PUSH      HL              ;
                LD        A,(HL)          ;GET THE HEX DIGIT
                LD        HL,CTBL         ;POINT AT CODE TABLE
                AND       0FH             ;MAKE SURE BITS 4-7 ARE 0
                ADD       A,L             ;FORM AN OFFSET
                LD        L,A             ;INTO THE TABLE
                LD        D,(HL)          ;RETRIEVE THE CODE TO D
                POP       HL              ;RESTORE
                POP       AF              ;
                RET
                ;
                ;THESE ARE THE SEVEN-SEGMENT CODES
                ;
CTBL            DEFB      3FH             ;0
                DEFB      06H             ;1
                DEFB      5BH             ;2
                DEFB      4FH             ;3
                DEFB      66H             ;4
                DEFB      6DH             ;5
                DEFB      7DH             ;6
                DEFB      07H             ;7
                DEFB      7FH             ;8
                DEFB      67H             ;9
                DEFB      77H             ;A
                DEFB      7CH             ;B
                DEFB      39H             ;C
                DEFB      5EH             ;D
                DEFB      79H             ;E
                DEFB      71H             ;F
```

Figure 8.14 *(Continued)*

So that SCAN can be called at any time, it begins by saving all CPU registers used. Several registers are then initialized and HL pointed at the display buffer. HXSG is then called and the seven-segment code for the hex digit in the buffer looked up in a table. Note how the hex digit's value is used to form the *address offset* into this table (for example, if HL = 4810 and the hex digit is 07, location 4817 will contain the seven-segment code for a 7).

Returning to SCAN, the code is output to the segment driver and digit 0 is turned on for 1 ms. Register A is rotated left to prepare to turn on the next digit. The buffer pointer is advanced and DJNZ used to test if all six digits have been output.

In actual use, the main software must be sure to include a CALL SCAN instruction in all program loops to ensure that the display is continually "refreshed." Failure to perform this call at least once every 5 to 10 ms will cause the display to flicker (and, of course, go dark if SCAN is not called at all). To write data to the display, the display buffer should be written to. For example, to show a 5 in digit 4:

```
LD      A,05
LD      (DSBF+4),A
```

Electrical Characteristics of the Ports.   The I_{OL} specification for the data ports is 2 mA and 250 μA for I_{OH}. This means that one standard TTL load or five LSTTL loads can be driven safely at each pin. In addition, port B can supply up to 1.5 mA at 1.5 V. This means that Darlington transistors can be driven and used to control high current loads such as mechanical or solid-state relays.

Three speed versions of the PIO are available. These are the 2.5-MHz Z-80 PIO, the 4-MHz Z-80A PIO, and the 6-MHz Z-80B PIO.

8.2 THE Z8430 COUNTER/TIMER CIRCUIT

As you read this section, look for the answers to these Key Concept questions:

8.2.1. What are the two operating modes of the Z-80 CTC?

8.2.2. What clock source is used as the time base when the CTC is operated in the counter mode?

8.2.3. In the counter mode one channel of the CTC can count as many as _____ external clock pulses.

8.2.4. When used in the timer mode, each count represents _____ or _____ system clock pulses dependent on the prescale factor.

The Z8430 counter/timer (or simply Z-80 CTC) is commonly used in Z-80 microcomputer systems for the generation of accurate time delays. In software this is typically done by forming counting loops that accumulate the time delay as the product of X passes through a loop Y T states long.

Programming the microprocessor to count backward from one million to zero may be one method of generating a time delay, but it hardly qualifies as an efficient use of the resources of the processor! The CTC, on the other hand, is designed specifically for just such a task.

The Z-80 CTC is programmable by the Z-80 to operate as a *counter* or a *timer*. As a counter it decrements an internal 8-bit counter each time an external clock signal (applied to CLK/TRG) makes an active transition. When the count passes from 1 to 0, the ZC/TO output pulses high for 1.5 system clock periods. At the same time, and if enabled, an interrupt request will be generated. And, like the PIO, the CTC is capable of supplying a (Z-80) mode 2 interrupt vector to the Z-80 during $\overline{\text{INTA}}$.

When programmed as a timer, the 8-bit counter is decremented once for every 16 (or 256) system clock pulses. In this mode the CLK/TRG input becomes a programmable trigger initiating the timer. A timing interval as short as 16 system clock states can be detected (2.7 μs with the Z-80B CTC).

The main features of the Z-80 CTC are:

1. Four individual programmable channels.
2. Three channels with ZC/TO outputs.
3. Each counter can be read by the CPU at any time.
4. Selection of counter or timer mode for each channel.
5. Programmable active trigger edge.
6. Standard Z-80 type interface with daisy-chain priority structure.

If you are comparing the Z-80 CTC with the Intel 8254, the main differences are:

1. The 8254 has only three channels.
2. The 8254 counters are all 16 bits wide.
3. The 8254 can be programmed to generate various wave shapes (strobes, pulses, square waves).

Interfacing the Z-80 CTC. Pin functions and pin numbers for the Z-80 CTC are shown in Fig. 8.15. Figure 8.16 illustrates typical connections when interfaced to a Z-80 microprocessor. Like the PIO, the CTC decodes $\overline{M1}$, $\overline{IORQ}$, and $\overline{RD}$ to identify the $\overline{IOW}$, $\overline{IOR}$, $\overline{INTA}$, and $\overline{M1}$ machine cycles. This was shown previously in Table 8.3. Note that a separate $\overline{RESET}$ input has been provided (unlike the PIO).

The CTC appears to the programmer as four I/O ports defined by the two channel select pins CS0 and CS1. However, only when the chip enable ($\overline{CE}$) input is low can the microprocessor access the CTC and the address decoder connected to this pin determines the specific port addresses. Table 8.6 summarizes the I/O read and write operations possible with the CTC. Note that the channel control lines ZC/TO and CLK/TRG cannot be read.

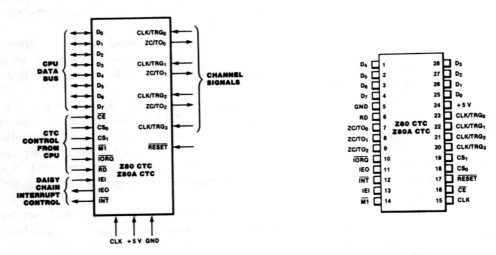

Figure 8.15 Pin functions and numbers for the Z-80 CTC. (Courtesy of Zilog, Inc.)

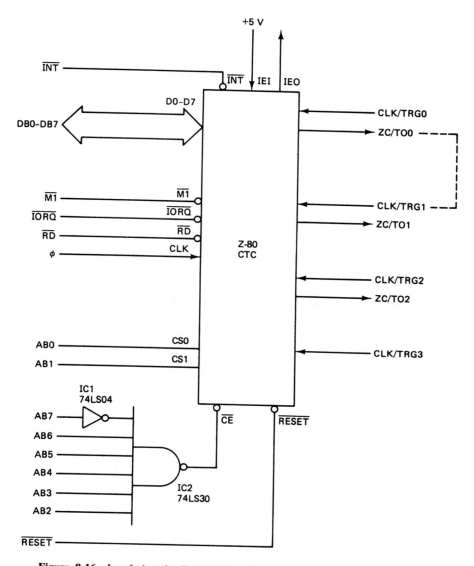

Figure 8.16 Interfacing the Z-80 CTC to the three-bus system architecture of the Z-80 microprocessor. The dashed line indicates how two counters can be cascaded to achieve larger counts (see Ex. 8.7).

Three of the CTC pins are dedicated to the daisy-chain interrupt structure. The technique used is identical to that discussed previously with the PIO (see Fig. 8.3). Any number of compatible devices can be added to the daisy chain. Chips farthest from the CPU have lowest priority.

Simultaneous interrupt requests within the CTC will be arbitrated such that channel 0 has highest priority and channel 3 lowest priority. When programming

TABLE 8.6 THE Z-80 CTC APPEARS TO BE FOUR I/O PORTS
TO THE MICROPROCESSOR

Figure 8.16 port address	CS1	CS0	$\overline{M1}$	$\overline{IORQ}$	$\overline{RD}$	Function
7C	0	0	1	0	0	Read channel 0 counter
	0	0	1	0	1	Write channel 0 control word
7D	0	1	1	0	0	Read channel 1 counter
	0	1	1	0	1	Write channel 1 control word
7E	0	1	1	0	0	Read channel 2 counter
	0	1	1	0	1	Write channel 2 control word
7F	1	1	1	0	0	Read channel 3 counter
	1	1	1	0	1	Write channel 3 control word

the interrupt vector, only bits 3–7 of channel 0 need to be specified as the CTC automatically inserts bits 1 and 2 (recall that bit 0 must be 0).

Programming the Z-80 CTC: Counter Mode.

The main difference between the counter mode and the timer mode is the source of the clock signal. When programmed as a counter, the CTC counts clock pulses applied to the CLK/TRG input. When programmed as a timer, the CTC counts *system* clock pulses.

Figure 8.17 flowcharts operation of the Z-80 CTC when operated in the counter mode. Two control words must be written. The first identifies the counter mode and the second is called the *time constant*. This 8-bit value will be loaded into the counting register and used as the base when decrementing begins. The remaining operations in the flowchart occur without CPU intervention and continue indefinitely until a reset or new control word is written.

After writing the two control words, the first active transition at the CLK/TRG input (programmable as either a rising or falling edge) will cause the counter to be decremented by 1. This is shown in Fig. 8.18. Note that the CLK/TRG transition must occur 210 ns before the rising edge of ϕ (for the Z-80A CTC). If this condition is not met, the counter will not be decremented until the next rising edge of ϕ. The CLK/TRG must also have a minimum pulse width of 200 ns (120 ns for the Z-80B CTC) and the trigger period must be at least twice the clock period.

When the Nth CLK/TRG pulse finally occurs, the ZC/TO output will pulse high for 1.5 periods of the ϕ clock. $\overline{INT}$ will also become active at this time if interrupts have been enabled. The base count is then automatically reloaded into the counter and the cycle repeated indefinitely.

When programming a counter (by writing to the desired channel port address), three types of control words are possible. These are shown in Fig. 8.19. Initially, the CTC control logic examines bit 0 of the control word. If this bit is a 0, the *interrupt vector* is assumed. If a 1, the *channel control word* is indicated. The interrupt vector need only be written to channel 0; the CTC automatically determines the address for the other channels, as shown in Fig. 8.19.

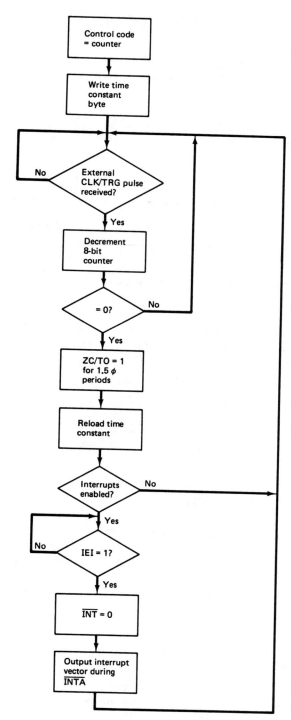

Figure 8.17 Flowchart of the Z-80 CTC operations when programmed for the counter mode.

Sec. 8.2   The Z8430 Counter/Timer Circuit

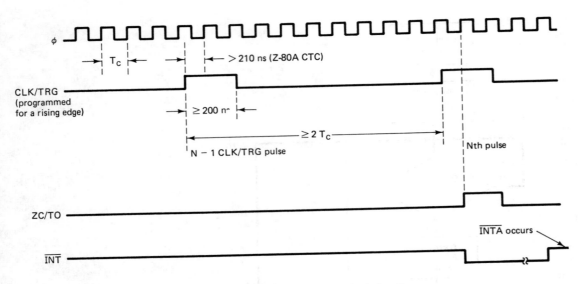

Figure 8.18 Counter-mode timing diagram.

Example 8.6

Assume that the address for the channel 0 ISR is stored in locations D8C0H and D8C1H. Write the interrupt initialization routine required for the Z-80 CTC interface in Fig. 8.16. What locations will store the ISRs for channels 1–3?

Solution. The program to initialize the CTC is as follows:

```
LD    A,0D8H      ;HIGH-ORDER ADDRESS
LD    I,A         ;TO REGISTER I
IM    2           ;INTERRUPT MODE 2
LD    A,0C0H      ;LOW-ORDER ADDRESS
OUT   (7CH),A     ;TO CTC CHANNEL 0
```

The other CTC channels will automatically be programmed for address D8C2H (channel 1), D8C4H (channel 2), and D8C6H (channel 3).

When bit 0 of the control word is a 1, the channel control word is indicated. Several characteristics of the CTC can then be specified, as Fig. 8.19 illustrates. Note that the prescaler value (16 or 256) and timer trigger are "don't cares" for the counter mode.

When bit 2 of the channel control word is a 1, the CTC is alerted to interpret the next channel write as a time-constant byte.

Example 8.7

Program the Z-80 CTC in Fig. 8.16 to count 1000 rising edges of the signal applied to a CLK/TRG input, generate an interrupt request, and repeat.

Solution. Using an 8-bit counter, 256 clock edges can be counted. Therefore, for this application two counters will have to be cascaded; that is, the ZC/TO output of one will be connected to the CLK/TRG input of another. This is shown in Fig. 8.16

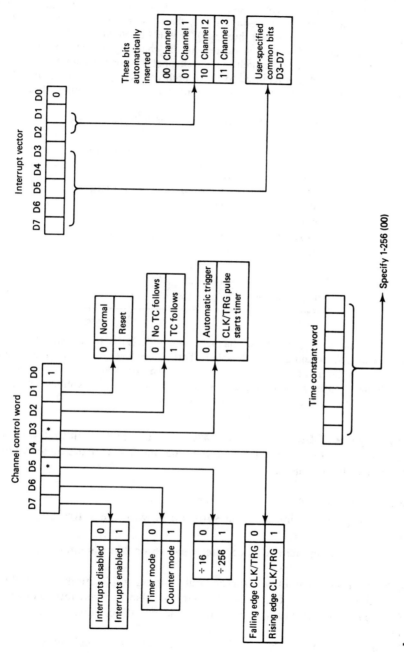

Figure 8.19 Three forms of the CTC control word are possible. The channel control word and time constant need to be written to each channel's port address. The interrupt vector should be written to channel 0 only.

*These bits are "don't cares" in the counter mode.

with a dashed line between ZC/TO0 and CLK/TRG1. The choice of channels 0 and 1 is arbitrary.

What time-constant value should we program for the channel 0 and 1 counters? If cascading resulted in a true 16-bit counter, the answer would be 03E8H (1000_{10}). However, when channel 0 passes through 0, it will be reloaded with its base count, not zero. The result is that we will decrement the channel 1 counter once each time the channel 0 counter is decremented to 0. If channel 0 is loaded with N0 and channel 1 with N1, the total clocks required to make both counters go to 0 (and the ZC/TO1 output pulse high) is N0 × N1. In this example we will choose N0 = 10 and N1 = 100.

The control word for each channel is found as follows:

	Channel 0	Channel 1
Interrupts	0 (disabled)	1 (enabled)
Mode	1 (counter)	1
Prescale	X	X
CLK/TRG edge	1 (rising)	1
Timer trigger	X	X
Time constant	1 (to follow)	1
Reset	0 (normal)	0
Control/vector	1 (control word)	1

The result is 01X1X101 for channel 0 and 11X1X101 for channel 1. Note that only interrupts for channel 1 are enabled. This is because only when the channel 1 counter passes through 0 will 1000 clock edges have occurred.

Figure 8.20 is a copy of the Z-80 program required. Locations D8C2H and D8C3H should be loaded with the desired ISR address.

Programming the Z-80 CTC: Timer Mode.
Figure 8.21 illustrates the operation of the Z-80 CTC when programmed for the timer mode. There are three differences when compared with the counter mode.

1. The clock source is φ and not an external signal.
2. The timing period is initiated via software or with the active edge of CLK/TRG.
3. The counter is decremented once after each 16 or 256 system clock pulses.

The timer mode is intended for accurate timing applications using the system clock as the time base. The counter mode can also be used this way (by connecting CLK/TRG to φ) but is best suited for counting pulses arriving at the CLK/TRG input.

Note that in the timer mode some initial counts cannot be obtained. For example, to time for 64 system clock periods a time constant of 4 with a prescale factor of 16 should be selected. However, a timing period of 65 system clock periods cannot

```
;PROGRAM TO INITIALIZE THE Z-80 CTC IN FIG. 8-16 TO
;CAUSE AN INTERRUPT REQUEST EVERY 1000 RISING EDGES
;OF THE SIGNAL APPLIED TO CLK/TRG0.
;
;ASSUME THE ISR ADDRESS IS STORED IN D8C2 AND D8C3.
;
;BEGIN BY PROGRAMMING CHANNELS 0 AND 1
;
LD      A,55H           ;CHANNEL 0 CONTROL WORD
OUT     (7CH),A         ;CHANNEL 0 CONTROL PORT
LD      A,0D5H          ;CHANNEL 1 CONTROL WORD
OUT     (7DH)A          ;CHANNEL 1 CONTROL PORT
;
;NOW THE TIME CONSTANT BYTES
;
LD      A,0AH           ;CHANNEL 0 GETS 10
OUT     (7CH),A         ;CHANNEL 0 CONTROL PORT
LD      A,64H           ;CHANNEL 1 GETS 100
OUT     (7DH),A         ;CHANNEL 1 CONTROL PORT
;
;COUNTING BEGINS WITH THE FIRST RISING EDGE AFTER
;THE CHANNEL 0 TIME CONSTANT HAS BEEN WRITTEN
```

Figure 8.20 Initialization program for Ex. 8.7.

be obtained. Due to the prescaler, the timing period must be a multiple of 16 or 256 system clocks.

A timing diagram for this mode is shown in Fig. 8.22. The timer is initiated by the active edge of CLK/TRG (in this case the rising edge). Note that 210 ns of lead time (for the Z-80A) is required between the active edge of the trigger and the rising edge of φ. If this condition is met, the timer will begin with the rising edge of the *second* clock pulse.

It is also possible to start the timer from software. In this case the timer begins with the second rising edge immediately following the time-constant write machine cycle.

In either case, the counter is decremented every 16 or 256 system clock pulses. When the count passes from 1 to 0, the ZC/TO output pulses high for 1.5 periods of φ and if enabled, $\overline{INT}$ is forced low. The time constant is now reloaded into the counter and the cycle repeats (that is, without an additional software command or CLK/TRG pulse). A reset command should be used to stop the timer.

Example 8.8

Design the hardware and write the software to utilize the Z-80 CTC as a one-shot. Applying an active-low pulse to the CLK/TRG input should produce a 3.6-s active-high pulse.

Solution. The Z-80 CTC has no provision for controlling the shape or pulse width of the ZC/TO output (as does the 8254 PIT). It is restricted to 1.5 system clock periods or 375 ns with a 4-MHz clock. This problem can be overcome by adding an external flip-flop as shown in Fig. 8.23. Pushing the button sets the flip-flop and starts the timer. When ZC/TO occurs, the flip-flop is clocked and the pulse terminated.

Unfortunately, 3.6 s is too long a period for one timer alone. For example, if the time constant is 256 and the prescaler is also set to 256, 65,536 clock periods will occur before ZC/TO0 goes high. At 4 MHz this is 0.016384 s, too short to be used for the one-shot. However, if the ZC/TO0 output is used as the clock signal for channel 1 programmed as a counter, the 3.6-s time delay can be realized.

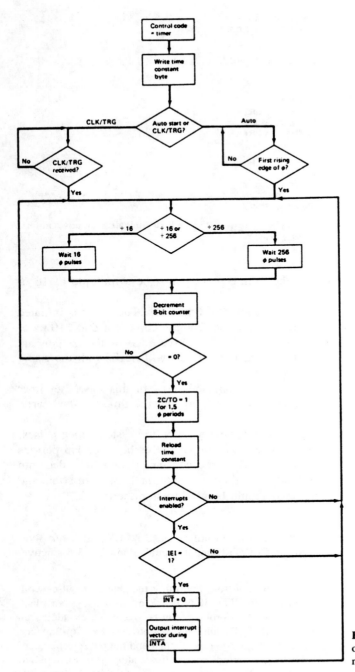

Figure 8.21 Flowchart of the Z-80 CTC operations when programmed for the timer mode.

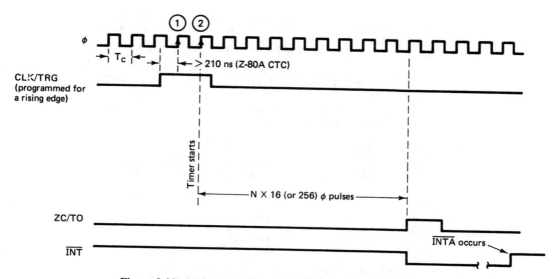

Figure 8.22 Timing diagram when the CTC is operated in the timer mode.

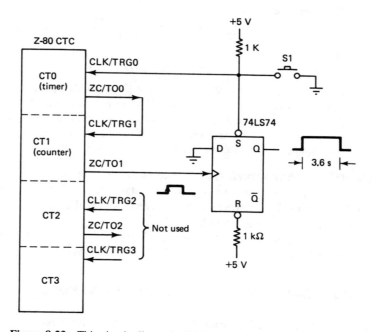

Figure 8.23 This circuit allows the Z-80 CTC to function as a one-shot.

```
;THIS PROGRAM CONVERTS THE Z-80 CTC AND HARDWARE
;SHOWN IN FIG. 8-23 TO A ONE-SHOT.  THE PULSE WIDTH
;IS FOUND AS
;               PW = (NO x N1 x P)/F
;
;NO AND N1 ARE THE TIME CONSTANTS FOR COUNTERS 0 AND 1,
;P IS THE PRESCALE FACTOR AND F IS THE SYSTEM CLOCK
;FREQUENCY.
;
;IN THIS EXAMPLE NO=250, N1=225, P=256 AND F= 4 MHZ.
;THE PULSE WIDTH IS 3.6 S.
;
LD      A,2DH           ;CHANNEL 0 IS A TIMER, P=256
OUT     (07CH),A        ;CHANNEL 0 CONTROL WORD
LD      A,55H           ;CHANNEL 1 IS A COUNTER
OUT     (07DH),A        ;CHANNEL 1 CONTROL WORD
;
;THE NEXT TWO WRITES SPECIFY THE TIME CONSTANTS
;
LD      A,0FAH          ;NO=250
OUT     (07CH),A        ;CHANNEL 0 TIME CONSTANT
LD      A,0E1H          ;N1=225
OUT     (07DH),A        ;CHANNEL 1 TIME CONSTANT
;
;THE CTC NOW RUNS INDEPENDENT OF THE CPU
;PRESSING THE SWITCH WILL PRODUCE A 3.6 S PULSE
```

Figure 8.24 Control program for the one-shot circuit in Fig. 8.23. The pulse width is 3.6 s assuming a 4-MHz system clock.

The "trick" now is to select time-constant values, N0 and N1, for CT0 and CT1 such that either

$$N0 \times N1 \times 256 = \frac{4,000,000}{1/3.6} = 14,400,000$$

or

$$N0 \times N1 \times 16 \ = 14,400,000$$

In either case, N0 and N1 are restricted to integers between 1 and 256. There are no solutions if the prescaler = 16, but if a prescale factor of 256 is chosen, then N0 = 250 and N1 = 225 will work (try it!—then see Prob. 8.19 to see how I found these).

Using these values, the program in Fig. 8.24 can be written. Note that once programmed, the circuit runs independent of the CPU.

Electrical Characteristics.   The ZC/TO outputs have drive capabilities of 2 mA in the low state and 250 μA in the high state. This allows them to safely drive one standard TTL load or five LSTTL loads. Each output is also capable of driving a Darlington transistor pair, sourcing 1.5 mA at 1.5 V.

There are three speed versions of the CTC: the Z-80 CTC (2.5 MHz), the Z-80A CTC (4 MHz), and the Z-80B CTC (6 MHz).

8.3 THE Z8410 DIRECT MEMORY ACCESS CONTROLLER

As you read this section, look for the answers to these Key Concept questions:

8.3.1. The Z-80 DMA performs sequential DMA cycles. What does this mean?

8.3.2. What are the two ways of requesting that a DMA transfer begin?

8.3.3. Which Z-80 DMA mode—byte, burst, or continuous—does not relinquish control of the system buses until all bytes have been transferred?

8.3.4. The DMA programming sequence should begin with a disable DMA command. This is accomplished by writing _____ H to register _____ .

Nearly all input/output interfacing is concerned with the transfer of data between system memory and the I/O devices. As we have seen, three techniques are commonly used to accomplish this transfer:

1. Programmed I/O
2. Interrupt-driven I/O
3. Direct memory access

Programmed I/O (also called polling) and interrupts both utilize the microprocessor to control the data transfer. As a result, the data transfer rate is relatively slow. This is due to the software overhead involved in setting up data pointers and byte counters and testing for the end-of-block condition.

The direct memory access or DMA technique replaces this software with hardware. A special DMA controller or *DMAC* manages the data transfer after receiving source and destination addresses from the processor. The advantage of this technique is that DMA transfers can occur at speeds approaching the access time of the memory. The disadvantage is that the CPU must suspend all operations while the DMAC controls the system buses. This means that interrupts will not be recognized and CPU-refreshed dynamic memories will not be refreshed.

Because the DMAC takes the place of the microprocessor during a DMA transfer, it must be compatible with the control signals of the processor. In the case of the Z-80, a special DMA processor is available from Zilog called the *Z-80 DMA*. This device is fully compatible with all control signals generated by the Z-80 and features:

1. Two MB/s DMA transfers using two clock cycle simultaneous transfers
2. One channel with 16-bit source and destination addresses
3. Transfer and/or search modes with byte masking
4. Byte, burst, and continuous DMA modes
5. Software- or hardware-initiated DMA requests
6. Direct Z-80 compatibility, including programmable mode 2 interrupt vector and daisy-chain priority structure
7. I/O-to-I/O, I/O-to-memory, memory-to-I/O, and memory-to-memory DMA transfers

Interfacing the Z-80 DMA. Pin functions and numbers for the Z-80 DMA are shown in Fig. 8.25. The most important characteristic to note is that all three system buses can be output by the DMA with exactly the same timing as output by the Z-80 processor. Because of this, the memory and I/O can be accessed by the DMA without these devices knowing that the CPU is not in control.

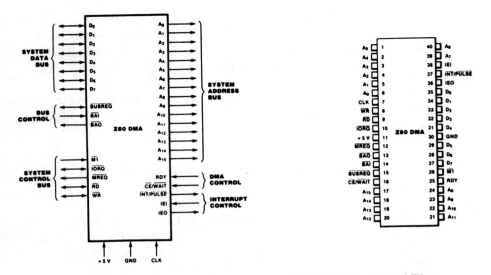

Figure 8.25 Pin functions and numbers for the Z-80 DMA. (Courtesy of Zilog, Inc.)

Note that $\overline{\text{IORQ}}$, $\overline{\text{RD}}$, and $\overline{\text{WR}}$ are also input signals. This enables the DMA to be accessed by the Z-80 as a single I/O port. $\overline{\text{M1}}$ and $\overline{\text{IORQ}}$ allow recognition of the Z-80 $\overline{\text{INTA}}$ condition ($\overline{\text{IORQ}} \cdot \overline{\text{M1}}$) and detection of the RETI instruction.

Figure 8.26 illustrates how the Z-80 DMA is interfaced to the Z-80 microprocessor. For non-DMA operations ($\overline{\text{BUSAKB}} = 1$) the $\overline{\text{CE/WAIT}}$ input acts as a normal *chip enable* and is driven by the address decoder IC1. In this case port FFH is decoded. When DMA is active, the I/O device can request *WAIT* states by pulling the DMA's $\overline{\text{CE/WAIT}}$ line low; the timing is identical to Z-80 WAIT state timing discussed in Chap. 4.

The DMA cycle is initiated by the DMA output signal $\overline{\text{BUSRQ}}$. The CPU responds with $\overline{\text{BUSAKB}}$ and tri-states all of its buses. In larger systems $\overline{\text{BUSAKB}}$ is also used to tri-state the bus buffers (see Fig. 4.27). In Fig. 8.26 this means that all three system buses to the left of the diagram become open circuits. The Z-80 DMA now controls these bus lines.

Two inputs are provided to synchronize the DMA to the speed of the peripheral. These are $\overline{\text{WAIT}}$ and RDY. $\overline{\text{WAIT}}$ functions as a normal WAIT state request input, as discussed previously. The RDY input can be connected to the peripheral's BUSY/READY status output. Only when RDY is high can DMA transfers take place.

Finally, the $\overline{\text{BAI}}$ and $\overline{\text{BAO}}$ bus acknowledge input and output are used for daisy-chaining several DMA devices, similar to the standard Z-80 daisy-chain interrupt structure. $\overline{\text{BAO}}$, connected to $\overline{\text{BAI}}$ of the next-highest-priority DMA, is output high when its $\overline{\text{BAI}}$ input is low, preventing lower-priority DMAs from generating a $\overline{\text{BUSRQ}}$.

Typical DMA Transfer. Figure 8.27 is a flowchart of the operation of the Z-80 DMA when programmed for the *burst* mode. Before the DMA transfer takes place,

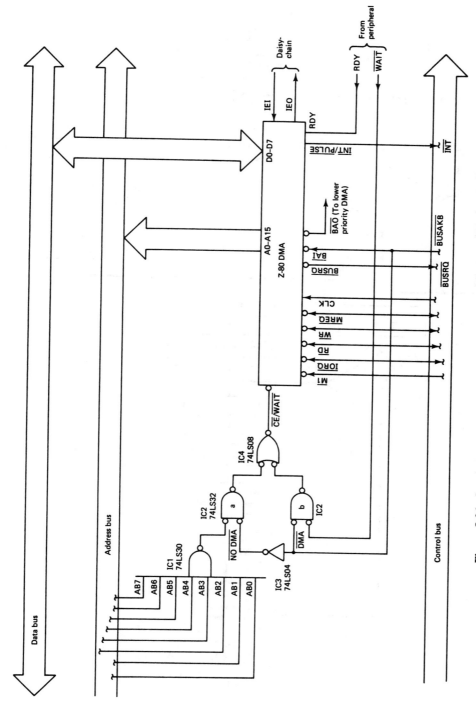

Figure 8.26 Interfacing the Z-80 DMA to the three-bus system architecture of the Z-80 microprocessor. The RDY and $\overline{\text{WAIT}}$ inputs are used to synchronize the DMA to the I/O device.

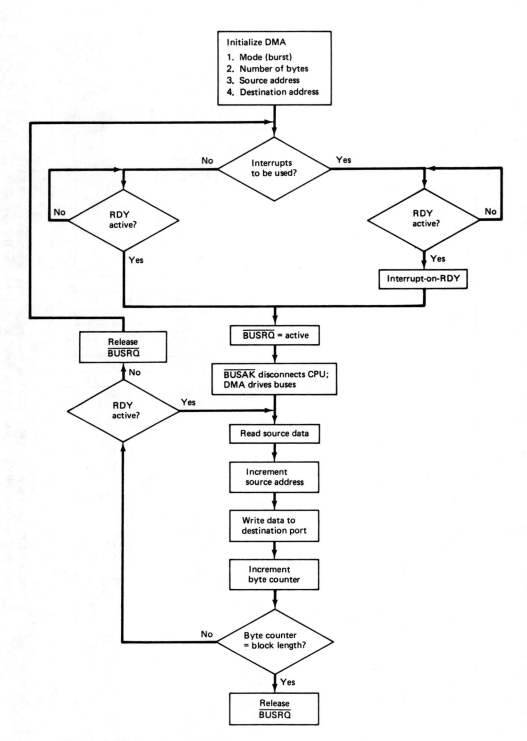

Figure 8.27 Flowchart of the DMA sequence when the Z-80 DMA is programmed for the burst mode.

control codes must be written to the DMA's I/O port, selecting the operating mode, number of bytes to transfer, and source and destination addresses.

The transfer sequence begins when the peripheral's READY flag becomes active. The DMA can be programmed to *interrupt on RDY*; the interrupt service routine then starts the DMA by writing a DMA enable command word, or begins the transfer as soon as READY is active. The flowchart shows both choices.

In either case the DMA asserts $\overline{BUSRQ}$ and the processor responds (within one machine cycle) with $\overline{BUSAK}$, relinquishing control of the system buses to the DMA. The data byte is then fetched from memory, brought into the DMA, and written to the I/O port. This is called "sequential" DMA—a read followed in sequence by a write. The byte counter is next incremented and compared with the block length. If more data is to be transferred, the RDY line is again sampled, and if found active, the cycle repeats.

You might recall from the discussion in Chap. 6 that this mode of DMA is called *burst* or *demand* DMA. As long as the RDY line remains high, data bytes will be transferred to the peripheral. Burst DMA is appropriate for filling a printer's buffer, for example. In this case, the buffer is filled by the DMA at memory access speed until full (RDY = inactive). The DMA cycle then ends while the printer empties the buffer. When RDY becomes active again, another DMA transfer begins.

The Z-80 DMA can also be programmed to operate in a *continuous* or *block* mode. The only difference is that after transferring a byte, if the RDY input is found inactive, the DMA idles waiting for the RDY condition. The buses are not released to the processor until the entire block has been transferred.

A third mode called *byte* or *single*-mode DMA can also be programmed. In this case a single byte is transferred, after which control of the buses is relinquished to the CPU— even if RDY remains active. In the latter case, one machine cycle will always be executed before the DMA again takes control of the buses for the next transfer.

Response Time and Transfer Rate.   As pointed out in Fig. 8.27, there are two ways that a DMA transfer can be requested. Both involve the RDY input. If the *interrupt on RDY* option is selected, an interrupt will be generated when RDY becomes active. The interrupt service routine can then enable the DMA and the transfer sequence will begin. Because of the interrupt response time and software overhead involved, this will be the slowest means of responding to RDY.

The other technique is to enable the DMA *before* RDY becomes active. In this case the DMA sequence will occur within one machine cycle (plus one T state) after RDY becomes active. In the worst case this will require 11 T states or 2.75 μs with a 4-MHz clock.

The transfer rate, on the other hand, refers to how fast data can be transferred to the I/O device. Using standard Z-80 timing and a sequential DMA technique (read a byte—write a byte), four clock cycles are required for each operation, or eight clock cycles per transfer. At 4 MHz this corresponds to 0.5 MB/s.

A unique feature of the Z-80 DMA is that the number of clock periods per read or write cycle can be programmed as two, three, or four. Therefore, the maximum transfer rate is obtained by programming two clock periods per cycle or four clock periods per transfer. In this case the transfer rate becomes 1 MB/s.

The fastest transfer speed of all is obtained if *simultaneous* DMA transfers are allowed. In this technique the $\overline{\text{MEMR}}$ and $\overline{\text{IOW}}$ control bus signals are active simultaneously (or $\overline{\text{MEMW}}$ and $\overline{\text{IOR}}$). Data is fetched from memory and written directly to the I/O device. This is the (only) technique used by Intel's 8237 DMAC and is illustrated in Fig. 7.39. The Z-80 DMA can also support this technique, but external hardware is required.

When simultaneous DMA transfers are used and the option of two clock periods per operation is programmed, the Z-80 DMA can transfer one byte every two clock periods. The transfer rate becomes 2 MB/s with a 4-MHz clock.

Of course, the memory devices and peripheral must be capable of keeping up with the DMA transfer rate. For memory this is not a problem. Even with only two clock periods per transfer, the memory has nearly 500 ns to fetch and output the data byte. This is quite slow by today's standards, where memory access times are commonly less than 200 ns.

For many peripherals, however, a data rate of 2 MB/s (or even 1 MB/s) will be too fast. In this case the RDY line can be used to synchronize the peripheral and DMA. Another option is to use the WAIT input to cause WAIT states while the I/O device processes the data byte.

The type of interfacing technique to use—polling, interrupts, or DMA—must be considered carefully. And even if DMA is selected, the type of DMA transfer to use—byte, burst, or continuous—must also be given careful consideration if maximum utilization of the resources of the processor is to be achieved.

Example 8.9

Determine, from an efficiency standpoint, which interfacing technique to use—polling, interrupts, or DMA—to interface a 5¼-inch double-density disk drive. Assume a Z-80A microprocessor.

Solution. A 5¼-inch double-density disk drive reads and writes data at a 250,000-bit/s rate. This corresponds to a new byte every 32 μs. Let's examine each interfacing technique for feasibility.

1. *Polling*: A programmed I/O technique would require a program similar to that shown in Fig. 6.14. Although developed for a parallel printer, the program is easily adapted to the READY flag of the floppy disk drive. In Ex. 6.6 the transfer period of this routine was shown to be 12.75 μs with a Z-80A. Therefore, this technique will work, although the processor will be dedicated to this single task.

2. *Interrupts*: If interrupts are used, the READY output of the floppy disk drive is used to generate the interrupt request. Control then branches to a special interrupt service routine (ISR) where a data byte is output to the disk drive. In principle the processor is now free to perform some other task, as opposed to polling the READY flag repeatedly as is done in the programmed solution. However, Fig. 8.28 illustrates that the interrupt service routine alone will require 49 T states.

```
;EXAMPLE OF A Z-80 INTERRUPT SERVICE ROUTINE FOR
;TRANSFERRING DATA TO A FAST PERIPHERAL.
;
;THE ALTERNATE REGISTERS ARE USED TO SAVE THE
;ENVIRONMENT AND SPEED UP THE HOUSEKEEPING.
;
;T STATES ARE SHOWN ALONG THE RIGHT MARGIN.

ISR   EXX                       ;GET TRANSFER PARAMETERS        [4]
      OUTI                      ;TRANSFER A BYTE, BUMP COUNTER  [16]
      JR         Z,DONE         ;TEST FOR END OF DATA           [7]
      EXX                       ;IF NOT THEN SAVE PARAMETERS    [4]
      EI                        ;REENABLE INTERRUPTS            [4]
      RETI                      ;RETURN CONTROL                 [14]
      ;
;TOTAL T STATES IS 49 OR 12.25 MICROSECONDS AT 4 MHZ
```

Figure 8.28 Sample Z-80 ISR for Ex. 8.9.

The response time will require an additional 20–43 T states (see Table 6.6). This is 23 μs (worst case)—marginally fast enough to keep up with the drive.

3. *DMA*: If the Z-80 DMA is used and READY used to start the transfer sequence (that is, no interrupt on ready), 11 T states (worst case) will elapse before the transfer and 8 more T states will be required assuming a sequential (with standard Z-80 timing) transfer. Therefore, 19 T states or 4.75 μs will be required. Certainly, the DMA technique is fast enough.

The choice of DMA mode still remains. If the continuous or block mode is selected, the DMA (and microprocessor) will idle for 27.25 μs until the READY flag is again set. Although this technique will work, it is analogous to polling and does not utilize the full resources of the processor.

The burst mode would be a better choice. After transferring the byte and finding READY low, control of the system buses will be released and the processor given 27.25 μs to work on some other task (one or two instructions could be executed per transfer). Programming the DMA for byte mode would work equally well.

Read/Write Registers. Although the Z-80 DMA appears to the programmer to be only one input and one output port, in fact it contains 21 writable registers and seven readable registers. Figure 8.29 lists the write registers, referred to as WR0 through WR6. Examining WR0, note that two ports are defined, A and B. One of these is chosen as the *source* port and the other becomes the *destination* port. For example, programming WR0 bit 2 to a 1 defines port A as the source and port B as the destination. Subsequent programming then allows you to define specific addresses for ports A and B.

Example 8.10

Assume that DMA is to be used to transfer data from memory beginning at location D800H to an output port. If 1000H bytes are to be transferred, write the Z-80 program required to program WR0. Assume that the circuit in Fig. 8.26 is used.

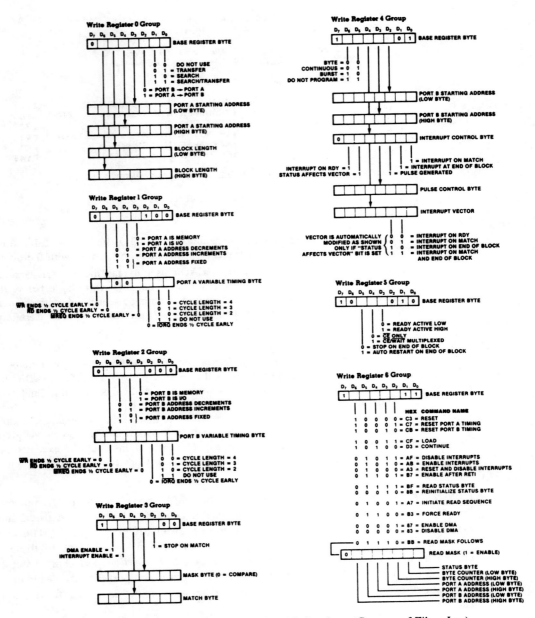

Figure 8.29 Z-80 DMA write register bit functions. (Courtesy of Zilog, Inc.)

Solution. WR0 actually consists of five registers. Bits 3 through 6, if set, specify that the following writes should be interpreted as the port A starting address and block length. The following codes should be written to WR0.

1. 01111101   (7D)   A → B transfer, address and block length to follow
2. 00000000   (00)   Port A starting address (low byte)
3. 11011000   (D8)   Port A starting address (high byte)
4. 11111111   (FF)   Block length (low byte)
5. 00001111   (0F)   Block length (high byte)

Note: One more byte is transferred than is specified. The initialization program can take advantage of the Z-80's *OTIR* instruction.

```
    LD   C,OFFH      ;C HOLDS DMA PORT ADDRESS
    LD   B,05H       ;5 BYTES TO PROGRAM
    LD   HL,CODES    ;POINT HL AT CODES
    OTIR             ;PROGRAM THE BYTES
DB  CODES            7DH,00,0D8H,0FFH,0FH
```

The following is a brief description of each of the writable registers.

WR0   Port A address, transfer or search, and source/destination definitions.

WR1   Port A controls. Note that timing can be shortened from the Z-80 standard four clock cycles per operation to two or three cycles per operation.

WR2   Port B controls.

WR3   Specifies the match byte when programmed for the search mode. The mask byte allows certain bits of the match byte to be masked (not considered).

WR4   Port B address and DMA mode. Also interrupt control, including the Z-80 mode 2 interrupt vector.

WR5   When the end-of-block condition occurs, the DMA can be programmed to reload the starting address automatically and begin again.

WR6   16 different commands can be given to the DMA. Refer to Fig. 8.30 for a description of each. Example 8.11 will show how these commands are used in a typical initialization routine.

The seven read registers are labeled RR0 through RR6 and their descriptions are provided in Fig. 8.31. These registers should not be read until one of two special read commands has been given (see Fig. 8.30):

1. *Read status byte*: This command causes the next CPU read operation to return the DMA status byte (the first register in the RR0 group).

2. *Initiate read sequence*: This command causes the next CPU read operation to return the first unmasked read register beginning with RR0. For example, if

WR6 code (hex)	Command	Action/Comment
C3	Reset	Do at power on
C7	Reset port A timing	Standard Z-80 timing
CB	Reset port B timing	Standard Z-80 timing
CF	Load	Load source address register (specified by WR0) and clear byte counter; load destination address register (specified by WR4) during the first count to the destination address
D3	Continue	Clear byte counter and continue DMA
AF	Disable interrupts	Simulate $\overline{\text{INTA}}$ for non Z-80 CPUs
AB	Enable interrupts	Do only at power on or with non Z-80 CPUs to simulate RETI
A3	Reset and disable interrupts	This and the AB control word simulate the RETI instruction for non Z-80 CPUs
B7	Enable after RETI	Use when interrupt-on-RDY is selected to allow subsequent interrupt requests
BF	Read status byte	Next I/O read will be status byte
8B	Reinitialize status byte	Reinitialize (set) the match-found and end-of-block status flags
A7	Initialize read sequence	Next I/O read will be first low order read register designated by read mask
B3	Force ready	Takes the place of external READY signal for memory-memory transfers
87	Enable DMA	If RDY is active, DMA will begin immediately with $\overline{\text{BUSRQ}}$
83	Disable DMA	Prevent DMA from requesting bus even if RDY = active
BB	Read mask follows	A 0 bit masks that read register; 2-byte command

Figure 8.30 When writing to the Z-80 DMA write register 6 (WR6), 16 different commands can be specified.

the *Read mask follows* command specifies the mask word 00011001 (see WR6 in Fig. 8.29), the read registers will be read in the following order:

RR0   Status byte
RR3   Port A address counter (low byte)
RR4   Port A address counter (high byte)

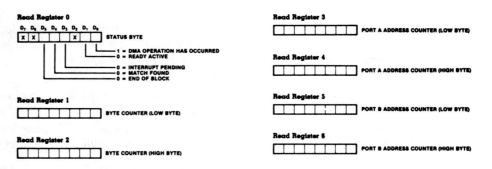

Figure 8.31 Z-80 DMA read register bit functions. (Courtesy of Zilog, Inc.)

Programming the Z-80 DMA. All registers of the Z-80 DMA must be programmed at power-on; none come up in a predictable state. Table 8.7 is the recommended initialization sequence. In the worst case, 35 bytes will be required. Note that the *Reset* command is given six times. This is done to guarantee a reset in the event that you are in the middle of a five-byte write to WR4 (the DMA would interpret the resets as addresses). All WR6 commands disable the DMA, except *Enable DMA*, and this command should be the last one programmed. In this way, if RDY is active, the DMA transfer can begin immediately.

Example 8.11

Program the Z-80 DMA (assuming the circuit in Fig. 8.26) for burst mode and to transfer 1000H bytes beginning at address D800H to output port 05. Initiate the transfer with an interrupt request when the RDY input goes *low* and generate a second interrupt at the end of the block. Determine addresses on page F8H to store the ISR jump vectors for the end-of-block and interrupt-on-RDY conditions.

Solution. The programming codes required are listed in Fig. 8.32 and follow the recommended sequence given in Table 8.7. Note in line 3 that port B (the I/O port) is temporarily assigned as the source. This is because the LOAD command loads a *fixed address* to a source port, not a destination port. In line 9, port B is indicated as a fixed address, and in line 15, the address is loaded from the address register to the address counter (where it is used as the DMA address). Line 16 redefines port A as the source and line 17 loads this address. In this way port B is defined as a fixed address and the destination port.

TABLE 8.7 INITIALIZATION SEQUENCE FOR THE Z-80 DMA

Initialization/Reinitialization Sequence	Maximum Number of Bytes for Z80 CPU
DISABLE DMA command	1
RESET command (multiple)	6
WR0 control bytes	5
WR1 control bytes	2
WR2 control bytes	2
WR3 control bytes	3
WR4 control bytes	5
WR5 control bytes	1
RESET PORT A TIMING command	1
RESET PORT B TIMING command	1
LOAD command	1
REINITIALIZE STATUS BYTE command	1
READ MASK FOLLOWS command	1
Read Mask control byte	1
INITIATE READ SEQUENCE command	1
FORCE READY command	1
ENABLE INTERRUPTS command	1
ENABLE DMA command	1
	35

Source: Zilog, Incorporated.

Line	Register	Code	Action/Comment
1	WR6	83	Disable DMA
2	WR6	C3	Reset (do 6 times)
3	WR0	79	Port B → A*, transfer no search
4	WR0	00	Port A address (lower)
5	WR0	D8	Port A address (upper)
6	WR0	FF	Block length (less 1, lower)
7	WR0	0F	Block length (upper)
8	WR1	14	Standard timing, address increments Port A is memory
9	WR2	28	Standard timing, address fixed, Port B is I/O
			Skip WR3 — no match required
10	WR4	D5	Burst mode, interrupt control byte follows, no upper address, Port B lower address follows
11	WR4	05	Port B lower address
12	WR4	72	Interrupt control byte: interrupt vector follows, interrupt on end of block and RDY, status affects vector
13	WR4	E0	Interrupt vector
14	WR5	82	No auto restart, no WAIT states, RDY active low
			Skip reset port A, B timing — reset already does this
15	WR6	CF	LOAD* — load source (port B) address registers and clear byte counter
16	WR0	05	Port A → B*, transfer no search
17	WR6	CF	LOAD* — load source (port A) address register
18	WR6	8B	Reinitialize status byte
19	WR6	BB	Read mask follows
20	WR6	3F	Mask port B high address
21	WR6	A7	Reinitialize read sequence — next read will be RR0
			Skip force ready — I/O port supplies RDY input
22	WR6	AB	Enable interrupts
23	WR6	87	Enable DMA — this command should be given in the ISR

*Refer to the text to explain these steps.

Figure 8.32 Programming codes for Ex. 8.11.

The interrupt control register is written in line 12. The *interrupt-on-RDY* and *interrupt-on-end-of-block* conditions are enabled with bits 1 and 6. By making bit 5 a 1, the interrupt vector will automatically be altered for these two conditions (status affects vector). Bit 4 of the interrupt control byte indicates that the interrupt vector follows, and this is given in line 13. Arbitrarily selecting E0H as the base, the *interrupt-on-RDY* condition will vector to F8E0H and the *interrupt-on-end-of-block* condition will vector to F8E4H (see WR4 in Fig. 8.29).

The programming codes end by enabling interrupts but not the DMA. Now as soon as RDY goes low, control is transferred to the ISR whose address is stored in F8E0. Presumably, this routine enables the DMA and a burst transfer occurs until RDY goes inactive. The DMA releases control of the buses and normal processing resumes. When the peripheral is ready for new data (RDY = 0), the DMA requests control of the buses and the transfer continues. Eventually, the entire block will be transferred and an interrupt generated (interrupt on end of block) vectoring to the ISR whose address is stored in F8E4H. This routine can define a new block or end the DMA.

The program to support the codes in Fig. 8.32 is very similar to the program given in Ex. 8.10 except that mode 2 interrupts should be specified and the I register loaded.

8.4 PERIPHERAL CONTROLLER BUS BUFFERING TECHNIQUES

When using the special family support devices, careful attention must be given to the bus buffers. The techniques required are the same whether the Z-80 family or the 8080/85 family of devices is being considered. Section 7.6 provides details on the techniques required. Please turn to this section if you have not read this material.

CHAPTER SUMMARY

1. The Z-80 microprocessor is supported by a number of special interfacing components. In addition, the Z-80 CPU module is compatible with all 8080 support devices. The Z-80 support devices are not compatible with the 8080 or 8085, however.
2. The Z-80 PIO provides two 8-bit programmable input or output ports, including two handshaking signals per port.
3. The PIO has four modes of operation, including input and output ports with handshaking, a bidirectional I/O port, and a bit-programmable I/O port.
4. As with all Z-80 support devices, a daisy-chain priority structure is implemented using Z-80 mode 2 interrupts.
5. The Z-80 CTC has four 8-bit timer/counter channels, each programmable as a timer or counter.
6. When operated as a counter, the CTC will decrement an 8-bit counter with each external clock pulse. When 0 count occurs, an interrupt can be requested and the ZC/TO output will pulse high.
7. When operated as a timer, the CTC will decrement an 8-bit counter with each system clock pulse. When 0 count occurs, an interrupt can be requested and the ZC/TO output will pulse high.
8. The Z-80 DMA provides sequential DMA transfers up to 1 MB/s and up to 2 MB/s with simultaneous transfers.
9. The DMA provides one channel with separately programmable 16-bit source and destination addresses.
10. The DMA can be programmed for byte, burst, or block mode and allows transfer or search operations. In the search mode a maskable match byte can be specified.

LAB PROJECTS

8.1. Study the schematic diagram of the microcomputer you are using to support this text/course and see if your computer uses a Z-80 PIO. If so, answer the following questions about the interface.
  (a) To what range of addresses is the chip mapped?
  (b) List the I/O devices (if any) connected to ports A and B.
  (c) List the operating modes for ports A and B.

8.2. Write a program to access your computer's PIO chip. For example, if a keypad and display are interfaced, write a program to read the keyboard and display the key's value. If a speaker is connected to one output bit, write a program to produce a tone. (Program 14 in Chap. 3 provides an example of a computer music program.)

8.3. Using Fig. 8.33 as a guide build the PIO matrix keyboard interface shown. Probs. 8.8 and 8.9 outline the necessary control software.

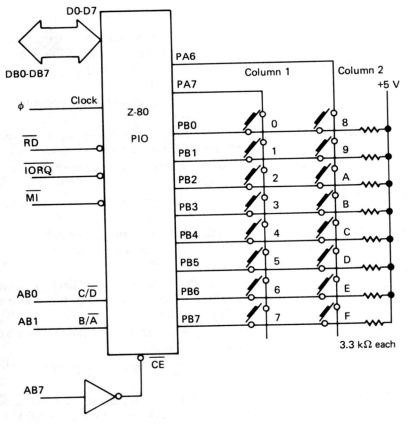

Figure 8.33 PIO interface for Lab 8.3 and Probs. 8.8 and 8.9.

8.4. Construct the mode 0 and mode 1 PIO parallel printer interface shown in Fig. 8.8. The program in Fig. 8.9 can be used to send (ASCII) data to the printer. A female DB-25 connector with long wires attached can be used to bring the printer signals to a breadboard.

8.5. Repeat Lab 8.1 for the Z-80 CTC.

8.6. Using a circuit similar to Fig. 8.16 program the Z-80 CTC:

   (a) as a one-shot triggered by the CLK/TRG input (see Probs. 8.17 through 8.19).

   (b) as a divide-by-N counter. Use a signal generator as the CLK input and observe the output on an oscilloscope (see Probs. 8.15 and 8.20).

QUESTIONS AND PROBLEMS

Section 8.1

8.1. The Z-80 port B control register is accessed when $C/\overline{D}$ is _____ and $B/\overline{A}$ is _____.

8.2. The Z-80 PIO and CTC do not use the CPU's $\overline{WR}$ signal. How is an I/O write cycle detected by these chips?

8.3. Write a program like Ex. 8.2 for the Z-80 PIO interface in Fig. 8.2. Have your program enable mode 2 interrupts on port A assuming a jump table at address C840H.

8.4. Refer to the Z-80 PIO interface in Fig. 8.2. Write a program that will cause the PIO to generate an interrupt when bits PA0, PA1, and PA4, each programmed as an input, are all low. Program the remaining bits of port A as outputs.

8.5. The program in Fig. 8.34 is written to control the PIO interface in Fig. 8.2. Answer the following questions about this program.

   (a) Which port—A or B—is being programmed?

   (b) What PIO mode is being programmed?

```
         IM     2

         LD     A,80H

         LD     I,A

INIT     LD     HL,CODES

         LD     B,5

         LD     C,F3H

         OTIR

CODES    DEFB   CFH, F0H, B7H, 3FH, 6EH
```

Figure 8.34 Program for Prob. 8.5.

(c) Under what conditions will an interrupt be generated?

(d) What is the interrupt vector address?

8.6. Specify the PIO programming sequence required for the following configuration. Assume the hardware interface in Fig. 8.2.

(a) Port A = mode 3, all bits are active-high inputs.

(b) Port B = mode 0.

(c) Port A low–order interrupt vector = 00.

(d) Port B interrupts disabled.

(e) Port A interrupt request should occur only if PA1, PA2, or PA7 is high.

8.7. Assume that port A of the Z-80 PIO interface in Fig. 8.2 is used to control an industrial process with bit definitions as shown in Fig. 8.35. Bits 0, 2, and 3 are active-high inputs, while bits 5 and 7 are active-high alarm outputs. Write two subroutines to supervise control of this process. Subroutine 1 should initialize the PIO, turn on power, and after a 10-s delay, turn on the heaters. Subroutine 2 should be called as an ISR if OVFLW or HIGH TEMP occurs. If an OVFLW condition occurs, cause the process to halt; if HIGH TEMP occurs, power-down the system.

8.8. Figure 8.33 shows a 16-key switch matrix interfaced to a Z-80 PIO. This circuit is similar to the memory-mapped interface in Chap. 6, Fig. 6.8. Answer the following questions about this interface.

(a) What *range* of I/O addresses does the PIO occupy?

(b) To read only column 1, PA6 must be _____ and PA7 must be
_____.

(c) If only key 6 is held down, what hex code will be read from PIO port B?

8.9. Write the software to control the keyboard interface in Fig. 8.33. Your program should have the following subroutines:

(a) INIT: Program the PIO chip so that port A is an output and port B an input. Any active-low input on port B should cause an interrupt to location 8000H.

(b) START: Program PA6 and PA7 low to enable both columns. Check that no keys are down (KREAD subroutine) and then enable interrupts.

(c) KREAD: Read port B and set flags (nonzero result means a key is down in the active column).

(d) ISR: When any key is pressed, control vectors here. This routine should call KREAD and encode the key pressed in register A.

8.10. Sketch a timing diagram for the PIO printer interface and control program shown in Figs. 8.8 and 8.9. Your diagram should include ARDY/$\overline{\text{ASTB}}$, $\overline{\text{STROBE}}$, BUSY/$\overline{\text{READY}}$, $\overline{\text{ACK}}$, $\overline{\text{BSTB}}$, and $\overline{\text{INT}}$.

D7	D6	D5	D4	D3	D2	D1	D0
OVFLW	X	HIGH TEMP	X	POWER ON	HEATERS ON	X	HALT PROCESS

Figure 8.35 PIO port A bit definitions for Prob. 8.7.

*8.11. Assume the PIO printer interface in Fig. 8.8 malfunctions in such a way that the PB0 input is always high. Which of the following would be symptoms of this problem?

    (a) The printer would miss characters because the CPU would be outputting data faster than it could be printed.

    (b) The message "PRINTER OFF LINE" would be output each time the printer was accessed.

    (c) Bus contention could occur each time the CPU attempted to read from the PIO chip.

8.12. What codes must be output to ports A and B in the PIO-controlled multiplexed display in Fig. 8.12 to cause the letter "F" to appear in the digit 2 position?

*8.13. If the digit 4 and digit 5 pins of IC6 in the multiplexed display in Fig. 8.12 were accidentally shorted together, what would the symptom of this problem be? Assume the software in Fig. 8.14 is used to control the interface.

8.14. Write a program for the multiplexed display in Fig. 8.12 to cause the message "CPU UP" to appear in the six displays.

Section 8.2

8.15. A Z-80 CTC is interfaced to a 4-MHz Z-80 microprocessor. A 2-MHz square-wave signal is connected to its CLK/TRG0 input.

    (a) When operated in the counter mode, what is the maximum time delay that can be programmed between successive ZC/TO0 output pulses?

    (b) Repeat (a) for the timer mode.

    (c) Repeat (a) if channels 0, 1, and 2 are cascaded and the output is taken at ZC/TO2.

8.16. Assume the CTC in Ex. 8.7 is programmed with the following time constants: channel 0 = E8H and channel 1 = 03H. How many clock edges will occur between ZC/TO1 output pulses?

8.17. Assuming the I/O ports shown in Fig. 8.16, write a program to initialize the CTC as follows:

    (a) Channel 0 timer mode, time constant = F9H, interrupts enabled, falling edge trigger, prescale = 256.

    (b) Channel 1 counter mode, time constant = B3H, interrupts enabled, rising edge trigger.

8.18. Calculate the width of the one-shot pulse produced by the CTC circuit in Fig. 8.23 when programmed as described in Prob. 8.17. Assume the system clock frequency is 4 MHz.

8.19. Write a BASIC program to find all possible time constant combinations of N0 and N1 that solve the equation

$$N0 \times N1 \times P = N$$

where N0 and N1 are integers between 1 and 256; P is a prescale factor, 16 or 256; and N is an integer describing the Z-80 CTC as a divide-by-N counter with channel 0 a timer, and channel 1 a counter, wired in cascade.

8.20. Calculate the frequency and duty cycle of output Q in Fig. 8.36. Assume

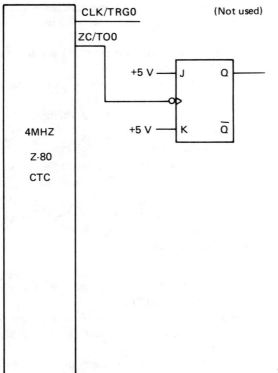

CLK/TRG0   (Not used)

ZC/TO0

+5 V — J   Q

+5 V — K $\overline{Q}$

4MHZ

Z-80

CTC

Figure 8.36   CTC circuit for Prob. 8.20.

channel 0 of the CTC is programmed as a timer with prescale factor = 16, time constant = 125, and automatic trigger.

8.21. Sketch a circuit diagram to interface a Z-80 PIO at I/O ports 40–43H and a Z-80 CTC at ports 44–47H using full decoding. Connect the daisy-chain interrupts such that the PIO has the highest priority.

Section 8.3

8.22. Which is faster, sequential or simultaneous DMA transfers? Why?

8.23. State the logic condition—active or inactive—of the Z-80 DMA RDY and $\overline{\text{WAIT}}$ inputs in order for a DMA transfer to take place.

8.24. With a cycle length of 4, calculate the length of time required by a Z-80 DMA to transfer a 16K-byte file to an I/O device assuming a 4-MHz clock and sequential DMA.

8.25. The program in Fig. 8.37 uses the Z-80 OTIR instruction to transfer a block of data from memory to an I/O device (in effect a DMA transfer using the Z-80 as the controller. Answer the following questions about this program.
  (a) What is the I/O port address?
  (b) What is the starting memory location?

```
                          LD      D,40H

                          LD      B,0

                          LD      C,5

                          LD      HL,1000H

              LOOP        OTIR

                          DEC     D
                                               Figure 8.37   Transfer program for Prob.
                          JR      NZ,LOOP      8.25.
```

(c) How many bytes will be transferred?

(d) Calculate the data transfer rate assuming a 4-MHz clock.

(e) How long will it take to transfer the entire block?

8.26. Assume a 16K-byte DMA transfer is to take place from I/O port 07H to memory beginning at address A000H using the Z-80 DMA. For each of the following, determine the specified bytes for the conditions listed.

	Register	No. of bytes to program	Condition
(a)	WR0	4	A → B transfer
(b)	WR1	1	Normal timing, 4 cycles
(c)	WR2	1	Normal timing, 4 cycles
(d)	WR4	5	Interrupt on RDY and end of block, burst, vector address 8040H
(e)	WR5	1	Active-high RDY, $\overline{CE}$/$\overline{WAIT}$ multiplexed, stop on end-of-block
(f)	WR6	1	Disable DMA

8.27. Calculate the worst-case 4-MHz Z-80A response (time from RDY active until the first instruction of the service routine) for each of the following:

(a) Polling

```
              LOOP        IN      A,(C)
                          RRA
                          JR      NC,LOOP
              ;service routine begins here
```

(b) Peripheral's READY flag used to generate a mode 2 interrupt.

(c) Peripheral's READY flag used to initiate a Z-80 DMA transfer (no interrupts).

Section 8.4

8.28. Assume the data bus of the Z-80 PIO in Fig. 8.2 is buffered with a bidirectional bus buffer (see for example, Fig. 7.50). What signals should be used to control the DIR and $\overline{E}$ inputs of the buffer?

KEY CONCEPT ANSWERS

8.1.1. lowest

8.1.2. AND, OR

8.1.3. $\overline{\text{STROBE}}$

8.1.4. Only one decoder/driver is required.

8.2.1. counter and timer

8.2.2. external clock applied to CLK/TRG input

8.2.3. 256

8.2.4. 16, 256

8.3.1. Data is read into the DMA and then written to the destination.

8.3.2. (1) When RDY becomes active, begin the DMA. This requires DMA to be enabled ahead of time. (2) Enable DMA after RDY becomes active (via an interrupt).

8.3.3. continuous

8.3.4. 83H, WR6

9

Serial I/O Techniques

All microcomputer input/output falls under one of two broad categories: *serial* or *parallel*. A parallel port is the most natural for the 8080, 8085, and Z-80 because they are designed for 8-bit parallel data transfers. All of their registers are 8 bits wide (or multiples of 8 bits) and the data bus is optimized for the handling of parallel data. Because of this, data bytes can be transferred at very high speeds. For example, the Z-80 *OTIR* instruction can transfer data to a parallel port at over 190,000 bytes per second.

However, the parallel port is not without its drawbacks. In most cases the high transfer speed requires some form of handshaking logic to synchronize the data transfer. In the case of a printer, the following are required:

1. One 8-bit parallel output port
2. One 1-bit input port to monitor BUSY/$\overline{\text{READY}}$
3. A device select pulse for the $\overline{\text{STROBE}}$ signal

This means (at least) that an 11-conductor cable will be required. The parallel port also tends to become *hardware specific*, with the result that a parallel port on one computer may not be compatible with a parallel port on another (for example, the $\overline{\text{STROBE}}$ signals might not match, or one might use the $\overline{\text{ACK}}$ signal and the other a BUSY/$\overline{\text{READY}}$ signal).

A *serial* I/O port transmits each data byte bit by bit. The immediate advantage to this technique is that only two conductors are required—the signal wire and ground—three wires if *full-duplex* operation (simultaneous transmission and reception) is to be allowed. Of course, we must decide how long each bit will persist and the order of the bits. These "rules" are referred to as the *serial communications protocol*. As you might imagine, several different protocols have been developed over the years.

The obvious penalty with a serial I/O port is a significant reduction in the data transfer rate. The most popular serial standard, *EIA RS-232D*, restricts the data rate to less than 2000 bytes per second and cable lengths less than 50 ft. Newer (and faster) standards have been proposed but have not (yet) gained RS-232D's popularity.

Despite this disadvantage, serial communications, and the RS-232D standard in particular, has become widely accepted. One of the reasons is the definition by the EIA committee of a "standard" serial port. By defining the protocol (right down to the pinning of the connector), users can be sure of compatibility between their equipment and an RS-232D serial port.

Another powerful feature of serialized data is that it can easily be converted to audio tones and transmitted over the switched telephone network. This is done with a *modem* and allows communications between computer equipment thousands of miles apart.

In this chapter we study *synchronous* and *asynchronous* serial I/O ports and the Intel 8251 USART and Zilog Z-80 SIO. These chips are used to convert data from parallel to serial, and vice versa. Common error detection and correction techniques are also discussed. The chapter concludes with an introduction to the common modem standards used in the telecommunications field.

9.1 ASYNCHRONOUS SERIAL COMMUNICATIONS

As you read this section, look for the answers to these Key Concept questions:

9.1.1. Asynchronous serial data is framed between a _____ bit and one or two _____ bits.

9.1.2. The serial data rate in bits-per-second is usually called the _____ rate.

9.1.3. The _____ is an integrated circuit designed to transmit and receive asynchronous serial data.

One of the most common applications for a serial I/O port is the interface of a keyboard on a video display terminal (VDT). In this circuit, each keystroke generates a 7-bit ASCII code which is converted to bit-by-bit serial and then transmitted to a computer over a two- or three-conductor cable. Because even the fastest typist cannot exceed data rates of 60 to 100 words per minute, it is a good match for the (relatively) slow transmission rate of the serial port.

Note an important characteristic of this interface. At some times the serial port will be required to transfer data at 10 to 20 characters per second, but at other times the data rate may be only 1 or 2 characters per second. Indeed, most of the time the keyboard is not in use and the data rate is zero. Because of this erratic data rate, an *asynchronous* communications protocol must be established.

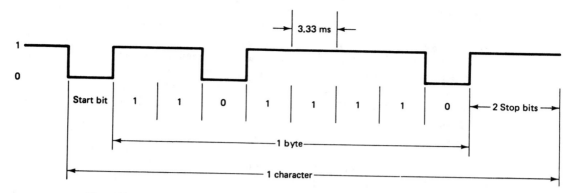

Figure 9.1 Standard asynchronous serial data format. The data byte is framed between the start bit and two stop bits. In this example the data byte is 7BH.

Start Bits, Stop Bits, and the Baud Rate.

The accepted technique for asynchronous serial communications is to hold the serial output line at a logic 1 level (called a "*mark*") until data is to be transmitted. Each character is required to begin with a logic 0 (called a "*space*") for one bit time. This bit is called the *start bit* and is used to synchronize the transmitter and receiver. Figure 9.1 illustrates how the data byte 7BH would look when transmitted in the asynchronous serial format. The data is sent least significant bit first and framed between a start bit (always a 0) and one or two stop bits (always a 1).

The start and stop bits carry no information but are required because of the asynchronous nature of the data. The data rate can be expressed as bits per second (bps) or characters per second (cps). The term "bits per second" is also called the *baud rate*.*

Example 9.1

Calculate the baud rate and character rate for the serial data shown in Fig. 9.1.

Solution. Because one bit persists for 3.33 ms, the bps rate is 1/3.33 ms = 300 bps or 300 baud. Because there are 11 bits per character, it will require 11 × 3.33 ms = 36.63 ms to transmit the entire byte. The character rate is therefore 1/36.63 ms = 27.3 cps.

Example 9.2

A VDT has 80 characters per line and 24 lines. At 300 baud, how long will it take to fill the screen of this terminal?

Solution. The total number of characters required is 80 × 24 = 1920. The total time is thus

$$\frac{1920 \text{ characters}}{27.3 \text{ cps}} = 70.3 \text{ s}$$

Note: A *memory-mapped* video display could fill this screen in less than 1 s.

---

* Baud rate actually refers to *signal events* per second. This is usually the same as the bits/s rate—but not always, as shown later in this chapter.

Generating and Recovering Asynchronous Serial Data. All microprocessors are capable of generating serial data without special hardware. For example,
consider the Z-80 program in Fig. 9.2. Assume that bit 0 of the DPORT is used as the
serial output pin. Each bit to be transmitted is rotated to the bit 0 position of the
accumulator and output. The DELAY subroutine determines the baud rate.

The 8085 microprocessor even has two pins devoted specifically for this task.
These are *SOD*, serial output data, and *SID*, serial input data. In this case an external
data port is not required (see Prob. 9.7).

Recovering the serial data requires a more complex program, but again no
special hardware is required. Assuming that a 1-bit input port is used, Fig. 9.3
flowcharts the process. The program begins by waiting for the one-to-zero transition
of the start bit. Once found, the middle of the bit is located by waiting for DELAY/
2 seconds. If the input bit is still 0, a valid start bit is assumed and the program
then waits for one additional bit time (thus sampling in the middle of all following
bits).

As each bit is read, it is rotated right—through the carry—and after eight
reads the entire byte has been recovered. The ninth read should return the first
stop bit, but if this bit is low, a *framing* error is indicated. If high, the data byte
can be saved and the program begins searching for the next start bit.

It has been implied in our discussion thus far that the receiver and transmitter
data rates are exactly matched. But is this necessary? Can we tolerate slight differences? For example, using software timing loops it is unlikely that the DELAY
subroutine in two different computers will be *exactly* the same.

Figure 9.4 illustrates the results of trying to recover data that is too fast or
too slow for the receiver. In either case, note how the error *accumulates*. If sampling
is done in the middle of the bit time, the maximum allowable error will cause the
ninth bit to be shifted $\frac{1}{2}$ bit time to the right or left. If all bits are shifted equally
(because of a data rate mismatch), the amount of error in one bit will be $\frac{1}{2}$ bit
time $\div\ 9 = \frac{1}{18}$ bit time. This means that the received and transmitted data rates
must match within 5.6%.

This is an interesting result. You might have guessed that the data rates had
to match exactly. This would be true if there were no start or stop bits. But because
of these bits, synchronization need only be held from the beginning of one start bit

```
;Z-80 SERIAL DATA TRANSMITTER PROGRAM
;
;BIT 0 OF THE DPORT IS THE SERIAL OUTPUT LINE.
;
        LD      C,DPORT     ;C HOLDS DATA PORT ADDRESS
        LD      B,0BH       ;11 BITS PER CHARACTER
        AND     A           ;CLEAR CARRY FOR START BIT
        RLA                 ;MOVE CARRY TO BIT 0
TRAN    OUT     (C),A       ;TRANSMIT THE BIT
        CALL    DELAY       ;HOLD FOR ONE BIT TIME
        RRA                 ;GET NEXT DATA BIT
        SCF                 ;SET CARRY FOR STOP BIT
        DJNZ    TRAN        ;DO FOR ALL 11 BITS
        RET                 ;AND THEN RETURN
```

Figure 9.2 Z-80 serial transmitter program. Bit 0 of the DPORT is used for the
serial output line.

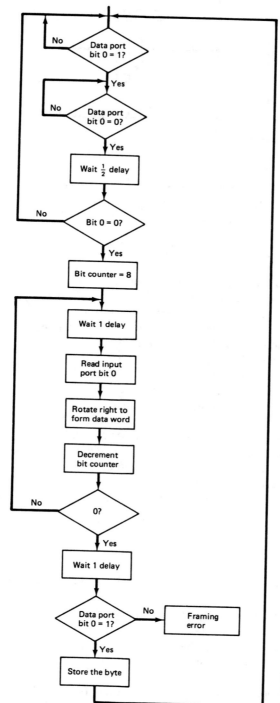

Figure 9.3 Flowchart of the process required to recover asynchronous serial data.

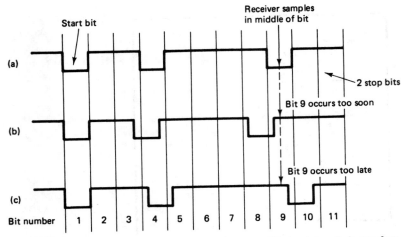

Figure 9.4 (a) Data transmitted at the proper rate; (b) the data rate is too fast; (c) the data rate is too slow.

to the beginning of the first stop bit. The technique *self-synchronizes* itself after each character. Of course, the price we pay for this is that each data byte must be increased in length by 3 bits or 37.5% (25% with only one stop bit). If these bits were not required, the character rate calculated in Ex. 9.2 would rise to 37.5 cps and the VDT screen could be filled in 52 s instead of 70 s.

In some cases a logic 1 might be delayed more than a logic 0 (or vice versa) when passing through the transmission medium. This can lead to individual bit errors rather than framing errors. Because of this, the rule of thumb is to try to match receiving and transmitting data rates to 1% or less.

Standard Asynchronous Serial Communications Protocols. As mentioned previously, protocols define certain rules that should be followed to help standardize the communications technique. An example is the adoption of a 0 start bit and logic 1 stop bits. Certain baud rates have also become standard and are listed in Table 9.1.

When setting up a serial port, several parameters must be specified. The most common are:

1. Data bits per character, usually five to eight
2. Stop bits, one or two
3. Parity bit, used to detect single bit errors, may be specified as odd or even or no parity (see Sec. 9.3)
4. Baud rate (see Table 9.1 for standard frequencies)

As an example, the old (and venerable) ASR-33 teletype (TTY) requires (1) 7 data bits, (2) 2 stop bits, (3) even parity, and (4) 110 baud.

The UART. Although reception and transmission of serial data can be done in software, programs that can adapt to the various protocols can become very long and tedious.

TABLE 9.1
COMMON BAUD
RATES FOR SERIAL
DATA
COMMUNICATIONS

Standard baud rates
75
110
150
300
600
1,200
2,400
4,800
9,600
19,200

They tie up the processor in timing loops, shuffling data bits and in general require time that might otherwise be spent more efficiently. For this reason, the semiconductor companies long ago designed the single-chip *universal asynchronous receiver/transmitter*, or UART.

Figure 9.5 is the block diagram of a common second-generation part, the General Instruments AY-5-1013. This chip provides a separate and independent transmitter and receiver of serial data. The two clock inputs (labeled *16X CLOCK*) determine the baud rate and should be chosen 16 times higher than the intended data rate. For example, if the transmitter should operate at 300 baud, the transmitter clock pin should receive a 4800-Hz square wave.

By dividing each bit time into 16 time periods, the UART is more accurately able to locate the center of each data bit. Some UARTs allow the clock to be 32 or 64 times the data rate.

Note that because of the separate receiver and transmitter circuits, full-duplex operation can occur. This would be particularly difficult to accomplish with the "software UART" discussed earlier.

I called the AY-5-1013 a *second-generation* part because it combines the receiver and transmitter functions in a single chip. However, unlike third-generation parts, all of its control functions must be hard-wired. That is, they are not directly programmable by the microprocessor. The following functions can be selected:

1. *Data word (DW1, DW2)*: allows 5 to 8 bits per data word
2. *Parity select (PS)*: odd or even parity
3. *Stop bits (SB)*: 1 or 2
4. *No parity (NP)*: no parity bit

In addition to these control functions, three status bits can be monitored. These are:

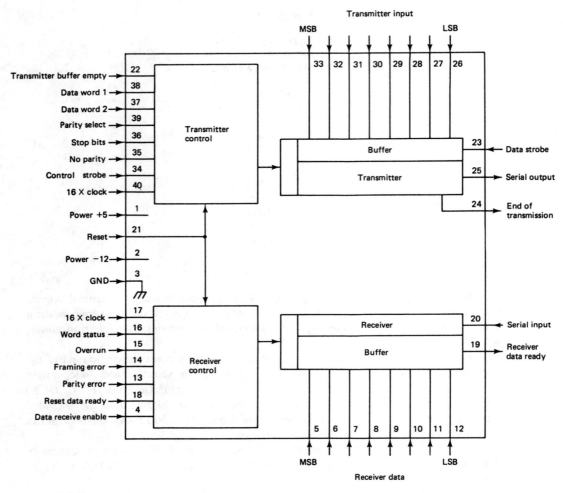

Figure 9.5 The AY-5-1013 UART. A separate transmitter and receiver are provided. Control functions are hard-wired.

1. *Transmitter buffer empty* (*TBE*): transmitter is ready for a new character
2. *Receiver data ready* (*RDR*): receiver has a character to be read
3. *End of transmission* (*EOT*): no character is being transmitted

Three other signals are provided to indicate error conditions. These are:

1. *Framing error* (*FE*): stop bit not received
2. *Parity error* (*PE*): received word's parity is incorrect
3. *Overrun* (*OR*) *error*: new received character has overwritten the preceding one

Figure 9.6 illustrates how the AY-5-1013 can be interfaced to the three-bus systems architecture of any of the CPU modules discussed in Chap. 4. To help understand this circuit, let's consider the sequence of events as one character is transmitted and received.

1. The status word (RDR, TBE, PE, FE, and OR) is tri-stated by the UART and enabled by the *STATUS WORD ENABLE* input. In this circuit, input port F1H becomes the status port.
2. The microprocessor monitors port F1H and tests bit 1, TBE. If high, a data byte is written to the UART transmitter at output port F0H. The $\overline{OUT\ F0}$ DSP ($\overline{DATA\ STROBE}$) causes the data byte to be latched and initiates transmission.
3. The UART automatically inserts the start bit, the 8 data bits, an even-parity bit, and 2 stop bits as hard-wired. The data rate will be $\frac{1}{16}$ of the clock rate.
4. Because the UART is *double buffered*, the TBE flag returns high as soon as the start bit is output, indicating that a second character can be loaded (however, it will not be transmitted until the first one is complete).
5. The microprocessor tests for a received character by reading the status port, in this case F1H. If the RDR flag is high, the receiver is holding a data byte.
6. The receiver outputs are not tri-stated by the AY-5-1013, and therefore an input port must be constructed using a 74LS244 buffer. Note that the $\overline{IN\ F0}$ DSP enables this buffer and resets the RDR flag (this avoids the overrun condition).

The software controlling the UART interface can also test the three error flags while waiting for TBE and RDR to be ready. However, in many cases these lines are ignored.

The interesting feature of the UART interface is that to the microprocessor, the data transfer appears to be parallel. It simply writes a byte to the transmitter (parallel) output port and reads a byte from the receiver (parallel) input port. The UART takes care of serializing the data, inserting start, stop, and parity bits, and controlling the data rate.

Usually, the UART is controlled with a simple polling routine, but interrupts and DMA can also be used. The latter two might be good choices due to the (relatively) long time period between ready signals.

Example 9.3

Refer to Program 9 in Chap. 3. This is a simple serial communications test program that causes the UART to transmit to itself (serial out must be connected to serial in). What changes should be made to this program to adapt to the circuit in Fig. 9.6?

Solution. The following equates should be changed.

```
SPORT    EQU   0F1H
DPORT    EQU   0F0H
TMSK     EQU   2
RMSK     EQU   1
```

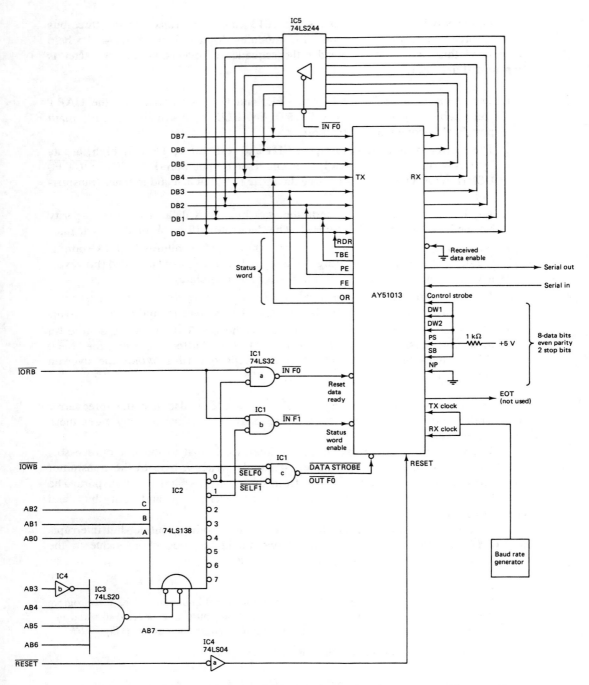

Figure 9.6 Interfacing the AY-5-1013 to the three-bus system architecture. One output port and two input ports are required.

Third-generation UARTs are programmable by the microprocessor similar to the techniques used with the 8255 PPI or Z-80 PIO. They are also more versatile than the AY-5-1013, allowing both asynchronous and synchronous serial formats. The Intel 8251 USART and Zilog Z-80 SIO circuits are discussed in detail in Secs. 9.4 and 9.5.

9.2 SYNCHRONOUS SERIAL COMMUNICATIONS

As you read this section, look for the answers to these Key Concept questions:

9.2.1. How does the transmission of synchronous serial data differ from asynchronous serial data?

9.2.2. The bisync protocol is _____ oriented but the SDLC format is _____ oriented.

The start and stop bits of asynchronous serial represent wasted overhead bits that reduce the overall character rate no matter what the baud rate. Even adding a parity bit can reduce the transfer rate by 10%.

But giving up the start and stop bits will require some means of synchronizing the data. How will we know when the data starts and when to sample it? In this section we examine two common synchronous serial protocols that answer these questions.

Bisync Protocol. Because there is no start bit, a special *sync* character is required in all synchronous serial formats. This character tells the receiver that data is about to follow. This requires the UART to have a special "hunt" or "search" mode so that the sync character can be found.

Because there is no stop bit, a clock signal usually accompanies the synchronous data to maintain synchronization. When synchronous serial data is to be transmitted over the telephone network, it is not possible to provide a separate clock channel. In this case a special *synchronous modem* is used that encodes the data and clock into a single signal. The receiving modem separates the data and clock signals.

Another difference when compared to asynchronous serial is that the clock rate is the same as the baud rate (that is, a 1X clock is used).

In the *bisync* protocol several special (ASCII) characters are used to control the data transfer, as shown in Table 9.2. Figure 9.7 illustrates one "frame" of a synchronous message. Just as asynchronous data is framed between start and stop bits, synchronous data is framed between special control codes. In Fig. 9.7 two sync characters are output followed by *STX*—start of text. Next, the data bytes follow. This block may consist of 100 or more data bytes or simply be other control codes. *ETX* signifies end of text. *BCC* is a block check character for error detection (see Sec. 9.3). *PAD* is the character output when no data is being transmitted and corresponds to the "mark" output in asynchronous serial.

Of course, the bisync protocol is simply a set of rules that everyone has

TABLE 9.2 SPECIAL CHARACTERS USED
IN THE BISYNC SYNCHRONOUS SERIAL PROTOCOL

Character	ASCII code	Description
SYNC	16	Sync character
PAD	FF	End of frame pad
DLE	10	Data link escape
ENQ	05	Enquiry
SOH	01	Start of header
STX	02	Start of text
ITB	0F	End of intermediate transmission block
ETB	17	End of transmission block
ETX	03	End of text

agreed to follow. It is not necessarily any better or worse than some other set of rules.

Example 9.4

Calculate the percentage of "wasted" bits using the bisync protocol compared to 8-data-bit, 2-stop-bit, 1-parity-bit asynchronous serial. Assume that the data block size is 100 bytes.

Solution. The overhead required for the asynchronous character is 50%. (4 extra bits for each byte). The bisync protocol requires six extra bytes (assuming a 16-bit BCC) for the 100-byte block. The overhead is 6%.

The consequences of the reduced overhead should be clear. For a given baud rate, synchronous data will have a considerably higher character rate.

Another not-so-obvious advantage of synchronous data is due to the UART clock rate being the same as the data rate (that is, the multiplier is 1, not 16). This means that for a given UART maximum operating frequency, the synchronous baud rate can be 16 times higher than the asynchronous rate.

Serial Data Link Control. This format was developed by IBM for use with their *Systems Network Architecture* (SNA) communications package. Figure 9.8 illustrates one frame of data using this protocol. It is similar to bisync but is not byte oriented.

The serial data link control (SDLC) receiver searches for the beginning flag (01111110) as its sync character. An 8-bit address field follows, allowing each frame to be addressed to a particular station among a network of stations. Next is

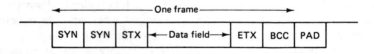

Figure 9.7 One frame of a synchronous message using the bisync protocol.

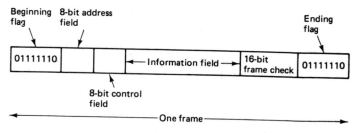

Figure 9.8 One frame of a synchronous message using the SDLC protocol.

an 8-bit control field with special control characters identified by a sequence of six or more logic 1s.

The information field can be of any format (that is, it does not have to consist of an integral number of bytes). The transmitter will automatically insert 0s in this field if five or more logic 1s should appear in sequence. This will avoid inadvertent control characters appearing in the information field. The receiver automatically deletes these 0s.

The 16-bit frame check is used for error detection similar to the BCC character in bisync. The frame ends with the ending flag.

SDLC is actually a subset of HDLC (high-level data link control), which is an international synchronous communications protocol. As with bisync, SDLC is simply a set of rules that have been agreed on for the transfer of serial data.

9.3 ERROR DETECTION AND CORRECTION

As you read this section, look for the answers to these Key Concept questions:

9.3.1. When one bit of a byte changes, the _____ of that byte must also change.

9.3.2. What is the advantage of the checksum versus single-byte parity for error detection?

9.3.3. The CRC method of error detection is similar to the checksum but is _____ oriented.

9.3.4. The Hamming code uses _____ parity bits to encode one byte of data.

Whenever data is transmitted between two points, it is important to be sure of the integrity of that data. This is true whether the data path is a 2000-mile telephone connection or a 2-inch trace on a PC board.

Errors can be handled in one of two ways.

1. *Error detection* using parity, checksums, or cyclic redundancy characters (CRC). If an error is detected, the receiver requests retransmission.
2. *Error correction* using the Hamming (or modified Hamming) codes. The most common forms detect multiple-bit errors and correct single-bit errors.

In this section we examine both methods and see how they can be implemented in a microcomputer environment.

Parity.   Perhaps the simplest scheme for detecting single-bit errors is to add a parity bit to each data byte transmitted. This *redundant checking bit* is chosen to make the total number of bits (including the parity bit) in the word odd or even.

Example 9.5

The following data bytes are ASCII characters encoded with an even-parity bit in the MSB position: D1,36,E5. Which of these bytes, if any, are in error?

Solution.   Convert each byte to binary:

$$D1 = 11010001$$
$$36 = 00110110$$
$$E5 = 11100101$$

Inspecting each byte, only E5 has an odd number of 1s and must therefore be in error. The actual bit in error, however, is unknown.

All UARTs are designed to implement parity automatically. When an error is detected, the PE flag is set. The receiver can then request another transmission if desired. Note that the UART takes no other action than to set its PE flag.

The inherent assumption behind parity is that a multiple-bit error is unlikely. In Ex. 9.5, if the data byte D1 was received as D2, the parity would still be correct, but two bits would be in error. It can be shown* that adding a parity bit improves the data integrity by a factor of 357. Quite an improvement for the price of an extra bit!

The use of parity is not restricted to serial communications channels. Indeed, the contents of RAM in most microcomputer systems today is protected by a ninth bit—the parity bit. Each time the CPU writes to memory, this bit is computed. When the byte (and parity bit) is read back, the parity is checked. If an error is detected, the machine is halted.

Checksums.   The main disadvantage to parity is that an extra bit is required for each data byte. This reduces the character rate (as do the asynchronous start and stop bits) and requires additional space or memory cells when the data is to be stored. A 64K memory will require 64K parity bits. When used with secondary memory devices such as disk drives and magnetic tape units, valuable storage space is required for the parity bit.

For this reason the *checksum* has become popular when transferring blocks of data. The checksum is a byte usually sent as the last byte in a block of data. The receiver calculates the checksum on the block of data received (including the checksum) and compares to the checksum byte. If the bytes do not compare, the transmitter is told to retransmit the block.

---

* William I. Fletcher, *An Engineering Approach to Digital Design* (Englewood Cliffs, N.J.: Prentice-Hall, Inc., 1980), p. 47.

The advantage is much less overhead compared to parity. For example, for a 256-byte block, one byte or ~4% is devoted to error checking. If parity is used, 256 extra bits are required or 32 extra bytes—12.5% of the block size.

There is another good reason for using the checksum. Errors introduced when data blocks are transmitted over the telephone network tend to occur in "bursts." For example, a lightning strike or a noisy switch may garble the received data for several milliseconds, causing multiple-bit errors to occur. Because the checksum character is characteristic of the entire block of data, it is more likely to detect these errors than the simpler parity scheme.

How is the checksum calculated? The byte needs to be representative of the entire data block. One way of doing this is to sum all of the bytes in the block. Any carries that are generated are ignored. The resulting byte is then complemented and incremented by 1 (that is, the *2's complement* is formed). The last two steps are done to make easier the receiver's job of testing the checksum byte.

Example 9.6

Calculate the checksum byte for the four hex data bytes 10, 23, 45, and 04.

Solution. The sum is calculated first.

$$
\begin{array}{r}
10 \\
23 \\
45 \\
\underline{04} \\
7C
\end{array}
$$

Inverting 7C and adding 1, we have

$$\overline{01111100} + 1 = 10000011 + 1 = 10000100 = 84H$$

Example 9.7

Assume that the following data bytes are received and the last byte is the checksum character: 10,23,45,04,84. Has the data been received correctly?

Solution. The receiver need only add the five data bytes:

$$
\begin{array}{r}
10 \\
23 \\
45 \\
04 \\
\underline{84} \\
1\ \ \overline{00}
\end{array}
$$

Because the carry is discarded, the result is 00. The data has been received correctly.

You should now be able to see why the 2's complement of the sum is formed. In this way, the receiver need only add all the bytes and test for a zero result. You should also be able to see that the checksum is not perfect. If the data byte 45H changed to 44H and the byte 04H to 05H, the check sum would still agree. However, the likelihood of a multiple-bit error that does not affect the checksum is very small.

Cyclic Redundancy Checks. The *cyclic redundancy check* (CRC) technique, like the checksum method, is used to detect errors in a block of data. It is commonly used when reading and writing data to a floppy disk and to ensure data integrity in programmable ROMs. It is universally used for detecting errors in synchronous data communications.

Unlike the checksum, the CRC method is not byte-oriented. Instead, the data block is thought of as a "stream" of serial data bits. The bits in this n-bit block are considered the coefficients of a *characteristic polynomial* (usually referred to as $M(X)$—"M of X"). $M(X)$ has the form

$$M(X) = b_n + b_{n-1}X + b_{n-2}X^2 + \cdots + b_1X^{n-1} + b_0X^n$$

where b_0 is the least significant bit (LSB) and b_n is the most significant bit (MSB).

Example 9.8

Calculate the data polynomial $M(X)$ for the 16-bit data stream 26F0H.

Solution. First visualize this data in binary form:

$$0\ 0\ 1\ 0 \quad 0\ 1\ 1\ 0 \quad 1\ 1\ 1\ 1 \quad 0\ 0\ 0\ 0$$

Now write this as $M(X)$:

$$M(X) = 0 + 0X^1 + 1X^2 + 0X^3 + 0X^4 + 1X^5 + 1X^6 + 0X^7$$
$$+ 1X^8 + 1X^9 + 1X^{10} + 1X^{11} + 0X^{12} + 0X^{13} + 0X^{14} + 0X^{15}$$

and eliminate the 0 terms:

$$M(X) = X^2 + X^5 + X^6 + X^8 + X^9 + X^{10} + X^{11} \tag{9.1}$$

Equation (9.1) is a unique polynomial representing the data in the 16-bit block. If one bit were to change, the polynomial would also change. The CRC bytes are found by applying the following equation:

$$\frac{M(X) \times X^n}{G(X)} = Q(X) + R(X) \tag{9.2}$$

In this equation $G(X)$ is called the *generator polynomial*. For the bisync protocol $G(X)$ is

$$G(X) = X^{16} + X^{15} + X^2 + 1 \tag{9.3}$$

The SDLC protocol uses

$$G(X) = X^{16} + X^{12} + X^5 + 1 \tag{9.4}$$

When this division is performed, the result will be a *quotient* $Q(X)$ and a *remainder* $R(X)$. The CRC technique consists of calculating $R(X)$ for the data stream and then *appending* this to the data block. The result, when $R(X)$ is again calculated by the receiver, should be $R(X) = 0$. Also note that because $G(X)$ is of power 16, the remainder, $R(X)$, cannot be of order higher than 15 and is thus represented by two bytes (no matter what the block length itself).

Example 9.9

Calculate the CRC bytes for the data block 26F0H using the bisync generator polynomial.

Solution. Figure 9.9 shows the arithmetic. The remainder is

$$R(X) = X^{15} + X^{13} + X^9 + X^8 + X^6 + X^4 + X^3 + X + 1$$

Expressed in binary this becomes (recalling that the coefficient of the highest power becomes the LSB)

$$1101 \quad 1010 \quad 1100 \quad 0101 = \text{DAC5H}$$

If the two bytes DAC5H are appended to the 26F0H data stream, the received CRC calculation should result in $R(X) = 0$, indicating that no errors have been detected. In practice, the CRC bytes can be generated by hardware or software. The division operations can be performed by a shift register and exclusive-OR gates. Although the CRC bytes can be calculated with software, more and more of the peripheral controller circuits are performing this function on-board. In this way the CRC generation and checking becomes transparent to the user.

The Hamming Code. In 1950 an article appeared in the *Bell System Technical Journal* entitled "Error Detecting and Error Correcting Codes." In this article, mathematician Richard Hamming described a technique that not only detected transmission errors but also *corrected* those errors. The resulting Hamming codes have become the basis for all error-correcting schemes in use today.

This seemingly impossible task is done by performing multiple parity checks on each data word. The additional bits are transmitted together with the data word. Figure 9.10 illustrates the technique for an 8-bit word. Four parity bits are required (labeled P0 through P3 in Fig. 9.10).

Note that each parity bit checks a different set of bits and each bit is included in at least two of the parity checks. In this example the data byte D6H would be transmitted as the 12-bit number 4D6H.

Figure 9.11 shows how the received word is tested. Four parity bits are again generated, but this time include the four check bits generated by the transmitter. For example, the low-order check bit is found by calculating the odd parity of data bits 0, 1, 2, 6, and 8.

To illustrate the technique, bit 7 in Fig. 9.11 is assumed in error and has become a 0. The four parity bits generated are referred to as the *error code*. Table 9.3 explains the significance of each of the 16 possible error codes. An error code of 0000 indicates no error detected.

In this example the error code is 1110 and data bit 7 has been correctly identified as the errant bit. If the true Hamming code is used, the error code should identify the actual bit position in error. Because of this the technique illustrated here is referred to as a *modified Hamming code*.

Although 4 additional bits represent a 50% storage penalty, the technique will detect and correct all single-bit errors and reportedly detect an average of 97%

$$\frac{M(X)\,X^{16}}{G(X)} = \frac{X^{27}+X^{26}+X^{25}+X^{24}+X^{22}+X^{21}+X^{18}}{X^{16}+X^{15}+X^2+1} =$$

```
                                                              X^11 + X^9 + X^6 + X^2 + X + 1
X^16 + X^15 + X^2 + 1 ) X^27 + X^26 + X^25 + X^24 + X^22 + X^21 + X^18
                        X^27 + X^26                  + X^13 + X^11
                        ─────────────────────────────────────────────
                               X^25 + X^24 + X^22 + X^21 + X^18 + X^13 + X^11
                               X^25 + X^24                  + X^11 + X^9
                               ──────────────────────────────────────────
                                             X^22 + X^21 + X^18 + X^13 + X^9
                                             X^22 + X^21       + X^8 + X^6
                                             ─────────────────────────────
                                                          X^18 + X^13 + X^9 + X^8 + X^6
                                                          X^18 + X^17       + X^4 + X^2
                                                          ─────────────────────────────
                                                                 X^17 + X^13 + X^9 + X^8 + X^6 + X^4 + X^2
                                                                 X^17 + X^16                        + X^3 + X
                                                                 ────────────────────────────────────────────
                                                                        X^16 + X^13 + X^9 + X^8 + X^6 + X^4 + X^3 + X^2 + X
                                                                        X^16 + X^15                              + X^2    + 1
                                                                        ────────────────────────────────────────────────────
                                                                  R(X) = X^15 + X^13 + X^9 + X^8 + X^6 + X^4 + X^3       + X + 1
```

Figure 9.9 Generating the CRC bytes from the bisync data stream 26F0H.

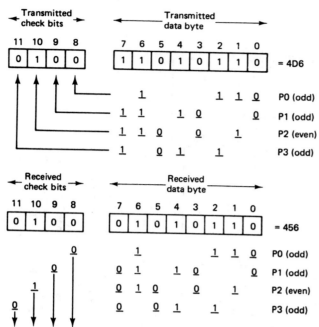

Figure 9.10 Four parity bits are required to encode one byte in the Hamming code.

Figure 9.11 The receiver computes an error code based on the four check bits and the data byte. An error code of 0000 indicates that no errors have been detected.

TABLE 9.3 ERROR CODES FOR THE 8-BIT MODIFIED HAMMING CODE TECHNIQUE IN FIG. 9.11

Error code	Bit in error
0000	No error detected
0001	Check bit 0
0010	Check bit 1
0011	Data bit 0
0100	Check bit 2[a]
0101	Data bit 1
0110	Data bit 3
0111	Data bit 6
1000	Check bit 3
1001	Data bit 2
1010	Data bit 4
1011	All data and parity set to 0
1100	Data bit 5
1101	Multibit error
1110	Data bit 7
1111	Multibit error

[a] All data and parity bits are set to a 1.

Sec. 9.3   Error Detection and Correction

463

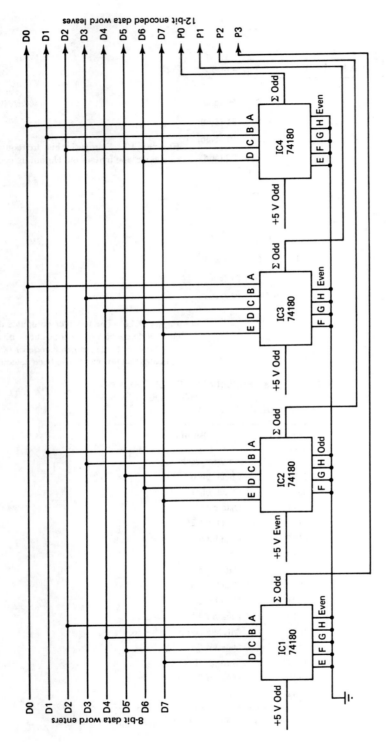

Figure 9.12 The check bits of the modified Hamming code can be generated using four 74180 parity generator/checkers. (Redrawn from "Error Checking and Correcting for Your Computer" by Gregory J. Walker, appearing in the May 1980 issue of BYTE magazine. Copyright © 1980 Byte Publications, Inc. Used with the permission of Byte Publications, Inc.

Figure 9.12 The check bits of the modified Hamming code can be generated using four 74180 parity generator/checkers. (Redrawn from "Error Checking and Correcting for Your Computer" by Gregory J. Walker, appearing in the May 1980 issue of BYTE magazine. Copyright © 1980 Byte Publications, Inc. Used with the permission of Byte Publications, Inc.

of all multiple-bit errors.* When extended to 16 bits, 5 check bits are required and the overhead reduced to 32%.

How can we implement such a system? The solution is quite simple. Using four 74180 parity generator/checkers the 12-bit encoded data word can be formed. This is shown in Fig. 9.12. Look carefully at the parity generator inputs and compare to the bits tested in Fig. 9.10. Using this circuit, 68 ns (worst case) is required to generate the 4 parity bits. This will increase the memory access time, possibly necessitating high-speed RAMs to store the parity bits.

Decoding the parity bits and correcting the proper bit is slightly more complex. Figure 9.13 illustrates the circuit. Again four 74180s are required and you should be able to see that the bits tested agree with those in Fig. 9.11.

The resulting 4-bit error code is used to enable a 74LS154 4-line to 16-line decoder. The output of this circuit is carefully wired to agree with Table 9.3. For example, if bit 7 is in error, the error code is 1110 and output 14 of the 74154 will go low. This level is inverted and causes the output of exclusive-OR gate IC6d to assume the opposite state (correcting the bit).

The *multiple-bit-error* output could be connected to the processor's interrupt input and cause the processor to refetch the last data byte or suggest that a memory test be run.

A considerably more elaborate version of the circuits in Figs. 9.12 and 9.13 is manufactured by Intel as the 8206 *Error Detection and Correction Unit.* This device will handle 16-bit data words and generate up to 8 check bits. It is designed to be interfaced between the microprocessor and system RAM. The check bits are generated during memory write operations and checked and corrected during memory read operations. The total time to detect and correct all single-bit errors is 67 ns.

9.4 THE INTEL 8251A USART

As you read this section, look for the answers to these Key Concept questions:

9.4.1. To the microprocessor, the 8251A appears to be _____ I/O ports.

9.4.2. List three different ways of developing a baud rate clock signal.

9.4.3. The _____ signal indicates that the USART has received a byte. _____ indicates that the USART is ready to accept another byte to transmit.

9.4.4. What is the function of the USART when operated in the hunt mode?

Intel supports its family of 8- and 16-bit microprocessors with the 8251A *universal synchronous/asynchronous receiver/transmitter* (USART). A third-generation part, the 8251A can be programmed by the microprocessor for synchronous or asynchronous serial communications. Also under program control are the number of bits per data word, the number of stop bits, and the choice of parity.

_____

* George J. Walker, "Error Checking and Correcting for Your Computer," *BYTE*, Volume 5 No. 5 (1980), p. 260.

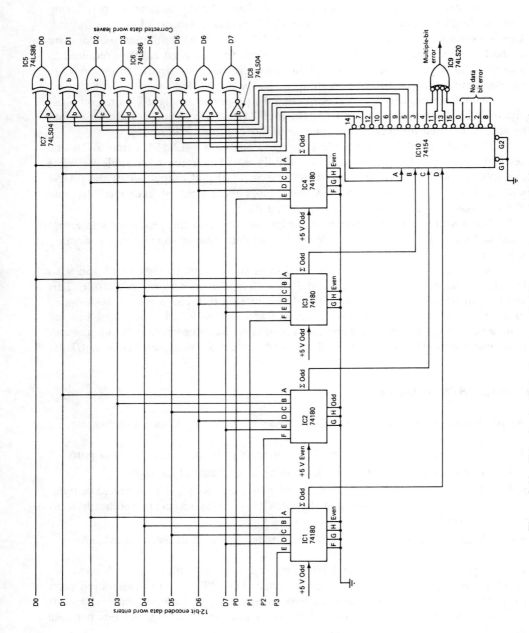

Figure 9.13 This circuit checks the error code bits, corrects any single-bit errors, and notifies the processor of any multiple-bit errors. (Redrawn from "Error Checking and Correcting for Your Computer", by Gregory J. Walker, appearing in the May 1980 issue of BYTE magazine. Copyright © 1980 Byte Publications, Inc. Used with the permission of Byte Publications, Inc.

When operated in the synchronous mode each frame is preceded by one or two sync characters as specified. These characters will automatically be inserted by the transmitter and searched for by the receiver when in the "hunt" mode.

All status signals can be monitored via an internal 8-bit input port. Flags for parity error, framing error, and overrun error are also provided.

The 8251A is an improved version of the 8251, the most significant difference being an increase in the asynchronous baud rate from 9600 to 19,200. In this section we see how the 8251A can be interfaced to the three-bus system architecture and provide several programming examples.

Interfacing the 8251A. A block diagram and pin description for the 8251A is provided in Fig. 9.14. Figure 9.15 illustrates a typical I/O-mapped interface. As with all Intel programmable I/O devices, the $\overline{CS}$ input must be low for the device to be selected. Normally, this is controlled by an address decoder as shown in the figure.

The C/$\overline{D}$ input selects the control functions or data functions of the USART as indicated in the control logic truth table in Table 9.4. In Fig. 9.15, ports 70H and 71H have been selected arbitrarily.

The CLK input is not related to the baud rate clocks but is required for internal timing. It must have a frequency at least 30 times higher than the data rate. For 19,200 baud this is 576 kHz. Usually, it is connected to φ2 of the 8080/85 system clock.

Figure 9.15 shows the two baud rate clock inputs, T×C and R×C connected together. This will cause the receiver and transmitter to operate at the same baud rate, as is usually desired. Under program control the clocks can be chosen as 1, 16, or 64 times the data rate. This allows the baud rate to be varied without changing the clock frequency.

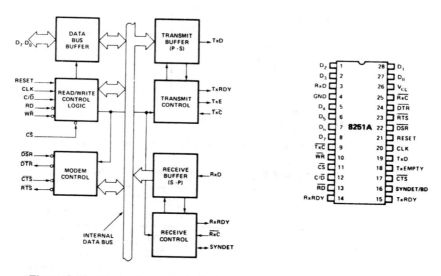

Figure 9.14 Block diagram and pin descriptions for the Intel 8251A USART. (Courtesy of Intel Corporation.)

Sec. 9.4   The Intel 8251A USART

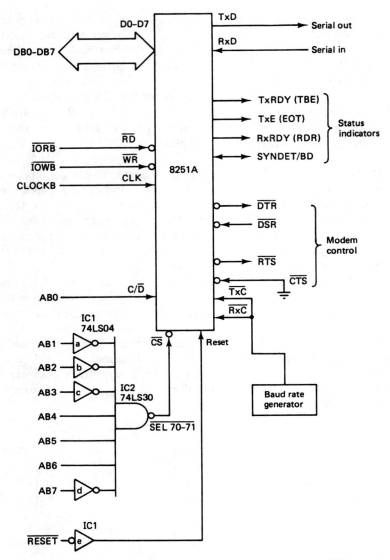

Figure 9.15 Interfacing the 8251A to the three-bus system architecture.

TABLE 9.4 8251A CONTROL LOGIC TRUTH TABLE

C/D̄	RD̄	WR̄	Figure 9.15 port address	Function
0	0	1	70H	Read data word
0	1	0	70H	Write data word
1	0	1	71H	Read status word
1	1	0	71H	Write status word

Example 9.10

What frequency is required for a baud rate of 1200 using a 16× clock signal? What is the baud rate if 64× is selected?

Solution. For 1200 baud the clock frequency must be $16 \times 1200 = 19,200$ Hz. If the USART is programmed for 64× operation, the baud rate becomes $19,200/64 = 300$ baud.

The block marked "baud rate generator" in Fig. 9.15 can be implemented in one of three ways.

1. *TTL oscillator*: This type of circuit requires three 74LS04 inverters and a crystal. Chapter 4 demonstrated its use as a microprocessor system clock generator. Although a very simple solution, its main disadvantage is that the frequency cannot be changed without changing the crystal time base.
2. *PIT oscillator*: The 8254 PIT was discussed in Chap. 7 and provides an elegant solution to the baud rate clock problem—elegant because different baud rates can be *programmed* by changing the initial count in a PIT register programmed as a square-wave generator (mode 3). See Probs. 9.24 and 9.25 for an interesting application of this idea.
3. *External baud rate generator*: The Motorola MC14411 shown in Fig. 9.16 provides 14 different baud rate clocks that can be jumped to the USART clock inputs. Note that the clock outputs can be programmed as 1×, 8×, 16×, or 64×, the desired baud rate.

Returning to Fig. 9.15, the 8251A supplies four status signals for external control. All of these can also be monitored internally via the status port. The more familiar names (developed in Sec. 9.1) are shown in parentheses. T×E indicates that the transmitter's buffer is empty and that no characters are being transmitted. This signal can be used to "turn the line around" for half-duplex operations (half-duplex is discussed in Sec. 9.7).

T×RDY and R×RDY indicate a ready condition for the transmitter and receiver. They could be used to request an interrupt or initiate a DMA transfer. They can also be tested by polling the internal status port.

SYNDET/BD is a signal that goes high when the sync character has been detected when operating in the synchronous mode. Note that this pin can also be programmed as an input. In this case it is used to provide the sync signal externally.

When used in the asynchronous mode, SYNDET/BD is an output that goes high to indicate a "break" condition. The break character is a constant logic 0 usually sent by the receiver to the transmitter to suspend transmission (perhaps due to an error condition).

Four modem control signals are also provided. These are $\overline{\text{DTR}}$ and $\overline{\text{RTS}}$, both outputs, and $\overline{\text{DSR}}$ and $\overline{\text{CTS}}$, both inputs. They are intended for handshaking applications and will be discussed in detail in Sec. 9.7. Note, however, that $\overline{\text{CTS}}$ must be low to enable the transmitter function of the 8251A. The $\overline{\text{DSR}}$ input is general purpose in nature and can be monitored via the status word.

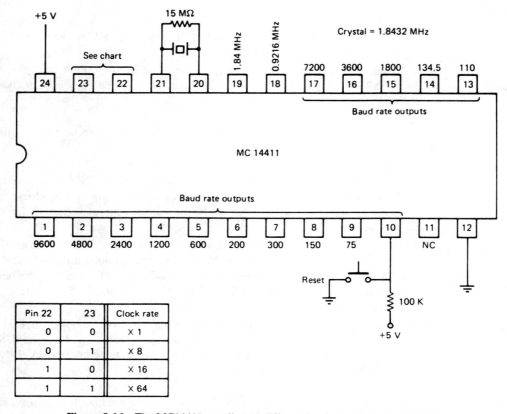

Pin 22	23	Clock rate
0	0	× 1
0	1	× 8
1	0	× 16
1	1	× 64

Figure 9.16 The MC14411 supplies 14 different baud rate clock signals. (From J. Uffenbeck, *Hardware Interfacing with the Apple II Plus*, Prentice-Hall, Inc., Englewood Cliffs, N.J., 1983.)

Programming the 8251A: Asynchronous Mode. When programming the 8251A, the following sequence must be followed:

1. Reset (either internal or external)
2. Mode instruction (specify the asynchronous mode)
3. Command instruction

Figure 9.17 describes the form of the mode and command instructions. A reset command must be used to start the initialization sequence. The following command (only) will be interpreted as a mode instruction. After the mode instruction has been written, all further writes will be interpreted as command instructions. *The only way to return to the mode instruction is to apply a reset pulse or write a command word with bit 6 high.*

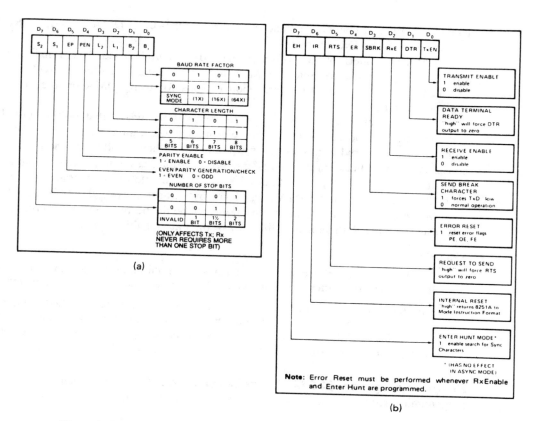

Figure 9.17 (a) Asynchronous mode instruction format; (b) synchronous or asynchronous command instruction format. (Courtesy of Intel Corporation.)

Example 9.11

Write the initialization routine required to program the 8251A USART in Fig. 9.15 for asynchronous transmission with 7 data bits, 2 stop bits, and odd parity. Select a $16\times$ clock and program $\overline{DTR}$ and $\overline{RTS}$ active.

Solution. The program is as follows:

```
MVI    A,40H    ;RESET
OUT    71H      ;COMMAND INSTRUCTION
MVI    A,0DAH   ;7 DATA, 2 STOP, ODD PARITY, 16×
OUT    71H      ;MODE INSTRUCTION
MVI    A,37H     ;RTS,ERROR RESET,DTR, ENABLE
OUT    71H      ;COMMAND INSTRUCTION
```

Although most applications will use the 8251A in a polled mode, interrupts and DMA can also be used. In an interrupt environment, $T\times RDY$ and $R\times RDY$ can be used to initiate the interrupt request. If this is done, note that the $T\times RDY$ output pin can be masked by making the $\overline{CTS}$ input high or by giving the transmit enable inactive command (command instruction bit 0 = 0). If DMA is used, T×RDY is connected to the DREQ input (of the 8237).

DMA and interrupts are often associated with high-speed data transfers and would seem incompatible with the slow data rates usually associated with serial I/O techniques. However, there are good reasons for using DMA or interrupts to control a serial port.

The inherently slow data rate of the serial port means that polling will be very wasteful of the resources of the microprocessor. Using interrupts or DMA, data can be transferred to the port only when needed, thereby allowing the processor considerable time between data transfers. For example, assuming a 10-bit character and a baud rate of 1200, more than 8300 μs is available between transmission of each character. Note that if DMA is used, the byte transfer mode should be selected.

When polling is used, the status register should be read and the appropriate bits tested. Figure 9.18 indicates the bit assignments for this register.

Example 9.12

Write a subroutine that outputs the contents of a print buffer to the 8251A interface in Fig. 9.15. The buffer begins at location BUF and terminates with a carriage return.

Solution. The program is given in Fig. 9.19. The T×RDY flag is polled and a data byte fetched from the buffer each time this flag is found high. After outputting the byte to the USART data port, the byte is compared against the ASCII code for a carriage return, and when a match is found, the subroutine returns.

Programming the 8251A: Synchronous Mode. The synchronous mode programming sequence consists of the following control port writes:

1. Reset (either internal or external)
2. Mode instruction (specify the synchronous mode and the number of sync characters)
3. One or two sync characters
4. Command instruction

As with the asynchronous mode, the mode instruction can only be written immediately after a reset. Following this instruction, the USART expects one or two sync characters. The next (and all following) writes will be interpreted as command instructions.

Figure 9.20 indicates the format for the mode instruction when the USART is operated in the synchronous mode. The command instruction format does not change and was given in Fig. 9.17(b).

After programming the USART for the synchronous mode, the serial output line will be high (marking) until $\overline{CTS}$ goes low. At this time the contents of the transmitter buffer will be serialized and output. Normally, this will be one or two sync characters.

Polling T×RDY, the processor can now output the data to be transmitted. If at any time the transmitter's buffer becomes empty, the SYNC characters will automat-

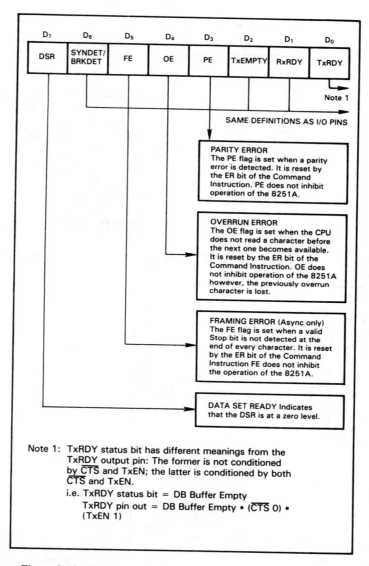

Figure 9.18 8251A status register. (Courtesy of Intel Corporation.)

ically be inserted. This is illustrated in Fig. 9.21. Also note that one bit is transmitted for each pulse of the baud rate clock (that is, the 16× and 64× clock options do not apply in the synchronous mode).

When receiving data the command instruction should specify "enter hunt mode." The USART will then test the incoming data after each bit is received for a match with the sync character. When a match is found, SYNDET/BD will go high, indicating character synchronization. Data can now be read by polling R×RDY.

```
;8251 PRINT BUFFER SUBROUTINE
;
;THIS PROGRAM EMPTIES A PRINT BUFFER STORED AT BUF
;TERMINATED WITH A CARRIAGE RETURN CHARACTER.
;
;THE HARDWARE IS SHOWN IN FIG. 9-15.
;
BUF      EQU    nnnn             ;PUT ADDRESS OF BUFFER HERE
CR       EQU    0AH              ;CARRIAGE RETURN MARKS BUFFER END
;
         LXI    H,BUF            ;POINT AT THE BUFFER
POLL     IN     71H              ;USART STATUS PORT
         RAR                     ;TEST TXRDY
         JNC    POLL             ;WAIT UNTIL READY
         MOV    A,M              ;FETCH A DATA BYTE
         OUT    70H              ;TRANSMIT THE BYTE
         CPI    CR               ;IS IT CR?
         JZ     DONE             ;IF YES THEN DONE
         INX    H                ;ELSE INCREMENT POINTER
         JMP    POLL             ;AND DO AGAIN
DONE     RET                     ;BUFFER IS EMPTY SO RETURN
```

Figure 9.19 Print buffer subroutine using polling for Ex. 9.12.

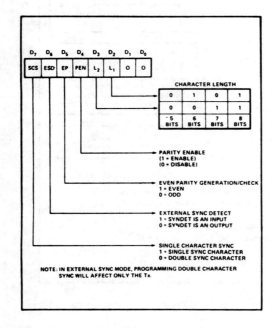

Figure 9.20 Synchronous mode instruction format. The command instruction format is the same as Fig. 9.17(b). (Courtesy of Intel Corporation.)

9.5 THE ZILOG Z-80 SIO AND Z-80 DART

As you read this section, look for the answers to these Key Concept questions:

9.5.1. In effect, the Z-80 SIO and DART include _____ separate UARTs in one package.

9.5.2. The Z-80 SIO includes _____ write registers and _____ read registers.

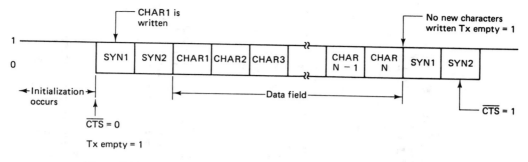

Figure 9.21 Synchronous data format when programmed for two sync characters.

9.5.3. List three ways of interfacing the PIO.

9.5.4. What is the function of the SIO when operated in the hunt mode?

For serial communications the Z-80 is supported by the *Z-80 SIO*, *serial input/ output controller* and the *Z-80 DART*, *dual asynchronous receiver/transmitter*. Both devices provide two separate and independent serial communications channels. This means that one channel can be programmed to communicate with a 19,200-baud VDT while the other is interfaced to a modem at 300 baud, for example.

The SIO has both asynchronous and synchronous capabilities, including compatibility with the bisync, SDLC, and HDLC synchronous protocols. Automatic CRC checking and generation is also provided in this mode. For asynchronous-mode-only applications, the Z-80 DART should be selected. It has all of the SIO's asynchronous capabilities and is pin-compatible with the Z-80 SIO/0 version of the SIO.

Similar to other Z-80 support devices, all control functions of the SIO and DART are programmable by the microprocessor. Several status registers are provided that allow monitoring of all important UART flags and error conditions. Also supported is the (standard technique for all Zilog peripheral controllers) Z-80 mode 2 interrupt scheme, including the daisy-chain priority structure.

Clock multipliers of $\times 1$, $\times 16$, $\times 32$, and $\times 64$ are programmable and data rates up to one-fifth of the system clock frequency are possible. A Z-80A SIO with a 4-MHz clock can operate at 800K baud in the synchronous mode and as high as 50K baud in the asynchronous mode ($\times 16$ clock).

Comparing the SIO and the DART. Figure 9.22 shows the pin assignments for the three versions of the SIO and the single version of the DART. As mentioned, the DART pinning is identical to the SIO/0 option except that pins 11 and 29 are labeled $\overline{\text{SYNCA}}$ and $\overline{\text{SYNCB}}$ on the SIO and $\overline{\text{RIA}}$ and $\overline{\text{RIB}}$ on the DART. In the asynchronous mode (the only mode of operation for the DART) these pins are general-purpose inputs that have no special function. Indeed, they could be connected to a ring indicator signal from a modem (hence the DART signal names).

When operated in the synchronous mode (the SIO) $\overline{\text{SYNCA}}$ and $\overline{\text{SYNCB}}$ signals indicate reception of valid sync characters. More details on the SYNC pins will be provided later in this section.

Sec. 9.5   The Zilog Z-80 SIO and Z-80 DART

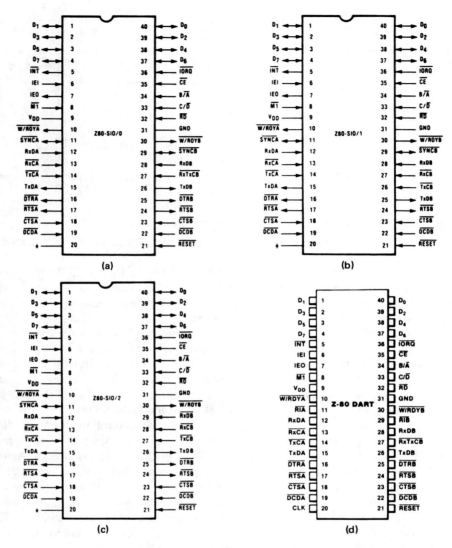

Figure 9.22 (a)–(c) Pin assignments for the three versions of the Z-80 SIO; (d) single version of the Z-80 DART. The SIO/0 and DART have identical pin assignments. (Courtesy of Zilog, Inc.)

The differences between the three versions of the SIO are:

1. The SIO/0 channel B receiver and transmitter have a common clock pin.
2. The SIO/1 lacks the $\overline{\text{DTRB}}$ signal.
3. The SIO/2 lacks the $\overline{\text{SYNCB}}$ signal.

Note that this means that channel B of the SIO/0 and the DART have a common transmitter and receiver clock but that channel A can have separate clocks. In the discussion to follow the Z-80 SIO/0 will be shown, but all comments regarding asynchronous operation apply equally to the Z-80 DART.

Interfacing the Z-80 SIO.

Interfacing the Z-80 SIO to the Z-80 microprocessor is straightforward, as illustrated in Fig. 9.23. All control signals are directly compatible with the Z-80. Internally, the SIO decodes $\overline{IORQ}$, $\overline{M1}$, and $\overline{RD}$ to generate $\overline{IOR}$, $\overline{IOW}$, and $\overline{INTA}$ (see Table 8.3). All communications between the Z-80 and the SIO is done using the bidirectional data bus, and to the processor, the SIO appears to be four parallel I/O ports.

The $B/\overline{A}$ input selects channel A or B and the $C/\overline{D}$ input determines if the control or data registers will be examined. The $\overline{CE}$ input must be low for all I/O read or write operations with the processor (it need not be low when transmitting or receiving data). Table 9.5 lists specific port addresses based on the address decoding in Fig. 9.23.

For variety, a more elaborate address decoder than is required is shown. This circuit generates three additional chip-enable signals that could be used with additional SIO chips or other peripheral controllers, such as the Z-80 PIO or CTC. If this is done, the IEI and IEO daisy-chain controls should be used to establish interrupt priorities. In Fig. 9.23 the SIO is given highest priority by wiring its IEI input to +5 V.

Examining the serial interfaces, two channels are provided labeled Channel A and Channel B. Note that each provides separate serial in and out lines and has independent clock inputs. The SIO/0 option shown has the channel B receiver and transmitter pins internally connected.

As mentioned in Sec. 9.4, the baud rate can be controlled by changing the clock multiplier ($\times 16$, $\times 32$, $\times 64$) without changing the baud rate clock frequency. The baud rate generator itself can be a crystal-controlled TTL oscillator, a Z-80 CTC programmed for a specific baud rate, or a special baud rate generator IC such as the Motorola MC14411. Because these options were discussed in detail in Sec. 9.4, that material will not be repeated here.

Four modem control signals are provided for each channel: two inputs and two outputs. These are used to establish a handshaking protocol between the serial peripheral and the SIO. More detail will be provided in Sec. 9.7. Note, however, that the signals are identical to those provided on the Intel 8251 except that $\overline{DSR}$ is replaced with $\overline{DCD}$ on the SIO.

If the auto enables function is selected, $\overline{DCD}$ and $\overline{CTS}$ become the receiver and transmitter enables, respectively. If disabled, they function as general-purpose inputs.

Each channel (of the SIO/0) also has two special-purpose control signals, $\overline{SYNC}$ and $\overline{W/RDY}$.

1. $\overline{SYNC}$ can be programmed to be an input or output signal when the SIO is operated in the synchronous mode. As an output it indicates valid sync characters are being received and could be used by non-Z-80 processors to initiate an interrupt request. As an input, $\overline{SYNC}$ allows an external signal to indicate synchronization and cause the SIO to begin capturing the synchronous data.

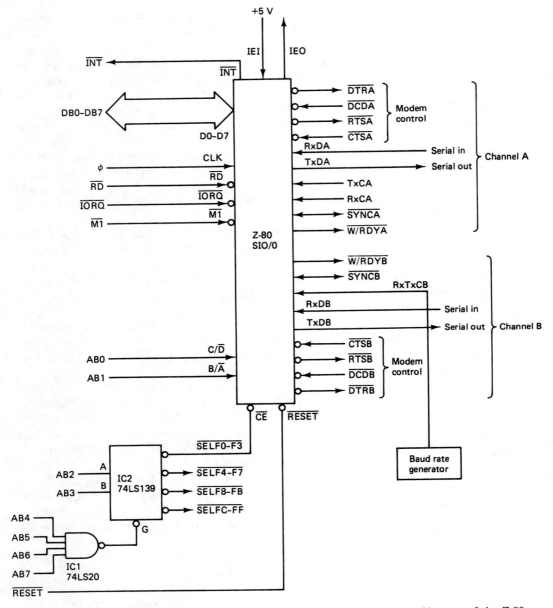

Figure 9.23 Interfacing the Z-80 SIO to the three-bus system architecture of the Z-80 microprocessor.

In the asynchronous mode $\overline{\text{SYNC}}$ is a general-purpose input that can be monitored via a status register. A typical application is to detect the ring signal output by a modem.

2. $\overline{\text{W/RDY}}$ is an output that can be programmed as an open drain *WAIT* request

TABLE 9.5 PORT ADDRESSES FOR THE Z-80 INTERFACE IN FIG. 9.23

B/$\overline{\text{A}}$	C/$\overline{\text{D}}$	$\overline{\text{IORQ}}$	$\overline{\text{RD}}$	Figure 9.23 port address	Function	
0	0	0	0	F0H	Data read	
0	0	0	1	F0H	Data write	Channel
0	1	0	0	F1H	Status read	A
0	1	0	1	F1H	Control write	
1	0	0	0	F2H	Data read	
1	0	0	1	F2H	Data write	Channel
1	1	0	0	F3H	Status read	B
1	1	0	1	F3H	Control write	

signal. It is used for block transfers to synchronize the data rate between the SIO and a DMA controller or the processor. It can also be programmed as a RDY signal compatible with the Z-80 DMA RDY input.

Programming the Z-80 SIO: Asynchronous Mode. Figures 9.24 and 9.25 describe the read and write registers of the Z-80 SIO. These are usually referred to as RR0–RR2 (read registers 0 through 2) and WR0–WR7 (write registers 0 through 7). Registers WR2 and RR2 can be accessed only when B/$\overline{\text{A}}$ = 1. This does not mean that the interrupt vector can be specified only for channel B. Rather, the interrupt vector is common to channels A and B and therefore need not be specified for both.

All other registers are duplicated for channel A and channel B. Note that WR6 and WR7 control the synchronous mode of operation exclusively and are not available in the Z-80 DART. In general, all bits dedicated to the synchronous mode are "do nothing" bits for the DART.

You may be wondering how eight write registers and three read registers can be accessed through one control port. The trick is to use WR0 as a *pointer register*. For example, by specifying D2–D0 as 010, RR2 will be accessed with the next control port read operation, and WR2 will be written to with the next control port write.

As with all programmable I/O devices, an initialization sequence must be followed before the device can be used. Figure 9.26 shows the suggested sequence for the SIO. As can be seen, WR0 must repeatedly be programmed to point at the desired register.

The SIO can be controlled using any of the familiar I/O techniques:

1. Polling
2. Interrupts
3. DMA

The particular scheme used affects the last steps of the initialization sequence. As an illustration, consider the following example, which will program the SIO for simple polling.

Sec. 9.5   The Zilog Z-80 SIO and Z-80 DART

479

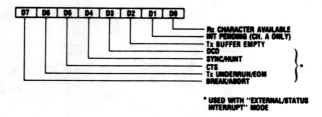

READ REGISTER 0

| D7 | D6 | D5 | D4 | D3 | D2 | D1 | D0 |

- Rx CHARACTER AVAILABLE
- INT PENDING (CH. A ONLY)
- Tx BUFFER EMPTY
- DCD
- SYNC/HUNT
- CTS
- Tx UNDERRUN/EOM
- BREAK/ABORT

* USED WITH "EXTERNAL/STATUS INTERRUPT" MODE

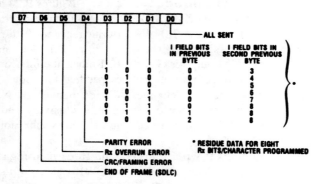

READ REGISTER 1†

| D7 | D6 | D5 | D4 | D3 | D2 | D1 | D0 |

- ALL SENT

	I FIELD BITS IN PREVIOUS BYTE	I FIELD BITS IN SECOND PREVIOUS BYTE
1 0 0	0	3
0 1 0	0	4
1 1 0	0	5
0 0 1	0	6
1 0 1	0	7
0 1 1	0	8
1 1 1	1	8
0 0 0	2	8

- PARITY ERROR
- Rx OVERRUN ERROR
- CRC/FRAMING ERROR
- END OF FRAME (SDLC)

* RESIDUE DATA FOR EIGHT Rx BITS/CHARACTER PROGRAMMED

† USED WITH SPECIAL RECEIVE CONDITION MODE

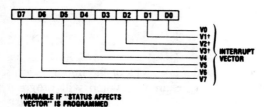

READ REGISTER 2

| D7 | D6 | D5 | D4 | D3 | D2 | D1 | D0 |

- V0
- V1†
- V2†
- V3† INTERRUPT VECTOR
- V4
- V5
- V6
- V7

†VARIABLE IF "STATUS AFFECTS VECTOR" IS PROGRAMMED

Figure 9.24 Z-80 SIO read register bit functions. (Courtesy of Zilog, Inc.)

WRITE REGISTER 0

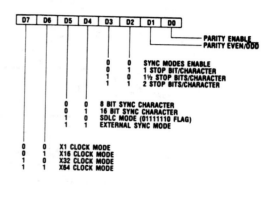

D7	D6	D5	D4	D3	D2	D1	D0	

0	0	0	REGISTER 0
0	0	1	REGISTER 1
0	1	0	REGISTER 2
0	1	1	REGISTER 3
1	0	0	REGISTER 4
1	0	1	REGISTER 5
1	1	0	REGISTER 6
1	1	1	REGISTER 7

0	0	0	NULL CODE
0	0	1	SEND ABORT (SDLC)
0	1	0	RESET EXT / STATUS INTERRUPTS
0	1	1	CHANNEL RESET
1	0	0	ENABLE INT ON NEXT Rx CHARACTER
1	0	1	RESET TxINT PENDING
1	1	0	ERROR RESET
1	1	1	RETURN FROM INT (CH-A ONLY)

0	0	NULL CODE
0	1	RESET Rx CRC CHECKER
1	0	RESET Tx CRC GENERATOR
1	1	RESET Tx UNDERRUN/EOM LATCH

WRITE REGISTER 4

D7	D6	D5	D4	D3	D2	D1	D0	

PARITY ENABLE
PARITY EVEN/ODD

0	0	SYNC MODES ENABLE
0	1	1 STOP BIT/CHARACTER
1	0	1½ STOP BITS/CHARACTER
1	1	2 STOP BITS/CHARACTER

0	0	8 BIT SYNC CHARACTER
0	1	16 BIT SYNC CHARACTER
1	0	SDLC MODE (01111110 FLAG)
1	1	EXTERNAL SYNC MODE

0	0	X1 CLOCK MODE
0	1	X16 CLOCK MODE
1	0	X32 CLOCK MODE
1	1	X64 CLOCK MODE

WRITE REGISTER 1

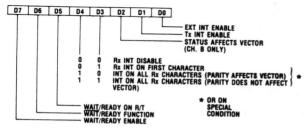

D7	D6	D5	D4	D3	D2	D1	D0	

EXT INT ENABLE
Tx INT ENABLE
STATUS AFFECTS VECTOR (CH. B ONLY)

0	0	Rx INT DISABLE
0	1	Rx INT ON FIRST CHARACTER
1	0	INT ON ALL Rx CHARACTERS (PARITY AFFECTS VECTOR)
1	1	INT ON ALL Rx CHARACTERS (PARITY DOES NOT AFFECT VECTOR)

* OR ON SPECIAL CONDITION

WAIT/READY ON R/T
WAIT/READY FUNCTION
WAIT/READY ENABLE

WRITE REGISTER 5

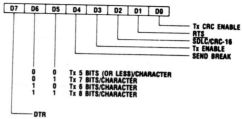

D7	D6	D5	D4	D3	D2	D1	D0	

Tx CRC ENABLE
RTS
SDLC/CRC-16
Tx ENABLE
SEND BREAK

0	0	Tx 5 BITS (OR LESS)/CHARACTER
0	1	Tx 7 BITS/CHARACTER
1	0	Tx 6 BITS/CHARACTER
1	1	Tx 8 BITS/CHARACTER

DTR

WRITE REGISTER 2 (CHANNEL B ONLY)

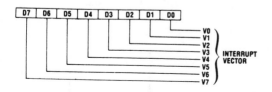

D7	D6	D5	D4	D3	D2	D1	D0	

V0
V1
V2
V3   INTERRUPT
V4   VECTOR
V5
V6
V7

WRITE REGISTER 6

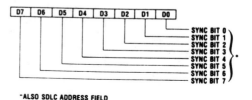

D7	D6	D5	D4	D3	D2	D1	D0	

SYNC BIT 0
SYNC BIT 1
SYNC BIT 2
SYNC BIT 3
SYNC BIT 4
SYNC BIT 5
SYNC BIT 6
SYNC BIT 7

*ALSO SDLC ADDRESS FIELD

WRITER REGISTER 3

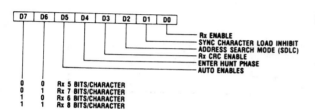

D7	D6	D5	D4	D3	D2	D1	D0	

Rx ENABLE
SYNC CHARACTER LOAD INHIBIT
ADDRESS SEARCH MODE (SDLC)
Rx CRC ENABLE
ENTER HUNT PHASE
AUTO ENABLES

0	0	Rx 5 BITS/CHARACTER
0	1	Rx 7 BITS/CHARACTER
1	0	Rx 6 BITS/CHARACTER
1	1	Rx 8 BITS/CHARACTER

WRITE REGISTER 7

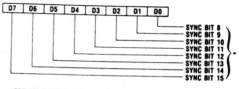

D7	D6	D5	D4	D3	D2	D1	D0	

SYNC BIT 8
SYNC BIT 9
SYNC BIT 10
SYNC BIT 11
SYNC BIT 12
SYNC BIT 13
SYNC BIT 14
SYNC BIT 15

*FOR SDLC IT MUST BE PROGRAMMED TO "01111110" FOR FLAG RECOGNITION

Figure 9.25 Z-80 SIO write register bit functions. Registers 6 and 7 are not available in the Z-80 DART. (Courtesy of Zilog, Inc.)

Sec. 9.5   The Zilog Z-80 SIO and Z-80 DART

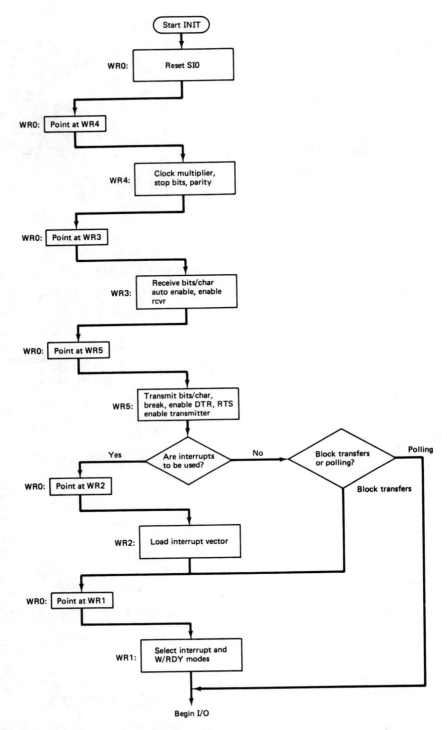

Figure 9.26 Suggested initialization sequence for the Z-80 SIO in the asynchronous mode.

Example 9.13

Determine the codes and write the program required to initialize channel B of the Z-80 SIO interface in Fig. 9.23 for asynchronous polled transfers. Use 8 data bits per character, odd parity, 1 stop bit, and a 64× clock multiplier. Disable the auto enables function.

Solution. Figure 9.27(a) lists the required sequence of codes. Figure 9.27(b) is the Z-80 control program which puts the OTIR instruction to good use.

Controlling the Z-80 SIO in the Asynchronous Mode

Polling. The simplest way to use the SIO (although not the most efficient) is with polling. Example 9.13 gives an example of the initialization required. Once initialized, receiving and transmitting programs must be written. Flowcharts for these programs are provided in Fig. 9.28.

Referring to the read register definitions in Fig. 9.24, bit 0 of RR0 is the receive data ready flag. When this bit is high, one to three data bytes are available to be read (the SIO has a three-character buffer). If bit 0 is not high, the $\overline{\text{DCD}}$ bit

	Register	Binary Code Required	Hex	Explanation
1.	WR0	00 011 000	18	Channel reset command sent to WR0.
2.	WR0	00 010 100	14	Reset status/interrupts and point at WR4.*
3.	WR4	11 XX 01 01	C5	64X clock, 1 stop bit, odd parity (trans and rcvr).
4.	WR0	00 010 011	13	Point to WR3.
5.	WR3	11 000001	C1	8 bits/char, $\overline{\text{DCD}}$ and $\overline{\text{CTS}}$ disable (auto enables disable), rcvr enable.
6.	WR0	00 010 101	15	Point to WR5.
7.	WR5	0 11 01000	68	No DTR or RTS, 8 bits/char, no break, trans enable.

*When any of the external lines $\overline{\text{DCD}}$, $\overline{\text{CTS}}$ or a Break condition occurs, the status bits of RR0 are latched. These bits should be reset during initialization. It is just as easy to do this with each write to WR0 and no harm is done. This is done in this example.

(a)

```
;Z-80 SIO ASYNCHRONOUS INITIALIZATION ROUTINE
;
;THIS PROGRAM INITIALIZES THE Z-80 SIO FOR 1 STOP
;BIT, ODD PARITY, 8 DATA BITS AND 64X CLOCK MODE.
;ALL MODEM CONTROL SIGNALS ARE DISABLED.
;
INSIO   LD      C,0F3H          ;CHANNEL B CONTROL PORT
        LD      B,7             ;7 BYTES TO PROGRAM
        LD      HL,CODES        ;POINT HL AT CODE TABLE
        OTIR                    ;OUTPUT THE CONTROL CODES
;
;I/O CAN BEGIN HERE
;
CODES   DB      18H,14H,0C5H    ;THESE ARE THE INITIALIZATION
        DB      13H,0C1H,15H    ;CODES
        DB      68H
```

(b)

Figure 9.27 (a) Control codes required for Ex. 9.13; (b) Z-80 initialization routine.

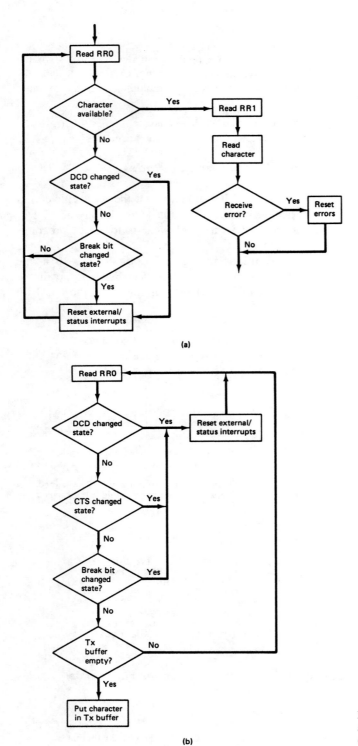

Figure 9.28 Z-80 SIO flowcharts for asynchronous mode polling: (a) receiver; (b) transmitter.

can be tested (this line is usually used by a modem to indicate that it has a valid carrier from the distant station) or the break condition tested. The break character is a continuous logic 0 level and is used to interrupt the transmitter.

When bit 0 goes high, RR1 should be read and its contents saved. As indicated in Fig. 9.24, this register stores the error conditions. Next the data character itself should be read, and after testing RR1 for errors, stored in a buffer. If errors did occur, retransmission can be requested. Note that RR1 *latches* the error bits, so that unless they are reset, they will still be there on the next read. An output write to WR0 with D5–D3 = 110 accomplishes this. Because the error bits are latched, it may be desirable to read a *block* of characters and then test for an error. This technique would be more appropriate when interrupts are used, as it would allow the processor maximum time between character reads.

Example 9.14

Assuming that the initialization routine in Fig. 9.27(b) has been executed, write a subroutine that polls the Z-80 SIO in Fig. 9.23 and returns with the received character in register A. If an error has occurred (parity, overrun, or framing error), return with the Z flag reset and all error bits reset. Assume that the modem control lines and the break character are not used.

Solution. The program is shown in Fig. 9.29 and follows the receiver flowchart in Fig. 9.28(a).

Note: See Prob. 9.29 for the corresponding polled transmitter program.

```
        ;Z-80 SIO ASYNCHRONOUS RECEIVER SUBROUTINE
        ;
        ;THIS PROGRAM READS ONE CHARACTER FROM CHANNEL B OF
        ;THE Z-80 SIO INTERFACE SHOWN IN FIG. 9-23.  POLLING
        ;IS USED AND THE CHARACTER READ IS RETURNED IN
        ;REGISTER A.   IF AN ERROR OCCURS THE SUBROUTINE
        ;RETURNS WITH THE Z FLAG RESET.
        ;
        LD      C,0F3H          ;CHANNEL B CONTROL PORT ADDR
        LD      A,00000000B     ;POINT WR0 AT RR0
        OUT     (C),A           ;PROGRAM WR0
POLL    IN      A,(C)           ;READ RR0 - CH. B STATUS PORT
        BIT     0,A             ;TEST RECEIVER READY FLAG
        JR      Z,POLL          ;WAIT FOR A CHARACTER
        ;
        ;GOT A CHARACTER - STORE IT AND TEST FOR ERRORS
        ;
        LD      A,00000001B     ;POINT WR0 AT RR1
        OUT     (C),A           ;PROGRAM WR0
        IN      A,(C)           ;ERROR STATUS TO A
        AND     70H             ;TEST BITS 4,5,6
        IN      A,(0F2H)        ;CHARACTER TO A
        RET     Z               ;NO ERRORS IF ZERO
        ;
        ;RESET ERROR FLAGS FOR NEXT READ
        ;
        LD      B,00110000B     ;RESET ERROR BITS
        OUT     (C),B           ;PROGRAM WR0
        RET                     ;RETURN WITH Z FLAG RESET
```

Figure 9.29 Receiver polling program for Ex. 9.14.

Interrupts. The flowchart in Fig. 9.26 indicates that WR2 and WR1 must also be initialized when using the SIO with interrupts. WR2 holds the base interrupt vector for both channels A and B. The SIO can be programmed to output this vector for all interrupt conditions or to output up to eight variations of the vector corresponding to different status conditions. Bit D2 of WR1 for channel B controls the selection.

Assuming that this bit is set, Table 9.6 lists the conditions tested and the resulting modifications to the interrupt vector. The external/status change refers to the modem input control signals $\overline{DCD}$ and $\overline{CTS}$, and the $\overline{SYNC}$ pin programmed as an input.

WR1 controls the interrupt mode. Using this register you control the source of the interrupts (receiver, transmitter, or special receive conditions) and whether to interrupt on all received characters or just the first. You can also program parity errors to alter the interrupt vector if desired.

Example 9.15

Modify the initialization codes given for the program in Ex. 9.13 to allow interrupt-driven I/O instead of polled I/O. Choose the codes such that all interrupts have their own address. The jump table base address is 1080H. Assume that the modem control signals are not used.

Solution. The seven codes specified in Ex. 9.13 need not be changed, but four additional codes will have to be added. These are shown in Fig. 9.30(a). Figure 9.30(b) shows the Z-80 program required.

Example 9.16

Specify jump table addresses for the interrupt sources initialized in Ex. 9.13.

Solution. Refer to Table 9.6 and use a base address of 1080H:

1080	Channel B transmitter buffer empty
1082	Not enabled

TABLE 9.6 EFFECT ON THE INTERRUPT VECTOR DUE TO ENABLING THE STATUS AFFECTS VECTOR, BIT D2 OF WR1

	V_3	V_2	V_1	
Channel B	0	0	0	Transmit buffer empty
	0	0	1	External/status change
	0	1	0	Receive character available
	0	1	1	Special receive condition[a]
Channel A	1	0	0	Transmit buffer empty
	1	0	1	External/status change
	1	1	0	Receive character available
	1	1	1	Special receive condition[a]

[a] Special receive conditions: parity error, Rx overrun error, framing error, end of frame (SDLC).

Source: Courtesy of Zilog Corporation.

	Register	Binary Code Required	Hex	Explanation
8.	WR0	00 010 010	12	Point to WR2.
9.	WR2	10000000	80	Interrupt vector.
10.	WR0	00 010 001	11	Point to WR1.
11.	WR1	XXX 10 110	16	Interrupt on all rcvd char, status affects vector, trans interrupts enabled, external interrupts (the modem control signals) disabled.

(a)

```
;Z-80 SIO ASYNCHRONOUS INITIALIZATION ROUTINE
;               (WITH INTERRUPTS)
;
;THIS PROGRAM IS SIMILAR TO FIG. 9-27(B) BUT INCLUDES
;INITIALIZATION FOR A Z-80 MODE 2 INTERRUPT VECTOR.
;
        IM      2               ;MODE 2 INTERRUPTS
        LD      A,10H           ;HIGH ORDER JUMP TABLE ADDRESS
        LD      I,A             ;TO REGISTER I
;
;THE REMAINDER IS THE SAME AS FIG. 9-27(B)
;
        LD      C,0F3H          ;CHANNEL B CONTROL PORT
        LD      B,0BH           ;11 BYTES TO PROGRAM
        LD      HL,CODES        ;POINT HL AT CODE TABLE
        OTIR                    ;OUTPUT THE CODES
        EI                      ;ENABLE INTERRUPTS
;
;I/O CAN BEGIN HERE
;
CODES   DB      18H,14H,0C5H    ;THESE ARE THE INITIALIZATION
        DB      13H,C1H,15H     ;CODES
        DB      68H,12H,80H
        DB      11H,16H
```

(b)

Figure 9.30 (a) Additional control codes required when initializing the Z-80 SIO for interrupts; (b) initialization program for Ex. 9.15.

1084	Channel B receive character available
1086	Channel B parity, overrun, or framing error

Note: The four addresses for channel A are not enabled.

Using the SIO with the initialization program given in Fig. 9.30(b), transmitter, receiver, and error routines would have to be located at the addresses stored in the jump table shown in Ex. 9.16.

Block transfer mode. At first the thought of transferring data to or from the SIO in blocks does not seem logical. However, what is intended is to have the SIO facilitate a block transfer without direct CPU intervention. Certainly, the transfer of individual bytes will occur (relatively) slowly, but if implemented properly the CPU will be free to perform other tasks while the block is being transferred.

Block transfers are more commonly done in the synchronous mode but can be done asynchronously as well. Two methods are possible.

1. *DMA controlled*: A Z-80 DMA can be programmed for byte mode transfers and the $\overline{W/RDY}$ output of the SIO programmed as a RDY signal to synchronize the transfer. In this way the transfer of data to the SIO will occur very rapidly and allow the CPU considerable time for alternate processing between each byte.

2. *Z-80 block transfer instructions*: The Z-80 has several block transfer instructions which should be capable of keeping up with even the fastest SIO baud rates. The SIO $\overline{W/RDY}$ output can be programmed to request *WAIT* states automatically and thereby synchronize the SIO and Z-80 CPU. Of course, this technique does not allow the processor to perform other tasks simultaneously, but does eliminate the need for polling and provides the highest transfer rate possible without going to the Z-80 DMA.

Control of the $\overline{W/RDY}$ pin is via bits 5–7 of WR1, as summarized in Fig. 9.31. Regardless of the block transfer technique, the SIO would normally be programmed to interrupt on the first character received, after which the block would be transferred until completion.

Using the Z-80 SIO in the Synchronous Mode.

As mentioned earlier in this chapter, synchronous communications involve more than deleting the start and stop bits of asynchronous serial. The receiving and transmitting stations must strictly adhere to a *protocol* governing the form of the data transfer.

The Z-80 SIO supports four such protocols:

1. Monosync
2. Bisync
3. External sync
4. SDLC

The first three are character-oriented, which means that the data field is made up of fixed-length characters (8 bits, for example). Figure 9.7 illustrated one frame of a bisync message. Monosync is identical except only one sync character is used.

If $D_7 = 0$	
And $D_6 = 1$	**And $D_6 = 0$**
READY is High	$\overline{WAIT}$ is floating

If $D_7 = 1$	
And $D_5 = 0$	**And $D_5 = 1$**
READY Is High when transmit buffer is full.	READY Is High when receive buffer is empty.
$\overline{WAIT}$ Is Low when transmit buffer is full and an SIO data port is selected.	$\overline{WAIT}$ Is Low when receive buffer is empty and an SIO data port is selected.
READY Is Low when transmit buffer is empty.	READY Is Low when receive buffer is full.
$\overline{WAIT}$ Is floating when transmit buffer is empty.	$\overline{WAIT}$ Is floating when receive buffer is full.

Figure 9.31 The W/RDY output is controlled by bits 5–7 of WR1. (Courtesy of Zilog, Inc.)

External sync allows an external signal (applied to the $\overline{SYNC}$ input) to start the transmission without using the sync characters.

When using the SIO in the synchronous mode, WR3–WR5 control the various options. Figure 9.32 indicates the bit selections for monosync, bisync, external sync, and the SDLC mode. Bits 4 and 5 of WR4 select one of these four modes. Of course, in the synchronous mode the clock multiplier must be specified as ×1 (bits 6 and 7 of WR4 = 00).

When operated as a transmitter the sync bytes are written to WR6 and WR7. The SIO will automatically insert these at the start of the message and whenever the transmitter buffer becomes empty. At the completion of the message the SIO will automatically send the CRC (or BCC) bytes if the transmitter CRC has been enabled (bit 0 of WR5).

In the receive mode the sync characters (to be searched for) should also be loaded into WR6 and WR7. Then when enabled, the receiver will be in the *hunt* mode. Assuming that the sync characters match, the receiver can be programmed to interrupt on the first character and the following characters can then be read using polling, interrupts, or block transfers (synchronized with $\overline{W/RDY}$).

If the SDLC protocol is selected, operation is similar. Figure 9.33 illustrates the bit definitions for WR3–WR5. Recall that SDLC is bit-oriented with the information field-framed between a beginning flag, an 8-bit address field, an 8-bit control field, and an ending field. This was shown in Fig. 9.8.

When the transmitter is initialized, the SIO will automatically supply the beginning flag (01111110) but the address byte and control byte must be written by the CPU. The information field follows. Any occurrence of five or more consecutive logic 1s will cause the SIO to insert a 0 automatically to prevent interpretation as a control code. At the completion of the message the CRC bytes will again be automatically inserted by the SIO.

In the SDLC receive mode, WR6 holds the address field and WR7 the flag character. The receiver will then be in the *hunt* mode until the first flag is received.

	BIT 7	BIT 6	BIT 5	BIT 4	BIT 3	BIT 2	BIT 1	BIT 0
WR3	00 = Rx 5 BITS/CHAR 10 = Rx 6 BITS/CHAR 01 = Rx 7 BITS/CHAR 11 = Rx 8 BITS/CHAR		AUTO ENABLES	ENTER HUNT MODE	Rx CRC ENABLE	0	SYNC CHAR LOAD INHIBIT	RX ENABLE
WR4	0	0	00 = 8-BIT SYNC CHAR 01 = 16-BIT SYNC CHAR 10 = SDLC MODE 11 = EXT SYNC MODE		0 SELECTS SYNC MODES	0	EVEN/$\overline{ODD}$ PARITY	PARITY ENABLE
WR5	DTR	00 = Tx 5 BITS (OR LESS)/CHAR 10 = Tx 6 BITS/CHAR 01 = Tx 7 BITS/CHAR 11 = Tx 8 BITS/CHAR		SEND BREAK	Tx ENABLE	1 SELECTS CRC-16	RTS	Tx CRC ENABLE

Figure 9.32 WR3–WR5 control operation of the Z-80 SIO when operated in the synchronous mode. (Courtesy of Zilog, Inc.)

Sec. 9.5   The Zilog Z-80 SIO and Z-80 DART

	BIT 7	BIT 6	BIT 5	BIT 4	BIT 3	BIT 2	BIT 1	BIT 0
WR3	00 = Rx 5 BITS/CHAR 10 = Rx 6 BITS/CHAR 01 = Rx 7 BITS/CHAR 11 = Rx 8 BITS/CHAR		AUTO ENABLES	ENTER HUNT MODE (IF INCOMING DATA NOT NEEDED)	Rx CRC ENABLE	ADDRESS SEARCH MODE	0	Rx ENABLE
WR4	0	0	1 0 SELECTS SDLC MODE		0	0	0	0
WR5	DTR	00 = Tx 5 BITS (OR LESS)/CHAR 10 = Tx 6 BITS/CHAR 01 = Tx 7 BITS/CHAR 11 = Tx 8 BITS/CHAR		0	Tx ENABLE	0 SELECTS SDLC CRC	RTS	Tx CRC ENABLE

Figure 9.33 Bit designations for WR3–WR5 when operating the SIO with the SDLC synchronous serial protocol. (Courtesy of Zilog, Inc.)

If WR3 bit 2 is set, the receiver then enters the address search mode, and finding an address match, the data transfer begins. Control is again via polling, interrupts, or block transfers. Any 0s inserted in the data stream by the transmitter will be deleted by the receiver.

9.6 REMOTE CONTROL APPLICATIONS FOR ASYNCHRONOUS SERIAL DATA

As you read this section look for the answer to this Key Concept question:

9.6.1. Using only a _____ conductor cable and two UARTs, _____ input and output lines can be controlled by a microcomputer.

Perhaps the principal advantage of serial communications is the simplicity of the data path—only a two- or three-conductor cable is required for many applications. Because of this we should not restrict the serial data link to computer peripherals such as printers, VDTs, and modems.

Figure 9.34 illustrates how a microcomputer and two UARTs can be used to control a remote solar heating system. The transmit channel of the remote UART is used to relay temperature information about the system. It uses an *analog-to-digital converter* to convert the temperature-sensitive voltage developed across the thermistor to an 8-bit digital word.

The receiver channel of the same UART is used to control the water flow by means of two solenoid-actuated valves. Provision has also been made to provide

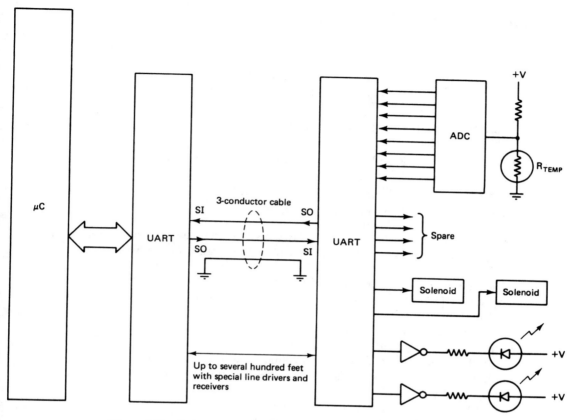

Figure 9.34 Serial data techniques can be extended to allow remote control applications.

status indicators at the remote site with two LED indicators. Four outputs remain available and can be used for other miscellaneous control functions.

The most interesting feature of the circuit is the fact that only a three-conductor cable is required at the remote site. Depending on the baud rate and voltages used on this cable, the distance between computer and remote site can be several thousand feet. In fact, if a transmitting and receiving *modem* are used, the computer could "call" the solar heating station from several thousand miles away and monitor and control its status.

Another possibility is to construct a network of *addressable* UARTs all connected in parallel with the transmission line. When the UART selected sees its address, it responds, while all others remain in the standby mode. The Motorola MC14469 is an *addressable asynchronous receiver/transmitter* (AART) designed exactly for this purpose. A 7-bit address code can be hard-wired allowing up to 128 such devices in the network. Clock generation is simplified by the inclusion of an on-board oscillator requiring only an external crystal.

9.7 SERIAL DATA INTERFACE STANDARDS

As you read this section, look for the answers to these Key Concept questions:

9.7.1. The R-232D standard specifies transmitters and receivers with _____-_____ inputs and outputs. RS-422 uses _____ transmitters and receivers.

9.7.2. What are the range of output voltages for a logic 1 and 0 in the R-232D standard?

9.7.3. Under the R-232D standard, all computer equipment is considered a _____ or a _____.

9.7.4. Why are handshaking signals required with a serial interface?

9.7.5. List the five handshaking signals provided in the RS-232D standard.

Because of the large number of manufacturers building data communications equipment, industry-wide standards must be adopted to ensure compatibility. These standards define the logic 1 and 0 voltage levels, maximum baud rates, maximum cable lengths, and even the type of connector to be used. But before we examine specific standards, let's consider the two basic electrical techniques for transmitting serial data.

Electrically, data is transmitted as either a *single-ended* signal referenced to ground or as a *differential* signal referenced between two conductors. TTL gates are single-ended. The input voltage is applied with respect to ground and the outputs are similarly referenced. An operational amplifier or op-amp, however, has differential inputs (usually labeled + and −) and a single-ended output. The op-amp responds only to the *difference* between its two input pins.

The advantage of the differential input is that noise impulses that tend to degrade the single-ended logic levels are common to both inputs of the differential receiver. But because the receiver responds only to the difference between its inputs, the noise pulses tend to be rejected. The result is that differential transmitters and receivers allow higher data rates for a given cable length than do single-ended techniques.

Table 9.7 compares the electrical characteristics of three common serial communications standards. Note that the data rates for the differential standards are considerably higher than for the single-ended standard.

The EIA RS-232D Standard

Electrical characteristics. RS-232D is the oldest (and most popular) of the three standards in Table 9.7. Nearly all VDTs, modems, and serial printers follow this standard. It was developed in the early 1960s as a standard governing the interconnection of terminals and modems.

The most striking feature about RS-232D is that the logic levels are *not* TTL-compatible. TTL is fine for short-distance cables of 5 to 10 ft, provided that the data rate is not too high. However, as the cable lengths increase, the capacitive and DC loading effects reduce the noise margins to an unacceptable level.

TABLE 9.7 COMMON SERIAL INTERFACE STANDARDS

Parameter	RS-232D	RS-422A	RS-423A
Line length (max.)[a]	50 ft	4000 ft	4000 ft
Frequency (max.)	20 kbaud/50 ft	10 Mbaud/40 ft 1 Mbaud/400 ft 100 kbaud/4000 ft	100 kbaud/30 ft 10 kbaud/300 ft 1 kbaud/4000 ft
Mode of operation	Single-ended input and output	Differential input and output	Single-ended output differential input
Logic levels			
0	$> +3$ to $+25$ V	$A < B$	$+4$ to $+6$ V
1	< -3 to -25 V	$A > B$	-4 to -6 V
Number of receivers allowed on one line	1	10	10
Input impedance	3–7 kΩ and 2500 pF	>4 kΩ	>4 kΩ
Output impedance	—	<100 Ω balanced	<50 Ω
Short circuit current	500 mA	150 mA	150 mA
Output-slew rate	30 V/μs	—	Controls provided
Receiver input voltage range	± 15 V	± 7 V	± 12 V
Maximum voltage applied to driver output	± 25 V	-0.25 to $+6$ V	± 6 V

[a] May be exceeded with proper design.

An RS-232D receiver will interpret a voltage more negative than -3 V as a logic 1 and a voltage more positive than $+3$ V as a logic 0. RS-232D transmitters are specified to output a voltage more negative than -5 V for a logic 1 and more positive than $+5$ V for a logic 0.* In this way 2 V of noise immunity is *guaranteed*. This should be compared with 0.4 V for standard TTL. Typical values for RS-232D logic 1s and 0s are ± 10 to ± 12 V.

The cable length for RS-232D at its maximum baud rate is not too impressive—50 ft maximum. However, it is common to find interfaces running at 1200 to 4800 baud with 1000 to 2000-ft cables.

Although it is possible to generate the RS-232D voltage levels with discrete parts, special *line drivers* and receivers have been developed that meet all of the requirements of the EIA specification. The most commonly used are the Motorola MC1488 and MC1489 shown in Fig. 9.35(a) and 9.35(b). The MC1488 accepts TTL-level inputs and converts these to RS-232D output voltages. The MC1489 performs the opposite function.

Figure 9.35(c) shows another option. The MAX232 is an RS-232D *transceiver*. This chip contains four RS-232D transmitters and receivers in a single package. It also contains a *charge pump* to generate the ± 12-V signal levels. This is an important

* The actual output voltage depends on the supply voltages used.

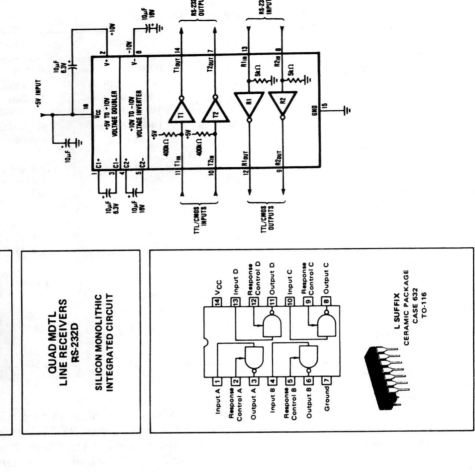

Figure 9.35 (a) MC1488 line driver; (b) MC1489 line receiver; (c) MAX232 line transceiver. (Courtesy of Motorola Semiconductor Products, Inc. and Maxim Integrated Products Inc.)

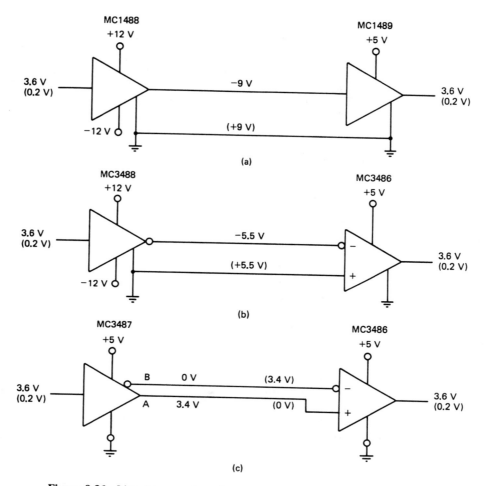

Figure 9.36 Line drivers and receivers are available to convert TTL levels to any of the three standards: (a) RS-232D; (b) RS-423A; (c) RS-422A.

advantage as it may eliminate the need to provide ±12-V power supplies (often required only for the RS-232D interface).

Figure 9.36(a) illustrates a typical RS-232D transmission line. Note the use of ±12-V power sources at the MC1488 end of the transmission line. The RS-422 and 423A circuits in (b) and (c) are discussed in more detail later in this section.

Signal designations. As mentioned earlier in this section, RS-232D was originally developed to standardize the interface between a modem and a terminal. This includes more than simply specifying the logic 1 and 0 voltage levels. Table 9.8 indicates the 25 signal names and pin assignments of the standard. These consist of four data pins—two for the main channel and two for a low-speed secondary channel—and a number of control signals supporting these two channels.

Figure 9.37 illustrates the two connectors that have become the ''de facto''

TABLE 9.8 SIGNAL DESIGNATIONS FOR THE RS-232D SERIAL INTERFACE STANDARD

Pin	Signal name	Data		Control	
		From DTE to DCE	To DTE from DCE	From DTE to DCE	To DTE from DCE
1	Protective ground				
2	Transmitted data	x			
3	Received data		x		
4	Request to send (RTS)			x	
5	Clear to send (CTS)				x
6	Data set ready (DSR)				x
7	Signal ground				
8	Data carrier detect (DCD)				x
9/10	Reserved for data set testing				
11	Unassigned				
12	Secondary data carrier detect				x
13	Secondary clear to send				x
14	Secondary transmitted data	x			
15	Transmit signal element timing				x
16	Secondary received data		x		
17	Receive signal element timing				x
18	Unassigned				
19	Secondary request to send			x	
20	Data terminal ready (DTR)			x	
21	Signal-quality detector (indicates probability of error)				x
22	Ring indicator				x
23	Data signal rate select (allows selection of two different baud rates)				x
24	Transmit signal element timing			x	
25	Unassigned				

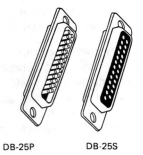

DB-25P   DB-25S

Figure 9.37 DB-25S socket connector and DB-25P plug connector universally used with all RS-232D communications ports.

standard for the mechanical interface to RS-232D. The DB-25S is a 25-pin socket connector designed to mate with a DB-25P plug connector. Note that these connectors are not part of the original RS-232D specification but are almost universally used with RS-232D ports today.

Now you might think that a 25-conductor serial interface cable defeats the purpose of serial communications in the first place (and you might be right!) but the full complement of RS-232D signals are very rarely required.*

In fact, for many interfaces only the *transmitted data*, *received data*, and *signal ground* wires are required. This flexibility in the choice of interface signals also leads to a great deal of confusion about RS-232D.

Technically, the standard classifies all computer equipment and related peripherals to be in one of two categories:

1. *Data terminal equipment* (DTE): printers, terminals
2. *Data communications equipment* (DCE): modems

Unfortunately, the term *microcomputer* is not included in this list. Of course, at the time of RS-232's inception there were no microcomputers and most computers were accessed via a terminal connected to a modem. The problem with the microcomputer is that in some cases it is a DTE (for example, when interfaced to a modem), but in others it is a DCE (when interfaced to a printer).

The main confusion centers around pin 2, transmitted data, and pin 3, received data. As Table 9.8 indicates, transmitted data is from the DTE and to the DCE. Similarly, received data is data from the DCE to the DTE. In other words, the definitions are from the DTE's point of view.

A typical RS-232D interface is shown in Fig. 9.38. The parallel data of the microcomputer is converted to serial by the UART, and its TTL levels are converted to RS-232D levels by the MC1488. The MC1489 converts incoming RS-232D levels to TTL levels for the UART receiver. Note that the interface cable simply patches the lines from the microcomputer to the terminal.

If the microcomputer's serial port was also wired as a DTE (DTE "talking" to DTE), the cable would have to be rewired to interchange pins 2 and 3. Such a cable is sometimes called a "null modem" (there is no DCE).

Handshaking. If the serial port of a microcomputer is adjusted to 1200 baud and a 1200-baud printer connected to this port, there would not appear to be a need for any handshaking signals. Indeed, this is one of the advantages of asynchronous serial data: the synchronization information is "built in" in the form of start and stop bits.

The problem occurs when the receiver must *process* the data before the next character occurs. A serial printer is a good example. At the end of each printed line a carriage return character must be sent. This will cause the print head to return to the left margin. Since this distance is relatively large compared to the

---

* Many microcomputers today use a nine-pin socket and plug to implement a subset of the RS-232D standard.

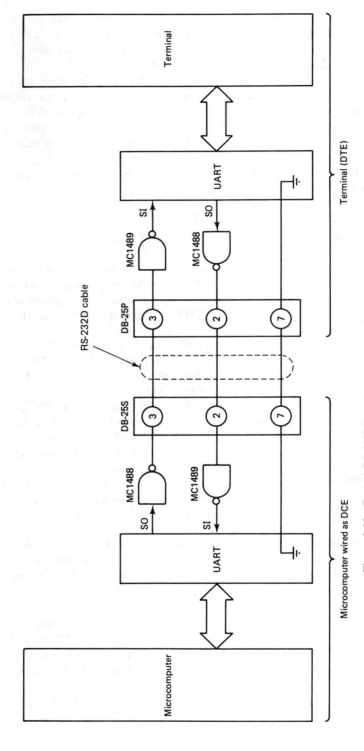

Figure 9.38 Typical RS-232D interface between a microcomputer wired as a DCE and a VDT wired as a DTE.

normal print increment of one character, more time will be required to position the print head properly.

If handshaking is not used, the transmitter simply monitors its TBE flag and *assumes* that the receiver can accept characters as fast as its UART can send them. After all, they are both running at the same baud rate. But if a carriage return character is sent, the print head may not have enough time to return to the left margin before the next character is received. The result is a "mysterious" letter printed right in the middle of the line.

Other examples of this problem are clear screen characters and the smooth scroll feature of some VDTs. Both require extra time between characters, which may not be available at the higher baud rates. The solution is a handshaking signal monitored by the transmitter before launching a new character down the serial data link. RS-232D provides five such signals specifically designed for modem control but applicable for nonmodem applications as well. The five lines are:

1. *Data carrier detect* ($\overline{DCD}$): This signal is output by the DCE and indicates that the modem has detected a valid carrier (marking level).
2. *Data terminal ready* ($\overline{DTR}$): This signal is output by the DTE to indicate that it is ready for communications. It can be used to switch on a modem.
3. *Data set ready* ($\overline{DSR}$): This signal is output by the DCE in response to $\overline{DTR}$ and indicates that the DCE is connected to the communications channel.
4. *Request to send* ($\overline{RTS}$): This signal is output by the DTE to indicate that it is ready to transmit data.
5. *Clear to send* ($\overline{CTS}$): This signal is output by the DCE and acknowledges $\overline{RTS}$. It indicates that the DCE is ready for transmission.

Because of RS-232's modem heritage, these signals all relate to establishing a communications link between a modem (DCE) and a terminal (DTE). Figure 9.39 indicates the handshaking that takes place. It is important to remember, however, that these signals are simply names reserved for various RS-232D pins. This means

		DTE	DCE	Comment
(pin 20)	1.	$\overline{DTR} \rightarrow 0$	–	DTE device announces it is ready.
(pin 6)	2.	–	$\overline{DSR} \rightarrow 0$	DCE device says, "OK, I am also ready." An acknowledgement.
(pin 4)	3.	$\overline{RTS} \rightarrow 0$	–	DTE device indicates it is ready to begin transmissions (receive or transmit).
(pin 8)	4.	–	$\overline{DCD} \rightarrow 0$	DCE device announces it has found a valid carrier.
(pin 5)	5.	–	$\overline{CTS} \rightarrow 0$	DCE says, "I am now ready to begin transmissions."

Monitoring the receiver and transmitter ready flags, data can now be exchanged between the DTE and DCE.

Figure 9.39 Modem control signals are used to provide handshaking between the DTE and DCE.

that a (nonmodem) peripheral can use any of these signals to indicate its BUSY/READY status. By monitoring the appropriate pin, the transmitter can be prevented from sending data even though the TBE flag of its UART indicates empty.

Both the 8251A USART and the Z-80 SIO provide for direct connections to the modem control signals (see Figs. 9.15 and 9.23). Consider first the 8251A. The $\overline{RTS}$ and $\overline{DTR}$ outputs of the USART can be set or reset by writing to the command register. The $\overline{DSR}$ input can be monitored as bit 7 of the status port. The $\overline{CTS}$ input, however, cannot be read, as the USART uses this line as a transmitter enable. Only when $\overline{CTS}$ is low is the transmitter enabled for sending serial data.

The Z-80 SIO $\overline{RTS}$ and $\overline{DTR}$ modem outputs can be set or reset by writing to WR5 of the appropriate channel. The SIO modem inputs are $\overline{DSR}$ and $\overline{CTS}$. These can be used in two ways. If auto enables are selected (bit 5 of WR3 set), $\overline{DCD}$ and $\overline{CTS}$ act as enables for the receiver and transmitter, respectively. If bit 5 of WR3 is reset, $\overline{DCD}$ and $\overline{CTS}$ can simply be monitored as bits 3 and 5 of RR0.

Example 9.17

Assume that a serial printer connects its BUSY/$\overline{READY}$ status signal to $\overline{DSR}$ of the 8251A interface in Fig. 9.15 or to $\overline{DCDB}$ of the Z-80 SIO interface in Fig. 9.23. Write the 8080/85 and Z-80 polled subroutines required to transmit data to the printer with handshake control. Assume that initialization has been completed.

Solution. Figure 9.40(a) is the 8080/85 solution and Fig. 9.40(b) the Z-80 solution. Both programs poll the printer's status (via $\overline{DSR}$ or $\overline{DCDB}$) before loading the transmitter's buffer with a character. In this way the printer receives a character only when it is ready.

Note: A printer is classified as a DTE and therefore should use $\overline{DTR}$ and $\overline{RTS}$ as status outputs. However, both the 8251A and Z-80 SIO output $\overline{DTR}$ and $\overline{RTS}$ and therefore these devices are also DTEs! The problem is solved by using the $\overline{DSR}$ (or $\overline{DCD}$) pins to carry the BUSY/$\overline{READY}$ flag.

Some printers transmit the ASCII characters 11H (*X-ON* or control Q) and 13H (*X-OFF* or control S) to synchronize data flow. In these cases the transmitted and received data lines (pins 2 and 3) will both be required. In addition to monitoring transmitter buffer empty, the computer must monitor its UART's receiver data ready flag to see if the printer has sent the X-OFF character.

In summary, a great deal of confusion surrounds the EIA RS-232D standard. This is due to it being an "old" standard based on a terminal-to-modem interface. When designing an RS-232D interface, the documentation supplied with each piece of equipment to be used should be studied carefully to determine the connections required. If it is determined that the handshaking logic supplied by the modem control signals is not required, the connections shown in Fig. 9.41 can be used to wire the DTE and DCE to a permanent "ready" condition.

The RS-422A and RS-423A Standards. RS-422A and RS-423A are newer electrical standards for serial communications designed to permit higher data rates over longer cables. As indicated in Table 9.7, RS-422A will operate at 100 kbaud with a 4000-ft cable and 10 Mbaud with a 40-ft cable. RS-423A is restricted to considerably

```
;8251A POLLED TRANSMITTER SUBROUTINE
;    (WITH DSR HANDSHAKING)
;
;THIS SUBROUTINE OUTPUTS THE DATA BYTE IN REGISTER B TO
;A SERIAL PRINTER INTERFACED TO THE 8251 SHOWN IN
;FIG. 9.15.   THE BUSY/READY FLAG OF THE PRINTER IS
;ASSUMED TO BE CONNECTED TO THE RS-232D SIGNAL DSR.
;
;ASSUME THE 8251 HAS BEEN INITIALIZED
;
;BEGIN BY TESTING THE PRINTER'S BUSY/READY STATUS
;
WDSR    IN      71H                 ;READ 8251 STATUS PORT
        RAL                         ;DSR TO CARRY
        JNC     WDSR                ;WAIT FOR PRINTER
        ;
        ;PRINTER IS READY - TEST TXRDY
        ;
WTXRDY  IN      71H                 ;READ 8251 STATUS PORT
        ANI     02H                 ;TXRDY IS IN BIT 1
        JZ      WTXRDY              ;WAIT FOR TXRDY
        ;
        ;PRINTER AND 8251 ARE READY - TRANSMIT THE BYTE
        ;
        MOV     A,B                 ;FETCH THE CHARACTER
        OUT     70H                 ;8251 DATA PORT
        RET                         ;DONE
```

(a)

```
;Z-80 SIO POLLED TRANSMITTER SUBROUTINE
;        (WITH DCD HANDSHAKING)
;
;THIS SUBROUTINE OUTPUTS THE DATA BYTE IN REGISTER B TO
;A SERIAL PRINTER INTERFACED TO THE Z-80 SIO SHOWN IN
;FIG. 9.23.   THE BUSY/READY FLAG OF THE PRINTER IS
;ASSUMED TO BE CONNECTED TO THE RS-232D SIGNAL DCD.
;
;ASSUME THE SIO HAS BEEN INITIALIZED AND CHANNEL B IS
;USED FOR THE INTERFACE
;
;BEGIN BY RESETTING EXTERNAL STATUS (REMEMBER THE SIO
;LATCHES ITS MODEM AND ERROR STATUS BITS)
;
        LD      C,0F3H              ;CHANNEL B CONTROL PORT
        LD      A,00010000B         ;POINT WR0 AT RR0 AND RESET STATUS
        OUT     (C),A               ;PROGRAM WR0
        ;
        ;NOW TEST THE PRINTER'S BUSY/READY STATUS
        ;
WDCD    IN      A,(C)               ;READ RR0
        BIT     3,A                 ;TEST DCD
        JR      NZ,WDCD             ;WAIT FOR PRINTER
        ;
        ;PRINTER IS READY - TEST TX BUFFER EMPTY
        ;
WTXB    IN      A,(C)               ;READ RR0
        BIT     2,A                 ;TEST TX BUFFER
        JR      Z,WTXB              ;WAIT UNTIL READY
        ;
        ;PRINTER AND SIO ARE READY - TRANSMIT THE BYTE
        ;
        LD      C,0F2H              ;CHANNEL B DATA PORT
        OUT     (C),B               ;OUTPUT THE BYTE
        RET                         ;DONE
```

(b)

Figure 9.40   (a) 8080/85 solution to Ex. 9.17; (b) Z-80 solution to the same problem.

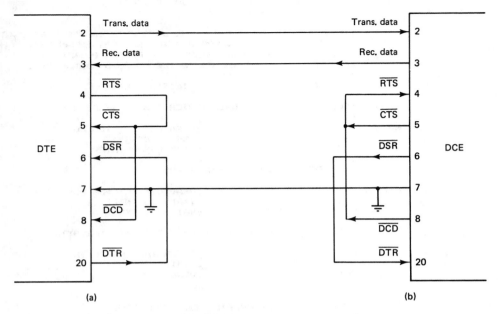

Figure 9.41 These connections will force the (a) DTE and (b) DCE to a permanently enabled condition. This should be done only if handshaking is not needed.

lower data rates due to its single-ended output. However, improved wave-shaping techniques and a differential receiver allow considerably faster data rates than RS-232D, also a single-ended output. Figure 9.36(b) and (c) illustrate typical line drivers and receivers for these new standards.

RS-422A and RS-423A actually describe only the electrical characteristics for yet another standard, *RS-449*. RS-449 was introduced in 1977 as a replacement for RS-232D. The most important specifications for this new standard are:

1. Two connectors are specified—one a 37-pin connector, the other a 9-pin connector. The 37-pin connector carries the main RS-449 signals, while the 9-pin connector carries the secondary channel signals.

2. The mechanical specifications for the connectors are defined in detail so that there can be no confusion. A latching mechanism is used that requires no special tools to engage or disengage (most DB-25 connectors require a screwdriver to tighten down two latching screws).

3. For data rates under 20 kbaud, either the RS-422A or RS-423A electrical standard may be used. For data rates above 20 kbaud, the balanced RS-422A specification must be followed.

RS-449, although offering a significant performance advantage over RS-232D, has not yet displaced RS-232D as the most popular standard. Certainly, the improved performance and standardization encourage manufacturers to introduce new equipment with this standard. However, because of higher costs and resistance to change, the conversion to RS-449 will probably go on for many years.

9.8 TELECOMMUNICATIONS

As you read this section, look for the answers to these Key Concept questions:

9.8.1. Bell 103 type modems use _____ _____ _____ to convert digital 1s and 0s into audio tones.

9.8.2. List the advantages of direct connect modems.

9.8.3. When is the baud rate not equal to the data rate in bits-per-second?

The serial communications techniques we have been discussing are commonly used to interface VDTs and printers to computer systems. However, serializing the data path also allows long-distance communications over the switched telephone network. This is referred to as *telecommunications*.

The effects of microelectronics and microcomputer technology are just beginning to be seen in this field. For example, consider the dialogue shown in Fig. 9.42

Typical Interaction Between Operator and Dialer (from Data Terminal)

Here is a typical exchange demonstrating auto dialing and modem responses:

1. Operator types ENQ (control E) followed by a carriage return (CR). This enables the dialer to automatically set the modem to speed (300 or 1200 bps) and parity of the terminal.
2. Dialer responds with HELLO: I'M READY followed by an asterisk (*), signaling the operator to respond with a keyboard command.
3. Operator types "D" (CR) indicating keyboard dial mode.
4. Dialer answers NUMBER?
5. Operator keys in the number to be dialed: (for example) 408_774_0810 (CR).
6. Dialer responds with 408_774_0810 and waits for acknowledgement.
7. Operator enters carriage return (CR) to command start of dialing.
8. During a normal connect sequence the dialer accesses the telephone line and when dial tone is detected, responds with:

   DIALING. . .
   RINGING. . .
   ANSWER TONE
   ON LINE

9. If the dial sequence fails, the dialer responds with an appropriate message, such as:

   NO DIAL TONE!
   BUSY!
   VOICE!
   FAILED CALL

Figure 9.42 Typical interaction between an operator and a modem equipped with an auto dialer. (Courtesy of Racal Vadic.)

between an "intelligent modem" interfaced to a terminal and an operator. Using a direct connection to the phone line, the operator need only specify to the modem the phone number of the distant station. The modem detects the dial tone, dials the number, detects the ringing or busy signal, and finally goes on line with the distant station.

One possible scenario would be to program the modem to place a call at 3 A.M. (when the phone rates are lowest) and retrieve and exchange a number of data files for the next business day—all without operator intervention. The result could be a sort of "electronic post office."

The backbone of all telecommunications is the *modem* itself. In this section we learn what a modem is and how it is interfaced to a microcomputer.

The Basics. Any attempt to transmit the serial data output by a UART directly over the telephone network is doomed to failure. This is because the phone system is optimized for *voice transmissions* and has a 300- to 3300-Hz bandwidth. A digital signal with 10- or 20-ns rise and fall times exhibits frequency components well into the hundreds of megahertz. The result of attempting to pass such signals through this low-pass filter (the phone network) would be a signal unrecognizable as a logic 1 or 0.

For this reason the modem was invented. A modem (*modulator–demodulator*) is designed to convert input serial data (usually in RS-232D levels) to audio frequencies within the bandpass of the telephone network. Figure 9.43 illustrates the basic concept. A technique called *frequency-shift keying* (FSK) is used by the modem to convert the binary 1s and 0s to two different sine-wave frequencies that can be passed by the telephone network.

Once converted to sine waves, the binary information can be transmitted through the telephone network just as a voice signal. The distant modem demodulates the signal, outputting the serial data in standard binary form.

A voltage-controlled oscillator (VCO) is used for the modulation process and a phase-locked loop (PLL) for the demodulation process. Thus a modem is made from a combination of linear and digital circuitry.

There are two basic types of modems, called *originate* modems and *answer* modems. The originate modem is used to originate the call, while an answer modem is used at the distant computer site to answer the call. For these two modems to communicate with each other simultaneously (called *full duplex*), two sets of frequencies are required. Specifications for the Bell 103 full-duplex 300-baud modem are given in Fig. 9.44. In this standard the originate modem transmits using the low set of frequencies and receives on the high set. The answer modem operates just the opposite.

The data rate for a 103-type modem is 300 bits per second (bps). The maximum standard data rate using FSK techniques and the frequency assignments shown in Fig. 9.44 is 600 bps. This can be verified by noting that the period for a 1070-Hz sine wave (the lowest frequency required) is $1/1070 = 0.93$ ms, while the period for a 1200-bps data rate (the next highest standard) is $1/1200 = 0.83$ ms—insufficient time for even one period of the 1070-Hz tone.

When interfacing to the telephone network, two techniques are possible:

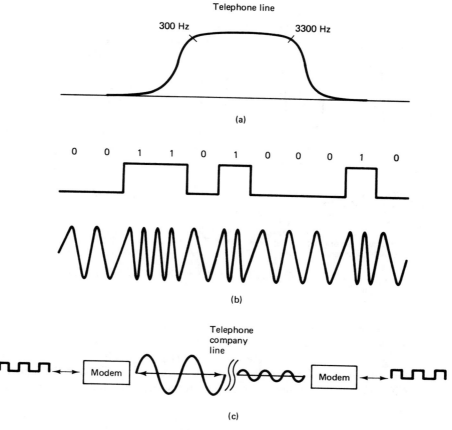

Figure 9.43 The telecommunications concept: (a) the switched telephone network has a 3000-Hz bandwidth; (b) using frequency-shift keying (FSK), the modem converts the binary 1s and 0s into two different-frequency sine waves; (c) these sine waves are transmitted over the telephone company lines.

1. *Acoustic coupling*: cradle, speaker, microphone
2. *Direct connect*

Acoustic coupling is the simplest to accomplish, requiring no special interface between the modem and telephone. The audio tones output by the modem are used to drive a loudspeaker acoustically coupled to the microphone of the telephone handset. The received tones are coupled from the handset earpiece to a microphone and hence to the modem receiver.

Acoustic coupling restricts operation to a manual mode. The operator must dial the call, wait for the distant carrier, and then place the handset in the acoustic coupler of the modem. The connection is also subject to external room noise, packing of the carbon microphone granules, and mechanical vibrations.

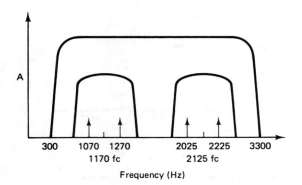

Specifications

Data:

Serial, binary, asynchronous, full duplex

Data transfer rate:

0 to 300 bps

Modulation:

Frequency shift-keyed (FSK) FM

Frequency assignment:

	Originating end	Answering end
Transmit	1070 Hz space	2025 Hz space
	1270 Hz mark	2225 Hz mark
Receive	2025 Hz space	1070 Hz space
	2225 Hz mark	1270 Hz mark

Transmit level:

0 to −12 dBm

Receive level:

0 to −50 dBm simultaneous with adjacent channel transmitter at as much as 0 dBm

Specifications and channel assignments for the full-duplex 300-bps asynchronous Bell 103/113 modem are shown in this illustration. The Bell 103 modem can transmit and receive the low or high band. The ability to switch modes has been termed "originate and answer." The Bell 113A/D operates only in the originate mode; the Bell 113B/C operates only in the answer mode.

Figure 9.44 Specifications for the 103 300-bps full-duplex modem standard. (Courtesy of Racal Vadic.)

Prior to 1976 a *direct access arrangement* (DAA) had to be leased from the telephone company when it was desired to use a direct connect modem. However, using a *registered protective circuit*, it is now possible to buy or build equipment that connects directly to the telephone company lines if it is registered with the FCC (Federal Communications Commission). All intelligent modems are direct connect.

Interfacing a 300-bps Modem. The 103-style modem has until recently been the "standard" for telecommunications. It offers full-duplex operation at 300 bps. A one-chip 103-style modem is available from Texas Instruments called the TMS99532. An interface to this circuit is shown in Fig. 9.45. The modem can be driven in two ways:

1. Directly by SERIAL OUT and SERIAL IN of a UART, USART, or SIO chip
2. From an RS-232D serial port using the MC1488 and MC1489 line receiver and line driver

The TMS99532 can be programmed to operate in the answer or originate mode via the four control pins SQT, ALB, A/O, and ATE. Table 9.9 summarizes the operating modes of the modem selectable by these four lines. These pins can be hard-wired or controlled by the output port of a PPI or PIO.

The chip features an on-board oscillator requiring only a 4.032-MHz external crystal. Figure 9.46(a) illustrates an acoustically coupled interface and Fig. 9.46(b)

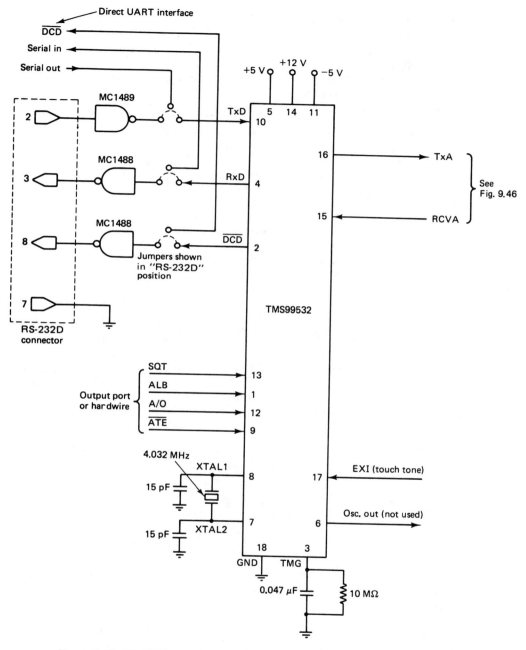

Figure 9.45 The TMS99532 is a single-chip 300-bps full-duplex modem. It can be interfaced directly to a UART chip or to the serial data lines of an RS-232D port.

TABLE 9.9 OPERATING MODES FOR THE TMS99532 300-BPS MODEM

Mode	Mode controls SQT ALB A/O ATE[a] (digital)	Transmitted data		Received data		Touch tones EXI[b] (analog)
		XMTD[b] (digital)	TXA (analog) (Hz)	RVCA[b] (analog) (Hz)	RCVD (digital)	
Answer	0 0 0 1	Mark = 1 → 2225 Space = 0 → 2025		Mark = 1270 → Space = 1070 →	1 0	×
Originate	0 0 1 1	Mark = 1 → 1270 Space = 0 → 1070		Mark = 2225 → Space = 2025 →	1 0	×
Answer, squelch	1 0 0 1	×	Disabled	Mark = 1270 → Space = 1070 →	1 0	×
Originate, squelch	1 0 1 1	×	Disabled	Mark = 2225 → Space = 2025 →	1 0	×
Analog loop back, answer	0 1 0 1	Mark = 1 Space = 0	Disabled	Disabled	1 0	×
Analog loop back, originate	0 1 1 1	Mark = 1 Space = 0	Disabled	Disabled	1 0	×
ALB test, answer	1 1 0 1	×	Disabled	Disabled	1	×
ALB test, originate	1 1 1 1	×	Disabled	Disabled	1	×
EXI as input	1 0 1 0	×	Same as EXI, inverted[c]	×	Three-state HBPF[d] active	External tone source
EXI as input[e]	1 0 0 0	×	Same as EXI, inverted[c]	×	Three-state LBPF[f] active	External tone source
2100 Hz[e] CCITT V.25 answer tone	0 0 0 0	×	2100	×	Three-state	×

[a] The following states are undefined and should not be used:

        0 0 1 0
        0 1 0 0
        0 1 1 0
        1 1 0 0
        1 1 1 0

[b] ×, don't care.
[c] Assumes ac coupling at EXI.
[d] High-bandpass filter.
[e] Typically not used in USA applications.
[f] Low-bandpass filter.
Source: Courtesy of Texas Instruments, Inc.

shows a direct connection. In either case external operational amplifiers are required to provide signal levels within telephone company specifications.

Note that the direct-coupled circuit is completely *isolated* from the phone line, as required by FCC regulations. There are four components to this circuit:

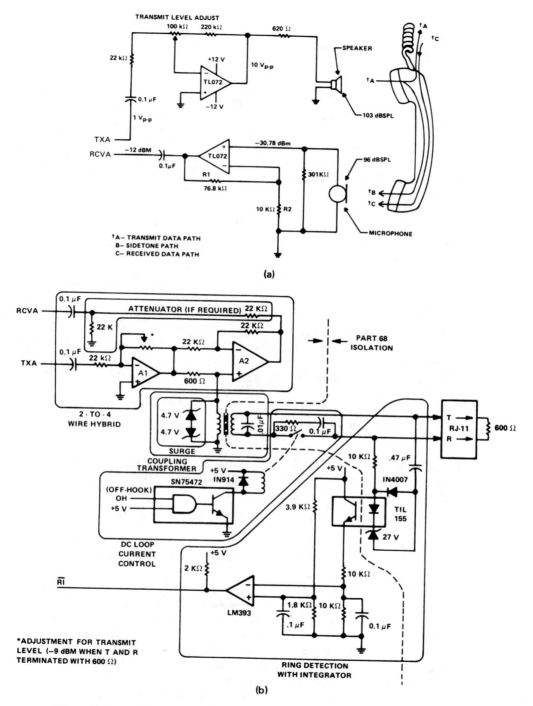

Figure 9.46 The output and input lines to the modem circuit in Fig. 9.45 can be (a) coupled acoustically to the phone line or (b) direct-connected. (Courtesy of Texas Instruments.)

1. Ring detector
2. Dc loop current control
3. Coupling transformer and surge protection
4. Two- to four-wire hybrid

Normally, the phone line rests at 48 V when the phone is "on hook" (not used). To ring the phone a 40- to 130-V rms at 17- to 33-Hz ring signal is superimposed on this level. In the modem's ring detector circuit, this signal causes the 27-V zener diode and infrared LED in the TIL 155 optocoupler to conduct. The inverting input of the LM393 comparator becomes more positive than the noninverting input and the $\overline{RI}$ signal goes low. This can be used to alert the control circuit to apply the OH (off-hook signal).

The 75472 relay driver allows the OH signal to "answer the phone" by closing the dc loop current switch. Note that the OH input can also be used to implement an *auto-dial* feature (see Prob. 9.41).

A 600-Ω transformer is used to couple the data signal onto and off of the 600-Ω phone line. Back-to-back zener diodes prevent excessive voltages (due to lightning, for example) from damaging the modem.

The transmit and receive signals are mixed onto a two-wire line by the phone company. These must be converted to separate receive (and ground) and transmit (and ground) signals for the modem. The two op-amps accomplish this function. The transmitted signal (TXA) is amplified by op-amp A1 but rejected by op-amp A2, a *differential amplifier* with 0 gain. However, to the received signal op-amp A2 appears to be a noninverting amplifier with 6-dB gain. The result is a circuit that separates the receive and transmit signals for the modem, but mixes them for transmission over the phone lines.

High-Speed Modems. The limitations of a 300-baud modem soon become apparent when the need to transmit large blocks of data occurs. For example, the time to transmit a 32K-byte ASCII file at 300 baud can be calculated as

$$32,768 \text{ characters} \times 9 \text{ bits/character} \times 1 \text{ s/300 bits} = 983 \text{ s}$$

This is over 16 minutes! Even at 600 baud over 8 minutes is required. What's more, data files of 32K bytes are not particularly long (the text for one chapter in this book typically runs over 75K bytes).

If half-duplex operation is acceptable, the FSK modulation technique can be extended to 1200 bps using 1200 Hz and 2200 Hz for the logic 1 and 0 frequencies respectively. This is the Bell 202 standard. However, for full-duplex operation at 1200 bps or higher, new modulation methods must be used.

Two related techniques have become popular. The first is called *phase-shift keying* or PSK. Unlike FSK, which switches the logic 1 and 0 carrier frequencies, PSK modulates the *phase* of a constant-frequency sine wave. If the demodulating circuitry can detect 90° of phase shift, the same sine wave can be transmitted in four different ways, depending on the amount of phase shift: 0°, 90°, 180°, or 270°.

The receiver compares the present sine wave with the previous one to measure this phase-angle difference. Because the same sine wave can be represented in four different ways, two binary bits—called *dibits*—can be used to describe the four phases. This is shown in Fig. 9.47.

When PSK is used for the modulating technique, the baud rate and data rate (in bps) are no longer the same. The baud rate is defined to be the number of signal events per second. With FSK this is the same as the baud rate, but with PSK one signal event is encoded with 2 bits of information. If the carrier frequency is such that 600 dibits are transmitted per second, the data rate is 1200 bps. Table 9.10 indicates the dibit definitions for Bell 212A and Racal Vadic VA3400 series full-duplex 1200-bps modems.

Depending on the sophistication of the receiver and transmitter circuitry, eight phase angle shifts will encode a *tribit*. At 600 baud this would accommodate an 1800-bps data rate.

Another technique similar to PSK is *quadrature amplitude modulation* or QAM.

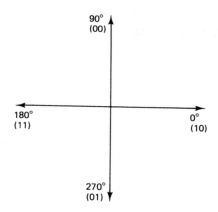

Figure 9.47 PSK results in four dibit patterns, corresponding to the four possible 90° phase shifts of the carrier wave.

TABLE 9.10 DIBIT PATTERNS FOR THE TWO POPULAR 1200-BPS MODEM STANDARDS

Dibit pattern	Phase shift (deg)
Racal Vadic VA3400	
00	90
01	270
10	0
11	180
Bell 212A	
00	90
01	0
10	180
11	270

In this modulating scheme four levels of amplitude are combined with four angles of PSK. The result is 16 possible combinations of phase and amplitude in a single phase shift and amplitude-modulated sine wave. This is shown in Fig. 9.48. Instead of dibits, a QAM modem transmits *quad bits* and a 600-Hz baud rate will accommodate a 2400-bps data rate.

Regardless of the modulating technique, PSK or QAM, the control circuitry is considerably more complex than that required for FSK. For example, Racal Vadic's VA4400 quad modem can be used as a Bell 103 FSK modem, a Bell 212A mode 1200-bps modem, a VA3400 mode 1200-bps modem, and a 2400-bps modem. It uses a built-in 16-bit microprocessor to perform the analog signal-processing functions for all four full-duplex modems.

CHAPTER SUMMARY

1. Serial data is transmitted one bit at a time. The data rate is measured in bits per second and called the baud rate.

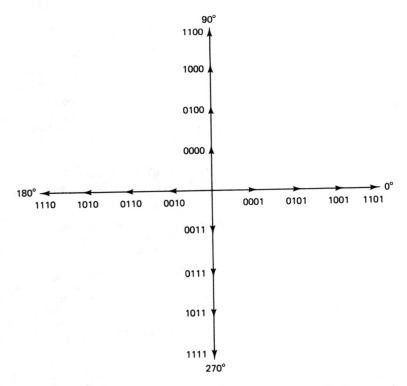

Figure 9.48 Using QAM, 16 combinations of phase shift and amplitude are possible. The resulting bit patterns are referred to as *quad bits*.

2. Serial data may be transmitted asynchronously with start and stop bits or synchronously with special sync characters identifying the start of data.

3. The UART is a universal asynchronous receiver/transmitter designed for converting parallel data to asynchronous serial data and vice versa. The UART usually requires a clock signal 16 times the desired baud rate.

4. The 8251A USART and Z-80 SIO are examples of programmable UARTs that also include synchronous serial data capabilities. The 8251A provides a single channel and the Z-80 SIO has two channels.

5. Error-detecting schemes include parity, checksums, and cyclic redundancy check characters. The (modified) Hamming code is an error-correcting technique. It requires four redundant bits for one byte of data but detects and corrects all single-bit errors and detects most multiple-bit errors.

6. Serial data techniques can be extended to remote control applications requiring only three signal wires.

7. When transmitting data over long lengths of cable, special line drivers and receivers should be used. Optimum performance is obtained from drivers with differential input and output stages.

8. The RS-232D standard defines a single-ended transmission technique limited to 20,000 baud with a 50-ft cable. Also defined are signal descriptions for a 25-pin connector, including several modem control lines that can be used for handshaking purposes.

9. A modem is a device that converts binary data into sine waves that can be passed over the switched telephone network. Frequency-shift keying is used for 300- and 600-baud modems, but phase shift modulation techniques are required for higher-speed devices.

10. A modem can be interfaced to the phone line using an acoustic coupler or a registered protective circuit.

LAB PROJECTS

9.1. Study the schematic diagram of the microcomputer you are using to support this text/course. If your computer includes a serial port, answer the following questions about this port.[1]
(a) What chip is used to implement the UART function?
(b) Determine the addresses for the control, status, and data input and output ports of your computer's UART.
(c) Locate the baud rate generator circuit. What baud rates are supported?
(d) Check to see if the serial port is RS-232D compatible.

---

[1] On some computers a *software UART* is used via one bit of an I/O port (see Fig. 9.49 and Probs. 9.5 through 9.8). The 8085 microprocessor has this feature built-in via its SID and SOD input and output pins (see Prob. 9.8).

(e) Is the port wired as a DCE or a DTE?

(f) Which modem-control signals are supported?

9.2. Write a program to cause your serial port to continually transmit the same character. Monitoring the serial output with an oscilloscope, switch the time base out of calibration and adjust so that one division equals one bit time. Sketch the output waveform (see Probs. 9.1 and 9.5.)[2]

9.3. Repeat Lab 9.2 but try the following changes:

(a) Add an even parity bit

(b) Add an odd parity bit

(c) Switch to higher and lower baud rates

9.4. Try interfacing two computers via their serial ports. One machine should be programmed as a transmitter and the other as a receiver (see Probs. 9.5 through 9.8).

9.5. Two PC's can be interfaced via their serial ports if a *null* modem cable is used. The diagram below shows two DTE's connected by such a cable.

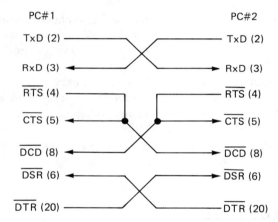

After you have wired the cable, connect the two PC's and use the BASIC program COMM to "talk" to each other. See if you can send a file from one machine to another. Experiment with the baud rate and communications parameters.

9.6. Using the cable described in Lab 9.5 and a communications program such as Crosstalk, link two computers together and practice sending files between the two. Several different protocols can be used: ASCII, X-modem, Kermit, etc.

---

[2] Most IBM PCs and compatibles come with a BASIC program called COMM. This progam can be used to access the PC's serial port if your trainer does not have one.

QUESTIONS AND PROBLEMS

Section 9.1

9.1. Sketch the output waveform of a UART transmitting the 7-bit ASCII letter "B" with even parity and 2 stop bits at 1200 baud.

9.2. Answer the following questions about the 7 data bit with parity, 2 stop bit, serial waveform shown in Fig. 9.50.
  (a) Calculate the baud rate.
  (b) Is even or odd parity being used?
  (c) Interpreted in ASCII, what is the character being sent?

9.3. Serial data can be saved on a cassette recorder if it is converted to audio form. One standard uses 8 cycles of a 2400-Hz sine wave for a logic 1 and 4 cycles of a 1200-Hz sine wave for a logic 0.
  (a) What is the equivalent baud rate of this standard?
  (b) Using 8 data bits, 1 stop bit, and no parity, how long would it take to store a 16K-byte file?

9.4. The circuit in Fig. 9.49 can be used to transmit and receive serial data. Answer the following questions about this circuit.
  (a) What is the port address of the receiver and transmitter?
  (b) What prevents the flip-flop from storing the input serial data?
  (c) Why is it important that the flip-flop be *rising-edge* triggered?

9.5. The following program can be used to transmit serial data using the interface shown in Fig. 9.49 (see Fig. 9.2 for the Z-80 equivalent program).

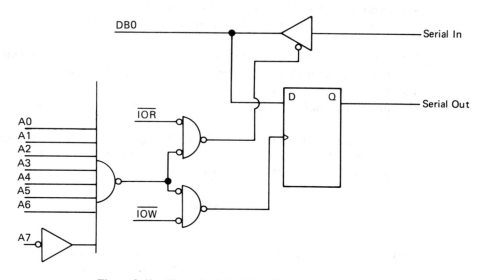

Figure 9.49 Circuit for Lab 9.1 and Probs. 9.4 through 9.7.

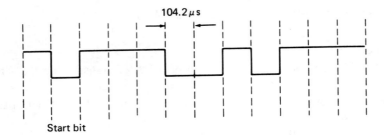

Figure 9.50 Serial waveform for Prob. 2.

```
              MOV    B,0BH     ;11 bits per character
              ANA    A         ;Clear carry flag
              RAL              ;Move carry to bit 0
       TRAN   OUT    DPORT     ;Transmit the bit
              CALL   DELAY     ;Hold for one bit time
              RAR              ;Next bit
              STC              ;Set carry for stop bit
              DCR    B         ;Bump bit counter
              JNZ    TRAN      ;Do for all 11 bits
              RET
```

(a) What is the purpose of the RAL (RLA) instruction?

(b) How can the program transmit 11 bits when register A is only 8 bits wide?

(c) Assume register A is loaded with 69H. What is the content of register A and the carry flag the *first* time the OUT instruction is executed?

(d) In (c), what are the contents of register A and the carry flag after all 11 bits have been transmitted?

9.6. Write an 8080/85 or Z-80 program that calls the serial transmitter described in Prob. 9.5 and transmits the 4K block of memory beginning at address A000H.

9.7. Write the matching 8080/85 or Z-80 serial-data receiver program for the interface in Fig. 9.49. use the flowchart in Fig. 9.3 as a guide.

9.8. Using the 8085's SID and SOD lines write serial transmitter and receiver programs similar to Figs. 9.2 and 9.3. Refer to Fig. 6.20 for the SID/SOD bit definitions.

9.9. Write a subroutine that polls the RDR flag of the UART interface shown in Fig. 9.6 and returns with the received character in register A. Register B should hold an error code as follows

00	→ no error
01	→ parity error
02	→ framing error
03	→ overrun

*9.10. Assume two computers are connected via a serial data link. Inadvertently, one user has set his baud rate to 300, and the other to 600. Which of the following would be symptoms of this problem?

(a) At the 300 baud terminal you would see each character repeated twice.
(b) Each system's UART would report *framing errors*.
(c) The data displayed on each system's screen would be "*garbage.*"
(d) Each terminal would receive the characters correctly, but the UARTs would report parity errors.

Section 9.2

9.11. Calculate the time to transmit an 8K-byte file at 1200 baud using the bisync synchronous serial protocol. Assume 256-byte data fields. Compare the result with the time required for asynchronous serial with 8 data bits, 2 stop bits, and even parity.

Section 9.3

9.12. For the bytes listed below, (a) calculate the checksum; (b) if all bytes are encoded with odd parity, determine which byte(s) are in error.

A7H, 09H, 6EH, C2H

9.13. Write a subroutine that adds an even-parity bit (in bit position 7) to the 7-bit character passed it in register C. Return the encoded byte in register C.

9.14. Write a subroutine to generate the checksum for a 256 byte block of data whose starting address is passed in the HL pair. Return with the checksum byte in register A.

9.15. Write a subroutine that tests the checksum of a 256-byte block of data whose starting address is passed in the HL pair. Return with the zero flag set if no error. The checksum byte is passed in register C.

9.16. Assume the data byte A5H is to be transmitted using the Hamming code described in Sec. 9.3.
(a) What is the 12-bit word to be transmitted?
(b) What is the error code if this byte is received as 3ADH?

9.17. A certain 8-bit computer uses the Hamming code as described in Sec. 9.3. If the code B27H is received, what is the (*corrected*) data byte?

9.18. If the 12-bit number B27H is input by the error correction and detection circuit in Fig. 9.13, determine the logic levels at the following points:
(a) 74154 A–D inputs
(b) 74154 0–15 outputs
(c) 74LS20 output
(d) IC7 and 8 outputs
(e) 74LS86 outputs D0–D7

9.19. Calculate the worst-case time required to detect and correct a single-bit error using the circuit in Fig. 9.13. Hint: Look up each chip's propagation delay time in a TTL data book.

Section 9.4

9.20. Write the 8080/85 initialization routine required to program the 8251A USART in Fig. 9.15 for the following:

(a) 16× clock

(b) 8 data bits

(c) even parity

(d) 1 stop bit

(e) $\overline{\text{DTR}}$ and $\overline{\text{RTS}}$ active

9.21. Assuming the USART has been programmed as described in Prob. 9.20, what is the baud rate if the transmitter and receiver clock frequencies are 307.2 KHz?

9.22. Describe the contents of the 8251A status register when programmed for the asynchronous mode and the following conditions apply:

(a) No errors detected

(b) The receiver has a character to be read.

(c) The transmitter is outputting a character and is not ready for new data.

(d) The break character has not been received.

(e) $\overline{\text{DSR}} = 0$

9.23. Assume the print buffer subroutine in Fig. 9.19 is used to send data from one computer to another via a serial data link. Write the corresponding receiver subroutine such that the received character is returned in register B. Ignore the error flags and assume the hardware interface in Fig. 9.15 applies.

9.24. In this program you are to design an interface to the three-bus architecture of the 8080/85 with the following features:

(a) 8255A mapped to I/O ports C0–C3H.

(b) 8254 mapped to I/O ports C4–C7H.

(c) 8251A mapped to I/O ports C8–C9H.

(d) Wire the 8254 so that it can be used as a baud rate generator for the 8251A. Use a 1.8432-MHz time base.

(e) Wire a 3-switch DIP switch to PC0–PC2 of the 8255A.

9.25. Write a control program for the interface described in Prob. 9.24 that allows the switch to select eight different baud rates as listed in the table below. Assume a 16× clock.

Switch value	Baud rate
0	110
1	300
2	600
3	1200
4	2400
5	4800
6	9600
7	19200

Section 9.5

9.26. Using the Z-80 SIO initialization routine in Fig. 9.27(b), determine the new codes to program for the following configuration:

(a) 16× clock

(b) 7 data bits

(c) no parity

(d) 1 stop bit

(e) receiver enabled by $\overline{DCD}$, transmitter by $\overline{CTS}$

(f) $\overline{DTR}$ and $\overline{RTS}$ active

(d) 1 stop bit

(e) receiver enabled by $\overline{DCD}$, transmitter by $\overline{CTS}$

(f) $\overline{DTR}$ and $\overline{RTS}$ active

9.27. Assuming the SIO has been programmed as described in Prob. 9.26, what is the baud rate if the transmitter and receiver clock frequencies are 38.4 KHz?

9.28. Answer the following questions about the Z-80 SIO interface in Fig. 9.23 and receiver subroutine in Fig. 9.29.

(a) Which channel of the SIO is being used?

(b) What is the port address corresponding to WR0?

(c) From which port should the in-coming character be read?

(d) How does the *calling* routine know if a parity, overrun, or framing error has occurred?

9.29. Write a subroutine to serially transmit the character passed in register A using channel B of the Z-80 SIO interface shown in Fig. 9.23. Assume the $\overline{DCD}$ and $\overline{CTS}$ inputs are permanently enabled and break is not used.

9.30. In this problem you are to design an interface to the three-bus architecture of the Z-80 with the following features:

(a) Z-80 PIO mapped to I/O ports C0–C3H.

(b) Z-80 CTC mapped to I/O ports C4–C7H.

(c) Z-80 SIO mapped to I/O ports C8–CBH.

(d) Wire the CTC so that it can be used as a baud rate generator for the SIO. Use a 1.8432-MHz time base.

(e) Wire a 3-switch DIP switch to PA0–PA2 of the PIO.

9.31. Write a control program for the interface described in Prob. 9.30 that allows the switch to select eight different baud rates as listed in the table in Prob. 9.25. Assume a 16× clock.

Section 9.6

9.32. At first it would seem that an 8-bit UART would be limited to monitoring/controlling the on/off status of 8 I/O devices. What is wrong with this logic? What are the limits?

Section 9.7

9.33. When not transmitting data ("marking"), the output of a serial port is a logic 1. In the RS-232D standard what voltage level would you expect to measure for this marking condition?

*9.34. A technician is troubleshooting an RS-232D interface. Spotting a 25-pin connector, his first job is to determine if the connector is wired as a DTE or a DCE. The technician responds, "That's easy. I'll just measure the voltage on pin 2." Is this correct? Explain.

9.35. Assume two computers are to be wired together to exchange data via their RS-232D serial ports. If both machines are wired as DTEs', how should the cable be wired? Assume $\overline{DTR}$ and $\overline{DSR}$ (only) are used for handshaking.

9.36. Explain how the four modem control signals of the 8251A USART or the Z-80 SIO should be connected to the BUSY/$\overline{READY}$ and $\overline{STROBE}$ handshaking signals of a serial printer.

9.37. Explain how the X-ON/X-OFF protocol can be used to synchronize the flow of data between two serial ports.

Section 9.8

9.38. Explain the following statement. For full-duplex operation, an answer and originate modem are required.

***9.39.** When operating half duplex, only one station can transmit at a time. Because of this, a terminal set for half duplex displays the operator's keystrokes as they are typed. However, when set for full duplex, the terminal expects the distant station to "echo" the keystrokes back. Assume you are troubleshooting such a system and find that each keystroke is repeated *twice* on the CRT screen. What do you think is wrong?

9.40. Determine the *data rate* for a 600-baud modem using
  (a) FSK
  (b) PSK (di-bits)
  (c) QAM (quad bits).

9.41. The OH input to the dc loop current control circuit in Fig. 9.46 can be used to implement a computer-controlled automatic dialing circuit. Figure 9.51 illustrates the timing required to dial the two-digit sequence "4" "3." Write a subroutine that pulses the OH line in Fig. 9.46 the appropriate number of times and with the proper interdigit timing to facilitate a computer-controlled auto dialer. Assume that the digit to be dialed is passed to the subroutine in register A, and that the OH input is connected to $\overline{DTR}$ of the 8251A interface in Fig. 9.15.

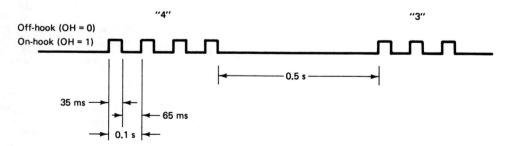

Figure 9.51 Telephone pulse timing required to dial the two-digit sequence "4" "3."

KEY CONCEPT ANSWERS

9.1.1. start, stop

9.1.2. baud

9.1.3. UART

9.2.1. Synchronous serial data does not use start and stop bits.

9.2.2. byte, bit

9.3.1. parity

9.3.2. The checksum requires less overhead and is more likely to detect burst errors.

9.3.3. bit

9.3.4. 4

9.4.1. 4 (2 input ports and 2 output ports)

9.4.2. TTL oscillator, 8254 PIT oscillator, baud rate generator chip (MC14411 for example)

9.4.3. $R \times RDY$, $T \times RDY$

9.4.4. The USART can be programmed to hunt for a special sync character indicating the start of synchronous serial data.

9.5.1. two

9.5.2. 8,3

9.5.3. polling, interrupts, DMA

9.5.4. The PIO can be programmed to hunt for a special sync character indicating the start of synchronous serial data.

9.6.1. 3,8

9.7.1. single-ended, differential

9.7.2. logic 1: -3 to -25 V logic 0: $+3$ to $+25$ V

9.7.3. DTE, DCE

9.7.4. The receiver must have time to process the received data.

9.7.5. $\overline{DCD}$, $\overline{DTR}$, $\overline{DSR}$, $\overline{RTS}$, $\overline{CTS}$

9.8.1. frequency-shift keying

9.8.2. automatic dialing, better signal coupling

9.8.3. PSK and QAM modems encode more than one bit for each signal event. With these modems, the data rate is greater than the baud rate.

10

Floppy and Hard Disk Drives

In Chap. 5 we spent a considerable amount of time studying RAM and ROM memory technologies. This type of memory is called *main memory*. Main memory is interfaced to the microprocessor in such a way that each memory location has its own unique address. Using its address, data, and control buses the microprocessor is then able to repeatedly fetch and execute program instructions stored in this unit.

Some computers can get by with a single program stored in one or more ROM chips. Microcomputer-controlled appliances like VCRs, dishwashers, and microwave ovens are good examples. Desktop computers, on the other hand, usually have a large amount of RAM into which applications programs are loaded via a disk drive.

Disk drives are referred to as *secondary* storage devices. Their purpose is twofold. One is to back up data that is stored in RAM, but will be lost when power is removed. The second is to provide a means to quickly load new applications programs into RAM. Two types of disk drives are in common use: *floppy* and *hard* or *fixed* disk drives.

In this chapter we will study the technology behind these two types of drives. We begin by learning how binary data can be stored on a magnetic disk. The components of a typical drive are then explained. It is here that the differences between a floppy and hard disk drive will become clear. Next, common disk drive terminology like tracks, sectors, cylinders, and clusters are explained. The popular data-encoding techniques—MFM and RLL—are also discussed. The chapter concludes with a discussion of the disk drive interface. This section identifies the industry standard interfaces that are used to mate the disk drive electronics to the disk controller.

10.1 STORING DATA ON A MAGNETIC DISK

As you read this section, look for the answers to these Key Concept questions:

10.1.1. Data to be stored on a magnetic disk must first be converted to _____ form.

10.1.2. The read/write head of a disk drive functions as a(n) _____ .

10.1.3. What are the two common sizes for floppy disks?

10.1.4. Why are the platters of a hard drive protected from the environment?

Although floppy disk drives and hard disk drives are quite different as far as data rates and storage capacities are concerned, the data recording technique used by the two drives is the same. Data to be written must first be converted to serial form. The data bits are then written by applying current pulses to a read/write head positioned over the surface of a spinning magnetic disk.

Flux Transitions. As shown in Fig. 10.1 the read/write head is actually an *electromagnet*. When a current pulse is applied to the head, the surface of the disk directly under the head becomes magnetized. Depending on the direction of the applied current, the flux lines produced will be oriented left to right, or right to left.

Note that each time a set of north or south poles face each other, the flux lines must reverse. Data is written to the disk by defining a *bit cell* within which a logic 1 or 0 is written. In the single density encoding scheme, a flux transition in the middle of the bit cell is interpreted as a logic 1, the absence of this transition as a logic 0. Each time a flux transition is to occur, the *direction* of the current through the read/write head must be reversed.[1]

In the play-back or read mode, the head acts as a magnetic pickup. Each time a flux transition occurs, a small voltage is induced in the head (recall Faraday's law: $v = N \, d\phi/dt$). *In this way, the original waveform can be recovered.*

The Media. The magnetic disk upon which the data is stored is called the *media*. Floppy disks use a Mylar disk coated with iron oxide, a magnetic compound. Because of the flexibility of the Mylar disk, the term "floppy" has been applied.

Figure 10.2 shows the two types of floppy disks in common use. The principal difference is the size of the disk—$3\frac{1}{2}''$ or $5\frac{1}{4}''$. Both use a Mylar disk enclosed in a protective jacket. The $3\frac{1}{2}''$ disks use a hard plastic package which makes these disks less "floppy" than their $5\frac{1}{4}''$ counterparts.

Hard drives use a rigid disk often made of aluminum. In low-end drives this disk is coated with iron oxide, similar to a floppy disk. High-end drives use a thin film-plated media which creates a much thinner and smoother surface. This, in turn, allows much higher bit densities than are possible with iron oxide-coated

---

[1] Be careful not to interpret each flux transition as a logic 1. Because of the need to maintain synchronization with the data, *clock* pulses are embedded within the data stream. Thus, some flux transitions may represent data, but others the synchronizing clock pulses. This is explained in more detail in Sec. 10.4.

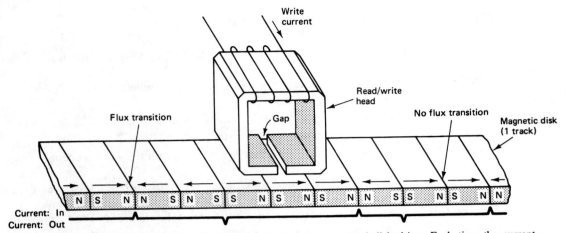

Figure 10.1 The read/write head of a floppy or hard disk drive. Each time the current reverses, a flux transition is recorded.

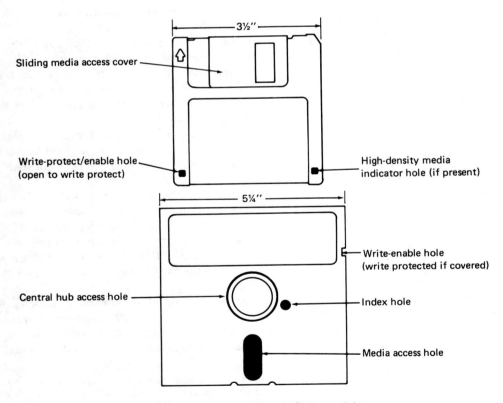

Figure 10.2 Comparing 3½″ and 5¼″ floppy diskettes.

disks. Plated media is also stronger, making it more tolerant of a "head crash," which can occur if the read/write heads contact the surface of the spinning disk.

Hard drives often use several disks—called "platters"—which are mounted in a sealed chamber. This is necessary because of the extremely close tolerance between the read/write head and disk surface. In a typical drive the head "floats" on a cushion of air only a few millionths of an inch thick. This allows the drive to store data at a density much higher than that of a floppy disk. It also means that the disk platters and read/write head must be protected from the environment. On this scale, even a human hair appears to be a "gigantic tree limb."

For these reasons the platters of a hard drive are not removable and become an integral part of the drive. In fact, if one of the platters becomes damaged, it usually means scrapping the entire drive.

10.2 THE COMPONENTS OF A DISK DRIVE

As you read this section, look for the answers to these Key Concept questions:

10.2.1. List the two types of motors used in a floppy disk drive.

10.2.2. What is the purpose of the tunnel erase head in a floppy or hard disk drive?

10.2.3. What are the typical disk rotation rates for floppy and hard disk drives?

10.2.4. Why do high-end hard drives use voice coil head positioners?

Floppy Disk Drives. Figure 10.3 highlights the major components of a 5¼″ floppy disk drive. The disk is rotated by the *spindle motor*—at 300 RPM. Unlike hard drives the spindle motor runs only when the disk is being accessed.

A second motor called the *stepper motor* is used to move the read/write head linearly across the surface of the spinning disk. The resolution of this motor determines the number of tracks—concentric circles—within which data is stored. A single voltage pulse applied to the stepper motor moves the head in or out by one track. Typical drives have 40 or 80 tracks per disk side.

The *read/write* head is actually three heads in one. This is shown in Fig. 10.4(a). The data head is in the center with *tunnel erase* heads mounted on each Typical drives have 40 or 80 tracks per disk side.

The *read/write* head is actually three heads in one. This is shown in Fig. 10.4(a). The data head is in the center with *tunnel erase* heads mounted on each side. The purpose of the latter is to clear the intertrack region of any flux transitions [Fig. 10.4(b)]. Nearly all disk drives today are *double-sided*. This means data can be written to both sides of the disk. Of course such drives require two read/write heads, with the disk sandwiched between the two.

Although not shown in Fig. 10.3, every floppy disk drive also includes a *logic board*. This printed circuit board contains the circuitry needed to translate the flux transitions into valid logic levels. Also included are circuits for controlling the various motors and sensors within the drive. Section 10.5 includes a discussion of the disk drive/computer interface.

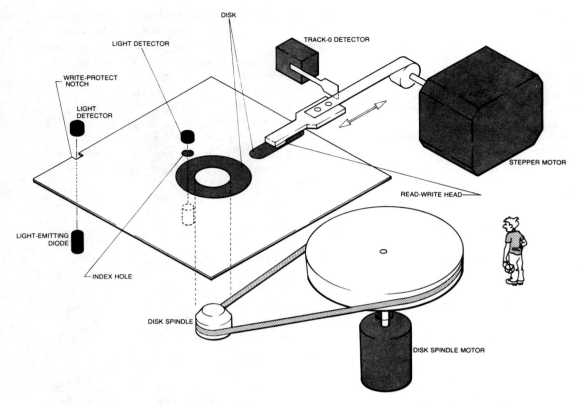

Figure 10.3 Mechanical design of a floppy disk drive. The spindle motor rotates the disk and a stepper motor is used to position the read/write head over the desired data track. (Courtesy of Reason Redacting.)

Hard Drives. Figure 10.5 identifies the major components of a hard disk drive. Note that unlike floppy drives, several disks or *platters* may be used, each of these with their own double-sided read/write head. Because of the sealed enclosure, the platters can be rotated at a much higher rate than that of a floppy, typically 3600 RPM.

Hard drives intended for microcomputers typically use $5\frac{1}{4}''$ or $3\frac{1}{2}''$ disk platters. This makes it possible to slide a hard drive into the space originally intended for a floppy drive. Because the disk platters are not removable, the choice of $5\frac{1}{4}''$ or $3\frac{1}{2}''$ is less important than it is with floppy drives. Generally speaking, a particular hard drive is chosen because of its capacity and speed, not the size of the disk platters.

Hard drives use two types of head positioners. Low-end drives—sometimes called XT class drives because they were made popular by the IBM XT computer— use *stepper motor* actuators. Pulses applied to this motor step the head in or out one track at a time.

The biggest problem with this type of head positioner is its sensitivity to temperature. As the disk platters heat and cool, the relative position of the (closely

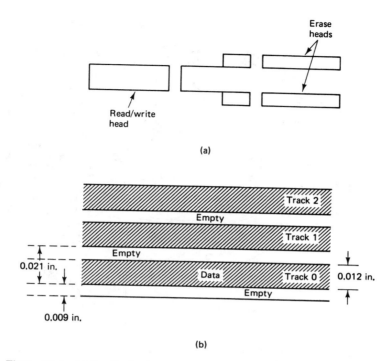

Erase heads

Read/write head

(a)

Track 2

Empty

Track 1

Empty

0.021 in.

Data   Track 0   0.012 in.

Empty

0.009 in.

(b)

Figure 10.4 (a) Read/write head with tunnel erase; (b) the path written by the head as the disk rotates. The dimensions shown are typical for a low-density 5¼" drive.

spaced) data tracks expand and contract. Unfortunately, the stepper motor has no way of tracking these variations. As a result, data errors can occur as the head is simply stepped out to what the drive "thinks" is the location of the desired track. This type of drive needs to be operated at a constant temperature to avoid these problems.

High-end hard drives—sometimes called AT class drives after the IBM AT computer—use a *voice coil* head positioner. Operating like the voice coil of a loudspeaker, the head is moved in and out dependent on the magnitude of current through a voice coil. There are no detent positions. This allows the head to be moved rapidly from one track position to another.

Voice coil drives require that one disk surface be dedicated to storing address marks. When a command is received to move to a particular track, the head is moved out until that address position is found on the dedicated surface. If that head position has moved because of temperature variations, the head will track it and no data errors will occur. Because voice-call drives receive feedback about the current head position, they are said to be *closed loop servo controlled*.

Another advantage to this type of drive is *automatic head "parking."* When power is removed, the read/write heads are automatically pulled back to a safe landing zone by a small spring.

Sec. 10.2   The Components of a Disk Drive

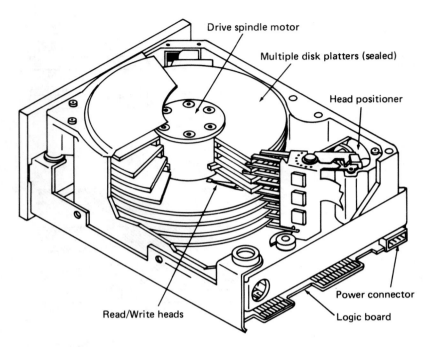

Drive spindle motor

Multiple disk platters (sealed)

Head positioner

Read/Write heads

Power connector

Logic board

Figure 10.5 Mechanical design of a typical hard disk drive. Note the use of several disk platters.

10.3 COMMON DISK DRIVE SPECIFICATIONS

As you read this section, look for the answers to these Key Concept questions:

10.3.1. Data is stored on a floppy or hard disk in concentric tracks with each track further divided into _____.

10.3.2. One cylinder corresponds to all _____ under the read/write heads at a given time.

10.3.3. What is the advantage of organizing the data on a disk into clusters?

10.3.4. What is meant by the interleave factor of a disk?

Sectors.   As the read/write head of a floppy or hard disk drive is stepped in and out across the surface of the disk, concentric data circles—*tracks*—are defined. This was shown in Fig. 10.4. To efficiently allocate space within these tracks, the DOS (*disk operating system*) further divides these tracks into *sectors*. This is shown in Fig. 10.6.

Under PC or MS-DOS, four different floppy disk formats have become standard. Table 10.1 lists the important parameters for these drives.

Example 10.1

Calculate the total number of sectors and storage capacity for a low density $5\frac{1}{4}''$ floppy disk drive.

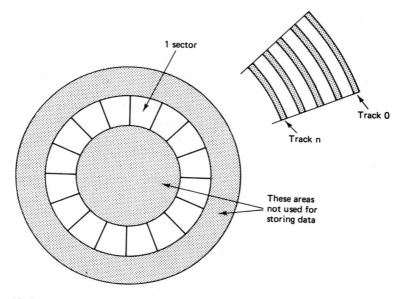

10.6 The surface of the disk is organized into tracks with several sectors per track.

TABLE 10.1 FLOPPY DISK DRIVE FORMATS

Drive size	$5\frac{1}{4}''$	$5\frac{1}{4}''$	$3\frac{1}{2}''$	$3\frac{1}{2}''$
Density	low	high	low	high
Tracks/side	40	80	80	80
Sides	2	2	2	2
Sectors/track	9	15	9	18
Bytes/sector	512	512	512	512
Total sectors	720	2400	1440	2880
Total capacity	360K[a]	1200K	720K	1440K

[a] 1K = 1024 bytes

Solution. The total number of sectors can be found as:

$$\text{Sectors} = \frac{\text{sectors}}{\text{track}} \times \frac{\text{tracks}}{\text{side}} \times \text{no. of sides}$$
$$= \quad 9 \quad \times \quad 40 \quad \times \quad 2 = 720 \text{ sectors}$$

The total disk capacity is then found as:

$$\text{Disk capacity} = \text{total sectors} \times \frac{\text{bytes}}{\text{sector}}$$
$$= \quad 720 \quad \times \quad 512 = 368,640 \text{ bytes}$$
$$= \quad 360\text{K} \ (1\text{K} = 1024 \text{ bytes})$$

Comparing the four drive types in Table 10.1 it is interesting to note that the $3\frac{1}{2}''$ drives are able to store more data than their $5\frac{1}{4}''$ counterparts. The smaller drives are actually storing data at a higher *bit density* (bits/in). This is an indication of the improved technology present in these (newer) drives.

Because there are so many different types of hard drives, it is hard to make up an all encompassing table for these drives. Depending on the encoding scheme and drive interface (explained in Secs. 10.4 and 10.5), several sector configurations are common. Some drives have 17 sectors/track, others 25 or 26, still others 34. Some drives have 4 platters and 8 heads, others 3 platters and 7 heads, etc. Only the number of bytes/sector (512) remains constant. Nevertheless, the formulas presented in Ex. 10.1 can be used to determine the capacity of any hard drive.

Example 10.2

Calculate the total number of sectors and disk capacity for a hard drive with 2 platters, 614 tracks/side, and 25 sectors/track.

Solution

$$\text{Sectors} = \frac{\text{sectors}}{\text{track}} \times \frac{\text{tracks}}{\text{side}} \times \text{no. of sides}$$

$$= \quad 25 \quad \times \quad 614 \quad \times \quad 4 = 61{,}400 \text{ sectors}$$

$$\text{Disk capacity} = \text{total sectors} \times \frac{\text{bytes}}{\text{sector}}$$

$$= \quad 61{,}400 \quad \times \quad 512 = 31{,}436{,}800 \text{ bytes}$$

$$= 29.98 \text{ MB } (1 \text{ MB} = 1{,}048{,}576 \text{ bytes})$$

Cylinders. The term *cylinder* is often applied when describing the capacity of a hard drive. A cylinder is defined as all tracks under the read/write heads at a given time, in effect, a three-dimensional area that traces out the shape of a *cylinder*. Each track on a hard drive can then be specified by its cylinder and head number. Figure 10.7 shows an example for a drive with three platters. Cylinder 0, head 5, for example, would then specify the outside track of the bottom-most disk surface.

Example 10.3.

Calculate the total number of cylinders and bytes for a hard drive with 8 heads, 940 tracks/side, and 17 sectors/track. Determine the number of bytes stored in each cylinder and the total capacity of the drive.

Solution. The number of tracks/side is the same as the number of cylinders. Thus this drive has 940 cylinders. Each cylinder stores:

$$\frac{17 \text{ sectors}}{\text{track}} \times \frac{8 \text{ tracks}}{\text{cylinder}} \times \frac{512 \text{ bytes}}{\text{sector}} = 69{,}632 \text{ bytes} = 68\text{KB}$$

The total storage capacity of the drive is therefore 940 cylinders $\times$ 68K bytes/cylinder = 63,920K bytes or 62.42 MB.

Clusters. It is the job of the DOS to manage the storage and retrieval of files on the disk. In order to do this job as efficiently as possible, DOS allocates the available storage space in *clusters*. Hard drives use either 4 or 8 consecutive sectors per cluster. This means that file space will be ''handed out'' in 2K or 4K increments.

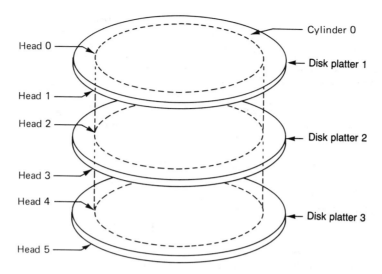

Figure 10.7 A cylinder encompasses all tracks under the read/write heads at a given time. In this example there are three platters and therefore six tracks/cylinder.

The advantage of clustering is to make it easier for the DOS to keep track of files. Instead of a 4K byte file being stored in eight different sector locations, it can be stored in one cluster. This file can thus be located more easily and faster. Of course files greater than 4K bytes will require additional clusters of disk space.

The disadvantage to clustering is wasted disk space. With 4K bytes per cluster, a file of only 10 bytes will require 8 sectors or 4K locations. Similarly, a 5K byte file will require 2 clusters and 8K total bytes of storage. But this may not be all bad. If new information is added to a file, as is common with database records, no additional disk space will be required until another cluster is needed.

Because floppy disks usually store smaller files than hard drives, the cluster size for a floppy is 1 sector/cluster for high-density drives and 2 sectors/cluster for low-density drives.

High- and Low-Level Formatting.
Before a floppy or hard disk can be used to store data, it must be *formatted*. This is a software process in which each sector on the disk is prepared so that it can be referenced by the DOS and used to store data.

The low-level format.
The first step is to perform a *low-level format*. It is here that the number of tracks and sectors/track are defined. In addition, the surface of the disk may be scanned to ensure that each track is capable of storing data.

Hard drives usually come with a *defect list* specifying those cylinders and head numbers that have been found incapable of reliably storing data. Figure 10.8 is an example of a printout that typically accompanies a drive. This drive has 4 heads and 615 cylinders. The results of several tests are shown. Near the bottom of the sheet one hard error is listed identifying head 3 cylinder 143.

The low-level format program will give you an opportunity to specify the

```
FINAL                    PASS DRIVE          REVISION - 1.5
----------------------------------------------------------------------
MODEL NO. 225-0      SERIAL NO. 3412939  DCU NO. 0         SYSTEM NO. 1
START DATE  5/06/87  TIME 20:28          STOP DATE  5/06/87  TIME 22:25
----------------------------------------------------------------------
     DATA     DATA     WRITE      REDUCE     PARK     STEP
     HEADS    CYLS     PRECOMP    WRT CUR    CYL      PULSE
                       CYLS                          RANGE
     0-3      0-614    256-614    N/A        670      5-200US
----------------------------------------------------------------------
SELECTS AVAILABLE          1  2  3  4      PASS
DE-SELECT                                  PASS
INDEX                                      PASS
TRACK 0                                    PASS
FULL CYLINDER                              PASS
STEP
  NOM        LOW          HIGH
  3MS        3MS          3MS              PASS
RECOVERY                                   PASS
START TIME
  NOM        LOW      HIGH       REV
  5.4SEC     6.3SEC   4.9SEC     5.8SEC    PASS
OUTSIDE MARGIN
  HEAD 0   HEAD 1   HEAD 2   HEAD 3
  36NS     38NS     36NS     36NS     LATE
  40NS     40NS     36NS     36NS     EARLY
  76NS     78NS     72NS     72NS     TOTAL
  PASS     PASS     PASS     PASS
INSIDE MARGIN
  HEAD 0   HEAD 1   HEAD 2   HEAD 3
  32NS     26NS     34NS     32NS     LATE
  30NS     26NS     32NS     30NS     EARLY
  62NS     52NS     66NS     62NS     TOTAL
  PASS     PASS     PASS     PASS
SEEK TEST                                  PASS
FORMAT                                     PASS
SINGLE TRACK ACCESS
  20.2MS                                   PASS
ROTATIONAL SPEED
  NOM          LOW          HIGH
  3600.6RPM    3599.9RPM    3599.9RPM      PASS
FORMAT                                     PASS
READ/WRITE TEST                            PASS
  TOTAL HARD ERRORS = 1
  TOTAL SOFT ERRORS = 0
HARD ERROR MAP :

HD    CYL     MFM BFI       HITS
----------------------------------------------------
3     143     6062          10

SEQUENCE REVISION 1.02
```

Figure 10.8 Hard drives usually come with a defect list taped to the drive. This drive has one hard error at head 3 cylinder 143. (Courtesy of Seagate Technologies.)

defective cylinders and head numbers so that these locations can be marked with invalid checksum figures. This will ensure that these tracks are not used by the DOS.

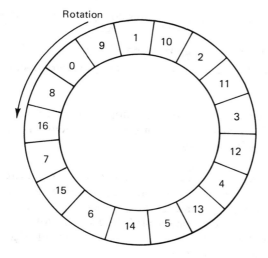

Rotation

Figure 10.9 A 17-sector disk with an interleave factor of 2.

Specifying the interleave. As the disk rotates, each sector passes one-by-one beneath the read/write head. Depending on the speed of the disk controller, the next sector may come up before the controller has had a chance to process the last sector. When this happens, an extra rotation of the disk will be required. Naturally this will add to the effective access time of the disk.

Figure 10.9 shows a 17 sector/track disk that has been formatted with an interleave factor of 2. The advantage is to give the controller "one sector's worth" of time before the next sector comes up. Although not as efficient as reading the disk sector-by-sector, it is much faster than waiting for an entire disk revolution. Usually the manufacturer of the disk controller will indicate the interleave required for the particular drive you are using.

The high-level format. The last step in the formatting process is to perform a high-level format. Under PC or MS-DOS, this is done with the command

FORMAT   C: /S/V

which will format drive C and copy the DOS system files to this disk. The high-level format program also sets up a blank *file allocation table* (FAT) and root directory. As files are written to the disk, these tables will then be updated to keep track of the exact sectors used by each file.

10.4 DATA ENCODING TECHNIQUES

As you read this section, look for the answers to these Key Concept questions:

10.4.1. What is meant by the term "bit cell?"

10.4.2. For each of the encoding techniques—FM, MFM, and RLL—what is the minimum and maximum number of missing pulses allowed in the data stream?

10.4.3. What is the data-rate relationship between FM, MFM, and RLL encoding?

10.4.4. Why is the unformatted capacity of a disk always greater than the formatted disk capacity?

In Sec. 10.1 we learned that data is stored on a floppy or hard disk as a series of *flux transitions*. Over the years several different encoding schemes have been developed utilizing these flux transitions to store data.

Single-Density. When data is encoded in single-density format, there is one clock pulse written for each data bit. Figure 10.10 provodes an example. At the top, the data pattern is shown as it would appear after having been converted from parallel to serial. Each bit persists for a period of time called the *bit cell*. All 5¼" single-density disk drives have a data rate of 125,000 bits/s. This requires a bit cell 8-μs wide.

The rules for single-density encoding are:

1. Begin each bit cell with a clock pulse.
2. If a logic 1 is to be stored, write a pulse in the middle of the bit cell. No pulse will represent a logic 0.

If you compare the data pattern in Fig. 10.10 with the FM-encoded data, you should be able to see how the rules for single-density data are applied. Also

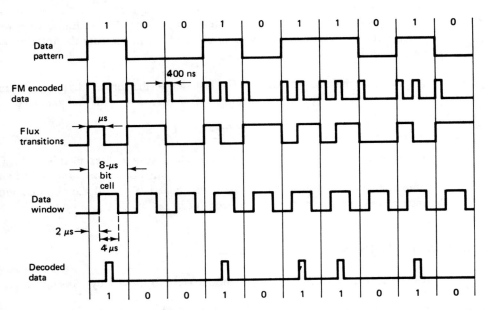

Figure 10.10 Single-density or FM encoding. Each bit cell begins with a clock pulse and two flux transitions (maximum) are required per cell.

note that each clock or data pulse becomes a *flux transition* when written to the disk.

Single-density encoding is also called FM (frequency modulation) encoding because a string of logic 1's will produce a different frequency than a string of logic 0's. That is, the data is encoded by *modulating* a carrier frequency.

FM encoding is said to be *self-clocking*. This is because the clock signal can be derived from the bit stream. Self-clocking is important because it is tolerant of slight variations in motor speed, as is likely to occur when moving a disk from one drive to another.

When the IBM-PC was first introduced, it used single-sided single-density encoding. This allowed a $5\frac{1}{4}''$ disk to store 160 KB of data. Today, single-density is considered obsolete and has been replaced by double-density and RLL encoding.

Double-Density. Single-density encoding requires a bit cell that can accommodate two flux transitions: one for the clock pulse and another for the data bit. Because the clock pulse carries no useful data information, this method is inefficient. In effect, it wastes 50% of the possible flux transitions.

Double-density encoding or *modified* FM (MFM) is 100% efficient because only one flux transition is required per data bit. Figure 10.11 compares the two encoding techniques. In Fig. 10.11(a) the data byte is encoded following the rules for single-density data. The resulting 8-bit data stream is 64-μs long.

In Fig. 10.11(b) the same data byte has been encoded following the rules for double-density encoding.

1. Write a logic 1 as a pulse in the middle of the bit cell as with single-density data.
2. Write a logic 0 as a pulse at the beginning of the bit cell (in the clock position) except when preceded by a logic 1. In this case, no pulse is written.

Studying the MFM data pattern in Fig. 10.11(b) we can note the following:

1. There is one flux transition (maximum) per data bit.
2. The maximum rate of change of flux transitions is the same as for FM data.
3. The bit cell is one-half the single-density cell size allowing two bits to be stored per single-density cell.
4. Because two bits are written in the time required for one single-density bit, the data rate for MFM is twice that of FM.

The MFM encoding process is really a software "trick." By eliminating the clock pulses associated with FM data, it is able to pack two data bits in the space previously required for one. No hardware changes are required of the disk drive. A drive used for writing single-density data can be used for double-density data as well. And because the flux transition rate is the same, special disks are not required.

RLL (Run Length Limited). FM encoded data requires a minimum of one pulse per bit cell (when storing a logic 0) and a maximum of two (when storing a logic 1).

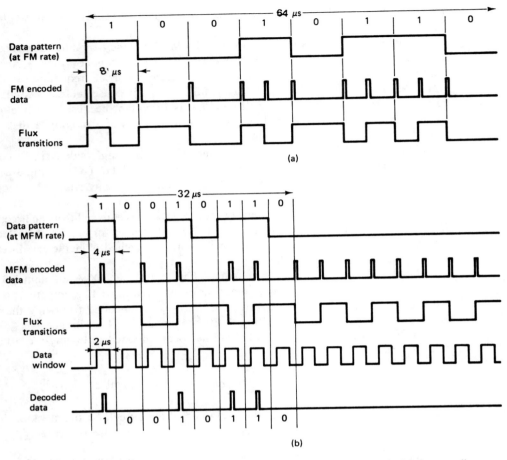

Figure 10.11 (a) Single-density encoding is compared with (b) double-density encoding. The latter requires only one flux change per data bit.

This means FM data is limited to a minimum of 0 missing pulses and a maximum of 1. We could describe this as *RLL 0,1*—run length limited with a minimum run length of 0 and maximum run length of 1. The term *run length* thus refers to the number of missing pulses.

Studying the MFM waveforms in Fig. 10.11(b), you can see a minimum run length of 1 (between two consecutive logic 1s or 0s) and a maximum of 3 (when storing the data pattern 101). MFM can thus be described as RLL 1,3.

Many hard drives today are using RLL 2,7. This is an encoding scheme that has a minimum run length of 2, and a maximum of 7. The rules for RLL 2,7 are shown in Table 10.2. Note that the data bits are not encoded individually, but rather as a *group*. Thus the data pattern 00 is encoded as a single pulse followed by three missing pulses. Studying this table you can see that there will always be at least two missing pulses, but no more than seven, no matter what the data pattern.

TABLE 10.2 RULES FOR RLL 2,7
ENCODING

Data bit group	RLL 2,7 encoding*
0 0	1 0 0 0
0 1	0 1 0 0
1 0 0	0 0 1 0 0 0
1 0 1	1 0 0 1 0 0
1 1 0 0	0 0 0 0 1 0 0 0
1 1 0 1	0 0 1 0 0 1 0 0
1 1 1	0 0 0 1 0 0

[a] A 1 indicates a data pulse, a 0 indicates
the absence of a pulse.

Figure 10.12 compares FM and RLL 2,7 encoded data. Note that three RLL data bits can be encoded in the space for one FM data bit. For example, the data pattern 101 is stored as one pulse, two spaces, one pulse, and again two spaces. Notice, however, that the pulse-to-pulse spacing is the same as that of the FM data.

When a hard drive is RLL encoded it can store three times as much data as the equivalent FM drive, and one and one-half times as much data as the equivalent MFM drive.

Example 10.4

A certain hard drive has been formatted to 10 MB using FM encoding. Determine the storage capacity of this drive when formatted using (a) MFM; (b) RLL 2,7.

Solution When formatted using MFM the capacity doubles to 20 MB. The same drive formatted with RLL 2,7 has a capacity of 30 MB.

In theory, any drive can be formatted to the RLL 2,7 specifications. Of course an RLL disk controller will be required to read and write this coding. Because of the long spacing between pulses (as many as seven), the timing for RLL drives is critical. Because of this, you should only use hard drives that have been certified by the manufacturer to be RLL compatible. Low-end drives may simply not be reliable enough for this complex encoding scheme.

Disk Drive Data Rates. The rate at which data can be read and written from a magnetic disk depends on the capabilities of the disk controller electronics, and the ability of the media to store flux transitions. The following example illustrates how the data rate can be calculated, based on the maximum allowable flux density.

Example 10.5

The specifications for a low density $5\frac{1}{4}''$ disk drive indicate a maximum flux density of 5162 flux changes per inch. The radius of the inside track (where maximum flux density occurs) is given to be 1.542 in. Calculate the maximum data rate in bits/s for this drive assuming double-density encoding.

Sec. 10.4   Data Encoding Techniques

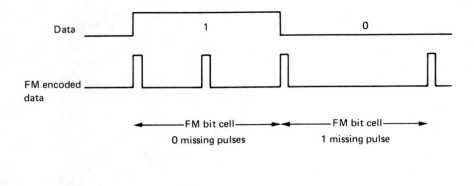

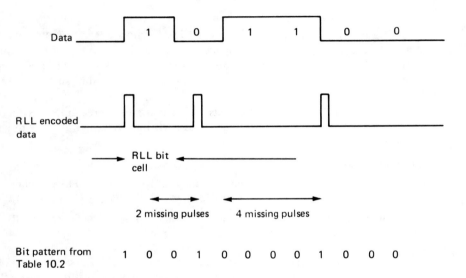

Bit pattern from   1   0   0   1   0   0   0   0   1   0   0   0
Table 10.2

Figure 10.12 Comparing the FM and RLL 2,7 encoding schemes. Three RLL data bits can be stored in the space required by one FM data bit.

Solution. The circumference of the inside track is:

$$C = 2 \times \pi \times 1.542 \text{ in} = 9.69 \text{ in}$$

The total number of flux changes per track is therefore:

$$5162 \text{ flux changes/in} \times 9.69 \text{ in} = 50,012$$

With one flux change per data bit, this represents 50,012 bits of data. Because the drive rotates at 300 RPM, the data rate can be calculated as:

$$\frac{50,012 \text{ bytes}}{\text{track}} \times \frac{300 \text{ tracks}}{\text{min}} \times \frac{1 \text{ min}}{60 \text{ s}} = 250,060 \text{ bits/s}$$

Low density MFM $5\frac{1}{4}''$ drives are usually specified at 250 Kbits/s.

Hard disks can tolerate flux densities twice that of floppy drives. In addition typical drives rotate at 3600 RPM—12 times faster than a low-density floppy drive. Data rates as high as 5 million bits/s (MFM) and 7.5 million bits/s (RLL) are common for these drives.

The effective data rate.   As we have seen, data to be stored on a disk is organized into tracks and sectors. Each sector is identified by its track number, side number, sector number, and several CRC bytes for error detection. These extra bytes add nothing to the data, but must be present for the DOS to locate individual sectors.

The effect of these extra bytes is to *lower* the apparent data rate of the drive to something less than that determined by the maximum allowable flux transitions. The following example illustrates.

Example 10.6

Calculate the effective data rate for a low-density $5\frac{1}{4}''$ floppy disk drive with MFM encoding. Assume 9 sectors/track, 512 bytes/sector, and 300 RPM.

Solution.   The effective data rate can be calculated as:

$$\frac{9 \text{ sectors}}{\text{track}} \times \frac{512 \text{ bytes}}{\text{sector}} \times \frac{8 \text{ bits}}{\text{byte}} \times \frac{300 \text{ tracks}}{\text{min}} \times \frac{1 \text{ min}}{60 \text{ s}}$$

$$= 184{,}320 \text{ bits/s} = 23{,}040 \text{ bytes/s} = 22.5 \text{ KB/s}$$

Table 10.3 provides several performance specifications for the various types of floppy disk drives. Note that in all cases the effective data rate is less than the rate at which the bits are actualy being written. This is due to the extra check bits that must be included with the data.

Several programs are available that measure a drive's effective data rate. If you run one of these programs, you may find the results even lower than those in Table 10.3. One reason is due to the fact that the DOS stores files wherever there is open space on the disk. If a file becomes *fragmented*, that is, stored in nonconsecutive sectors throughout the disk, it will take even longer to read or write that file.

Another factor affecting the effective rate is the *disk interleave*. A drive with an interleave factor of 3 will have to wait for every third sector before reading or

TABLE 10.3 FLOPPY DISK PERFORMANCE SPECIFICATIONS

Drive size Density	$5\frac{1}{4}''$ low	$5\frac{1}{4}''$ high	$3\frac{1}{2}''$ low	$3\frac{1}{2}''$ high
Encoding	MFM	MFM	MFM	MFM
Disk speed (RPM)	300	300	300	300
Data rate (bits/s)	250,000	500,000	250,000	500,000
Data rate (bytes/s)	30.5K[a]	61K	30.5K	61K
Effective data rate[b] (bytes/s)	22.5K	37.5K	22.5K	45K

[a] 1K = 1024 bytes

[b] Based on the number of bytes per sector and sectors per track given in Table 10.1.

writing data. Naturally this will increase the length of time required to read or write a file, and therefore decrease the effective data rate.

Formatted and unformatted disk capacity. Hard drives are often rated in terms of their formatted and unformatted disk capacities. At 5 million bits/s and 3600 RPM (16.67 ms/track), a hard drive can read or write 16.67 ms × 5,000,000 bits/s = 10,416 bytes/track. If this drive has 820 tracks/side and 3 sides, the total unformatted capacity of the drive will be:

$$820 \text{ tracks/side} \times 3 \text{ sides} \times 10,416 \text{ bytes/track} = 24.44 \text{ MB}$$

However, when this same drive is formatted by DOS with seventeen 512 byte sectors/track, the disk capacity becomes:

$$\frac{820 \text{ tracks}}{\text{side}} \times 3 \text{ sides} \times \frac{17 \text{ sectors}}{\text{track}} \times \frac{512 \text{ bytes}}{\text{sector}} = 20.42 \text{ MB}$$

The difference is again due to the extra check bits written by the DOS to help keep track of each individual sector. Don't be fooled by a hard drive's unformatted disk capacity. The same drive, once formatted, will always end up with several million fewer bytes.

10.5 THE DISK DRIVE INTERFACE

As you read this section, look for the answers to these Key Concept questions:

10.5.1. List the three main parts of a floppy disk drive interface.

10.5.2. What is the SA-450 standard disk drive interface?

10.5.3. List the two types of hard drive interfaces.

10.5.4. What is the SCSI bus?

Floppy Drives. Floppy disk drive interfaces consist of three parts:

1. Read, write, and control logic circuits mounted on a card (the *logic board*) on the disk drive.

2. Data and power cables.

3. Disk drive controller interface board.

The disk drive logic board is a combination of digital and analog circuits. It converts the serial data from the computer into current pulses which are applied to the read/write head. In the playback mode the flux transitions are detected and converted into voltage pulses.

It is the job of the floppy disk controller (FDC) to encode and decode these pulses (all floppy drives uses MFM encoding). As you might imagine, special floppy disk formatter/controller LSI chips are available for this purpose. The typical chip used with the IBM-PC family of computers is the NEC765. It will accept 15 different commands such as *format a track*, *read a track*, *write data*, *restore to track 0*, etc. These high-level commands make the FDC software much easier to write as the "nitty gritty" details are handled by the controller chip.

All four types of floppy drives described in this chapter—high- and low-density $5\frac{1}{4}''$ and $3\frac{1}{2}''$ drives—use the same electrical interface known as the *SA-450*. This interface was invented by Shugart Associates in the 1970s. It uses a 34-pin data cable between the disk drive and disk controller and a 4-pin power cable (+12 V, +5 V, and 2 ground pins).

Perhaps the most important feature of the SA-450 interface is that any manufacturer's compatible drive can be plugged into any other manufacturer's compatible disk controller card. Be careful with high-density drives, however. Because they read and write data at a 500-kHz rate (low-density drives operate at 250 kHz), low-density drives will be incompatible with high-density FDCs.

Hard Drives.   There are two popular hard disk drive interface specifications. These are: *ST-506/412* and *ESDI*.

ST-506/412.   This interface was designed by Seagate Technologies in the early 1980s. Like the SA-450 standard floppy interface, it defines a set of signals to be exchanged between the logic board of a hard drive and the hard drive controller. Three cables are required—data, control, and power. When so equipped, any ST-506 drive and controller can be connected together without fear of compatibility problems.

When installing a hard drive, it is necessary to "tell the DOS" the type of drive you have (i.e., number of heads and sectors per track). This is usually done via a *setup* program with the parameters stored in battery-backed CMOS RAM. In this way each time the computer is booted, it can read the parameter table and know the type of hard drive installed. Drives of this type are usually formatted with 17 sectors/track (MFM) or 25–26 sectors/track (RLL).

The ST-506/412 interface performs the encoding and decoding process on the disk controller card. The flux transition signals are then sent—via a 12–18″ data cable—to the drive. Unfortunately, as disk drive data rates increase and timing therefore becomes more critical (especially with RLL controllers), the ST-506/412 interface becomes limited. Most manufacturers of large capacity drives (70 MB or more) are switching to the ESDI standard interface.

ESDI.   This standard was established by Maxtor Corporation in 1983. It stands for *Enhanced Small Device Interface*. Unlike ST-506/412 drives, ESDI drives perform the encoding and decoding of the data at the drive itself. A disk controller card and data cable are still required, but the cable no longer carries the flux transition data.

The effect of this is to allow the drive to operate at much higher data rates. Typical ESDI drives can support a 1-to-1 interleave factor and are usually formatted with 34–36 512-byte sectors/track using RLL encoding. This means the effective data rate is at least twice that of an ST-506/412 MFM drive which is limited to 17 sectors/track.

Another feature of the ESDI interface is a built-in high-level command processor,

The disk controller can automatically interrogate the drive and determine such things as drive type and defect list. This simplifies the low-level formatting process.

SCSI. SCSI ("scuzzy") is the acronym for *small computer system interface.* Unlike ST-506/412 and ESDI, SCSI is not specifically a hard drive interface. Instead, it defines a bus standard to which all types of I/O devices—floppy and hard drives, scanners, mice, plotters, etc.—can be interfaced.

In a typical implementation, a SCSI host adapter is installed in the computer, which can then control seven other SCSI adapter cards, each connected to some type of I/O device. If you want to install a SCSI hard drive, you first install the SCSI host adapter card. This card is then connected—via cables—to a hard drive which has an embedded SCSI controller. Note that this drive may actually be an ST-506/412 or ESDI drive, but with its drive electronics modified to include the SCSI controller.

The purpose of the SCSI standard is to create a uniform I/O bus to which any SCSI-compatible peripheral may be interfaced—independent of the type of device or computer. In this way, a "slotless" computer (one that cannot be internally expanded) with an SCSI host adapter and connector on the back can be interfaced to many different I/O devices.

At present, the SCSI standard is not truly standard, with each manufacturer implementing it with their own special "flavor." This is expected to change as the concept becomes more popular.

CHAPTER SUMMARY

1. Floppy and hard disk drives are the most common types of secondary storage devices used in a computer system.
2. Floppy disk drives are a removable $5\frac{1}{4}''$ or $3\frac{1}{2}''$ flexible diskette. Both high- and low-density versions are available.
3. Hard drives use a rigid nonremovable platter mounted in a sealed chamber.
4. Data is stored on a magnetic disk as a series of flux transitions located in concentric tracks.
5. Floppy drives spin at 300 RPM while hard drives operate at speeds as high as 3600 RPM.
6. Floppy drives have only a single double-sided read/write head. Hard drives have several disks with a separate read/write head for each.
7. Each data track is divided into 512 byte sectors. The number of sectors/track varies from 9 for low density floppy drives to 34–36 for RLL-encoded ESDI hard drives.
8. All tracks under the read/write heads at a given time are referred to as a cylinder.
9. Before a disk can be used, it must be formatted so that each individual track and sector is identified.

10. Two different schemes are in popular use for encoding the data to be stored on a magnetic disk. These are modified FM (MFM) and run length limited (RLL).

11. RLL encoding achieves a 50% higher storage capacity and data rate than MFM.

12. Disk drives are connected to a computer through an industry standard interface. Floppy drives use the SA-450 interface, while hard drives use the ST-506/412 or ESDI interface.

QUESTIONS AND PROBLEMS

Section 10.1

10.1. In what ways are floppy disk drives and hard drives similar? In what ways are they different?

10.2. What is meant by the term flux transition? How is a flux transition written to the disk?

Section 10.2

10.3. Compare the time required for one revolution of a disk at
  (a) 300 RPM and
  (b) 3600 RPM

*10.4. You are troubleshooting a floppy disk drive and note that the disk does not spin when accessed. Which drive motor would you suspect as the problem?

10.5. Low density 5¼″ floppy drives have 40 tracks/side and 48 tracks/inch.
  (a) If the inside track has a radius of 1.542 in., calculate the radius of the *outside* track.
  (b) Using this result calculate the amount of area on the 5¼″ disk used for storing data.
  (c) Compare this to the total area of the disk.

*10.6. You are troubleshooting a computer equipped with a hard drive and note the following problem. Each morning when first turned on, the DOS reports a BOOT FAILURE and the machine will not boot up. However, after the computer has been on for 30 minutes, it boots normally. What do you think is the cause of this problem? The drive uses a stepper-motor head positioner.

Section 10.3

10.7. A certain hard drive has 4 heads and 612 cylinders. How many tracks per disk side does this drive have?

10.8. If the hard drive in Prob. 10.7 is formatted using MFM to have 17 sectors/track, how many total sectors does this drive have?

10.9. An RLL hard drive has 5 heads, 1022 cylinders, and thirty-four 512-byte sectors/track.

(a) Calculate the number of bytes stored per cylinder.

(b) Calculate the total capacity of the drive.

10.10. A high-density $3\frac{1}{2}''$ floppy disk stores 1440K bytes. Express this capacity in bytes and MB.

10.11. The defect map accompanying a hard drive indicates that cylinder 347 head 3 is bad. If the drive is formatted with 17 sectors/track, how many total bytes correspond to this defect?

10.12. Assume you have created a short data file of only 10 bytes. When the directory command is given, DOS reports that the file is actually 1024 bytes long. Explain.

Section 10.4

10.13. Why does a hard drive formatted with 34 sectors/track have a data transfer rate twice that of a drive formatted with only 17 secors/track? Assume both drives operate at the same RPM rate.

10.14. True or false: The maximum flux transition rate for MFM-encoded data is the same as that for FM data.

10.15. A certain hard drive has 4 heads, 612 cylinders, and is formatted with 17 sectors/track. If the disk spins at 3600 RPM, calculate the *effective data rate* for this drive in K bytes/s.

10.16. If the drive in Prob. 10.15 can transfer data at 5,000,000 bits/s, calculate the formatted and unformatted disk capacities.

Section 10.5

10.17. Specify the standard interface—SA-450, ST-506/412, or ESDI—for each of the following applications.

(a) 20 MB hard drive formatted with 17 sectors/track

(b) $3\frac{1}{2}''$ high-density floppy disk drive

(c) 90 MB hard drive formatted with 34 sectors/track

KEY CONCEPT ANSWERS

10.1.1. serial

10.1.2. electromagnet

10.1.3. $3\frac{1}{2}''$ and $5\frac{1}{4}''$

10.1.4. Impurities in the air can easily damage the read/write head and magnetic disk

10.2.1. spindle and head stepper motor

10.2.2. remove any flux transitions that may have been written between the data tracks

10.2.3. floppy: 300 RPM; hard: 3600 RPM

10.2.4. insensitive to temperature, faster, automatic head parking

10.3.1. sectors

10.3.2. tracks

10.3.3. faster access of files and fewer storage units per file

10.3.4. The relative location of each sector within a track. With an interleave of 2, consecutive sectors are located every second sector.

10.4.1. A timing window corresponding to the time allocated to one data bit.

10.4.2. FM: 0,1   MFM: 1, 3   RLL: 2, 7

10.4.3. MFM = 2 × FM data rate, RLL = 1.5 × MFM data rate.

10.4.4. To format the disk each sector requires several overhead bytes to describe the sector number, track number, side number, and CRC.

10.5.1. logic board, data and power cables, FDC card

10.5.2. standard defining the signals exchanged between a floppy disk drive and the FDC.

10.5.3. ST-506/412 and ESDI

10.5.4. a standard I/O bus to which compatible peripherals can be interfaced.

11

Microcomputer Control Applications and Troubleshooting Techniques

In this book we have studied several aspects of microcomputer input/output. These have included:

Serial and parallel data ports

Software control techniques

Special-purpose programmable I/O controllers

But believe it or not, one point has not been discussed! That is, what do we do with all of the I/O pins our interfaces have provided? For example, adding an 8255A PPI chip provides the microcomputer with 24 programmable I/O pins. Presumedly, we can use these to control or monitor the "outside world"—but how, exactly?

Perhaps we are building a microprocessor-controlled vending machine and need to detect a switch closure and then turn on a relay. Can the PPI drive the relay directly, and how do we test for the switch closure? Figure 11.1 illustrates the problem in general terms. The microcomputer "lives and breathes" TTL voltage levels, but the same can hardly be said for most real-world sensors and controllers. Some form of converter is required between the microprocessor and the real world.

This converter can generally be considered to fit into one of two categories:

1. Converters to monitor or control the real-world device's ON/OFF status
2. Converters that change the computer's digital signals to analog signals compatible with the real-world device

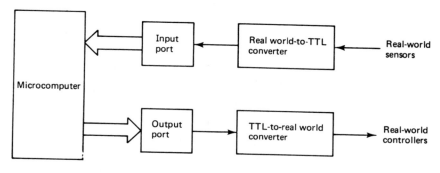

Figure 11.1 Interfacing a microcomputer to the real world.

An example of the first would be a circuit that allowed a microcomputer to turn a 120-V ac light on or off. An example of the second would be a circuit that allows the computer to output 47.9 V (or any other voltage within some range) to the light controlling its brilliance.

In this chapter we study the microprocessor as a *controller* and learn how it can be made compatible with the (non-TTL) real world.

But now imagine that you have designed and built a microcomputer controller, perhaps to monitor and control the functions of a solar heating system. You have interfaced sensors for measuring the inside and outside water temperatures, sensors for monitoring the level of water in the holding tank, and solenoids for controlling the water flow. A complex controller program has been written and stored in an EPROM. Finally, the moment of truth arrives—power is applied to the circuit. What happens? Unless you are very lucky, probably nothing.

But what could be wrong? A hardware problem, or is there a bug in the software? Unfortunately, there are no easy answers. The microprocessor, while providing the designer with an extremely powerful design tool, can also be the source of much anguish and frustration. A simple wiring error such as crossing the A0 and A1 address lines will stop the processor dead in its tracks—and without any obvious clues.

The last section of this chapter deals with microprocessor *troubleshooting techniques*—from a discussion of the logical steps to follow when approaching a "dead" computer, to the tools required, and how to use them.

11.1 DETECTING THE PRESENCE OF AN ANALOG SIGNAL: THE COMPARATOR

As you read this section, look for the answers to these Key Concept questions:

11.1.1. The LM334 produces an output _____ that is directly proportional to _____.

11.1.2. State the input conditions required to cause the output of the LM393 to be (a) an open circuit; (b) a short circuit to ground.

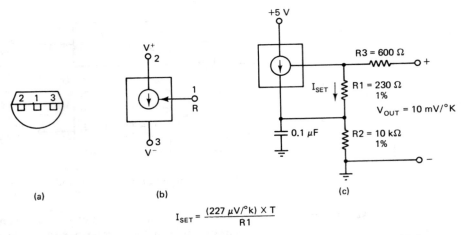

+5 V

V+
2

1
R

3
V−

2 1 3

R3 = 600 Ω

I_{SET} R1 = 230 Ω
               1%

V_{OUT} = 10 mV/°K

0.1 μF   R2 = 10 kΩ
             1%

(a)   (b)   (c)

$$I_{SET} = \frac{(227 \, \mu V/°k) \times T}{R1}$$

Figure 11.2 LM334 three-terminal temperature-dependent current source: (a) the package outline; (b) the schematic symbol; (c) a typical application.

It is not always necessary to know the exact value of an analog input signal. For example, Fig. 11.2 shows the LM334 three terminal current source. It produces an output current that is directly proportional to temperature in degrees Kelvin (the Kelvin temperature scale is 273 degrees higher than the Celsius scale). At 72°F (22°C), $V_{OUT} = (22° + 273°) \times 10$ mV/°K = 2.95 V.

Using the LM334, we could design a computer interface that warns when the temperature is too high or too cold.

Example 11.1

Assume that the LM334 is to be used to indicate a "temperature too high" condition. What output voltage is produced by a temperature of 100°F or higher?

Solution. The conversion is

$$°K = \left[(100° - 32°) \times \frac{5}{9} \right] + 273° = 311°$$

Therefore, a voltage of 3.11 V or more corresponds to 100°F or higher.

Of course now we need a circuit that can be set to detect a voltage of 3.11 V or higher. Such a circuit can be built using an *analog comparator*. A data sheet for the National Semiconductor LM393 dual comparator is shown in Fig. 11.3. Similar to a digital comparator, the LM393 compares the voltages applied to its (+) and (−) inputs and produces the following results: If $V(+) > V(-)$, then V_{OUT} = open circuit, but if $V(+) < V(-)$, then $V_{OUT} = 0$ V. By pulling the output to +5 V through a resistor, TTL compatibility can be achieved.

Example 11.2

Design an interface to a microcomputer input port using the LM334 temperature sensor and the LM393 analog comparator. A logic 1 input should indicate a temperature > 100°F.

LM193/LM293/LM393, LM193A/LM293A/LM393A, LM2903
Low Power Low Offset Voltage Dual Comparators

General Description

The LM193 series consists of two independent precision voltage comparators with an offset voltage specification as low as 2.0 mV max for two comparators which were designed specifically to operate from a single power supply over a wide range of voltages. Operation from split power supplies is also possible and the low power supply current drain is independent of the magnitude of the power supply voltage. These comparators also have a unique characteristic in that the input common-mode voltage range includes ground, even though operated from a single power supply voltage.

Application areas include limit comparators, simple analog to digital converters; pulse, squarewave and time delay generators; wide range VCO; MOS clock timers; multivibrators and high voltage digital logic gates. The LM193 series was designed to directly interface with TTL and CMOS. When operated from both plus and minus power supplies, the LM193 series will directly interface with MOS logic where their low power drain is a distinct advantage over standard comparators.

Advantages

- High precision comparators
- Reduced V_{OS} drift over temperature

- Eliminates need for dual supplies
- Allows sensing near ground
- Compatible with all forms of logic
- Power drain suitable for battery operation

Features

- Wide single supply
  Voltage range   2.0 V_{DC} to 36 V_{DC}
  or dual supplies   ±1.0 V_{DC} to ±18 V_{DC}
- Very low supply current drain (0.8 mA)—independent of supply voltage (1.0 mW/comparator at 5.0 V_{DC})
- Low input biasing current   25 nA
- Low input offset current   ±5 nA
  and maximum offset voltage   ±3 mV
- Input common-mode voltage range includes ground
- Differential input voltage range equal to the power supply voltage
- Low output   250 mV at 4 mA
  saturation voltage
- Output voltage compatible with TTL, DTL, ECL, MOS and CMOS logic systems

Schematic and Connection Diagrams

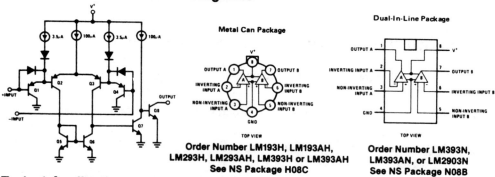

Metal Can Package

TOP VIEW

Order Number LM193H, LM193AH, LM293H, LM293AH, LM393H or LM393AH
See NS Package H08C

Dual-In-Line Package

TOP VIEW

Order Number LM393N, LM393AN, or LM2903N
See NS Package N08B

Typical Applications (V+ = 5.0 V_{DC})

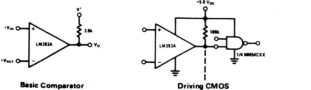

Basic Comparator

Driving CMOS

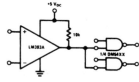

Driving TTL

Figure 11.3   LM393 voltage comparator. (Courtesy of National Semiconductor Corporation.)

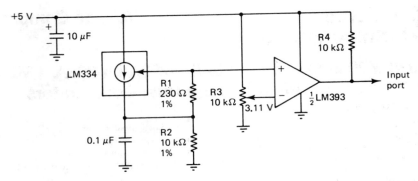

Figure 11.4 This circuit will produce a logic 1 output whenever the LM334 temperature exceeds 100°F. The 10-kΩ potentiometer allows the switching threshold of the comparator to be varied.

Solution. Figure 11.4 shows the circuit. The 10-kΩ potentiometer is adjusted to produce 3.11 V at the (−) input and if the LM334 output should ever exceed this value, the comparator output will become an open circuit and be pulled to a logic 1 by the 10-kΩ resistor R4.

The analog comparator is very useful for detecting a voltage level and converting this information into a TTL-compatible logic 1 or 0. It can be used to monitor a number of real-world sensors such as photocells, strain gauges, thermistors, and other *transducers* (devices that convert a physical phenomenon to an analog voltage). The LM393 is particularly useful, as it will allow up to a 36-V differential between its (+) and (−) inputs.

11.2 ON/OFF CONTROL OF ANALOG PERIPHERALS

As you read this section, look for the answers to these Key Concept questions:

11.2.1. What is the maximum high-level output voltage for the 7406 open collector buffer?

11.2.2. What is the purpose of the clamp diodes in the 75416 series of peripheral drivers?

11.2.3. Why do solid-state relays incorporate opto-couplers?

11.2.4. Commercial solid-state relays may be _____-_____ switching or _____ switching.

Many real-world peripherals require high voltages and currents incompatible with the TTL output capabilities of a typical microcomputer output port. Examples are 5-V 100-mA dc relays, 120-V ac solenoids, 12-V 2-A indicator lamps, and 20- to 30-V dc pulses for EPROM programmers.

TABLE 11.1 BUFFER AND INTERFACE GATES WITH OPEN-COLLECTOR OUTPUTS

DESCRIPTION	HIGH-LEVEL OUTPUT VOLTAGE	LOW-LEVEL OUTPUT CURRENT	TYPICAL DELAY TIME	TYP POWER PER GATE	DEVICE TYPE AND PACKAGE −55°C to 125°C	DEVICE TYPE AND PACKAGE 0°C to 70°C
HEX BUFFERS/DRIVERS	30 V	40 mA	13 ns	21 mW		SN7407 J, N
	30 V	30 mA	13 ns	21 mW	SN5407 J, W	
	15 V	40 mA	13 ns	21 mW		SN7417 J, N
	15 V	30 mA	13 ns	21 mW	SN5417 J, W	
HEX INVERTER BUFFERS/DRIVERS	30 V	40 mA	12.5 ns	26 mW		SN7406 J, N
	30 V	30 mA	12.5 ns	26 mW	SN5406 J, W	
	15 V	40 mA	12.5 ns	26 mW		SN7416 J, N
	15 V	30 mA	12.5 ns	26 mW	SN5416 J, W	
QUADRUPLE 2-INPUT POSITIVE-NAND BUFFERS	15 V	16 mA	13.5 ns	10 mW	SN5426 J	SN7426 J, N
	15 V	8 mA	16 ns	2 mW		SN74LS26 J, N
	15 V	4 mA	16 ns	2 mW	SN54LS26 J, W	
	5.5 V	60 mA	6.5 ns	41 mW	SN54S38 J, W	SN74S38 J, N
	5.5 V	48 mA	12.5 ns	24.4 mW	SN5438 J, W	SN7438 J, N
	5.5 V	24 mA	19 ns	4.3 mW		SN74LS38 J, N
	5.5 V	12 mA	19 ns	4.3 mW	SN54LS38 J, W	
QUADRUPLE 2-INPUT POSITIVE-NOR BUFFERS	5.5 V	48 mA	11 ns	28 mW	SN5433 J, W	SN7433 J, N
	5.5 V	24 mA	19 ns	5.45 mW		SN74LS33 J, N
	5.5 V	12 mA	19 ns	5.45 mW	SN54LS33 J, W	

Source: Courtesy of Texas Instruments, Inc.

DC Control

The open-collector buffer. When the control voltage and current requirements are not too high, standard 7400-family TTL open-collector buffers can be used. We first discussed the open-collector gate in Chap. 4, where its capability to perform the "wired-OR" function was taken advantage of. In this section we are more interested in the buffer's ability to pull the output to levels other than +5 V.

Table 11.1 lists the capabilities of the 7400 family of open-collector buffers. Note that voltages as high as 30 V can be switched. Also remember that in the low state the buffer must be capable of *sinking* current from the controlled device and its pullup resistor. This current can be as high as 60 mA with the 74S38.

Figure 11.5 illustrates several typical control applications for open-collector buffers. Note that in all cases the buffer is required to sink the ON current of the controlled device and withstand the power supply voltage in the OFF state. The clamp diode in the relay driver circuit is needed to protect the buffer's output transistor when the relay is turned off. The sudden reduction to zero of current in the relay coil causes a *back emf* to be developed as the magnetic field in the relay coil collapses [$V_L = L(di/dt)$]. The diode clamps the output pin to +12 V. When larger

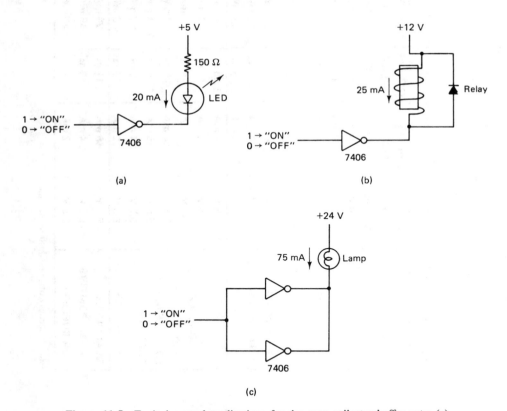

Figure 11.5 Typical control applications for the open-collector buffer gate: (a) LED driver; (b) relay driver; (c) lamp driver.

TABLE 11.2 SN75400 FAMILY OF PERIPHERAL DEVICES

DRIVERS WITH LOGIC GATES

Military Temperature Range (−55 C to 125°C)

SWITCHING VOLTAGE	MAX RECOMMENDED OUTPUT CURRENT	DRIVERS PER PACKAGE	INTERNAL CLAMP DIODES	LOGIC GATE FUNCTION				PACKAGE OPTIONS
				AND	NAND	OR	NOR	
20 V	300 mA	2	—	SN55450B				J
				SN55451B	SN55452B	SN55453B	SN55454B	JG
30 V	300 mA	2	—	SN55460				J
				SN55461	SN55462	SN55463	SN55464	JG
55 V	300 mA	2	—	SN55470				J
				SN55471	SN55472	SN55473	SN55474	JG

Commercial Temperature Range (0°C to 70°C)

SWITCHING VOLTAGE	MAX RECOMMENDED OUTPUT CURRENT	DRIVERS PER PACKAGE	INTERNAL CLAMP DIODES	LOGIC GATE FUNCTION				PACKAGE OPTIONS
				AND	NAND	OR	NOR	
15 V	300 mA	2	—	SN75430				J, N
				SN75431	SN75432	SN75433	SN75434	JG, P
20 V	100 mA	2	—			SN75441		J, N
	300 mA	2	—	SN75450B				J, N
				SN75451B	SN75452B	SN75453B	SN75454B	JG, P
30 V	300 mA	2	—	SN75460				J, N
				SN75461	SN75462	SN75463	SN75464	JG, P
	500 mA	2	—	SN75401	SN75402	SN75403	SN75404	NE
35 V	500 mA	4	YES		SN75437			NE
55 V	300 mA	2	—	SN75470				J, N
				SN75471	SN75472	SN75473	SN75474	JG, P
			YES	SN75476	SN75477	SN75478	SN75479	JG, P
	350 mA	2	YES	SN75446	SN75447	SN75448	SN75449	JG, P
	500 mA	2	—	SN75411	SN75412	SN75413	SN75414	NE
			YES	SN75416	SN75417	SN75418	SN75419	NE

Source: Courtesy of Texas Instruments, Inc.

currents must be switched, buffers may be paralleled as shown in the lamp–driver interface in Fig. 11.5(c).

The 75400 family of peripheral drivers. Table 11.2 lists the current and voltage capabilities of the SN75400 family of peripheral drivers with logic gates and Fig. 11.6 shows the pinouts for the 75416 series. These devices are open-collector buffers but with considerably higher current capabilities than the standard TTL buffers. Even higher current devices are available in the ULN series (not shown in Table 11.2). These buffers use *Darlington* output transistors to achieve output sink currents as high as 1.5 A.

The 75416 series of drivers shown in Fig. 11.6 include all four logic functions and are characterized for applications to 500 mA. Clamp diodes for transient suppression when driving inductive loads (relays) are built into the package. Note that six pins in each package are devoted for use as a heat sink and ground.

Sec. 11.2   On/Off Control of Analog Peripherals

- **Characterized for Use to 500 mA**
- **No Output Latch-Up at 55 V (After Conducting 500 mA)**
- **High-Voltage Outputs (100 V Typical)**
- **High-Speed Switching**
- **Output Clamp Diodes for Transient Suppression (500 mA, 70 V)**
- **TTL- or MOS-Compatible Diode-Clamped Inputs**
- **P-N-P Inputs Reduce Input Current**
- **Standard Supply Voltage**
- **Suitable for Hammer-Driver Applications**
- **Available in the 14-Pin NE Package**
- **2-Watt Power Dissipation Capability**

description

Series 75416 dual peripheral drivers are designed for use in systems that require high output voltage, high current, and fast switching times. The SN75416, SN75417, SN75418, and SN75419 provide AND , NAND, OR, and NOR functions respectively. The devices have diode-clamped inputs as well as high-current, high-voltage inductive clamp diodes on the outputs. Each device has a 2-watt power dissipation capability.

Series 75416 drivers are characterized for operation from 0°C to 70°C.

schematics of inputs and outputs

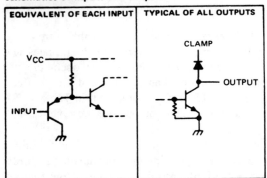

SN75416

FUNCTION TABLE (EACH AND DRIVER)

INPUTS		OUTPUT
A	S	Y
L	L	L
L	H	L
H	L	L
H	H	H

H = high level
L = low level

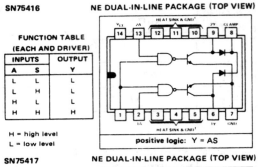

positive logic: Y = AS

SN75417

FUNCTION TABLE (EACH NAND DRIVER)

INPUTS		OUTPUT
A	S	Y
L	L	H
L	H	H
H	L	H
H	H	L

H = high level
L = low level

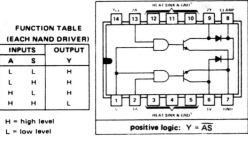

positive logic: Y = $\overline{AS}$

SN75418

FUNCTION TABLE (EACH OR DRIVER)

INPUTS		OUTPUT
A	S	Y
L	L	L
L	H	H
H	L	H
H	H	H

H = high level
L = low level

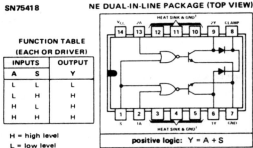

positive logic: Y = A + S

SN75419

FUNCTION TABLE (EACH NOR DRIVER)

INPUTS		OUTPUT
A	S	Y
L	L	H
L	H	L
H	L	L
H	H	L

H = high level
L = low level

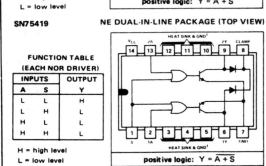

positive logic: Y = $\overline{A + S}$

†Heat-sink pins are internally connected to pin 7.

Figure 11.6 SN75416 series of peripheral drivers. (Courtesy of Texas Instruments.)

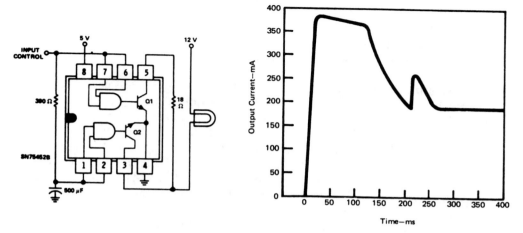

Figure 11.7 (a) Using the SN75452B as a lamp driver; (b) lamp current versus time. The surge current is limited to less than 400 mA. (Courtesy of Texas Instruments.)

Variations on the 75416 series include:

1. Eight-pin packages for lower current devices (SN75476–479)
2. Eight-pin packages for devices without clamp diodes and no common gate pins (SN75451B–454B)

One application for these drivers is to control high-current lamps. Initially, this would seem to be a trivial problem. However, because a lamp's "cold" resistance can be as much as 10 times less than its "hot" resistance, care must be taken to avoid an initial inrush of current that could destroy the driver.

Figure 11.7(a) illustrates an application for the SN75452B as a lamp driver with warm-up circuit. A graph of current versus time is shown in Fig. 11.7(b). Note that both gates in the 75452B are used in this design. When the input control is first applied, only Q1 is ON, as the 500-μF capacitor holds the AND gate inputs low and Q2 OFF. The surge of current is limited by the 18-Ω resistor. Now as the capacitor charges, Q2 turns ON and the load current is shifted to Q2. During this time the lamp filament is heating up and its resistance increasing. The effect is to limit the initial surge to a safe value protecting the lamp and driver.

AC Control

Electromechanical relays. The electromechanical relay (EMR) has been the workhorse of the control industry for many years. By providing sets of switched contacts, both ac and dc devices can be controlled. Several circuits can be switched simultaneously by providing parallel sets of contacts. The contacts are usually described as *normally open* (N.O.) or *normally closed* (N.C.).

Depending on the control current, relays can be driven directly by a TTL gate [see Fig. 11.5(b)] or with a special peripheral driver (see Fig. 11.6). Some low current relays are even available in DIP packages and can be plugged into standard IC sockets.

Disadvantages of the EMR include finite lifetime, corrosion of the contacts, arcing, contact bounce, and slow operation.

Hybrid solid-state relays.   The solid-state relay (SSR) was developed to solve the problems associated with the EMR. Two types of SSR are popular: *isolated* and *nonisolated*. Figure 11.8 shows an example of a nonisolated SSR. A peripheral driver is used to control the current flow through a diode bridge. When ON, current passes through the bridge and develops a voltage across the 0.1-μF capacitor. When this voltage reaches a trigger threshold, the 2N4992 AST (asymmetrical trigger) "fires" the TRIAC, causing a nearly short circuit to appear between its MT1 and MT2 terminals. Because the TRIAC will conduct in both directions, MT1 and MT2 resemble the normally open contacts on a conventional EMR.

The advantages to this relay include no moving parts, no contact bounce, fast operation (usually < 1 μs to activate), TTL level compatibility and logic gate control.

Once fired the TRIAC will remain ON until its load current falls below a small "holding" value. This means that when the control signal is removed, the ac load will not be turned OFF until the next zero crossing of the line voltage. This is ideal for ac control applications because it eliminates transients that would be produced by an abrupt turnoff. It also eliminates the arcing problem that is associated with EMRs. Of course, this same feature makes the SSR totally unsatisfactory for controlling dc devices (why?).

There are two main disadvantages to this circuit. The first is a problem that plagues all solid-state devices. High-voltage transients can destroy the TRIAC. This circuit is especially susceptible because it is connected directly to the main lines, where these transients are initiated. The second problem is the lack of isolation between the control circuit (the peripheral driver) and the 120-V ac mains. If a component should fail, say one of the diodes, it might become a short circuit passing

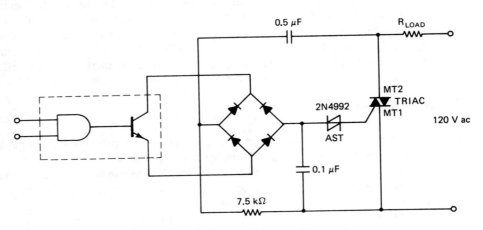

Figure 11.8 Nonisolated hybrid solid-state relay.

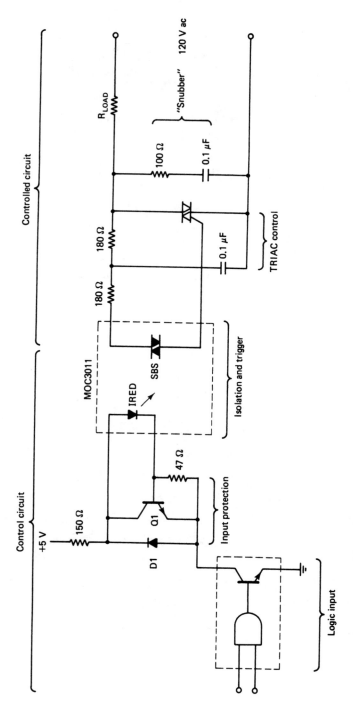

Figure 11.9 Isolated hybrid solid-state relay. The control and controlled circuits are separated by the infrared light path.

557

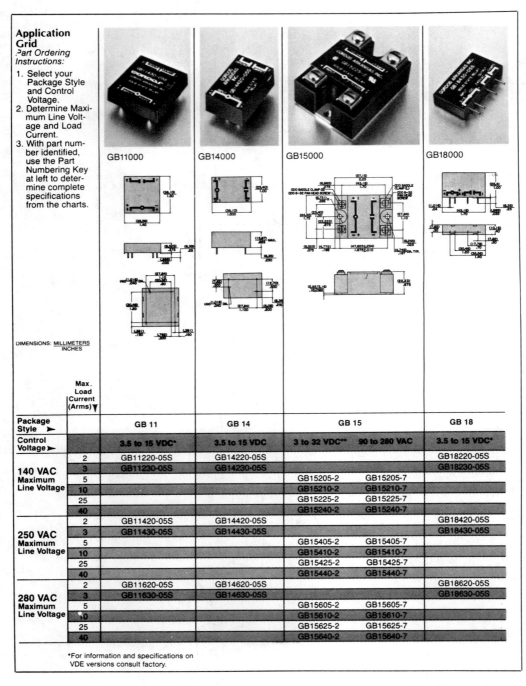

Application
Grid
*Part Ordering
Instructions:*
1. Select your
   Package Style
   and Control
   Voltage.
2. Determine Maxi-
   mum Line Volt-
   age and Load
   Current.
3. With part num-
   ber identified,
   use the Part
   Numbering Key
   at left to deter-
   mine complete
   specifications
   from the charts.

DIMENSIONS: MILLIMETERS
INCHES

GB11000   GB14000   GB15000   GB18000

Package Style ▶	Max. Load Current (Arms) ▼	GB 11	GB 14	GB 15		GB 18
Control Voltage ▶		3.5 to 15 VDC*	3.5 to 15 VDC	3 to 32 VDC**	90 to 280 VAC	3.5 to 15 VDC*
140 VAC Maximum Line Voltage	2	GB11220-05S	GB14220-05S			GB18220-05S
	3	GB11230-05S	GB14230-05S			GB18230-05S
	5			GB15205-2	GB15205-7	
	10			GB15210-2	GB15210-7	
	25			GB15225-2	GB15225-7	
	40			GB15240-2	GB15240-7	
250 VAC Maximum Line Voltage	2	GB11420-05S	GB14420-05S			GB18420-05S
	3	GB11430-05S	GB14430-05S			GB18430-05S
	5			GB15405-2	GB15405-7	
	10			GB15410-2	GB15410-7	
	25			GB15425-2	GB15425-7	
	40			GB15440-2	GB15440-7	
280 VAC Maximum Line Voltage	2	GB11620-05S	GB14620-05S			GB18620-05S
	3	GB11630-05S	GB14630-05S			GB18630-05S
	5			GB15605-2	GB15605-7	
	10			GB15610-2	GB15610-7	
	25			GB15625-2	GB15625-7	
	40			GB15640-2	GB15640-7	

*For information and specifications on
VDE versions consult factory.

Figure 11.10 Typical package outlines and specifications for commercial solid-state relays.
(Courtesy of Gordos Arkansas, Inc.)

120 V ac to the peripheral driver. Obviously not intended for 120 V ac, the peripheral driver could be destroyed and pass the ac on to the output port of the computer and on to the data bus and memory, and so on.

Figure 11.9 shows an improved SSR that includes a "snubber circuit" for suppressing transients on the line and uses an *opto-coupler* to isolate the control circuit from the controlled circuit. The digital input is also protected against excessive currents and reverse voltages by D1 and Q1.

The peripheral driver allows logic gate control of the relay and is used to sink the ON current of the IRED (infrared-emitting diode). The Motorola MOC3011 is an optically triggered silicon bilateral switch (SBS). This device provides 7500 V minimum isolation between the SBS and IRED. The only path between control circuit and controlled circuit is through the light emitted by the IRED.

The SBS is used like the AST to trigger the TRIAC into conduction. For low current and voltages less than 250 V, the SBS can be used by itself to control the ac load. The *RC* "snubber" suppresses high-frequency transients that can damage the TRIAC or trigger it into conduction.

Commercial solid-state relays. Rather than having to build your own SSR, several types are available with all components encapsulated in one package. These devices usually have four terminals: two for the output contacts and two for the control circuit. Figure 11.10 shows the Gordos Arkansas GB series of zero-voltage turn-on SSRs. The GB1500 devices are rated to switch currents as high as 40 A.

Generally, two types of commercial SSRs can be purchased. These are called *zero-cross switching* or *random switching*. Zero-cross switching relays do not switch on until the first zero crossing of the line voltage after the control signal is applied. Random-switching relays switch on immediately after receipt of the control signal.

The zero-crossing technique is desirable when driving incandescent lamps due to the inrush of current when power is first applied. If this current is not limited, it can easily burn out the switching device in the SSR. On the other hand, zero-crossing relays are reputed to be the worst case for switching inductive loads (motors, for example). This is due to large transient currents set up when the motor is first turned on. Application Note SSR 110 prepared by Gordos Arkansas, Inc. explains this problem in detail and shows that optimum switching for an inductive load should occur at the 90° point of the input sinusoid.

11.3 INTERFACING A DIGITAL-TO-ANALOG CONVERTER

As you read this section, look for the answers to these Key Concept questions:

11.3.1. What determines the step size for a digital-to-analog converter (DAC)?

11.3.2. Because only two different resistor values are required, the _____ _____ is the most popular form of DAC.

11.3.3. Explain how a microcomputer interfaced to a DAC can be used to synthesize an analog waveform.

Sec. 11.3   Interfacing a Digital-to-Analog Converter

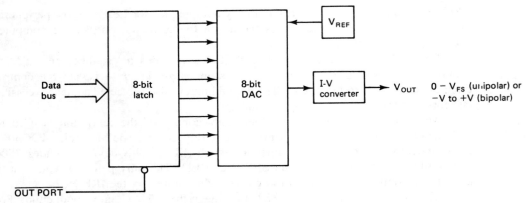

Figure 11.11   Digital-to-analog converter system.

The peripheral drivers and open-collector buffers discussed in Sec. 11.2 allow a microcomputer to provide ON/OFF control of a peripheral. But what if the application requires the microcomputer to output a sine wave or a complex waveform such as speech or music? In this case some means of converting digital bits and bytes to a continuous analog signal must be found.

The Digital-to-Analog Conversion process.   Figure 11.11 illustrates the major components required in a digital-to-analog converter system. The latch stores the digital word output by the computer and presents it to the *digital-to-analog converter* (DAC). This circuit, using a stable reference voltage or current, converts the binary data to an analog current. Finally, a current-to-voltage converter changes this current to a unipolar or bipolar voltage.

Of course, to truly be an analog signal, the output voltage must be capable of assuming any value between 0 V and some full-scale value. If the DAC in Fig. 11.11 has 10 V full scale and receives 8-bit input words, 256 values can be output by the DAC between 0 and 10 V. Figure 11.12 shows the result (not drawn to scale) of programming the DAC to generate a sine wave.

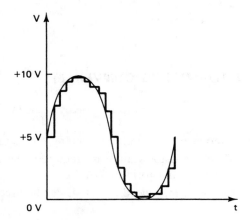

Figure 11.12   Using a DAC to generate a sine wave. The finite step size and conversion time cause a staircase-shaped output waveform.

Studying Fig. 11.12, we can list two properties of an "ideal" DAC:

1. Infinitely small step size
2. Instantaneous conversion time

Example 11.3

Calculate the step size of the 8-bit DAC shown in Fig. 11.11 assuming that full-scale output is 10.0 V. Calculate the output voltage when the binary input is 3CH.

Solution. The step size is found by dividing the full-scale output voltage by the number of steps.

$$\text{step size} = V_{FS}/2^n = 10 \text{ V}/256 = 0.0390625 \text{ V}$$

When the input is 3CH (60_{10}), 60 steps are indicated and V_{out} must be 60×0.0390625 V = 2.34375 V. Another way to express this is 60/256 of full scale or 60/256 × 10 V = 2.34375 V.

How many bits do you think are required for the "ideal" DAC? I think it should be obvious that the more bits a DAC inputs, the smaller its step size. As the step size shrinks to zero, the number of input bits must increase to infinite. Unfortunately, a DAC with an infinite number of input bits would require a package with an infinite number of pins!

Example 11.4

What is the maximum output voltage of the 8-bit DAC in Fig. 11.11 if V_{FS} = 10.0 V?

Solution. Strangely enough, it is *not* 10 V! Consider why. When the most significant bit is turned on, 5.0 V is output ($V_{FS}/2$), the next bit adds half of this or 2.5 V ($V_{FS}/4$), the next bit 1.25 V ($V_{FS}/8$), the next bit 0.625 V ($V_{FS}/16$), and so on. Each bit adds half of the preceding bit's contribution. An infinite number of bits will be required to reach full scale. So what will the maximum output be? The maximum input is FFH and this produces an output of 255/256 × 10 V = 9.960375 V. The general rule is that the maximum output will always be one step less than full scale.

The step size of a DAC is referred to as its *resolution*. An 8-bit DAC with 10 V full scale has a resolution of 39.1 mV. Adding 4 bits, a 12-bit DAC has 2.4-mV resolution. The accuracy of a DAC is usually expressed as a percentage. Most DACs are specified as accurate to $\pm\frac{1}{2}$ LSB (least significant bit). For an 8-bit DAC this means 1 part in 512 or ±0.19%. The 12-bit DAC is accurate to 1 part in 8192 and has an accuracy of ±0.012%.

The other property of an "ideal" DAC is the conversion time. This depends on the conversion technique. Most DACs use a form of the *R-2R ladder* shown in the switched voltage DAC in Fig. 11.13(a). The binary inputs control switches D0–D2 connected to a voltage reference. Figure 11.13(b) and (c) shows the circuit analysis steps in realizing the contribution due to bit D0 (the only switch assumed closed). At each node in the ladder (A, B, or C) the current splits exactly in half, "seeing" a resistance of 2R to ground in either direction [see Fig. 11.13(c)].

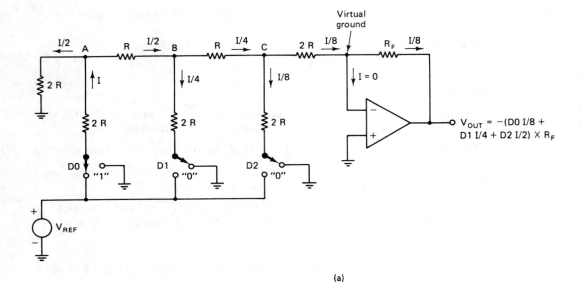

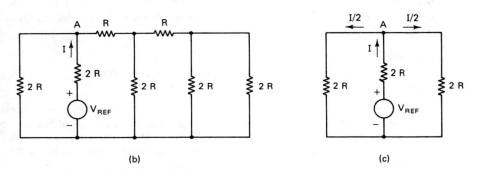

Figure 11.13 (a) Switched voltage R-2R DAC; (b) equivalent circuit at node A when switch D0 (only) is closed; (c) at each node the current splits exactly in half.

The operational amplifier (op-amp) is used to sum the current contributions of each bit. Because the current splits at each node, the contribution due to D0 is reduced to $I/2$ at node A, $I/4$ at node B, and $I/8$ at node C. This current is then forced through the feedback resistor to develop V_{OUT}. Making R_F adjustable allows V_{FS} to be set to any desired value within the saturation limits of the op-amp. Applying superposition, the output voltage will be

$$V_{OUT} = -\left[\left(D0 \times \frac{I}{8}\right) + \left(D1 \times \frac{I}{4}\right) + \left(D2 \times \frac{I}{2}\right)\right] \times R_F$$

Although other techniques for digital-to-analog conversion have been developed (see Prob. 11.12), the R-2R ladder is used in the majority of DACs today. Because only two different resistor values are required, it lends itself well to integrated techniques.

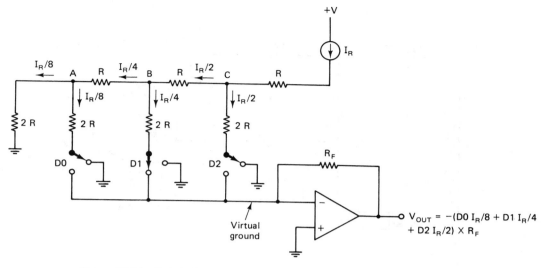

Figure 11.14 Switched-current DAC. The current in each leg is constant independent of the digital input.

Figure 11.14 shows a switched-current DAC similar to that found in the Motorola MC1408 8-bit DAC. A reference current is injected into the ladder splitting by exactly one-half at each node. Because the switch connects each leg of the ladder to virtual ground (through the op-amp) or actual ground, the current in each leg of the ladder is constant independent of the digital input. This increases the speed of conversion because the junction capacitances of the resistors need not be continually charged and discharged.

The effect of conversion time can be seen in Fig. 11.12 by the flat part of the step in the output waveform. If the sinusoid changes too fast, the DAC output will have to change by more than one step to keep up causing a very "herky jerky" output. Eventually, the resemblance to a sine wave will be lost entirely. Because the output voltage "settles" to a particular value, the conversion time is usually called the *settling time* on most DAC data sheets. Values typically range from 100 ns to more than 1.5 µs.

Interfacing the MC1408 DAC. The MC1408 is an 8-bit DAC, popular because of its simplicity and low cost. Motorola manufactures three accuracy versions, labeled the 1408L8, 1408L7, and 1408L6. These parts have 8-, 7-, and 6-bit accuracies, respectively. A microcomputer interface using one output port of the 8255A PPI is shown in Fig. 11.15.

Comparing Fig. 11.15 with Fig. 11.11, an LM336 precision zener diode is used to establish a 2-mA reference current. The output of the DAC is a current which is converted to a voltage by the op-amp. The output voltage is given by

$$V_{OUT} = 2 \text{ mA} \times \frac{\text{binary input}}{256} \times 5 \text{ k}\Omega$$

Sec. 11.3   Interfacing a Digital-to-Analog Converter

563

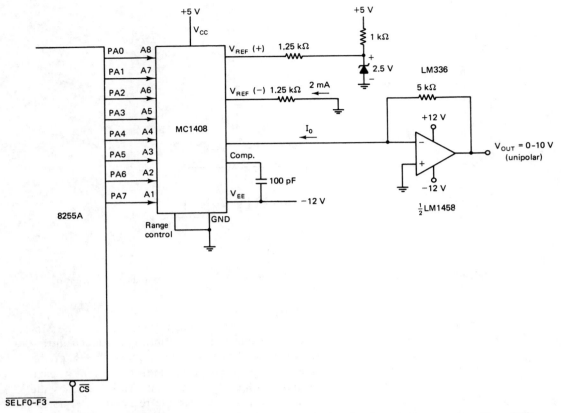

Figure 11.15 The MC1408 8-bit DAC can be interfaced to a microcomputer with an 8-bit output port. In this example one port of the 8255A PPI is used.

Because the full-scale output current is 2 mA, the full-scale output voltage is 10 V. The MC1408 has a 300-ns typical settling time.

Example 11.5

Write an 8080/85 program to synthesize the 1-kHz sine wave shown in Fig. 11.16. Use 12 samples per period.

Solution. The DAC must produce a new output voltage every 1 ms/12 = 83.3 μs. The value of the voltage to output can be found from

$$V_{OUT} = 5 \text{ V} + 3 \text{ V} \sin \theta \qquad \text{where } \theta = 0°, 30°, 60°, \text{ etc.}$$

These values are shown in the table in Fig. 11.16.

Figure 11.17 is the 8080/85 program. It begins by programming port A of the 8255A as a simple output port. Register B is used to count the bytes to be output per cycle. The HL pair is used as a pointer into the sine-wave data table. After each value is output, it is held for 83 μs (27 μs in the program loop and 56 μs in the HOLD subroutine).

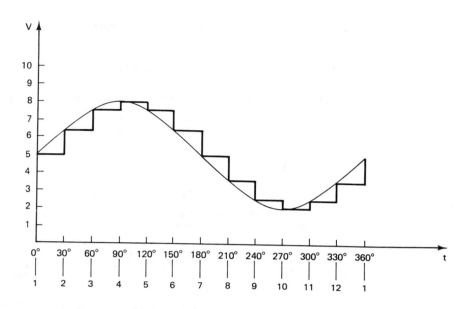

θ (deg)	$\sin \theta$	V_{OUT}	Hex code
0	0	5 V	80
30	0.5	6.5 V	A6
60	0.866	7.6 V	C3
90	1.0	8 V	CD
120	0.866	7.6 V	C3
150	0.5	6.5 V	A6
180	0	5 V	80
210	−0.5	3.5 V	5A
240	−0.866	2.4 V	3D
270	−1.0	2 V	33
300	−0.866	2.4 V	3D
330	−0.5	3.5 V	5A

Figure 11.16 1-kHz sine wave to be synthesized in Ex. 11.5. Twelve samples are output per cycle distributed every 30°.

The sine wave produced by the program in Ex. 11.5 will be rather crude due to the few samples per cycle. By increasing the number of samples, the output can be made to resemble more closely the desired sine wave. Of course, the time delay in the loop will ultimately limit the number of samples per cycle.

A number of interesting applications are suggested by the program in Fig. 11.17. For example, a complex waveform displayed on an oscilloscope could be photographed and then duplicated by storing the proper values in a table. Outputting these codes to the DAC should reproduce the original waveshape. In this way patterns of speech could be synthesized.

```
;8080/85 1KHZ SINE WAVE SYNTHESIZER PROGRAM
;
;THIS PROGRAM USES THE MC1408 DAC INTERFACE SHOWN
;IN FIG. 11-15.  THE OUTPUT IS A 6V P-P SINE WAVE
;CENTERED ON 5V DC.  THE DAC PRODUCES A NEW OUTPUT
;VOLTAGE EVERY 30 DEGREES.
;
;PORT A OF THE 8255 MUST FIRST BE PROGRAMMED AS AN OUPUT
;
        MVI     A,80H           ;MODE 0 CONTROL WORD
        OUT     0F3H            ;8255 CONTROL PORT
;
;12 VALUES WILL BE OUTPUT PER CYCLE STORED IN A TABLE
;CALLED SINE
;
NEW     MVI     B,0CH           ;COUNTER
        LXI     H,SINE-1        ;POINT AT TABLE LESS 1
;
;FETCH DATA FROM TABLE AND OUTPUT TO DAC.  8085 T STATES
;ARE SHOWN IN THE RIGHT MARGIN.
;
LOOP    INX     H               ;ADVANCE POINTER        [6]
        MOV     A,M             ;FETCH BYTE             [7]
        OUT     0F0H            ;OUTPUT TO DAC          [10]
        CALL    HOLD            ;1 KHZ TIME DELAY       [18]
        DCR     B               ;BUMP COUNTER           [4]
        JNZ     LOOP            ;DO ALL 12 VALUES       [7/10]
        JMP     NEW             ;THEN BEGIN A NEW CYCLE [10]
;
;TOTAL T STATES FOR ONE LOOP IS 55 OR 27.5 MICROSECONDS
;WITH A 2 MHZ CLOCK.  THE HOLD SUBROUTINE THUS REQUIRES
;83.3 MICROSECONDS (1000 MICROSECONDS / 12 SAMPLES) -
;27.5 MICROSECONDS = 55.8 MICROSECONDS OR 112 T STATES.
;
HOLD    MVI     C,7             ;STANDARD DELAY ROUTINE [7]
WAIT    DCR     C               ;                       [4]
        JNZ     WAIT            ;                       [7/10]
        RET                     ;                       [10]
;
;DATA VALUES FOR THE DAC - SEE FIG. 11-16.
;
SINE    DB      80H,0A6H,0C3H
        DB      0CDH,0C3H,0A6H
        DB      80H,5AH,3DH
        DB      33H,3DH,5AH
        END
```

Figure 11.17 8080/85 program to control the DAC in Fig. 11.15 and synthesize a 1-kHz 6-V p-p sine wave.

A touch-tone dialer could similarly be implemented by storing values for each numeral in a code table. This is particularly interesting because the tones used are actually two different frequencies summed together. Rather than doing this summing with an analog circuit, the computer can add values from two different tables synthesizing the waveshape directly.

Interfacing the DAC1200.   When the resolution of an 8-bit DAC is insufficient, a 10- or 12-bit DAC can be selected. An example of such a DAC is the National Semiconductor DAC 1200 shown in Fig. 11.18. This device is unique because in addition to providing 12 bits of resolution, it also contains an internal reference and current-to-voltage converter. The only external support required is a latch for the data bits.

National Semiconductor

DAC1200, DAC1201 12-Bit Digital-to-Analog Converters

General Description

The DAC1200 series of D/A converters is a family of precision low-cost converter building blocks intended to fulfill a wide range of industrial and military D/A applications. These devices are complete functional blocks requiring only application of power for operation. The design combines a precision 12-bit weighted current source (12 current switches and 12-bit thin-film resistor network), a rapid-settling operational amplifier, and 10.24V buffered reference.

Input coding is complementary binary. In all instances, a logic "low" ($\leq 0.8V$) turns a given bit ON, and a logic "high" ($\geq 2.0V$) turns the bit OFF. Output format may be programmed for bipolar ($\pm 10V$) or unipolar (0 to 10V) operation using internally supplied thin-film resistor pin strap options. Current mode operation is also available from 0 to 2 mA.

The entire series is available in hermetically sealed 24-lead DIP.

Features

- Circuit completely self-contained
- Both current and voltage-mode outputs
- Standard power supplies: $\pm 15V$ and $+5V$
- Internal buffered reference: 10.24V
- 0 to 2 mA, $\pm 10V$ or 0 to 10V output by strapping internal resistors; other scales by external resistors
- $\pm 1/2$ LSB linearity
- Fast settling time: 1.5 μs in current mode
  2.5 μs in voltage mode
- High slew rate: 15 V/μs
- TTL and CMOS compatible complementary binary input logic
- 12 bit linearity
- Standard 0.6'' 24-pin DIP package

Block and Connection Diagrams

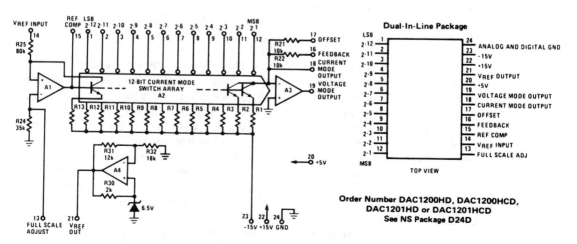

Figure 11.18 Description and block diagram of the National Semiconductor DAC1200. (Courtesy of National Semiconductor Corporation.)

Sec. 11.3   Interfacing a Digital-to-Analog Converter

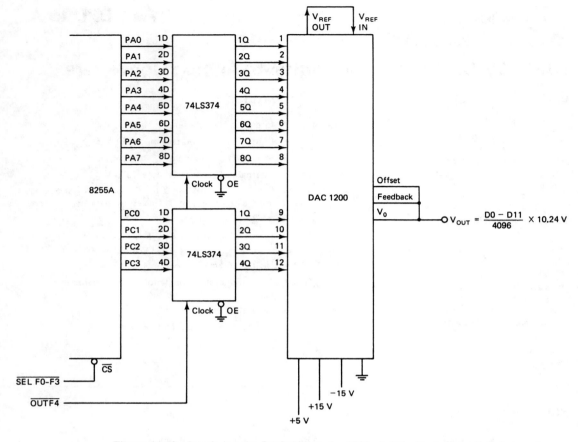

$$V_{OUT} = \frac{D0 - D11}{4096} \times 10.24 \text{ V}$$

Figure 11.19 Interfacing the DAC1200 to the 8255. A "double-buffering" technique is required to prevent "glitches" (momentary voltage spikes) in the DAC output.

Of course, we do have one problem. How do you interface a 12-bit DAC to an 8-bit microprocessor? Answer—very carefully! Actually, the problem is not as difficult as it might seem. Figure 11.19 shows a method using port A and the lower portion of port C of an 8255A PPI. The control program outputs the low 8 bits of the 12-bit data to port A and the high 4 bits to port C (lower). A second buffer is required between the PPI and the DAC to prevent a "glitch" from being generated as the DAC first receives the low 8 bits and then the high 4 bits.

An OUT F4 command loads the two 74LS374s with the PPI data and transfers it as one 12-bit word to the DAC. The price we pay for the *double buffering* is the additional time required to fetch the extra 4 bits, output them to port C, and then clock the 74LS374 buffers.

Using ±15-V power supplies, the full-scale output voltage is 10.24 V (set by the internal reference). Note that the feedback resistors for controlling V_{FS} are provided internally at pins 16 and 17 and need only be connected to the V_{OUT} pin.

The step size can be found as $V_{FS}/2^n = 10.24$ V/4096 = 2.5 mV. The settling time using the internal current-to-voltage converter is 2.5 μs.

Example 11.6

Write an 8080/85 subroutine to transfer the 12 bits of data stored in two sequential memory locations to the DAC interface in Fig. 11.19. Assume that the address of the first byte is passed in the HL pair.

Solution. The program is as follows:

```
MOV   A,M          ;GET LOW BYTE
OUT   0F0H         ;OUTPUT TO PORT A
INX   H            ;POINT TO HIGH 4 BITS
MOV   A,M          ;MOVE TO A
OUT   0F2H         ;OUTPUT TO PORT C
OUT   0F4H         ;LOAD LATCHES AND TRANSFER TO DAC
RET
```

The interface in Fig. 11.19 is truly remarkable. It provides microcomputer control of an output voltage from 0 V to 10.24 V with 4096 steps of 2.5 mV each! No external components are required except ±15-V power sources.

11.4 INTERFACING AN ANALOG-TO-DIGITAL CONVERTER

As you read this section, look for the answers to these Key Concept questions:

11.4.1. List the three types of common analog-to-digital converters (ADCs).

11.4.2. Feedback converters can be controlled by a _____ or _____ _____ technique.

11.4.3. Which type of analog-to-digital converter is often used in digital voltmeters?

11.4.4. The ADC0809 is an _____-bit ADC with _____ separate analog inputs.

The analog comparator is useful to detect when some analog threshold level has been exceeded. However, in many cases it is desirable to know the exact voltage, or the exact temperature, or the exact pressure felt by a transducer. Consider an interface designed to measure room temperature every 5 minutes for 24 hours. This would require 288 data samples. Using conventional analog techniques, all of this data could be recorded by hand or a chart recorder could be used. In either case, analysis of the data will require going back through selected data points.

Now assume that an interval timer is programmed to interrupt a microprocessor once every 5 minutes and request that an analog-to-digital converter sample its temperature sensor. The data point read can be stored in memory or on magnetic disk. The data can then be analyzed by writing an appropriate program. In fact, the data can even be analyzed as it is input, if desired.

In this section we look at three common techniques for analog-to-digital conversion and show how to interface an eight-channel converter to the three-bus system architecture.

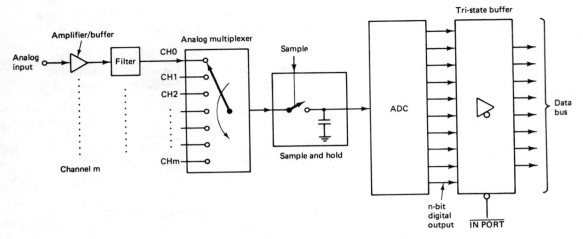

Figure 11.20 Multichannel data acquisition system.

The Analog-to-Digital Conversion Process.

The analog-to-digital converter (ADC) is actually just one part of what is called a *data acquisition system*. Refer to Fig. 11.20. Because the amplitude of the analog signal output by many transducers is usually quite small, amplification is required before it can be converted to digital form. This amplifier should have a high input resistance so that the signal being measured is not affected by the data acquisition system.

After amplification the signal is passed through a filter to reject any noise or other undesirable signals that may be present. The resulting amplified and filtered signal is applied to one of the inputs of an analog *multiplexer*. This circuit behaves like a rotary switch routing the selected input signal on to the ADC. This technique allows the data acquisition system to monitor several analog signals at once.

If the signal is changing rapidly in time, a *sample-and-hold* circuit can be used to temporarily hold a sample of the analog signal long enough for the ADC to convert it to digital. A set of tri-state buffers is provided so that the digital output can be gated directly onto the microprocessor data bus.

Depending on the design, all of the components in Fig. 11.20 may be integrated into a single chip or you may have to build the system out of several chips.

For the moment, let us turn our attention to the ADC. In many cases, this circuit and the tri-state buffers are sufficient to form a useful data acquisition system. Unlike the DAC in which the conversion process is fairly standard for all types, there are three popular techniques for converting analog signals to digital. These are called *open loop*, *feedback*, and *integrating* converters.

The open-loop "flash" converter.

Figure 11.21 illustrates a flash converter for 2 bits. This converter is so named because it converts its analog input to a digital output after propagation delay times through the analog comparators and logic gates (in a "flash"). The circuit is open-loop because there is no feedback between input and output. Like a logic gate, the output appears within a propagation delay after the input is applied.

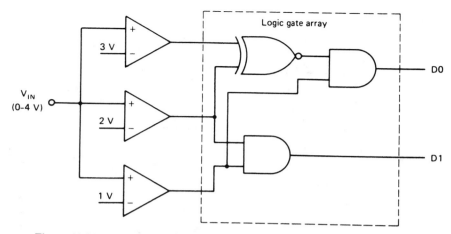

Figure 11.21 "Flash" converter. Three comparators are used to detect the three possible voltage steps: 1 V, 2 V, and 3 V. The logic gates convert the comparator outputs to standard binary code. (From J. Uffenbeck, *Hardware Interfacing with the Apple II Plus*, Prentice-Hall, Inc., Englewood Cliffs, N.J., 1983.)

Note that a separate comparator is required for each voltage step possible. For two bits there are three voltage levels (not counting 0), and in general $2^n - 1$ comparators are required for an *n*-bit converter. The logic gate array is needed to produce standard 1–2–4–8 binary code from the nonstandard output of the comparators. The advantage to this type of ADC is a very high-speed operation. For example, TRW manufactures an 8-bit flash ADC called the *TDC1018*. This converter can operate at speeds up to 125 million conversions per second. It is ECL (emitter-coupled logic)-compatible and intended for high-resolution graphics displays used in image processing.

The obvious disadvantage to the flash converter is that the number of comparators double for each additional bit. Although only 255 comparators are required for an 8-bit ADC, 4095 comparators are required for a 12-bit converter. For this reason flash converters are usually expensive and reserved for specialized applications.

Feedback converters. Feedback ADCs are considerably slower than flash converters but much less costly. Figure 11.22 shows how the MC1408 interface described in Sec. 11.3 is modified to become an ADC interface. The only (hardware) addition is an analog comparator used to compare the MC1408 DAC output with the unknown analog input voltage. What makes this circuit work is the software.

The conversion process is begun by outputting a value to port A of the 8255A (call this "guess 1"). The MC1408 and LM1458 convert this guess to a voltage which is then compared with the unknown input voltage by IC2A. If "guess 1" is too small, the comparator output will be low; if too big, the comparator output will be high. By monitoring PC0, the control program can adjust its guess up or down until the binary code output to the DAC corresponds to the unknown voltage.

Two algorithms (programming techniques) are commonly used to control the

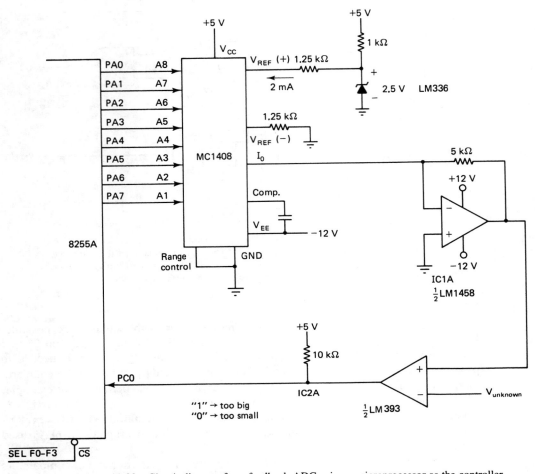

Figure 11.22 Circuit diagram for a feedback ADC using a microprocessor as the controller.

feedback ADC and are flowcharted in Fig. 11.23. The *tracking* converter diagrammed in Fig. 11.23(a) simply increments or decrements a counter using the comparator output to tell it which way to go. Figure 11.24 shows the output of the LM1458 (IC1A) in Fig. 11.22 as it attempts to "track" the input signal. The program begins by guessing that the input is $V_{FS}/2$ and because this is too low, slowly ramps up until it "locks" on the input signal. Now as the input slowly changes, the converter tracks these changes, faithfully reproducing the input signal.

However, note what happens when the input makes a sudden change. The tracking converter falls out of lock and does not regain lock until the signal returns to a more constant level. Thus we see that the tracking converter is good for tracking slowly changing signals (say, temperature levels over a long time period) but is inadequate for signals that make rapid transitions (say, music or speech waveforms).

We can imagine a worst-case scenario for the tracking ADC in which the input makes a sudden transition from V_{FS} to near 0 V. The control program will begin decrementing the output code to the DAC but could require as many as 256 cycles before lock is again found. Assuming that approximately 25 μs is required to test the comparator output at PC0 and output a new code, 256 × 25 μs = 6.4 ms will be required to regain lock.

The trouble with the tracking converter is that the algorithm used to control it is too simpleminded. A ''smarter'' approach is taken in the *successive approximations* flowchart in Fig. 11.23(b). This technique requires only eight cycles to converge on the unknown voltage. It begins by turning on bit 7, the most significant bit, and outputs this value (80H) to the DAC. If the comparator output goes high, it means that this value was too big and bit 7 should then be reset. If the comparator output is low, bit 7 is left on.

The cycle now repeats working on bit 6 (but keeping bit 7 on or off, as determined previously). After eight cycles all 8 bits will have been tested and the DAC output will be within 1 LSB (least significant bit) of the unknown input voltage.

Studying Fig. 11.24 you can see that the successive approximations converter does not try to ''follow'' the input signal. Instead, the software begins a conversion cycle and eight cycles later the conversion has ended. The ability of this converter to return an accurate representation of the input voltage depends on the speed of conversion. If the input changes too rapidly, the converter can be ''fooled,'' as shown in the second sample in Fig. 11.24.

Without getting too deep into communications theory, there is a *sampling theorem* which states that you need only sample a waveform twice per cycle to be able to reproduce that waveform. Thus we should not put too much emphasis on a

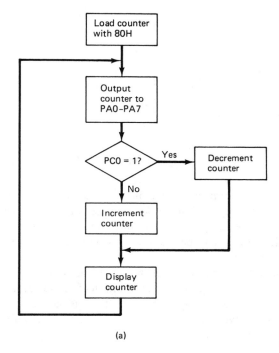

(a)

Fig. 11.23 Flowcharts for the (a) tracking ADC and (b) successive approximations ADC.

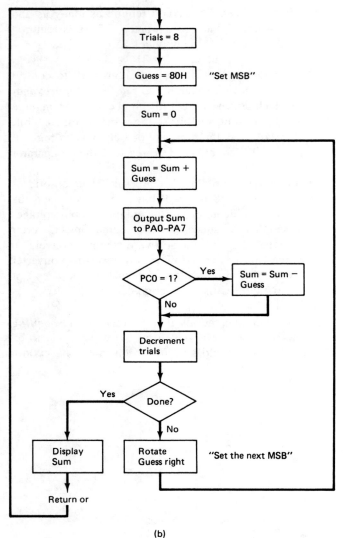

Trials = 8

Guess = 80H   "Set MSB"

Sum = 0

Sum = Sum + Guess

Output Sum to PA0–PA7

PC0 = 1? —Yes→ Sum = Sum − Guess

No

Decrement trials

Done? —Yes→

No

Display Sum

Rotate Guess right   "Set the next MSB"

Return or

(b)   **Fig. 11.23** (*Continued*)

converter's ability to track a waveform but rather on its ability to return an accurate sample of that waveform. If the input signal does change rapidly, a sample-and-hold circuit can be used to hold the sample constant until the conversion is complete. As long as at least two such samples can be taken per cycle of the input waveform, the wave shape can be reproduced.

Assuming approximately 50 μs per bit, 0.4 ms would be required to converge on the input signal using the successive approximations technique. Note that this value does not depend on the input voltage (that is, there is no worst case). In general, for n bits n conversions will be required for convergence (compared to 2^n for the tracking design).

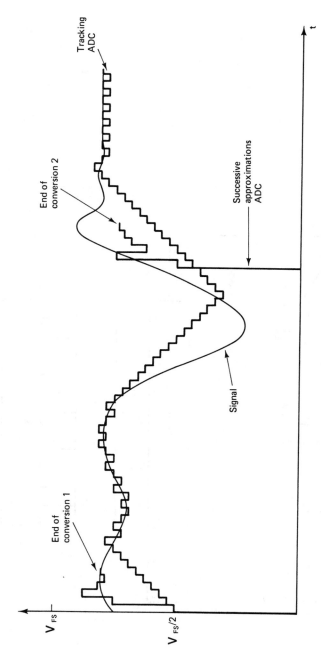

Figure 11.24 A tracking ADC follows a slowly changing input signal but falls out of lock when the input makes rapid transitions. The successive approximations ADC does not try to follow the input signal but converges on the digital code after eight cycles.

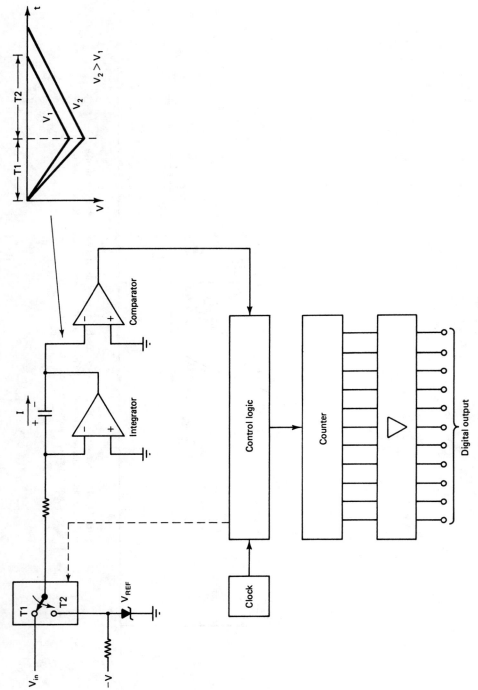

Figure 11.25 Integrating or dual-slope technique for analog-to-digital conversion.

Finally, before ending our discussion of feedback converters, you should realize that both the tracking and successive approximations converters can be built without requiring a microprocessor controller. A special *successive approximations register* (SAR) is available for that technique. A simple up/down counter can also be used to implement the tracking converter (see Prob. 11.16).

The integrating converter.   The integrating converter, or as it is more often called, the *dual-slope* converter, is commonly used in digital voltmeters, multimeters, and panel meters. Figure 11.25 illustrates the concept. The conversion begins with the electronic switch in the T1 position and the counter reset to zero. The input voltage causes the capacitor connected to the op-amp to charge at a rate dependent on the magnitude of the input voltage.

After T1 seconds have elapsed, the switch is moved to position T2 by the control logic. Because the reference voltage is of the opposite polarity to V_{in}, the capacitor now discharges. The control logic also starts the counter at this time. When the capacitor has fully discharged, the comparator output level switches and the counter is halted. The value in the counter is directly proportional to the input voltage:

$$V_{in} = \frac{T2}{T1} \times V_{REF}$$

As shown in Fig. 11.25, the higher the input voltage, the greater the charge stored on the capacitor during T1. During T2 this voltage is discharged, but at a *constant rate* dependent on V_{REF}. This means that larger voltages will require more time to discharge and the equation above can be used to calculate V_{in}. The technique is analogous to measuring the quantity of water in a bucket by measuring the time it takes to empty the bucket through a fixed-diameter hose. As long as the time to fill the bucket is kept constant, the longer it takes to empty it, the more water in the bucket.

Dual-slope converters are quite slow, requiring anywhere from 1 to 200 ms for one conversion. For this reason they are most often used in digital panel meters—faster conversion times could not be noted by the human eye. The main advantages to the technique are its simplicity (which translates into low cost) and its relative immunity to noise. Because the sampling period (T1) is so long, it is a good assumption that any noise that is present will add to the signal as much as it subtracts. This means that the voltage stored on the capacitor at the end of T1 seconds represents the *average* value of the input signal over this time interval.

Some dual-slope converters make T1 a multiple of 16.6 ms (1/60 Hz), thus averaging out any 60-Hz noise riding on the level being measured. The data collected by a flash or feedback converter can also be averaged over a 16.6-ms time period, but additional software is required. Data from the dual-slope converter is averaged in real time.

ADC0808, ADC0809 8-Bit μP Compatible A/D Converters With 8-Channel Multiplexer

General Description

The ADC0808, ADC0809 data acquisition component is a monolithic CMOS device with an 8-bit analog-to-digital converter, 8-channel multiplexer and microprocessor compatible control logic. The 8-bit A/D converter uses successive approximation as the conversion technique. The converter features a high impedance chopper stabilized comparator, a 256R voltage divider with analog switch tree and a successive approximation register. The 8-channel multiplexer can directly access any of 8-single-ended analog signals.

The device eliminates the need for external zero and full-scale adjustments. Easy interfacing to microprocessors is provided by the latched and decoded multiplexer address inputs and latched TTL TRI-STATE® outputs.

The design of the ADC0808, ADC0809 has been optimized by incorporating the most desirable aspects of several A/D conversion techniques. The ADC0808, ADC0809 offers high speed, high accuracy, minimal temperature dependence, excellent long-term accuracy and repeatability, and consumes minimal power. These features make this device ideally suited to applications from process and machine control to consumer and automotive applications. For 16-channel multiplexer with common output (sample/hold port) see ADC0816 data sheet. (See AN-247 for more information.)

Features

- Resolution — 8-bits
- Total unadjusted error — ± 1/2 LSB and ± 1 LSB
- No missing codes
- Conversion time — 100 μs
- Single supply — 5 V_{DC}
- Operates ratiometrically or with 5 V_{DC} or analog span adjusted voltage reference
- 8-channel multiplexer with latched control logic
- Easy interface to all microprocessors, or operates "stand alone"
- Outputs meet T^2L voltage level specifications
- 0V to 5V analog input voltage range with single 5V supply
- No zero or full-scale adjust required
- Standard hermetic or molded 28-pin DIP package
- Temperature range −40°C to +85°C or −55°C to +125°C
- Low power consumption — 15 mW
- Latched TRI-STATE® output

Block Diagram

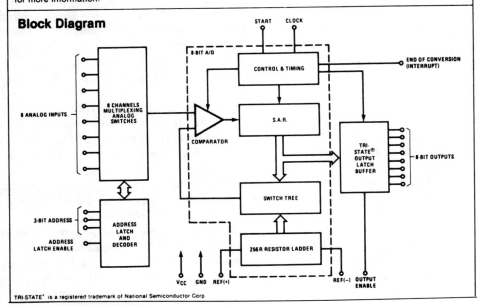

TRI-STATE® is a registered trademark of National Semiconductor Corp

Figure 11.26   Features and block diagram of the National Semiconductor ADC0809 eight-channel ADC. (Courtesy of National Semiconductor Corporation and Prentice Hall, Inc.)

Interfacing the ADC0809 Eight-Channel ADC.

In one integrated circuit the National Semiconductor ADC0809 provides nearly all of the components needed to build a complete data acquisition system. A block diagram is shown in Fig. 11.26. At a given time, any one of eight separate input signals can be sampled as selected by the three address input lines. The selected channel is converted to an 8-bit digital word after a typical conversion time of 100 μs. Tri-state output latches/buffers are built in to allow direct connection with the data bus of a typical microcomputer. An external 5.00-V reference voltage is required and this determines the absolute accuracy. A 10- to 1280-kHz clock signal must also be provided.

Internally, the ADC uses the *successive approximations* technique for analog-to-digital conversion. A successive approximations register, R-2R resistor ladder, and analog comparators are all included on the chip. With the 5-V reference, the input voltage is limited to 0 to 5 V.

Figure 11.27 shows the pinouts and the timing for the control signals. The conversion process is begun by pulsing the ALE (address latch enable) input high. This loads the selected address into the multiplexer and gates the signal on one of the eight-channel inputs into the comparator. Applying a START pulse begins the conversion. The EOC (end of conversion) output is low as the internal successive approximations register accumulates the 8-bit binary code. The rising edge of EOC indicates that the conversion is complete and the data byte can be read. Applying an active-high pulse to OE (output enable) places this data on the eight data bus lines which are normally in a tri-state condition.

The ADC0809 can be interfaced directly to the three-bus system architecture without the need for special I/O chips such as the 8255A PPI or Z-80 PIO. A typical interface is shown in Fig. 11.28. Address lines AB0–AB2 select one of eight input channels. An I/O write instruction to any port address 30–37H (corresponding to channels 0 through 7) will generate a START and ALE pulse beginning the conversion for the selected channel. Note that no data is actually transferred with this instruction.

Once the conversion has begun, the EOC output can either be polled or used as an interrupt to the processor. The interface in Fig. 11.28 uses the latter approach. The rising edge of EOC, indicating data available, clocks the D flip-flop setting its Q output and requesting an interrupt. The processor acknowledges the interrupt by asserting $\overline{INTAB}$ and this signal is used to reset the flip-flop for the next EOC.

The interrupt service routine (ISR) must execute an I/O read instruction from any of the eight input port addresses 30–37H. This will pulse OE and place the data byte onto the data bus.

A simple TTL oscillator is sufficient for the clock signal. Using the values in Fig. 11.28, the clock frequency is approximately 500 kHz. An LM336-5 precision zener diode is used for the 5.00-V reference. The additional diodes and resistors compensate for voltage drifts in the LM336 with temperature.

Example 11.7

Assume that an analog signal on channel 3 of the ADC interface in Fig. 11.28 is to be converted to digital and the result stored in a memory location called TEMP. Write the interrupt service routine required.

Sec. 11.4   Interfacing an Analog-to-Digital Converter   **579**

Connection Diagram

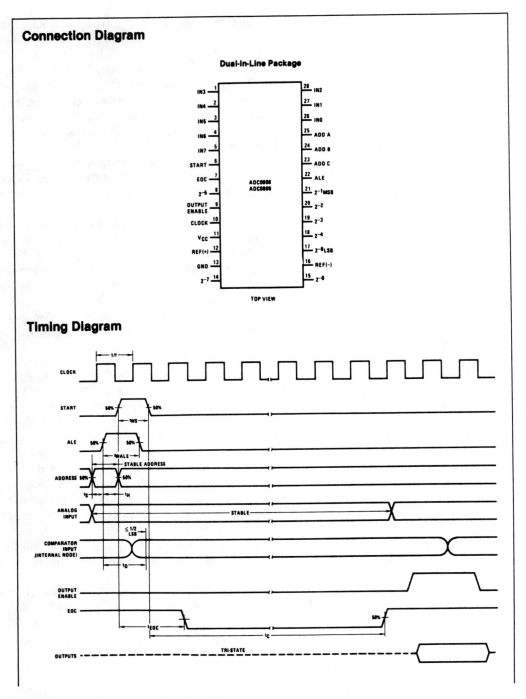

Figure 11.27 Connection diagram and timing relationships of the ADC0809 control signals. (Courtesy of National Semiconductor Corporation and Prentice-Hall, Inc.)

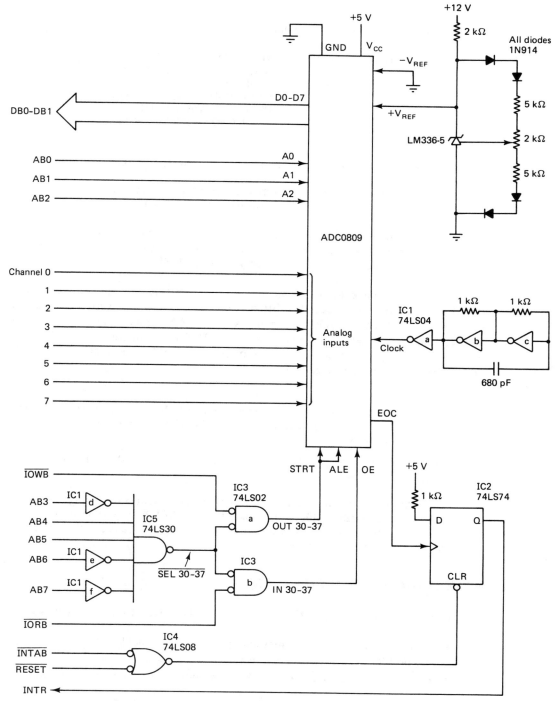

Figure 11.28 Interfacing the ADC0809 to the three-bus system architecture. Eight input and eight output ports are required. This circuit uses an interrupt-driven technique to control data transfers.

Sec. 11.4   Interfacing an Analog-to-Digital Converter

581

Solution. The program is as follows.

```
ISR    PUSH    PSW      ;MAKE TRANSPARENT
       IN      30H      ;READ DATA BYTE—ANY ADDRESS 30–37H
       STA     TEMP     ;STORE RESULT
       OUT     33H      ;START CONVERSION FOR NEXT CYCLE
       POP     PSW      ;RESTORE ENVIRONMENT
       EI               ;ENABLE FOR NEXT EOC PULSE
       RET
```

The main program can execute the following code to start the process.

```
       OUT     33H      ;START CONVERSION FOR CHANNEL 3
       EI               ;ENABLE INTERRUPT STRUCTURE
```

The processor can now perform some other task. Every 100 μs it will be interrupted to perform the ISR. The most recent value of the analog input on channel 3 can be found by reading the contents of memory location TEMP.

One disadvantage to using the 8080/85 I/O instructions in this example is that the port address is fixed. If a different channel is to be converted, a new ISR must be written. This is not a problem with the Z-80 microprocessor. The port address can be passed in register C and an *OUT* (*C*),*r* instruction used. If the interface is changed to become memory-mapped, the 8080 and 8085 can pass the port address in a register pair.

Example 11.8

Assume that an LM334 temperature sensor (see Sec. 11.1) is connected to channel 3 and the ISR in Ex. 11.7 executed. If memory location TEMP contains 9CH, what is the temperature of the sensor?

Solution. $9CH = 156_{10}$ and thus $V_{in} = 156/256 \times 5.0$ V $= 3.05$ V. This corresponds to $305°K = 32°C = 90°F$.

Note: Machine code to convert 9CH to 90°F could be written by storing the possible temperatures in a table with the hex code found in TEMP used as an *index* into the table. Alternatively, a program written in BASIC could easily *calculate* the temperature directly from the number stored in TEMP.

11.5 TROUBLESHOOTING TECHNIQUES

As you read this section, look for the answers to these Key Concept questions:

11.5.1. When troubleshooting a microcomputer system, the first task is to isolate the problem to _____ or _____.

11.5.2. Explain the role of a test ROM when booting up a computer for the first time.

11.5.3. What is the difference between the state and timing modes as applied to a logic analyzer?

It would be nice if a microcomputer system could be designed, constructed, and used without having to spend long hours tracking down bad connections, design errors, and software bugs. It would also be nice if we did not have to pay taxes. But both being inevitable, it is probably wise to prepare for the eventuality and become familiar with basic microcomputer troubleshooting techniques. As Murphy* has said, *"Anything that can go wrong, will."*

When faced with any troubleshooting problem, the goal is to isolate the problem area. What part of the system is working and which parts are not? A good starting point is to determine if the problem is due to a *hardware* failure or a *software* bug. For example, a "new" computer being booted up for the first time may appear "dead" if a wrong code has been programmed into its bootstrap PROM. Several hours could easily be spent looking for an apparent hardware problem that is not there.

Separating hardware from software problems can result in a lot of "finger pointing" if the hardware designer and programmer have too much confidence in their work. I can remember thinking that I surely had a bad microprocessor chip when my first machine language programs caused the system to "crash" repeatedly.

In new systems, test PROMs from similar systems should be used so that the software is known to be good. If this is not possible, a very simple test PROM should be programmed that will cause an unmistakable pattern to appear on the system buses.

An example of the "wrong way" of developing system software would be to try to write a complete DOS (disk operating system) without first testing the disk primitives such as load the head, locate track 00, and read or write a sector of data. Because the program would have to be so complex, it would be very difficult to isolate any problems to hardware or software.

When software problems are indicated, special aids are available. These include debuggers that allow instructions to be *traced* in a single-step mode displaying all CPU registers after each instruction (see the discussion on DDT in Sec. 3.2).

Another software debugging tool is called the *breakpoint*. This is a special instruction inserted into a program to cause control to be transferred to a routine that displays the contents of all microprocessor registers at the time of the breakpoint. It is similar to the trace technique but allows known good sections of the program to be executed at normal speeds. Because they occupy only one byte of memory, the RST instructions are usually used for breakpoints in 8080/85 and Z-80 microcomputer systems. The DDT program included with CP/M supports the insertion (and automatic deletion) of breakpoints in 8080/85 programs.

When hardware problems are indicated, several tools are also available for locating the fault. The most common of these are:

1. Multimeter
2. Logic probe
3. Oscilloscope

* Well-known pessimist.

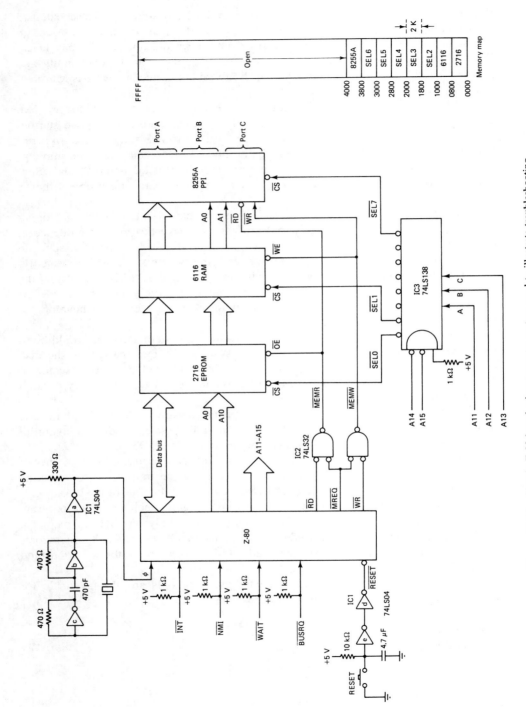

Figure 11.29 Simple Z-80-based microcomputer system used to illustrate troubleshooting techniques.

4. Signature analyzer
5. Logic analyzer

In this section we examine these hardware troubleshooting tools and see how they are used to locate faults in microcomputer systems.

Hardware Troubleshooting Tools

Multimeter. Each connection in a new microcomputer system should be tested for *continuity* before any of the ICs are placed in their sockets and power is applied. The ohms function of the multimeter can be used for this purpose. Some of the newer meters emit a "beep" to indicate continuity and help make this task less tedious. Each connection should be checked off against a wiring list or schematic diagram of the system.

When it has been determined that all connections are correct, the power supply voltages should be measured using the voltmeter function of the meter. Perform this measurement at the power source terminals *and* at the power pins of each IC socket (you do not want +12 V going to all of the TTL chips!).

Logic probe. When troubleshooting a digital system, a logic probe is useful for two measurements:

1. Check for valid logic levels.
2. Detect pulses.

When bringing up a new system, a logic probe can be used to verify that the system clock is running. Note, however, that you will be unable to verify the actual voltage levels of the clock or its exact frequency.

A logic probe is most effective if the processor can be *single-stepped*. In Chap. 4 we saw circuits that permitted single-stepping by forcing the processor to execute one machine cycle and then enter a *WAIT* state. In this WAIT state all data, address, and control bus signals are "frozen" and can readily be tested with a logic probe.

Example 11.9

Figure 11.29 shows the schematic diagram for a simple Z-80 microcomputer system with 2K RAM, 2K EPROM, and 24 I/O lines. The memory map is also shown (note that the 8255A is memory-mapped). Write the code for a simple Z-80 TEST EPROM that could be executed in the single-step mode to verify basic system operation.

Solution. Because the system is so simple, the TEST PROM might do best to exercise the address decoding and read/write logic. One possibility would be to perform a memory read from each of the three devices (2716, 6116, and 8255A), a memory write to the RAM, and finally a memory read from an address not decoded. Figure 11.30(a) shows one possible program.

ADDR	CODE	STMT	SOURCE	STATEMENT	
		0001	;Z-80 TEST PROGRAM FOR THE HARDWARE IN FIG.11-29		
		0002	;		
>0000		0003	ORG	0000	;RESET WILL START PROGRAM
		0004	;		
'0000	3AFF07	0005 LOOP	LD	A,(07FFH)	;GENERATE SEL0 AND MEMR
'0003	3AFF0F	0006	LD	A,(0FFFH)	;GENERATE SEL1 AND MEMR
'0006	3A0038	0007	LD	A,(3800H)	;GENERATE SEL7 AND MEMR
'0009	32FF0F	0008	LD	(0FFFH),A	;GENERATE SEL1 AND MEMW
'000C	3AFFFF	0009	LD	A,(0FFFFH)	;ALL SELECTS SHOULD BE HIGH
'000F	C30000'	0010	JP	LOOP	;NOW SINGLE-STEP WHILE LOOPING

ERRORS=0000

(a)

PROM ADDRESS	DATA
0000	3A
0001	FF
0002	07
0003	3A
0004	FF
0005	0F
0006	3A
0007	00
0008	38
0009	32
000A	FF
000B	0F
000C	3A
000D	FF
000E	FF
000F	C3
0010	00
0011	00

Figure 11.30 (a) Test EPROM program for the Z-80 system in Fig. 11.29; (b) the EPROM hex codes.

(b)

Figure 11.30(b) shows the hex codes for the TEST PROM as they would be stored starting at location 0 of the 2716 EPROM. Pushing RESET should start the program. The $\overline{\text{MEMR}}$ and $\overline{\text{MEMW}}$ lines should be pulsing from high to low (the logic probe will show this as a steady logic 1 with the pulse indicator flashing) and the $\overline{\text{SEL0}}$, $\overline{\text{SEL1}}$, and $\overline{\text{SEL7}}$ decoder outputs should also be pulsing.

Example 11.10

Sketch a machine cycle timing diagram for the program in Fig. 11.30(a). Indicate the contents of the address and data buses for each cycle.

Solution. The diagram is shown in Fig. 11.31. Note that the addresses have been chosen to allow each address and data bus line to be tested for a logic 1 and logic 0 condition.

Without a single-step circuit the contents of the buses in Fig. 11.29 will appear only as pulse indications on the logic probe. This will prove that none of the data

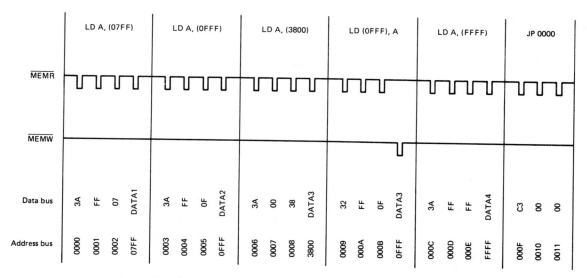

LD A, (07FF)				LD A, (0FFF)				LD A, (3800)				LD (0FFF), A				LD A, (FFFF)				JP 0000		

Data bus: 3A FF 07 DATA1 | 3A FF 0F DATA2 | 3A 00 38 DATA3 | 32 FF 0F DATA3 | 3A FF FF DATA4 | C3 00 00

Address bus: 0000 0001 0002 07FF | 0003 0004 0005 0FFF | 0006 0007 0008 3800 | 0009 000A 000B 0FFF | 000C 000D 000E FFFF | 000F 0010 0011

Figure 11.31 Machine cycle timing diagram for the TEST program in Fig. 11.30(a).

or address lines are "stuck" high or low but is not as conclusive as could be found by stepping the processor through each machine cycle shown in Fig. 11.31.

A single-step circuit is not shown in Fig. 11.31 but was presented in Fig. 4.31 for the Z-80. Using this circuit the following steps should be followed.

1. With the single-step switch in the RUN position, start the program running by pushing the RESET switch.
2. Switch to the single-step position.
3. Find your "place" in the program by monitoring $\overline{\text{MEMW}}$ with the logic probe. It will go low only once for each loop through the program.
4. Having found the memory-write machine cycle, trace the program by pushing the STEP switch, examining the buses with the logic probe and verifying the addresses and data for each cycle.
5. The memory read cycle from address FFFF should cause all of the decoder outputs to be high (this is the only cycle for which this will occur).

Assuming that this program runs correctly, more elaborate programs can now be written that read and write data to the RAM and program the 8255A for simple I/O operations. If these programs check out, the system can be declared functional and you can begin writing the application programs.

Oscilloscope. Compared to the logic probe the oscilloscope lets you "see" the logic pulses. Problems such as marginal voltage levels and excessive ringing can readily be spotted. However, the main advantage in using the oscilloscope is the ability to compare the timing between two signals (assuming a dual trace). If $\overline{\text{SEL1}}$ must go low during $\overline{\text{MEMW}}$ low, the oscilloscope can show the relationship between these two signals exactly.

The oscilloscope is not too effective, however, when it comes to monitoring the content of the data and address bus lines. This is because all eight data bus and all 16 address bus lines need to be examined at once (for that matter, the logic probe is not too effective at reading these buses either).

Generally, the oscilloscope is used when the timing between two signals must be observed or when the electrical characteristics of a signal are in question.

Signature analyzer. Signature analysis is a troubleshooting technique developed by Hewlett-Packard specifically for microcomputer systems. A signature analyzer is used much like a conventional digital voltmeter touching a probe to various nodes in the circuit. At each node a "characteristic signature" is displayed. This is a four-digit number made up of the numerals 0–9 and (for clarity) the letters A, C, F, H, P, or U. Comparing the measured signature against a predetermined value on a schematic diagram (much as voltages are recorded on an analog schematic), a technician can quickly isolate defective components.

The basis of the technique is to note that at any circuit node a serial stream of pulses will be observed over time. If this stream is repetitive, a CRC character can be generated representative of the data block (see Sec. 9.3 for a discussion of CRC).

The signature analyzer has three inputs. These are START, STOP, and CLOCK. START and STOP are signals used to tell the analyzer when to begin and end the CRC calculation. The rising or falling edge of the CLOCK signal is used to cause the analyzer to sample the logic level at the circuit node.

For signature analysis to be most effective, the signature at each node in the circuit must be known (before the system needs troubleshooting!). This is best designed in by the manufacturer who can then identify a logical sequence to follow when an incorrect signature is found. However, in a known good microcomputer system, signature analysis can be used by recording the signatures at important nodes. Note that it will be important to document the program used to produce this signature and the CLOCK, START, and STOP signal definitions.

Realistically, few users will take the time to record signatures on functioning equipment. Determining the important nodes to be tested and developing test programs that exercise these nodes requires a knowledge of the system unique to the manufacturer. For these reasons, signature analysis tends to be restricted to equipment that supports the technique by design.

Logic analyzer. The logic analyzer is the most sophisticated (and most expensive) tool available for troubleshooting the microcomputer. It is available with anywhere from eight to over 40 input channels. Unlike an oscilloscope, the logic analyzer does not display its input signals in real time. Instead, it stores this information in a semiconductor memory, usually allowing 16 to 1024 words of storage (that is, a 40-channel analyzer would have storage capabilities for 1024 40-bit words).

The stored data can be displayed as a conventional voltage waveform (without rise and fall times) using the *timing mode*. It can also be displayed as binary,

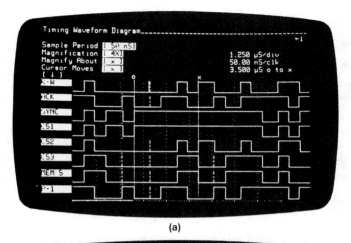

(a)

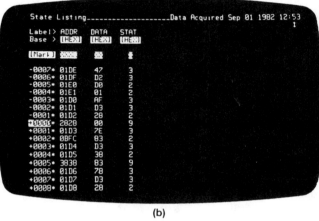

(b)

Figure 11.32 (a) In the timing mode, voltage waveforms versus time are displayed by the logic analyzer. An internal clock determines the sampling period. (b) In the state mode, data can be displayed in binary, octal, hex, ASCII, or disassembled mnemonic form. In this example, 28 channels are used. (Courtesy of Hewlett-Packard.)

octal, hex, ASCII, or disassembled mnemonics in the *state mode*. Recalling the logic probe example, we essentially performed a state-mode analysis. However, it was neccessary to single-step the processor manually to collect the data and then record it on paper to reconstruct the data and address bytes.

Figure 11.32(a) shows an example of the display produced by a Hewlett-Packard model 1630 logic analyzer when operated in the timing mode. Note that each channel can be assigned a label, making analysis of the display much simpler. The sample period is similar to the horizontal sweep rate of a conventional oscilloscope and controls the resolution of the data stored.

Figure 11.32(b) illustrates the display produced when operated in the state mode. Again, labels have been used to simplify interpretation. Note that in this case ADDR represents 16 input channels, DATA represents eight input channels, and STAT represents four input channels. The operator has chosen to display the data in a hex format.

A very powerful feature of most logic analyzers is the ability to *trigger* on a

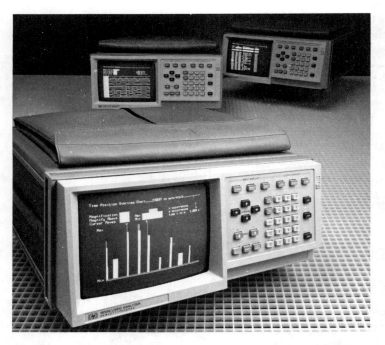

Figure 11.33 Front panel of the HP 1630 logic analyzer. (Courtesy of Hewlett-Packard.)

particular data word. Using this feature, you can, for example, specify data collection to begin when $\overline{\text{MEMR}}$ is low, the address bus contains 2800H, and the data bus contains 3EH. In addition, data can be collected in either a pre (before) or post (after)-trigger mode. This can be seen in Fig. 11.32(b), where the trigger word is highlighted in reverse video (ADDR = 2828). Seven data samples are shown before the trigger word and eight samples after the trigger word.

The logic analyzer is itself a microcomputer system programmable by a front-panel keyboard. Operation is simplified due to various control menus placed on the screen by the instrument. Figure 11.33 shows the calculator-like front panel of the Hewlett-Packard model 1630. Note that the roll keys allow the data on the screen to be scrolled up or down so that all of the stored data can be examined by the operator.

The most difficult part about using a logic analyzer is the setup. For example, the state display in Fig. 11.32(b) requires that 28 probes be connected to the microcomputer system under test for the address, data, and control bus signals. Next, the proper operating mode must be selected via the front panel. Of particular importance is the clock signal. In the timing mode this is usually an internally generated signal that determines when to sample the input data. The HP 1630 will allow clock samples as fast as every 20 ns or as slow as one each millisecond.

Selecting a 20-ns sample period might be a good choice when looking for close timing problems, but will restrict the timing period to 1024 samples × 0.02

μs/sample $= 20.48$ μs. Depending on the microprocessor's clock frequency, this may not be enough time to see more than two or three complete instructions. On the other hand, selecting a 1-ms sample period will store 1.024 s of data, possibly resulting in waveforms so compressed as to be unreadable.

In the state mode the clock signal is supplied externally. This is because it is desirable to take the data samples synchronously with a particular clock signal. Two examples will help illustrate.

Example 11.11

Describe the connections required to connect a logic analyzer in the state mode to the Z-80 system shown in Fig. 11.29. Assuming that the TEST EPROM used to obtain the machine cycle timing diagram in Fig. 11.31 is used, explain the resulting state display.

Solution. Using the labels ADDR, DATA, and STAT (where STAT = $\overline{\text{MEMR}}$ and $\overline{\text{MEMW}}$, in that order) the display is shown in Fig. 11.34. We assume that a trigger word of ADDR = 0000 has been selected (although with the roll feature of the HP 1630, this is not essential). Note that the clock must be connected to $\overline{\text{MREQ}}$ (and programmed for a rising edge trigger) so that data samples are recorded for both memory read and write cycles. Also note that the data is essentially identical to that shown in Fig. 11.31 (but has been found a lot more quickly!).

ADDR	DATA	STAT ($\overline{\text{MEMR}}$ $\overline{\text{MEMW}}$)
0000	3A	1
0001	FF	1
0002	07	1
07FF	DATA1*	1
0003	3A	1
0004	FF	1
0005	0F	1
0FFF	DATA2	1
0006	3A	1
0007	00	1
0008	38	1
3800	DATA3	1
0009	32	1
000A	FF	1
000B	0F	1
0FFF	DATA3	2
000C	3A	1
000D	FF	1
000E	FF	1
FFFF	DATA4	1
000F	C3	1
0010	00	1
0011	00	1
0000	3A	1
⋮	⋮	⋮

Figure 11.34 Logic analyzer display in the state mode for the TEST program in Fig. 11.30(a). $\overline{\text{MREQ}}$ is used as the clock source. STAT = 1 (01–memory read) or 2 (10–memory write).

ADDR	DATA	STAT (MEMR MEMW)
0FFF	DATA3	2
0FFF	DATA3	2
0FFF	DATA3	2
:	:	:

Figure 11.35 Changing the logic analyzer clock from $\overline{\text{MREQ}}$ to $\overline{\text{MEMW}}$ results in only one data sample per program loop.

Example 11.12

If the clock input to the logic analyzer is changed from $\overline{\text{MREQ}}$ to $\overline{\text{MEMW}}$ in Fig. 11.29, what will the state display become?

Solution. The display is shown in Fig. 11.35. There is only one memory write cycle per loop through the program and this occurs when the LDA (0FFF),A instruction is executed. The address bus contains 0FFF and the data bus the data byte read in the preceding instruction.

Summary. Before you attempt to troubleshoot a microcomputer system, be sure that you understand its operation. Get a copy of the system monitor in PROM. Be sure that you are familiar with the system memory map. Although a number of sophisticated troubleshooting tools are available, you must understand the system to make effective use of these tools. Often, TEST PROMs will have to be programmed to exercise selected portions of the hardware. A little luck won't hurt either!

CHAPTER SUMMARY

1. The output of an analog comparator will switch from one TTL level to another when the input voltage to the comparator exceeds some threshold. In this way the microprocessor can monitor the ON/OFF status of analog peripherals.

2. Analog peripherals usually require ON/OFF control voltage and current levels incompatible with standard TTL. However, for dc control applications, standard 7400 family open-collector buffers or 75400 series peripheral drivers can be used.

3. When a microprocessor must control the ON/OFF status of an ac peripheral, electromechanical relays or solid-state relays are the best choice.

4. An important design consideration for a microprocessor controller is to ensure isolation between the high-voltage ac-controlled circuit and the low-voltage TTL control circuit. This is typically accomplished with an opto-isolator.

5. Nearly all digital-to-analog converters use the R-2R ladder technique because of the requirement for only two matched resistors.

6. When interfacing a 12-bit DAC, double buffering is required to avoid "glitches" in the DAC output.

7. There are several techniques for converting analog signals to digital. Among these are the "flash" converter intended for high-speed applications, the feed-

back converter used in most microprocessor-controlled ADCs, and the integrating converter used in most digital voltmeters.

8. Complete data acquisition systems are available on a single silicon chip. These are designed to interface directly with a microprocessor and offer as many as 16 separate analog input channels.

9. Troubleshooting a microprocessor is very complex due to the mix of hardware and software in a standard system. When a ''new'' system is being tested, a special TEST EPROM should be programmed that can be used to isolate hardware problems.

10. A number of tools are available for troubleshooting microprocessor hardware. These include the multimeter, logic probe, oscilloscope, signature analyzer, and logic analyzer.

11. The logic analyzer is the most sophisticated troubleshooting tool available but requires a thorough understanding of the system being tested and the analyzer itself.

LAB PROJECTS

11.1. Light activated relay:
  (a) Using one bit of an available input port, construct the photocell input circuit shown in Fig. 11.36. Adjust the potentiometer so that the output switches reliably when covered and uncovered by your thumb (see Prob. 11.2).
  (b) Using one bit of an available output port, construct a relay control circuit. Fig 11.5(b) shows an example of a circuit using an open collector buffer. Fig. 11.37 shows another method that does not require an output port (see Probs. 11.6 and 11.7).

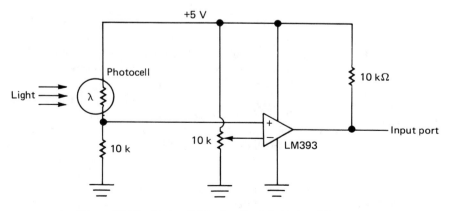

Figure 11.36 Photocell interface for Lab 11.1 and Prob. 11.2.

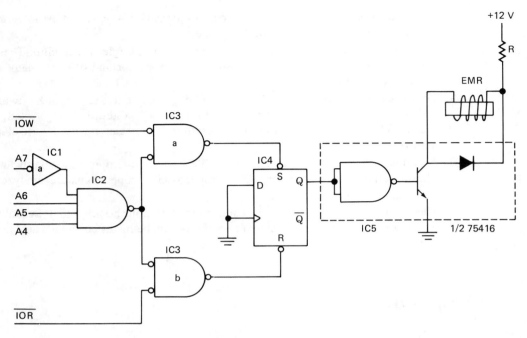

Figure 11.37 Relay driver circuit for Lab 11.1 and Probs. 11.6–7.

(c) Write a program to activate the relay when the photocell is covered for one or two seconds. Have the relay stay on until the next time the cell is similarly covered.[1]

11.2. Computer controlled lamp dimmer:

(a) Construct the solid-state relay circuit shown in Fig. 11.9 using an MOC3011. Use an 12-V ac signal for the source and a 12-V incandescent lamp as the load. An open-collector buffer can be substituted for the 75416 relay driver. Connect the input of this buffer to one bit of an available output port. Test to be sure you can turn the lamp on and off via software.

(b) Use a comparator like the LM393 to generate a 60-Hz TTL-compatible square wave from a 6-V or 12-V ac transformer. Connect this signal to one bit of an available input port.

(c) Write a program to detect zero crossings of the line voltage (rising or falling edges of the 60-Hz square wave), enter a time delay, and then activate the SSR turning on the lamp for the remainder of the half-cycle. The brilliance of the bulb can be controlled by selecting different

---

[1] Conventional push-button switches will wear out, especially when exposed to heavy use. The circuit in Fig. 11.36 can be put to good use replacing such switches. If the photocell is mounted behind a piece of glass, it will still be accessible, but should have an unlimited life.

time delays. Be sure to observe the waveforms across the lamp, TRIAC, 60-Hz square wave, and computer output port using an oscilloscope.

11.3. Synthesizing a sine wave:
  (a) Construct a DAC interface like that shown in Fig. 11.15.
  (b) Write a program to cause the output to ramp from 0 V to 10 V and back down again, repeating. Observe this waveform on an oscilloscope. Measure the step size.
  (c) Using a program similar to that in Fig. 11.17, write a program to synthesize a 1-kHz sine wave. Try adding more samples to produce a ''cleaner'' waveform.
  (d) Connect the op-amp output to an LM386 driving a loudspeaker. Modify your program from part (c) to emulate a European police siren as described in Prob. 11.14.

11.4. Digital voltmeter/thermometer:
  (a) Modify the DAC circuit described in Lab 11.3 to become a feedback ADC (see Fig. 11.22).
  (b) Write a program to control the interface following the tracking or successive approximations flowcharts given in Fig. 11.23(a) and (b). Have your program output the hex value of the result to the displays on your computer.
  (c) Modify the program from part (b) to display the *decimal* value of the input voltage (the easiest way to do this is to set up a data table). Check your interface with a conventional digital voltmeter.
  (d) Monitoring the voltage across an LM334 (see Fig. 11.2), convert your voltmeter into a digital thermometer (again a data table may be the easiest way to do this).

QUESTIONS AND PROBLEMS

Section 11.1

11.1. True or false: The output of the LM393 in Fig. 11.36 will be +5 V whenever the voltage applied to its V(+) input exceeds the voltage applied to its V(−) input.

11.2. Assume the resistance of the photocell in Fig. 11.36 varies from 1 kΩ in bright daylight to 1 MΩ in darkness. At dusk the cell's resistance is 10 kΩ. To what resistance value should the 10 kΩ pot be adjusted to cause the circuit's output to be low from dusk to daylight?

Section 11.3

*11.3. Study the driver circuits in Fig. 11.38 and identify the design error in each.

11.4. One bit of a microcomputer output port is to be used to control a 24-V dc mechanical relay. The pull-in current of the relay is 35 mA. Sketch the

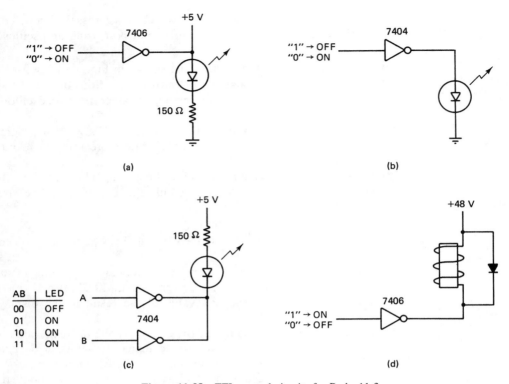

Figure 11.38 TTL control circuits for Prob. 11.3.

schematic diagram of a circuit that uses a TTL open-collector buffer to interface this relay and microcomputer.

11.5. Using the graph of I versus time in Fig. 11.7(b), calculate the "cold" and "hot" resistance of the incandescent lamp.

11.6. Answer the following questions about the EMR interface shown in Fig. 11.37.

(a) To turn on the relay the flip-flop must be _____.

(b) If the relay has a pull-in current of 150 mA and the coil is rated at 9 V, calculate the value of the series dropping resistor R.

(c) What is the range of I/O addresses to which this circuit will respond?

(d) Give an example of an instruction that will turn the relay on.

*11.7. Which of the following could be a cause for the relay in Fig. 11.37 to be "stuck" on?

(a) A solder splash has shorted the output of IC3a to ground.

(b) The collector–emitter junction of the driver transistor in IC5 is shorted.

(c) The series-dropping resistor has burned out, becoming an open circuit.

11.8. What is the purpose of the bridge rectifier in the hybrid SSR in Fig. 11.8?

11.9. Answer the following questions about the SSR in Fig. 11.9.

(a) What logic condition is required to turn the relay on?

(b) Assuming the IRED drops 3.0 V, calculate the current through the IRED.

(c) Explain how Q1 and D1 protect the IRED. If Q1 comes on when its VBE = 0.6 V, what is the maximum current that can be forced through the IRED?

Section 11.3

11.10. Calculate the smallest output voltage for an 8-bit and a 12-bit DAC each with V_{FS} = 10.0 V.

11.11. Calculate all currents and the output voltage for the R-2R DAC in Fig. 11.13 if D2 D1 D0 = 101. Assume V_{REF} = 3.0 V, R = 1 kΩ, and R_F = 8 kΩ. (*Hint*: Find I0 then I2, then use superposition.)

11.12. Calculate the output voltage for the *weighted resistor DAC* in Fig. 11.39 assuming VR = 1 V and D3 D2 D1 D0 = 0101. Why do you think the R-2R DAC is preferable?

11.13. Answer the following questions about the MC1408 PPI interface in Fig. 11.15.

(a) What is the purpose of the LM336.

(b) What is the function of the op-amp?

(c) What is the maximum output voltage for the circuit as shown?

11.14. Write a program to synthesize a European police siren using an 8-bit DAC. Your program should produce 1 s of a 1 kHz tone, and then 1 s of a 500-Hz tone, repeating. Use the program in Fig. 11.17 as a subroutine.

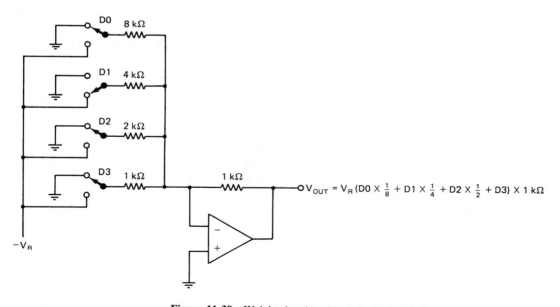

Figure 11.39 Weighted resistor DAC for Prob. 11.12.

Section 11.4

11.15. Compare the worst-case conversion time for an 8-bit tracking ADC and an 8-bit successive approximations ADC. Assume 25 μs conversion time per bit.

11.16. Sketch the schematic diagram of an 8-bit ADC using an 8-bit DAC, up-down counter, and analog comparator. Indicate where the analog input is applied and the digital output retrieved.

11.17. Refer to the feedback ADC in Fig. 11.22. If the analog input voltage is 6.25 V and the digital output is 9EH, determine the logic level on the output of the analog comparator.

11.18. Write a program to convert the feedback ADC in Fig. 11.22 into a tracking ADC per the flowchart in Fig. 11.23(a).

11.19. Write a program to convert the feedback ADC in Fig. 11.22 into a successive approximations ADC per the flowchart in Fig. 11.23(b).

*11.20. Assume a tracking routine has been written for the ADC circuit in Fig. 11.22. In testing you find that the program continually converges on FFH, regardless of the analog input voltage. Which of the following could be a cause of this problem?
   (a) The output of the LM393 is "stuck" high.
   (b) The reference current is set too high.
   (c) The output of the LM1458 is shorted to ground.

11.21. Answer the following questions about the ADC0809 interface in Fig. 11.28.
   (a) What is the I/O port address of the channel 5 analog input?
   (b) Give an example of a command that will cause a conversion to begin for channel 5.
   (c) What signal indicates to the microprocessor that the conversion for channel 5 has been completed?
   (d) Give an example of a command that can be used to read the converted data for channel 5.

Section 11.5

11.22. Answer the following questions about the microcomputer system shown in Fig. 11.29.
   (a) How much ROM does this system have?
   (b) How much RAM does this system have?
   (c) What is the *range* of port addresses to which the 8255A will respond?
   (d) Each of the $\overline{SEL}$ outputs of the 74LS138 is active for _____ consecutive bytes.

*11.23. With the test program in Fig. 11.30 running, you are checking the microcomputer system in Fig. 11.29. You find $\overline{MEMR}$ to be pulsing but $\overline{MEMW}$ appears to be stuck low. List at least three possible causes for this problem. What action would you take to prove or disprove each problem? Assume all chips are socketed.

*11.24. You are tracing the test program in Fig. 11.30(a). Watching the address bus you see 0000, 0001, 0002, and then 07FFH. Is this correct? Explain.

*11.25. Assume the A15 and A14 address lines in the microcomputer system shown in Fig. 11.29 have become shorted. Will the test program in Fig. 11.30(a) detect this problem? Explain.

*11.26. Assume that a microcomputer system you have been using for several months suddenly goes "dead." The system uses a machine language monitor in PROM, hex keypad, and seven-segment LED displays. In its dead state it will not respond to the keypad, and although the displays are lit, they do not change. What steps and tools would you use to troubleshoot this problem?

*11.27. If the dead system described in Prob. 11.26 is being booted up for the very *first* time, how would you modify your troubleshooting procedure?

11.28. Write a simple test program for the 8255A in Fig. 11.29. Have your software program the 8255A for mode 0 with each port programmed to follow a binary count sequence. A logic probe can then be used to verify correct operation.

11.29. What *mode*, timing or state, should be selected to cause a logic analyzer to display the $\overline{MEMR}$ and $\overline{MEMW}$ waveforms shown in Fig. 11.31?

*11.30. You have connected a logic analyzer to an 8080/85 or Z-80 microcomputer. Using the state mode, you program the analyzer to begin collecting data after a system reset (address bus = 0000). Explain the data shown below. What do you think is wrong with this system?

ADDR	DATA	STAT	$\overline{(MEMR\ MEMW)}$
0000	FF		1
274E	00		2
274D	01		2
000F	FF		1
274C	00		2
274B	01		2
000F	FF		1

KEY CONCEPT ANSWERS

11.1.1. current, temperature

11.1.2. $V(+) > V(-)$, $V(-) > V(+)$

11.2.1. 30 V

11.2.2. When used to drive a relay, the diodes protect the output transistor from the inductive voltage spike created when the current in the relay coil collapses.

11.2.3. They provide isolation between the control and controlled circuit.

11.2.4. zero-cross, random

11.3.1. The number of bits.

11.3.2. R-2R ladder

11.3.3. Samples of the desired output voltage can be stored in a table and then output to the DAC.

11.4.1. Open loop, feedback, and integrating or dual-slope

11.4.2. tracking, successive approximations

11.4.3. dual-slope

11.4.4. 8, 8

11.5.1. hardware, software

11.5.2. The test ROM can put a known pattern on the buses allowing the basic pieces of the system (address decoders, buffers, control logic gating) to be easily tested.

11.5.3. Timing mode: data is displayed as voltage waveforms. State mode: data is displayed as the hex, ASCII, or instruction mnemonic equivalent.

12

Introduction to the 8086 16-Bit Microprocessor

"Just when you think you understand the picture, the picture changes." This was the key line in an advertisement that ran on television several years ago. Anyone who has studied electronics soon learns this (sad?) lesson. It took only two years for the 8-bit microprocessor to replace the early 4-bit chips. Now we have 16-bit, 32-bit, even 64-bit microprocessors. Clock speeds have gone from 1 or 2 MHz to over 30 MHz today. By the time you sit down and study one chip, it has been obsoleted by another!

Or has it? Although this book is written around the 8080, 8085, and Z-80, what we have really been studying is *microprocessor technology*. What is a RAM chip, a ROM, and how do we connect these parts to a microprocessor? How do we interface a parallel printer, or monitor a temperature sensor, or control a mechanical relay? What if your software doesn't run as expected? How do you go about trouble-shooting it? This is what microprocessor technology is all about.

As you read this chapter and study the 16-bit 8086 microprocessor, you will find all of the concepts studied in the previous chapters still apply. The memory and I/O interfaces still require address decoders and buffers. Output ports are still built from latches, input ports from tri-state gates.

The main difference is the *width* of the data bus. Sixteen bits of data can now be fetched from memory instead of eight. The internal registers are also 16 bits wide. This allows more data to be manipulated at a given time. The result is faster program execution.

Electrically, the 8086 appears similar to the 8085. It uses a multiplexed address/data bus and an 8085-like set of control signals—ALE, $M/\overline{IO}$, $\overline{RD}$, $\overline{WR}$, and $\overline{INTA}$. Twenty address lines are provided. This means the 8086 can potentially access as much as 1 MB of memory.

The 8086 is a good 16-bit chip to study. Its 8-bit cousin, the 8088 was used by IBM in its PC and XT computers. In addition the more powerful 80286, 80386, and 80486 microprocessors are all *object-code compatible*. This means programs written for the 8086 can be run on these processors without change. This makes the 8086 a good stepping-off point.

In this chapter we will first develop a CPU module for the 8086, learning about the support chips required. The programming model is presented next. Here you will learn about the internal registers available to the programmer. The instruction set is then surveyed and two examples of a program to fill a block of memory are presented.

The software sections are followed by discussions on memory and I/O interfacing. Included is an 8255A interface that provides three 16-bit input/output ports. The chapter concludes with a brief description of the other chips available in the 8086 family. These include the 8-bit 8088, the 16-bit 80286, and the 32-bit 80386 and 80486.

12.1 8086 HARDWARE DETAILS AND BASIC SYSTEM TIMING

As you read this section, look for the answers to these Key Concept questions:

12.1.1. The 8086 is divided into two separate processors called the _____ and _____ .

12.1.2. When used with the 8087 numeric coprocessor, the 8086 should be operated in the _____ mode.

12.1.3. List the three types of 8086 memory read/write cycles.

12.1.4. Each 8086 machine cycle requires _____ T states.

We began this book with a description of the stored program digital computer. It works by storing program instructions in a separate memory unit from which the CPU fetches commands arranged in a logical sequence. The process is called "fetch and execute."

The 16-bit 8086 still follows this basic principle. Where it differs from most 8-bit microprocessors is that it assigns two separate processors for the job. These are called the *execution unit* (EU) and the *bus interface unit* (BIU). Figure 12.1 illustrates this organization in a block diagram.

The BIU fetches instructions from memory and transfers data between the execution unit general registers and the outside world. The EU decodes the instructions and executes them.

The Queue. A unique feature of the 8086 is the use of an *instruction prefetch queue*. This is a six-byte (four-byte in the 8088) first-in, first-out storage area in the BIU used to save instructions that are pending execution in the EU. Because the queue will normally hold the next instruction to be executed, the fetch and execute phases of the classic stored program computer can *overlap*. While the EU is executing one instruc-

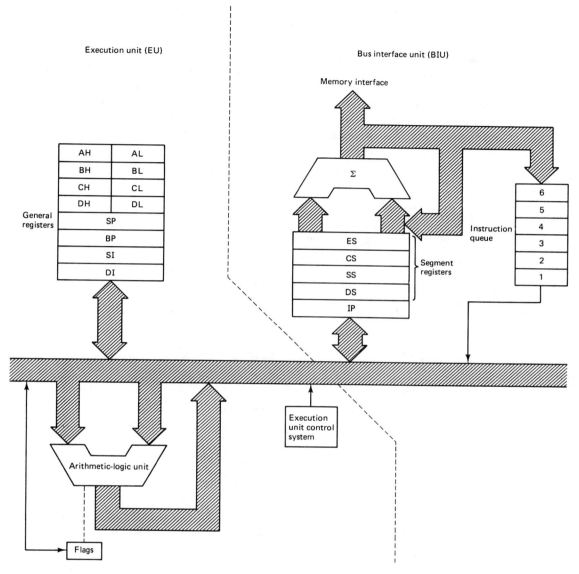

Execution unit (EU)

Bus interface unit (BIU)

Memory interface

General
registers

AH	AL
BH	BL
CH	CL
DH	DL
SP	
BP	
SI	
DI	

Σ

ES
CS
SS
DS
IP

Segment
registers

Instruction
queue

6
5
4
3
2
1

Execution
unit control
system

Arithmetic-logic unit

Flags

Figure 12.1 Block diagram of the 8086 microprocessor. The chip is made up of two processors: the execution unit (EU) and the bus interface unit (BIU).

tion, the BIU can be fetching another, ensuring that the queue will always be full and that no time will have to be spent waiting for an instruction fetch. This technique of allowing the fetch and execute cycles to overlap is also called "*pipelining.*"

It is interesting to note that the 8086 and 8088 differ only in the BIU. The BIU is 16 bits wide in the 8086 but 8 bits wide in the 8088. Not only does this technique decrease instruction execution times, it simplifies the task of redesigning the 8086 into an 8088—only the BIU need be redesigned.

The Min and Max Mode. The signal names for the 40-pin 8086 are given in Fig. 12.2. In order to maintain a 40-pin package and still provide 20 address lines, 16 data bus lines, and several control and status signals, nearly every pin of the 8086 is time *multiplexed*. This is a scheme in which a pin carries one type of signal during one time period and a different signal during another.

Consider first the data/address bus. These lines are labeled AD0–AD15 and

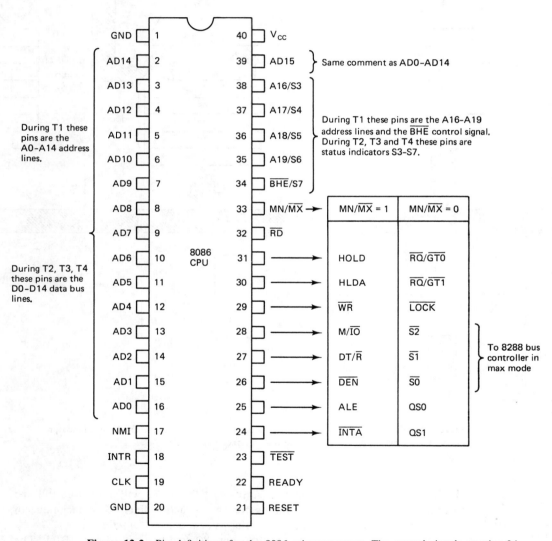

Figure 12.2 Pin definitions for the 8086 microprocessor. The control signals on pins 24 through 31 change depending on the mode of operation.

A16/S3–A19/S6. Like the 8085, AD0–AD15 and A16–A19 hold a valid address when pin 25, ALE (address latch enable), is high. When ALE is low, these lines carry the 16 data bus lines and status information on S3–S6.

A second group of multiplexed pins is controlled by the MN/$\overline{\text{MX}}$ input. When this pin is high, the *min mode* is selected and pins 24 through 31 take on the control signal definitions shown under the column MN/$\overline{\text{MX}}$ = 1 in Fig. 12.2. When operated in the min mode the 8086 presents a control bus similar to that of the 8085 and requires only an address latch and clock generator to form a CPU module (see Sec. 12.2).

When MN/$\overline{\text{MX}}$ is low, the *max mode* of operation is selected. This mode is intended for more complex applications in which the 8086 is supported by the 8087 numeric data processor and the 8089 I/O processor. The control signals on pins 24–31 change to become those shown under the column MN/$\overline{\text{MX}}$ = 0 in Fig. 12.2. In this mode a special bus controller (the 8288) is required to develop the memory and I/O control bus signals (see Sec. 12.2).

One of the philosophical changes Intel has made in developing its family of 16-bit microprocessors is to share the processing among several specialized *coprocessors*. These are optional processors that can be used to speed up math and I/O processing. In simpler (min mode) systems these chips can be omitted.

Memory Organization.

As mentioned, the 8086 (and 8088) has a 20-bit address bus. This allows the processor to access 2^{20} or 1,048,576 memory locations. But what is a memory location for a 16-bit microprocessor? Is it a 16-bit word or an 8-bit byte?

Figure 12.3(a) and (b) illustrates the two common ways for organizing the memory space of a 16-bit microprocessor. Both memories store 1,048,576 bytes (1 MB). The difference is that the organization in Fig. 12.3(a) can be accessed as a byte or a word while the organization in Fig. 12.3(b) must be accessed as a 16-bit word only. The 8086 uses the technique in Fig. 12.3(a).

Operation codes for the 8086 are all 8 bits in length, with the second through fifth bytes specifying the operand. Several instructions are only a single byte in length. Thus it is logical for the 8086 to be able to access its memory as a byte or a word.

There are actually three types of memory cycles:

1. Word access on AD0–AD15
2. Even-addressed byte on AD0–AD7
3. Odd-addressed byte on AD8–AD15

Table 12.1 helps explain how the 8086 identifies which type of memory access it is performing. The $\overline{\text{BHE}}$ (bus high enable) control bus signal—multiplexed with the S7 status signal—must be latched when ALE is high. This signal is then combined with A0 to determine the type of memory access. Be sure that you understand the consequences of this encoding. The A0 address line no longer connects to the memory devices. Instead, it is combined with $\overline{\text{BHE}}$ to generate an ODD BYTE SEL and EVEN BYTE SEL pair of control signals. This concept should become clearer when we study memory and I/O interfacing in Sec. 12.5.

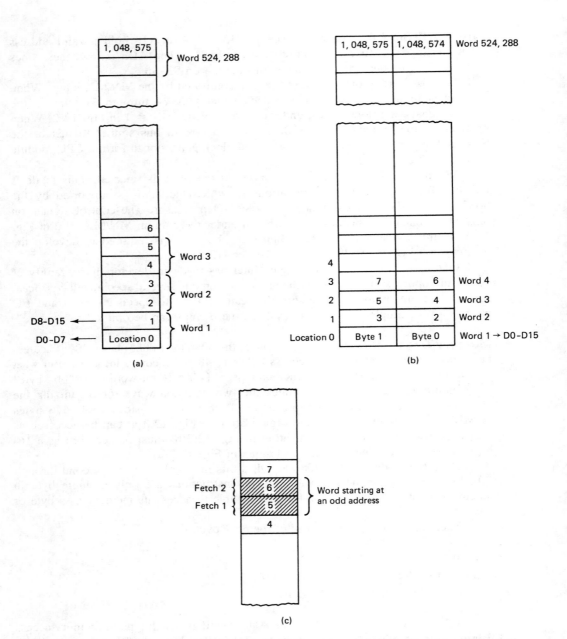

Figure 12.3 (a) and (b) Two methods for organizing a 16-bit memory; (c) a 16-bit word is stored at an odd address, causing the 8086 to perform two fetches to retrieve the full word.

TABLE 12.1 8086 MEMORY ACCESS ENCODING

BHE	A0	Action
0	0	Access 16-bit word
0	1	Access odd byte to D8–D15
1	0	Access even byte to D0–D7
1	1	No action

From a speed standpoint it is most advantageous for the 8086 to access the memory as 16-bit words. In this way one memory cycle brings two bytes into the BIU via AD0–AD15. However, referring to Table 12.1, this can happen only when A0 is low (that is, the word must be stored at an *even address*). If a 16-bit word is stored beginning at an *odd address*, two memory cycles will be required to fetch both bytes. This is illustrated in Fig. 12.3(c).

The BIU handles the job of determining the type of memory access automatically and the programmer need not be concerned except to be aware that four extra clock states are required for words stored at odd addresses. Indeed, the 8088 suffers this speed penalty with every memory access because its data bus is only 8 bits wide.

A memory with a 20-bit address will also cause us to "rethink" our memory-map nomenclature. Figure 12.4 shows such a map divided into 16 "64K pages." Note that five hex digits are required to describe any one address. This is a convenient

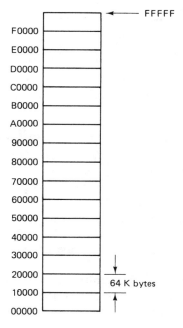

Figure 12.4 Memory map for the 1 MB of memory accessible by 8086 and 8088 microprocessors. Sixteen pages of 64K bytes each are provided.

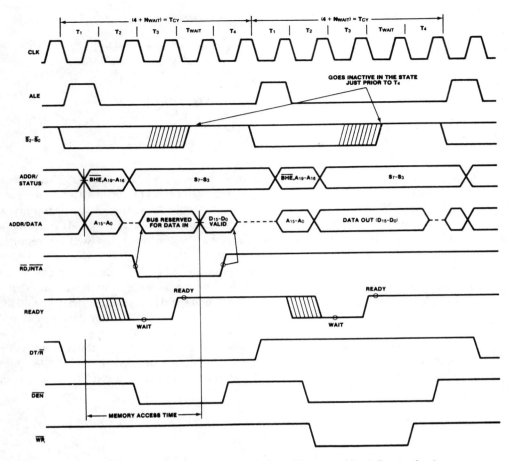

Figure 12.5 8086 basic system timing. (Courtesy of Intel Corporation.)

way of drawing the map because the most significant hex digit increments by 1 with each new (64K) page.

Basic System Timing. Figure 12.5 illustrates 8086 system timing. Each machine cycle consists of four T states (plus any WAIT states if requested). All read or write cycles begin with an ALE pulse, which should be used to latch AD0–AD19 for a memory address, AD0–AD15 for an I/O address, and $\overline{\text{BHE}}$ to determine if a word or byte is to be accessed.

In the max mode status signals $\overline{\text{S0}}$, $\overline{\text{S1}}$, and $\overline{\text{S2}}$ are decoded by the 8288 bus controller to provide the I/O and memory control signals. The eight possible "status words" are listed in Table 12.2. Note that the control bus output by the 8288 is similar to that of the 8080.

In the min mode $M/\overline{\text{IO}}$ can be combined with $\overline{\text{RD}}$ and $\overline{\text{WR}}$ to decode memory and I/O operations. The result is a control bus nearly identical to that of the 8085.

The 8086 (and 8088) provide two signals for controlling data bus buffers.

TABLE 12.2 8288 STATUS WORDS BASED ON THE $\overline{S0}$, $\overline{S1}$, AND $\overline{S2}$ MAX MODE STATUS SIGNALS

$\overline{S2}$	$\overline{S1}$	$\overline{S0}$	Processor state	8288 active output
0	0	0	Interrupt acknowledge	$\overline{INTA}$
0	0	1	Read I/O port	$\overline{IORC}$
0	1	0	Write I/O port	$\overline{IOWC}$ (also advanced $\overline{IOWC}$)
0	1	1	Halt	None
1	0	0	Code access	$\overline{MRDC}$
1	0	1	Read memory	$\overline{MRDC}$
1	1	0	Write memory	$\overline{MWTC}$ (also advanced $\overline{MWTC}$)
1	1	1	Passive	None

These are DT/$\overline{R}$ (data transmit/receive) and $\overline{DEN}$ (data enable). $\overline{DEN}$ is low whenever the processor is using its data bus and can be used to enable a set of bidirectional bus buffers. DT/$\overline{R}$ is normally used to control the *direction* of data through the buffers. When DT/$\overline{R}$ is low, the buffers should be enabled to input data off the system data bus lines.

The status signals S3–S7 are multiplexed with A16–A19 and $\overline{BHE}$. They hold valid status information when ALE is low. The S3 and S4 status outputs indicate which segment register (see Sec. 12.3) is in use for the current bus cycle. S5 reflects the status of the internal interrupts enabled flag bit, S6 = 0, and S7 is a spare status bit.

The remaining min mode control bus signals have functions similar to their counterparts in the 8080 and 8085. This group includes HOLD, HLDA, and $\overline{INTA}$.

In the max mode, $\overline{RQ/GT0}$ and $\overline{RQ/GT1}$ are intended for use with the 8087 numeric data processor. These lines are bidirectional and allow the coprocessor to request control of the buses when it must access system memory. The 8086 grants control of the buses by pulsing these lines for one clock cycle. The $\overline{LOCK}$ signal is also intended for the 8087 coprocessor. When active it indicates that the 8087 should not attempt to gain control of the system buses. This is necessary when updating information in memory that the 8087 will in turn be processing. It is used in conjunction with the *LOCK* instruction.

QS0 and QS1 are status signals also intended for the 8087. They are used by the 8087 to synchronize its queue with that of the 8086.

The $\overline{TEST}$ input can be monitored in software (with the *WAIT* instruction). If this line is found high, the 8086 will idle until $\overline{TEST}$ = 0. This signal is again intended for the 8087. When the 8086 needs a result from the 8087, it can execute a *WAIT* instruction to ensure that the calculation has been completed by the 8087 before continuing.

The READY input provides a means to synchronize the processor to slow memories, as does the same signal on the 8080 and 8085. RESET forces the 8086 to fetch its next instruction from memory location FFFF0H. Normally, a jump instruction would be stored here, transferring control to the main program.

There are two interrupt inputs, labeled INTR and NMI. INTR can be masked by resetting the interrupt enable flag bit. The NMI input is nonmaskable. Like the 8080 INTR input, the interrupting device must supply an 8-bit "type" number during $\overline{\text{INTA}}$. The 8086 multiplies this number by 4 and fetches a four-byte jump address from that location (and the next three consecutive bytes) as the location of the interrupt service routine. The first 1K of memory is reserved for interrupt jump addresses corresponding to the 256 possible type numbers. The NMI input automatically retrieves its ISR address from location 00008H–0000BH.

Example 12.1

An interrupting device gates 03 onto AD0–AD7 when $\overline{\text{INTA}}$ is low. Where should the interrupt jump address be located in memory?

Solution. The address is found as $3 \times 4 = 12 = 0CH$. The jump address should be stored in 0000CH–0000FH.

Note: Section 12.3 will explain the segment registers and show how four bytes can be combined to form the 20-bit physical address.

Interrupt requests can also be initiated via software and this technique is discussed in Sec. 12.4.

Special Support Chips. Because of the dual and specialized nature of many of the 8086 signals, Intel has developed several support devices designed to simplify the task of building an 8086 microcomputer system. Figure 12.6 identifies these chips by function and part number.

The 8086 requires an external clock signal and this function is provided by the 8284 clock generator. The 8286 is an octal data transceiver similar to the 74LS245. The 8282 is an octal latch specifically designed to demultiplex the address/data bus of the 8086. It is similar to the 74LS373. Note that three latches are required for the 20-bit address bus. The 8288 bus controller is required in all max mode designs and it decodes $\overline{S0}$, $\overline{S1}$, and $\overline{S2}$ to provide the system control bus.

Also shown in Fig. 12.6 are the optional coprocessors designed to enhance system throughput. The 8087 numeric data processor (NDP) executes special instructions prefixed by an *ESCAPE* command. These include exponential, logarithmic, and trignometric math functions. The 8087 can speed up the calculation of these functions by a factor of 100 or more. For example, a square-root routine written for the 8086 will require 19,600 μs with a 5-MHz 8086 but only 36 μs with a 5-MHz 8087 NDP!

The 8089 has two dedicated I/O channels that can function independent of the 8086 processor. The 8089 can be operated as a DMA controller or as a programmable peripheral controller device. What separates the 8089 from other peripheral controllers is its own built-in instruction set, which allows it to transfer data to or from the processor's I/O and memory.

In conclusion, we can say that the 8086 still follows the principles set down in Chap. 1 for a stored program computer. However, it allows the basic fetch and execute cycles to be overlapped through the use of two separate processors, called

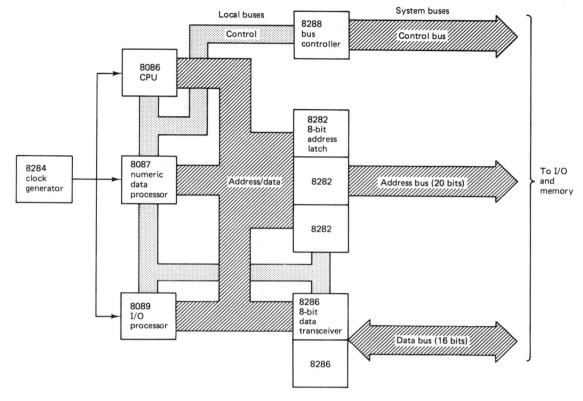

Figure 12.6 The 8086 is supported by several special ICs designed to interface with the specialized local buses of the processor.

the EU and BIU. Externally, the three bus system architecture is still followed but is broken into a specialized set of *local* buses and a conventional set of *system* buses. This is shown in Fig. 12.6.

12.2 MIN AND MAX MODE CPU MODULES FOR THE 8086

As you read this section, look for the answers to these Key Concept questions:

12.2.1. What is the purpose of the 8284 in an 8086 microcomputer system?

12.2.2. What signal is provided by the 8086 to demultiplex the address/data bus?

12.2.3. What two signals are used by the 8086 to control the data bus buffers?

12.2.4. In which operating mode is the 8288 bus controller required?

The CPU module has been consistently emphasized throughout this book. It is this module that provides all bus signals to the microcomputer system. It must develop the system clock signal, provide a means for resetting the processor, allow interrupts and DMA activities, and for the special case of the 8086 (and 8088), demultiplex the address and data bus lines. Bus buffering must be incorporated to allow for reliable system expansion without loading problems.

In this section we will examine the two ways in which an 8086 CPU module can be formed. These are based on the min and max modes of operation. Once the CPU module has been defined, we can proceed to interface memory and I/O to complete the job of designing an 8086-based microcomputer system. This is the subject of Sec. 12.5.

The Min Mode.   The min and max modes of the 8086 operation are sufficiently different that the designer must choose one operating mode and design the system to that mode. Figure 12.7 shows a CPU module based on the min mode of operation. In this mode the 8086 develops its own set of control bus signals (without the 8288) and provides a bus interface very similar to that of the 8085.

Consider the following points about this circuit:

1. The 8284 is used to develop the system clock signal. The clock frequency generated will be one-third of the external crystal frequency. The clock signal itself has a 30% duty cycle and switches between 0 and 4.5 V. The 8284 also accepts *WAIT* requests via the READY input and synchronizes these to the system clock. The RESET circuit functions similar to those described in Chap. 4 and provides for a power-on reset function.

2. The 20-bit address is demultiplexed with three 8282 octal latches. ALE is used to strobe data into the latches and data is stored with the falling edge of this signal. Note that $\overline{BHE}$ is also latched by ALE.

3. The data bus is buffered by two 8286 octal transceivers. As mentioned before, $\overline{DEN}$ and DT/$\overline{R}$ are output by the processor specifically for the purpose of controlling these buffers.

4. The control bus signals are identical to those of the 8085 (except that M/$\overline{IOB}$ must be inverted) and are buffered with one 74LS244.

5. The INTR, NMI, and HOLD inputs are active high and therefore held low with 1-kΩ resistors. The HLDA output is buffered and is available for DMA applications.

The control bus could be decoded to provide an ''8080-like'' control bus if desired (this was done for the 8085 CPU module in Fig. 4.26). Another option is to include the decoding as part of the address decoding logic associated with the memory or I/O interface.

Table 12.3 compares the 8286 electrical capabilities with those of the more familiar 74LS245. If we allow a V_{OL} of 0.45 V, the 8286 exceeds the specifications of the 74LS245 in all categories except for I_{IH}.

Table 12.4 provides a similar comparison between the 8282 octal latch and the 74LS373. Again, if the higher V_{OL} level is acceptable, the 8282 exceeds the capabilities of the 74LS373.

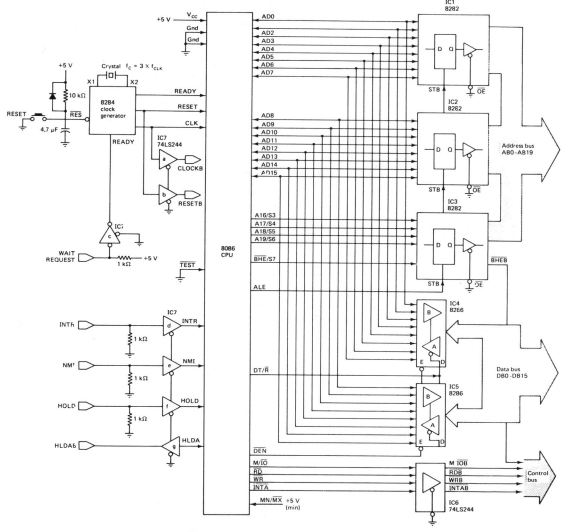

Figure 12.7 Min mode 8086 CPU module.

TABLE 12.3 COMPARING THE
ELECTRICAL SPECIFICATIONS OF THE 8286
AND 74LS245 OCTAL TRANSCEIVERS

	8286	74LS245
I_{OL}	32 mA at 0.45 V	12 mA at 0.4 V
I_{OH}	5 mA at 2.4 V	3 mA at 2.4 V
I_{IL}	0.2 mA	0.2 mA
I_{IH}	50 μA	20 μA

TABLE 12.4 COMPARING THE ELECTRICAL
SPECIFICATIONS OF THE 8282
AND 74LS373 OCTAL LATCHES

	8282	74LS373
I_{OL}	32 mA at 0.45 V	12 mA at 0.4 V
I_{OH}	5 mA at 2.4 V	2.6 mA at 2.4 V

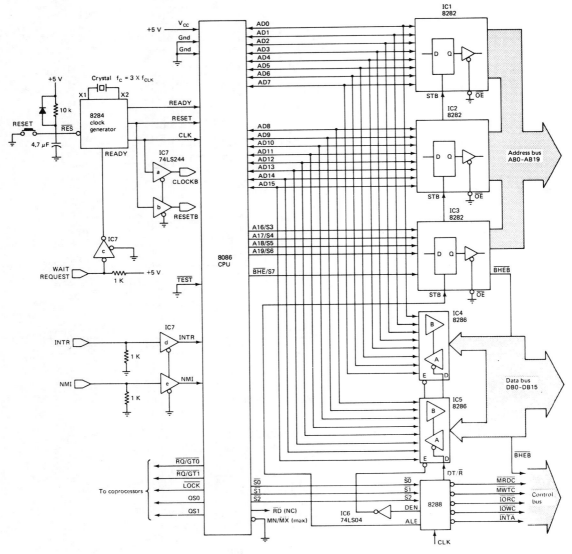

Figure 12.8 Max mode 8086 CPU module.

The Max Mode. Figure 12.8 illustrates a CPU module for the 8086 when operated in the max mode. The clock, data bus, and address bus connections do not change from the min mode diagram in Fig. 12.7. However, the former control bus signals, ALE, DT/$\overline{\text{R}}$, $\overline{\text{DEN}}$, M/$\overline{\text{IO}}$, $\overline{\text{WR}}$, and $\overline{\text{INTA}}$, plus the HOLD and HLDA pins, all have new signal names. This was shown in Fig. 12.2 (see pins 24 through 31). Five of these eight signals become special control signals for the 8087 and 8089 coprocessors. These are $\overline{\text{RQ}}/\overline{\text{GT0}}$, $\overline{\text{RQ}}/\overline{\text{GT1}}$, $\overline{\text{LOCK}}$, QS0, and QS1.

The remaining three signals are now called $\overline{\text{S0}}$, $\overline{\text{S1}}$, and $\overline{\text{S2}}$ and are decoded by the 8288 to provide the new max mode control bus $\overline{\text{MRDC}}$, $\overline{\text{MWTC}}$, $\overline{\text{IORC}}$, $\overline{\text{IOWC}}$, and $\overline{\text{INTA}}$. Note that these are in an "8080-like" form. The 8288 also generates the buffer control signals lost when the max mode was selected. This includes DT/$\overline{\text{R}}$, DEN, and ALE. Note that the 8288 outputs DEN, not $\overline{\text{DEN}}$.

The HOLD and HLDA signals appear to be lost. Actually, they are renamed $\overline{\text{RQ}}/\overline{\text{GT0}}$ and $\overline{\text{RQ}}/\overline{\text{GT1}}$ (request/grant). Other local bus masters (such as the 8089 I/O processor) can request (and be granted) control of the local bus via these two pins.

12.3 A PROGRAMMING MODEL FOR THE 8086

As you read this section, look for the answers to these Key Concept questions:

12.3.1. Explain the difference between 8086 registers AH, AL, and AX.

12.3.2. In which 8086 memory segment are the instruction codes stored?

12.3.3. Explain the difference between a logical address and a physical address.

12.3.4. The instruction MOV AX,(BP)+6 uses the _____ addressing mode and copies the word pointed to by register BP + 6 in the _____ segment to register AX.

As an 8086 programmer you are less interested in the electrical interface required between the 8086 and its support chips and more interested in the size and number of registers and how the instruction set is used to manipulate data within these registers. In this section we develop this programming model and survey the instruction set in Sec. 12.4.

Internal Register Array. One view of the internal architecture of the 8086 has been presented in Fig. 12.1. In this model the 8086 is broken into two processors, called the EU and BIU. Note that each processor has a set of registers. In the BIU these are called the *segment registers* and will be discussed in detail in the next subsection. The registers of the EU form the *programming model*. Figure 12.9 provides a closer look.

Perhaps one of the most interesting features of the 8086 register array is that it is not too different from the 8080/85 set of registers. These are shown shaded in Fig. 12.9 and their 8080/85 names are enclosed in parentheses. The main differences are:

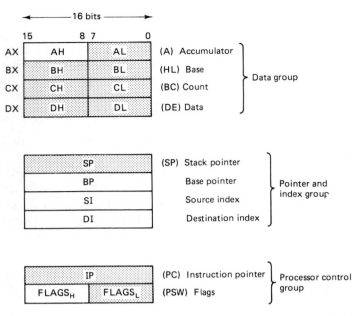

Figure 12.9 8086 programming model. The shaded registers are the 8080/85 equivalents.

1. The 8086 accumulator is 16 bits wide.
2. The 8086 has two 16-bit index registers and a 16-bit pointer register not present in the 8080/85.
3. The 8086 flag word is 16 bits wide.

Recalling the 8086's ability to manipulate bytes as well as 16-bit words, the four data registers (AX, BX, CX, and DX) can be read as a word or a high or low byte. For example, CH represents the 8 high-order bits of 16-bit register CX. Similarly, CL represents the low 8 bits of this register.

The stack pointer register performs the same function as it does in the 8080/85. A new addition is register BP, which can be used as a second stack pointer. This is useful for passing parameters to a subroutine on the stack. Register BP can point at the parameters without disturbing the stack pointer itself (and the subroutine return address).

Registers SI and DI are used as pointers for the indirect and indexed addressing modes. For example, a typical instruction might move the data byte pointed at by the source index (SI) to the memory location pointed at by the destination index (DI).

The 8080/85's program counter is called the *instruction pointer* (IP) in the 8086, but performs nearly identically. It points to the next instruction or operand to be brought into the prefetch queue.

A unique feature of the 8086 is that many of its instructions require that

TABLE 12.5 GENERAL REGISTERS WITH DEDICATED USES

Register	Dedicated operation
AX	Word multiply, word divide, word I/O
AL	Byte multiply, byte divide, byte I/O, translate, decimal arithmetic
AH	Byte multiply, byte divide
BX	Translate
CX	String operations, loops
CL	Variable shift and rotate
DX	Word multiply, word divide, indirect I/O
SP	Stack operations
SI	String operations
DI	String operations

specific registers be used. The use of the SI and DI registers as source and destination pointers has already been mentioned. Table 12.5 indicates the assignments for all of the registers. Until we examine the instruction set, these definitions may not be too meaningful, but the point to note is that the programmer is not always free to use any register that he or she wishes when developing an 8086 program.

The 8086 flag word is shown in Fig. 12.10. To simplify the conversion of 8080/85 programs to the 8086, the low 8 bits of the flag word are identical to those of the 8080/85. Three of the four new flag bits are actually *control* flags. When the TF flag is set, the 8086 operates in the single-step mode, branching to the address stored in 00004–00007 after each instruction. This can be a routine to display the contents of the various registers to aid in software debugging.

The IF flag, when set, enables interrupts on the INTR input. The DF flag is used with the string or block instructions. When set, the memory pointer decrements after each transfer; if reset, the pointer increments.

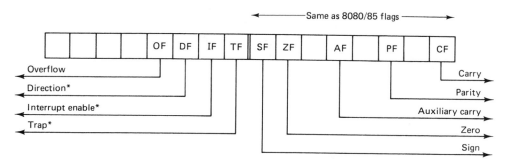

*These three flags can be set or reset to control the operation of the processor. The remaining flags are status indicators.

Figure 12.10 8086 flag word.

Sec. 12.3 A Programming Model for the 8086

617

Overflow is a new status flag. When set it represents an error condition, due to a math operation causing the sign bit to change.

Segment Registers.   Although Fig. 12.4 shows the 1-MB address space of the 8086 as a linear sequence of 8-bit memory locations, the memory is not actually used in this way. Instead, only four 64K pages or *segments* are active at any given time. This is shown in Fig. 12.11. The four segment registers of the BIU are used as pointers to location 0 of each four segments, called the *code*, *data*, *stack*, and *extra* segments.

By segmenting its memory the 8086 can devote one segment to the program op-codes (the code segment), another for program data (the data segment), another for the stack (the stack segment), and a fourth as an extra segment.

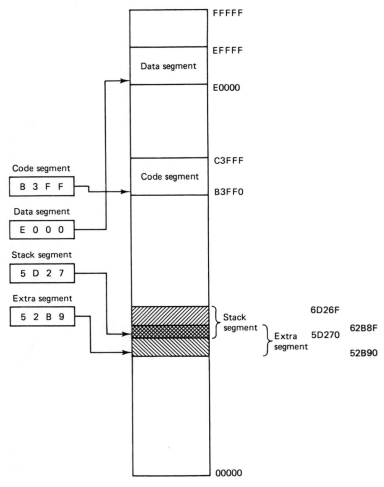

Figure 12.11   The full 1 MB of 8086 memory space is accessed in 64K byte segments. Only four segments are active at a given time, determined by the segment registers in the BIU.

The segment registers also allow the 16-bit EU registers to be used as memory pointers even though the memory address is 20 bits long. The "trick" is to force the low 4 bits of the segment address to be 0. Thus in Fig. 12.11 the code segment register contains B3FF but should be interpreted as pointing to address B3FF0. Similarly, the extra segment register points at 52B90.

Example 12.2

Referring to Fig. 12.11, calculate the starting and ending address of the stack segment of memory.

Solution. Forming the 20-bit address by appending four 0s to the stack segment register, the starting address is 5D270. The last address can be found by adding FFFFH (that is, 64K).

$$
\begin{array}{r}
5D270 \\
+\,0FFFF \\
\hline
6D26F
\end{array}
$$

The four 64K segments can be located anywhere within the 1-MB memory space of the 8086 but must begin at an address divisible by 16 (that is, the low 4 bits must be 0). As Fig. 12.11 illustrates, the location of the segments can result in any order, including disjoint, partially overlapping, and fully overlapping.

Because of the memory segmenting, there are two types of memory address associated with each program. These are called the *logical address* and the *physical address*. The logical address ranges from 0 to 65535 (FFFFH) and corresponds to the 64K locations within one segment. When developing small programs, these are the only addresses that the programmer need worry about.

The physical address corresponds to the actual address output by the 8086 on the AD0–AD19 address lines. This address is formed by combining the logical address as an *offset* to the base segment address.

Example 12.3

If register SI = 0005H, what memory location will be accessed as the string source using the segment definitions shown in Fig. 12.11?

Solution. String operations work on data in the data segment. To calculate the string address, add the contents of register SI to the data segment register with four appended 0s.

$$
\begin{array}{r}
DS \rightarrow E0000 \\
+\ \ 0005 \\
\hline
E0005
\end{array}
$$

The byte will be fetched from physical address E0005H.

Once the segment registers have been loaded, the programmer need not be concerned with the physical address. In Ex. 12.3 the source of data is simply thought of as offset by 0005 locations from the start of the data segment (wherever that is in the physical address space).

Instruction fetches work in a similar manner. If register IP = 2600, then

TABLE 12.6 DEFAULT MEMORY SEGMENT ASSIGNMENTS FOR EACH TYPE OF MEMORY REFERENCE

Type of memory reference	Default segment	Alternate segment	Offset (logical address)
Instruction fetch	CS	None	IP
Stack operation	SS	None	SP
Variable	DS	CS, ES, SS	Effective address
String (source)	DS	CS, ES, SS	SI
String (destination)	ES	None	DI
BP used as base register	SS	CS, ES, SS	Effective address

using the contents of the code segment register in Fig. 12.11, the next fetch will come from

$$\begin{array}{r} \text{CS} \rightarrow \text{B3FF0} \\ + \quad 2600 \\ \hline \text{B65F0} \end{array}$$

One of the advantages of the logical address concept is that programs can be dynamically relocated to run anywhere within the 1-MB address space of the processor. This is because *the logical address is always the same*, *no matter what the physical address*. This also has advantages when working with large data files of similar information. A whole new set of data can be operated on with the same program simply by changing the contents of the data segment register to the address of the new data file.

Just as all of the general registers have dedicated uses depending on the instruction being executed (see Table 12.5), each type of physical memory reference has a dedicated segment register. The default segment assignments are shown in Table 12.6. For example, all instruction fetches use the code segment (CS) with the offset supplied by register IP. String sources are accessed from the data segment (DS) with register SI supplying the offset. String destinations are accessed with ES as the segment address and DI as the offset. Note that the segment register for some types of memory references can be changed from the default setting obtained at power-on.

Summarizing the 8086's segmented memory, we can say:

1. The physical address is 20 bits long.
2. The logical address is 16 bits long.
3. The physical address is formed by adding the logical address as an offset to the segment address (with four appended 0s).
4. The segment address must begin at an address that is a multiple of 16.
5. The segment address will vary depending on the segment register to be used.

In the remainder of this chapter the term ''offset'' will mean the logical address within a particular 64K segment.

Addressing Modes. The 8086 expands on the four addressing modes of the 8080/ 85 (and six of the Z-80) to include the nine modes listed in Table 12.7. The table indicates where the data to be manipulated is obtained from or written to and which registers are involved. Also shown is a sample 8086 mnemonic and a symbolic interpretation of the instruction. For example, in the immediate addressing mode, the instruction MOV AX,1000H loads the AX register with the 16-bit word 1000H.

The first four addressing modes should be familiar from their 8080/85 and Z-80 equivalents. The *register indirect* mode is similar to the 8080/85's use of the HL pair but can use the SI, DI, BX, or BP registers. Instructions using the indexed addressing mode must supply a displacement in addition to the offset in the SI or DI pointer registers.

The *relative* addressing mode is used with the transfer instructions to transfer

TABLE 12.7 ADDRESSING MODES OF THE 8086 MICROPROCESSOR

Mode	Physical memory location	Examples (using MOV)	
		Mnemonic	Symbolic
Immediate	Within instruction + code segment	MOV AX,1000H	$10 \rightarrow$ AH $00 \rightarrow$ AL
Register	In register + code segment	MOV BX,DX	DL $\rightarrow$ BL DH $\rightarrow$ BH
Direct	Address + segment	MOV 8000H,BX	BL $\rightarrow$ (8000) BH $\rightarrow$ (8001)
Register indirect	SI + segment DI + segment BX + segment BP + segment	MOV CX,(BX)	(BX) $\rightarrow$ CL
Indexed	SI + displacement + segment DI + displacement + segment	MOV AL,(SI)+6	(SI+6) $\rightarrow$ AL
Relative	Displacement + IP + code segment	JMP target	Displacement + IP $\rightarrow$ IP
Based	BX + displacement + segment BP + displacement + segment	MOV (BX)+6,AL	AL $\rightarrow$ (BX+6)
Based and indexed	BX + SI + segment BX + DI + segment BP + SI + segment BP + DI + segment	MOV DX,(BX+DI)	(BX+DI) $\rightarrow$ DL (BX+DI+1) $\rightarrow$ DH
Based and indexed with displacement	BX + SI + displ. + segment BX + DI + displ. + segment BP + SI + displ. + segment BP + DI + displ. + segment	MOV (BX+DI)+5,DX	DL $\rightarrow$ (BX+DI+5) DH $\rightarrow$ (BX+DI+6)

Notes:

1. All operands of the form destination, source
2. Parentheses indicate the contents of memory addressed by the operand
3. In all cases the operand specifies an offset that must be added to the proper segment register contents to form the physical address
4. Table 12.6 indicates the default segment register to be used depending on the type of memory reference

control ahead or behind the present instruction pointer location. This allows position independent code within a given segment. Both the relative and indexed addressing modes are also supported by the Z-80.

There are three new addressing modes not available with the 8080/85 or Z-80. The *based mode* is similar to the indexed mode but uses the BX or BP registers plus a displacement to locate the data. The *based and indexed mode* (without displacement) forms the offset by adding the contents of BX or BP to the contents of SI or DI. The offset is then combined with the segment register to form the physical address. The *based and indexed with displacement mode* is similar but allows the instruction to supply a displacement as well.

12.4 PROGRAMMING THE 8086

As you read this section, look for the answers to these Key Concept questions:

12.4.1. The indirect I/O instructions use register _____ to hold a 16-bit port address.

12.4.2. Which CPU registers store the result of the instruction MUL BX?

12.4.3. Which type of jump instruction is required to transfer control to a program in a different code segment?

12.4.4. What is a software interrupt?

The mnemonics used in Table 12.7 give an indication of the form and complexity of the 8086 instruction set. The mnemonics themselves are similar to those of the 8080/85 but are more general purpose. For example, the 8086 *MOV* op-code replaces such 8080/85 op-codes as *LXI, LDA, STA, MVI,* and *STAX*. This makes it simpler to form the desired instruction (somewhat like the Z-80 instruction set).

Because the 8080/85 registers can be considered a subset of the 8086 register set, it is possible to convert 8080/85 programs to run on the 8086 using a *translator*. This is a program that accepts 8080/85 assembly code and outputs 8086 assembly code. The resulting programs are not as efficient and require more memory than an 8086 program designed specifically for the purpose. However, it is a quick way of upgrading large numbers of 8080/85 programs to the more powerful 8086.

Several new operations are possible with the 8086 that were not available with the 8080/85. These include:

1. Byte and word multiply and divide instructions
2. Block moves and compares
3. Byte translations
4. Software interrupts
5. Program loop instructions (for example, loop until zero)
6. Multiprocessor or coprocessor coordination
7. Nondestructive bit testing

Because of the large number of instructions and addressing modes (there are over 1000 different variations of the 8086 instruction set), hand assembly of 8086 programs is extremely tedious. Serious work should be attempted only using an editor and 8086 assembler.

In this section we briefly examine the various instruction groups and look at example instructions within each group. We will conclude this section by writing two versions of the block fill program from Chap. 3.

Data Transfer Group. Table 12.8 lists the form of the instructions in the data transfer group. In general, each instruction could use any of the addressing modes listed in Table 12.7 (except relative). The MOV instructions allow 8- or 16-bit data to be moved between registers, or between memory and the CPU registers. Note that the segment registers are loaded in this way.

The XCHG command is similar to the 8080/85 instruction XCHG but can be used to exchange 8- or 16-bit registers or an 8-bit register with a memory location.

LAHF and SAHF allow the 8086 to access the 8080/85 flag word directly, assisting in the conversion of these programs to the 8086.

The 8086, like the 8080/85, has only two I/O instructions. However, these instructions may be used in two ways. In the *direct* mode the I/O instructions are similar to those of the 8080/85, inputting or outputting 8- or 16-bit data from register AL or AX to the 8-bit port or consecutive ports whose address is carried by AD0–AD7.

TABLE 12.8 DATA TRANSFER GROUP OF INSTRUCTIONS

General mnemonic	Sample	Description of operation
MOV dest,source	MOV DS,AX	Put a copy of AX in DS
PUSH source	PUSH BX	Push BX onto stack top
POP dest	POP ES	Pop stack top into ES
PUSHF	Same[a]	Push flags onto stack top
POPF	Same[a]	Pop stack top into flag register
XCHG op1,op2	XCHG AL,BL	Exchange contents of AL and BL
LAHF	Same[a]	Copy 8080/85 flags into AH
SAHF	Same[a]	Copy AH into the 8080/85 flags
IN acc,port	IN AL,DX (indirect)	Input a byte to AL from the port whose address is in DX
OUT port,acc	OUT 27H,AX (direct)	Output AX to port 27H and 28H
LEA dest,source	LEA DX,TABLE	Load DX with the address of TABLE
LDS dest,source	LDS DX,TABLE	Load DX with (TABLE) and (TABLE+1) Load DS with (TABLE+2) and (TABLE+3)
LES dest,source	LES CX,TABLE	Load CX with (TABLE) and (TABLE+1) Load ES with (TABLE+2) and (TABLE+3)
XLAT	XLAT TABLE	AL is replaced with (BX+AL)

[a] Use the general mnemonic.

In the *indirect* mode register DX is used to hold a 16-bit port address and data may be 8 or 16 bits wide. This mode can accommodate up to 65,536 unique I/O ports. Data is still required to flow through the accumulator, however. A significant advantage to the indirect mode is that the port address can be changed by the program [unlike the 8080/85 but similar to the Z-80's OUT (C),r].

TABLE 12.9 ARITHMETIC GROUP OF INSTRUCTIONS

General mnemonic	Sample	Description of operation
ADD dest,source	ADD DX,BX	Replace DX with DX+BX
ADC dest,source	ADC DX,BX	Replace DX with DX+BX+CF
SUB dest,source	SUB CX,1000H	Replace CX with CX−1000H
SBB dest,source	SBB CX,1000H	Replace CX with CX−1000H−CF
INC dest	INC DI	Replace DI with DI+1 (flags affected)
DEC dest	DEC CL	Replace CL with CL−1
NEG dest	NEG AX	Replace AX with the 2's complement of AX; set OF if AX = 8000H or 0080H
CMP dest,source	CMP AX,BX	Set flag based on AX−BX
MUL source	MUL BX	Unsigned multiply—BX times AX; store the result in DX and AX
IMUL source	IMUL BX	Signed multiply—BX times AX; store the result in DX and AX
DIV source	DIV BX	Unsigned division—DX,AX by BX; store the result in AX and the remainder in DX
IDIV source	IDIV BX	Signed division—DX,AX by BX; store the result in AX and the remainder in DX
CBW	Same[a]	Convert signed AL byte to signed AX word
CWD	Same[a]	Convert signed word in AX to signed double word in AX,DX
DAA	Same[a]	Adjust AL after the addition of two packed BCD numbers
DAS	Same[a]	Adjust AL after the subtraction of two packed BCD numbers
AAA	Same[a]	Adjust AL after the addition of two unpacked BCD numbers
AAS	Same[a]	Adjust AL after the subtraction of two unpacked BCD numbers
AAM	Same[a]	Adjust AX after the multiplication of two unpacked BCD numbers
AAD	Same[a]	Adjust AX after the division of two unpacked BCD numbers

[a] Use the general mnemonic.

There are three load commands that can be used to fill CPU registers with the address or contents of memory locations. LDS and LES are 32-bit load operations, filling the ES or DS segment registers and a general register. LEA loads the destination operand with the *address* of the source operand.

The XLAT instruction uses register AL as an 8-bit offset pointer into a table with base address in BX. The byte found replaces the byte in register AL.

Arithmetic Group. Table 12.9 summarizes the arithmetic group of instructions. The add and subtract (with and without carry or borrow) are similar to those of the 8080/85 but work on 8- or 16-bit data. Also note that the accumulator does not have to be used as the destination or source of data.

The INC and DEC instructions are also similar to those of the 8080/85. Because the 16-bit increments (or decrements) affect all flags, 16-bit counters can easily be tested for 0 (unlike the 8080/85's INX or DCX instructions).

The multiplication and division instructions require specific registers for one of the operands and the result, as shown in Fig. 12.12. Either signed or unsigned operations are possible on 8- or 16-bit data. It is interesting to note that a 5-MHz 8086 8-bit multiplication will require approximately 16 μs. The Z-80 8-bit multiplication routine developed in Chap. 3 as Program 5 requires approximately 100 μs (at 4 MHz).

The CBW and CWD instructions are used with the multiplication and division instructions to extend signed bytes into words and signed words into double words maintaining the proper sign.

The decimal adjust instructions are used after addition and subtraction instructions to ensure that register AL contains a valid BCD number.

The ASCII adjust instructions work with unpacked BCD numbers (one digit/byte). They are used after any of the four math operations to adjust the accumulator to an unpacked BCD number with the most significant four bits 0.

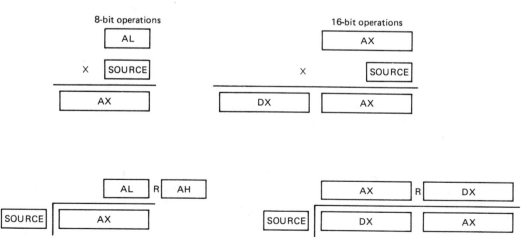

Figure 12.12 The multiply and divide instructions require one of the operands and the result to be in dedicated registers.

TABLE 12.10 BIT MANIPULATION GROUP OF INSTRUCTIONS

General mnemonic	Sample	Description of operation
NOT dest	NOT BX	Replace BX with $\overline{\text{BX}}$
AND dest,source	AND BX,CX	Replace BX with the bit-by-bit result of BX·CX
OR dest,source	OR DL,80H	Replace DL with the bit-by-bit result of DL+80H
XOR dest,source	XOR SI,SI	Replace SI with the bit-by-bit result of SI + SI (in this case, clear SI)
TEST dest,source	TEST BX, 8000H	AND BX bit by bit with 8000H and set the flags accordingly—BX does not change
SHR dest,count	SHR AX	Shift AX logically right CX times—zeros are shifted in on the left
SAR dest,count	SAR BX	Shift BX arithmetic right CX times—bits equal to the original high-order bit are shifted in on the left
SHL/SAL dest,count	SHL BL	Shift BL left CX times—zeros are shifted in on the right
ROR dest,count	ROR DX	Rotate DX right CX times
RCR dest,count	RCR AH	Rotate AH right through the carry CX times
ROL dest,count	ROL (BX)	Rotate (BX) left CX times
RCL dest,count	RCL BX	Rotate BX left through the carry CX times

Bit Manipulation Group.   This group includes the logical NOT, AND, OR, and XOR instructions as shown in Table 12.10. The operations are performed bit by bit and can specify 8- or 16-bit operands. As with the math operations, neither the source nor the destination need be the accumulator.

The TEST instruction is a nondestructive AND setting the flags depending on the result.

The shift instructions shift the contents of a register or memory location but without wraparound. The rotate instructions are circular and the carry flag can be included. A unique feature of these instructions is that the number of rotates or shifts can be programmed in register CL. This allows up to 255 shifts or rotates with one instruction.

Transfer Group.   The 8086 fetches instructions from memory using CS as the segment register and IP as the offset. The transfer group of instructions allows these two registers to be changed under program control. Table 12.11 lists the instructions in this group.

Two types of JMP instruction are possible. In the *direct* mode the instruction supplies the JMP address. In the *indirect* mode a general register holds the address. Direct mode JMPs can be *short*, *near*, or *far*. Short JMPs supply an 8-bit displacement

TABLE 12.11 TRANSFER GROUP OF INSTRUCTIONS

General mnemonic	Sample	Description of operation
JMP JMPS, JMPF target	Same[a]	Transfer control to the address specified by target (short, near, or far jump)
Jcond target	JNZ target	IF ZF = 0 transfer control to the address specified by target (short jump only)
LOOP target	Same[a]	Decrement CX and transfer control to the address specified by target if CX $\neq$ 0, else continue (short jump only)
LOOPE/LOOPZ target	Same[a]	Decrement CX and transfer control to the address specified by target if CX $\neq$ 0 and ZF is set (short jump only)
LOOPNE/LOOPNZ target	Same[a]	Decrement CX and transfer control to the address specified by target if CX $\neq$ 0 and ZF is reset
JCXZ target	Same[a]	If CX = 0, transfer control to the address specified by target
CALL, CALLF target	Same[a]	Push IP (and CS for a far CALL) onto the stack and transfer control to the address specified by target (near or far CALL only)
RET, RETF optional value	RET 4	POP the stack top into IP (and CS for a far CALL) and add 4 to SP
INT type	INT 1	Transfer control to the address stored in 1 × 4 = 00004 through 00007; push IP and the flags onto the stack
INTO	Same[a]	If the OF flag is set, transfer control to the address stored in 00010 through 00013
IRET	Same[a]	POP the stack top into the flags, IP and CS

[a] Use the general mnemonic.

that is added to register IP to form the new address. This allows transfers up to 127 bytes ahead or 128 bytes backward from the present IP value.

Near JMPs supply a 16-bit displacement. This allows a transfer up to +32,767 bytes or −32,768 bytes relative to register IP.

Far JMPs are a third type of direct JMP requiring five instruction bytes: one for the op-code, two for the new IP value, and two for the new CS value. This is the only (direct) JMP that allows you to move to a new code segment.

Indirect JMPs can be near or far. A near indirect JMP uses one of the general registers to supply a 16-bit offset. Thus the mnemonic JMP BX is interpreted as "Transfer control to the instruction whose offset address is found in register BX."

Far indirect JMPs use four consecutive memory locations (a double word) to identify the new code segment and index pointer. The first two bytes are loaded into register IP, the second two into the CS register.

A number of conditional JMPs can also be specified as indicated in Table

TABLE 12.12 CONDITIONAL TRANSFER GROUP
OF INSTRUCTIONS

Mnemonic	Condition
	Signed Operations
JG/JNLE	Greater/not less nor equal $((SF + OF) + ZF) = 0$
JGE/JNL	Greater or equal/not less $(SF + OF) = 0$
JL/JNGE	Less/not greater nor equal $(SF + OF) = 1$
JLE/JNG	Less or equal/not greater $((SF + OF) + ZF) = 1$
JO	Overflow $(OF = 1)$
JS	Sign $(SF = 1)$
JNO	Not overflow $(OF = 0)$
JNS	Not sign $(SF = 0)$
	Unsigned Operations
JA/JNBE	Above/not below nor equal $(CF + ZF) = 0$
JAE/JNB	Above or equal/not below $(CF = 0)$
JB/JNAE	Below/not above nor equal $(CF = 1)$
JBE/JNA	Below or equal/not above $(CF + ZF) = 1$
	Either
JC	Carry $(CF = 1)$
JE/JZ	Equal/zero $(ZF = 1)$
JP/JPE	Parity/parity even $(PF = 1)$
JNC	Not carry $(CF = 0)$
JNE/JNZ	Not equal/not zero $(ZF = 0)$
JNP/JPO	Not parity/parity odd $(PF = 0)$

12.12. Note that all of these instructions are *short direct* jumps and that most instructions have two mnemonics saying the same thing: for example, "Jump if greater than" or "Jump if not less than nor equal to."

Similar to the Z-80 instruction DJNZ, the LOOP instruction transfers control to the target address until register CX is 0. The conditional loop instructions transfer control if CX $\neq$ 0 and the specified condition is met.

The JCXZ instruction should be used before a LOOP command when the contents of CX is unknown. If this is not done and CX = 0, 65,536 loops could occur until the instruction completes.

The CALL instruction can be near (within the segment) or far (outside the current segment). It can also be direct (address in instruction) or indirect (address in a register). The far version requires that four bytes be pushed onto the stack saving register IP and CS. The RET instruction must also be near or far, so that the data on the stack is handled correctly. RET instructions can specify an optional number such as RET 5. This value is added to register SP after popping CS and IP to form the stack address. It allows parameters to be passed onto the stack and then discarded after the subroutine has been executed.

Interrupts. The 8086 has three sources of interrupts:

1. Hardware initiated
2. Software initiated
3. Processor initiated

Regardless of the source, all interrupts must furnish an 8-bit type number. This number is multiplied by 4 by the 8086 to determine the interrupt service routine (ISR) address from a 1K-byte table beginning at address 00000. Figure 12.13 shows this interrupt-pointer table. Note that each entry in the table is four bytes long to accommodate a new instruction pointer and a new code segment.

Hardware-initiated interrupts can be maskable—INTR—or nonmaskable—NMI. Maskable interrupts supply an 8-bit type number during $\overline{\text{INTA}}$ and can be

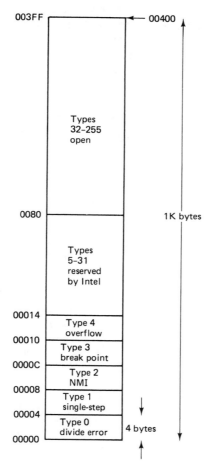

Figure 12.13 The interrupt-pointer table reserves four bytes of memory for each of 256 type numbers. Note that some of the type numbers are reserved for future use by Intel Corp.

masked by resetting the IF bit in the flag register. Nonmaskable interrupts automatically generate a type 2 interrupt (that is, the address of the ISR is assumed stored in locations 00008–0000B). This interrupt cannot be masked.

Software interrupts are given with the *INT type* instruction, causing control to be transferred to the address stored in the appropriate table entry. INTO is a special software interrupt instruction. It will cause a type 4 interrupt if an overflow condition exists; if not, control proceeds to the next instruction.

The 8086 will generate a type 0 interrupt if a divide error occurs (such as division by 0 or a result too large for the destination register). If the TF flag is set, the 8086 will generate a type 1 interrupt after each instruction. This can be used for debugging purposes.

The op-code for a type 3 interrupt is a single byte, allowing this special software interrupt to be used as a "breakpoint." In practice, you would place an INT 3 instruction at a test point in your program, causing control to transfer to a routine in which the CPU registers could be examined. The process is then repeated, moving the breakpoint farther into the program until all bugs have been found.

Regardless of the source of the interrupt, the processor will push the 16-bit flag word, the CS segment register, and register IP onto the stack when the interrupt occurs. Because the flags are included, the special IRET instruction must be used to terminate the ISR.

TABLE 12.13 STRING GROUP OF INSTRUCTIONS

General mnemonic	Sample	Description of operation
MOVSB/MOVSW	MOVSB	Move the byte or word pointed at by SI and DS to the memory location pointed at by DI and ES. Increment SI and DI if DF = 0, else decrement these registers.
CMPSB/CMPSW	CMPSW	Compare the byte or word pointed at by SI and DS to the word pointed at by DI and ES. Increment SI and DI if DF = 0, else decrement these registers.
SCASB/SCASW	SCASB	Compare AL or AX with the contents of the memory location pointed at by DI and ES. Increment DI if DF = 0, else decrement DI.
LODSB/LODSW	LODSW	Load the sequential bytes or words pointed at by SI and DS to AX. Increment SI if DF = 0, else decrement SI.
STOSB/STOSW	STOSB	Store AL or AX at the memory location pointed at by DI and ES. Increment DI if DF = 0, else decrement DI.
REP	REP MOVSW	Repeat MOVSW until CX = 0
REPE/REPZ	REPZ CMPSW	Repeat CMPSW until CX = 0 or the memory locations do not compare
REPNE/REPNZ	REPNZ SCASB	Repeat SCASB until CX = 0 or a match is found

String Group. Table 12.13 lists the instructions in the string or block group. Three basic operations are possible:

1. Move a byte or a word from one location to another.
2. Compare a byte or a word in one memory location with that in another.
3. Scan memory and compare with the contents of the accumulator.

Instructions in this group use the following registers for dedicated functions:

1. DS and SI for the physical source address
2. ES and DI for the physical destination address
3. CX as a repetition counter
4. Accumulator for the scan value and the destination for load operations and the source for store operations

The REP prefix in front of MOVSB/MOVSW, LODSB/LODSW, or STOSB/STOSW will cause the instruction to repeat until CX = 0. The direction flag (DF) determines if the pointer registers are incremented or decremented. Using REP, entire blocks of data can be moved with a single instruction.

REPE and REPNE can be used with CPMSB/CMPSW and SCASB/SCASW and will cause the instruction to repeat until CX = 0 or a match is or is not found. When the loop terminates, the flags can be tested to determine if a match was found.

Processor Control Group. The processor control instructions are shown in Table 12.14. These instructions primarily allow various flags to be set or reset.

TABLE 12.14 PROCESSOR CONTROL GROUP OF INSTRUCTIONS

General mnemonic	Description of operation
STC	Set carry flag
CLC	Clear carry flag
CMC	Complement carry flag
STD	Set direction flag
CLD	Clear direction flag
STI	Set interrupt-enable flag
CLI	Clear interrupt-enable flag
HLT	Halt until interrupted or reset
WAIT	Idle until the $\overline{\text{TEST}}$ input = 0
ESC	Escape to external processor
LOCK	Lock buses during next instruction
NOP	No operation

The ESC and LOCK instructions are used with the 8087 NDP coprocessor. Commands intended for the 8087 are prefixed by an ESC alerting the 8087 to read the next instruction. In the meantime the 8086 goes on to the following instructions. When the 8087 result is needed by the 8086, it executes a WAIT instruction idling until its $\overline{\text{TEST}}$ input, driven by the 8087, is found low, indicating that the result is ready. The NDP stores the result in memory by requesting control of the buses (via $\overline{\text{RQ}}/\overline{\text{GT0}}$) and performing a direct memory access.

Any instruction preceded by LOCK has total control of the system buses during its activities. This prevents the 8089 or 8087 processors from reading or writing data to a block of RAM that the 8086 is updating.

An Example: Two 8086 Block Fill Programs. So that we might gain some appreciation of how the 8086 is programmed, we will develop two 8086 programs for filling a block of memory with a constant. This operation might be required to initialize a block of memory or clear the screen of a memory-mapped video screen.

The block fill problem was first solved with the 8080/85 and Z-80 as Program

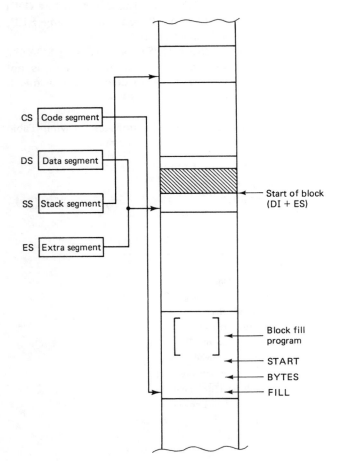

Figure 12.14 Memory usage for the 8086 block fill programs in Fig. 12.15.

7 in Chap. 3. The 8080/85 solution appears in Fig. 3.13 and the Z-80 solution in Fig. 3.14. The objective of the program is to fill a block of memory (up to 64K bytes) with a special character. The starting address of the block is assumed stored in a memory location called *START*. The number of bytes in the block is stored in another memory location, called *BYTES*. The byte to be written is stored in a third memory location called *FILL*.

Figure 12.14 shows how the memory is assumed to be organized for the problem. The physical addresses of the segments do not matter. However, the block to be filled is assumed to be within the data segment. The DI register will be used as the destination pointer. This presents a problem because DI is normally the offset for the ES segment (see Table 12.6). This can easily be overcome by making ES = DS.

Figure 12.15(a) shows version 1 of the 8086 block fill program. The PUSH DS, POP ES sequence makes ES = DS for the reasons just mentioned. Next, AL,

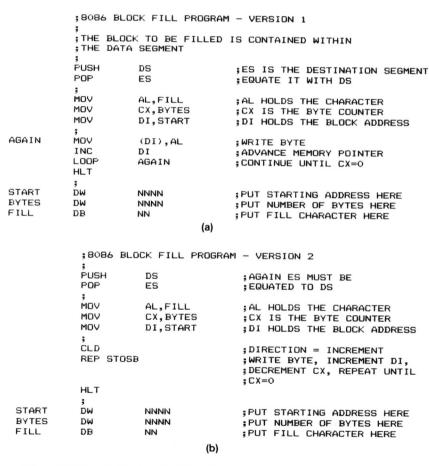

```
;8086 BLOCK FILL PROGRAM - VERSION 1
;
;THE BLOCK TO BE FILLED IS CONTAINED WITHIN
;THE DATA SEGMENT
;
        PUSH    DS              ;ES IS THE DESTINATION SEGMENT
        POP     ES              ;EQUATE IT WITH DS
        ;
        MOV     AL,FILL         ;AL HOLDS THE CHARACTER
        MOV     CX,BYTES        ;CX IS THE BYTE COUNTER
        MOV     DI,START        ;DI HOLDS THE BLOCK ADDRESS
AGAIN   ;
        MOV     (DI),AL         ;WRITE BYTE
        INC     DI              ;ADVANCE MEMORY POINTER
        LOOP    AGAIN           ;CONTINUE UNTIL CX=0
        HLT
        ;
START   DW      NNNN            ;PUT STARTING ADDRESS HERE
BYTES   DW      NNNN            ;PUT NUMBER OF BYTES HERE
FILL    DB      NN              ;PUT FILL CHARACTER HERE
```
(a)

```
;8086 BLOCK FILL PROGRAM - VERSION 2
;
        PUSH    DS              ;AGAIN ES MUST BE
        POP     ES              ;EQUATED TO DS
        ;
        MOV     AL,FILL         ;AL HOLDS THE CHARACTER
        MOV     CX,BYTES        ;CX IS THE BYTE COUNTER
        MOV     DI,START        ;DI HOLDS THE BLOCK ADDRESS
        ;
        CLD                     ;DIRECTION = INCREMENT
        REP STOSB               ;WRITE BYTE, INCREMENT DI,
                                ;DECREMENT CX, REPEAT UNTIL
                                ;CX=0
        HLT
        ;
START   DW      NNNN            ;PUT STARTING ADDRESS HERE
BYTES   DW      NNNN            ;PUT NUMBER OF BYTES HERE
FILL    DB      NN              ;PUT FILL CHARACTER HERE
```
(b)

Figure 12.15 (a) Version 1 of the 8086 block fill program using the LOOP instruction; (b) version 2 using the REP and STOSB instructions.

CX, and DI are loaded with the program variables. The contents of AL are then written to the destination address, DI is incremented, and the LOOP instruction used to decrement automatically the counter (CX) and transfer control back to location AGAIN until all bytes have been written.

Figure 12.15(b) is version 2 of the same program. It is essentially the same as version 1 but uses the STOSB instruction and the REP prefix to automatically write the byte, decrement the CX counter, and increment the DI pointer until CX = 0.

Comparing the four versions of this program, the 8080/85 routine requires 14 instructions, the Z-80 requires seven instructions, version 1 for the 8086 requires nine instructions and version 2 requires eight.

The 8086 does not compare as well as we might think it should. This is due to the instructions required to get the segment registers pointing to the right locations, load the dedicated registers for the LOOP and STOSB instructions, and finally fill the block.

12.5 8086 MEMORY AND I/O INTERFACING

As you read this section, look for the answers to these Key Concept questions:

12.5.1. What signals are provided by the 8086 to allow selection of the even and odd memory banks?

12.5.2. Will the 8086 operate successfully with only an even or only an odd bank of memory?

12.5.3. Is it necessary to interface 8-bit I/O chips like the 8255A in pairs, so that even and odd I/O ports are provided?

Although the 8086 has a 16-bit data bus, it is capable of accessing memory (and its I/O devices) as bytes or words. The A0 address line and $\overline{\text{BHE}}$ control signal define the type of access to occur. This was shown in Table 12.1. In this section we show how to design the hardware to accommodate this byte or word access and interface to the CPU modules in Figs. 12.7 and 12.8.

Interfacing a 16K-Word Memory. Figure 12.16 illustrates a 16K-*word* memory using 16K × 1 static RAM chips. The memory is organized as two banks of 16K bytes. RAMs 0–7 supply the even-addressed byte and RAMs 8–15 supply the odd-addressed byte. By selecting both banks simultaneously, a 16-bit word can be read.

Example 12.4

For what range of addresses will the signal $\overline{\text{MEM SEL}}$ in Fig. 12.16 be active?

Solution. The address decoder consists of IC1 and IC2 and it tests address lines AB15–AB19. These lines must all be low for $\overline{\text{MEM SEL}}$ to be active. The range of addresses is thus

$$\text{0000 0XXX XXXX XXXX XXXX}$$

or 00000H–07FFFH. This corresponds to the low 32K bytes of the first 64K segment in the 1-MB address space.

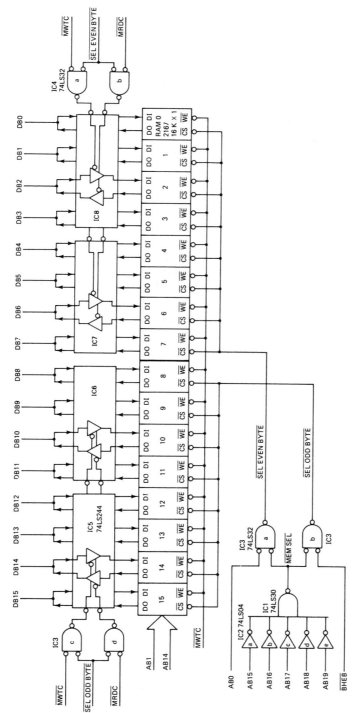

Figure 12.16 Max mode 16K-word 8086 memory module.

The $\overline{\text{MEM SEL}}$ signal is combined with AB0 and $\overline{\text{BHE}}$ to form the even- and odd-byte select signals. This is consistent with the decoding of A0 and $\overline{\text{BHE}}$ in Table 12.1. Note that because of the even/odd bank arrangement, each bank stores every other byte. For example, the even bank stores bytes 0, 2, 4, 6, . . . , 32,764, 32,766.

The 2167 RAMs have separate data in and out pins requiring the 74LS244 buffers (IC4–7) to convert this into a bidirectional bus. Note that the buffers must also be separated into an even bank and an odd bank and can only be enabled if the address matches and a memory read or memory write cycle is taking place (this ensures that the memory is not enabled by an I/O address).

Although not shown, all of the control and address bus signals are assumed buffered as they enter the memory module. The control signals shown are for a max mode system, but the module could be redesigned for a min mode if desired.

Interfacing the 8255A PPI.   The 8086 I/O operations may transfer 8- or 16-bit data quantities. The particular instruction used determines the number of bits to be input or output. Again, A0 and $\overline{\text{BHE}}$ are used to determine the byte or word selected.

Because of the byte input/output capability, all of the 8080/85 support devices discussed in Chap. 7 can be used with the 8086. This is an important point. There is no need to redesign the PPI, or PIT, or USART, to accommodate the 16-bit 8086. By exchanging bytes with these devices they can be used directly.

Figure 12.17 shows an I/O interface between the 8086 max mode CPU module and two 8255As. This design will allow 16 bits of data to be exchanged between an I/O device and the 8086. Be sure to note, however, that a single 8255A could also be interfaced if 8-bit I/O operations were sufficient.

The port decoding is similar to the memory interface in the last section using AB0 and $\overline{\text{BHE}}$ to select an even set of ports and an odd set of ports. IC1 and IC2 determine the specific port address.

Example 12.5

Determine the 8255A port addresses in Fig. 12.17 for *direct* I/O instructions and for *indirect* I/O instructions.

Solution.   The direct I/O instructions supply an 8-bit fixed address as part of the instruction on AB0–AB7. The decoding in Fig. 12.17 will cause $\overline{\text{PORT SEL}}$ to be active over the range.

$$\text{AB7–AB0} = 00000\text{XXX} = 00\text{H} - 07\text{H}$$

IC3 combines the $\overline{\text{PORT SEL}}$ signal with AB0 and $\overline{\text{BHE}}$ to produce $\overline{\text{EVEN PORT SEL}}$ and $\overline{\text{ODD PORT SEL}}$. There will be four combinations of each of these signals because they do not include AB1 and AB2. For example, $\overline{\text{EVEN PORT SEL}}$ will be active if the direct port address is 0, 2, 4, or 6. Similarly, $\overline{\text{ODD PORT SEL}}$ will be active if the direct port address is 1, 3, 5, or 7.

Because AB1 and AB2 are used to select one of four ports within the 8255, the four combinations of the $\overline{\text{EVEN PORT SEL}}$ and $\overline{\text{ODD PORT SEL}}$ signals correspond to ports A, B, and C and the control port of the 8255A. This is shown more clearly in Table 12.15.

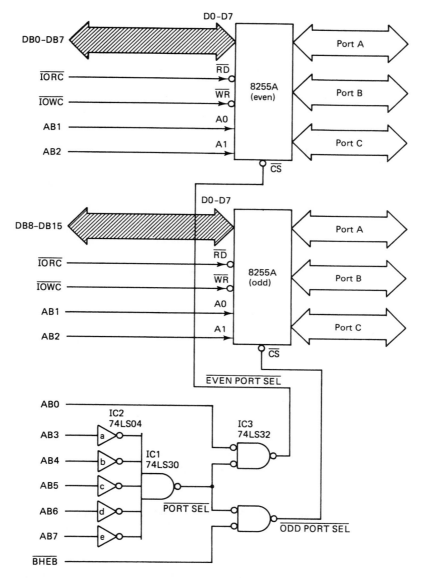

Figure 12.17 Interfacing the 8255A PPI to the 8086 max mode CPU module. Two 8255As are required for 16-bit I/O operations.

When indirect I/O instructions are given, register DX is used to hold a 16-bit port address. Because AB8–AB15 are not decoded in Fig. 12.17, this circuit is *partially decoded* for indirect I/O instructions. This means that in addition to ports 0–7, ports 0100H–0107H, 0200H–0207H, . . . , FF00H–FF07H will all respond to indirect I/O instructions.

TABLE 12.15 8255 PORT ADDRESSES FOR THE INTERFACE IN FIG. 12.17

AB7–AB3	AB2	AB1	AB0	BHE	Port	Description	Comment
00000	0	0	0	1	0	Port A	Even port on
00000	0	1	0	1	2	Port B	DB0–DB7
00000	1	0	0	1	4	Port C	
00000	1	1	0	1	6	Control port	
00000	0	0	1	0	1	Port A	Odd port on
00000	0	1	1	0	3	Port B	DB8–DB15
00000	1	0	1	0	5	Port C	
00000	1	1	1	0	7	Control port	
00000	0	0	0	0	0 and 1	Port A	Even port
00000	0	1	0	0	2 and 3	Port B	on DB0–DB7
00000	1	0	0	0	4 and 5	Port C	and odd port
00000	1	1	0	0	6 and 7	Control port	on DB8–DB15

Normally, both 8255As would be programmed identically, allowing 16-bit data transfers with the I/O device.

Example 12.6

Write the 8086 initialization routine required to program both 8255As in Fig. 12.17 for mode 0 with port A an output and ports B and C inputs.

Solution. The direct or indirect mode can be used. By using register AX, both PPI chips can be programmed simultaneously. The program is as follows:

```
MOV   DX,0006H    ;DX POINTS AT THE EVEN CONTROL PORT
MOV   AX,8B8BH    ;CONTROL WORD DUPLICATED IN AL AND AH
OUT   DX,AX       ;WRITE AL TO EVEN PPI AND AH TO ODD PPI
```

Note that when the OUT DX,AX instruction is executed, AB0 and $\overline{BHE}$ will both be low, enabling the control port of both 8255As simultaneously.

Example 12.7

Write an 8086 program to input a byte from port B of the even PPI chip and output this byte to port A of the odd PPI chip in Fig. 12.17.

Solution. The program is very simple.

```
IN   AL,02    ;READ PORT B OF THE EVEN PPI
OUT 01,AL    ;WRITE THE BYTE TO PORT A OF THE ODD PPI
```

Note that the contents of AL is automatically put on AD8–AD15 for the odd port address.

12.6 THE 8086 FAMILY OF MICROPROCESSORS

As you read this section, look for the answers to these Key Concept questions:

12.6.1. The external data bus width of the 8088 is _____ bits, but internally all CPU registers are _____ bits wide.

12.6.2. When operated in the _____ _____ mode the 80286 appears to be a fast 8086 microprocessor.

12.6.3. To be compatible with OS/2, the 80286 and 80386 must be operated in the _____ _____ address mode.

As mentioned in the introduction, the 8086 is a "stepping-off" point. Behind, it leaves the 8-bit 8080 and 8085 microprocessors, ahead, it leads the way to the more powerful 80286 and the 32-bit 80386 and 80486. In this section we present a brief overview of the other processors in the 8086 family.

The 8088. In 1979, when Intel first introduced the 8086, the microcomputer industry had not yet standardized a particular CPU. The CP/M operating system was popular on S-100 machines, the Apple II$^+$ was becoming a standard in the education market, and Tandy was announcing an improved version of its TRS-80 computer based on the Z-80. There didn't seem to be a place for this new 16-bit chip.

Someone at Intel then came up with a clever idea. Why not design an *8-bit* version of the 8086? Externally, it would have an 8-bit data bus, electrically appearing very similar to the 8085. But internally, it would be an 8086. That is, all of the CPU registers would be 16 bits wide, and the chip would execute the complete instruction set of the 8086. Thus was born the 8088 microprocessor.

You might wonder, "Why an 8-bit 8086?" One advantage of the 8-bit data bus is the fact that memory can be added 8 bits at a time, instead of 16, as is required by the even/odd memory bank arrangement of the 8086. With 64K memory chips selling for $10–$20 apiece at the time, this was a significant consideration.

Figure 12.18 compares the pinouts for the 8088 and 8086. The two chips are nearly identical with the following exceptions:

1. Address lines A8–A15 are not multiplexed on the 8088.
2. The 8088 data bus is just 8 bits wide (AD0–AD7).
3. There is no need for the $\overline{BHE}$ signal on the 8088; it is replaced by SS0, a status signal.
4. M/$\overline{IO}$ of the 8086 is changed to IO/$\overline{M}$ on the 8088 (to be 8085 compatible).

When operated in the min mode, the bus structure of the 8088 is identical to that of the 8085. Because of this, all of the 8085 peripherals, such as the 8755A 16K EPROM with I/O, and the 8155 2K RAM with timer and parallel I/O, are directly compatible with the 8088. This allows a min mode 8088 microcomputer system to be built with only a few ICs.

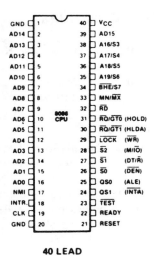

40 LEAD

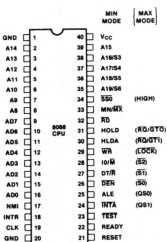

| | MIN MODE | { MAX MODE } |

Figure 12.18 Pin comparisons between the 8086 and 8088 microprocessors. (Courtesy of Intel Corporation.)

Bus timing is essentially the same as that of the 8086 except that four additional T states are required when fetching 16-bit operands. This causes the 8088 to be somewhat slower than the 8086. Both processors are object code compatible, and programs written for one chip will run without changes on the other.

In 1981 IBM selected the 8088 as the CPU chip for their new family of PCs. And, as they say, the rest is history.

The 80286. In 1983 Intel announced a successor for its 8086/8088 microprocessors called the 80286. Housed in a new 17-pin per side, 68-pin surface mount package, the 80286 has a 24-line address bus and a 16-bit data bus. This allows the chip to access 16,777,216 8-bit memory locations (i.e., 16 MB). The 286 (as it is known) is upward compatible with the 8088 and 8086. This means that software written for these processors will run without change on the 286. The reverse is *not* true.

The 80286 has two modes of operation called *real address mode* and *protected virtual address mode*. In the former case, the processor presents an architecture which is identical to that of the 8086. In fact, in this mode the chip is limited to the 8086's 20-bit memory address and resulting 1 MB of memory space. Due to internal improvements, however, the 80286 can be as much as 2.5 times faster than an 8086 operated at the same clock speed.

When the 80286 is switched to protected mode (via a software command), the chip takes on a new personality. All 24 address lines become active and several *memory management* and *data protection* features can now be accessed. This allows the 80286 to be used in a multitasking environment in which several programs simultaneously share the CPU. Protected mode programs are assigned one of four privilege levels, with level 0 the most privileged and level 3 the least. Programs at a given privilege level can only access data and code at the same or a numerically higher privilege level. In this way, a program failure by one user cannot "bring down" the entire system.

When run in the protected mode, each user program "thinks" it has access to 1 gigabyte (1024 MB) of memory. If a program calls for an address that is not available in the 16 MB of physical memory, the 286 swaps some of its physical memory with program instructions on disk. This technique is known as *virtual memory*. The advantage, of course, is to allow program developers to write extremely large programs, even though the physical memory is limited to 16 MB.

PC-DOS and MS-DOS are currently the most popular operating systems for the 8086 family of microprocessors. Neither supports the concept of multitasking or virtual memory. When the 80286 is used with these operating systems, it is always used in the real address mode, in effect, functioning as a "fast" 8086.

The successor to PC-DOS and MS-DOS is OS/2 (operating system 2). OS/2 is a multitasking operating system that allows several programs to run simultaneously. This is done by presenting the user with several on-screen "windows." Within each window a separate program can be run. OS/2 requires a protected mode 80286 or higher level processor and will not run on 8086 or 8088 based machines.

The 80386. In 1985 the 32-bit 80386 microprocessor was announced by Intel. Built with CMOS technology, the 386 has 280,000 transistors but draws less current (400 mA) than an 8086! The chip comes in a pin-grid array package that features 132 pins.

The 386 is a true 32-bit microprocessor. It has 32 bit address and data bus lines and all internal CPU registers are also 32 bits wide. This allows access to 2^{32} or 4 gigabytes of physical memory. In the virtual memory mode a 46-bit address is supported. This allows the software to "think" that 64 terabytes (64 million megabytes) of memory exist!

The 386 has three operating modes. In the first, called *real mode*, the chip performs as a fast (units with clock speeds over 30 MHz are available) 8086. In this mode the 386 is limited to 1 MB of memory and only one program may run at a time. This is the PC-DOS mode.

The second mode of operation is called *protected virtual mode* and causes the 386 to perform as an 80286 complete with virtual memory and multitasking capabilities. This is the mode used by OS/2.

The final operating mode is called the *virtual real mode*. In this mode the 386 appears to be multiple 8086s, each with access to 1 MB of memory, but "protected" from each other. That is, if one user crashes his or her program, the other users are unaffected. In effect, the virtual real mode allows several programs to run simultaneously with the task switching done in hardware, not software.

In 1988 the 80386SX appeared. This is a 16-bit version of the 80386. Internally the chip is a 386 with 32-bit data registers. But externally, it features a 16-bit data bus. Another difference is that the 386SX supports only a 24-bit address bus. For these reasons, the 386SX is comparable in speed to a 286.

The 80486. The 80486 is not so much a new microprocessor as it is a refinement of an "old" one—the 80386. It features over one million transistors and provides two to four times the software performance of the 386, all the while providing object code compatibility as far back as the 8086 and 8088 microprocessors.

The 486 brings mainframe performance to the microcomputer. With a clock frequency of 33 MHz, the chip can do 20 million instructions per second (MIPs)! This is accomplished by streamlining many of the frequently used instructions to a single clock cycle. In addition, an 8K byte cache memory is incorporated on-board. This memory is used to hold anticipated instructions and data, thereby reducing the need to perform external memory cycles. Another advantage of the 486 is a built-in 80387 numeric coprocessor, which in effect allows the 486 to perform floating-point math operations on-board.

At present 486-based PCs are very expensive—over $15,000 for a base system. However, with a performance level more than 50 times that of the original IBM PC, that price might just be a bargain!

CHAPTER SUMMARY

1. The 8086 and 8088 are organized internally as two processors called the execution unit (EU) and the bus interface unit (BIU).

2. The 8086 and 8088 both follow the basic principle of fetch and execute, but the instruction prefetch queue and pipeline architecture allow these two cycles to overlap, increasing processor throughput.

3. Both the 8086 and the 8088 can be operated in a min mode or a max mode. In the min mode the processor generates all of its control bus signals and presents a bus interface similar to that of the 8-bit 8085.

4. When operated in the max mode, both processors require the 8288 bus controller to generate the control bus signals.

5. The 8087 numeric data processor and 8089 I/O processor are intended for

use with max mode 8086 or 8088 systems. They provide the processor with more complex and faster math and I/O capabilities.

6. The 8086 and 8088 have a 20-bit address bus, allowing each processor to access 1 MB of memory.

7. The 1-MB memory space of the 8086 and 8088 is divided into 64K segments called the code, data, stack, and extra segments. Addresses within a given segment are 16 bits long and referred to as the logical address or offset.

8. Memory addresses are formed by combining the segment address (always a multiple of 16) with the logical address to form the physical 20-bit memory address.

9. The 8086 can access memory as a 16-bit word, an 8-bit byte at an odd address, or an 8-bit byte at an even address.

10. The 8088 has an 8-bit data bus and can only access bytes of memory.

11. The programming model for the 8086 and 8088 includes all of the registers of the 8080/85 plus a 16-bit accumulator, 16-bit flag register and three 16-bit pointer/index registers.

12. The 8086 and 8088 instruction sets include data transfer, arithmetic, bit manipulation, transfer, string, and processor control groups of instructions. There are nine addressing modes.

13. I/O operations can be direct with the port address fixed by the instruction, or indirect with register DX holding a 16-bit I/O address. The 8086 can input or output 8- or 16-bit data words.

14. The 8086 is upward compatible with a family of 16- and 32-bit microprocessors. This includes the 80286, 80386, and 80486.

15. The PC- and MS-DOS operating systems will run on any 8086 based computer. OS/2, the successor to DOS, requires a protected mode 80286 level processor or higher.

LAB PROJECTS

12.1. If you have access to an 8086 family computer, answer the following questions about your system.
   (a) Which microprocessor chip is used?
   (b) What is the system clock frequency?
   (c) How much total RAM does your system have?
   (d) How much total ROM?
   (e) How are the memory chips organized (256K $\times$ 1, 32K $\times$ 8, etc.)?
   (f) Make a list of all of the I/O ports in your computer.

12.2. Sketch a *memory map* for your computer identifying the RAM and ROM blocks. Identify the size of any "open" areas.

12.3. [1] Start DEBUG and at the "–" prompt type "R". You should see a display of all of the 8086 CPU registers and the flags. The instruction pointed to by register IP will also be shown. Type "A100" to begin assembling instruction mnemonics at logical address 0100H. Enter the following program.

```
0100    MOV     AX,0000
0103    MOV     CX,8000
0106    DEC     AX
0107    MOV     BX,AX
0109    LOOP    0106
010B    INT     3
```

12.4. With the program in Lab 12.3 loaded, give the command "U100 LC" to unassemble (U) the program beginning at address 100H with a length (L) of 12 (0CH) bytes.

(a) Examine the program listing. Note that DEBUG has determined the hexadecimal object code for each instruction.

(b) For another view of the program type "D100 LC." This command will display (D) 12 bytes of memory beginning at address 100H. Note that the display is shown in hex and its ASCII equivalent.

12.5. There are several ways of running and testing the program.

(a) Press the "T" key for trace. The first instruction will execute and DEBUG will then display all CPU registers. Repeatedly pressing "T" will cause one instruction at a time to execute.

(b) Type "G=100" to run the program at full speed beginning at address 100H. In this example the program will stop at the INT 3 (breakpoint) instruction, displaying all CPU registers (note that CX has been counted down to 0).

(c) Type "G=100 109" to run the program at full speed beginning at address 100H but halting at address 109H.

(d) Type "RIP" to examine register (R) IP. Enter the value 0100 to point this register to the beginning of the program. Now type "G" to run the program at full speed starting at the address in register IP.

12.6. If you have written a program with DEBUG, you can save it with the N and W commands.

(a) Type "N TEST" to name the program TEST.

(b) The number of bytes to be written must be stored in the 32-bit register pair BX:CX. In this example 12 bytes must be written. Use "RBX" to set BX to 0 and RCX to make CX=000CH.

(c) Type "W" to write the (12 byte) file to the disk.

12.7. A saved file can be retrieved by loading it when DEBUG is first started. Type "DEBUG TEST" to start DEBUG and load the file TEST.

---

[1]*Note*: The MS-DOS operating system includes the utility DEBUG.COM. This program can be used to enter 8086 instruction mnemonics to memory. The resulting program can then be traced or run at full speed. All of the CPU registers can be examined and modified.

QUESTIONS AND PROBLEMS

Section 12.1

12.1. What is the advantage of having the fetch and execute cycles of a microcomputer *overlap*? What makes this possible in a 8086 CPU?

12.2. If you intend to use the 8087 numeric coprocessor, then the 8086 must be wired for the _____ mode.

12.3. The following logic levels/hex equivalents are observed on the buses of an 8086 microprocessor during an instruction cycle:

address bus: D8000H

data bus: 1234H

control bus: $M/\overline{IO} = 1$, $\overline{RD} = 0$, $\overline{WR} = 1$, $\overline{BHE} = 0$

(a) Is this a byte or word access?

(b) From memory or an I/O device?

(c) Read or write cycle?

12.4. Describe the contents of the address, data, and control buses (see Prob. 12.3 for an example) if the 8086 is writing the byte 73H to memory location 80001H.

12.5. The 8086 can access 1 MB of memory. How many 64K *pages* is this?

*12.6. Planning to add 64 KB of memory to an 8086 computer system, you purchase eight 64-KB DRAM chips. Unfortunately, this will not work. Explain why.

12.7. If an interrupt driven peripheral gates the type number C6H onto the data bus during $\overline{INTA}$, from which group of memory locations will the address of the ISR be fetched?

Section 12.2

12.8. Refer to the min mode 8086 CPU module in Fig. 12.7. Assume the 8086 is performing a memory read cycle and determine the logic level of the following control signals during the T3 clock cycle.

(a) $DT/\overline{R}$

(b) $\overline{DEN}$

(c) ALE

(d) $M/\overline{IO}$

(e) $\overline{RD}$

(f) $\overline{WR}$

*12.9. Refer to the max mode 8086 CPU module in Fig. 12.8. Assume the $\overline{OE}$ inputs of the three 8282 chips are inadvertently tied to +5 V instead of ground. How would this affect the operation of the CPU module?

Section 12.3

12.10. How do the 8086's four pointer and index registers differ from the four data registers?

12.11. Assume register CS = 3800H and register IP = 0100H. Calculate the *logical* and *physical* addresses pointed to by register IP.

12.12. Sketch a diagram similar to Fig. 12.11 showing the starting and ending physical addresses for each 8086 memory segment if CS = 1000H, DS = 8800H, SS = 57F0H, and ES = 5FFFH.

12.13. Using the segment assignments given in Prob. 12.12, calculate the physical address of the memory operand in each of the following 8086 instructions:

    (a) MOV (0200H),AH

    (b) MOV (BP),AH   (assume BP = A800H)

    (c) MOV (SI)+6,AH   (assume SI = C010H)

    (d) JMP 089EH   (089E is the target address)

12.14. Determine the addressing mode for each of the instructions in Prob. 12.13.

12.15. True or false: Because each of the four 8086 memory segments is 64K bytes in length, a minimum of 256K of memory (64K × 4) is required in an 8086-based computer.

Section 12.4

12.16. Write an 8086 program to load register AX with B370H, register BH with the contents of memory location D800H in the data segment, and SI with a copy of the data in register CX. Identify the addressing mode of each instruction you use.

12.17. What is wrong with each of the following 8086 instructions?

    (a) MOV BL,AX

    (b) MOV DX,FE000H

    (c) INC (AX)

    (d) IN AX,8000H

12.18. What is the I/O port address for the 8086 program shown in Fig. 12.19?

12.19. Under what condition will the 8086 program in Fig. 12.19 escape the loop?

12.20. Determine the contents of AX after each of the following programs has been run.

(a) MOV	AL,80H	**(b)** MOV	AX,C879H
MOV	BL,63H	MOV	BL,D9H
MUL	BL	DIV	BL

12.21. Answer the following questions about the block move program shown in Fig. 12.20.

    (a) What value is loaded into the DS and ES segment registers?

    (b) Register SI points to the block starting address in the data segment. What is this (logical) address?

```
                        ; INPUT TEST PROGRAM
                        ;
                        MOV        DX,00C3H
              INPUT     IN         AL,DX
                        TEST       AL,40H
                        JNE        INPUT
                        ;
                        ;PROGRAM CONTINUES
```

Figure 12.19 Program for Probs. 12.18 and 12.19.

```
                    ;BLOCK MOVE PROGRAM
                    ;
                    MOV       AX,8000H
                    MOV       DS,AX
                    MOV       ES,AX
                    MOV       SI,SOURCE
                    MOV       DI,DEST
                    MOV       CX,0080H
                    CLD
                    REP MOVSW
                    HLT
           SOURCE   DW        1000H
           DEST     DW        0C000H
```

Figure 12.20   Program for Prob. 12.21.

```
           MOV       CX,8000H

   OUTER   MOV       BX,0

   INNER   INC       BX

           JNZ       INNER

           LOOP      OUTER

           RET
```

Figure 12.21   Program for Prob. 12.22.

   (c) Register DI points to the block destination address in the extra segment. What is this (logical) address?

   (d) Register CX is the byte/word counter. How many words are transferred by this program?

12.22. The program shown in Fig. 12.21 functions as a time delay routine. The program is made up of an inner loop and an outer loop.

   (a) How many times are the instructions in the inner loop executed for each outer loop pass?

   (b) How many times will the LOOP instruction be executed?

   (c) Calculate the total number of times the inner loop instructions are executed.

12.23. Code the 8-bit addition problem, Program 1 in Fig. 3.1, for the 8086.

12.24. Code the 32-bit addition problem, Program 3 in Fig. 3.4, for the 8086.

Section 12.5

12.25. Answer the following questions about the 8086 memory interface in Fig. 12.16.

   (a) How many total bytes does this interface provide?

   (b) Which RAM chip—RAM0–RAM15—stores bit 5 of the byte at location 06A83H?

   (c) $\overline{MWTC}$ is connected in common to all RAM chips. If a write cycle to the even bank occurs, what prevents data from also being written to the odd bank?

   (d) Which memory bank—even, odd, or both—will be accessed for the instruction MOV AL,0005H?

*12.26. Assume the 8086 memory interface in Fig. 12.16 has been wired incorrectly.

The data bus connections—DB0 and DB1—are interchanged. What would the symptom of this problem be?

12.27. Show how to expand the 8086 memory in Fig. 12.16 to 64K bytes using additional 2167 SRAMs. Map your design to cover the address range 00000–0FFFFH.

12.28. True or false: All 8086 I/O instructions use register AX and input or output 16 bits of data.

12.29. Give an example of an 8086 instruction to input data from port C of the odd 8255A in Fig. 12.17.

12.30. Give an example of an 8086 instruction to output data to 16-bit port B of the 8255A in Fig. 12.17.

12.31. Sketch a circuit diagram showing an 8254 PIT interfaced to a max mode 8086. Map the PIT to cover even port addresses from 08H to 0EH.

KEY CONCEPT ANSWERS

12.1.1. BIU, EU

12.1.2. max

12.1.3. even byte, odd byte, and 16-bit word access

12.1.4. 4

12.2.1. The 8284 generates the clock signal.

12.2.2. ALE

12.2.3. $\overline{\text{DEN}}$ and DT/$\overline{\text{R}}$

12.2.4. max

12.3.1. AX is the 16-bit accumulator. The high-order 8 bits can be accessed as register AH and the low-order 8 bits as register AL.

12.3.2. code

12.3.3. The logical address is the 16-bit offset (0–64K) within a segment. The physical address is the 20-bit address output by the 8086.

12.3.4. based, stack

12.4.1. DX

12.4.2. DX:AX

12.4.3. far jump

12.4.4. an interrupt initiated by the instruction INT n where n is the type number.

12.5.1. A0 and $\overline{\text{BHE}}$

12.5.2. No. Both even and odd banks must be present.

12.5.3. Even and odd banks are required only when interfacing memory.

12.6.1. 8,16

12.6.2. real address

12.6.3. protected virtual

Answers to Selected Problems

Chapter 1

1.3. Control bus: S1 = memory, S2 = write, S3 = memory; address bus: 16; data bus: 26

1.5. 2^{24} = 16,772,216 (16 MB)

1.7. (a) 1111 1110, 254
    (b) 0001 0011, 19
    (c) 1100 1100 0000 0000, 52,224
    (d) 1111 1110 0000 0010 0111 1100, 16,646,780

1.8. (a) 1011, 13H
    (b) 0110 0011, 63H
    (c) 1111 1011, FBH
    (d) 1110 0001 0001 1101, E11DH

1.11. (a) −42
    (b) −113
    (c) −61
    (d) +102

1.13. (a) "&"
    (b) "d"
    (c) "BEL"
    (d) "ESC"

1.17. key 5 or 0101

1.19. B192; 13 address lines

1.21. 13FFH

1.23. 33H; "3"; INX SP

1.25. M1: memory read (op-code fetch); M2: memory read (port address); M3: I/O read

1.27. 8

1.29. Change location 0001 from 32H to 26H.

1.32. 2 T states or 500 ns

Chapter 2

2.4. instruction fetch

2.5. input read and output write

2.7. 9 pulses on $\overline{\text{MEMR}}$

2.8. false

2.12. true

2.13. The $\overline{\text{M1}}$ signal is provided.

2.15. true

2.18. C3 + 3D = 00; S = 0; Z = 1; CY = 1, AC = 1; P = 1

2.20. A = 10H + C9H = D9H; Z = 0; S = 1; P = 0; CY = 0; AC = 0

2.22. 1.916 ms

2.24. C3 + 3D = 00; S = 0; Z = 1; CY = 1; H = 1; P/V = 0

2.26. P/V = 1

2.31. 07FDH

2.33. (a) S = 0; Z = 0; H = 1; P/V = 0; CY = 0

2.39. 0701H

2.41. 0711

Chapter 3

3.2. 24 μs and 22 μs

3.4. EA; 1A; 21; 1A

3.5. 16FF; 2BH

3.7. 7.8 kHz and 0.6 Hz

3.8. 0.008 Hz, CMA

3.9. DE = F420H

3.14. Each byte is ANDed with itself.

3.16. 18.75 μs

3.17. F4 = −12

3.19. CF34

3.20. 108.75 μs

3.21. 16,777,215

3.29. E = B7H

3.31. A = DDH

Chapter 4

4.2. 667 KHz

4.3. 4

4.8. 10 loads in the high state and 5 loads in the low state

4.9. 0.7 V; 0.3 V

4.12. 75 UL, and 15 UL (high)/(low)

4.14. $V_{NH} = 0.7$ V; $V_{NL} = 0.5$ V

4.17. $3291\Omega \geq R \geq 261$ Ω

4.21. **(b)** bidirectional data bus buffer

4.22. **(a)** clock generator

4.24. Single-step to the I/O write machine cycle.

4.31. The single-step switch would have no effect.

4.32. The computer would operate normally until the single-step switch was pushed.

Chapter 5

5.1. **(b)** secondary storage

5.8. tRD = 75 ns

5.9. tRD = 120 ns

5.13. Both flip-flops would be permanently SET.

5.16. BFFFH

5.17. 24K; unused

5.22. **(a)** volatile

5.23. 8 chips for either design

5.26. **(b)** 8K bytes

5.27. Invert AB14 before connecting to IC1A.

5.29. 2732A: 0000–0FFFH and 8000–8FFFH

5.30. 7000–73FFH;

5.31. 260 ns

5.32. **(b)** DD00–DDFFH; active-low; 256 bytes

5.37. PROM data = D, E, B, F

5.39. $\overline{ROM1} = \overline{A15}\ \overline{A14}\ \overline{A13}$; 1

5.46. 1.92%

Chapter 6

6.3. OUT   A,3CH
       OUT   27H
       OUT   28H

6.10. **(a)** Use a logic probe to monitor the OUTFF and INFF DSPs.

6.12. C800–CBFFH

6.15. 03H (because column 1 is given priority)

6.19. BUSY/$\overline{\text{READY}}$; peripheral; when high peripheral is busy and cannot accept new data;

6.21. (a) I/O-mapped

6.23. NUMB is limited to 255.

6.25. 58 T states

6.26. 51 T states

6.29. true

6.37. When an NMI occurs, interrupts are automatically disabled.

6.39. The RST 7.5 input is rising edge-triggered;

Chapter 7

7.2. FCH through FFH

7.7. (a) 0BH

7.13. The program is identical to Fig. 7.9 with the following changes:
  (1) OUT   0F2H becomes STA FF02H.
  (2) The column access codes are 02H for col1 and 01H for col2.
  (3) IN   0F1H becomes LDA   FF00H.
  (4) COL2 DB   7,8,9,A,B,C,D,E,F.

7.17. (b) 11 10 001 0 → E2H

7.18. (d) 16.3845 ms

7.24. The IR6 is a lower priority so no interrupt request will be generated. If interrupts an enabled, the 8085 will allow lower priority interrupts to interrupt higher priority interrupts.

7.26. Assuming the IR3 service routine has enabled interrupts, IR5 will be accepted because it has a higher priority. After servicing IR5, IR3 is resumed.

7.34. 198 μs (8080) or 172 μs (8085)

Chapter 8

8.3. IM   2   ;mode 2 interrupts
      LD   A,C8H   ;high-order address
      LD   I,A   ; to register I
      LD   A,40H   ;low-order address
      OUT (F1H),A ;port A interrupt vector

8.5. (b) mode 3

8.12. Port A = 04H

8.15. (a) 128 μs
      (b) 16,384 μs
      (c) 8.388608 s

8.16. 696 pulses

8.18. 2.85 s

8.20. F = 1 KHz

8.24. 32.768 ms

8.25. (d) 190,476 bytes/s

8.26. (a) 6DH, 07H, FFH, 3FH

8.27. (a) 9.75 μs

(b) 10.75 μs

(c) 2.75 μs

Chapter 9

9.3. (b) 9 min 6 s

9.6.

```
        LHLD  1000H        ;Number of bytes to transmit
        XCHG               ;in DE.
        LHLD  A000H        ;Starting address in HL
LOOP    MOV   A,M          ;Fetch a byte
        CALL  SER_TRAN     ;Convert to serial and transmit
        INX   H
        DCX   D            ;Bump byte counter
        MOV   A,D          ;Test for D = E = 0
        ORA   E            ;
        JNZ   LOOP         ;Repeat
```

9.11. 55.3 s *vs* 81.9 s

9.17. Data bit 0 is in error.

9.18. (e) D7–D0 = 26H

9.19. 153 ns

9.21. 19,200 baud

9.23.

```
POLL  IN    71H      ;Get USART status
      ANI   2        ;Test RxRDY
      JZ    POLL     ;Wait for a character
      IN    70H      ;Now read it
      MOV   B,A      ;Save in B
      RET
```

9.32. 256 Input/output combinations are possible.

Chapter 10

10.3. (c) 16.7 ms

10.4. spindle motor

10.5. 47%

10.8. 41,616

10.9. (a) 87,040 bytes /cylinder

(b) 84.83 MB

10.10. 1.40625 MB

10.11. 8704 bytes

10.15. 510 KB/s

10.16. 25,500,000 bytes (unformatted)
21,307,392 bytes (formatted)

Chapter 11

11.2. 5 k

11.5. Rcold = 14 Ω; Rhot = 62 Ω.

11.6. (b) R = 20 Ω

11.9. (b) 10 mA

11.10. 39 mV and 2.44 mV

11.12. V_{OUT} = .625 V

11.13. (c) 9.96 V

11.15. 6.4 ms and 0.2 ms

11.27. Wiring errors may now be present.

Chapter 12

12.2. max

12.4. address bus = 80001H;

12.6. Even and odd banks must always be added.

12.11. physical address = 38100H;

12.12. code segment: 10000–1FFFFH

12.13. (a) data segment: 88200H

12.17. (a) moving 16-bit data to an 8-bit register

12.20. (a) 3180H
(b) 6DECH

12.22. (c) 2,147,483,648

APPENDIX A.1

Instruction		Code	Bytes	T States 8085A	T States 8080A	Machine Cycles
ACI	DATA	CE data	2	7	7	F R
ADC	REG	1000 1SSS	1	4	4	F
ADC	M	8E	1	7	7	F R
ADD	REG	1000 0SSS	1	4	4	F
ADD	M	86	1	7	7	F R
ADI	DATA	C6 data	2	7	7	F R
ANA	REG	1010 0SSS	1	4	4	F
ANA	M	A6	1	7	7	F R
ANI	DATA	E6 data	2	7	7	F R
CALL	LABEL	CD addr	3	18	17	S R R W W*
CC	LABEL	DC addr	3	9/18	11/17	S R•/S R R W W*
CM	LABEL	FC addr	3	9/18	11/17	S R•/S R R W W*
CMA		2F	1	4	4	F
CMC		3F	1	4	4	F
CMP	REG	1011 1SSS	1	4	4	F
CMP	M	BE	1	7	7	F R
CNC	LABEL	D4 addr	3	9/18	11/17	S R•/S R R W W*
CNZ	LABEL	C4 addr	3	9/18	11/17	S R•/S R R W W*
CP	LABEL	F4 addr	3	9/18	11/17	S R•/S R R W W*
CPE	LABEL	EC addr	3	9/18	11/17	S R•/S R R W W*
CPI	DATA	FE data	2	7	7	F R
CPO	LABEL	E4 addr	3	9/18	11/17	S R•/S R R W W*
CZ	LABEL	CC addr	3	9/18	11/17	S R•/S R R W W*
DAA		27	1	4	4	F
DAD	RP	00RP 1001	1	10	10	F B B
DCR	REG	00SS S101	1	4	5	F*
DCR	M	35	1	10	10	F R W
DCX	RP	00RP 1011	1	6	5	S*
DI		F3	1	4	4	F
EI		FB	1	4	4	F
HLT		76	1	5	7	F B
IN	PORT	DB data	2	10	10	F R I
INR	REG	00SS S100	1	4	5	F*
INR	M	34	1	10	10	F R W
INX	RP	00RP 0011	1	6	5	S*
JC	LABEL	DA addr	3	7/10	10	F R/F R R†
JM	LABEL	FA addr	3	7/10	10	F R/F R R†
JMP	LABEL	C3 addr	3	10	10	F R R
JNC	LABEL	D2 addr	3	7/10	10	F R/F R R†
JNZ	LABEL	C2 addr	3	7/10	10	F R/F R R†
JP	LABEL	F2 addr	3	7/10	10	F R/F R R†
JPE	LABEL	EA addr	3	7/10	10	F R/F R R†
JPO	LABEL	E2 addr	3	7/10	10	F R/F R R†
JZ	LABEL	CA addr	3	7/10	10	F R/F R R†
LDA	ADDR	3A addr	3	13	13	F R R R
LDAX	RP	000X 1010	1	7	7	F R
LHLD	ADDR	2A addr	3	16	16	F R R R R
LXI	RP,DATA16	00RP 0001 data16	3	10	10	F R R
MOV	REG,REG	01DD DSSS	1	4	5	F*
MOV	M,REG	0111 0SSS	1	7	7	F W
MOV	REG,M	01DD D110	1	7	7	F R
MVI	REG,DATA	00DD D110 data	2	7	7	F R
MVI	M,DATA	36 data	2	10	10	F R W
NOP		00	1	4	4	F
ORA	REG	1011 0SSS	1	4	4	F
ORA	M	B6	1	7	7	F R
ORI	DATA	F6 data	2	7	7	F R
OUT	PORT	D3 data	2	10	10	F R O
PCHL		E9	1	6	5	S*
POP	RP	11RP 0001	1	10	10	F R R
PUSH	RP	11RP 0101	1	12	11	S W W*
RAL		17	1	4	4	F
RAR		1F	1	4	4	F
RC		D8	1	6/12	5/11	S/S R R*
RET		C9	1	10	10	F R R
RIM (8085A only)		20	1	4	–	F
RLC		07	1	4	4	F
RM		F8	1	6/12	5/11	S/S R R*
RNC		D0	1	6/12	5/11	S/S R R*
RNZ		C0	1	6/12	5/11	S/S R R*
RP		F0	1	6/12	5/11	S/S R R*
RPE		E8	1	6/12	5/11	S/S R R*
RPO		E0	1	6/12	5/11	S/S R R*
RRC		0F	1	4	4	F
RST	N	11XX X111	1	12	11	S W W*
RZ		C8	1	6/12	5/11	S/S R R*
SBB	REG	1001 1SSS	1	4	4	F
SBB	M	9E	1	7	7	F R
SBI	DATA	DE data	2	7	7	F R
SHLD	ADDR	22 addr	3	16	16	F R R W W
SIM (8085A only)		30	1	4	–	F
SPHL		F9	1	6	5	S*
STA	ADDR	32 addr	3	13	13	F R R W
STAX	RP	000X 0010	1	7	7	F W
STC		37	1	4	4	F
SUB	REG	1001 0SSS	1	4	4	F
SUB	M	96	1	7	7	F R
SUI	DATA	D6 data	2	7	7	F R
XCHG		EB	1	4	4	F
XRA	REG	1010 1SSS	1	4	4	F
XRA	M	AE	1	7	7	F R
XRI	DATA	EE data	2	7	7	F R
XTHL		E3	1	16	18	F R R W W

Machine cycle types:

F	Four clock period instr fetch
S	Six clock period instr fetch
R	Memory read
I	I/O read
W	Memory write
O	I/O write
B	Bus idle
X	Variable or optional binary digit

*All mnemonics copyrighted © Intel Corporation 1976.

DDD	Binary digits identifying a destination register
SSS	Binary digits identifying a source register
RP	Register Pair

B = 000, C = 001, D = 010 Memory = 110
E = 011, H = 100, L = 101 A = 111

BC = 00, HL = 10
DE = 01, SP = 11

*Five clock period instruction fetch with 8080A.

†The longer machine cycle sequence applies regardless of condition evaluation with 8080A.

•An extra READ cycle (R) will occur for this condition with 8080A.

Appendix A.1 ' 8080/85 Machine Cycle and T State Summary. (Courtesy of Intel Corporation.)

APPENDIX A.2

CONSTANT DEFINITION

0BDH	} Hex	
1AH		
105D	} Decimal	
105		
72Q	} Octal	
72Q		
11011B	} Binary	
00110B		
'TEST'	} ASCII	
'A' 'B'		

OPERATORS

(,)
*, /, MOD, SHL, SHR
+, -
NOT
AND
OR, XOR

STANDARD SETS

A	SET	7
B	SET	0
C	SET	1
D	SET	2
E	SET	3
H	SET	4
L	SET	5
M	SET	6
SP	SET	
PSW	SET	6

FLAG BYTE STANDARD FORMAT

7	6	5	4	3	2	1	0
S	Z	0	C	0	P	1	C

ACCUMULATOR*

80 ADD B	88 ADC B	90 SUB B	98 SBB B	A0 ANA B	A8 XRA B	B0 ORA B	B8 CMP B
81 ADD C	89 ADC C	91 SUB C	99 SBB C	A1 ANA C	A9 XRA C	B1 ORA C	B9 CMP C
82 ADD D	8A ADC D	92 SUB D	9A SBB D	A2 ANA D	AA XRA D	B2 ORA D	BA CMP D
83 ADD E	8B ADC E	93 SUB E	9B SBB E	A3 ANA E	AB XRA E	B3 ORA E	BB CMP E
84 ADD H	8C ADC H	94 SUB H	9C SBB H	A4 ANA H	AC XRA H	B4 ORA H	BC CMP H
85 ADD L	8D ADC L	95 SUB L	9D SBB L	A5 ANA L	AD XRA L	B5 ORA L	BD CMP L
86 ADD M	8E ADC M	96 SUB M	9E SBB M	A6 ANA M	AE XRA M	B6 ORA M	BE CMP M
87 ADD A	8F ADC A	97 SUB A	9F SBB A	A7 ANA A	AF XRA A	B7 ORA A	BF CMP A

PSEUDO INSTRUCTION

ORG	Adr
END	
EQU	D16
SET	D16
DS	D16
DB	D8
DW	D16
IF	D16
ENDIF	
MACRO	[ ]
ENDM	

MOVE (cont)

58 MOV E,B	60 MOV H,B	68 MOV L,B	70 MOV M,B	78 MOV A,B
59 MOV E,C	61 MOV H,C	69 MOV L,C	71 MOV M,C	79 MOV A,C
5A MOV E,D	62 MOV H,D	6A MOV L,D	72 MOV M,D	7A MOV A,D
5B MOV E,E	63 MOV H,E	6B MOV L,E	73 MOV M,E	7B MOV A,E
5C MOV E,H	64 MOV H,H	6C MOV L,H	74 MOV M,H	7C MOV A,H
5D MOV E,L	65 MOV H,L	6D MOV L,L	75 MOV M,L	7D MOV A,L
5E MOV E,M	66 MOV H,M	6E MOV L,M		7E MOV A,M
5F MOV E,A	67 MOV H,A	6F MOV L,A	77 MOV M,A	7F MOV A,A

ROTATE†

07	RLC
0F	RRC
17	RAL
1F	RAR

CONTROL

00	NOP
76	HLT
F3	DI
FB	EI

MOVE

40 MOV B,B	48 MOV C,B	50 MOV D,B
41 MOV B,C	49 MOV C,C	51 MOV D,C
42 MOV B,D	4A MOV C,D	52 MOV D,D
43 MOV B,E	4B MOV C,E	53 MOV D,E
44 MOV B,H	4C MOV C,H	54 MOV D,H
45 MOV B,L	4D MOV C,L	55 MOV D,L
46 MOV B,M	4E MOV C,M	56 MOV D,M
47 MOV B,A	4F MOV C,A	57 MOV D,A

RESTART

C7	RST 0
CF	RST 1
D7	RST 2
DF	RST 3
E7	RST 4
EF	RST 5
F7	RST 6
FF	RST 7

STACK OPS

C5	PUSH B
D5	PUSH D
E5	PUSH H
F5	PUSH PSW
C1	POP B
D1	POP D
E1	POP H
F1	POP PSW*

SPECIALS

EB	XCHG
27	DAA*
2F	CMA
37	STC†
3F	CMC†

INPUT/OUTPUT

D3	OUT	} D8
DB	IN	

JUMP

C3	JMP	
C2	JNZ	
CA	JZ	
D2	JNC	
DA	JC	
E2	JPO	} Adr
EA	JPE	
F2	JP	
FA	JM	
E9	PCHL	

CALL

CD	CALL	
C4	CNZ	
CC	CZ	
D4	CNC	
DC	CC	} Adr
E4	CPO	
EC	CPE	
F4	CP	
FC	CM	

RETURN

C9	RET
C0	RNZ
C8	RZ
D0	RNC
D8	RC
E0	RPO
E8	RPE
F0	RP
F8	RM

LOAD IMMEDIATE

01	LXI B,	
11	LXI D,	} D16
21	LXI H,	
31	LXI SP,	

DOUBLE ADD†

09	DAD B
19	DAD D
29	DAD H
39	DAD SP

LOAD/STORE

0A	LDAX B
1A	LDAX D
2A	LHLD Adr
3A	LDA Adr
02	STAX B
12	STAX D
22	SHLD Adr
32	STA Adr

MOVE IMMEDIATE

06	MVI B,	
0E	MVI C,	
16	MVI D,	
1E	MVI E,	} D8
26	MVI H,	
2E	MVI L,	
36	MVI M,	
3E	MVI A,	

Acc IMMEDIATE*

C6	ADI	
CE	ACI	
D6	SUI	
DE	SBI	} D8
E6	ANI	
EE	XRI	
F6	ORI	
FE	CPI	

INCREMENT**

04	INR B
0C	INR C
14	INR D
1C	INR E
24	INR H
2C	INR L
34	INR M
3C	INR A
03	INX B
13	INX D
23	INX H
33	INX SP

DECREMENT**

05	DCR B
0D	DCR C
15	DCR D
1D	DCR E
25	DCR H
2D	DCR L
35	DCR M
3D	DCR A
0B	DCX B
1B	DCX D
2B	DCX H
3B	DCX SP

D8 = constant, or logical/arithmetic expression that evaluates to an 8 bit data quantity.

* = all Flags (C, Z, S, P, AC) affected

D16 = constant, or logical/arithmetic expression that evaluates to a 16 bit data quantity.

† = only CARRY affected

Adr = 16 bit address

** = all Flags except CARRY affected; (exception: INX & DCX affect no Flags)

Appendix A.2 8080/85 Hexadecimal Instruction Set Index. (Courtesy of Intel Corporation.)

Instruction Set

The Z80 microprocessor has one of the most powerful and versatile instruction sets available in any 8-bit microprocessor. It includes such unique operations as a block move for fast, efficient data transfers within memory or between memory and I/O. It also allows operations on any bit in any location in memory.

The following is a summary of the Z80 instruction set and shows the assembly language mnemonic, the operation, the flag status, and gives comments on each instruction. The *Z80 CPU Technical Manual* (03-0029-01) and *Assembly Language Programming Manual* (03-0002-01) contain significantly more details for programming use.

The instructions are divided into the following categories:

☐ 8-bit loads

☐ 16-bit loads

☐ Exchanges, block transfers, and searches

☐ 8-bit arithmetic and logic operations

☐ General-purpose arithmetic and CPU control

☐ 16-bit arithmetic operations

☐ Rotates and shifts

☐ Bit set, reset, and test operations

☐ Jumps

☐ Calls, returns, and restarts

☐ Input and output operations

A variety of addressing modes are implemented to permit efficient and fast data transfer between various registers, memory locations, and input/output devices. These addressing modes include:

☐ Immediate

☐ Immediate extended

☐ Modified page zero

☐ Relative

☐ Extended

☐ Indexed

☐ Register

☐ Register indirect

☐ Implied

☐ Bit

8-Bit Load Group

Mnemonic	Symbolic Operation	S	Z	H	P/V	N	C	Opcode 76 543 210	Hex	No. of Bytes	No. of M Cycles	No. of T States	Comments
LD r, r'	r ← r'	•	•	•	•	•	•	01 r r'		1	1	4	
LD r, n	r ← n	•	•	•	•	•	•	00 r 110 / – n –		2	2	7	
LD r, (HL)	r ← (HL)	•	•	•	•	•	•	01 r 110		1	2	7	
LD r, (IX + d)	r ← (IX + d)	•	•	•	•	•	•	11 011 101 / 01 r 110 / – d –	DD	3	5	19	
LD r, (IY + d)	r ← (IY + d)	•	•	•	•	•	•	11 111 101 / 01 r 110 / – d –	FD	3	5	19	
LD (HL), r	(HL) ← r	•	•	•	•	•	•	01 110 r		1	2	7	
LD (IX + d), r	(IX + d) ← r	•	•	•	•	•	•	11 011 101 / 01 110 r / – d –	DD	3	5	19	
LD (IY + d), r	(IY + d) ← r	•	•	•	•	•	•	11 111 101 / 01 110 r / – d –	FD	3	5	19	
LD (HL), n	(HL) ← n	•	•	•	•	•	•	00 110 110 / – n –	36	2	3	10	
LD (IX + d), n	(IX + d) ← n	•	•	•	•	•	•	11 011 101 / 00 110 110 / – d – / – n –	DD 36	4	5	19	
LD (IY + d), n	(IY + d) ← n	•	•	•	•	•	•	11 111 101 / 00 110 110 / – d – / – n –	FD 36	4	5	19	
LD A, (BC)	A ← (BC)	•	•	•	•	•	•	00 001 010	0A	1	2	7	
LD A, (DE)	A ← (DE)	•	•	•	•	•	•	00 011 010	1A	1	2	7	
LD A, (nn)	A ← (nn)	•	•	•	•	•	•	00 111 010 / – n – / – n –	3A	3	4	13	
LD (BC), A	(BC) ← A	•	•	•	•	•	•	00 000 010	02	1	2	7	
LD (DE), A	(DE) ← A	•	•	•	•	•	•	00 010 010	12	1	2	7	
LD (nn), A	(nn) ← A	•	•	•	•	•	•	00 110 010 / – n – / – n –	32	3	4	13	
LD A, I	A ← I	↕	↕	0	IFF	0	•	11 101 101 / 01 010 111	ED 57	2	2	9	
LD A, R	A ← R	↕	↕	0	IFF	0	•	11 101 101 / 01 011 111	ED 5F	2	2	9	
LD I, A	I ← A	•	•	•	•	•	•	11 101 101 / 01 000 111	ED 47	2	2	9	
LD R, A	R ← A	•	•	•	•	•	•	11 101 101 / 01 001 111	ED 4F	2	2	9	

Comments (register encoding for r, r'):

r, r'	Reg.
000	B
001	C
010	D
011	E
100	H
101	L
111	A

NOTES: r, r' means any of the registers A, B, C, D, E, H, L.
IFF the content of the interrupt enable flip-flop, (IFF) is copied into the P/V flag.

For an explanation of flag notation and symbols for mnemonic tables, see Symbolic Notation section following tables.

Appendix B.1 Z-80 Instruction Set Description. (Courtesy of Zilog, Inc.)

16-Bit Load Group

Mnemonic	Symbolic Operation	S	Z	H	P/V	N	C	Opcode 76 543 210	Hex	No.of Bytes	No.of M Cycles	No.of T States	Comments
LD dd, nn	dd ← nn	•	•	X	•	X	•	•	•	00 dd0 001 – n – – n –		3	3	10	dd Pair 00 BC 01 DE 10 HL 11 SP
LD IX, nn	IX ← nn	•	•	X	•	X	•	•	•	11 011 101 00 100 001 – n – – n –	DD 21	4	4	14	
LD IY, nn	IY ← nn	•	•	X	•	X	•	•	•	11 111 101 00 100 001 – n – – n –	FD 21	4	4	14	
LD HL, (nn)	H ← (nn + 1) L ← (nn)	•	•	X	•	X	•	•	•	00 101 010 – n – – n –	2A	3	5	16	
LD dd, (nn)	dd$_H$ ← (nn + 1) dd$_L$ ← (nn)	•	•	X	•	X	•	•	•	11 101 101 01 dd1 011 – n – – n –	ED	4	6	20	
LD IX, (nn)	IX$_H$ ← (nn + 1) IX$_L$ ← (nn)	•	•	X	•	X	•	•	•	11 011 101 00 101 010 – n – – n –	DD 2A	4	6	20	
LD IY, (nn)	IY$_H$ ← (nn + 1) IY$_L$ ← (nn)	•	•	X	•	X	•	•	•	11 111 101 00 101 010 – n – – n –	FD 2A	4	6	20	
LD (nn), HL	(nn + 1) ← H (nn) ← L	•	•	X	•	X	•	•	•	00 100 010 – n – – n –	22	3	5	16	
LD (nn), dd	(nn + 1) ← dd$_H$ (nn) ← dd$_L$	•	•	X	•	X	•	•	•	11 101 101 01 dd0 011 – n – – n –	ED	4	6	20	
LD (nn), IX	(nn + 1) ← IX$_H$ (nn) ← IX$_L$	•	•	X	•	X	•	•	•	11 011 101 00 100 010 – n – – n –	DD 22	4	6	20	
LD (nn), IY	(nn + 1) ← IY$_H$ (nn) ← IY$_L$	•	•	X	•	X	•	•	•	11 111 101 00 100 010 – n – – n –	FD 22	4	6	20	
LD SP, HL	SP ← HL	•	•	X	•	X	•	•	•	11 111 001	F9	1	1	6	
LD SP, IX	SP ← IX	•	•	X	•	X	•	•	•	11 011 101 11 111 001	DD F9	2	2	10	
LD SP, IY	SP ← IY	•	•	X	•	X	•	•	•	11 111 101 11 111 001	FD F9	2	2	10	
PUSH qq	(SP – 2) ← qq$_L$ (SP – 1) ← qq$_H$ SP ← SP – 2	•	•	X	•	X	•	•	•	11 qq0 101		1	3	11	qq Pair 00 BC 01 DE 10 HL 11 AF
PUSH IX	(SP – 2) ← IX$_L$ (SP – 1) ← IX$_H$ SP ← SP – 2	•	•	X	•	X	•	•	•	11 011 101 11 100 101	DD E5	2	4	15	
PUSH IY	(SP – 2) ← IY$_L$ (SP – 1) ← IY$_H$ SP ← SP – 2	•	•	X	•	X	•	•	•	11 111 101 11 100 101	FD E5	2	4	15	
POP qq	qq$_H$ ← (SP + 1) qq$_L$ ← (SP) SP ← SP + 2	•	•	X	•	X	•	•	•	11 qq0 001		1	3	10	
POP IX	IX$_H$ ← (SP + 1) IX$_L$ ← (SP) SP ← SP + 2	•	•	X	•	X	•	•	•	11 011 101 11 100 001	DD E1	2	4	14	
POP IY	IY$_H$ ← (SP + 1) IY$_L$ ← (SP) SP ← SP + 2	•	•	X	•	X	•	•	•	11 111 101 11 100 001	FD E1	2	4	14	

NOTES: dd is any of the register pairs BC, DE, HL, SP. (PAIR)$_H$, (PAIR)$_L$ refer to high order and low order eight bits of the register pair respectively,
qq is any of the register pairs AF, BC, DE, HL. e.g., BC$_L$ = C, AF$_H$ = A.

Exchange, Block Transfer, Block Search Groups

Mnemonic	Symbolic Operation	S	Z	H	P/V	N	C	Opcode 76 543 210	Hex	No.of Bytes	No.of M Cycles	No.of T States	Comments
EX DE, HL	DE ↔ HL	•	•	X	•	X	•	•	•	11 101 011	EB	1	1	4	
EX AF, AF'	AF ↔ AF'	•	•	X	•	X	•	•	•	00 001 000	08	1	1	4	
EXX	BC ↔ BC' DE ↔ DE' HL ↔ HL'	•	•	X	•	X	•	•	•	11 011 001	D9	1	1	4	Register bank and auxiliary register bank exchange
EX (SP), HL	H ↔ (SP + 1) L ↔ (SP)	•	•	X	•	X	•	•	•	11 100 011	E3	1	5	19	
EX (SP), IX	IX$_H$ ↔ (SP + 1) IX$_L$ ↔ (SP)	•	•	X	•	X	•	•	•	11 011 101 11 100 011	DD E3	2	6	23	
EX (SP), IY	IY$_H$ ↔ (SP + 1) IY$_L$ ↔ (SP)	•	•	X	•	X	•	•	•	11 111 101 11 100 011	FD E3	2	6	23	
LDI	(DE) ← (HL) DE ← DE + 1 HL ← HL + 1 BC ← BC – 1	•	•	X	0	X	①	0	•	11 101 101 10 100 000	ED A0	2	4	16	Load (HL) into (DE), increment the pointers and decrement the byte counter (BC)
LDIR	(DE) ← (HL) DE ← DE + 1 HL ← HL + 1 BC ← BC – 1 Repeat until BC = 0	•	•	X	0	X	0	0	•	11 101 101 10 110 000	ED B0	2 2	5 4	21 16	If BC ≠ 0 If BC = 0

NOTE: ① P/V flag is 0 if the result of BC – 1 = 0, otherwise P/V = 1.

Exchange, Block Transfer, Block Search Groups (Continued)

Mnemonic	Symbolic Operation	S	Z	Flags H	P/V	N	C	Opcode 76 543 210 Hex	No. of Bytes	No. of M Cycles	No. of T States	Comments
					①							
LDD	(DE) ← (HL) DE ← DE − 1 HL ← HL − 1 BC ← BC − 1	•	•	X 0 X	‡	0	•	11 101 101 ED 10 101 000 A8	2	4	16	
LDDR	(DE) ← (HL) DE ← DE − 1 HL ← HL − 1 BC ← BC − 1 Repeat until BC = 0	•	•	X 0 X	0	0	•	11 101 101 ED 10 111 000 B8	2 2	5 4	21 16	If BC ≠ 0 If BC = 0
			②		①							
CPI	A − (HL) HL ← HL + 1 BC ← BC − 1	‡	‡	X ‡ X	‡	1	•	11 101 101 ED 10 100 001 A1	2	4	16	
			②		①							
CPIR	A − (HL)	‡	‡	X ‡ X	‡	1	•	11 101 101 ED	2	5	21	If BC ≠ 0 and A ≠ (HL)
	HL ← HL + 1 BC ← BC − 1 Repeat until A = (HL) or BC = 0							10 110 001 B1	2	4	16	If BC = 0 or A = (HL)
			②		①							
CPD	A − (HL) HL ← HL − 1 BC ← BC − 1	‡	‡	X ‡ X	‡	1	•	11 101 101 ED 10 101 001 A9	2	4	16	
			②		①							
CPDR	A − (HL)	‡	‡	X ‡ X	‡	1	•	11 101 101 ED	2	5	21	If BC ≠ 0 and A ≠ (HL)
	HL ← HL − 1 BC ← BC − 1 Repeat until A = (HL) or BC = 0							10 111 001 B9	2	4	16	If BC = 0 or A = (HL)

NOTES: ① P/V flag is 0 if the result of BC − 1 = 0, otherwise P/V = 1.
② Z flag is 1 if A = (HL), otherwise Z = 0.

8-Bit Arithmetic and Logical Group

Mnemonic	Symbolic Operation	S	Z	Flags H	P/V	N	C	Opcode 76 543 210 Hex	No. of Bytes	No. of M Cycles	No. of T States	Comments
ADD A, r	A ← A + r	‡	‡	X ‡ X	V	0	‡	10 **000** r	1	1	4	r Reg.
ADD A, n	A ← A + n	‡	‡	X ‡ X	V	0	‡	11 **000** 110 ← n →	2	2	7	000 B 001 C 010 D
ADD A, (HL)	A ← A + (HL)	‡	‡	X ‡ X	V	0	‡	10 **000** 110	1	2	7	011 E
ADD A, (IX + d)	A ← A + (IX + d)	‡	‡	X ‡ X	V	0	‡	11 011 101 DD 10 **000** 110 ← d →	3	5	19	100 H 101 L 111 A
ADD A, (IY + d)	A ← A + (IY + d)	‡	‡	X ‡ X	V	0	‡	11 111 101 FD 10 **000** 110 ← d →	3	5	19	
ADC A, s	A ← A + s + CY	‡	‡	X ‡ X	V	0	‡	**001**				s is any of r, n, (HL), (IX + d),
SUB s	A ← A − s	‡	‡	X ‡ X	V	1	‡	**010**				(IY + d) as shown
SBC A, s	A ← A − s − CY	‡	‡	X ‡ X	V	1	‡	**011**				for ADD instruction.
AND s	A ← A ∧ s	‡	‡	X 1 X	P	0	0	**100**				The indicated bits
OR s	A ← A ∨ s	‡	‡	X 0 X	P	0	0	**110**				replace the **000** in
XOR s	A ← A ⊕ s	‡	‡	X 0 X	P	0	0	**101**				the ADD set above.
CP s	A − s	‡	‡	X ‡ X	V	1	‡	**111**				
INC r	r ← r + 1	‡	‡	X ‡ X	V	0	•	00 r **100**	1	1	4	
INC (HL)	(HL) ←(HL) + 1	‡	‡	X ‡ X	V	0	•	00 110 **100**	1	3	11	
INC (IX + d)	(IX + d) ← (IX + d) + 1	‡	‡	X ‡ X	V	0	•	11 011 101 DD 00 110 **100** ← d →	3	6	23	
INC (IY + d)	(IY + d) ← (IY + d) + 1	‡	‡	X ‡ X	V	0	•	11 111 101 FD 00 110 **100** ← d →	3	6	23	
DEC m	m ← m − 1	‡	‡	X ‡ X	V	1	•	**101**				m is any of r, (HL), (IX + d), (IY + d) as shown for INC. DEC same format and states as INC. Replace **100** with **101** in opcode.

General-Purpose Arithmetic and CPU Control Groups

Mnemonic	Symbolic Operation	S	Z	Flags H	P/V	N	C	Opcode 76 543 210	Hex	No. of Bytes	No. of M Cycles	No. of T States	Comments
DAA	Converts acc. content into packed BCD following add or subtract with packed BCD operands.	↕	↕	X ↕ X	P	•	↕	00 100 111	27	1	1	4	Decimal adjust accumulator.
CPL	A ← Ā	•	•	X 1 X	•	1	•	00 101 111	2F	1	1	4	Complement accumulator (one's complement).
NEG	A ← 0 − A	↕	↕	X ↕ X	V	1	↕	11 101 101 01 000 100	ED 44	2	2	8	Negate acc. (two's complement).
CCF	CY ← C̄Ȳ	•	•	X X X	•	0	↕	00 111 111	3F	1	1	4	Complement carry flag.
SCF	CY ← 1	•	•	X 0 X	•	0	1	00 110 111	37	1	1	4	Set carry flag.
NOP	No operation	•	•	X • X	•	•	•	00 000 000	00	1	1	4	
HALT	CPU halted	•	•	X • X	•	•	•	01 110 110	76	1	1	4	
DI ★	IFF ← 0	•	•	X • X	•	•	•	11 110 011	F3	1	1	4	
EI ★	IFF ← 1	•	•	X • X	•	•	•	11 111 011	FB	1	1	4	
IM 0	Set interrupt mode 0	•	•	X • X	•	•	•	11 101 101 01 000 110	ED 46	2	2	8	
IM 1	Set interrupt mode 1	•	•	X • X	•	•	•	11 101 101 01 010 110	ED 56	2	2	8	
IM 2	Set interrupt mode 2	•	•	X • X	•	•	•	11 101 101 01 011 110	ED 5E	2	2	8	

NOTES: IFF indicates the interrupt enable flip-flop.
CY indicates the carry flip-flop.
★ indicates interrupts are not sampled at the end of EI or DI.

16-Bit Arithmetic Group

Mnemonic	Symbolic Operation	S	Z	Flags H	P/V	N	C	Opcode 76 543 210	Hex	No. of Bytes	No. of M Cycles	No. of T States	Comments
ADD HL, ss	HL ← HL + ss	•	•	X X X	•	0	↕	00 ss1 001		1	3	11	ss Reg.
ADC HL, ss	HL ← HL + ss + CY	↕	↕	X X X	V	0	↕	11 101 101 01 ss1 010	ED	2	4	15	00 BC
SBC HL, ss	HL ← HL − ss − CY	↕	↕	X X X	V	1	↕	11 101 101 01 ss0 010	ED	2	4	15	01 DE
ADD IX, pp	IX ← IX + pp	•	•	X X X	•	0	↕	11 011 101 01 pp1 001	DD	2	4	15	pp Reg.
ADD IY, rr	IY ← IY + rr	•	•	X X X	•	0	↕	11 111 101 00 rr1 001	FD	2	4	15	rr Reg.
INC ss	ss ← ss + 1	•	•	X • X	•	•	•	00 ss0 011		1	1	6	
INC IX	IX ← IX + 1	•	•	X • X	•	•	•	11 011 101 00 100 011	DD 23	2	2	10	
INC IY	IY ← IY + 1	•	•	X • X	•	•	•	11 111 101 00 100 011	FD 23	2	2	10	
DEC ss	ss ← ss − 1	•	•	X • X	•	•	•	00 ss1 011		1	1	6	
DEC IX	IX ← IX − 1	•	•	X • X	•	•	•	11 011 101 00 101 011	DD 2B	2	2	10	
DEC IY	IY ← IY − 1	•	•	X • X	•	•	•	11 111 101 00 101 011	FD 2B	2	2	10	

ADD HL, ss / ADC HL, ss / SBC HL, ss registers:
00 BC, 01 DE, 10 HL, 11 SP

ADD IX, pp registers:
00 BC, 01 DE, 10 IX, 11 SP

ADD IY, rr registers:
00 BC, 01 DE, 10 IY, 11 SP

NOTES: ss is any of the register pairs BC, DE, HL, SP.
pp is any of the register pairs BC, DE, IX, SP.
rr is any of the register pairs BC, DE, IY, SP.

Rotate and Shift Group

Mnemonic	Symbolic Operation	S	Z	Flags H	P/V	N	C	Opcode 76 543 210	Hex	No. of Bytes	No. of M Cycles	No. of T States	Comments
RLCA		•	•	X 0 X	•	0	↕	00 000 111	07	1	1	4	Rotate left circular accumulator.
RLA		•	•	X 0 X	•	0	↕	00 010 111	17	1	1	4	Rotate left accumulator.
RRCA		•	•	X 0 X	•	0	↕	00 001 111	0F	1	1	4	Rotate right circular accumulator.
RRA		•	•	X 0 X	•	0	↕	00 011 111	1F	1	1	4	Rotate right accumulator.
RLC r		↕	↕	X 0 X	P	0	↕	11 001 011 00 [000] r	CB	2	2	8	Rotate left circular register r.
RLC (HL)		↕	↕	X 0 X	P	0	↕	11 001 011 00 [000] 110	CB	2	4	15	r Reg.
RLC (IX + d)	r,(HL),(IX + d),(IY + d)	↕	↕	X 0 X	P	0	↕	11 011 101 11 001 011 − d − 00 [000] 110	DD CB	4	6	23	000 B, 001 C, 010 D, 011 E, 100 H, 101 L, 111 A
RLC (IY + d)		↕	↕	X 0 X	P	0	↕	11 111 101 11 001 011 − d − 00 [000] 110	FD CB	4	6	23	
RL m	m = r,(HL),(IX + d),(IY + d)	↕	↕	X 0 X	P	0	↕	[010]					Instruction format and states are as shown for RLC's. To form new opcode replace [000] of RLC's with shown code.
RRC m	m = r,(HL),(IX + d),(IY + d)	↕	↕	X 0 X	P	0	↕	[001]					

Mnemonic	Symbolic Operation	S	Z	H	P/V	N	C	Opcode 76 543 210	Hex	No.of Bytes	No.of M Cycles	No.of T States	Comments
RR m	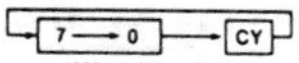 [7→0]→CY m = r,(HL),(IX + d),(IY + d)	↕	↕	X	0	X	P	0	↕	[011]				
SLA m	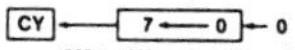 CY←[7←0]←0 m = r,(HL),(IX + d),(IY + d)	↕	↕	X	0	X	P	0	↕	[100]				
SRA m	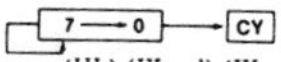 [7→0]→CY m = r,(HL),(IX + d),(IY + d)	↕	↕	X	0	X	P	0	↕	[101]				
SRL m	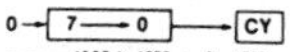 0→[7→0]→CY m = r,(HL),(IX + d),(IY + d)	↕	↕	X	0	X	P	0	↕	[111]				
RLD	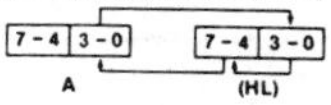 [7-4 3-0] [7-4 3-0] A (HL)	↕	↕	X	0	X	P	0	•	11 101 101 / 01 101 111	ED / 6F	2	5	18	Rotate digit left and right between the accumulator and location (HL). The content of the upper half of the accumulator is unaffected.
RRD	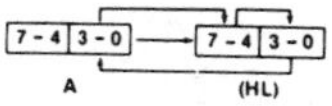 [7-4 3-0] [7-4 3-0] A (HL)	↕	↕	X	0	X	P	0	•	11 101 101 / 01 100 111	ED / 67	2	5	18	

Bit Set, Reset and Test Group

Mnemonic	Symbolic Operation	S	Z	H	P/V	N	C	Opcode 76 543 210	Hex	No.of Bytes	No.of M Cycles	No.of T States	Comments
BIT b, r	$Z \leftarrow \bar{r}_b$	X	↕	X	1	X	X	0	•	11 001 011 / 01 b r	CB	2	2	8	
BIT b, (HL)	$Z \leftarrow (\overline{HL})_b$	X	↕	X	1	X	X	0	•	11 001 011 / 01 b 110	CB	2	3	12	
BIT b, (IX + d)ₓ	$Z \leftarrow (\overline{IX+d})_b$	X	↕	X	1	X	X	0	•	11 011 101 / 11 001 011 / — d — / 01 b 110	DD / CB	4	5	20	
BIT b, (IY + d)ₓ	$Z \leftarrow (\overline{IY+d})_b$	X	↕	X	1	X	X	0	•	11 111 101 / 11 001 011 / — d — / 01 b 110	FD / CB	4	5	20	
SET b, r	$r_b \leftarrow 1$	•	•	X	•	X	•	•	•	11 001 011 / [11] b r	CB	2	2	8	
SET b, (HL)	$(HL)_b \leftarrow 1$	•	•	X	•	X	•	•	•	11 001 011 / [11] b 110	CB	2	4	15	
SET b, (IX + d)	$(IX+d)_b \leftarrow 1$	•	•	X	•	X	•	•	•	11 011 101 / 11 001 011 / — d — / [11] b 110	DD / CB	4	6	23	
SET b, (IY + d)	$(IY+d)_b \leftarrow 1$	•	•	X	•	X	•	•	•	11 111 101 / 11 001 011 / — d — / [11] b 110	FD / CB	4	6	23	
RES b, m	$m_b \leftarrow 0$ m = r, (HL), (IX + d), (IY + d)	•	•	X	•	X	•	•	•	[10]					To form new opcode replace [11] of SET b, s with [10]. Flags and time states for SET instruction.

Register/Bit reference (right column):

r	Reg.
000	B
001	C
010	D
011	E
100	H
101	L
111	A

b	Bit Tested
000	0
001	1
010	2
011	3
100	4
101	5
110	6
111	7

NOTES: The notation m_b indicates bit b (0 to 7) or location m.

Jump Group

Mnemonic	Symbolic Operation	S	Z	H	P/V	N	C	Opcode 76 543 210	Hex	No.of Bytes	No.of M Cycles	No.of T States	Comments
JP nn	$PC \leftarrow nn$	•	•	X	•	X	•	•	•	11 000 011 / — n — / — n —	C3	3	3	10	
JP cc, nn	If condition cc is true PC ← nn, otherwise continue	•	•	X	•	X	•	•	•	11 cc 010 / — n — / — n —		3	3	10	
JR e	$PC \leftarrow PC + e$	•	•	X	•	X	•	•	•	00 011 000 / — e-2 —	18	2	3	12	
JR C, e	If C = 0, continue	•	•	X	•	X	•	•	•	00 111 000 / — e-2 —	38	2	2	7	If condition not met.
	If C = 1, PC ← PC + e											2	3	12	If condition is met.
JR NC, e	If C = 1, continue	•	•	X	•	X	•	•	•	00 110 000 / — e-2 —	30	2	2	7	If condition not met.
	If C = 0, PC ← PC + e											2	3	12	If condition is met.
JP Z, e	If Z = 0 continue	•	•	X	•	X	•	•	•	00 101 000 / — e-2 —	28	2	2	7	If condition not met.
	If Z = 1, PC ← PC + e											2	3	12	If condition is met.
JR NZ, e	If Z = 1, continue	•	•	X	•	X	•	•	•	00 100 000 / — e-2 —	20	2	2	7	If condition not met.
	If Z = 0, PC ← PC + e											2	3	12	If condition is met.
JP (HL)	$PC \leftarrow HL$	•	•	X	•	X	•	•	•	11 101 001	E9	1	1	4	
JP (IX)	$PC \leftarrow IX$	•	•	X	•	X	•	•	•	11 011 101 / 11 101 001	DD / E9	2	2	8	

Condition codes (right column):

cc	Condition
000	NZ non-zero
001	Z zero
010	NC non-carry
011	C carry
100	PO parity odd
101	PE parity even
110	P sign positive
111	M sign negative

Jump Group (Continued)

Mnemonic	Symbolic Operation	S	Z		H		P/V	N②	C	Opcode 76 543 210 Hex	No.of Bytes	No.of M Cycles	No.of T States	Comments
JP (IY)	PC ← IY	•	•	X	•	X	•	•	•	11 111 101 FD 11 101 001 E9	2	2	8	
DJNZ, e	B ← B – 1 If B = 0, continue If B ≠ 0, PC ← PC + e	•	•	X	•	X	•	•	•	00 010 000 10 – e – 2 –	2 2	2 3	8 13	If B = 0. If B ≠ 0.

NOTES: e represents the extension in the relative addressing mode.
e is a signed two's complement number in the range < –126, 129 >.
e – 2 in the opcode provides an effective address of pc + e as PC is incremented
by 2 prior to the addition of e.

Call and Return Group

Mnemonic	Symbolic Operation	S	Z		H		P/V	N	C	Opcode 76 543 210 Hex	No.of Bytes	No.of M Cycles	No.of T States	Comments
CALL nn	(SP – 1) ← PC_H (SP – 2) ← PC_L PC ← nn	•	•	X	•	X	•	•	•	11 001 101 CD – n – – n –	3	5	17	
CALL cc, nn	If condition cc is false continue, otherwise same as CALL nn	•	•	X	•	X	•	•	•	11 cc 100 – n – – n –	3 3	3 5	10 17	If cc is false. If cc is true.
RET	PC_L ← (SP) PC_H ← (SP + 1)	•	•	X	•	X	•	•	•	11 001 001 C9	1	3	10	
RET cc	If condition cc is false continue, otherwise same as RET	•	•	X	•	X	•	•	•	11 cc 000	1 1	1 3	5 11	If cc is false. If cc is true.
RETI	Return from interrupt	•	•	X	•	X	•	•	•	11 101 101 ED 01 001 101 4D	2	4	14	
RETN[1]	Return from non-maskable interrupt	•	•	X	•	X	•	•	•	11 101 101 ED 01 000 101 45	2	4	14	
RST p	(SP – 1) ← PC_H (SP – 2) ← PC_L PC_H ← 0 PC_L ← p	•	•	X	•	X	•	•	•	11 t 111	1	3	11	

cc	Condition
000 NZ	non-zero
001 Z	zero
010 NC	non-carry
011 C	carry
100 PO	parity odd
101 PE	parity even
110 P	sign positive
111 M	sign negative

t	p
000	00H
001	08H
010	10H
011	18H
100	20H
101	28H
110	30H
111	38H

NOTE: [1]RETN loads IFF_2 → IFF_1

Input and Output Group

Mnemonic	Symbolic Operation	S	Z		H		P/V	N	C	Opcode 76 543 210 Hex	No.of Bytes	No.of M Cycles	No.of T States	Comments
IN A, (n)	A ← (n)	•	•	X	•	X	•	•	•	11 011 011 DB – n –	2	3	11	n to $A_0 \sim A_7$ Acc. to $A_8 \sim A_{15}$
IN r, (C)	r ← (C) if r = 110 only the flags will be affected	↕	↕	X	↕	X	P	0	•	11 101 101 ED 01 r 000	2	3	12	C to $A_0 \sim A_7$ B to $A_8 \sim A_{15}$
INI	(HL) ← (C) B ← B – 1 HL ← HL + 1	X	①↕	X	X	X	X	↕	X	11 101 101 ED 10 100 010 A2	2	4	16	C to $A_0 \sim A_7$ B to $A_8 \sim A_{15}$
INIR	(HL) ← (C) B ← B – 1 HL ← HL + 1 Repeat until B = 0	X	1	X	X	X	X	↕	X	11 101 101 ED 10 110 010 B2	2 2	5 (If B≠0) 4 (If B=0)	21 16	C to $A_0 \sim A_7$ B to $A_8 \sim A_{15}$
IND	(HL) ← (C) B ← B – 1 HL ← HL – 1	X	①↕	X	X	X	X	↕	X	11 101 101 ED 10 101 010 AA	2	4	16	C to $A_0 \sim A_7$ B to $A_8 \sim A_{15}$
INDR	(HL) ← (C) B ← B – 1 HL ← HL – 1 Repeat until B = 0	X	1	X	X	X	X	↕	X	11 101 101 ED 10 111 010 BA	2 2	5 (If B≠0) 4 (If B=0)	21 16	C to $A_0 \sim A_7$ B to $A_8 \sim A_{15}$
OUT (n), A	(n) ← A	•	•	X	•	X	•	↕	X	11 010 011 D3 – n –	2	3	11	n to $A_0 \sim A_7$ Acc. to $A_8 \sim A_{15}$
OUT (C), r	(C) ← r	•	•	X	•	X	•	↕	X	11 101 101 ED 01 r 001	2	3	12	C to $A_0 \sim A_7$ B to $A_8 \sim A_{15}$
OUTI	(C) ← (HL) B ← B – 1 HL ← HL + 1	X	①↕	X	X	X	X	↕	X	11 101 101 ED 10 100 011 A3	2	4	16	C to $A_0 \sim A_7$ B to $A_8 \sim A_{15}$
OTIR	(C) ← (HL) B ← B – 1 HL ← HL + 1 Repeat until B = 0	X	1	X	X	X	X	↕	X	11 101 101 ED 10 110 011 B3	2 2	5 (If B≠0) 4 (If B=0)	21 16	C to $A_0 \sim A_7$ B to $A_8 \sim A_{15}$
OUTD	(C) ← (HL) B ← B – 1 HL ← HL – 1	X	①↕	X	X	X	X	↕	X	11 101 101 ED 10 101 011 AB	2	4	16	C to $A_0 \sim A_7$ B to $A_8 \sim A_{15}$

NOTE: ① If the result of B – 1 is zero the Z flag is set, otherwise it is reset.
② N Flag is 1 if data bit is 1, otherwise N Flag is 0.

Input and Output Group (Continued)

Mnemonic	Symbolic Operation	S	Z		H	P/V	N	C	Opcode 76 543 210 / Hex	No.of Bytes	No.of M Cycles	No.of T States	Comments
OTDR	(C) ← (HL) B ← B – 1 HL ← HL – 1 Repeat until B = 0	X	1	X	X	X	X	↕ X	11 101 101 ED 10 111 011	2 2	5 (If B ≠ 0) 4 (If B = 0)	21 16	C to $A_0 \sim A_7$ B to $A_8 \sim A_{15}$

Summary of Flag Operation

Instruction	$\frac{D_7}{S}$	Z		H		P/V	N	$\frac{D_0}{C}$	Comments
ADD A, s; ADC A, s	↕	↕	X	↕	X	V	0	↕	8-bit add or add with carry.
SUB s; SBC A, s; CP s; NEG	↕	↕	X	↕	X	V	1	↕	8-bit subtract, subtract with carry, compare and negate accumulator.
AND s	↕	↕	X	1	X	P	0	0 }	Logical operations.
OR s, XOR s	↕	↕	X	0	X	P	0	0 }	
INC s	↕	↕	X	↕	X	V	0	•	8-bit increment.
DEC s	↕	↕	X	↕	X	V	1	•	8-bit decrement.
ADD DD, ss	•	•	X	X	X	•	0	↕	16-bit add.
ADC HL, ss	↕	↕	X	X	X	V	0	↕	16-bit add with carry.
SBC HL, ss	↕	↕	X	X	X	V	1	↕	16-bit subtract with carry.
RLA, RLCA, RRA; RRCA	•	•	X	0	X	•	0	↕	Rotate accumulator.
RL m; RLC m; RR m; RRC m; SLA m; SRA m; SRL m	↕	↕	X	0	X	P	0	↕	Rotate and shift locations.
RLD; RRD	↕	↕	X	0	X	P	0	•	Rotate digit left and right.
DAA	↕	↕	X	↕	X	P	•	↕	Decimal adjust accumulator.
CPL	•	•	X	1	X	•	1	•	Complement accumulator.
SCF	•	•	X	0	X	•	0	1	Set carry.
CCF	•	•	X	X	X	•	0	↕	Complement carry.
IN r (C)	↕	↕	X	0	X	P	0	•	Input register indirect.
INI; IND, OUTI; OUTD	X	↕	X	X	X	X	1	•	Block input and output. Z = 0 if B ≠ 0 otherwise Z = 0.
INIR; INDR; OTIR; OTDR	X	1	X	X	X	X	1	• }	
LDI; LDD	X	X	X	0	X	↕	0	•	Block transfer instructions. P/V = 1 if BC ≠ 0, otherwise P/V = 0.
LDIR; LDDR	X	X	X	0	X	0	0	• }	
CPI; CPIR; CPD; CPDR	X	↕	X	X	X	↕	1	•	Block search instructions. Z = 1 if A = (HL), otherwise Z = 0. P/V = 1 if BC ≠ 0, otherwise P/V = 0.
LD A, I, LD A, R	↕	↕	X	0	X	IFF	0	•	The content of the interrupt enable flip-flop (IFF) is copied into the P/V flag.
BIT b, s	X	↕	X	1	X	X	0	•	The state of bit b of location s is copied into the Z flag.

Symbolic Notation

Symbol	Operation
S	Sign flag. S = 1 if the MSB of the result is 1.
Z	Zero flag. Z = 1 if the result of the operation is 0.
P/V	Parity or overflow flag. Parity (P) and overflow (V) share the same flag. Logical operations affect this flag with the parity of the result while arithmetic operations affect this flag with the overflow of the result. If P/V holds parity, P/V = 1 if the result of the operation is even, P/V = 0 if result is odd. If P/V holds overflow, P/V = 1 if the result of the operation produced an overflow.
H	Half-carry flag. H = 1 if the add or subtract operation produced a carry into or borrow from bit 4 of the accumulator.
N	Add/Subtract flag. N = 1 if the previous operation was a subtract.
H & N	H and N flags are used in conjunction with the decimal adjust instruction (DAA) to properly correct the result into packed BCD format following addition or subtraction using operands with packed BCD format.
C	Carry/Link flag. C = 1 if the operation produced a carry from the MSB of the operand or result.

Symbol	Operation
↕	The flag is affected according to the result of the operation.
•	The flag is unchanged by the operation.
0	The flag is reset by the operation.
1	The flag is set by the operation.
X	The flag is a "don't care."
V	P/V flag affected according to the overflow result of the operation.
P	P/V flag affected according to the parity result of the operation.
r	Any one of the CPU registers A, B, C, D, E, H, L.
s	Any 8-bit location for all the addressing modes allowed for the particular instruction.
ss	Any 16-bit location for all the addressing modes allowed for that instruction.
ii	Any one of the two index registers IX or IY.
R	Refresh counter.
n	8-bit value in range < 0, 255 >.
nn	16-bit value in range < 0, 65535 >.

ABSOLUTE MAXIMUM RATINGS*

Temperature Under Bias	$0°C$ to $+70°C$
Storage Temperature	$-65°C$ to $+150°C$
All Input or Output Voltages	
With Respect to V_{BB}	$-0.3V$ to $+20V$
V_{CC}, V_{DD} and V_{SS} With Respect to V_{BB}	$-0.3V$ to $+20V$
Power Dissipation	1.5W

NOTICE: Stresses above those listed under "Absolute Maximum Ratings" may cause permanent damage to the device. This is a stress rating only and functional operation of the device at these or any other conditions above those indicated in the operational sections of this specification is not implied. Exposure to absolute maximum rating conditions for extended periods may affect device reliability.

D.C. CHARACTERISTICS (T_A = 0°C to 70°C, V_{DD} = +12V ±5%, V_{CC} = +5V ±5%, V_{BB} = −5V ±5%, V_{SS} =0V; unless otherwise noted)

Symbol	Parameter	Min.	Typ.	Max.	Unit	Test Condition
V_{ILC}	Clock Input Low Voltage	$V_{SS}-1$		$V_{SS}+0.8$	V	
V_{IHC}	Clock Input High Voltage	9.0		$V_{DD}+1$	V	
V_{IL}	Input Low Voltage	$V_{SS}-1$		$V_{SS}+0.8$	V	
V_{IH}	Input High Voltage	3.3		$V_{CC}+1$	V	
V_{OL}	Output Low Voltage			0.45	V	I_{OL} = 1.9mA on all outputs,
V_{OH}	Output High Voltage	3.7			V	I_{OH} = -150µA.
$I_{DD(AV)}$	Avg. Power Supply Current (V_{DD})		40	70	mA	
$I_{CC(AV)}$	Avg. Power Supply Current (V_{CC})		60	80	mA	Operation
$I_{BB(AV)}$	Avg. Power Supply Current (V_{BB})		.01	1	mA	T_{CY} = .48 µsec
I_{IL}	Input Leakage			±10	µA	$V_{SS} \leqslant V_{IN} \leqslant V_{CC}$
I_{CL}	Clock Leakage			±10	µA	$V_{SS} \leqslant V_{CLOCK} \leqslant V_{DD}$
I_{DL} [2]	Data Bus Leakage in Input Mode			-100	µA	$V_{SS} \leqslant V_{IN} \leqslant V_{SS}+0.8V$
				-2.0	mA	$V_{SS}+0.8V \leqslant V_{IN} \leqslant V_{CC}$
I_{FL}	Address and Data Bus Leakage During HOLD			+10	µA	$V_{ADDR/DATA}$ = V_{CC}
				-100		$V_{ADDR/DATA}$ = V_{SS} + 0.45V

CAPACITANCE (T_A = 25°C, V_{CC} = V_{DD} = V_{SS} = 0V, V_{BB} = −5V)

Symbol	Parameter	Typ.	Max.	Unit	Test Condition
C_ϕ	Clock Capacitance	17	25	pf	f_c = 1 MHz
C_{IN}	Input Capacitance	6	10	pf	Unmeasured Pins
C_{OUT}	Output Capacitance	10	20	pf	Returned to V_{SS}

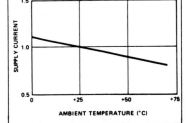

Typical Supply Current vs. Temperature, Normalized[3]

NOTES:
1. The RESET signal must be active for a minimum of 3 clock cycles.
2. ΔI supply / ΔT_A = -0.45%/°C.

Appendix C.1   8080A Electrical Specifications. (Courtesy of Intel Corporation.)

A.C. CHARACTERISTICS (8080A) ($T_A = 0°C$ to $70°C$, $V_{DD} = +12V \pm 5\%$, $V_{CC} = +5V \pm 5\%$, $V_{BB} = -5V \pm 5\%$, $V_{SS} = 0V$; unless otherwise noted)

Symbol	Parameter	Min.	Max.	-1 Min.	-1 Max.	-2 Min.	-2 Max.	Unit	Test Condition
t_{CY}[3]	Clock Period	0.48	2.0	0.32	2.0	0.38	2.0	μsec	
t_r, t_f	Clock Rise and Fall Time	0	50	0	25	0	50	nsec	
$t_{\phi 1}$	∅$_1$ Pulse Width	60		50		60		nsec	
$t_{\phi 2}$	∅$_2$ Pulse Width	220		145		175		nsec	
t_{D1}	Delay ∅$_1$ to ∅$_2$	0		0		0		nsec	
t_{D2}	Delay ∅$_2$ to ∅$_1$	70		60		70		nsec	
t_{D3}	Delay ∅$_1$ to ∅$_2$ Leading Edges	80		60		70		nsec	
t_{DA}	Address Output Delay From ∅$_2$		200		150		175	nsec	$C_L = 100$ pF
t_{DD}	Data Output Delay From ∅$_2$		220		180		200	nsec	
t_{DC}	Signal Output Delay From ∅$_2$ or ∅$_2$ (SYNC, WR, WAIT, HLDA)		120		110		120	nsec	$C_L = 50$ pF
t_{DF}	DBIN Delay From ∅$_2$	25	140	25	130	25	140	nsec	
t_{DI}[1]	Delay for Input Bus to Enter Input Mode		t_{DF}		t_{DF}		t_{DF}	nsec	
t_{DS1}	Data Setup Time During ∅$_1$ and DBIN	30		10		20		nsec	
t_{DS2}	Data Setup Time to ∅$_2$ During DBIN	150		120		130		nsec	
t_{DH}[1]	Data Holt time From ∅$_2$ During DBIN	[1]		[1]		[1]		nsec	
t_{IE}	INTE Output Delay From ∅$_2$		200		200		200	nsec	$C_L = 50$ pF
t_{RS}	READY Setup Time During ∅$_2$	120		90		90		nsec	
t_{HS}	HOLD Setup Time to ∅$_2$	140		120		120		nsec	
t_{IS}	INT Setup Time During ∅$_2$	120		100		100		nsec	
t_H	Hold Time From ∅$_2$ (READY, INT, HOLD)	0		0		0		nsec	
t_{FD}	Delay to Float During Hold (Address and Data Bus)		120		120		120	nsec	
t_{AW}	Address Stable Prior to WR	[5]		[5]		[5]		nsec	
t_{DW}	Output Data Stable Prior to WR	[6]		[6]		[6]		nsec	
t_{WD}	Output Data Stable From WR	[7]		[7]		[7]		nsec	
t_{WA}	Address Stable From WR	[7]		[7]		[7]		nsec	$C_L = 100$ pF: Address, Data
t_{HF}	HLDA to Float Delay	[8]		[8]		[8]		nsec	$C_L = 50$ pF: $\overline{WR}$, HLDA, DBIN
t_{WF}	WR to Float Delay	[9]		[9]		[9]		nsec	
t_{AH}	Address Hold Time After DBIN During HLDA	-20		-20		-20		nsec	

A.C. TESTING LOAD CIRCUIT

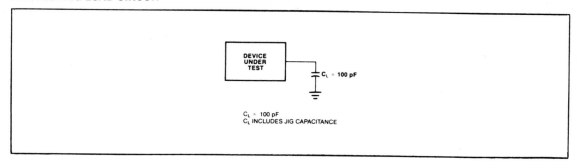

DEVICE UNDER TEST

$C_L = 100$ pF

$C_L = 100$ pF
C_L INCLUDES JIG CAPACITANCE

WAVEFORMS

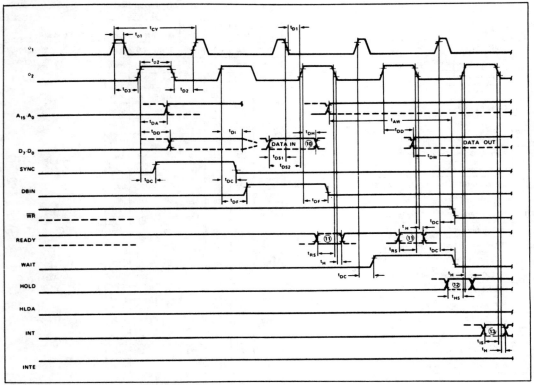

NOTE:
Timing measurements are made at the following reference voltages: CLOCK "1" = 8.0V,
"0" = 1.0V; INPUTS "1" = 3.3V, "0" = 0.8V; OUTPUTS "1" = 2.0V, "0" = 0.8V.

ABSOLUTE MAXIMUM RATINGS*

Ambient Temperature Under Bias .... 0°C to 70°C
Storage Temperature .... −65°C to +150°C
Voltage on Any Pin
  With Respect to Ground .... −0.5V to +7V
Power Dissipation .... 1.5 Watt

*NOTICE: Stresses above those listed under "Absolute Maximum Ratings" may cause permanent damage to the device. This is a stress rating only and functional operation of the device at these or any other conditions above those indicated in the operational sections of this specification is not implied. Exposure to absolute maximum rating conditions for extended periods may affect device reliability.

D.C. CHARACTERISTICS

8085AH, 8085AH-2: (T_A = 0°C to 70°C, V_{CC} = 5V ±10%, V_{SS} =0V; unless otherwise specified)*
8085AH-1: (T_A = 0°C to 70°C, V_{CC} = 5V ±5%, V_{SS} = 0V; unless otherwise specified)

Symbol	Parameter	Min.	Max.	Units	Test Conditions
V_{IL}	Input Low Voltage	−0.5	+0.8	V	
V_{IH}	Input High Voltage	2.0	V_{CC} +0.5	V	
V_{OL}	Output Low Voltage		0.45	V	I_{OL} = 2mA
V_{OH}	Output High Voltage	2.4		V	I_{OH} = −400µA
I_{CC}	Power Supply Current		135	mA	8085AH, 8085AH-2
			200	mA	8085AH-1 (Preliminary)
I_{IL}	Input Leakage		±10	µA	0 ≤ V_{IN} ≤ V_{CC}
I_{LO}	Output Leakage		±10	µA	0.45V ≤ V_{OUT} ≤ V_{CC}
V_{ILR}	Input Low Level, RESET	−0.5	+0.8	V	
V_{IHR}	Input High Level, RESET	2.4	V_{CC} +0.5	V	
V_{HY}	Hysteresis, RESET	0.25		V	

A.C. CHARACTERISTICS

8085AH, 8085AH-2: (T_A = 0°C to 70°C, V_{CC} = 5V ±10%, V_{SS} = OV)*
8085AH-1: (T_A = 0°C to 70°C, V_{CC} = 5V ±5%, V_{SS} = 0V)

Symbol	Parameter	8085AH[2] (Final) Min.	Max.	8085AH-2[2] (Final) Min.	Max.	8085AH-1 (Preliminary) Min.	Max.	Units
t_{CYC}	CLK Cycle Period	320	2000	200	2000	167	2000	ns
t_1	CLK Low Time (Standard CLK Loading)	80		40		20		ns
t_2	CLK High Time (Standard CLK Loading)	120		70		50		ns
t_r, t_f	CLK Rise and Fall Time		30		30		30	ns
t_{XKR}	X_1 Rising to CLK Rising	25	120	25	100	20	100	ns
t_{XKF}	X_1 Rising to CLK Falling	30	150	30	110	25	110	ns
t_{AC}	A_{8-15} Valid to Leading Edge of Control[1]	270		115		70		ns
t_{ACL}	A_{0-7} Valid to Leading Edge of Control	240		115		60		ns
t_{AD}	A_{0-15} Valid to Valid Data In		575		350		225	ns
t_{AFR}	Address Float After Leading Edge of READ (INTA)		0		0		0	ns
t_{AL}	A_{8-15} Valid Before Trailing Edge of ALE [1]	115		50		25		ns

*Note: For Extended Temperature EXPRESS use M8085AH Electricals Parameters.

Appendix C.2 8085AH Electrical Specifications. (Courtesy of Intel Corporation.)

A.C. CHARACTERISTICS (Continued)

Symbol	Parameter	8085AH[2] (Final)		8085AH-2[2] (Final)		8085AH-1 (Preliminary)		Units
		Min.	Max.	Min.	Max.	Min.	Max.	
t_{ALL}	A_{0-7} Valid Before Trailing Edge of ALE	90		50		25		ns
t_{ARY}	READY Valid from Address Valid		220		100		40	ns
t_{CA}	Address (A_{8-15}) Valid After Control	120		60		30		ns
t_{CC}	Width of Control Low ($\overline{RD}$, $\overline{WR}$, $\overline{INTA}$) Edge of ALE	400		230		150		ns
t_{CL}	Trailing Edge of Control to Leading Edge of ALE	50		25		0		ns
t_{DW}	Data Valid to Trailing Edge of $\overline{WRITE}$	420		230		140		ns
t_{HABE}	HLDA to Bus Enable		210		150		150	ns
t_{HABF}	Bus Float After HLDA		210		150		150	ns
t_{HACK}	HLDA Valid to Trailing Edge of CLK	110		40		0		ns
t_{HDH}	HOLD Hold Time	0		0		0		ns
t_{HDS}	HOLD Setup Time to Trailing Edge of CLK	170		120		120		ns
t_{INH}	INTR Hold Time	0		0		0		ns
t_{INS}	INTR, RST, and TRAP Setup Time to Falling Edge of CLK	160		150		150		ns
t_{LA}	Address Hold Time After ALE	100		50		20		ns
t_{LC}	Trailing Edge of ALE to Leading Edge of Control	130		60		25		ns
t_{LCK}	ALE Low During CLK High	100		50		15		ns
t_{LDR}	ALE to Valid Data During Read		460		270		175	ns
t_{LDW}	ALE to Valid Data During Write		200		120		110	ns
t_{LL}	ALE Width	140		80		50		ns
t_{LRY}	ALE to READY Stable		110		30		10	ns
t_{RAE}	Trailing Edge of $\overline{READ}$ to Re-Enabling of Address	150		90		50		ns
t_{RD}	$\overline{READ}$ (or $\overline{INTA}$) to Valid Data		300		150		75	ns
t_{RV}	Control Trailing Edge to Leading Edge of Next Control	400		220		160		ns
t_{RDH}	Data Hold Time After $\overline{READ}$ $\overline{INTA}$	0		0		0		ns
t_{RYH}	READY Hold Time	0		0		5		ns
t_{RYS}	READY Setup Time to Leading Edge of CLK	110		100		100		ns
t_{WD}	Data Valid After Trailing Edge of $\overline{WRITE}$	100		60		30		ns
t_{WDL}	LEADING Edge of $\overline{WRITE}$ to Data Valid		40		20		30	ns

WAVEFORMS

CLOCK

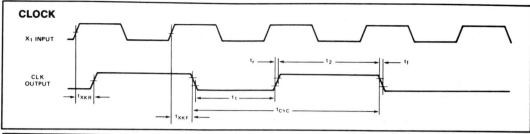

READ

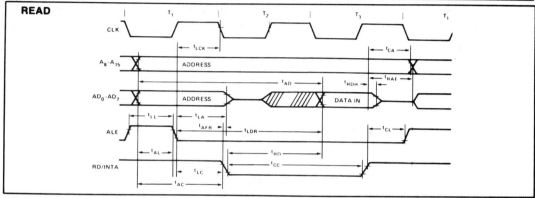

WRITE

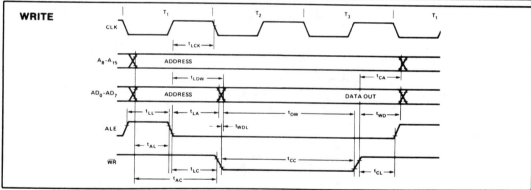

HOLD

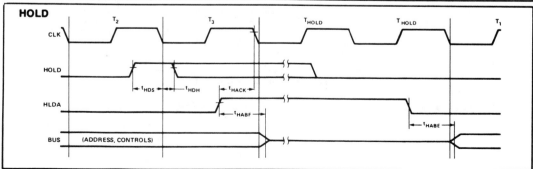

CPU Timing The Z80 CPU executes instructions by proceeding through a specific sequence of operations:

- Memory read or write
- I/O device read or write
- Interrupt acknowledge

Instruction Opcode Fetch. The CPU places the contents of the Program Counter (PC) on the address bus at the start of the cycle (Figure 5). Approximately one-half clock cycle later, $\overline{MREQ}$ goes active. When active, $\overline{RD}$ indicates that the memory data can be enabled onto the CPU data bus.

The basic clock period is referred to as a T time or cycle, and three or more T cycles make up a machine cycle (M1, M2 or M3 for instance). Machine cycles can be extended either by the CPU automatically inserting one or more Wait states or by the insertion of one or more Wait states by the user.

The CPU samples the $\overline{WAIT}$ input with the falling edge of clock state T_2. During clock states T_3 and T_4 of an $\overline{M1}$ cycle dynamic RAM refresh can occur while the CPU starts decoding and executing the instruction. When the Refresh Control signal becomes active, refreshing of dynamic memory can take place.

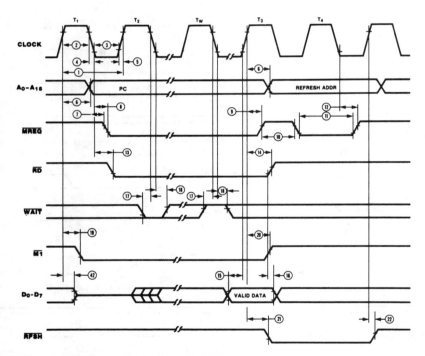

NOTE: T_W–Wait cycle added when necessary for slow ancilliary devices.

Figure 5. Instruction Opcode Fetch

Appendix C.3   Z-80 Electrical Specifications. (Courtesy of Zilog, Inc.)

CPU Timing (Continued)

Memory Read or Write Cycles. Figure 6 shows the timing of memory read or write cycles other than an opcode fetch ($\overline{M1}$) cycle. The $\overline{MREQ}$ and $\overline{RD}$ signals function exactly as in the fetch cycle. In a memory write cycle, $\overline{MREQ}$ also becomes active when the address bus is stable. The $\overline{WR}$ line is active when the data bus is stable, so that it can be used directly as an R/W pulse to most semiconductor memories.

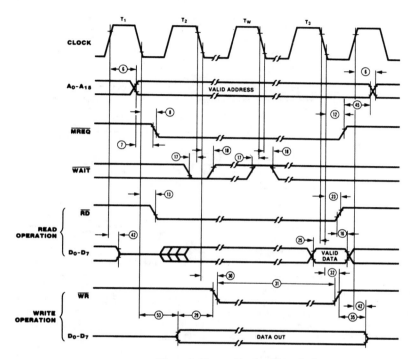

Figure 6. Memory Read or Write Cycles

Input or Output Cycles. Figure 7 shows the timing for an I/O read or I/O write operation. During I/O operations, the CPU automatically inserts a single Wait state (T_w). This extra Wait state allows sufficient time for an I/O port to decode the address from the port address lines.

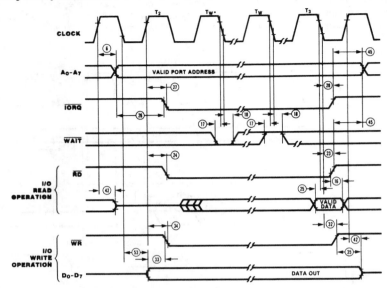

NOTE: T_w• = One Wait cycle automatically inserted by CPU.

Figure 7. Input or Output Cycles

Interrupt Request/Acknowledge Cycle. The CPU samples the interrupt signal with the rising edge of the last clock cycle at the end of any instruction (Figure 8). When an interrupt is accepted, a special $\overline{M1}$ cycle is generated. During this $\overline{M1}$ cycle, $\overline{IORQ}$ becomes active (instead of $\overline{MREQ}$) to indicate that the interrupting device can place an 8-bit vector on the data bus. The CPU automatically adds two Wait states to this cycle.

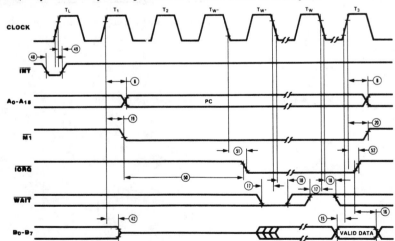

NOTE: 1) T_L = Last state of previous instruction.   2) Two Wait cycles automatically inserted by CPU(•).

Figure 8. Interrupt Request/Acknowledge Cycle

AC Characteristics	Number	Symbol	Parameter	Z80 CPU Min	Z80 CPU Max	Z80A CPU Min	Z80A CPU Max	Z80B CPU† Min	Z80B CPU† Max
	1	TcC	Clock Cycle Time	400*		250*		165*	
	2	TwCh	Clock Pulse Width (High)	180*		110*		65*	
	3	TwCl	Clock Pulse Width (Low)	180	2000	110	2000	65	2000
	4	TfC	Clock Fall Time	—	30	—	30	—	20
	5	TrC	Clock Rise Time		30		30		20
	6	TdCr(A)	Clock ↑ to Address Valid Delay	—	145	—	110	—	90
	7	TdA(MREQf)	Address Valid to $\overline{MREQ}$ ↓ Delay	125*	—	65*	—	35*	—
	8	TdCf(MREQf)	Clock ↓ to $\overline{MREQ}$ ↓ Delay	—	100	—	85	—	70
	9	TdCr(MREQr)	Clock ↑ to $\overline{MREQ}$ ↑ Delay	—	100	—	85	—	70
	10	TwMREQh	$\overline{MREQ}$ Pulse Width (High)	170*		110*		65*	
	11	TwMREQl	$\overline{MREQ}$ Pulse Width (Low)	360*	—	220*	—	135*	—
	12	TdCf(MREQr)	Clock ↓ to $\overline{MREQ}$ ↑ Delay	—	100	—	85	—	70
	13	TdCf(RDf)	Clock ↓ to $\overline{RD}$ ↓ Delay	—	130	—	95	—	80
	14	TdCr(RDr)	Clock ↑ to $\overline{RD}$ ↑ Delay	—	100	—	85	—	70
	15	TsD(Cr)	Data Setup Time to Clock ↑	50		35		30	
	16	ThD(RDr)	Data Hold Time to $\overline{RD}$ ↑	—	0	—	0	—	0
	17	TsWAIT(Cf)	$\overline{WAIT}$ Setup Time to Clock ↓	70	—	70	—	60	—
	18	ThWAIT(Cf)	$\overline{WAIT}$ Hold Time after Clock ↓	—	0	—	0	—	0
	19	TdCr(M1f)	Clock ↑ to $\overline{M1}$ ↓ Delay	—	130	—	100	—	80
	20	TdCr(M1r)	Clock ↑ to $\overline{M1}$ ↑ Delay		130		100		80
	21	TdCr(RFSHf)	Clock ↑ to $\overline{RFSH}$ ↓ Delay	—	180	—	130	—	110
	22	TdCr(RFSHr)	Clock ↑ to $\overline{RFSH}$ ↑ Delay	—	150	—	120	—	100
	23	TdCf(RDr)	Clock ↓ to $\overline{RD}$ ↑ Delay	—	110	—	85	—	70
	24	TdCr(RDf)	Clock ↑ to $\overline{RD}$ ↓ Delay	—	100	—	85	—	70
	25	TsD(Cf)	Data Setup to Clock ↓ during M_2, M_3, M_4 or M_5 Cycles	60		50		40	
	26	TdA(IORQf)	Address Stable prior to $\overline{IORQ}$ ↓	320*	—	180*	—	110*	—
	27	TdCr(IORQf)	Clock ↑ to $\overline{IORQ}$ ↓ Delay	—	90	—	75	—	65
	28	TdCf(IORQr)	Clock ↓ to $\overline{IORQ}$ ↑ Delay	—	110	—	85	—	70
	29	TdD(WRf)	Data Stable prior to $\overline{WR}$ ↓	190*	—	80*	—	25*	—
	30	TdCf(WRf)	Clock ↓ to $\overline{WR}$ ↓ Delay		90		80		70
	31	TwWR	$\overline{WR}$ Pulse Width	360*	—	220*	—	135*	—
	32	TdCf(WRr)	Clock ↓ to $\overline{WR}$ ↑ Delay	—	100	—	80	—	70
	33	TdD(WRf)	Data Stable prior to $\overline{WR}$ ↓	20*	—	-10*	—	-55*	—
	34	TdCr(WRf)	Clock ↑ to $\overline{WR}$ ↓ Delay	—	80	—	65	—	60
	35	TdWRr(D)	Data Stable from $\overline{WR}$ ↑	120*		60*		30*	
	36	TdCf(HALT)	Clock ↓ to $\overline{HALT}$ ↑ or ↓	—	300	—	300	—	260
	37	TwNMI	$\overline{NMI}$ Pulse Width	80	—	80	—	70	—
	38	TsBUSREQ(Cr)	$\overline{BUSREQ}$ Setup Time to Clock ↑	80	—	50	—	50	—

* For clock periods other than the minimums shown in the table, calculate parameters using the expressions in the table on the following page.
† Units in nanoseconds (ns). All timings are preliminary and subject to change.

	Number	Symbol	Parameter	Z80 CPU		Z80A CPU		Z80B CPU†	
AC Characteristics (Continued)				Min	Max	Min	Max	Min	Max
	39	ThBUSREQ(Cr)	$\overline{BUSREQ}$ Hold Time after Clock ↑	0	—	0	—	0	—
	40	TdCr(BUSACKf)	Clock ↑ to $\overline{BUSACK}$ ↓ Delay		120		100		90-
	41	TdCf(BUSACKr)	Clock ↓ to $\overline{BUSACK}$ ↑ Delay	—	110	—	100	—	90
	42	TdCr(Dz)	Clock ↑ to Data Float Delay	—	90	—	90	—	80
	43	TdCr(CTz)	Clock ↑ to Control Outputs Float Delay ($\overline{MREQ}$, $\overline{IORQ}$, $\overline{RD}$, and $\overline{WR}$)	—	110	—	80	—	70
	44	TdCr(Az)	Clock ↑ to Address Float Delay	—	110	—	90	—	80
	45	TdCTr(A)	$\overline{MREQ}$ ↑, $\overline{IORQ}$ ↑, $\overline{RD}$ ↑, and $\overline{WR}$ ↑ to Address Hold Time	160*		80*		35*	
	46	TsRESET(Cr)	$\overline{RESET}$ to Clock ↑ Setup Time	90	—	60	—	60	—
	47	ThRESET(Cr)	$\overline{RESET}$ to Clock ↑ Hold Time	—	0	—	0	—	0
	48	TsINTf(Cr)	$\overline{INT}$ to Clock ↑ Setup Time	80	—	80	—	70	—
	49	ThINTr(Cr)	$\overline{INT}$ to Clock ↑ Hold Time	—	0	—	0	—	0
	50	TdM1f(IORQf)	$\overline{M1}$ ↓ to $\overline{IORQ}$ ↓ Delay	920*		565*		365*	
	51	TdCf(IORQf)	Clock ↓ to $\overline{IORQ}$ ↓ Delay	—	110	—	85	—	70
	52	TdCf(IORQr)	Clock ↑ to $\overline{IORQ}$ ↑ Delay	—	100	—	85	—	70
	53	TdCf(D)	Clock ↓ to Data Valid Delay	—	230	—	150	—	130

* For clock periods other than the minimums shown in the table, calculate parameters using the following expressions. Calculated values above assumed TrC = TfC = 20 ns.
† Units in nanoseconds (ns). All timings are preliminary and subject to change. All timings assume equal loading on pins with 50 pF.

Footnotes to AC Characteristics

Number	Symbol	Z80	Z80A	Z80B
1	TcC	TwCh + TwCl + TrC + TfC	TwCh + TwCl + TrC + TfC	TwCh + TwCl + TrC + TfC
2	TwCh	Although static by design, TwCh of greater than 200 µs is not guaranteed	Although static by design, TwCh of greater than 200 µs is not guaranteed	Although static by design, TwCh of greater than 200 µs is not guaranteed
7	TdA(MREQf)	TwCh + TfC – 75	TwCh + TfC – 65	TwCh + TfC – 50
10	TwMREQh	TwCh + TfC – 30	TwCh + TfC – 20	TwCh + TfC – 20
11	TwMREQl	TcC – 40	TcC – 30	TcC – 30
26	TdA(IORQf)	TcC – 80	TcC – 70	TcC – 55
29	TdD(WRf)	TcC – 210	TcC – 170	TcC – 140
31	TwWR	TcC – 40	TcC – 30	TcC – 30
33	TdD(WRf)	TwCl + TrC – 180	TwCl + TrC – 140	TwCl + TrC – 140
35	TdWRr(D)	TwCl + TrC – 80	TwCl + TrC – 70	TwCl + TrC – 55
45	TdCTr(A)	TwCl + TrC – 40	TwCl + TrC – 50	TwCl + TrC – 50
50	TdM1f(IORQf)	2TcC + TwCh + TfC – 80	2TcC + TwCh + TfC – 65	2TcC + TwCh + TfC – 50

AC Test Conditions:
V_{IH} = 2.0 V
V_{IL} = 0.8 V
V_{IHC} = V_{CC} -0.6 V
V_{ILC} = 0.45 V
V_{OH} = 2.0 V
V_{OL} = 0.8 V
FLOAT = ±0.5 V

NEC
NEC Electronics U.S.A. Inc.
Microcomputer Division

μPD2167-2
μPD2167-3
16,384 x 1-BIT STATIC RAM

Description

The μPD2167 is a 16,384-word by 1-bit static MOS RAM. Using a scaled-NMOS technology, its design provides the easy-to-use features associated with non-clocked static memories.

The μPD2167 has a three-state output and offers a standby mode that features an 83% savings in power consumption. The μPD2167 requires a single +5 volt supply and is fully TTL-compatible. It features equal access and cycle times and, because of its fully static operation, it requires no external clocks or timing strobes. It is packaged in a standard 20-pin, 300 mil DIP.

Features

☐ 16384 x 1 organization
☐ Fully static memory — no clock or timing strobe required
☐ Equal access and cycle times
☐ Single +5v supply
☐ Automatic power-down
☐ Standard 20-pin DIP, 300 mil
☐ All inputs and output directly TTL-compatible
☐ Separate data input and output
☐ Three-state output
☐ Power dissipation: 180 mA max (active)
    30 mA max (standby)

	Access time	R/W Cycle time
μPD2167-2	70ns	70ns
μPD2167-3	55ns	55ns

Pin Configuration

Pin Names

A_0-A_{13}	Address Inputs
$\overline{WE}$	Write Enable
$\overline{CS}$	Chip Select
D_{IN}	Data Input
D_{OUT}	Data Output
V_{CC}	Power (+5v)
V_{SS}	Ground

Truth Table

$\overline{CS}$	$\overline{WE}$	Mode	Output	Power
H	X	not selected	High Z	Standby
L	L	write	High Z	Active
L	H	read	D_{OUT}	Active

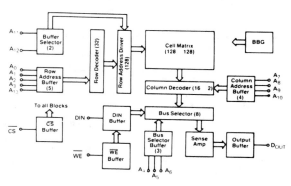

Absolute Maximum Ratings*
$T_a = 25°C$

Temperature under bias	−10°C to +85°C
Storage temperature	−65°C to +150°C
Voltage on any pin with respect to ground	−3.5v to +7v
D.C. output current	20mA
Power dissipation	1.2w

* Comment: Exposing the device to stresses above those listed in Absolute Maximum Ratings could cause permanent damage. The device is not meant to be operated under conditions outside the limits described in the operational sections of this specification. Exposure to absolute maximum rating conditions for extended periods may affect device reliability.

Capacitance
$T_a = 25°C$, f = 1.0 MHz

Parameter	Symbol	Max.	Unit	Conditions
Input Capacitance	C_{IN}	5	pF	$V_{IN} = 0V$
Output Capacitance	C_{OUT}	6	pF	$V_{OUT} = 0V$

This parameter is sampled and not 100% tested.

Appendix D.1 Specifications for the 2167 RAM. (Courtesy of NEC Electronics, Inc.)

DC Characteristics
$T_a = 0°C$ to $+70°C$, $V_{CC} = +5v \pm 10\%$

Parameter	Sym	Min	Typ	Max	Unit	Test Conditions
Input load current all input pins	I_{LI}			10	μA	V_{CC} = max, V_{IN} = GND to V_{CC}
Output leakage current	I_{LO}		0.1	50	μA	$\overline{CS}$ = V_{IH}, V_{CC} = max, V_{OUT} = GND to V_{CC}
Operating current	I_{CC}			170	mA	T_A = 25°C $\quad V_{CC}$ = max, $\overline{CS}$ = V_{IL}, output open
				180	mA	T_A = 0°C
Standby current	I_{SB}			30	mA	V_{CC} = min to max, $\overline{CS}$ = V_{IH}
Peak Power-On current	I_{PO}①		35	70	mA	V_{CC} = GND to V_{CC} min. $\overline{CS}$ = Lower of V_{CC} or V_{IH} min.
Input low voltage	V_{IL}	−3.0		0.8	V	
Input high voltage	V_{IH}	2.0		6.0	V	
Output low voltage	V_{OL}			0.4	V	I_{OL} = 8 mA
Output high voltage	V_{OH}	2.4			V	I_{OH} = −4 mA
Output short circuit current	I_{OS1}		−150		mA	V_{OUT} = GND
Output short circuit current	I_{OS2}		150		mA	V_{OUT} = V_{CC}

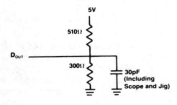

Figure 1 – Output Load

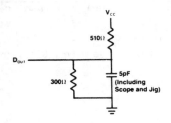

Figure 2 – Output Load for t_{HZ}, t_{LZ}, t_{WZ}, t_{OW}

AC Characteristics
$T_a = 0°C$ to $+70°C$, $V_{CC} = +5V \pm 10\%$

Parameter	Symbol	μPD2167-3 min	typ	max	μPD2167-2 min	typ	max	Unit	Notes
Read Cycle									
Read cycle time	t_{RC}	55			70			ns	
Address access time	t_{AA}			55			70	ns	①
Chip select access time	t_{ACS}			55			70	ns	②
Output hold from address change	t_{OH}	5			5			ns	
Chip select to output in low Z	t_{LZ}	10			10			ns	
Chip deselect to output in high Z	t_{HZ}	0		40	0		40	ns	
Chip select to power up time	t_{PU}	0			0			ns	
Chip deselect to power down time	t_{PD}		30			30		ns	
Write Cycle									
Write cycle time	t_{WC}	55			70			ns	
Chip select to end of write	t_{CW}	45			55			ns	
Address valid to end of write	t_{AW}	45			55			ns	
Address setup time	t_{AS}	0			0			ns	
Write pulse	t_{WP}	35			40			ns	
Write recovery time	t_{WR}	10			15			ns	
Data valid to end of write	t_{DW}	25			30			ns	
Data hold time	t_{DH}	10			10			ns	
Write enabled to output in high Z	t_{WZ}	0		30	0		35	ns	
Output active from end of write	t_{OW}	0			0			ns	

Notes:
① $\overline{CS}$ valid prior to or coincident with address transition
② Address valid prior to or coincident with $\overline{CS}$ transition low

2164A FAMILY
65,536 × 1 BIT DYNAMIC RAM

	2164A-15	2164A-20
Maximum Access Time (ns)	150	200
Read, Write Cycle (ns)	260	330
Page Mode Read, Write Cycle (ns)	125	170

- **HMOS-D III technology**
- **Low capacitance, fully TTL compatible inputs and outputs**
- **Single +5V supply, ±10% tolerance**
- **128 refresh cycle/2 ms $\overline{RAS}$ only refresh**
- **Compatible with the 2118**

- **Extended page mode, read-modify-write and hidden refresh operation**
- **Inputs allow a −2.0V negative overshoot**
- **Industry standard 16-pin DIP**
- **Compatible with Intel's microprocessors and DRAM controllers**

The 2164A is a 65,536 word by 1-bit N-channel MOS dynamic Random Access Memory fabricated with Intel's HMOS-D III technology for high system performance and reliability. The 2164A design incorporates high storage cell capacitance to provide wide internal device margins for reduced noise sensitivities and more reliable system operation. Moreover, high storage cell capacitance results in low soft error rates without the need for a die coat. HMOS-D III process employs the use of redundant elements.

The 2164A is optimized for high speed, high performance applications such as mainframe memory, buffer memory, microprocessor memory, peripheral storage and graphic terminals. For memory intensive microprocessor applications the 2164A is fully compatible with Intel's DRAM controllers and microprocessors to provide a complete DRAM system.

Multiplexing the 16 address bits into the 8 address input pins allows the 2164A to achieve high packing density. The 16 pin DIP provides for high system bit densities, and is compatible with widely available automated testing and insertion equipment. The two 8-bit TTL level address segments are latched into the 2164A by the two TTL clocks, Row Address Strobe ($\overline{RAS}$) and Column Address Strobe ($\overline{CAS}$). Non-critical timing requirements for the $\overline{RAS}$ and $\overline{CAS}$ clocks allow the use of the address multiplexing technique while maintaining high performance.

The non-latched, three state, TTL compatible data output is controlled by $\overline{CAS}$, independent of $\overline{RAS}$. After a valid read or read-modify-write cycle, data is held on the data output pin by holding $\overline{CAS}$ low. The data output is returned to a high impedance state, by returning $\overline{CAS}$ to a high state. Hidden refresh capability allows the device to maintain data at the output by holding $\overline{CAS}$ low while $\overline{RAS}$ is used to execute $\overline{RAS}$-only refresh cycles. Refreshing is accomplished by performing $\overline{RAS}$-only cycles, hidden refresh cycles, or normal read or write cycles on the 128 address combinations of addresses A_0 through A_6, during a 2 ms period.

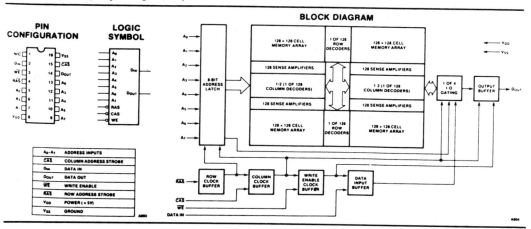

Appendix D.2   Specifications for the 2164A 64K DRAM. (Courtesy of Intel Corporation.)

Glossary

Access time   For a memory chip, the time from receipt of the memory address until valid data is output.

Accumulator   Data register within the CPU. All 8080 and 8085 I/O instructions use this register.

Active high   The signal is present (TRUE) when the output voltage is high.

Active low   The signal is present (TRUE) when the output voltage is low.

Address bus   The set of signal lines used by the CPU to indicate the memory or I/O port address that is to be accessed for the current machine cycle.

Address decoder   A logic circuit that produces an active output only when the address applied to its inputs is within a specified range.

Addressing modes   The list of methods by which a computer can specify a memory address. For example, direct and indirect.

Analog signal   An electrical signal that may take on an infinite number of values over time.

ADC (analog-to-digital converter)   A circuit with one analog input and n digital outputs. The binary output code can vary from 0 (OV input) to $2^n -1$ (the full scale input voltage).

ASCII   American Standard Code for Information Interchange, 7-bit code for the letters of the alphabet, numbers, punctuation symbols, and several control characters.

Assembler   A computer program that inputs instruction mnemonics (the source code) and outputs the binary equivalent (the object code).

Assembly language programming   A way of programming a computer using instruction mnemonics native to the particular CPU used. (*Example*:   Z-80 assembly language programming.)

Asynchronous   A type of logic design in which the outputs change whenever the circuit inputs change. There is no synchronizing signal.

Asynchronous serial communications   A method of sending data serially with each character framed between a start and stop bit.

Baud rate   For serially transmitted data, the number of signal events per second (usually the same as the number of data bits per second, except for high speed modems which encode more than one bit per signal event).

Bi-directional bus   A type of bus over which data can flow in two directions. (*Example*:   The data bus of a microprocessor.)

BCD (binary coded decimal)   A method of representing decimal numbers in binary with four bits for each decimal digit. (*Example*:   27 = 0010 0111.)

Bit   One binary digit.

Breakpoint   Software troubleshooting technique in which the program runs at full speed until the breakpoint is encountered. The CPU registers can then be examined, and the breakpoint moved further into the program.

Buffer   A type of logic circuit used to "clean up" a digital signal restoring the original logic 1 and logic 0 voltage levels and sharpening the pulse rise and fall times.

Bus   A collection of signal lines devoted to a common purpose.

Byte   8 bits.

CPU (central processing unit)   That portion of a digital computer that controls overall operation of the computer and in which all calculations and decisions are performed.

Checksum   An error detection scheme in which data is transmitted in blocks accompanied by a checking byte computed as the sum of the data bytes.

Chip   An integrated circuit.

Clock signal   The signal that specifies system timing for a synchronous logic circuit. The frequency of this signal thus determines the speed of that system.

CMOS (complementary metal-oxide semiconductor)   A type of digital circuit technology employing n- and p-channel field-effect transistors. CMOS circuits are best known for their low power consumption.

Control bus   The set of signal lines used by the CPU to indicate the current machine cycle type (memory or I/O) and direction (read or write).

CP/M (control program for microcomputers)   Popular disk operating system for microcomputers based on the 8080, 8085, and Z-80 8-bit microprocessors.

CRC (cyclic redundancy check)   Improved error detection scheme similar to the checksum but non-byte oriented.

Cylinder   For a hard drive, all tracks under the read/write heads at a given time. The total number of cylinders is equal to the number of tracks on one disk surface.

Data bus   The set of signal lines used to transfer data between the CPU and its memory unit and I/O devices.

DSP (device select pulse)   Derived from the address and control buses, the DSP is a signal used to activate an input or output port.

DAC (digital-to-analog converter) A circuit with n binary inputs and one analog output. The output voltage can vary from 0 V to some full-scale value in 2^n discrete steps.

DMA (direct memory access) An I/O technique in which the CPU is disconnected from its buses and a special DMA controller (DMAC) is used to directly route data between the I/O device and system memory.

DOS (disk operating system) A control program that manages the overall operation of a magnetic disk-based computer system.

DIP (dual in-line package) A type of through-hole IC package in which the leads are arranged in two parallel rows on each side of the case.

DRAM (dynamic RAM) A type of read/write semiconductor memory that uses a capacitor as the storage cell. DRAMs must be repeatedly refreshed or their data will be lost.

E^2PROM (electrically erasable programmable ROM) A type of ROM that can be programmed and erased electrically without removing the chip from its socket.

Fanout A measure of the number of gate inputs another logic gate can drive without exceeding its I_{OL} or I_{OH} specifications.

Flags Internal microprocessor flip-flops whose outputs are set or reset depending on the result of the last computer instruction.

FM (frequency modulation) Single-density encoding scheme used by magnetic disks.

Full duplex Serial communications technique in which each modem can simultaneously transmit and receive data.

Half duplex Serial communications technique in which the receiver and transmitter share the signal line. When using half duplex, only one modem can transmit at a time.

Handshaking logic A digital interface in which the sender and receiver of data exchange BUSY/READY signals to synchronize the data transfer.

Hexadecimal A base-16 number system convenient with digital circuits because one hexadecimal digit exactly represents four binary bits.

I/O (input/output) device A device such as a printer or a keyboard through which a computer may input or output information.

I/O (input/output) port The electrical interface to which an I/O device is connected.

Interrupt See interrupt line.

Interrupt driven A computer interface that is controlled via interrupts.

Interrupt line An input line monitored by the CPU. When this line is active, the current program is suspended and a special interrupt service routine (ISR) is run. Upon completion of the ISR, the interrupted program is resumed.

Interleave   Relative location of consecutive sectors on a magnetic disk. With an interleave of 3, consecutive sectors are located every third sector.

I_{OH} The high-level-output source current.

I_{OL} The low-level-output sink current.

K (kilo)   In binary 1024. (*Example*:   A 64K byte memory [64KB]).

Label   A name given to a memory location.

Latch   Logic circuit made up of flip-flops and designed to store digital data. (*Example*:   An 8-bit latch can be used as a microcomputer output port.)

Logic probe   A digital tester with LED indicators for a logic 0, a logic 1, and a pulsing condition.

Machine cycle   A computer operation in which an address is output and data transferred. (*Example*:   A memory-read machine cycle.)

Mask   A software term used to describe a combination of bits chosen to force selected bits of the operand low thus hiding their effect.

M (mega)   In binary, 1,048,576. (*Example*:   A 2 million byte/second data rate [2 MB/s].)

Memory   A digital circuit capable of storing a logic 1 or a logic 0.

Memory map   A drawing showing the type, size, and address location of the memory circuits in a computer.

Memory mapped I/O   An interfacing technique in which the I/O devices are wired to respond to memory addresses rather than I/O addresses.

Microcomputer   A digital computer system using a microprocessor chip as the CPU.

Microprocessor   An integrated circuit containing all of the logic of the central processing unit of a computer.

MS-DOS (Microsoft disk operating system)   Popular disk operating system for microcomputers based on the 8086 series of 16 and 32-bit microprocessors.

Mnemonic   Abbreviation for a computer instruction.

Modem (modulator/demodulator)   A device used to convert serial data into audio tones suitable for transmission over the telephone network.

MFM (modified FM)   Double-density encoding scheme used by magnetic disks.

Noise immunity   The ability of a logic circuit to reject and not respond to noise riding on its inputs, measured in volts.

Object code   The binary form of a computer program ready to run.

Op-code (operation code)   Mnemonic for a computer instruction specifying the type of operation that is to occur.

Open collector (or open drain) A type of logic circuit in which the high output level corresponds to an open circuit. The outputs of such circuits are commonly wired together to perform the wired-OR function via an external pull-up resistor.

Operand The memory location or CPU register to be accessed by the current instruction.

Parity An error detection scheme in which a checking bit is added to each data character such that the total number of 1s in the character is always even (even parity) or always odd (odd parity).

Peripheral An I/O device such as a keyboard or a printer.

Polling An I/O technique in which the CPU continually checks the I/O device to see if it is ready. Also called programmed I/O.

Port See I/O port.

Program counter CPU register holding the address of the next instruction to be fetched and executed.

PROM (programmable read-only memory) A type of ROM that can be programmed with the desired data. (*Example*: Mask- or fusible-link programmable.)

Propagation delay time See switching time.

Protocol A set of rules that have been developed to standardize the transmission of data between two systems.

RAM (random access memory) Main memory that can be read from or written to by the CPU.

Read cycle That portion of a computer instruction in which data is input to the CPU from memory or an I/O device.

ROM (read-only memory) A type of memory from which the CPU can only read but not write; often used for "booting up" the computer.

Refresh The process of recharging the bit cells in a DRAM.

Register A set of flip-flops wired with a common clock line and used to store several bits of data.

RS-232D Electronics Industries Associates (EIA) standard governing serial data transmission. Specified are logic 1 and 0 voltage levels, data rates, signal descriptions, and connector pinouts.

RLL (run length limited) Encoding scheme used by magnetic disks. RLL-encoded disks achieve a 50% greater bit density and transfer rate than MFM encoded disks.

Schmitt trigger A type of logic circuit that switches at two different input voltage levels depending if the input is high, going low, or low, going high. This property allows the circuit to reject noise and ringing on the input signal.

Sector For a magnetic disk, a portion of a track used for storing data. (*Example*: A low-density MS-DOS-formatted $5\frac{1}{4}''$ floppy disk has nine sectors per track and 512 bytes per sector.)

Serial data transmission A method of sending digital data one bit after the other on a single wire.

Signed binary number A binary number in which the most significant bit, if set, represents a negative number.

Software The instructions that form a computer program.

SSR (solid-state relay) A semiconductor circuit equivalent to a mechanical relay but with no moving parts.

Source code A form of a computer program in which the instructions are written in a high level form. (*Example*: Instruction mnemonics.)

Stack A last-in first-out area of RAM set aside for storing temporary data via the PUSH and POP instructions. The stack is also used to store subroutine return addresses.

Start bit With asynchronous serial data, a synchronizing bit, always a logic 0, identifying the start of a serial character.

SRAM (static RAM) A type of read/write semiconductor memory that uses a flip-flop as the storage cell.

Stop bit With asynchronous serial data, a synchronizing bit, always a logic 1, identifying the end of a serial character.

Subroutine A program within a program that can be called whenever needed by the main program. Because subroutines can be used several times within the same program, their use helps minimize the total number of instructions required by that program.

Switching time The time required for a logic circuit to switch from one logic state to the other—also called the propagation delay time.

Synchronous A type of logic design in which all circuit outputs switch at the same instant synchronized to a common clock signal.

Synchronous serial communications A method of sending data serially without start and stop bits.

T state One period of the system clock signal.

Track Circular path scanned by the read/write head of a magnetic disk. (*Example*: A $5\frac{1}{4}''$ MS-DOS-formatted floppy disk has 40 tracks per side.

TTL (transistor-transistor-logic) A type of saturating digital circuit technology employing bipolar transistors; available as a complete catalog line of logic gates, flip-flops, and counters.

Tri-state A type of logic circuit capable of producing three different output states: high-, low-, and open-circuit. The latter state is often referred to as the tri-state.

Truth table For a digital circuit, the list of all possible inputs and the corresponding circuit outputs.

Two's complement A method of representing negative numbers formed by complementing all bits in the byte or word and adding one.

V_{OH} The high level output voltage produced by a logic circuit.

V_{OL} The low level output voltage produced by a logic circuit.

UV EPROM (ultraviolet erasable programmable ROM)   A type of ROM that can be electrically programmed, but erased via exposure to ultraviolet light.

UART (universal asynchronous receiver–transmitter)   An IC used to transmit and receive serial data.

Wait state   Extra T state added to an instruction to give the memory or I/O device additional time to respond with data.

Write cycle   That portion of a computer instruction in which data is output from the CPU to memory or an I/O device.

Index

Accumulator, 2, 52, 55
Acoustic coupling, 505–6, (*illus.*), 509
Addition
    8-bit, 79–83
    32-bit binary, 84–86
    32-bit decimal, 86–89
Address decoder, 220–21, 224–26, 231–35
Addressing modes
    8080 and 8085 microprocessors (*table*),
      67
    8086/88 microprocessors (*table*), 621
    Z-80 microprocessor (*table*), 68
Analog-to-digital converter (ADC), 570
    ADC0809 interface, 578–82
    dual-slope, 576–77
    flash, 570–71
    successive approximations, 573–75
    tracking, 571–73
Archival storage, 194
Arithmetic logic unit (ALU), 2
ASCII (*table*), 11

Baud rate, 447, 450, (*table*), 451
Bi-directional bus buffer, 167–69
Binary number system, 7–9

Bisync, 455–56, 488
Bounce, switch, 270
Breakpoint, 583
Buffer (*see* bus)
Bus, 6, 19
    bandwidth, 157
    buffering
      effect on I/O timing, 260
      effect on memory timing, 222–23
      bi-directional, 167–69
      latches (*table*), 266
      open collector gates, 164–67, 552–53
      for peripheral controller chips, 382–
        83
      tri-state gates, 164–65
    loading of, 156–57
    reflections on, 157–60
    S-100, 33–34
    termination, 159–60

Central processing unit (CPU)
    8080 CPU module, 36–42, 160, (*illus.*),
      173
    8085 CPU module, 42–46, 160, (*illus.*),
      175

Central processing unit (CPU) (*Contd.*)
  8086 CPU module, 611–15
    max mode (*illus.*), 614
    min mode (*illus.*), 613
  Z-80 CPU module, 46–49, (*illus.*), 176
Checksum, 458–59
Clock
  baud rate, 469–70
  generator
    8224, for 8080 systems, 148–49
    8284, for 8086/88 systems, 610–11
  microprocessor, 146–47
  specifications
    8080 microprocessor, 148–50
    8085 microprocessor, 148, 150
    Z-80 microprocessor, 150–52
Cluster, 530
Comparator, analog, 547–50, 593
Compiler, 14–16
Complementary metal oxide semiconductor
  (CMOS), 16–17
  logic level specifications, 155
Computer
  8085 microcomputer system (*illus.*), 320
  single-board, 33
  Z-80 microcomputer system (*illus.*), 584
Computer codes, 10–12
Control bus, 4, 19, (*illus.*), 41
Conversions
  BASIC program, 27
  BCD-to-binary, 93–98
  BCD-to-seven segment, 408–12
  hexadecimal-to-ASCII, 105–9
Counter/timer circuit, Z-80 CTC (*see* Zilog
  Z-8430 CTC)
CP/M, 128
  function numbers, 135, (*table*), 136
Cyclic redundancy check (CRC), 460–61
Cylinder, 530

Daisy chain, 295–96
Data analyzer (*see* logic analyzer)
Data bus, 4, 19
Data communications equipment (DCE),
  497–98
Data terminal equipment (DTE), 497–98
Decoder, address, 220–21, 224–26, 231–
  35
Device select pulse (DSP), 260, 265

Dibits, 511
Differential line driver/receiver, 492–95
Digital-to-analog converter (DAC), 559–63
  DAC1200 interface, 566–69
  MC1408 interface, 563–66
  R-2R ladder, 561–63
Direct memory access (DMA), 299–302,
  363
  response time, 368–70, 429–31
  transfer rate, 368–70, 429–31
Direct memory access controller
  Intel 8237, 363–82
  Zilog Z-8410 DMA, 424–37
Disk drive
  data rates, 537–40
  floppy, 525
  hard, 526
  interfaces, 540–42
Disk operating system (DOS), 127–28
Display, 6-digit multiplexed, 408–13
Double density encoding, floppy disk, 535
DRAM (*see* RAM, dynamic)
Dynamic debugging tool (DDT), 132–35

Editor, 130–31
EPROM (*see* Read only memory)
E²PROM, 210–14
Error correction, 461–65
Error detection, 457–61

Fetch and execute principal, 4
Flags
  8080/85 microprocessor (*illus.*), 53
  8086/88 microprocessor (*illus.*), 617
  Z-80 microprocessor, (*illus.*), 56
Floppy disk, 523–24
Floppy disk drive
  mechanical design, 525–26
  performance specifications, (*table*), 539
  read/write head, 525, (*illus.*), 527
  types, (*table*), 529
Formatting
  high level, 533
  low level, 531–33
Framing error, 448
Frequency counter, 112–116, 348–50
Frequency modulation, FM, 534–35
Full duplex, 504

Games, NIM, 116–21

Hamming code, modified, 461–65
Hand assembly, 14, 69
Handshaking logic, 274–75, 497–500 (*see
    also* Intel 8255A mode 1, Zilog Z-
    8420 modes 0 and 1, and RS-232D)
Hard drive, 526–27
Hexadecimal number system, 7–10
Hysteresis, 154, 164

Index register, 55, 82–83, 616
Input/output, 2, 257–60
    8-bit input port design, 260–62
    8-bit memory mapped input port design,
        268–69
    8-bit output port design, 262–65
    1-bit I/O port using the 8085's SID and
        SOD lines, 110–12
    16-bit 8086 I/O port design, 636–38
Instruction cycles (*see* Machine cycles)
Instruction set
    8080, 8085, and Z-80 microprocessors
        (*see also* Appendices A and B)
        addressing modes, 66–68
        arithmetic group, 59
        bit manipulation group, 66
        branch group, 60
        data transfer group, 58–59
        exchange, block transfer and search
            group, 65–66
        logical and rotate group, 59–60
        stack, I/O and machine control group,
            62–65
    8086/88 microprocessor
        addressing modes, 621–22
        arithmetic group, 625
        bit manipulation group, 626
        data transfer group, 623–25
        processor control group, 631–32
        software interrupts, 629–30
        string group, 631
        transfer group, 626–28
Intel:
    2764 EPROM, 207–10
    2817 E²PROM, 210–14
    8080 microprocessor, 36

Intel (*Contd.*)
    8085 microprocessor, 42
        three-chip microcomputer system, 319–
            21
    8086 microprocessor, 602
    8087 numeric data processor, 610
    8088 microprocessor, 639
    8089 I/O processor, 610
    8203 DRAM controller, 240
    8224 system clock generator, 41, 148–50
    8228 system controller, 610, 615
    8237 programmable DMA controller
        (DMAC), 362
    8251A universal synchronous/asynchro-
        nous receiver/transmitter (USART),
        465
    8254 programmable interval timer (PIT),
        341
    8255A programmable peripheral interface
        (PPI), 321
        bit set/reset mode, 328
        mode 0, 324
        mode 1, 330
        mode 2, 336
    8259A programmable interrupt controller
        (PIC), 351
    8755A 16K EPROM with I/O, 314
    80286 microprocessor, 640
    80386 microprocessor, 641
    80386SX microprocessor, 642
    80486 microprocessor, 642
Interpreter, 14–16
Interrupt pointer table, 8086/88 (*illus.*), 629
Interrupt service routine (ISR), 282, (*illus.*),
    292
Interrupts, 281–98
    direct, 289
    with the 8086/88
        hardware, 610, 629–30
        software, 630
    8255A mode 1, 330
    indirect, 289–90
    priority, 293–96
    response time, 290–91, 430–31
    transfer rate, 291–93, 430–31
    vectored, 287–88
    with the Z-80 PIO, 397–400
IOR line, 26, 233–34
IOW line, 26, 234–35

Keypad matrix, 270–73, 385, 438

Label, 85
Lamp dimmer, 594
Lamp driver, 553–55
Latch, (table), 266
Line driver/receiver, 493–95
Loading, 156–57
Logic analyzer, 18–19,
Logic gates, symbology, 171–72
Logical address, 619
Loudspeaker, driving, 121

Machine cycles
  (table), 5
  timing diagrams, 21–23
  8080 (illus.), 39
  8085 (illus.), 46
  8086 (illus.), 608
  I/O read cycle, 258
  I/O write cycle, 258
  memory read cycle, 196
  memory write cycle, 197
  as a troubleshooting aid, 587
  Z-80 (illus.), 49
Main memory, 192
Memory
  access time, 25, 196
  buffers, effect of, 222–23
  byte-wide universal memory site, 217–19
  interfacing
    8-bit, 219–44
    16-bit, 634–36
  organization, 216–17, 605
  segments, for the 8086/88, 618–20
Memory map, 19–20, 202–203
Memory mapped I/O, 265, 267, 304
MEMR line, 22, 25–26, 196
MEMW line, 22, 25–26, 197
Microprocessor (see also computer and central processing unit)
  definition, 1
  three-bus architecture, 4–5
  timing, 23, 25–26
Mnemonics, 13
Modem, 503–12
Modified frequency modulation (MFM), 535

Motherboard, 33
Motorola
  MC1488 line driver, 493–95
  MC1489 line receiver, 493–95
Multiplication
  8086/88 instructions, 624–25
  Z-80 program, 89–93
Multitasking, 278

National Semiconductor
  ADC0809, eight channel analog-to-digital converter, 578–82
  DAC 1200, 12-bit digital-to-analog converter, 566–69
  DS75491/DS75492 display controllers/drivers, 408–10
  LM393 analog comparator, 548–50, 593
Nibble, 7
Noise immunity, 154–56
Null modem, 497, 514

Object code, 14, 69–70
One-shot, using the Z-80 CTC, 421–24
Op-code, 4, 21, 69,
Open collector bus buffer, 164–67, 552–53
Operand, 69
Opto-coupler, 559
Output port (see input/output)

Parallel input/output controller, PIO (see Zilog Z-8420)
Parity, 458
Peripheral drivers, 553–55
Physical address, 619
Polling, 275–78
  response time, 279–81
  transfer rate, 279
Printer control program
  using CP/M function calls, 135–38
  using interrupts, 291–93, 403–406
  using polling, 276, 328–29
Printer interface, parallel, 276, 328, 336, 404
Priority
  interrupts, 294–97
  polling, 353–56

Priority interrupt controller (PIC), 351
Program counter, 4
Programmable array logic (PAL), 233–35
Programmable DMA controller, DMAC,
    362
Programmable interval timer, PIT, 341
Programmable peripheral interface, PPI,
    321
Programmed I/O (*see* polling)
Programming
    assembly language, 12–14
    definition of, 5
    high level language, 14–16
    machine language, 12–14
Programming model
    8080 microprocessor, 51
    8085 microprocessor, 55
    8086 microproessor, 615
    Z-80 microprocessor, 55

Quadrature amplitude modulation (QAM),
    511–12
Queue, 602–604

Random access memory, RAM (*see also*
    memory)
    applications, 202
    dynamic, 214–16
        interfacing, 236–44
        timing (*illus.*), 237
    static, 214
        interfacing, 226–35
    test circuit, 246–47
    test program, 248
Read only memory, ROM (*see also* mem-
    ory)
    applications, 202
    electrically erasable (E^{2}PROM),
    electrically programmable (EPROM),
        207–10
    field-programmable, 204
    fusible-link, 205–206
    interfacing, 220–26
    mask programmable, 204
Reflections, 157–60
Refresh, 238–40 (*see also* Intel 8203 DRAM
    controller)
Register, 13, 51–52

Relay driver
    electromechanical, 267, 528–33
    solid-state, 533–37
Remote control, 490–91
Reset, 152–54
    Z-80 jump-on-reset circuit, 183–84
Response time (*see* polling, interrupts, or
    DMA)
RS-232D, 446
    electrical specifications, 492–94
    handshaking signals, 497–500
    signal descriptions, 495–97
RS-422A, RS-423A, 500, 502
RS-449, 502
Run length limited (RLL), 535–37

Secondary storage, 193–94
Sector, floppy disk, 528–30
Segment registers, 618–20
Serial data
    asynchronous, 446–55
    synchronous, 455–56
Serial data link control (SDLC), 456, 488
Signature analysis, 588
Single-board computer, 33
Single-density encoding, floppy disk, 535
Single-step
    circuits, 179–83
    as a troubleshooting aid, 585
Solid-state relay, 533–37
Source code, 14
SRAM (*see* RAM, static)
Stack, 52, 62–63, 294
Stack pointer, 52, 616
Start bit, 447
Status
    8080 status word, 39–40
    8085 status bits, 46
    8086/88 status signals, 608–609
Stop bit, 447
Switch (*see* keypad matrix)

Temperature, sensing, 548–50, 595
Termination, bus, 159–60
Texas Instruments
    SN74LS240, LS241, LS244, specifica-
        tions, 161–63

Texas Instruments (*Contd.*)
  SN75400, peripheral driver family, 553–55
  TMS99532, full duplex modem, 506–10
Time delays
  hardware (*see* Intel 8254 and Zilog Z-8430)
  software, 103
Timing, microprocessor (*see* machine cycles)
Track, floppy disk, 528–29
Transfer rate (*see* polling, interrupts, or DMA)
Transistor-transistor-logic (TTL), 16
  logic level specifications (*table*), 155
TRIAC, 556–59
Tri-state buffers, 164–65
Twisted pair, 160
Twos complement binary numbers (*table*), 12
  to calculate the checksum, 458–59
  with indexed instructions, 68,
  with relative jump instructions, 60, 89, 627

Universal asynchronous receiver/transmitter (UART), 451–55
Universal synchronous/asynchronous receiver/transmitter (*see* Intel 8251A)

Von Neuman, 2

Wait states:
  for processor single-step, 178–83
  for slow memories, 199–201
Word, 605

Zilog:
  Z-80 microprocessor, 46
    system with 2K RAM, 2K ROM, and 24 I/O lines (*illus.*), 584
  Z-80 dual asynchronous receiver/transmitter, DART (*see* Z-80 SIO)
  Z-80 serial input/output controller (Z-80 SIO), 474–90
    asynchronous mode programming, 479–88
    block transfers, 487
    interrupts, 486
    polling, 483
    synchronous mode programming, 488–90
  Z-8410 direct memory access controller (Z-80 DMA), 424–37
  Z-8420 parallel input/output controller (Z-80 PIO), 394–413
    mode 0, 400
    mode 1, 401
    mode 2, 404
    mode 3, 406
  Z-8430 counter/timer circuit (Z-80 CTC), 413–24
    counter mode, 416
    timer mode, 420